SAINTS, SINNERS AND SCALAWAGS

Thibaut de Saint Phalle

SAINTS, SINNERS AND SCALAWAGS

A LIFETIME IN STORIES

by

Thibaut de Saint Phalle

To my old friend Ben Gifford
With best regards

Thibaut

Boca Grande
12/04

HOBBLEBUSH BOOKS

ISBN: 0-9636413-8-7
Library of Congress Control Number: 2003115313

Designed and composed in Adobe Caslon Pro at Hobblebush Books

Printed in the United States of America

Published by
HOBBLEBUSH BOOKS
17-A Old Milford Road · Brookline, New Hampshire 03033
www.hobblebush.com

CONTENTS

My family goes back to the 9th century in France and before what became France—we were prominent in the Crusades and the liberation of Jerusalem— in the 20th century my father and five brothers created an international bank, which disappeared in the Great Depression of 1929—as children we spent every summer in my grandfather's chateau in France—he raised racehorses—there were always 30 children there every summer

Problems of getting an education without money during the Depression years— after my father lost all his money, I put myself through college and law school on scholarships and part-time jobs—tutoring the Sulzberger children—a second family at The New York Times

Joining the New York Bar and the United States Navy on the same day— midshipman school—Air Combat Intelligence School in Rhode Island—Panama and Latin America—combat with the 45th Division in Sicilian invasion— Patton's message—decoration in lieu of court-martial—explaining our work in Sicily to the Air Corps—joining the OSS—how to blow up a strategic war plant—avoiding a parachute landing in France to liberate Burma

General Wingate wouldn't wait—learning Chinese at sea—joining General Chennault in China—intelligence and sabotage operations in East China—a snow leopard hunt through Afghanistan—landing spies in Formosa— establishing an intelligence network on Chinese junks for U.S. submarines— coping with a feudal society in China—living in a Chinese cemetery—an attempted assassination fails—buying a wife for my sergeant—getting a plane from Chennault to fly home via Jerusalem, Cairo, Rome, the Riviera, Paris and London—family reunion in Paris

PREFACE

*T*HIS BOOK IS NOT SO much a memoir as a collection of stories about the people and places that were important in my life and that helped to make me who I am. The reader will travel with me —by ship and by aircraft—to China, Japan, France, Britain, the Middle East, the former Soviet Empire, and, of course, the United States, where I have spent most of my life.

Because this book is about my life and my career, I have, purposefully, not spoken more about my wife Mariana and about the nine children we have together and dearly love. This new century is theirs to conjure with. I have no doubt they will handle it well.

Of the saints, sinners and scalawags I have described, there are few saints—my paternal grandmother, my godmother, a Benedictine monk. There are many sinners, perhaps because it is more interesting to chronicle people's bad deeds than their good ones, and their motives are more fascinating. There are also a few certified scalawags, mostly in politics and the Church, persons whose behavior appears so at variance with what they have sworn to uphold.

All of them taught me a great deal. They taught me both what to do, and what to avoid doing. They brought understanding, appreciation, love, but nevertheless not envy, into my life.

Human existence is, after all, an immense learning process. The richness of human relationships is what makes it all worthwhile.

If the reader has enjoyed sharing these adventures with me, then I shall have accomplished what I set out to do.

—Thibaut de Saint Phalle
Boca Grande, Florida
November, 2003

ACKNOWLEDGMENTS

Unlike my other writings, this book has been written over many years, so that the stories and events recounted, all of which are true, are not dependant on a more distant memory.

I am indebted to many for secretarial assistance, but in particular my former secretary in Paris, Regine Hess, and especially Linda Preston who gave me so many hours of her time in typing and organizing the manuscript.

My Uncle Alexandre, proprietor of the Chateau of Cudot in France, spent many days with me visiting family chateaus, reviewing archives, and just talking of past historical events.

My wife, Mariana, has been both interested and patient in what I have been trying to accomplish. Daughter and granddaughter of writers, she kept me rewriting where needed.

To Sid Hall, my editor and publisher, I am most grateful for trying to teach a writer of longhand a few rudiments of technology. He is a great editor and a wonderful publisher.

*To those men and women I met along the way
who followed in their lives the dictates of their
hearts, this book is respectfully dedicated.*

SAINTS, SINNERS AND SCALAWAGS

Life was meant to be lived, and curiosity must be kept alive.
One must never, for whatever reason, turn his back on life.

—Eleanor Roosevelt (1961)

Happy who, like Ulysses, a glorious voyage made.

—Joachim du Bellay (*Les Regrets*, 1559)

When you come to a fork in the road, take it.   —Yogi Berra

I

THE PAST AS PROLOGUE

Cruce Deo, Gladio Regi, Jungor
"I pledge my cross to God, and my sword to the king."
—Family Crest

E *LEVEN HUNDRED YEARS* of recorded history. That is a long time for any family. One of my uncles, Alexandre, discovered in his research on the noble families of France that any family could survive without losing its recorded history for a maximum of two generations of unsuccessful offspring. If there were a third in a row, the family name would vanish. Added to the possibility that in any generation there might not be any male heirs, the likelihood of a continued recorded history is not very high. With the exception of the Toulouse-Lautrec clan of southwestern France, I am told the Saint Phalle family goes back in its recorded history further than any other in the country.

Eleven hundred years of recorded history is a long time for any family.

No one knows for sure where the name comes from or how the family was related to the saint who lived in the 5th century. The saint appeared to have been a Gaul from a family that lived in the southern mountains of France, a Roman citizen. Attila the Hun's army had suddenly come through the gap between the Rhine and Danube Rivers, had overwhelmed the Roman garrisons, sacked Rome and ravaged Gaul as far as the Mediterranean. Returning home, the army took this young Gaul with them as a slave. Passing through Troyes on their way north, they sold the boy to an abbot who had been warned in a dream that tribesmen would be passing by with a young slave whom he should buy.

The boy became a monk, succeeded the abbot on his death, and became a saint. His name was Fal or Fidolo (faithful) in Medieval Latin. Only later in 836 is there a written record of a Saint Phalle (spelled "Fale") in the region. Later, this family built a huge castle near Troyes, where Joan of Arc—leading the Dauphin to be crowned at Rheims as Charles VII—stayed with an army of 30,000 men.

There is a modern sequel to this story. In 1987, I was sent by President Reagan to work with the new Hungarian government established after Hungary's liberation from the control of the Soviet Union. The

3

Communist government had ruled by decrees issued by individual ministries—there were some 3,500 economic decrees. While reviewing these, to determine which should be scrapped, kept or modified, I had spent ten days on Lake Balaton in Hungary as a guest of the ministers who had their weekend retreats there. Asked one day why I had now come to Hungary, I replied that since my ancestor had been kidnapped by the Hungarians in 455, it was only natural that I should repay the favor by assisting at the new Hungarian liberation from foreign tyranny.

It was not to be expected that a family would survive for so long. Examination of the archives shows that family members, taking their oath seriously, fought in every war, crusade or insurrection in which Frenchmen were ever involved. They were not generals or marshals of France, but captains and colonels, the ones who most frequently died in battle. Some, in their quiet way, were heroes. In Alexandre Dumas' *Three Musketeers*, d'Artagnan is patterned after the colonel in command of that king's musketeers, Claude de Saint Phalle. In the battle of Mons en Pucelle in 1304, the king of France, Philippe III, le Hardi, was captured by the Flemish and shouted for his kinsman and godson to save him. Saint Phalle charged the enemy and liberated his king—hence, the battle cry. As a result of that battle and the end of that particular war between Flanders and France, an enclave of northern France, including the three cities of Lille, Roubaix and Tourcoing, great industrial and textile centers, were ceded to France.

In the 1940s and '50s, I represented several of the region's textile firms as an international lawyer. I was advised by my clients that this part of France shouldered 70 percent of the French income tax burden and since the Saint Phalles were responsible for their not being part of Belgium, would I please do something about this disproportionate tax!

In the Middle Ages, between the kingdom of France and the much larger province of Champagne there was a large fiefdom held by the Courtenay family, covering some three Departments of modern day France. Pierre de Saint Phalle, as hereditary Seneschal of Champagne and therefore the administrator of the province, had been sent there by Thibaut III, Count of Champagne, to negotiate a boundary dispute between the king of France, Louis VI, Courtenay and Champagne. Pierre also negotiated a marriage between his son, Andre, and Jeanne de Seignelay, whose mother was a Courtenay. Jeanne brought to her marriage to Andre, as her dowry, the fortress of Cudot, which has been in the family until very recently. This same Courtenay refused to marry his daughter to the king's son. Many years later, his descendants of the same name, the family having fallen on hard times, wrote to the king of France Louis XIII asking for a pension. Cardinal Richelieu, who never missed a chance to humble the nobles, wrote back a curt reply: "How can it be that you would ask a favor of the king, when your ancestor refused to allow his daughter to marry the son of the king of France?"

Perhaps the greatest role played by the family took place during the first Christian Crusades. A Saint Phalle was in charge of the fortresses established by the Crusaders, which are today in Israel, Bodrum in Turkey, Lindos in Rhodes, all great fortresses of the period, established to protect the gateways to Jerusalem. Add to this a kinsman who became emperor of Jerusalem. This was probably a great opportunity for dedication and courage, since both king and the Cross were involved.

I can only hope that when Pope John Paul II apologized for the behavior of the Crusaders in the Middle East, he was not referring to those first three Crusades in which my family played an important role, since these were sponsored by Saint Bernard, founder of the Benedictine Order, and by Saint Louis, king of France. It might have been preferable to apologize for the Albigensian Crusade of the 14th century when so many good Christians of the Cathar sect were burned at the stake at the behest of Saint Dominic and the Church of Rome. I am not proud that members of my family, as indeed most of the nobles of Champagne, participated in this Crusade as well. But having studied what life must have been like in the draughty castles of northeastern France in the Middle Ages, it is not surprising that my ancestors went off each spring to warmer climates, leaving their wives in charge of the castles, farms and villages in the hope of returning at the end of the summer laden with booty from Italy, southern France or the Middle East.

It must be remembered that during this period of war and plunder in the 10th to 15th centuries, the kingdom of France was very small. The province of Champagne, until it became part of France in the 11th century, was rich and powerful by comparison. The Saint Phalles were hereditary seneschals of Champagne, and were therefore rich in lands and castles, related to the kings of France and the counts of Champagne. These men were not only leaders in war; Count Thibaut IV of Champagne was the foremost poet of his day.

All these, of course, are periods long since consigned to the history books. By the turn of the 20th century there were only two branches of the family left, the issue of two brothers who had divided the remaining family properties between them in the early 18th century, the one moving to central France, to Montgoublin, the other remaining in the north at Cudot in the Yonne, an hour's drive by car from Paris. The brother who went to Montgoublin in 1720 was not exactly welcomed. A few days after his arrival with a new young wife, while sitting at dinner, the crystal chandelier fell on the table from the high ceiling, narrowly missing them both.

Gradually, as often happens, the two branches of the family drifted apart. The elder branch, with the title of marquis, remained in Montgoublin. My grandfather was the last of the younger branch. Like many in his family, he had graduated from the École Polytechnique, the M.I.T. of France, and had then taken up a military career. Invalided out of the service when still young, he had decided to move from Chennevieres on the Marne near Paris to the Chateau de Huez not far from Montgoublin. Not untypically, he did not marry until he was 29. It was his mother who suggested that it was high time that he do so. She offered to select a wife for him and called upon her close friend the Marquise de Chabannes La Palice who had two daughters, to suggest that perhaps her son and the oldest daughter might make a good match. Since the Chabannes and Saint Phalle families were already connected by marriage, the idea pleased my grandmother's friend, and mother and son journeyed for a weekend to La Palice, where Pierre and Henriette appeared to get along well, leading to an invitation for a visit in the other direction. The younger sister, Catherine, then age 17, accompanied Henriette and her mother to Huez. Some weeks later, my great grandmother asked Pierre whether he wanted to pursue the matter further. Pierre was embarrassed to tell his mother that while he thought the older daughter had all the qualities that he might wish to find in a wife, he was in love with her younger sister. This presented a problem because, in those days, mothers of good families expected to marry off the oldest daughter first. Nevertheless, my great grandmother wrote to her friend, who spoke to the young girl. Catherine's reaction: "I do love Pierre, but my sister comes first." The two girls then discussed the matter openly. The older sister said she felt that if Pierre wished to marry Catherine she should accept, because he would make her an excellent husband. After two years' engagement insisted upon by Catherine's mother to allow the older daughter to marry first, Pierre and Catherine were married in 1884. My grandfather could not have found a more perfect wife. She gave him seven sons and one daughter, supported him in all his ideas, loved him and nursed him until his death at the age of 80 and managed to live the life of a saint in her little community while never appearing surprised by anything she was told by her sophisticated daughters-in-law. Every

My paternal
grandmother
comes
from one
of the most
influential
families in
Frrench
history.

morning during her married life, winter or summer, she walked to the Catholic church, one kilometer away, to attend Mass.

Pierre and Catherine spent their lives together at Huez, near Nevers in central France, some four hours by train from Paris. There my grandfather brought up his seven sons himself, teaching them mathematics, Latin, Greek, history, religion and French literature. This was very unusual for someone of his generation and of the social world in which he lived.

My grandfather felt that French education was too narrow and did not stress religion sufficiently. This led to his decision that his children would not attend schools. He would educate his seven sons himself. He taught them mathematics and Latin literature and history, and above all, a strong moral code. One was expected to behave as a gentleman and no excesses were tolerated. One believed in God and went to Mass regularly; one respected one's father and mother, and obeyed instructions; politeness was a given; hard work in anything one did was expected; one never lied.

My father and his six brothers are educated at home and never attend school.

Years later when I spent much time with my father and was counsel for two of my uncles in their business ventures, I realized what it means never to have attended school. School is the place where one learns about human nature, both the good and the bad: cruelty, greed, envy, pride, avarice, as well as good manners, kindness, friendship, generosity. If you never go to school, you don't get the opportunity to find out about human nature, how to avoid the bad and seek out the good. My uncles, and I am quite sure my father as well, were constantly being blindsided by traits of human nature that they had not encountered when they were young. The British system of taking boys from good families at the age of seven and putting them in Dickensian boarding schools where they are subjected to every taunt, suffering and humiliation possible, in order to toughen their character for later life, has a good deal to recommend it, because it teaches one not only the art of survival, but self-discipline. I myself learned more about human nature from one year in an English boarding school in Bermuda at the age of 14, than I would have thought possible. Unpleasant, certainly, but very useful in later life. I have always surmised that Jimmy Carter, in whose administration I served, must have been kept from school when he was a youngster by his mother, Miss Lillian, because he appeared during his presidency to have the same difficulty in judging people. He reminded me of my uncles, all admirable men, but altogether lacking the capacity to understand others' reactions.

The second great conclusion that my grandfather reached was that the United States was the country of the future. Quite remarkable in a man who had never been to the United States and whose only knowledge of the country came from reading constantly in his old chateau in the depths of the French countryside. Having made this discovery, my grandfather put it to the test with his sons. As each reached the age of 16, he was sent to the United States to make his fortune, armed with a one-way steamer ticket, $100, which I suppose in those days was real money, and a letter of introduction to a great business leader whom my grandfather had heard of through his reading, but of course had never met. Looking back on it now, his choice of suitable business leaders was interesting.

My
grandfather
sends all
his boys to
America to
make their
future there.

The oldest son, Francois, was sent to Philadelphia just before the turn of the century. The letter he carried was addressed by my grandfather to the chairman of the Baldwin Locomotive Works in Philadelphia. Baldwin was a natural choice. It supplied locomotives all over the world, from Brazil to Russia. It was indeed one of the marvels of the new American industrial productivity. Francois fitted well in Philadelphia, and in due course married Helen Voorhees, daughter of Baldwin's president, whose forbears had come from Holland with the "Pennsylvania Dutch" settlers two centuries earlier. It was not a bad way to achieve business success.

The second son, Bernard, was sent to Chicago to the McCormick Company, whose reaper was then revolutionizing agricultural production all over the world. I had always felt sorry for Bernard. My grandfather didn't like him much because he was slow, methodical, not as quick as the others. Chicago at the turn of the century was not an easy place for an unsophisticated and highly religious young Frenchman to find his way. After a short time, Bernard took advantage of an opportunity to become a McCormick dealer in Roubaix in the north of France. There he married a strapping blond daughter of a local noble family, with whom he had some seven children.

Thibaut, the next, who died in World War I, had been in frail health and was therefore exempted from work in the United States.

The fourth son, my father, Fal, was ready to go in 1911. My grandfather's choice for him was again an interesting one. This was shortly after the money panic of 1907, when J. P. Morgan single-handedly saved the United States from financial disaster. The great Morgan received a nice letter from my grandfather, noting how he had saved the country, and asking him to teach my father to be a banker of international reputation in his mold. I often used to ask my father—when I was young and he was my close friend and model—how he had ever managed, landing in the United States without speaking a word of English. Evidently, he had found a small rooming house in the French section of West 23rd Street in Manhattan and had then gone to 23 Wall Street, home of the Morgan Bank, on foot. The guard there discovered that he couldn't understand English. He had sense enough to take him up to the foreign department where he and his letter were delivered to the great J. P. Morgan. In those days, there was no wait for employment if you were introduced. So my father began his life in the United States at the Morgan Bank, putting himself through law school at night and gradually making friends in the social world, where French was spoken. It must have been a lonely life of adjustment, terminated all too early by the advent of World War I in 1914.

The Past as Prologue

Rules on nationality and immigration have a tendency to change when governments need manpower to fight in wars. In France, ever since the Franco-Prussian War of 1870, successive governments were obsessed by *revanche,* the chance to get back Alsace and Lorraine taken by the Germans by the peace treaty of 1871. In order not to allow the disadvantage in population to grow further, the French government allowed only one male member of a family to emigrate. Since my Uncle Francois had already become an American citizen, my father's change of citizenship was not recognized by France, and in 1914 he was called upon to return to his native land to join the army. He went, but he never forgave the French for forcing him to come back and abandon the career and the life he had painfully created for himself in his new country. Wounded three times in the war, he was decorated twice for bravery. On one suicide mission for which he had volunteered, he received a bullet in his neck, which fortunately hit a gold medal of the Virgin my mother had given him when they became engaged.

They were married on May 5, 1916 with the New York social pages announcing: "American heiress marries French hero of the trenches." The romantic implications were apparent even though the truth might have been stretched. My mother was certainly very beautiful but no heiress; my father longed only for the war to end so that he could resume his life as an American.

My father marries an American girl raised in Europe.

Although an American, my mother had been raised in Europe. My grandmother was one of three beautiful daughters of a Belgian contractor named Guidet, who installed the wooden Guidet bricks in Manhattan's streets. When my grandmother ran off at the age of 17 with

Gustavus Abeel Duryee, a handsome but penniless young playboy of the period, her wealthy father disinherited her.

My grandfather's forebears had come to the United States from Holland with Hendrick Hudson, and his father had equipped his own regiment, the Duryee Zouaves, to fight for the North from New York in the Civil War. Dressed in the uniform worn by the French army for the conquest of Algeria in 1830, they must have added a good deal of color to the army fighting in Virginia. Although my grandmother always referred to him as a "nincompoop" and the marriage hadn't lasted, my sister and I thought of grandfather Duryee as rather rakish. He managed never to work a day in his life and ended his days in the south of France taken care of by a Russian countess who thought only of making him content. In a world dedicated to material success, he hadn't done too badly. In any event, my grandmother had three children by him, then divorced him and went off to live in Italy and Switzerland. She destroyed her son by catering to his every whim, disliked her younger daughter, but found in my mother a worthy successor to her own determination to hold her own in life, no matter what the odds. When World War I broke out, she had gone to France under Anne Morgan as her deputy in the American Red Cross. When Morgan returned home, my grandmother became head of the American Red Cross in France. She received repeated decorations from a grateful French government. After the war she married Sam Auchincloss of the well-known New York clan, but he was weak and drank too much, and so she put him in an English nursing home and left him. She used to tell me he was the love of her life. I was very fond of this American grandmother. She was tough, ruthless, unforgiving, but a lady through and through.

My mother and father's marriage should have been very successful. My mother was very beautiful, intelligent, pragmatic, fun to be with and as determined as her mother. My father was very serious, very much of a gentleman, contemplative and religious, and very much of an intellectual. After a formal dinner, he would seek out the most attractive woman in the room, take her to a corner and spin for her fanciful tales of the hereafter. He always treated women with great respect. They felt safe with him and pleased to be admired for their intellect whether deserved or not.

For my father, any economic theory, which he thought correct, must inexorably result in a predictable chain of events, which would cause certain listed securities either to rise or fall. Security movements to him were the result of laws, not the psychology of the investing public. For my mother, the securities business was predictable in a very different manner. If you were attractive, glamorous, wealthy and dealt with the movers and shakers of this world, you would know what they knew, what they thought would happen, either to the stock market as a whole, or to individual securities which were of interest to one's friends, and one's judgment could be adjusted accordingly. My father had the theories (which could, of course, be adjusted to facts as known), but my mother was practical: if you knew what would happen, you could forget the theories. So long as they were together, they were a marvelous combination. My mother tempered my father's imagination; my father gave international and intellectual credibility to the business prospects of the likes of Durant of GM and Walter Chrysler, who otherwise might have had difficulty in the 1920s being accepted in the world of international finance, which was not yet centered in the United States.

My parents' success in society and in the business world enabled them to build an Italian villa at 23 East 83rd Street in Manhattan and to spend a year in Italy choosing furniture for it. I remember well the outside of the house. It was made of pink sandstone with a front door of massive oak which my parents had found in some Italian castle. Above the door were two pink stone Venetian lions. The first floor windows were bottled glass. To get into the house one walked down a few steps. Inside was a terra cotta floor, the elevator, and a magnificent curved stone staircase leading upstairs. On the next floor was the formal living room with curtains which could be drawn across the windows in the evening. Opposite was the dining room with a huge fireplace along one wall and a massive oak dining table with velvet covered chairs from an Italian castle. At the end of this room was an Italian fountain, and beyond, French doors leading to a garden terrace.

The floor above was my parents' floor with the master bedroom and bath in the back and a French boudoir sitting room in the front. It was there that my mother received her friends during the day. It was there that my sister, Alix, and I came down in the evening to spend a short time with my parents before they set out for dinner or went downstairs to receive their guests.

The third floor was where my sister and I and our governess each had our bedrooms.

After my parents furnished the house, it was frequently featured in magazines like *House and Garden, Vogue,* and *Town and Country.*

In the morning I would leave for Bovee School with my father a little before eight. The school was on 63rd Street and 5th Avenue. My father and I would go by bus—sitting, if there were room, on the top deck in the front row. It was my one chance to be with him quietly and I looked forward to it each morning when I woke up. As a small boy I didn't know why, but I was so very proud of my father and pleased to be his son and have him take me to school. David Rockefeller and Claiborne Pell—my school friends—were delivered to school by a governess, not like me, by their father. My father opened offices of his brokerage and banking house on each of the great French liners. He had brought each of his brothers into the firm. There was even talk in financial circles of the de Saint Phalle Bank as a 20th century successor to the Rothschilds. My father, Fal, managed New York; Alexandre, Paris; Claude, Germany, Switzerland and Poland; even Francois was taken out of the Baldwin Locomotive Works to head international corporate finance. Why did it all end?

It is hard to think back now on what life was like for those who had the means to enjoy it in the 1920s, particularly those, like my parents, who were at home and very much part of Society on both sides of the Atlantic Ocean, whether Paris, London or New York. The war had cost well over two million lives in Britain, France and Germany. The battles in the trenches had caused incredible suffering to those on the front lines. The wealth of all three nations had been to a great extent wiped out. Those who had survived wanted only to enjoy life, to love and be loved, to make money and spend it without regard for the future, to make up for the lost years of the war.

My parents were very much a part of this post-World War world. My father had become a highly successful stockbroker and investment banker. My mother had beauty, endless energy, spoke French and Italian like a native. My father was admired for his business success. My mother was an envied hostess. She made friends easily. She was intelligent, always well-dressed, loved people and parties, ready to take part in any activity, whether an opening at the Metropolitan Opera, a weekend in Cannes, a cruise on George Baker's yacht in the Caribbean, the opening of La Scala in Milan. She had done the Cresta Run in St. Moritz on a bobsled with the Duke of Spoleto, nephew of Italy's king. Rumor had it she had even flown under the Brooklyn Bridge in a small plane.

While Europe was trying to reconstruct itself from the ravages of four bitter years of war, the United States had become very wealthy from supplying the Allies with the weapons they needed. The country had entered the war in April 1917 on the side of Britain and France but its losses had not been great. After the war, with the adoption of Prohibition in the United States, Europe had become for Americans a playground, and for American business an opportunity. Paris became the divorce capital of the world. Donald Harper, an uncle of mine by marriage—his two daughters married two of my father's brothers—moved his law practice from Atlanta to Paris and became wealthy by counseling American women on how to shed their husbands while enjoying life in the French capital. Paris was excitement—for the rich, for intellectuals and writers, for all those who wanted to enjoy life. This was the city of Hemingway's *The Sun Also Rises*.

As always, there are few simple reasons for eventual failures or successes. Luck always plays its part. Looking back at my parents' experience, there were a number of factors, most of which could have been turned around had they realized their dependence on each other for their extraordinary success as a couple.

My mother had wanted to have numerous children, as her mother-in-law had. These two women had quickly established a special bond between them. To my French grandmother, my mother was sophistication personified. My mother was her window to the wide world, a world which was not her world, but which she enjoyed through the endless stories my mother brought to her in her chateau at Huez. When my mother was there, my grandmother brought her breakfast in bed and sat beside her all morning, vicariously sharing in my mother's life. My grandfather pretended to be outraged by this waste of time and its nefarious effect on the good order of his household. But he was very proud of what his sons were accomplishing and recognized that my mother's role, while he could not understand it, was very significant. He thought her success as a woman in a male society was the result of American influence.

Unfortunately, after two healthy babies, my younger brother was stillborn. Not being able to have further children, my mother diverted her life's purpose away from family and towards her own self-satisfaction. Beautiful and desirable, she was very much sought after. She became an integral part of Society at home, whether in New York, Paris, St. Moritz or the Riviera. As my mother enjoyed social events more, my father enjoyed them less and spent more time working. This was unfortunate for both of them. My mother had less time to advise him in business because she was away more often. My father spent less time with successful business associates and their wives, who were up-to-date with international events as they occurred. This kept him from being as aware as he should have been of economic trends.

It was not that we were abandoned as children. My sister and I had a very happy childhood. We lived in a beautiful house in New York, went to France each spring on an ocean liner, spent two months of the summer in Huez with our grandparents and our cousins, then spent a month in St. Moritz. As a child, one of my fondest memories was boarding the train in Paris, getting into bed and waiting for that wonderful mournful sound of the engine's whistle as the train was getting underway. I remember also the stop at Basel where they changed engines in the middle of the night. We loved our month at the Palace Hotel in St. Moritz. My father would take us for long walks in the mountains.

In those days the children of those fortunate enough to have money all had governesses. My sister and I were probably more fortunate than most children we knew because we had as our governess a wonderful woman from Ghent in Belgium who was intelligent, well-educated, sophisticated, and quietly determined to make sure that we would be well-read, fluent in several languages, competent in mathematics and history, and, like her, have a well-developed code of honor. Although physically attractive, she had never married. My sister and I used to think that this was because she had never met a man whom she thought worthy of her affection. We used to think she was secretly in love with my father, whom she held out to me as a model to be emulated. When she spoke to him, which was rarely, she always addressed him in French and it was always "Monsieur le Comte."

To us she was a guide, a friend, a teacher, a model. She had no need to be strict with us. Even learning from her was a pleasure to be shared. While Mimi, as we called her, was insistent that we spend time with friends our own age, we were more than happy to do things with her. Since my mother spent relatively little time with us, she would tell our governess to take us on trips whenever there was a chance to do so. So we went skiing in Switzerland—the three of us—explored the Riviera, visited Washington, spent time in museums and at the opera.

My mother was also very special to us then. She always made it a point to be in St. Moritz with my father when we were there, and took care to spend time with us. We always came to see her when she was having her breakfast in bed. She would tell us what she had been doing the night before and who was doing what in the social swirl of St. Moritz. We would plan our day and what we might do together. Come what may, she always spent a whole day a week just with us and then we would go on an adventure somewhere, a train ride to another town for lunch, a picnic up the mountain—something fun that is a special treat with one's mother. When my father was free, he joined us. When we were in New York or Paris, my mother would always spend one day a week with us. Our allowance was only 25 cents a week, but we would go off with her to spend it and as likely as not she might add a little or a lot more to buy something really nice. In Paris we went to Rumpelmayer's and had a chocolate ice cream or a cake at the end of the afternoon. My sister and I were extremely close as children. We talked endlessly together, she who was intellectual as my father was, and I the younger brother telling her endless stories about what I would accomplish when I grew up. When we went to Europe each spring on one of the great ocean liners, my mother would have ordered for us for shipboard delivery enough milk, heavy cream, eggs and thick bacon to make sure we would not lack anything by way of an American breakfast on board.

My mother was a tiny woman. She was 5´2˝ in height and wore size 3 shoes made especially for her in Perugia, Italy. She had a small Voisin motorcar which my father had bought for her in Paris and which she had brought back to New York in 1927. She would get in first and sit in the middle, then my sister and I would get in on either side of her. The chauffeur would cover us with a rug and then painfully get in the front seat which was only covered by a kind of tarpaulin to keep out the rain. My mother communicated with the chauffeur through a speaking tube hung on the side of the back of the car, or *tonneau*, as it was called. There was a single flower in a vase on either side which was changed every day and gave a freshness to the interior. My mother would say, "Here we are like three bugs in a rug," and tell the chauffeur to drive down 5th Avenue and stop at Schwarz if it was nearing Christmas time.

The best part of the summer was always the time we spent with my French grandparents. I had twenty-six first cousins on my father's side of the family and many of them were of the same age. With my grandfather we learned to ride and to feed the racehorses. There were three Shetland ponies at Huez and in the mornings all the grandchildren in turn were given riding lessons by my grandfather. When we could ride bareback without a halter, directing the pony with our knees, we were graduated to the racehorses.

My grandmother's rules were quite strict. Children should amuse

My granfather raises and trains racehorses at his chateau.

themselves, in their own way, exercising their imagination. There were endless simple things to do in or around a large house, with a vegetable garden, two ponds, a stream, a wood of endless acres, horse barns, a farm, and other children to play with. Every afternoon at four, my grandmother would take out a large illustrated Bible full of pictures and teach her grandchildren for an hour.

With my grandmother we learned about religion, and gardens, and strange medications which she used indiscriminately but very effectively on the horses, the grandchildren, and the sick of the farm and even the village, whom she visited every afternoon. She had a face which reflected the radiant beauty within her. She never was cross with us, although she was very firm, and we were all very careful not to cause her pain because she was so special to us.

As each child reached the age of four, he or she was given a small wheelbarrow painted the color of his choice and initialed. He also received a bucket and a shovel. Then at ten one received a bigger wheelbarrow. When a child was not there, the wheelbarrows, all twenty-eight of them, were hung on the walls of the carriage house under the barn. The first thing any child did when he or she arrived at Huez was to go with "grandmère" and bring down his or her wheelbarrow. When the war ended in Europe, the first thing I did was to go to Huez, despite the fact that both my grandparents were dead. There on the carriage house wall, I found all the wheelbarrows lined up, those of the dead as well as those of the living, waiting for the children to claim what was theirs. Not even the Germans who occupied the chateau for five years during World War II had touched them.

When we were older—eight or more—we received bicycles. When the uncles were there, particularly the younger ones who then became children themselves, uncles and grandchildren played a game which one of the uncles had invented, in the big round graveled yard in front of the chateau. The game consisted of riding bicycles around obstacles placed in the yard. Anyone who hit the obstacle or otherwise committed an error went to the end of the line. The head of the line was always the Kaiser and the person at the end was always Adolf. In the late 1920s and early '30s, no one paid attention to Hitler's pretensions in Germany. The uncles enjoyed themselves at Huez as much as we did. They had been very close as children since they did everything together and had never been away at school. They left their cares behind, paid no attention to their wives except to join in the teasing at meal time, became boys again, and played games with the grandchildren. They also took us fishing at nearby lakes and taught us how to swim. The system here was simple. It consisted of putting a rope under the child's arms, attaching it to a bamboo fishing pole, and throwing the child in the deep water near the dam. If the child started sinking, he was pulled up. But all of us soon learned to swim this way. The uncles were made of stern stuff. My grandfather had never spoiled them, and they in turn were stern with us. We loved it. They insisted that my grandfather not electrify the chateau. Oil lamps were more restful and made everyone retire early.

My Uncle Alexandre was generally the ringleader in all these games. He spent more time at Huez than the others because he lived in Paris and was particularly devoted to my grandmother, as she was to him. As a child, he had always been in trouble with his father because if he could find a shortcut to his studies, he would seize it, and grandpère did not take very well to having his authority flouted at any time. Alexandre once told me that his father had once given him a difficult mathematical problem to solve. It was a problem given to the students in their last term at the École Polytechnique because the answer was so impossibly difficult. Alexandre had gone to the attic and found both the problem and the answer in my grandfather's notebooks. The next day, after pretending to study all night, he gave his father the correct answer. His father had waited until the afternoon to call him into his study. "You have done something quite remarkable, Alexandre. Now tell me, please, how you arrived at this answer."

After some minutes of an attempted explanation, Alexandre was forced to admit that he had found his father's notebooks and simply taken the answer without studying the problem.

"Very well, then. Since you do not care to learn, I will not teach you anymore. You can spend your time playing with the boys in the village."

During the rest of the week while the others were studying with their father, Alexandre was left by himself. Finally, he went to his mother and the following week Alexandre was allowed to resume his lessons.

"I have never forgotten this lesson my father gave me," Alexandre told me. "I saw myself abandoned by my father, left to work like the farmers in the village. It was a terrible experience."

My grandfather's third original idea, after his decision about the inadequacy of the French educational system and his conclusion that the United States would be the country of the future, was to decide to raise racehorses in an area of France where this had never been tried before. The French, as we all know, are great traditionalists. One eats asparagus, or salt-fed lamb, or melons from such and such a date to such and such, never one day longer. One goes to the Riviera (or to Normandy or Brittany) in August but not in July; one doesn't go abroad except on business because French is not spoken and the food is poor; the United States is New York, New Orleans (for the food, and the Frenchness), San Francisco (because of its sophistication). The rest of the country is Indian country, with cowboys roaming the plains; the South should have won the Civil War, but Grant is the general studied at the French War College; the United States will someday turn to the Pacific as its sphere of interest and remove its troops from Europe because, after all, the Americans are Anglo-Saxons and hence unreliable allies in the long run. In France one need not have any curiosity about the rest of the world or ask foreigners what they think, because one simply knows. My grandfather was a great exception to the usual thinking in his country, his class and his generation. He was a genuine innovator. It is hard to understand where genetically he acquired this trait. Certainly not from the Saint Phalles. They had always been satisfied to serve God and country, and to prepare for the next world while living in this one. But the soil in this part of France was rich. It was where the famed Charollais beef came from. Why wouldn't racehorses be as happy there as in Normandy?

My grandfather Pierre had an uncanny eye to judge the condition of a racehorse. One day when the uncles were young, he had taken his wife and children as a treat to Longchamps in Paris. There he had bet and won every race. In no uncertain terms, Catherine had told him he had done great wrong in front of his children, and she made him promise never to bet again. He never did. When my father and one of the uncles later had racehorses, they would consult him frequently. He knew what he was talking about when it came to horses.

Next to the chateau, Pierre had some thirty-six stalls built for the horses. He also designed and built an exercise track. The fields on either side of the chateau had horses and cows in them. If one was lucky enough to occupy one of the ground floor bedrooms, it was likely that, if the wooden blinds were not closed in the morning, a horse might poke its head in looking for sugar. With many children about, cows, horses, a barnyard full of life, flowers and vegetable gardens, Huez was a very happy place in the summertime.

One of the reasons we children were so happy there is that we were left to our own devices. Aside from wheelbarrows, bicycles and horses to ride, there were no toys and no organized games, no croquet or tennis or golf. We invented games and each family had a weekly newspaper with cartoons which we exchanged on Saturdays.

It has meant for me a lifetime relationship with my French cousins and those American ones who also spent summers there. In France, where we spent summers, there were still big chateaus with farms attached during this time, and children were apt to be left there during the summer. This is where friendships for life were made. It was also where boys and girls of thirteen to fifteen begin to feel for a cousin of the opposite sex those first sentiments of love and the first pangs of desire. In that world of local gentry it can be said that the French always fall in love with their cousins. It is a love of notes exchanged, kisses stolen in the hay loft, seats claimed in the dining room at meals, swims, rides and walks taken together to exchange confidences. It was a particularly lovely time of life for those who were fortunate enough to have shared in it.

Part of the charm of that period of my life was that we were all terrified of my grandfather. When he growled, which was not infrequently, the whole house came to attention. The maids were silent in the kitchen, the dogs disappeared under the dining room table, and the children took to the outdoors. Only his wife, Catherine, remained totally unconcerned. At lunch, if my grandfather engaged in a tirade against one of his sons or against a daughter-in-law, my grandmother would bide her time and then say, "That's quite enough, Pierre." He would then immediately change the subject. He never argued or fought with her. To us, she was our protectress. And she took great care during the course of the summer to spend time with us individually, to know us better, and to impart wisdom and guidance related to our own capacity to understand. To me, she was God, and the Church, and goodness and generosity of spirit, all combined. I loved her dearly.

All of us have memories of our childhood that our parents would never guess. One of mine—when I was about eight—occurred at my grandfather's chateau. As usual, the twenty or so children in the house were seated at the smaller round table in one corner of the large, paneled dining room, while the parents and my grandparents, some dozen of them, sat at the beautiful polished oak table in the center of the room. As was his prerogative, my grandfather was talking, this time about a politician who was running for the Chamber of Deputies from our Department, the Nievre. "It was a poor choice," he said. "The man is too young, too inexperienced, to serve the nation adequately." I listened carefully, as did the other children. Could he be 15 we thought, or even 20? To be 20 was to be very wise in our calculations of wisdom and experience. As the discussion of the elders continued, we discovered that the candidate was 68. The French, like the Chinese, have a particular respect for age. How different in the United States with its reverence for youth!

How many people, in looking back on their life in the 20th century from the 21st, are able to call on a collective memory of a time prior to the French Revolution or the birth of the United States? My earliest recollection was when I was four years old on the terrace outside my grandfather's chateau in France on a summer day, being lifted up by my nurse and placed on the lap of a very old woman, whom I was later told was 104 years old, my great great great grandmother, who was born in Paris in 1818. What I remember quite clearly even today at the start of the 21st century was the stories she would tell me—this very old, small, fragile woman dressed in white and wearing a white bonnet—about sitting on her own father's lap when she was my age—her father who wore knee britches and a green velvet jacket covered with sunburst medals because he was a minister on Louis XVIII's cabinet. Her father would tell her stories—and now she passed them on to me—of the balls, which he had attended in Versailles as a young man before the terrors of the French Revolution of 1789. These stories were very vivid to her then, and now she made them equally vivid to me—a little boy sitting on her lap as she had sat on her father's knees in 1822. So I had strayed back at the age of four into a world of pageantry and pleasure antedating the American Revolution or the demise of the Ancien Regime in France. I hated to be taken off the old lady's lap.

My grandparents only had one daughter, Genevieve, to make up for the seven sons. She was beautiful, talented and brought up with boys— a hellion. I remember her once arriving at Huez in a bright red racing car, which her brothers had bought for her. When she was 18, she had gone to the United States visiting brothers in New York, Philadelphia and Washington, each of whom gave a party for her. When she came back, she went to see her father in his study to tell him quietly that if what he and her mother had taught her about earning the life hereafter was correct, she intended to become a Benedictine nun. "I love life too much," she said, "not to seize everything it has to give. If I do that, I am sure to get into trouble. But you have taught me to love the Lord and now I will spend my life in his service." It was a terrible blow for my grandfather, even more so than for my grandmother who could take

I absorb
French
history and
the Roman
Catholic
religion.

pride that her daughter wished to give her life to God. I accompanied the two of them in their Ballot motorcar in September 1928 to Dourgne in the south of France when my godmother Genevieve, after a full year of preparation, took her final vows. I was only ten. I had never seen my grandfather weep before and was frightened. But I had a private meeting with my godmother after the ceremony—she in her black gown and white veil looking ever so happy. I wanted then and there to stay at Dourgne. To please me, I was allowed to spend a week in the monastery, getting up three times in the night to pray as the monks did. The peace of that monastery made a profound impression on me.

The Past as Prologue

In 1928, my mother and father decided to move to Paris where the headquarters of the international banking operations of the family firm, de Saint Phalle & Co., were to be centered at the Place Vendome. My mother rented an enormous and beautiful house on the Place des Etats Unis, which was subsequently to become notorious as the headquarters of the Gestapo in Paris during World War II. It had a large garden in the back and the most beautiful formal circular staircase I have ever seen. It belonged to the Marquise de Brantes, a rather famous Frenchwoman who had for years been the mistress of a Chinese marshal who ruled Manchuria. When he died, I am told, she returned to Paris with the red lacquer bed they had shared and redesigned her bedroom to resemble a Chinese royal tent with black silk-covered walls. It was certainly effective as a conversation piece. The master bathroom was also effective. The bathtub was in the center of a huge room, a tiled octagonal pool with a fountain. None of the normal facilities were apparent. They were located in separate cubicles at the end of the room on either side of an enormous dressing table. There were also couches and divans on either side of the pool. It was a reception room rather than a bathroom.

My father and his brothers establish an international banking operation.

Neither my sister nor I had wanted to spend a winter in Paris. In the winter we felt like Americans. School was always easy and we had our friends in New York. My parents had huge dinner parties each week, generally white-tie affairs. When the guests came, we sat at the railing above the staircase and watched them arrive. My favorite recollection was that of Andre Citroen, the famous automobile manufacturer, arriving one evening. He had so many medals that he had pinned the ones that did not fit on the front of his tailcoat onto his trousers. We were very impressed. Another memory of that winter in Paris was being sent to a French school, the École de Normandie. As an American whose sole exposure to education was the Bovee School on Fifth Avenue in New York where I spent my days with Pells, Morgans and Rockefellers, I was totally unprepared for the French educational system, even in a school supposedly as Americanized as the École de Normandie. At the age of ten, my classmates were studying Greek, Latin and algebra. I understood nothing of what was going on, was desperately homesick, and at the first available opportunity, packed a small bag and stood at the side of the road outside the gates until someone appeared who was going to Paris and would take me there. Twice my mother took me back quietly; twice I repeated the same performance. My father was purposely kept unaware of what was going on. But after the second attempt at escape, Monsieur Daudet, the headmaster, called my father to tell him he would not accept his son's return because the boy was quite evidently incapable of being educated. My father was furious. To save the day, my mother declared that there must be something seriously wrong with me physically, and took me to the American hospital to have my appendix out. This is always a safe way for mothers to protect their offspring from angry fathers, since the appendix is a totally useless organ and might just as well be taken out before it has occasion to become inflamed and burst. So the day was saved. After I recovered, I was sent to the Lycée Louis le Grand in Paris. That was an even worse horror because the boys there were even further advanced than those at the École de Normandie. I was happy when in the fall of 1929 my parents returned to New York.

Aside from school, my sister and I were not unhappy in Paris. In addition to our beloved governess, the house was awash in help. My mother had her personal maid who accompanied her everywhere she went. My father had his valet. There was also a maitre d'hotel (who spoiled us with little sandwiches), footmen in livery, a cook and kitchen maid, and a laundress.

Little then did I know that the family bank had taken its first great hit through its financing of the great Swedish match king, Ivar Kreuger. When Kreuger's firm went bankrupt and he supposedly killed himself in a private airplane on the way from Stockholm to London, both the family firm and its clients lost a great deal of money. The following year my Uncle Francois claimed that he saw Kreuger in Britain, but before he could get to him, the man had disappeared in a crowd. The only client of my father's who escaped the carnage was a very rich Boston lady who told my father she would not invest unless she met the man. She then went to Stockholm. There, she discovered that he was endeavoring to grow palm trees on his Swedish estate. She returned to Boston and advised my father that anyone who was silly enough to grow palm trees in Scandinavia could not be trusted with inherited money from Boston. How right she was!

My father returned to New York in the summer of 1929 and rented for the family, at 907 5th Avenue on the corner of 72nd Street, a floor-through apartment for $18,000 a year, a vast sum of money in those days. He had become convinced, as the financial pressure on him grew and as his relationship with my mother became more distant, that the only way their life together could recover a certain harmony was for him to keep up a style of living which he thought she required. How much better it would have been if he could have sacrificed his pride and quietly told her how bad things had become at the firm! I am convinced she would have responded. But he kept his situation as much a secret as he could. On our return by ship from Europe that fall, my mother was aghast at what he had done. We returned just in time for the Great Crash of October 1929, which finished what the Kreuger affair had started: the end of the de Saint Phalle banking empire. Neither my father nor my uncles understood what was happening. They lost not only their own wealth but also that of my grandfather who, in his pride in his sons' achievements, had given them his money to invest. My father never recovered from this disaster and took refuge in the Rosicrucian religion. His dressing room that year was my bedroom. On the dresser was a wonderful figure of Christ, emblem of this simple and strange religion, with beams of light shining forth. I remember that my bed was a great four-poster, and that my father, as he was dressing for dinner, would tell me stories of the great business leaders of the day. He was very kind to me that year. Perhaps he knew what difficult days would lie ahead for his children and wanted this last year to be a pleasant one. I was unaware of his financial difficulties; I attended the Buckley School, was first in my class and promoted at mid-year to the class above. The events of Wall Street failed utterly to penetrate the school. I was a serious child. I remember that winter reading a four-volume history of the United States Navy and a book on the origins of the First World War. I never could get enough to read.

In the spring of 1930, my sister and I were asked one day to join my mother and father for dinner. After dinner we sat in the library and looked at folders outlining the charms of Brioni, an island in the Adriatic, Majorca off the coast of Spain, and Bermuda. In those days, islands were considered as inexpensive places to go to weather the Crash. We were proud to be consulted and would have chosen Brioni, but it was decided that we should go to Bermuda because my mother could go back and forth easily and my father would be able to visit. So spring saw us on the *Queen of Bermuda* headed for what turned out to be a two-year stay. My mother rented a house near the Inverurie Hotel in Paget and secured the services of a retired English Protestant pastor to teach us mathematics and English literature.

For my mother this was a difficult time, but she made friends everywhere she went. In Bermuda in those days, there were no cars, only carriages and bicycles and, consequently, the island seemed much bigger than it does today. It was also much more fun. My sister and I were given bicycles, and for $50 I got a skiff that next summer when we moved to a white stucco house known as the Windsor Cottage which was the furthermost house on the road beyond the golf club at Tucker's Town. We also became good practicing Catholics that summer because my sister and I were made to bicycle to church in Hamilton every Sunday morning, a trip, there and back, of twenty miles. That summer was very special for me: I lived in a small one-room buttery off of the main house, I read Conan Doyle, I went fishing at night with the Portuguese fishermen, I slept in my boat, I paid no attention to my mother, and I fell in love with the daughter of a neighbor who subsequently married a justice of the Supreme Court. No one would have predicted this fate for her then. She wore freckles, was a tomboy and a tennis player, with big grey eyes and a mischievous grin. I was mad about her.

In the fall, my father's financial worries were, if anything, more acute, and my mother decided to return to the United States. So Alix and I were shipped to boarding school in Somerset on the other side of the island, near Gibb's lighthouse. There was a boy's school and, on the other side of a newly built railroad trestle, a girl's school. Somers College, as it was known, was run by an Anglican reverend and his wife (surely from the Scottish Church) and strictly sought to pattern itself after the more famous English public schools. My housemaster, Mr. Kerry, was a sadist who flogged the boys whenever an excuse justified this. But I must say I learned how to speak, read and write the English language properly, how to do mathematics using pounds, shillings and pence, and above all how to be self-disciplined. There were good times as well. I became one of two house prefects, and became adept at bicycle polo, a fiercely destructive game where one sought to swing one's mallet between the spokes of the opponent's bicycle to prevent him from reaching the ball. We also caught huge sharks at night with a line and chain and a hook six inches long. The great event of the year was

24

the opening of the railroad, which went from one end of Bermuda to the other. The line passed through the school grounds. The opening of the railroad featured the governor, in tailcoat and top hat, riding in a handcar propelled by two enormous blacks, from one end of the line to the other. As the governor passed through Somers College, we stood in our school blazers and caps and shouted, "Hip, hip hooray!" It was all very English.

I look back to my days at Somers College with nostalgia. As compared to the French system of education, the English seem to have great advantages. It was less learning than adjusting to a code of expected behavior. A boy in England had to learn self-discipline, self-control, and how to ignore pain. He had to learn to speak the English language properly, to respect his parents, to be loyal to his country, and to be dismissive of foreigners.

As I reflect now on the various schools that I briefly attended under three different national systems of education—the American, the French, and the English—it seems clear to me that each is designed to bring about a quite different result. In the United States, a man is not educated. He is trained for a profession, be it law, medicine, the sciences, business. This means he wastes his time through high school and college and then studies extremely hard to learn what from then on will be his profession. It means further that upon retirement there may be nothing for him to enjoy doing outside of playing golf, because he is not truly an educated person and is not at home with books. He must have people to talk to or games to play.

The English system sought to accomplish something quite different. Its purpose was twofold: to train a man who might later go off to the far-flung lengths of an Empire, to be self-disciplined and in control of his emotions at all times. The British and Japanese are not dissimilar in this regard. The other purpose is, of course, to teach students how to read, write and spell the English language correctly. This means that an educated man in England can enjoy his literature, both before and after retirement.

In France education has to be earned. Napoleon, who created the educational system, as he created the legal system and much else in modern France, was a Corsican who had had to earn his French mathematical education to become an artillery officer. The system ruthlessly winnows out those who cannot learn. None of the nonsense of Affirmative Action or rigged tests to allow the unprepared to participate. All children are treated alike in the educational system. If you can't pass the examinations given each year, you learn a trade. The best trade schools are in France. It is not a class system but a strict aptitude system. It means that an educated man in France is truly educated, but it does not assure either his self-discipline as in Britain or make him a truly competitive professional in his chosen line of work as in the United States.

In the spring of 1932, Alix and I returned to the United States. My parents by then had a small apartment on East 67th Street opposite the police station. I slept on a couch in the living room, and my sister had a cot in my mother's dressing room. My father was spending his evenings, when there were no dinners my parents had to go to, with his Rosicrucian friends, while my mother dined with rich Americans or with White Russians or Italians.

In 1932, my mother was only 40 years old. She was still a very beautiful woman. My father had been totally thrown off balance by the disaster which had overtaken the family firm into which he had brought his brothers. Like an incandescent candle, the firm had succeeded beyond anyone's imagination. It had now failed just as quickly and my father and his brothers—and their father—had lost everything. Unlike money in Wall Street, my father believed he had a personal obligation to his clients and those of his firm. Somehow he would get back on his feet, reestablish his business reputation, and make his clients whole. But there was no way he could accomplish this in the economic situation which was worsening everyday. He might have said to my mother: "We had a wonderful experience which we created together. Now together we will turn the situation which has befallen us around. We can only succeed if we bring this about by working together." It didn't happen that way. My father went back to being a stockbroker.

My mother had gone to work at the Salon Moderne at Saks Fifth Avenue where her rich friends bought very expensive clothes, relying on her judgment and her taste. She was still a leader of Society, and was paid handsomely to advertise products like Bisquick or Pond's Cold Cream. Her ability to make money was unaffected by the Depression. But she philosophized that my father was at fault for not being able to support her and for not having seen what was going to happen to the stock market, putting money aside and creating trusts for her and the children when he could have. She had concluded that it was a man's duty to support his wife and children. Yes, she would work, but she would not let him forget what he had done to her and to his children.

Naturally, my parents' successful business friends were of no help. They declared my father a loser and recommended that my mother divorce him.

My mother's reaction was very unfortunate. With her good looks, her standing, and her energy and determination, my mother could have kept the ship afloat and given my father the moral support he so badly needed. But the pressure was too great. Despite the efforts of each of my parents to keep their marriage intact, they were continuing to drift apart.

It was easy to see that the four of us could not continue to live in a tiny New York apartment. Alix and I were sent to France for a year to stay with my grandparents.

Huez was not the same as it had been. My grandfather had had to sell all his racehorses, and all the grooms were gone except old Gaby, who as a young boy had been his orderly when grandpère was a cavalry officer serving as Marshall Foch's aide de camp in World War I. He had been with him ever since, in charge of the stables. He had taught the uncles, as he later taught the grandchildren, how to care for horses. He was now in his 70s and as loyal as ever. My grandfather spent much time alone in his study, reading his precious *Revue des Deux Mondes* and trying to bring a degree of rational thinking to what had happened to his sons, and so clearly, through their misfortunes, to himself.

My grandfather decided Alix and I were hopelessly backward in our education and that he would have to remedy this situation promptly. After all, he had done it once with his own children. Why would it be any more difficult to educate two American grandchildren? My grandmother thought this a good idea because activity would cure his melancholy. To our consternation, he plunged into this challenging effort with remarkable determination. He had found in the attic two copies of *Caesar's Commentaries* written in old French of the 18th century. Even though the accompanying dictionary was clearly inadequate, he blithely assigned to us the first three pages as homework for the next day. We had only Ritchie's *First Steps* going back to 1930 at Buckley and Miss Hewitt's and were obviously unprepared for Caesar. Nevertheless—and this shows what fear of the instructor can do—by the time we returned to the United States, Alix and I had not only mastered all of *Caesar's Commentaries* but could converse with each other in Latin. As a result, I was able to take the Latin Comprehensive Examination several years later and enter Harvard that year as the first student in 25 years to have

My grandfather undertakes my education.

received a grade of 100 percent in this college board test. This shows what fear can do to instill learning. There were times, indeed, when I thought we would not survive. When we failed a weekly test—which was frequently—my grandfather would let out a roar heard in the village. My grandmother would burst in to tell him of some disaster in the kitchen or at the farm, and while he was gone, my sister and I would leap out of the window and head for the woods behind the chateau to be gone for the rest of the day. We not only learned Latin, we learned psychology and the art of survival.

Riding with my grandfather, on the other hand, was a joy. He still had two riding horses and at 78 still rode two hours a day. Since he did not like to ride alone and we were the only members of the family at Huez for most of that year, grandpère would take me with him. He not only taught me the finer points of riding and caring for a horse, but he would talk to me about himself, stories from his life, his philosophy, his love of God and his country. I began to learn a little of what this frightening old man was really made of. He even had a sardonic sense of humor. He was the mayor of the local village and before election time, as we rode through the countryside included in the electoral district, my job was to note how many of the voters addressed him: "Good morning, mayor"—a no vote—with those who addressed him: "Good morning, Count"—a clear yes.

I feared the old man but I loved and respected him as well. And I thought that if he lived long enough, he would also want to take credit later on for what I might be able to accomplish, as he had years earlier, in the case of his sons.

When we left Huez in the spring of 1933, I did not realize that I would never see my grandfather and grandmother alive again. By the time we left, they were our roots and a substitute for our parents. Although my mother had come over to be with us at Christmas, selling her remaining jewelry to pay for the trip and bringing gifts from New York, including, to my grandfather's particular horror, a plum pudding and hard sauce, our ties to the United States and home once again had been cut.

When we returned to New York, little had changed for the better. My mother had, in a final expenditure of capital, rented the James Forrestal cottage in Long Island for the summer.

One day that August my father called me into the library of the cottage.

"Do you want to go to work or continue to go to school?" he asked.

"I don't know what work is, and I don't particularly like school, but I think I would prefer school."

"Then figure it out for yourself."

That was the last discussion I ever had with my father on this subject. I still have a perfect memory of that day—it was the sudden realization that I would have to sink or swim on my own. I was as unprepared at barely 14 as I suspected my father must have been when he left for the United States at 16 in 1911.

The Chateau de Cudot in Yonne, France was in the author's family since the 13th century. It had been a fortress since Roman days. It was destroyed by the English during the Hundred Years War, and rebuilt from the ground up in the 16th century.

The St. Phalle family coat of arms is on the ceiling of the Palace of Versailles, along with the coats of arms of other French noble families who fought in the Crusades.

The author's great, great, great, great grandfather, the Duc de Mortemart, in his court regalia. He would tell his baby daughter held on his knee stories of the Court of Versailles before the French Revolution. She in turn told these same stories to the author as he rested in her lap when she was 104 years of age.

As a child, the author spent summers with his grandparents at the
Chateau de Huez in Nievre, France, where his grandfather
raised and trained racehorses.

This photo of Genevieve de Saint Phalle, the author's aunt and godmother, was taken on the day of her final vows as a Benedictine nun at Dourgne, France in 1928.

The author's father and mother attend the races in Longchamps, Paris, in October of 1928. They moved from New York to Paris in 1927.

II

THE STUDY YEARS

I *HAVE NEGLECTED SO FAR* to say very much about my sister except to say how very close we were as children. That is, indeed, very true. We were alone or with our governess a good deal of the time. We were sufficiently close in age—one and one-half years apart—that we were reaching stages of maturity at approximately the same time. My sister was far more intellectual than I. She could hold philosophical discussions with my father, whereas these bored me. I was interested in history, especially military history. I read books like the *Origins of World War I* and books on the Civil War when I was twelve. I read everything I could find on French history, English history, and European history. I found American history less interesting because it was more about economics than about people and why they did what they did. When I talked to my father it was about people; when my sister talked to him it was about ideas. I was pragmatic, very much like my mother; Alix was much more like my father, and I am sure he was fonder of her than of me, although he didn't show it. As far as I was concerned, I think he was terribly disappointed by my failure to "stick it out" at the College de Normandie. In his world, no matter how great the pain, you "saw it through." He didn't understand why every time I went away to school or to camp, I immediately had a temperature of 103 degrees, brought on by homesickness. His father would not have accepted this kind of behavior from his sons, and my father didn't see why he should. While I was always first in my class, as indeed my sister was, I think my father suspected that I would never be tough enough to cope with life. He did not understand where my extreme sensitivity came from, because it was not apparent on my mother's side of the family and certainly not on my father's side either. I was the original homebody. Now, in 1933, my home was shattered, my parents were headed for divorce court, and my father had cast me out on my own. I now did the obvious. I talked to my mother.

My mother immediately took charge. She had wanted me to go to St. Paul's in New Hampshire, but that school would obviously not take me because I had not filled their requirements, as my educational experience had been bizarre, to say the least: in turn, Bovee, no school in France, Buckley, no school, a year at Somers College, in Bermuda, then no school again in France. Where was the record of scholastic accreditation required by American schools? My mother decided she would have to find a school which for one reason or another would be interested in taking on a special student as an intellectual challenge. On top of this, the school would have to have enough of an endowment to give her son a scholarship.

Pomfret School in Connecticut proved to be the answer. Through friends of my parents, an introduction to Halleck Lefferts, headmaster of Pomfret, was arranged. He had just come East from being headmaster at the Thatcher School in California. He was as unlike an Eastern headmaster of the time as it was possible to be: laid-back, informal, open and friendly. Very intelligent, he had come to take over a famous old school that had fallen on difficult times because a remarkable headmaster had died and been succeeded by the school chaplain, who was totally unable to maintain discipline. As a result, the boys had taken up drinking, going off on weekends without authorization, and paying no attention to their studies. Worse, the students were unable to get into the colleges that their fathers had attended. Since I had obtained excellent grades whenever I had gone to school, Lefferts could at any rate count on one of his fifth-formers being able to pass the college boards and be accepted in college. Lefferts also agreed that the school would absorb room and board for the two years I would be spending at Pomfret. My mother had obtained the recommendation of a Pomfret resident, Admiral Luis Florez, a naval aviator and one of the authentic heroes of the U.S. Navy's Bureau of Aeronautics, who had proved willing to put in a good word for me. So that is how I started at Pomfret as a fifth-former in the fall of 1933, along with some twenty members of the original second-form class who had survived that far.

American boarding school was a new experience for me. Keeping up with my studies would be no problem because American schools were so far behind those in Europe. In terms of social relationships, it was a different world for me. My classmates had not traveled as I had. They came from very similar, upper middle-class backgrounds. They had been together at Pomfret already several years. They were also older than I. In accordance with boarding school practice at the time, we had one Jewish boy and one English boy on scholarship. There were two Catholics, DeWitt Alexandre, who would be captain of the football team, and myself, who wouldn't be captain of anything. What I did do for the school was to win all the academic prizes and get into Harvard with two 100s, one 90, and one 85 on my college entrance examinations. Above all, I finally conquered my homesickness, but it took the loss of my home to do it. In this I must also credit the members of my class. They didn't understand me, but they accepted me even though I was really joining them too late to "belong." They had at once great integrity and a sense of humor. They were uncomplicated and unemotional. I liked them.

Intellectually, the faculty was, in my view, uninteresting, with only one exception: a brilliant professor of French, German, Greek and advanced Latin named Aldis Hatch. Aldis became my friend, gave me employment doing research on a book he was writing on Ovid in the summer of my senior year, and stimulated my intellectual curiosity. He was that unfortunate rare man, the hermaphrodite who is drawn to both men and women but whose appetite is great in both directions. At Pomfret he left the boys alone but seduced two of the faculty wives, so far as I could detect without the knowledge of their husbands. I also discovered later that he had come to Pomfret from a small Midwestern college after recovering from a bullet wound received from a faculty colleague whose wife had become his mistress. Aldis was well aware of his problem: In our senior year he told me he had decided to marry a very nice, wholesome daughter of a New Yorker who had moved to Pomfret on his retirement. But first he would finish his book on which I would help him. In return he promised me a monthly salary for the summer and house parties which he would organize on weekends with girls he knew at Arthur Murray's dance studios in New York who would be delighted to spend weekends on the Cape. For twenty-five dollars a month—yes, twenty-five dollars a month—Aldis rented a four-bedroom house at Dennis on Cape Cod. The work I was given to do was not arduous, the weekends fun, the Arthur Murray dance teachers more than willing to teach me dancing and other social graces, and my last summer before Harvard went swiftly by.

My mother had gone to Europe that summer with my sister. My father remained in New York trying to recoup his fortunes in a brokerage firm where my youngest uncle, Andre, was working. On weekends my father generally went to Newport, attended dinner parties with the older set and played bridge for high stakes in the hope of winning.

When I left Aldis on the Cape at the end of the summer, I thought I had earned enough to need no additional pocket money for my first term at Harvard. But I would not be able to spend anything in the meantime. I had an invitation to go to Newport for tennis week, and I thought I would go and try to see my father at the same time. Aldis was going off to Pomfret to become formally engaged to his girl.

The following year he married her. They had two boys. When the war broke out, Aldis joined the Office of Strategic Services. While he was away in London, his wife caught one of their little boys masturbating, which is normal at that age. But she saw the boy becoming like the father, who had caused her so much suffering, and she took a knife and killed both her sons. She was acquitted on the grounds of temporary insanity. Hers became one of the famous stories on the nature of violence in the courses on psychology. Not having heard the story, and not having seen Aldis since that summer on the Cape, I was in Washington on my way into the OSS building to pick up my travel orders one night in 1943 when I saw Aldis coming out wrapped in a great cloak. He murmured something and passed on into the night. His face was ravaged and gaunt. I do not know what happened to him thereafter.

I took a night bus trip from the Cape to Newport, Rhode Island. In Newport, I walked up Bellevue Avenue on a Friday morning around nine o'clock, up the driveway to the Fosdick house, and rang the doorbell. An impeccably dressed butler came to the door. "I would like to see Mr. de Saint Phalle. I am his son," I said. "Just a minute, I will see if his Lordship is awake." I was not asked to come in. My father came down in his silk dressing gown which had surely been purchased for him at Charvet, Paris and given to him by my mother for Christmas in 1928 before the Depression. "I'm rather short of funds," I added. "I thought I'd see how you were fixed." "I have no money either," he said and turned back into the house. I was on my way to spend tennis week at Governor Sherman's house. His daughter was coming out the following week and had invited me. I spent a glorious week going to balls each night.

Sunday night I went down to the Fall River line pier. The line carried passengers by ship from Fall River to Newport and then on to New York. In return for free transportation, I agreed to take my turn at stoking the ship's furnace, while my friends with whom I had been enjoying the week were sleeping soundly in their cabins. At barely seventeen, one takes life as it comes. It meant nothing to me to have gone from evenings of white tie and tails, champagne and eighty-piece orchestras to stoking a furnace at sea.

When I graduated from Pomfret I was intellectually very advanced for my age. In terms of social maturity, I knew very little. One of my Pomfret classmates and I had decided that we would room together at Harvard. His name was Barker Slade. He came from Barrington, Rhode Island, where his father owned a small textile mill which he had sold after retiring. His parents had expressed the wish to meet me, so I spent a weekend in Barrington after graduation. Following dinner on Saturday night, I asked Mr. Slade if there was a Catholic church in Barrington to which I could go on Sunday morning. Once in bed that evening there was a knock on the door of the guest room and Barker came in. "My father wants to know," he said, "if your father is in domestic service." "No, he was a banker, and is now a stockbroker in New York. Why do you ask?" "Because up here the Catholics we know are domestic servants or work in the mills." A great deal has changed in New England since 1935! I was astounded to learn that there were prejudices against Catholics and Jews among Americans who were both educated and wealthy. Curiously, I had never up to this time of my life run across religious prejudice in my family on either side of the ocean or anywhere else in Europe or in New York. I would be made aware of this later during my law school days when I tutored the Sulzberger children on weekends. I had never run across racial prejudice, either, because in those days there were relatively few blacks in the North and there were, of course, no Hispanics. Religious intolerance and racial prejudice which I see so often today was then a surprising discovery for me. Because the United States today is making much more of an effort to become a multiracial society than Europe, Japan, China or the Soviet Union, race relations in the country have tended to become more open but also more difficult. I later discovered just how difficult when I would become counsel to the government of Haiti.

Barker and I had a suite of rooms on the top floor of Strauss Hall in the Yard. It had two bedrooms and a living room with a fireplace. At that time Harvard College was considered one of the largest private colleges in the nation. Our class set a new record for Harvard. There were 1000 students. Today, when there are so many more colleges and universities in the nation, and so many more students, one thousand students would not be considered a large class. After we had been there a day or so, I received a visit from the head of the Latin Department inviting me to join his class in Medieval Latin. It was a great honor for a freshman and would have taught me the link between Latin and the Romance languages of today, but I thanked him and refused. In those

Harvard gives me its maximum scholarship grant.

39

The
Study
Years

I write
my first
book, on
the French
Revolution.

days, freshmen had to take a number of core courses: European history, economics, English literature, one language. I proposed to major in history and made my only real effort of the year in Professor Merryman's European history course, where in the second semester one had the chance to write a treatise equivalent to a book. I chose to write a life of Maximilian Robespierre, a medical doctor, and the last and most ruthless survivor of the Revolutionary leaders after he had executed the others. I spent long hours in the stacks of Widener Library reading newspapers from the time of the French Revolution. What an incredible repository of knowledge is Widener! They not only had the newspapers of Paris of the period, but of Lyon, Marseilles, Bordeaux and other cities. I became lost in the debates of the day. I felt I knew not only Robespierre, the demoniac purist doctor, but Danton, the Girondists, and many others. There was a prize given for the best treatise. I made the finals but didn't win. At the end of the year, while I was on the dean's list, my grades certainly didn't justify the very large scholarship which I had been given on the basis of my entrance examinations.

Why was I so irresponsible as to allow this to happen when I had always done so well in my studies? With my incoming record I had been expected to be one of the leaders of my class in scholarship. I suppose part of the problem was my immaturity and that I had managed so easily to make enough money to meet my basic needs in college. The friends I had made at Harvard were no help to me either. They came from solid, closely-knit families largely untouched by the economic depression and college to them was essentially a period of time to be enjoyed, to make friends for life, to engage in sports, to learn a little, to pass unobtrusively from childhood to maturity.

It would have helped if there had been an older man with whom I could have talked and who could have advised me. But there wasn't. My father was of no help to me. He was lost in his new religion, was trying to make enough money to pay the creditors of the Saint Phalle firm—he was the only one of the brothers who had refused to accept the bankruptcy of the firm to clear the partnership debts which he considered to be his personal obligation. He managed to do so by playing bridge at the Racquet and Tennis Club in New York every afternoon for high stakes and going to the horse races where he often won on Saturdays. He was an excellent bridge player, had a keen mathematical sense, and an unusual power of concentration. But his own father, after educating his sons in a code of honor and a strong work ethic, had never given them advice or guidance afterward. And my father simply assumed that

I could take care of myself as he had when he came to the United States at 16, not speaking any English, and having to make his way in a strange country. My mother, who had been of such help to me in getting into Pomfret, now assumed that since I was in college, I would be able to function well on my own, without advice or help from her.

I have often wondered why I was so stupid. I had the opportunity despite all odds to attend Harvard and to learn from great scholarly minds in fields that had always been of interest to me. How could it happen that a man who has since then spent a lifetime trying to learn would fail to take advantage of spending four years at one of the great universities of the world? I had the chance and I didn't take it. Why? It is easy to say that I was unprepared for the freedom that college gave me to do anything I wanted. Since I did not have money to spend in my new freedom, I should at least have concentrated on my studies. Instead I probably rebelled against the hand I had been dealt. I did take up rowing and made the freshman light-weight crew which was a new and exciting experience. I went to Boston parties and I wrote my book on the French Revolution, but I wasn't growing as a person and I didn't really feel at home with myself. It was a confused time for someone who couldn't find himself. At the end of the year, the dean explained to me that my scholarship would be cut and that I would have to do better the next year if I wanted to have it renewed. Even this did not shake me into concentration.

My freshman summer, the Harvard placement bureau arranged for me to try out for the job of tutor and teacher of sailing for a family that owned a property on Jackson Lake in Wyoming. The job paid very well. My only sailing experience had come that spring when a group of us chartered a schooner called the *Heart's Desire* to cruise down to New London for the Harvard-Yale boat races. Aside from grounding the boat in South Boston on our way out of the harbor and running out of fuel coming back in a dead calm just south of the canal, the trip had been great fun. There were several good sailors aboard and they taught me what they could of nautical terms.

In any event, I survived the summer successfully. Mrs. Berol was extremely nice to me. Her son, Kenneth, whose tutor I was, had attended a sailing camp on Long Island the summer before. He knew far more than I did. But I was older. I had gone down to Brentano's before taking the Northern Pacific to Billings, Montana, where the Berols would meet me. I had bought all the books on sailing I could find and then read them assiduously all the way out on the train, trying to remember words like gaff, luff, mizzen, stem, cleat, centerboard, clew, reef, block, and their application. Imagine my consternation when I discovered the Snipe we were to sail had arrived in kit form. "Since you have been to sailing school, Kenneth," I said, "let's see how much you learned last year. I am going to let you unpack the crate, step the mast, install the fittings where they belong, attach the rudder and attach the sails." Then I sat on the dock and watched him. Thank God, he had been taught well. Often that summer I wondered whether that lovely woman, his mother, knew how little I knew about sailing. I didn't dare tell her until two years later, but then she gave an evasive answer in a kindly way and I am still not sure. At any rate, Ken and I learned together that summer that winds on a large mountain lake could blow from one direction, and then turn around suddenly and blow from the opposite direction, sometimes with great force.

The Berol ranch had been grandfathered out of the Jackson Hole State Park. It was right on the lake with a glorious view of the Tetons across the way. The whole region was then very wild. There were horses to ride, guests to sit around the fireplace with in the evenings. Imagine spending a summer like that and getting paid for it! At the end of the summer we even went to Sun Valley for a few days of rainbow trout fishing in the Snake River with a guide named Slim who was able to cast a fly 100 yards away and bring in a fish with each cast! Sun Valley had just opened the year before as a ski resort. The local cowboys with their legs in parentheses wanted to be ski instructors. They tried to teach me lassoing while I tried to help them simulate telemarks and christies. Neither of us made great progress!

I returned to New York at the end of the summer, fit, tanned and exhilarated, to find my mother and sister just returned from Europe and my father living in a one-room studio apartment on East 57th Street. My mother and sister had spent the summer with English friends of my mother's in Cannes. My sister was in love with a young man from Philadelphia whom she had met there. She had had trouble adjusting to the sophistication of life among the English expatriates of the Riviera, but my mother was at home there. She hated to return to her work in New York.

One afternoon my father took me to the races and gave me $20 to bet with. We studied the *Morning Telegraph* carefully before going. I was determined to make the $700 I needed to supplement my reduced scholarship. I let the first race go by, ignored the steeplechase that followed (horses fall) and bet half the twenty in the third race, recovering

$100. I then waited until the seventh race to bet on a beautiful roan named Grog. The horse was last at the stretch when, all of a sudden, it took off to win by two lengths. The $100 I had bet turned into $800. I subsequently used to tell my classmates at college that I went to Harvard on a daily double! So are the wages of sin sometimes rewarded. Now that I think back to those days, it seems extraordinary that tuition at Harvard was only $400 a year and rent only a little more. After that experience, I learned little at Harvard my second year except in math and history. I made the varsity lightweight crew, I learned lovemaking from the Polish girls of Lawrence, Massachusetts, and I disgraced myself with my tutor, Professor Crane Brinton, an eminent expert on modern French history. He asked me one day at what period of time in history I would have liked to live. I told him in the Germany of Bismarck. "Why?" he asked. "Because," I said, "that was a period of time where there was real leadership in the country and people felt they were creating a new country out of old feudal baronies. There was a feeling of strong national accomplishment in which everyone could share." Once again, I had neglected to take the opportunity to appreciate what this learned historian of French culture could have taught me. My only great learning experience that year was William Langer's course on modern Europe. A man who understood historical trends exceptionally well, he would turn out to be a most remarkable adviser to the State Department during World War II and its aftermath.

At the end of the year, I was as dissatisfied with myself as was the dean with my limited accomplishments. I had not improved much on my academic record. And although we had fielded a lightweight crew that beat the varsity regularly at its course length, and later won at Henley, I did not have the money to go, and I had to bow out. The dean suggested that perhaps I should take a leave of absence for a year to gain further maturity. He did not renew my scholarship.

I determined to take another road and went down to New York to find a job and put myself through law school at night. With two years of college completed, I was eligible. With my mother's help I went to see William Woodward, chairman of the Central Hanover Bank, and consequently started there as a runner in the spring of 1937. The other runners had just graduated from college. We delivered securities and loan documents from one end of Wall Street to the other, exchanged financial gossip with bankers and traders, and wondered why the Japanese were buying all the used steel structures they could find, including the Elevated Railroad running down Manhattan's Third Avenue. Little

When my scholarship is not renewed after my sophomore year, I return to New York and go to law school at night.

43

did we know that New York's steel was being used by the Japanese to build the naval vessels with which they would attack Pearl Harbor four years later.

In the fall, I started evening classes in law at New York Law School. I was living with my father in his studio, working late into the night while he slept on the other side of the room. I think we both felt equally melancholy. The Depression of 1937 had succeeded the Great Depression. On top of that, there was a strong impression among the Europeans my father knew and dined with that it was only a matter of time before war would break out in Europe. My father talked to me of the hereafter and the satisfaction his religion gave him. He expressed admiration for me because I was doing what he had done when he first came to the United States. But this meant little to me. I was not learning enough going to school at night. I felt at 18 that my life had been a failure.

Then one day I went to Columbia to see if I could transfer to the law school there. I met a young man in the college dean's office named Sam Beach. "What a fool you've been," he said, as he listened to my story. Then he suggested that if I could get my father to guarantee a loan for tuition, he would let me transfer to Columbia. If I could do two years of undergraduate courses in one and get straight A's, he would convert the loan into a scholarship and also give me a scholarship to the law school the following Fall. This seemed not an impossible challenge, but a way of extricating myself from my own stupidity. I persuaded my father to sign the note and transferred to Columbia. To me this was not attending college: it was spending a year to get back into the mainstream of my life. I reached out and grabbed the opportunity with both hands. At the end of the academic year, I had my straight A's, conversion of the loan and the assurance of a scholarship at the law school. I had finally regained my self-esteem.

I had also met a remarkable French girl who had landed a job at Macy's and become in a few months a buyer of foreign items, and a vice president. She was not beautiful but had extraordinary charm and energy, staying up dancing until four in the morning, then showing up for work in earrings and sneakers the next day. Young men from Europe and America took her out for dinner every night, but I lived with her in her New York apartment. I would study accounting, economics, and history while waiting for her to come home. On weekends I tutored in the country with the Berols. It was a suitcase life, but I felt I was making my way and was too busy not to be happy. My sister was in school in

Europe; my mother appeared to have regained her balance, had a nice apartment, and a man she loved in Europe. All in all, it was a good year. When law school began in the fall, "Miss Macy" married a rich Frenchman and I went back to my father's small apartment.

I have always thought that the law is one of the noblest of professions. When I was only five or thereabouts, adults would ask me, as they are apt to do to small boys, what I wanted to be when I grew up. No policeman, fireman or bus driver for me! I always answered, "I want to be a lawyer." Often I would then be asked, "And why do you want to be a lawyer?" Again the same response, "I want people to do what I want them to do." The lawyer as key adviser, that was what I wanted to be. Neither my father nor my sister could ever make decisions; my mother could, and so could I. To advise decision-makers on what action they should take I deemed a splendid profession. Later on, when I became for some years a so-called "doctor" of sick companies, I sometimes had to make very rapid decisions on my own and then take direct responsibility for them, rather than just give advice on what action should be taken. But this was different, because there weren't that many options available. I had no fear of making business decisions and did it well. The experience taught me that the business had to be saved, costs had to go down, and revenues up no matter how; financing had to be put in place regardless of promises or immediate costs. Other business lawyers have found that once you become addicted to making business decisions, it is impossible to go back to being just an adviser. But that is a much later part of my story.

All the way through school when I thought about the future I saw myself, with a vast knowledge of law and economics, advising kings and presidents about how to solve the problems faced by rulers. When I came face to face with Anglo-Saxon jurisprudence, the law became quite another matter. I had no patience with law as custom. If a rule was good enough to become law, it should be stated as such. How could elected state court judges ever be trusted to declare what the law was, particularly where the facts were complicated? Their training, especially in the cities, came from their attendance at the political clubhouses. They understood human nature and human reactions rather than rules of law. The law as an attempt by lawyers to persuade judges and jurors that a fact was something other than what seemed apparent; the importance of intent in changing a predictable decision; the concept of equity as a force able to reverse decisions in law were all concepts which appeared alien to me. I wanted clarity in the law because it seemed to me that people had the right to understand what would be the consequences of their acts. In that I was a Cartesian.

Even today, I am appalled at the thought that we need to produce over 25,000 lawyers *a year* in the United States to determine the law for clients when there are only 42,000 lawyers in all of Japan. Law in our country is a game and too much of an exercise that encourages contentiousness, because no law is clear and all laws can be questioned or circumvented. In law school my particular *bête noire* was Mr. Justice Felix Frankfurter who boasted that he was only deciding the law of the case on the set of facts before him. What arrogance, it seemed to me, to accept a ten-year wait for a Frankfurter decision and have it limited to its own facts. My heroes were Holmes, Brandeis, and Cardozo, and Justice Black, men who were not so much deciders of narrow issues, but philosophers of the law, aware of their responsibilities to draw lines clearly, and explain for the future, not only why they had decided as they had, but how their decision might serve as a future guide for other litigants. I particularly admired what Napoleon Bonaparte had done in France in personally supervising the work of the commission which created the Napoleonic Code out of the innumerable laws and regulations which made up the law prior to the French Revolution. Napoleon had insisted that the law should be simple and understandable to non-lawyers as well as lawyers. I also admired the English system which requires that specially trained lawyers—barristers—try cases and that judges be chosen from among the barristers.

I recall very clearly something which occurred in my third-year course on evidence. This course was taught by Professor Michael, a mathematical genius who taught in algebraic terms, as though law were an equation. One day he turned to the best scholar in the class and asked him, "Mr. Moorehead, how would you define a fact?" Moorehead replied, "A fact is something that is demonstrably true." As usual, when Moorehead answered a question in class, we were all impressed. Not for nothing had he compiled the best record ever, before or since, by any Columbia Law School student. "That, Mr. Moorehead, is the stupidest answer I have ever heard." Then he turned to the class and said, "Don't ever forget this. A fact is no more and no less than what the judge deciding the case thinks it is." I never forgot that statement.

What kind of legal system is it that even a truth is subject to interpretation? How often in Anglo-Saxon jurisprudence have facts been stretched beyond all logic because of judges' or jurors' prejudices and the trial lawyer's capacity to play up to these. Later, when I had as a partner Barent Ten Eyck, who had been in charge of appeals for the New York District Attorney's office under Tom Dewey, I used to plead with Barry to keep his argument as simple as possible for fear that the judge might not have his mental agility or legal sophistication and hence would not be able to follow his argument. Patent cases, tax cases, anti-trust cases, particularly tax the mind of a trial judge who is not an expert in these highly specialized matters. I have always preferred the civil law system, where business cases are tried by a panel of businessmen and judges and criminal cases are handled first by an examining magistrate and then by a panel of judges. The theory of cross-examination in the common law system of Anglo-Saxon jurisprudence is great for the lawyers who know how to use it effectively before juries, but is it sensible to have lawyers bring out the facts rather than judges trained for that purpose?

Alas, there is little Cartesian analysis in Anglo-Saxon jurisprudence. For me, who had always been very successful in my studies whenever I applied myself, receiving only a high B average in my first year of law school, represented intense humiliation. In some ways it was excusable because every weekend—Friday evenings, Saturdays and Sundays—I was tutoring to make enough money to stay in school. So at least two full days out of seven I was unable to study. It was then that I discovered that the easiest way to learn throughout one's life is to teach, because you cannot teach if you haven't grasped the subject. From then on, whenever I could find a friend to tutor before exams, I would do so, and we both benefited. I would get an A and he would pass a course he otherwise would have failed.

The student body at the Columbia Law School was either selected by or assigned to a Moot Court society. The purpose of the Moot Courts, in addition to making for friendships within the class, was to teach court procedures by having students from each court compete with one another in handling appellate cases: that is to say, presenting briefs and arguing the appeals. There were Irish courts, Jewish courts, an Ivy League court, Black courts, etc. Each group had a history and great pride despite its undemocratic composition. In my three years, the Ivy Court—my court—had exercised enormous influence in the school. Each year a member of this court was selected to run the competition. In my final year I was elected to do so. The competition was intense within the court in choosing those who would represent the court in the intercourt competition during the second year, and if they won, qualify for the finals in the third year. One of my roommates, John

Bainbridge, and I were chosen to represent the Kent Moot Court the second year, made the finals, and won the competition the third year, largely due to John's imposing presence—6′7″ and a booming voice that seemed to mesmerize our panel of judges, two from the U.S. Court of Appeals, and Chief Justice Stone from the Supreme Court, the former dean of the Columbia Law School.

My final two years at the law school, three friends and I shared an apartment on 114th Street near the school. They were all three very different from me and from each other. John Bainbridge was a product of Harvard, Class of 1938, where he had been a champion swimmer. His father was a well-known gynecologist in New York who had been a Navy doctor in World War I and inspired the fear of God in us when we visited John in their country place in Bethel, Connecticut. John should have been an English poet. He identified himself with Charles Lamb and would read snatches of his essays to Dick Keresey at night before going to sleep. I was not sure that Dick understood Lamb's philosophy, but he was delighted to think that John thought he did.

Dick Keresey had the best legal mind of the four of us and didn't understand why the study of law was not simpler for us. He made the *Law Review* at the end of our first year and was gone much of the time after that. He also became chief justice of our Moot Court our final year. He was a loner in his studies, and quick. A product of Dartmouth, it seemed to us that he resembled most an Irish storyteller, a troubadour with brains. He also had great wit, i.e., not the subtlety of an Irish poet. He was also coarse, pugnacious and ambitious. He thought the three of us too civilized, but we in turn suggested that he would never make it with the girls we knew on Park Avenue.

I remember once lying under the bed trying not to laugh while Keresey was above trying to persuade a girl I liked that she was ready for seduction.

Keresey and I were skiers. Whenever in the winter I could get away on a weekend from tutoring, we would drive up to Rutland, Vermont. We would stay at Mrs. Flood's where we could get a wonderful bed and breakfast, all for a dollar a night apiece. We would go up to the top of Pico's Peak on skins and ski down. There was a 14-year-old girl skiing there whom we would try to catch on the downhill run. We never did catch the young blonde with the flying pigtails. Her name was Andrea Mead, and she later turned out to be the best skier in America and won an Olympic gold medal.

Jack Tuohy was quite another sort. Jack and I shared one bedroom,

48

while Dick and John had the other. Jack had gone to Yale, sang in the glee club, made the squash team, and was never sure what he wanted to be or where he wanted to go. He was, however, one of the luckiest men I have ever met and one of the very nicest in a great Yale tradition of gentlemen. Jack would join the Air Corps in our last year. He wasn't there for graduation and if he had been, he wouldn't have known what he planned to do. He wasn't sure he wanted to be a lawyer at all. In World War II, he became a B-25 pilot flying from the islands north of Australia. One day as pilot of the lead plane of a group of B-25s on a cloudy day in the South Pacific, the clouds suddenly lifted and Jack saw the whole Japanese fleet lying below. I was in New York briefly then. The *World-Telegram* that night had big headlines: "Tuohy and friends catch Japs napping; sink carrier and cruiser." When the war ended, Jack had a girl whose father was a director of the Long Island Lighting Company. To please his daughter, he offered Jack a job as a lawyer for the company. Jack took the job but eventually married someone else. Some years later when he had become its general counsel, the firm needed to find a new president. There were two equally competent executive vice presidents. The board of directors was unable to choose between them. To keep them both, they chose Jack as president. He subsequently became chairman. It was a very good choice. It was impossible not to like Jack or not respect him. He was such a thorough gentleman and so quietly competent. We used to joke among ourselves that Jack would eventually without wanting it, become president of the United States—a little like Howard Taft or the first George Bush. I would certainly have voted for him. He had both common sense and sound judgment. The four of us were the best of friends and have remained so ever since.

There was an additional member of our group of very close friends. He was a class ahead of us. His name was Bill Beinecke, whose family had made a fortune in the S&H Green Stamps given away against grocery store purchases. We forgave him his wealth and the Beinecke Library at Yale, and he humored us by participating in our efforts to balance out our having to work far too much through exaggerated efforts at play. Bill has been a close friend of mine it now seems forever.

At the end of July 1939, I became 21. I was upset at what I thought was happening in France, because it seemed to me the politicians running the country were unrealistic about the military situation. To make it worse, the generals they had chosen reflected their own incompetence. Relying on the Maginot line of defense when it didn't cover Belgium was a military absurdity, particularly when one remembers that in

World War I, the Germans had invaded France through Belgium. And there was no Albert I as king of the Belgians, but a weak King Leopold. I stayed up all night at the house my mother had rented from the writer, Alice Leone Moats, in Turtle Bay, that wonderful square block of old houses and gardens in Manhattan's 48th to 49th Streets. I reflected on the unhappy fact that I had so far accomplished so little. I determined that I should have to do something to trigger my future. Since at 21 I had the right to choose to be French as well as American, I decided then and there to write a formal letter to the French Consulate declaring that I chose to be French. I fully expected that a day or two later I would receive a personal letter from Paul Reynaud, the prime minister, thanking me for my gracious gesture. Instead, a month later, I received a printed form with my name inserted inviting me to present myself forthwith for transportation to Martinique where I would undergo military training. No thank you, no appreciation, only a convocation to military service. The war then, for me, took on a more immediate meaning. Romantic notions yielded to blatant self-interest. I sent back a note requesting a delay to carry on my legal studies and was advised that I could have until June 1940. I was to sail for France, as it turned out, on the voyage the liner *Normandie* would have taken, if it had not burned at the dock in June of that year. To complete my come-uppance, my father, when I told him what I had done, would not speak to me for three months. "As a result of your stupidity," he said, "your children will now have the same right to be French, and all my efforts to rid myself of participation in those European wars of revenge will come to nothing." Neither of us really foresaw the political changes yet to come.

With the fall of France in June 1940, I persuaded my three law school roommates that this signified the end of civilization. It would be up to us to save the nation which would shortly be engulfed in war. Two chose the Navy, as I did; the other, John Tuohy, decided he would look silly in bellbottom trousers and chose the Army Air Corps. All of us signed up. The three of them went off shortly for training, whereas I, who had been the instigator of this patriotic gesture, was turned down by the Navy physical because my eyesight without glasses was inferior to 15/20. You can imagine the reaction from my three friends. Alas, it was too late for them.

It was still possible, after the fall of France and until the United States entered the war against Germany in December 1941, to exchange letters with people in France. One day I received a letter from an aunt in Paris, who had heard that I had volunteered for the United States

Navy. She sent me a long missive urging me to choose another branch of the service on the grounds that naval warfare had not brought success to the family. As she explained it, one of my naval officer ancestors, Xavier de Saint Phalle, at 19 a midshipman in the French navy, had been eaten, while some years later, his crew drank the blood of his brother, also a naval officer. It was a very sobering story. It appears that the admiral commanding the French flotilla, which had discovered New Caledonia in the year 1857, had sent his young officer Xavier with a group of men to fetch water from a spring located on an island in the bay of Noumea. Ambushed and killed by a group of cannibals, Xavier had his heart taken from his body and sent to the cannibal chief on the mainland as a special offering, for the young man had evidently fought bravely. His younger brother's fate was equally unfortunate. Designated to command the French fleet off Tampico in the days after France had imposed the Emperor Maximilian on Mexico, Gaston de Saint Phalle, youngest commodore (captain of frigates) in the Navy, had died of malaria and because he was a senior officer, his body had been stuffed into a cask, the cask filled with tequila, and a ship detached to take the officer back to Brest for burial. At sea the inevitable happened. Sailors at sea will sooner or later venture into the hold to find anything edible or imbibable. The cask was tapped. As air entered the cask, my ancestor's remains were added to the liquid. At voyage's end, both the tequila and a good bit of the commodore had vanished. When the charges were read to the crew assembled on deck for the court-martial, it is said that many fled to the side to be violently sick. Truly no comfort to me as I sought to serve my country in the United States Navy! I would later bear this story in mind as I sailed my small fleet junks along the coast of China.

In June of 1941, we graduated from the Columbia Law School. One of my three roommates had already left for active service and was in advanced flight training, two others were in midshipman school, while I still routinely went down to 90 Church Street, the New York Naval District Headquarters, to try to memorize the eye charts twice in succession as required to be accepted for officers' training. All of us wondered where we would be a year later. The war in Europe was going badly for the Allies. President Roosevelt, it was known, was doing everything he could think of to help the British navy to assure the supply line between the United States and Britain. We considered ourselves fortunate to have been allowed to finish our studies before being called up. To me the war probably seemed closer than to the others because of my close

The Study Years

51

French family ties and, of course, my weekends and vacations spent with the Sulzberger family in White Plains outside New York City.

I had been very fortunate during my three years in law school to obtain a job for weekends, vacations and the summers with the family of Arthur Sulzberger, publisher of *The New York Times*. It took me away from my studies at the law school which I could ill afford to miss, but it was an extraordinary opportunity to spend time with a remarkable

family. My specific job was to be the tutor for Punch—Arthur, Jr.—the only boy in the family, but in fact I often tutored the two oldest girls, Marian and Ruth, in helping them to be accepted in the college of their choice. I was very much accepted as a member of the family. For three years Arthur and Iphigene Sulzberger and their four children were my family.

Iphigene Sulzberger was the daughter of the legendary Adolf S. Ochs who had started as the publisher of *The Chattanooga Times* and subsequently purchased control of the *New York Times*. She was also the niece of the owner of the *Washington Post*. Had she been a man, she would have been publisher of the *Times*. She had married Arthur Hays Sulzberger. He was intelligent, extremely thoughtful, and very sensitive. I admired him greatly, looked up to him, and learned from him the nature of responsibility. I like to think that he became my friend. I know

he wanted me to come and work for him at the *Times* and remain, what I had become, a close friend of his entire family. As we drove together back and forth to White Plains on weekends, he would discuss with me what he saw as the problems and opportunities for the *Times* and what he was trying to accomplish. He often said he hoped that I would marry his elder daughter, Marian, and come and work for him at the paper. He was particularly fond of her and she of him. I was very fond of Marian but was certainly not ready for marriage to anyone at that time. I am happy to say that Marian and I have remained very close friends. The four years it had taken me to get through college and law school while tutoring every weekend, holidays and summers had been a great effort. I was anxious at last to practice my profession and to have money in my pocket which would make it possible to lead a civilized existence.

Every weekend while I was at Hillandale, the Sulzberger property in Westchester, there would either be a *Times* correspondent from abroad or visiting dignitaries from Washington or London. The conversations were rewarding. Both Arthur and Iphigene Sulzberger felt particularly concerned, not only because of the plight of the Jews in Germany, but because they were convinced that it would only be a question of time before the United States would be drawn into war.

One of the frequent weekend guests was the English actress, Madeleine Carroll. I thought she was the most beautiful woman I had ever seen. With her blonde hair with a hint of red in it, her large, soft gray eyes, her English complexion, and a Botticelli figure, she could have been his Venus. I would have done anything for her. I used to take her to Mass on Sundays. When we arrived at the small church in White Plains, there would be a tremor in the congregation. One day the priest, who was one of the first with an hourly program on the radio, came down to our pew after Mass asking her to autograph his missal. "As one actor to another, Miss Carroll," he said. "Please autograph this for me."

Charles Merz, editor of the *Times,* and his talented wife were generally at Hillandale on weekends. There might also be a European ambassador or two or more of our ambassadors on a return visit. If there were a foreign correspondent of the *Times* in town, he, too, would be invited to come. Since I was considered part of the family, it was a unique opportunity for me to learn what was really happening in the world outside. Every week, it seemed, brought new signs of European disintegration. One could only observe, make comments, try to understand the consequences of events occurring almost too quickly to be able to grasp them fully. Would the Soviet Union halt the German invasion? When would the onslaught on the Western front begin? Would Franco bring Spain into the war? Would those few British fighter pilots be able to prevent an invasion of the Nazis? At the end of each weekend, I wondered what would be discussed next Friday evening as a result of the week's events.

I also learned that correspondents were people of prejudice themselves. Some, it seemed to me as I listened to what they had to say, secretly applauded what was happening and slanted their conclusions accordingly. There were some who saw the Russians as the principal enemy rather than the Germans. There were many more who thought little of either French or English political or military capability. Then there were those like Herbert Matthews who had strong leftist views because of their experience in the civil war in Spain in 1937. These men had ceased, it seemed to me, to be journalists. They were political protagonists. Their views colored their accounts. Much later, when the Castro Revolution took place in Cuba, it seemed to me unbelievable that Herbert Matthews' accounts of that Revolution could be accepted as credible. I would find the same situation in China at the end of World War II during the time I spent with Theodore White in Chungking and which I will talk about later. There was a certain similarity of thinking between Herb Matthews and Teddy White. Both had a horror of autocratic regimes, which they found both corrupt and oppressive. Because of this, any alternative seemed better. The result: autocrats of the left were seen as agricultural reformers, i.e., White's view of Mao Tse-tung in 1945; Matthews' view of Castro in Cuba in 1962. Both views were quite false. I believe in both cases it came not only from the dislike of oppression from the right but from a total failure to understand the nature of Communism as the ultimate tyranny. In the 1940s, Americans did not yet understand the Stalin regime. Russia was far away. What was occurring there was not reported. Even the liquidation of the farmers and their forced move to communes were glossed over. It took a long time for the true nature of the Communist state to become apparent. In the meantime, journalists such as Matthews and White were convincing intellectual Americans to see leftist regimes in a way that was quite inaccurate. Even in 1940 at the Sulzbergers, I could see that these and other ideological correspondents were giving flawed presentations to the public through the press. I used to discuss these questions with Arthur Sulzberger as we drove back and forth to town. He was extremely concerned about the fate of the Jews in Europe and was doing all he could to make sure the government was aware of their plight. But he was also concerned about the future. "I am not a Zionist, Thibaut. To me this is not a racial but a religious issue. Hitler's declaration that the Jews are a separate race from the Aryans of Europe will cause permanent problems for the future. Jews in Germany had probably been more integrated into the community than anywhere else in Europe. Now, as a result of the horrors that are occurring in Germany, many Jews will insist on a homeland after the war. This will cause new and terrible problems because if a Jewish state is created in Palestine—and the Jews who survive the holocaust will want such a state—what will happen to the people who are there? What will be the position of men like me who do not want to see a Jewish state? Men like me are Americans who happen to believe in the Jewish religion." He might have added that there was little cultural affinity between the great German Jewish families of the United States with the Jewish groups who had more recently come from Poland and Russia and who were now demanding a Jewish homeland.

So here was I, a French Catholic so to speak, philosophizing with the publisher of the country's greatest newspaper about what was one of the terrible atrocities of all time—the holocaust taking place in Germany and wherever the Nazi troops went—and how to arouse the world to stop it, yet being aware that another racial disaster would succeed it. Arthur was an American of Jewish religion and culture, just as I was an American, but of Catholic religion and French culture. He would show me the letters he received at the *Times* from Zionist groups even then, attacking him and the newspaper for not immediately favoring a homeland for the Jewish people. It was an emotional issue to which rational thought could not bring a sensible answer. Those Jewish groups in America who were demanding a Jewish homeland were taking the position that the pogroms of Russia and Poland, and the devastating treatment of Jews in Germany, might be repeated again, unless the Jews were allowed to have a homeland carved out of someone else's territory in the Middle East. This is the legacy we are left with today.

To the Jewish leaders of New York City in the 1940s, the Lehmans, the Sulzbergers, the Strauses, and all the other great German Jewish families who represented the artistic and cultural tradition of a great city, it was inconceivable that they should be thought of as a foreign religion or a distinct, unwanted race. I began suddenly to recall phrases I had overheard in Paris: "He is a good banker, but of course he's a Protestant." Now here it was: "They're a serious banking house, but 'Jewish.'" Would I be expected to marry a Catholic girl? To work for a "Christian" law firm? To avoid having non-American partners? I will come back to this later when I talk about my friend, Margaret Mead, and her reaction to my firstborn son. We are a very long way—even today—from finding solutions to religious and racial prejudice. But in 1940–41, the persecution of Jews in Europe by the Nazis was an outrage which too often became lost in a consideration of how Europe itself was to survive.

The final year of law school is always a trying period even when war is not threatening. In February, the visits to law firms start, as well as the rumors about who may be invited to join and why. After the visits, then the wait for the letters of invitation or rejection, endless discussions with friends about interviews experienced, what should we have said that we didn't say, done that we didn't do? At last my decision was made: I was offered a job and accepted it, at Chadbourne, Wallace, Parke & Whiteside. In June, right after taking the bar examinations, I started work at the munificent salary of $2,100 a year. I felt like a rich man!

I get a real job at last as a lawyer, my chosen profession.

Tom Chadbourne, senior partner and founder of the firm was 6´7˝, a giant of a man. His hair had turned snow-white when he was in his early 20s. He had married one of the great beauties of the day. His forte was the Cuban sugar industry. He represented all the big sugar companies in the United States, as well as Cuba. To this he had added the mining companies, Phelps-Dodge, Anaconda, Asarco, Patino Mines and others. Wallace had been attorney general of Montana, a fiefdom of Anaconda. The American Tobacco Company and both airlines and airplane manufacturers, many of whom were offshoots of General Motors, also became clients of the firm as it grew. Eastern Airlines, TWA, North American Aviation, Sperry were all clients. William Parke was the trust and estates partner; George Whiteside the principal trial partner. It was a well-balanced firm of some 85 lawyers, a big firm in those days. Rumor in the firm had it that when Tom Chadbourne had amassed enough industrial clients, he invited himself to lunch at one of the city's major banks and told the chairman his partners couldn't understand why his firm did not represent the bank. He was told the bank was quite satisfied with its counsel. The next year, Chadbourne returned with the same request. This time the chairman became angry and told him the matter was not open for discussion. "My partners thought that might be your reaction, so we consulted our clients. They are equally disturbed that we do not handle work for your bank. Since together they represent a good proportion of your deposits, I suggest you reconsider my suggestion." Chadbourne was given the business, and the firm subsequently became counsel to the bank.

Two friends from law school and I took an apartment together at 323 East 19th Street in Manhattan. It was a fourth floor walk-up, but once inside, it had great charm. There was one huge room in the center, three bedrooms and a den at the corners, a large fireplace and a small circular steel stairway that went to a terrace on the roof. The apartment belonged to a *Time* correspondent and his wife. It was nicely furnished with mementos from previous assignments. The rent, $240 per month, split three ways, was easily affordable. For the first time in my life I felt secure.

Jim McDonnell of the very social Murray-McDonnell clan of New York and Southampton was the type of Irishman about whom young girls and their mothers dream all through the night. Dark hair, black eyes, boyish grin, a gift of gab and a love of dancing, he had it all. He was also very intelligent and very religious. As a young man he had had a very unfortunate love affair and had decided perhaps for safety's sake, as well as a love of God, to become a monk. Two years into the seminary, he realized he had too much passion to be right for the priesthood and joined us at the law school. Poor Jim, he would go to a party, take a woman home to spend the night with her, then return the next day, and for three days stay in his room reflecting on his sins and his weakness as a man.

Mac Smith, on the other hand, was a fine example of what the New South was going to turn out to be. His parents came from a small town in North Carolina near Fayetteville. His father was the local doctor. They were a very Christian family who had settled there before the Revolutionary War. They knew every great family in the South. Their forebears had fought in the Revolutionary War and in the War Between the States. It was as though both these events had occurred yesterday. They knew every battle, every commander, every brave exploit, who had fallen where. In our last year of law school, Mac, who was president of the Moot Court from the Old South, decided that I knew nothing of the history of my country and that single-handedly he would fill the gap. In his old car, the three of us proceeded through every battle site from 1778 to 1781 and 1861 to 1865—from Washington south to Charleston, South Carolina. Mac never drew a breath the whole time. From the "Swump Fox" to General Lee by way of Stonewall Jackson and Nathan Forrest, we lived through it all. It made a great impression on me that here were people who had the same love of God and of country that my grandparents in France had had. How different these Southerners seemed to be from the New Yorkers I knew, with their materialism and lack of interest and knowledge of the country's past. By the time I returned to New York, I had fallen in love with a girl from Chatham Hall School, written her every day, promised to be her escort for the St. Cecilia Ball in Charleston, and was ready to swear undying fealty to the Old South.

The three of us—while an odd trio—were very happy together. In those days, there were many young Southern girls working as models in New York. They lived at the Barbizon, fought off the advances of textile manufacturers and dress designers, and looked forward whenever possible to coming down to 19th Street where they could cook fried chicken and black-eyed peas for John McNeil Smith while he sat in his big chair and played classical music for them. There were never fewer than three. Jim and I observed these scenes with outright envy.

This whole period of my life was very chaste. In law school I was lost in my work and was happy with my friends. At Chadbourne, I was learning a new trade, realizing that I knew nothing about the practical aspects of being a lawyer, despite three years of constant work learning about the law. At law school I had had one serious but very chaste romantic interlude with the daughter, Eleanor, of the leading Catholic family in the city, the Hoguets. Mr. Hoguet was of Belgian ancestry but his wife was a Lynch, which made the family acceptable to the archbishop. I met them playing tennis. At one of the weekend parties in Mt. Kisco, New York, where the family spent the summer, one of the guests turned up one day with a friend who was an apostate. I did not know what this meant, but there were murmurs around the court, and Mrs. Hoguet, I later learned, had called the archdiocese in New York to find out if it was acceptable to invite an apostate to stay for lunch.

There were five boys in the family and three girls. Ellie was the next to youngest. She brought me books by French poets. I sent individual red roses to her house at 47 East 92nd Street. We kissed discreetly and spoke to one another as though we were Heloise and Abelard. It was intellectual and romantic and generally unsatisfactory both to Ellie's brothers, who were practical and unemotional, and to my own roommates, who thought I was wasting precious time.

Our earlier law school apartment on 114th Street was surrounded by similar ten-story buildings. In the middle was a courtyard, where from time to time an old Italian with what we considered to be a magnificent tenor voice would sing Neapolitan melodies and arias from his homeland. My roommates thought it appropriate to invite him in my name to sing at the ball the Hoguets were going to give for their daughter, Eleanor, on her 18th birthday. At the stroke of midnight, the doorbell rang and our tenor entered in Italian operatic garb, and before he could be stopped, bounded up the staircase in full voice. Neither Hoguet parent was amused. The tenor did not sound anywhere near as good as he did in the concrete well of our building on 114th Street, and it took me some time to recover from that fiasco. I then had to suffer through several Hoguet family dinners. Mr. and Mrs. Hoguet were always in evening dress at these affairs. There would also generally be a visiting prelate. It was here that I met two popes: Pius XII and Cardinal Montini of Milan who would become Paul VI. Even then Paul was spoken of as a certain future pope with all the necessary qualities to be a great leader of the church. Little did I know that I would someday play a minor role in American-Vatican strategy in Indochina during the papacy of Pius XII.

Anyway, nothing came of my budding romance with Eleanor. She subsequently married a Belgian Catholic from Atlanta, Paul de Give. I think Mrs. Hoguet was relieved. Like the Archbishop, who once declared to my aunt that the French were not worthy of being Catholics, Mrs. Hoguet looked upon me with a certain amount of disquiet, particularly in view of my parents' divorce and my own lack of inheritance.

When Sunday morning, December 7th, 1941 came, Mac, Jim and I were sitting in our apartment reading the Sunday papers. We heard the news on the radio, looked at each other, and suddenly realized that our new careers as lawyers, which we had been enjoying for perhaps six months, had abruptly come to an end.

World War II threatens my career as it begins.

III

FROM THE LAW TO WAR

O N *DECEMBER 8TH, 1941*, I was due to go out to the Sperry plant in Long Island City. This plant had already long since reached its mathematical capacity for further expansion. It was filled with machinery working day and night to produce mechanisms and products based on the principle of the gyroscope for steering ships, airplanes and bombs on a prescribed course and guiding bombs accurately to their destination—Sperry products were essential to the Allies in the war against Germany. The company at this time had also filed more applications in the patent office than any other industrial company in the United States. It was a company run by engineers and mathematicians. It was in the forefront of American technology. That Monday morning there was a feeling around the luncheon table in the executive dining room that all that the company had been striving for in supplying the Allies would now be put to the test in making it possible for the United States to recover militarily from the previous day's disaster at Pearl Harbor. There was electricity in the air at Sperry that day. We could all feel it. Many of the executives were graduates of the Naval Academy and served as Navy pilots and engineers. They longed to get into service. I was present because for several months I had been drawing contracts for Sperry's acquisitions of small engineering companies.

The law is an exciting learning experience.

In the big and well-staffed law firms of the day, young lawyers just out of law school were normally put in the library where they prepared memoranda of law for the partners and senior associates. These memoranda were carefully preserved in the firm's library where they were properly indexed as to subject matter. In this way partners might find the studies they had made years ago, but which might still be relevant to another client's needs. For six months, I had been working in the library for two partners in the corporate department to which I had been fortunate enough to be assigned, Stannard Dunn and Alexander B. Royce.

Alex and Stan were total opposites. Royce was brilliant, lazy, a born negotiator, but not a student of the law. Stan Dunn was a plodder, had no personality with clients, never played politics. It had taken the senior management at Sperry, his principal client, several years to appreciate how good their counsel was. He was never unprepared. His knowledge of the law was such that every possible legal problem which might come up in any transaction was always predicted and acted upon in advance. His clients were, therefore, never taken by surprise. When there was a contract to prepare, he always made it clear to me that we would prepare the first draft, not the other lawyer. This was easy to do, he said, because most lawyers were lazy. Doing the first draft meant that you could put in all the provisions that were helpful to your client instead of having to try to add them later by amending the other lawyer's draft—never an easy thing to do.

From the Law to War

Working with Royce was fun. What interested him was not the law but the personality of his client, the adversary, and the opposing lawyer. He might not have at his fingertips an answer to the legal questions which might be encountered, but he certainly knew the players, what his client really wanted and would settle for, how far he could push the other lawyer and *his* client. Clients loved him because he took such special care with them. He told me once that clients couldn't tell whether their lawyer had really done a good job for them or not. How could they, unless they were lawyers themselves? In this he was right. It was only when I myself became a business executive and was a client that I realized how insufficient most legal advice is, even that of large and supposedly knowledgeable firms.

Law is handling clients.

One day, as we were working together on an acquisition, Alex told me the story of how he had become counsel for the Patinos. It was in 1934. He had just been made a partner because the firm could no longer afford to give him a salary. Even though the firm was no longer making money, there were always in the reception room at the entrance to the firm's offices beautiful flowers on the receptionist's desk and a beautiful recent college graduate from Vassar to greet visitors. One day the receptionist had come to him in anguish. "There is a man outside, Mr. Royce, who is dressed in an old sheepherder's coat and dungarees. His English is hardly understandable. He wants to see Mr. Chadbourne. I told him Mr. Chadbourne was in Europe. 'Never mind,' he said, 'get me Mr. Wallace.' I told him Mr. Wallace was dead. 'Then get me Parke.' I couldn't let Mr. Parke see him. He would never forgive me. Shall I call the police?"

"Never mind," said Royce. "I'll see him. I have nothing better to do."

The "client" turned out to be Antenor Patino. Patino was a sheep-herder in the mountains of Bolivia. One day, while chasing his sheep, he had spotted a rock formation with traces of minerals that he had not run across before. He had had sense enough to take samples of the ore, go down to the nearest town, and see a lawyer. The lawyer checked and found it was tin. He filed the claims for Patino, but told him to take his savings and go to New York. He recommended to him that he go to the Chadbourne firm because it represented all the leading mining companies.

"Mr. Patino," said Royce, "come back tomorrow. I will have every-thing ready for you." As soon as Patino had gone, Royce called the firm's correspondent in Bolivia and checked the story. The next day he was ready.

"Mr. Patino," he said, "we must have a corporation for you. I suggest we call it 'Patino Mines and Enterprises Incorporated Consolidated.' That will impose respect. You will, of course, be chairman and president. If you wish, I will act as vice president, secretary and treasurer." Mr. Patino admitted that the name fitted his sentiments exactly. And so one of the world's most successful mining companies was formed and Alexander Royce became overnight a very rich man, as well as one of the principal partners in the firm.

The entire Patino family, wife, brother, sister and children, had all left Bolivia and come to the United States before eventually settling in Paris. They were not used to wealth. The women promptly covered themselves with rich jewels. The men took expensive mistresses and frequented the best watering holes of the Mediterranean. If they got into trouble—and they did—the Chadbourne firm's best legal special-ists were at their disposal. It was not long before Patinos married into the finest European families. Antenor, under the guidance of Alexander B. Royce, became a legendary "father" figure. The family created corpo-rate business problems worldwide, and tax, custody, legitimacy, foreign funds control, and estate questions enough to satisfy countless lawyers in the firm. Foundations were created, politicians were rewarded, new diplomatic ties negotiated. It was splendid.

I originally had worked principally for Stan Dunn in doing legal research. I couldn't figure out why he needed me, because he himself would spend every evening at the firm, generally in the library, and Saturday and Sunday as well. He had bought a house in New Hampshire many years earlier and installed his wife there. He himself lived in a small bachelor apartment in Tudor City. It was rumored that one year he had even forgotten to go home for Christmas. The law was his passion. If there were a legal problem that he didn't know the answer to, he would spend hours in the library simply to find the answer for his own satisfaction. It sometimes happened that I might mention to him some problem that I was researching for someone else. Two days later I would find on my desk a memorandum from Stan Dunn giving me his analysis on this same problem. He would have done my job for me. It was not as though he had the time to do all this. Sperry, which had been a small naval engineering company a short time earlier, was now the 10th largest corporation in the United States and growing very fast. He constantly had to go to Washington or even to London on Sperry business.

From the Law to War

On my return from Long Island City on December 8th, Stan Dunn was waiting for me. "I don't have time for you to keep on doing research in the library," he said. "The company will now have to grow much faster. We will have to bid on all the engineering talent available in this country. We will be buying small companies at the rate of maybe three a week to get their engineers. I don't have time to do this myself because the Washington military and political bureaucracy will be growing at the same pace or faster, and it will take all my time to negotiate the appropriate military contracts with governments to make it possible for the company to keep fulfilling its expanding military obligations. If you need me, come in on Sundays when I will be able to catch up with office work. Otherwise, I will leave you memos of what you should do. I know you will make mistakes, but that is unimportant. Get the job done and do it fast. I have told the key company executives that I have given you this additional responsibility. You will work directly with John Sanderson, the chief financial officer. Each of my memos to you will tell you who else you are to work with at the company, and who will have to clear any decisions you want to make. Good luck. It will be an adventure."

Law is negotiating the purchase of companies.

And so it was. My days were spent at the small tool-making and engineering companies in the Housatonic Valley of Connecticut and older industrial areas of New England negotiating acquisition agreements. My nights were spent at the office drawing up documents. And when I had any spare time, I was continuing my efforts to get into the Navy. I now found the same eye chart twice in a row at 90 Church Street and so passed my physical by memorizing it. It was now only a question of getting into midshipman school. I went down to Washington where my friend and law school classmate, Jim McDonnell, had found a job in the Navy at the Bureau of Aeronautics. There I met Admiral de Florez again. He was kind enough to support my application for Air Combat Intelligence, but he held out little hope because it was limited to older and senior officers. My friend, McNeil Smith, had applied for the Navy bomb-disposal service. My other friends had already disappeared into military training schools or direct to the Pacific.

In March 1942, I was sworn in on the same day as an ensign in the United States Naval Reserve and as a member of the bar of the state of New York. I was temporarily leaving the one and joining the other.

My two months of midshipman training took place at Fort Schuyler in the Bronx. From time to time, I would call Stan Dunn to check on work I hadn't been able to finish. He seemed to think that I was already facing the Japanese. It was embarrassing to tell him that I had been playing touch football for two hours that afternoon. I certainly didn't miss the office. I was learning a new trade among a very different group of young men my age. We were all very curious about what the future would hold out for us, but we were too busy during the day to think very much about it.

What was happening to the country in those early months of the war? To many of us, particularly in the East of the country who had been convinced for some time that sooner or later we would have to be called into military service, it was like a release. There was a job to be done; we would have to do it. Because of the way the Japanese had acted, there were no reservations and, curiously enough, no criticism of President Roosevelt for leaving the country so unprepared. The isolationists, once so strong, had disappeared overnight. We were young. Most of us had no wives to worry about. We had no thoughts about death. Those of us who were young professionals were being allowed to get away from office work, which was often uninspiring to most newly-minted young lawyers. I had just been lucky. The country was extraordinarily unified in a determination to get on with the war. There was unanimity in thinking that Roosevelt would be a great war leader. Because we would now be fighting alongside the USSR, even the leftists who were so strong in Hollywood and the press pushed each other to get behind the war effort. Only in Washington, that sleepy city of some 250,000 people, did there seem to be an inability to understand the need to get moving quickly.

Roosevelt used to refer to Georgetown, the elite suburb of Washington which had been a city before Washington was chosen as the country's capital, as a place of cave dwellers. The rich lived there in lovely old houses along with some members of Congress, and present and former State Department officials for whom a diplomatic note was a formal step indeed. The arrival of the New Deal and all its young men from Harvard eager to change the focus of the country was one shock which could perhaps be ignored in Georgetown. But the advent of war was something else, particularly for the Southerners, who made up such a large percentage of our officer corps. Even Georgetown would now have to cease to be an oasis for gentlemen of culture and refinement.

Shortly after Pearl Harbor, in January 1942, a cousin of mine, Francis Harper, had become engaged to a girl from Virginia. He asked me to be an usher at his wedding, which was to take place at her mother's house in Georgetown. I went to Washington for five days. I lived in the capital as though no war was going on and the horrors of Bataan and Corregidor were merely fictional tales invented by the press. There were luncheon parties, dinner parties and a dance every night. I remember one evening in particular, a party given by the aunt of the bride, at her Georgetown house. Around 11 o'clock a guest arrived wearing the dress uniform of the Marine Corps. The butler, aghast, went up to our hostess and said, "Madam, there is a soldier in the house. What should I do?" The "soldier" in question was the commandant of the Marine Corps, who had taken a few minutes from his duties to pay his respects.

Washington would be very much changed in the months that followed.

I have often thought that one of the great strengths of the United States has been the pretense that there is no central government and that the administration of the country is the result of a compact entered into by the states and by the people to limit the powers of the federal government. We had disproved that temporarily during the Civil War in 1861. But the chimera has persisted. Even to this day, despite a constant increase in the size and reach of the federal government, national politicians still claim that they are taking the central government off the backs of the people. This always evokes a favorable response, yet growth of government continues relentlessly as before, regardless of which political party is in office.

As World War II got underway, there was a massive movement of power towards Washington. To Roosevelt's everlasting credit and certainly for the first time in the country's history, he chose remarkably able men to lead the country, both on the military and on the administration side. Such men as Marshall, Eisenhower, Nimitz, Halsey, MacArthur, Bradley and Patton would certainly have to be considered extraordinary men by any country's standards.

All the great national policy determinations of the period were very far removed from my little world. In June, upon graduation from midshipman school, four of us in my class were selected to go on to Quonset Point, Rhode Island, near Newport, to join there at the Naval Air Station the more senior officers who had had their preliminary training at Quonset. Because there was no room at the Air Station for us, we received unlimited mileage gas ration cards and were allowed to live off the base. I found us a house by the Jamestown Bridge, a beach house of the 1910 era with four square rooms downstairs and four square bedrooms and one bath upstairs. Since the house was only used in the summer, its walls upstairs didn't go all the way to the ceiling. This was a real challenge in communal living for four young men who thought they were spending the last two months of their life here on earth and who were determined to enjoy it to the utmost as a consequence.

Walter Kiel, our eldest, had been a newspaperman in Florida. He was married to a former starlet from Hollywood whom he had met on an earlier newspaper assignment. She was beautiful, very sweet and had graciously undertaken to act as housemother and cook for the four of us. Unfortunately, as soon as we left for classes in the morning, she took to the bourbon and by dinnertime, she showed the effects of the day's activities. Vincent, from New Orleans, was a tall, dark-skinned would-be playboy, who lived for amorous intrigue. Carl Solberg, a foreign editor of *Time* magazine, was engaged to a nice New York girl who came up for weekends. He was the most serious of the group. He kept us advised of what was happening outside of our small, intense world. Then there was me, convinced that the South Pacific lay ahead, that I would not return for years if at all, and that every minute counted. Under the circumstances, all of us got along remarkably well, as did our respective wives, fiancées and visiting girlfriends who were with us over that two-month period. It was harder for our visiting women because they had to spend the days together without us. They also came from very different backgrounds and had different interests. But they made a great effort to get along with each other and be loving with us. As I look back on that period, it seems surprising to me how well it had all worked out. It was a little like having been cast in a play. The actors have been called in. They haven't been given their lines. But they have been told the play will only run for two months. It is up to the actors to improvise.

At last the day of our graduation came. I was first in my class and expected an assignment to the Marines at some beachhead in Southeast Asia. Instead, Keith had that job and I was sent to an air squadron based in the 3rd Naval District in Panama. I never found out why I was given what I considered to be a very dull assignment until years later I met in Princeton, New Jersey, the former woman naval lieutenant at Quonset Point who was responsible for filling the slots for our class. She laughed it off by saying: "I liked you. I thought you were too young to die."

Was this one more instance of luck in a decision which could not have been predicted but undoubtedly affected my future and perhaps even my life?

Panama was a lesson in frustration. The commanding officer of my squadron was one of the very few bad Annapolis graduates I ever ran across in the Navy Officer Corps. This man was tough, crude, coarse, dishonest and, on top of it all, a born coward. Based at the air base of Coco Solo on the Atlantic side of the Panama Canal, the squadron's job was to guard the approaches to the canal through which so much American shipping had to pass on its way to the Pacific. The whole region was filled with German submarines. My job was to keep track, as best we could, of the submarine sightings and of the ships that had been hit and sunk. The record was dismal in 1942. Our planes were old OS2Us, planes that had been designed to be catapulted off the decks of battleships and heavy cruisers of the prewar period. They were slow, 90 knots maximum, and carried only one bomb. If they were caught in the frequent tropical storms of the area, they would be lucky to get home. Yet they had to protect merchant ships throughout the Caribbean area as they headed to or from the canal. The pilots were young reserve officers who in most cases had been sent to Panama as the final part of their Navy training. Like all officers and men on the base, they disliked the commanding officer heartily. I once, at his request, had to go to his apartment to fetch some papers. Under the bed were half a dozen new tires that he was selling in the lucrative Panama market. Worse yet, when from time to time a lucky hit was registered on a German submarine, he would claim in the reports that it was either his kill or his assist. He only flew to get his flight pay and then only on selected missions where there was little danger of turbulence. I was very happy, when after a few months, I was transferred to Albrook Field, on the other side of the canal, where the Navy had a small group of officers attached as liaison to the Army Air Corps. My commanding officer there, also an Annapolis graduate, was as different from my former squadron commander as it was possible to be. He had been passed over for promotion, not because he was not a capable officer—he was—but because while serving on a ship where he had been the mess officer, he had had an unfortunate experience with a Congressional inspection team. During the visit, he had used his own funds to supplement the fare in the wardroom. There had been a report filed in the Congress that the officers on the ship lived too well, and he had taken the blame. At least that was his story, and I have no reason to doubt it. Incidents of that sort can destroy an officer's career in peacetime. It had given this officer a hearty dislike for civilian government. I suppose that at this stage of the way, with experienced officers lacking in a Navy expanding exceedingly rapidly, it was logical to send the best officers where the danger was greatest and leave the others to defend places like the canal, where there was little likelihood of a Japanese attack. The naval war, after all, was in the Pacific. And that is where I had expected to be.

This was little consolation to me or to my friend, Louis Auchincloss, who would become a famous author. I had known Louis in New York. He had graduated from the University of Virginia Law School the same year I had graduated from Columbia Law. Louis and I would meet for dinner at the Hotel Panama in Panama City once a month. Louis dreamed even then of being a writer. After a few martinis and a reasonably good dinner, we would each take pen in hand. He would write a letter, which I would sign, asking for a transfer to the Pacific war area. I would write a letter for him. Both of us would mail the letters before returning to our respective bases so that wisdom might not cause us to change our minds. The procedure had to follow naval regulations. The letters were addressed to the secretary of the Navy but sent via the officer in charge of our immediate unit, and then through the officer commanding the naval district. We could get by the first, but time after time our letters would come back from the district marked, "Refused." We would redouble our efforts at our next dinner to think up better reasons.

At any rate, Panama City had much more to offer than Colon on the Atlantic side of the canal. In the first place, there was a social life in Panama with dinners at the country club and an opportunity to meet from time to time with the Panamanian elite. My friend, John Tilney, had persuaded his commanding officer at naval headquarters to let him learn Spanish. For this purpose, he was allowed to live off the base with a Panamanian family who had semi-adopted him. As a result, he went to parties in town where the American military were not invited. So he had an opportunity to live in an environment other than the world of frustrated officers wishing to be elsewhere. Through him, I was often invited to dinners in town.

You can imagine what Panama was like in 1942. It had become an enormous tropical depot of officers and enlisted men, together with all the paraphernalia of war that was being transported through the canal from one ocean to the other. Sooner or later, everyone one knew was likely to pass through or to stop there for further training. I discovered my former law school roommate, Dick Keresey, one day based with his PT boat squadron on the island of Balboa in Panama Bay. We were delighted to find each other again. I envied the spirit among the officers and men in his squadron. The officers were all reservists like us. The chief petty officers ran the squadron, but every man aboard—regular Navy or reservists—had a sense of mission that was unique and very different from the shore-based Navy of which I was a part. They were only in Panama for advanced training and would shortly be pushing on to the Pacific.

With all the equipment, the food and the supplies passing through the canal, it was certain that great local fortunes were being made. The richest woman in Panama of the time was a redheaded Irish Panamanian of somewhat dubious parentage who controlled all the sales of liquor, wines and beer in the canal zone. You can imagine what a profitable trade that was, in a small country where thousands of men found either that this was the first alcohol they had had in weeks at sea or the last opportunity they would have for a drink until they came back to San Francisco at war's end. I remember one extraordinary night when I attended a party at this woman's penthouse apartment eight floors above her brewery in downtown Panama City. From the terrace, one could see the canal in the distance, and beyond, the bay and the Pacific Ocean shimmering in the tropical moonlight. Towards midnight, I found myself with a young Marine Corps captain, an Army general and our hostess as the last remnants of a big party. At this point my hostess asked me to come to her bedroom where she began to dance with a shrunken head which she had taken from her night table. "Sit down beside me," she said, "and I will tell you a story. I came to Panama some twenty years ago as a young girl. I have had three husbands, who have left me a very wealthy woman. One left me and went back to the States, number two drowned in the canal, and the third, who went home, took me to Guayaquil in Ecuador on our honeymoon. I told him I wanted him to buy me a shrunken head. That is an art that only the Indians of Ecuador still practice. As you can see from Jimmy here, the head is perfect, even to the blue eyes and the red hair. They take the skin off the head and shrink the bones through a secret process. Then they mummify the head in some way. The sale of shrunken heads is forbidden in Ecuador, but in a port city you can find anything if you take the trouble to look for it. In a little shop in a back alley near the docks, I found Jimmy. I fainted dead away at the sight of him. You see, he had been my lover in this very bed two years earlier. Reminded me of my home in Ireland, he did."

Imagine this scene: From the terrace outside, eight stories above the port city of Panama with the orange, green and blue lights of the "blue moon" bars three to a block—and beyond them the white lights of the canal and the dock area where the work of loading and unloading the cargo ships never ceased, twenty-four hours a day, and beyond that the bay shining in the moonlit night, and still beyond that, the ships, dark dots on the sea, and still beyond, the outline of Balboa Island near the horizon. And inside, dancing in her bare feet on the white marble floor this thirty-five year old woman, her curvaceous body laced into a white evening dress, dancing to the sounds of the music from the blue moon bars below mixing with the sounds of competing rumbas played too loud, and holding to her lips this tiny head of a long-dead red-headed Irishman. This was truly the mood of Panama of the time: the drinking, the womanizing, the deaths and the violence, and the promise of more of the same, and then the Latin music and the beauty of the tropical night. To a young man from New York who longed to be elsewhere, sitting on a white fur rug covering the big bed with its white satin sheets, this was a slice of the rawness of life itself.

Stupidly then, I left my friend with the young Marine captain, and the general dropped me back at Albrook Field in his staff car on his way home.

Fortunately for me, the boredom of my life at Albrook Field was lifted for a time. Perhaps because my letters were more persuasive than his, Louis Auchincloss had disappeared southward. I missed his company. Orders by chance came down from the admiral's office that one of the Albrook liaison officers was to be sent, accompanied by a young ensign from headquarters, on a mission to surrounding countries to determine whether a squadron of Navy airplanes on a rotating basis could be based there. The idea was an excellent one. Rather than have advanced training at Pensacola, why not have such training within flying range of the Panama Canal? In this way, more mature flyers could be moved out of the area and towards the fighting front or on the carriers at sea. Luckily for me, the seniors in my unit preferred the tennis courts of Albrook and the "blue moon" girls of the city to an adventure of this sort, and I was eventually chosen to go.

Our mission countries included Colombia, Ecuador, Guatemala, Honduras, Costa Rica, Peru, Nicaragua, the Galapagos and the San Andres Islands. The young ensign who accompanied me had just completed his Ph.D. studies in anthropology. The location of airfields certainly held no interest for him. I sometimes had the impression during our voyage that the choice of Ensign Bober might have been dictated by a desire to get him out from underfoot at headquarters. Still, the Navy had to take what it could get in my case, as well as his. I did not think I would ever get him back from the Galapagos Islands. Aside from a penal colony in one small island, the whole area had been untouched since the days of Charles Darwin. In Talara, Peru, he had found oil sumps filled with well-preserved parts of mastodons and mammoths, which he tried to send back to the Brooklyn Museum of Natural History.

The purpose had been two-fold: to locate places where the airfields could be converted for use by fighter pilots if they were not already equipped with lights and radio equipment or the runways were not sufficient in size, composition or direction; secondly, to determine whether and at what price the local authorities would be willing to allow our Navy fighter planes to use the airport facilities.

Our first stop was in Colombia. We went there by a Navy Amphibian PBY, a type of long-range, high-wing aircraft used by the Navy for long-range reconnaissance missions. It took us to Cartagena, possibly the most interesting old city in the Western Hemisphere. Our job there for the Navy presented no special problems. Our pilots knew what they needed to make sure of from a technical standpoint and there was little for us to negotiate. So Ensign Bober and I disappeared into the city and spent several days thinking that we were back in the 17th century when Cartagena was an important stopover for the Spanish galleons engaged in the gold trade and a port of call for the pirates who then infested the coast of Colombia.

I get a chance to learn about Central America.

Guatemala was then under the control of General Jorge Ubico. He was extremely proud of the cleanliness of his capital city located in a region of mountains and lakes. The city regulations even required small boys to run after the carriages in the streets with bucket, pan and brush to pick up horse droppings.

In Nicaragua, the Marines were well established. An amusing observation we made was that the local GIs could register their women with the local police authorities. If they were then found in the company of other men, they were subject to arrest or fine.

The most interesting part of our trip was certainly Peru and the Galapagos Islands. In Talara, Peru, while Ensign Bober reconnoitered for mammals of a bygone era, I spent time on Louis Auchincloss's yacht. I use the term advisably. It appeared that when the war broke out, Freddie Prince of the Armour meat-packing family in Chicago had felt it his duty as a loyal citizen to give his sea-going yacht to the Navy for the duration. The Navy, not knowing what to do with the yacht, had sent it down to Ecuador where it served as a vessel on which to train young midshipmen from that country. I was invited to spend a Sunday on the yacht by Louis. The wardroom contained the original oil paintings which had been there in Prince's day. There were no showers, but baths with gold faucets. Perhaps because of the atmosphere, which was certainly not naval, the commanding officer had drafted the Ecuadorian midshipmen to serve as cooks and mess boys. It was a foregone conclusion that someone at naval headquarters in Quito, the capital of Ecuador, would complain to the U.S. Navy in Washington and that Louis would be transferred again. According to the story, as it was later recounted to me, there was a complaint made, the yacht was transferred to Norfolk, Virginia, and the captain was given orders to police the sea lanes at night with no lights showing. There, the inevitable happened: the ship was cut in two one night by an American destroyer. It was said that Louis was the officer of the deck at the time and that he managed to step across to the destroyer, saluting smartly, and calling out with the appropriate etiquette: "Permission to come aboard, sir." He now denies it, but it is a great story in the best naval tradition.

Our only moment of anxiety occurred in Honduras where a kind of smuggler chieftain controlled Trujillo, the principal city on the coast, not far from the Bay Islands. This man invited us for dinner dressed in a naval uniform with large epaulets similar to what Nelson might have worn. His officers were similarly dressed. Behind each chair was a man fully armed. The admiral, himself, for I believed he called himself that, was critical of the United States, demanded that he be given naval shore patrol vessels if he was asked to make the airfield available, and highly praised the manners of the German submarine commanders he had met. We were glad to get away from that particular place.

I was sorry that I did not have a chance to visit the Bay Islands. They are located off the coast of Honduras, but they belong to Columbia. In the 16th and 17th Centuries, the islands had been occupied by pirates who used them as a supply base and as an area safe enough to keep their captive English women, most of whom had been taken off merchant ships that the pirates had seized. As a result, the women of these islands are famous today throughout Latin America for their blonde hair tinted with red and their English complexions. Many of them marry diplomats from the Central and South American countries. During the war, there was an American officer based on the island who was to keep an eye out for German submarines and radio the nearest base if he saw one. As one can imagine, it was a highly prized assignment.

It was not long after I had completed my report on this trip that I received my orders to report back to Washington for transfer to the Amphibious Forces.

Now the U.S. Navy is justly a very proud institution. Junior officers are supposed to follow orders swiftly and exactly. They are not to make suggestions or offer encouragement or advice. They are, above all, not to criticize their commanding officers or to demand a transfer to another command. I had violated a code of behavior and had earned appropriate punishment. What would be more appropriate than transferring a naval officer to an Army invasion force. If he didn't come back, it would be no great loss.

When I arrived back in Washington, I immediately went to find Jim McDonnell at the Bureau of Aeronautics to ask him about my new assignment. He tried to be positive. He told me the idea of assigning Air Combat Intelligence officers to amphibious landings represented a new development in technological assistance of which the Navy was proud. It would be an experiment, but the function was a needed one. The need had been amply demonstrated by the amphibious landings to date. Since the Navy was responsible for getting the troops ashore and assuring sufficient fire power until artillery units and tanks could be landed, this meant that Navy ships' guns and Navy air squadrons would have to replace artillery during the early days of any invasion. The Navy already had trained shore fire control officers—men who could be sent ashore in the assault waves with equipment with which to maintain communication with the ship's gunnery officers. But so far in the war, nothing had been done to coordinate air strikes against the enemy to assist the assault units. This new group to which I had been assigned would, if the system proved workable, be the forerunner of similar Air Combat Intelligence units who would take part in all future invasions. The Navy realized that the Allies were still in retreat around the world and that it would be some time before forward operations could be undertaken. But it wanted to be ready. For this purpose some thirteen ACI officers had been selected who would train with one U.S. division earmarked for an early planned landing operation somewhere in the world. In North Africa there had been no need for air support because when the Americans landed in Morocco, the French chose not to fire back. The next amphibious landing would be different.

In the ACI Amphibious Force unit there would be one officer assigned to the divisional command, responsible for coordination with the air commander on the assault command ship, as well as with the ACI officers participating in the landing. Each of the three infantry assault regiments would have an ACI officer assigned to it, as would each of the three battalions in each regiment, for a total of thirteen naval officers. Our unit would train with the 45th Infantry Division, a National Guard division from Oklahoma, Colorado and Arizona, and would eventually go into combat with it. It was certainly a novel assignment for naval officers. I looked forward to it, particularly since this represented a new concept in naval warfare due in large part, I suppose, to what would turn out to be the necessity of painfully recapturing a whole host of islands in order to reach Japan proper.

Our group of thirteen quickly developed a wonderful esprit de corps. Tom McFadden, our divisional officer, had been a trial lawyer in New York and a partner of Bill Donovan, hero of World War I and was currently head of the Office of Strategic Services, the American intelligence organization. He was a good choice, very organized, very methodical, with a good sense of humor and never subject to panic. He was the elder statesman of the group and it was very reassuring to have him in charge. The three regimental ACI officers were quite different. They were approaching their forties, yet were full of the devil. One had been running a mill in Rhode Island, one was in a textile business in Georgia which his family had owned for several generations, the third came from Seattle, Washington, where his father had made a fortune in the lumber business leaving a wife at his death who, as a result of an accident, was in a coma with nurses around the clock, no chance of recovery, but depleting the family fortune at a remarkable rate. Our group at the battalion level was much younger, lieutenants (junior grade) or ensigns. We had two lawyers, a government bureaucrat, a contractor, a manufacturer of fasteners, an accountant, an organizer of pack-trips in the Sierra Mountains. I suppose this was a typical group of naval reservists. The important thing was that all of us, young and old, looked upon this assignment as both a challenge and a lark. It didn't seem to have occurred to us that participation in an amphibious landing would be a highly dangerous occupation.

Each one of us was given a chief petty officer who was a highly experienced radioman. This was essential because the radio would be the key to voice communication with the naval aircraft which would serve as artillery on the landing. The ship's gunfire officers could be directed at targets ashore that could be seen from ships instead of having ships lob shells several miles inland. It was much more sensible to use planes to blast a troop concentration or strafe a convoy of troops inland.

In my case, the chief radioman assigned to me had had the best chief petty officer's job in the entire Navy. He had been the radioman on Admiral King's assigned aircraft. Since Admiral King, the chief of naval operations, detested flying, the crew's only duties were their four hours of flying time a month to qualify for flight pay. The rest of the time they simply stood by in case the admiral wanted to go somewhere by air. Occasionally, but not frequently, they may have taken important personages on a trip. It was marvelous duty for a chief petty officer who didn't want to do anything anyway. Unfortunately, my chief radioman had made a young girl in Washington pregnant, and her mother had written a personal note to King as chief of naval operations to inquire how a man of his standing and reputation would have as staff on his aircraft such a monster. The Navy in selecting suitable punishment had sent the poor man to be my radioman. When he arrived at Norfolk, he was thirty pounds overweight and obviously had taken no outdoor exercise in years. He did not know what awaited him. And since my life might depend upon his capacity to act, I was not about to show him any special kindness. I fully intended that he should get to be in top physical condition even if I had to cause his death in the process.

Life on maneuvers with the Army was not an easy occupation. We had first been sent for specialized training at Virginia Beach, south of Norfolk. There we practiced with landing craft, going up the Chesapeake every weekend for a bivouac and to undergo bombardment by Navy 8-inch and 14-inch guns to see how we reacted to bombing conditions. This activity in the mud and snow of winter where we were not allowed to make fires and the ground was forever wet was not pleasant. There were few laughs. Once we staged a landing on a beach in the Chesapeake. As we "hit the beach," we found newspaper boys meeting us with a call to "Get your *New York Times* here." It must have taken a certain amount of courage to market Sunday papers to a group of thoroughly soaked officers and men, armed to the teeth, landing on

My role in the 45th Division— using Naval airplanes as artillery the shore on a snowy morning. I thought it a remarkable example of American initiative.

Eventually, we joined our respective Army units. The company commanders in my battalion were an interesting sample of the West: a sheep rancher, a liquor runner for Al Capone from Mexico to Chicago, an oil wild-catter—tough men, but very able leaders, independent, but fiercely loyal to the men in their units. Our intelligence officer had a master's degree from Northwestern. The battalion commander was a West Pointer who might have qualified for the role of John Wayne in a movie featuring infantry landings in Normandy. These men's attitude was very new to me. They were very competent, no-nonsense individuals, products of their past civilian activities, further hardened by three years of training under all sorts of conditions: from desert training in Arizona in the summer to midwinter conditions at Pine Camp, northern New York State.

Our first effort together consisted of extensive Army maneuvers in western Virginia in the late fall of 1942. Our 45th Division did not behave according to the rules of the exercise. Too many of the officers and men came from the South. Told that they faced a largely black division from the North, they simply mounted their bayonets and charged the enemy. It broke up the maneuver. We did not even get the chance to use the squadron of Navy planes from Norfolk which was to participate with us.

The weeks that followed saw us gradually finding the rhythm of our life and work together. We were each given a naval squadron for different types of maneuvers all over the United States. We learned to work with the planes and to guide them to the objectives the battalion commander needed to have destroyed. We became accepted by our Army peers who began to recognize our usefulness.

When the day dawned for our great embarkation, we were ready. Mine turned out to be the lead vessel in a fleet of 3600 ships headed we knew not where. My entire battalion of roughly 1000 men was on this ship. The captain, discovering that I was a naval officer, called me to his cabin and notified me that I would be expected to stand watch. I had not been trained to do this. Navy regulations were of no help. They belonged to sailing days, containing such archaic instructions as "Wake the captain in the event of a change in wind." Fortunately, on any ship the quartermaster chief petty officer is worth his weight in gold. There were radars on all the ships. The lead ship in the convoy could see whether any ship was veering to port or starboard or gaining or losing way on the other ships. With 3600 vessels close together and constant changes in speed and direction to avoid possible submarines, these nights on watch were both fascinating and terrifying. Every few minutes a voice would come across the P.A. system ordering one ship or another to get back into line. There were no lights anywhere, only the red glow around the radar. In rough seas, it took all one's powers of concentration to remain on course. The hiss of so many vessels going through the water is unforgettable to me even today. I thought we would never reach land.

We passed at last into the Mediterranean and scattered into various ports along the Algerian coast. We still had no idea what would be our ultimate destination. On an invasion, no one except the key commanders knows the location of the landing.

In Oran, after two weeks at sea, the men were not allowed ashore. I was allowed to go because I was given the privileges of a deck officer, which I had earned during the passage across. I was delighted because it would give me the opportunity to speak French and study the reaction of the French to the war in Europe and their feelings toward the Americans, as well as the Germans. I was lucky. In the first restaurant I came to, I found an old friend from childhood in New York, Alex de Pourtales, who, like me, was half-French, half-American. I had not seen him in perhaps ten years, but in that atmosphere we were both delighted to see each other again. He was having lunch with two well-dressed young women and an older man in French uniform. "Come and join us, Thibaut," he said. He introduced me to his friends and I had lunch with them.

"I am going on maneuvers this afternoon, Alex, but we are due back in Oran in a week from today. Let's make a date now to meet together in this same restaurant then."

I was delighted to have met a friend so quickly. I had no idea how long I would be staying in Oran, but it would have been lonely by myself, and I didn't know whether the rest of the ACI group would meet up before we all left for the unknown.

That afternoon our flotilla began to meet up for landings further down the coast. Ours would be the invading division faced by three U.S. divisions. The British and Canadian forces would be trying the same tactic some miles away.

The invasion turned out to be a total disaster. As we plunged ashore from our landing craft, we saw no one. We had landed in the wrong place, some miles from the "enemy." The planes didn't show up on time either, and when they did, I had no targets to give them from the co-ordinates on my map. It was not comforting to think that wherever the real invasion would take place, such errors might be made again. But it was awesome to see all the naval cruisers and destroyers passing along the shore behind us ready to lend support if this had been the real thing.

We camped for the week, all 18,000 men of the division, on the grounds of an old battlefield of the 1942 campaign. The ground had not been properly cleared. There was debris everywhere. In practicing digging a foxhole, I even uncovered the bones of a man's leg. Needless to say, I then dug elsewhere. The worst, however, was the voice of Lili Marlene at 10 o'clock at night. The nights were very warm and as we lay close together under that clear Sahara sky, we listened to that voice calling us almost by name.

"This song is dedicated to the men of the First Battalion of the 157th Regiment of the 45th Division. I am playing for you the lovely song: 'Don't Sit Next to Anyone Else But Me Under the Old Apple Tree.' Isn't it sad that you will never see that tree or that girl again? She will not wait for you. And you will never return. For we know where you are going and we are waiting for you."

Her voice was delicate, haunting and very sad. Her effect on the men, however, was to stir their anger, rather than fear. I noticed that the men were unusually quiet that week. Perhaps it was because they were so far away from home facing a test they had been well trained for and yet were not able to predict how they would perform when it actually happened. And lastly, they knew there was no turning back.

I was glad, as I'm sure the men were, when we packed our gear and went back to the landing craft and to our ship. Everything had been checked and rechecked, inspected, greased, packed for the next landing, which would be for real.

Oran seemed like civilization after the desert. I hastened to my ap-pointment. Alex was there with two very beautiful young French girls. They had arrived early and had already had quite a bit of champagne. It was a warm, clear and very beautiful day. From the way Alex was look-ing at one of the girls and holding her close, it was easy to see how the afternoon would go. They all three seemed so young and so happy. I wondered how long I would be allowed to stay with them and just relax, to eat and drink wine, dance, and just have a good time, joking and laughing as though tomorrow would be a repetition of today. My date was lovely and very promising.

It didn't last very long. Halfway through the lunch, just as it was clear that the young French girl Alex had brought for me would make me forget the past few months and the long trip across, a group of shore patrol sailors came up to the second floor of the restaurant where we were sitting and called out: "If there are any men here from P.A. 140, you are requested to return to your ship immediately."

I promised my friends that I would return as soon as I could and went back to the ship. The ship's crew and the Army men were lying all over the foredeck, lounging and playing cards. I could see on the bridge the captain and a man wearing a polished helmet liner painted with three stars. The general wore what appeared from below to be beige silk jodhpurs and cavalry boots. The captain took his megaphone and introduced General Patton.

The men were paying no attention. Some were even trying to continue their card games.

"In 72 hours, men, you will all be dead." The three star voice roared out across the deck. The card games stopped. The men were all attention now.

"This battalion has been selected to be the hinge between the three U.S. divisions on the west, and the two British and one Canadian division on the east. This is a very special honor which has been granted you. Why? Because when you land, you will find the Hermann Goering SS Division, which I consider to be the best division in the German army, fully mechanized and at full tank strength. Your mission is to go as far as you can before you are all wiped out. It is of the utmost importance to the invasion that you keep the forces opposite you occupied for as long as possible to afford the armies on either side to consolidate their position and get their armor ashore. You are not to take any prisoners. The whole civilized world is looking to you. God bless you."

Then he turned to the captain.

"Captain, set sail."

Patton went ashore. The lines to shore were let go. The ship pulled out into the channel. There was a total silence among the troops on deck. Nobody wanted to be the first to speak. I thought of the lovely girl waiting for me whom I would never see again.

The next three days were the most extraordinary days I would ever spend. Imagine being on a vessel at sea carrying a thousand men who have been chosen to die within 72 hours. No reprieve, no appeal possible. The ship is headed toward the point where your destiny will end. How do you spend the limited time you still have?

There were Masses almost all day long. Our chaplain was a Catholic Maryknoll monk who had been with the battalion ever since I joined it. He talked with a broad Irish brogue, had a great wit and loved to drink whiskey, rather more than less. The first night in Oran he had been brought on board in a cargo net. Now all this changed. He was a priest preparing a thousand young men to meet their maker. He listened, he spoke, he prayed with some; he heard confessions; he gave the sacrament to those who wanted it; he accepted letters and messages to loved ones; he made promises. He was everywhere. All of a sudden he had taken on a great dignity as well as humanity. He was a priest.

Everyone wrote letters and postcards who could write. I saw a Scripto pencil worth 10 cents sell for thirty dollars. Money was worthless, but a pencil would send a message home with a last thought for mom, or Mary, or Jane or whoever. It was important.

One of the most interesting things that occurred during this 72-hour period—the lifetime allowed us by General Patton—was the men's reaction to Patton's order not to accept anyone's surrender. You must remember that this was the most highly trained division in the U.S. Army. Toughened by a year of constant wartime maneuver exercises, these men were in top physical condition, trained to kill with bayonet or knife, mean, and ready for any order to kill an enemy. Yet, curiously, some could not accept that no prisoners would be taken. As a result, if I walked on the deck, men would come up to me and say, "Lieutenant, I have just heard the Nazis caught some of our paratroopers, poured gasoline over them, and set fire to them." On a sealed vessel, nobody could get any news. The rumors of German atrocities were simply created spontaneously by men who were trying to adjust to the idea that they should kill other men in cold blood who asked to lay down their arms.

The poker games went on as before. I watched one Army officer on deck through the porthole in our cabin put an end to one poker game, seizing both the cards and the money. Through the open porthole, I heard one of the men say, "That bastard will never make it to the beach." I believed him, and it turned out that way.

The five officers, the four platoon commanders and the battalion's intelligence officer that I shared a cabin with, were very quiet. We were all trying to imagine how we would truly behave when the moment came. In the wardroom a packing case of huge dimensions had been opened. Laid out on mess tables and taking up a goodly portion of the room was a model scale of our landing site, the point of land, the village behind, the pill boxes and other defensive fortifications, the beaches on either side of the point, the roads beyond the village that we might never reach. Twice a day we met there with the colonel, who explained what each platoon would be responsible for. We spent hours reviewing the times of embarkation starting at midnight and what men and equipment each landing craft would contain. We also received the order on which craft would land and on which beach. So clear were our minds that we could each have recited these decisions in every detail. It had the beauty of a complex mathematical exercise.

As the French say: *L'homme propose, mais Dieu dispose*—"Man proposes, but the Lord disposes."

The day after we left Oran the weather changed. It was obvious to every one of us who had ever been to sea that some terrible storm was brewing in the Mediterranean. The next morning the sky was red. All day long the storm intensified. I wondered how they would even be able to get the small landing craft into the water. We now had twenty-four hours to go before the landing. The waves were building up constantly. About a third of our battalion was made up of Indians, Apaches from Arizona, Cherokees, even Utes from Colorado. On the way across the Atlantic, I used to see them standing silently as far forward as they could go on the foredeck, gazing silently and motionlessly toward the horizon in front of the ship. I had the impression that their forebears sitting loosely on their horses must have looked out in the same manner toward the horizon on the great western plains looking for a herd of buffalo or unfriendly men. Now they looked out to sea and noticed the waves building up. This was a very different scene from what they were used to. They could see it would be bad even though they didn't understand it. They simply understood instinctively more than the white men because they understood nature better. Toward dusk, everyone on the ship was becoming concerned. All of us who had major responsibilities on the landing were hopeful that somehow it would be postponed. But how can you possibly postpone an invasion that requires hundreds of ships, thousands of men, and attacks by planes taking place before the landings from dozens of airfields?

As night came, it became clear that this storm would be the worst in many decades—40 years as it later turned out. As night fell, our cabins' lights were extinguished. We knew that by midnight the landing craft would have to be lowered from the ship's sides. Putting a thousand men in small craft, lowering them to sea, and letting them circle the ship until just before dawn so that they could land before daybreak involved an extraordinary feat of logistics. In my case, I had to synchronize my equipment, landing in the assault wave with my battalion commander, while my chief petty officer radioman would land with the jeep in the fourth wave, by which time hopefully the beach would be secure enough for him to get his jeep ashore and drive it someplace where it would be reasonably secure. The whole operation had by its very nature to be completely hit or miss. Would my landing craft get to shore? If not, who would replace the battalion commander? Who would replace me in directing the aerial artillery? I had a squadron of Navy fighter airplanes from a carrier lying offshore. Would my jeep land safely with its radio equipment intact and dry? Would my radioman have time to strip off the protective coatings and get into radio contact with the assault ship commanding—and hence with the air commander—so that we could coordinate the air attack with the squadron commander? Would the enemy allow us the time to do all this? Would any of us even get ashore in this raging storm? If we did, what opposition would we meet? I kept thinking of what Patton had said: "Gentlemen, in 72 hours you'll all be dead."

I must say that when the Navy decides to organize a last supper, they do it well. Beginning at 11 o'clock p.m., the mess hall was ready to serve a meal that would have done any restaurant proud. There were soups, meats, vegetables, cakes, ice cream, and coffee in abundance. The only trouble was that the ship was pitching tremendously, and that we had to force ourselves to eat, knowing that for the next three days at least we would have to subsist on K-rations—those little boxes of chewing gum, raisins, artificial eggs and protein biscuits. At midnight, we began to gather on the deck to prepare, each with his group, for embarkation in the landing craft. It was very dark on the ship. Outside, the night was black. There was thunder, lightning, and occasional heavy rain. As I arrived on deck, I could see nothing. There was no shore visible. Only these enormous white caps shining in the dark and the waves smashing against the sides of the ship. It did not seem possible to me that we would ever be able to reach the water, much less stay afloat for the next four hours, until it was time to land. No one in my group spoke. Everyone knew what he had to do. Each one of us had on a life vest, carried his pack on his back, helmet on top, and held his rifle in his hand. Each individual was lost in his own thoughts. The only question was immediate survival. I don't think any one of us thought that if we managed miraculously to reach shore, we would then be face to face with the German Goering Division. It might perhaps have been worse if the night had been calm and we could have reflected on what awaited us.

I shall never forget that night. As a starter, try putting on a thirty-pound pack, then jumping into a small boat with thirty other men in the dark, get down in a knee-bent position to withstand the shock of the boat hitting the water, feel the sides of the boat hitting the sides of the ship as it swings with the rocking motion of the ship in the heavy seas, wondering whether the descent will ever end, then suddenly feel the smashing of the boat's bottom as the first wave hits it. With extraordinary agility, the crew of the landing vessel got us away from the ship before a new wave would destroy our landing craft against its side. Then the engine took us temporarily to safety. I managed to reach the side, where the wind could temporarily keep me from being sick. But the small diesel fumes took care of that. As we looked back at the ship, we could see that some of the landing craft were being overturned against the side of the ship as they were being lowered. I wondered whether my jeep would make it. The storm seemed to be getting worse all the time. In the boat there were a few oaths from time to time, but the only pervading sound was the vomiting and the retching of men who could not stop being sick. It was an endless four hours. There was no impression that there were any other ships nearby. It was as though some six thousand vessels making up the Sicilian Armada had all sunk in the storm. The landing craft's crew was magnificent. They managed somehow to keep us afloat, and just before dawn was about to come, they automatically took their allotted positions to make a run for the beach where it was thought to lay ahead in the darkness. I don't know how they managed it. All of a sudden, in the dark, we found ourselves in a long triple line of landing craft, all headed in the same direction.

After a while, we heard the sound of the surf and then saw the white foam on the rocks of the shore. The beach at Gela where our battalion landed was narrow and surrounded by rocks. Further down in both directions, where the three U.S. divisions would land, the 1st, 3rd and 9th, as well as the rest of the 45th, and where the two British divisions and the Canadian division would land, the beach was wide. But for us, there was only a narrow gap, tricky to get through even on a calm night. My landing craft did not quite make it. We hit a ledge lying just off the beach. We managed to get out of the landing craft but waded through waist-high water to get to shore. At that point, we would not have cared if there were lions and tigers in wait for us on the sand. We were too far gone to put up much resistance. Yet there was light. The town of Gela in the distance was aflame. Ships' guns had opened up on the shore batteries. There were huge flashes of light from behind us. We began to feel that in the pandemonium which was beginning to take place, there would perhaps be some way each of us would be able to move forward, taking advantage of any cover available.

From the Law to War

My battalion commander was superb. His company commanders had fanned out as directed as soon as they had landed. To our increasing surprise, there seemed to be little resistance. We were slowly making progress inland. Something must have happened to change the scenario that Patton had outlined to us. We didn't find out until much later what had happened. The day before our landing, the Hermann Goering Division had been moved to the area where the three major U.S. divisions would land. The Germans would almost succeed in throwing back the landing there. It would be necessary to bring U.S. destroyers close to shore where they could fire on individual German tanks approaching the beach. The survival of my battalion had nothing to do with the courage of its men or the skill of its officers. It was only once again a question of luck.

As the sun rose, the GIs began to notice that men were trying to surrender and that they were Italians rather than Germans. Before realizing this and accepting attempts at surrender, there were a few prisoners executed. The GIs' understanding always amazed me. The American is not methodical and ruthlessly effective like the German. But he will use his instinct better. As the sun came out, the men noticed that certain of the enemy were wearing medals that shone in the sunlight. These were the chests you aimed at. On the second day, I captured an Italian general who complained bitterly that our men only fired at the officers. Unfortunately for them, they had worn their medals.

In the late morning I found my jeep. My poor chief must have lost ten pounds in the night, but his equipment was working. We communicated with the assault commander and were promised a squadron for thirty minutes in two hours' time. By that time, we had identified the pillboxes that were holding up any advance. This time communication was excellent. In two passes the pillboxes were gone. The battalion commander couldn't believe it. We sent the planes on and agreed on a time schedule to be monitored in case of later need. There was one sad note to the help given us by the planes. A squadron of Messerschmidts had appeared briefly over the beach. As one of our fighters pulled up from the target, it was caught by a German fighter and shot down, too low for

An Italian Division is substituted for the best armored division in the German army.

the pilot to escape by parachute. I discovered later it was my friend, Bill Walsh, with whom I had played so much poker on our U.S. maneuvers.

The essential part of a landing operation is to never let men move faster than their ability to get ashore the equipment they will need to allow for a further advance. You must allow ammunition to get ashore; you must also try as quickly as possible to establish enough of a beachhead to allow reinforcements to land in comparative safety and as quickly as possible increase the firepower of the men ashore. It sounds very simple in theory. In practice for our battalion, everything worked out with comparative ease. The Germans had no interest in us because they were being successful to our left. The Italians had no interest in fighting. The second day when we took some five thousand prisoners, the Italians came up with signs saying, "We're going to New York. You're going to Rome." It was hard to believe that men around us were still being killed. We were not prepared for what was happening.

The first night ashore, I had dug a foxhole a mile or two from the beach. A lad of five or six years old came and joined me. I gave him half my K-ration kit. I spoke Spanish to him and he answered me in Italian. We managed fine that way. As he tried the canned egg, he said sadly: "You don't eat very well in the United States, either." He didn't know what was happening and wanted to walk back to Gela through U.S. and enemy lines in the middle of the night. I tried but could not dissuade him. He said his mother would be very angry if he didn't return home. I hope he made it.

Late the same night, the battalion commander picked up word on his radio that we should expect an enemy parachute drop on our lines. At three in the morning, we began to see parachutes dropping from the sky above us and inland far beyond us. Before we realized that the drop was our own 82nd Airborne Division, many of the paratroopers were shot by our own men. In the dark it was quite impossible to detect friend from foe. What courage these paratroopers had. To jump out of a plane in the night is bad enough; to depend upon accurate navigation in the middle of a terrible storm with very high winds to land where one is supposed to is demanding accuracy which cannot exist. I would reflect later, as I prepared to be parachuted into France, what special courage is demanded of those who join this service. What saved us from a worse disaster that night was the realization that the voices shouting to each other in the dark as the men landed were speaking English rather than German. As soon as light came, the problem was solved. It was good to have the 82nd with us in our march further inland.

Seeing the signs carried by the Italian prisoners made me realize the true senselessness of war. In the space of four days, we had been told by the general commanding the invasion of Sicily that we had no chance of survival; we had then sought to make peace with our maker; we had survived a terrible storm and succeeded in getting to shore; we had fought a night-time action against our own paratroopers; now the general we were fighting complained that we were concentrating our fire on officers, while our Italian prisoners were carrying signs boasting they were headed for New York. Humor and ridicule must certainly be the antidote to military action or senseless bravery. Fortunately, none of the men in my battalion had the opportunity to reflect on this senselessness. For a few days, they all knew that they would eventually be matched against the German Wehrmact and that was when the real test would come.

I shall not describe the next two days. Our units, as we speeded inland, became separated. I spent one afternoon leading an anti-tank unit. My jeep vanished in the turmoil, but we did not need the support of planes. By the end of the second day, my battalion had taken Ragusa, a city of 36,000 people. There was room now for the tanks to land. There was no longer any need for me to stay with the battalion.

As you can imagine, there was pandemonium in the streets. We had no heavy equipment, no tanks, yet the GIs were surrounded by people in the streets who welcomed them as liberators—no one seemed to be in charge on the American side. As often happens in an unplanned advance, we had simply advanced beyond any battalion headquarters. I found a Monsignor in the principal square, and together we located a balcony from which to speak. He spoke to the crowd below, told them many other troops were coming, that there would be fighting, and to go home to wait and avoid danger. I left him and went back to find my battalion commander. By now the tanks would be coming ashore on the beaches behind us. We had passed an airfield. There would no longer be any need for Navy air support. It did not take me long to find my battalion commander. He hurriedly wrote out some notes to be mailed home. We shook hands and he gave me permission to return to the ship. On the way back, I found my jeep and an angry chief who felt he had now expiated all his prior sins. By the third day, we had turned over our radio jeep to a communications unit and had gone back to our troopship. I had hardly slept in four days and had had little to eat, but the job was done and the beachhead by some miracle was secure.

I must have arrived back aboard my troopship around 5:00 p.m. The

86

captain asked me to report to him, and I gave him as complete a report as I could, stressing the excellent job done by the Navy men running the landing craft and the prompt manner in which Navy planes had eliminated the fortifications holding up our advance. I had time afterwards to go below, take a shower and put on my naval officer's uniform. By the time I reached the wardroom for dinner, I was almost too tired to stand.

On the ship one could not imagine what had been going on ashore. With the exception of Army material still being unloaded for transportation to the beach, it was as though the ship was still in Oran. There had been no German air attacks on the ship; the ship's officers and men carried on their duties quietly, efficiently and without discussion. In the wardroom, steaks were served that night. The mess boys wore clean whites and gloves. Beside me was a young ensign. When he was served, he remarked to the mess boy, "What, steak again?"

I don't know what happened to me then. I have only lost my temper to that degree one other time in my life. All I remember is that I got up, pulled the young ensign to his feet, held the front of his uniform tight with my left hand, while I hit him as hard as I could with my right fist. He went down like a rock. All of a sudden there was total silence in the wardroom. This is sacred officers' territory, and no one ever behaves that way in the wardroom of a U.S. naval ship—no matter what the provocation.

The captain's voice: "Executive officer, take this man below." I was ushered out, taken down to Sick Bay, given an injection, and immediately fell fast asleep in a bunk while an armed enlisted man stood outside my door for the night.

The next morning I was summoned by the captain. "I can give you a general court-martial," he said.

There was no point in arguing. He was totally in his rights. I had no explanation and no excuse.

"I will reflect upon what I shall do," he went on. "I have a copy of a message from Admiral Kirk on the command ship stating that the nine ACI battalion officers displayed extraordinary gallantry and devotion to duty and would be recommended for a merit citation. But this is my ship, and you have disgraced it. Go back to your duties, and I will decide what action I will take in due course."

A captain of a naval vessel at sea can do essentially anything he chooses to do. He is responsible for the safety of his ship and the actions of all its officers and men. He cannot allow or excuse what had happened the night before because those who had not observed what happened would immediately have heard it from others. Relationships between officers must meet the exact standards of the Navy or discipline fails.

I ended up making a public apology and getting a reprimand, following a statement given out on the public address system by the captain, stating the facts, the outrageous behavior of one of his officers, the conditions ashore and finally the expression from the admiral of the success of our ACI mission. Luckily, the young ensign I had hit was not popular with the ship's crew.

So this event lapsed into history. But all the way home, I had the midnight or 4:00 a.m. watch. We brought back on our return via Oran a full complement of German prisoners who would be sent to the Mideast to work on the farms replacing the men who had gone off to war. These men, too, would crowd the foredeck as the American Indians had done on the way over to Europe. But for these Germans, who had been led to believe that the seas were filled with German submarines, the concern was different. All the way across, they were looking for a periscope to rise, signaling either a rescue at sea or a sinking of the ship. On our way home, we traveled alone. It was believed that frequent changes in speed and course would perhaps be safe travel in a large group. Furthermore, there were few warships to spare for convoy duty when there were no troops aboard.

When we returned to Norfolk, we were reunited with our other ACI group. None had been killed, one grievously wounded, but his life would be saved by a new antibiotic that had just appeared in hospitals for the most difficult cases. It was called penicillin and was hailed as a miracle drug.

My three particular friends within the ACI group—who have remained friends throughout my life—were Henry Shoemaker from Seattle, Ike Livermore of California and Lou MacMurran of Newport News. They were all three very different, each unusually interesting in his own way.

Henry's family had originated in Philadelphia. He had gone to Princeton, was remarkably good looking and a splendid athlete. His mother had been put away in a hospital for the incurably ill where she would remain in a semi-comatose state for the rest of her life. His father had died shortly after the parents' divorce. Henry had never married, preferring to remain the bachelor in constant demand. Because of the unhappy relationship between his parents, Henry went so far as to spend every year from Christmas to New Year's at the Park Avenue apartment of the woman who had written, *A House is not a Home.* Henry would arrive on Christmas Eve with presents for all the girls and stay until New Year's Day. He would point out to me that this was a very quiet time at the apartment and since he had no more family than the girls there, he enjoyed making Christmas a happy time for them. Henry and I would spend much time together in China. Then we would meet up much later in Geneva in the 1970s. Henry by that time would be golf champion of Geneva and happily married to a particularly warm and attractive Austrian woman by whom he had a daughter. It was just unfortunate that with all the qualities in the world, Henry was one of those persons responsible for his own bad luck. In our work together later, he passed his luck on to me.

Lou MacMurran had been a real-estate developer in Newport News. His passion was politics and he was the ultimate people-person, a quality that one often finds in successful real-estate operators because they must understand people's needs and are able to relate to them. When we returned from Sicily, Lewis asked me to accompany him to visit the governor's mansion in Richmond. He had two purposes in mind: to brief the governor on the invasion, but also to introduce him to a young woman he thought of marrying. He wanted frankly to see, if I understood it correctly, how she might look in the governor's mansion and whether the current occupant would like her. On the way across to Europe and on the return trip, Lewis was working his way through the Encyclopedia Britannica. Armed with an outstanding memory, there was not much he didn't know on our return from the A's through the C's. In those days in Virginia, politics were of one party and that party was controlled by the Byrd family. They were gentlemen all, but very able politicians as well. Richard Byrd, the admiral, had become a friend after I had met him when I was working at the Sulzbergers. He had taught me that when he spent that winter alone with his men in their underground bunkers, the only way that he could keep them from fighting with each other was to force them to focus their dislike and frustrations on him. He would cut out all ice cream one week, then meat, then eggs. He would adopt exercise rules and then modify them on a whim, have curfews that didn't make sense, anything to keep the men from taking out their frustrations on each other. I thought at the time he had great courage to risk his own life that way. Lewis never married the girl, nor did he reach the governor's mansion—but he became president of almost every worthwhile organization in his native state of Virginia.

Ike Livermore was perhaps my closest friend. At 6´6˝ he was not the tallest of five sons in this well-known San Francisco family. He was a great outdoorsman. Before the Navy took him, he used to run pack trips in the High Sierra Mountains each summer with mules as the beasts of burden. In Sicily, he found more mules than he had thought existed. I think he would have gladly stayed there if he had been allowed to organize a mule-train to climb the mountains in the interior and take the Germans from the rear.

When we returned to Washington, the Bureau of Aeronautics asked Ike and me to visit the various Army Air Corps installations in order to discuss our experiences in Sicily and how the Air Corps might find it helpful to train a similar group of officers to maintain air-ground liaison where Navy planes might not be available. We were given a black F-70 night fighter-bomber and a remarkable pilot called Colonel Mears to take us to different sections of the country where there were Air Corps training bases. It was a great experience for us, and we stretched it out as long as we could.

Like Jack Tuohy, whom I have spoken about earlier, Ike was destined to make good choices and to be given the chance to make them. He had married, just before we went to Sicily, Dina Pennoyer, the granddaughter of J. P. Morgan, who was as outgoing and positive as he always was. Many years later, after serving as treasurer of a lumber company in California, he was invited by the new governor of the state, Ronald Reagan, to serve as his commissioner of natural resources, easily the most important job in the state administration. Ike asked the governor why, since he had not actively participated in his campaign. "I am told you are an officer of a lumber company and also president of the Sierra Club. Any man who can balance those two activities is the man I need in this job."

"Will you let me run the department as I wish?"

"I want you to report to me once a week so I know what you are doing, but I will not interfere. I have too many other things to do."

Ike accepted and later told me the governor never interfered with the way he ran the commission. I decided then that Reagan had a capacity to pick good men and then leave them alone. Roosevelt had had that same capability and used it well. As William Pitt had once said, "The essence of good government is to find good men at an early age, put them in positions of power, and then leave them alone." In 18th century England, as in wartime Washington, it was easier because the good men were anxious to serve.

Through Admiral King's efforts, it had been decided that each one of us would be attached to the staff of the commanding general in each theater of war and be responsible for preparing air-ground support plans and operations. Then at the last moment, Admiral King had been persuaded by the Marine Corps colonel or his staff that naval officers should be on ships, not on the ground. Our orders were cancelled. I had been slated to join General Alexander's staff in Italy. It would have been a glorious experience.

From the Law to War

Admiral King cancels my orders and I join the OSS. It's back to school.

As a result, most of us went to Navy carriers or land-based squadrons. With Jim McDonnell's help, I was introduced to the Office of Strategic Services (the OSS) and selected to take their four months' training program prior to joining a group called the Jedburghs to be parachuted behind the lines in Europe.

The OSS training was interesting, principally because the trainees came from many different countries, speaking many different languages, sometimes not in addition to English. I remember my first three-day indoctrination exercise very well. It was headed by a professor of Psychiatry at Harvard and took place somewhere in eastern Virginia. We were shown a series of silent films where one man was asking questions of another. We were then asked to answer a series of questions about the conversation. We were taken to rooms where acts of violence had taken place and given only minutes to study everything in the room and then give a written analysis of what had occurred and why. Finally, I remember that we were taken outside where there was a small stream running through a field. I went there with a group of some ten men, none of whom spoke a common language. The problem was to get across the stream without anyone getting wet. There was an instructor with a stopwatch present. The purpose was to see who could exercise initiative and leadership under impossible conditions. There were other similar exercises during the three-day period.

The next two months I spent with a group of so-called Special Operations men. The purpose here was to learn how to blow up bridges or buildings. The most intriguing part of the last day's exercise was to be divided into groups that would go down the river into the Marine Corps base at Quantico, avoid detection, and wire one of the bridges with explosives. This type of realistic training was supposed to make us ready for similar operations in enemy territory. With this group there was plenty of action every day, but very little intellectual stimulation. I enjoyed it because I was in excellent physical condition, and it interested me to try to determine just what countries my classmates came from.

I would not have wanted to run across any of them on a dark night. For some reason, in the man-to-man combat exercises, I was always paired with a very tall Greek who seemed to have far less difficulty practicing lethal exercises on me than I on him. The instructor kept telling me that I was smarter and quicker, but there seemed to be obvious limits to these advantages in close combat practice.

The next and last OSS school was for men who would be dropped behind the lines, either on intelligence or on sabotage missions. We were directed to meet in a Washington area barracks, being sure to arrive in civilian clothes. Each of us before meeting the other was given nondescript clothing and personal effects. We were advised at the same time that throughout our stay we would be expected to learn as much as possible about the other members of the class. We should create a role for ourselves which should be always consistent so that others would accept that we were just who we said we were. The purpose here was to teach each individual to play a role for a full two-month period. The lesson that I learned was to remember that if you are required to play the role of some other person under cover, be sure always to choose to be someone whose background, expertise, mannerisms, education, even intonation and accent conform as near as possible to your own. We were told that part of our job was to learn as much as we could about our thirty classmates, examining any correspondence, and keeping a notebook about what we had been able to learn. Since no one could be given away by the clothes he wore and each person left purposeful clues, it was not as easy as it may sound even to determine which country each man had originated from. With so many countries obviously represented in the group, it was difficult to even classify nationalities by accents. When you consider that we were constantly engaged in day-long activities together, the task of playing the role of someone else was difficult. To make matters even more complicated, at the end of the first month we were told we could have a three-day pass, but each of us was assigned another member of the class to spend the weekend with. To this day, I have no idea of the nationality, background or profession of the person with whom I went on this furlough. If I were asked, I would probably have guessed a Yugoslav headwaiter, but I have never seen this man again.

Have you ever tried to go off on a weekend of fun with someone you don't really know, who obviously from his accent comes from a foreign country? You have agreed together to go to New York. This is where you come from. But you cannot call or see anyone you know. You are both in remarkable physical condition. For a month you have been engaged in constant physical activity outdoors. At night you dreamed of glorious meals in the company of beautiful women. Now your tastes will be put to the test. It was a curious weekend. We stayed at the Hotel Pennsylvania near the station. We laughed a good deal, easily found dates, and ate well. We returned to Virginia exhausted, but ready to face another month in the woods. I knew no more about my weekend friend than before except that he enjoyed a good time, good food, and good-looking women.

We decided on New York, stayed at a large midtown West Side hotel, had some good meals, a great deal of sleep, saw several movies, went dancing at Roseland, and otherwise learned nothing about each other. Obviously, I could not call any New York friends. It was probably the most bizarre weekend I will ever spend. Out of desperation for something new and relaxing to do, we even spent half of one night practicing opening the doors of various hotel rooms, having just completed a lock-picking and safe-cracking course given by an old Frenchman who really knew his business. Many years later, when I was a senior partner of Coudert Brothers, the great international law firm, I remember arriving in Paris to have lunch with Charlie Torem, the senior partner in charge of this office, which had been opened long before the turn of the century. Charlie was having a fit. He could not open his safe. He was expecting an important and very wealthy woman client in the afternoon who was coming to execute a new will. The old will, which she would want to destroy, was in Charlie's safe. I lay down on the floor of his office, persuaded him to keep quiet long enough to hear the tumblers, and opened the safe that a French expert called in that morning had been unable to open. I think for the first time in his life my partner was speechless. "Any time you are in trouble over here," I told him, "just call on the New York office for help." Sometimes one learns a trade one should never know anything about.

The last day of our stay in this camp, the faculty offered us a magnificent dinner with a long cocktail hour in advance, excellent white and red wines at dinner, followed by brandy and cigars. When the director invited us to sit down, each one of us in turn took his place in an armchair at the end of the living room while the others dissected where he might have come from and what he had been doing in civilian life. Extraordinary that so many of these men with whom we had shared two months of life in a remote camp in the Virginia woods remained a complete mystery. We were totally unprepared for this end to the

*From
the Law
to War*

Fighting
the
enemy in
Pittsburgh.
It is us.

evening. Most of us had had too much to eat and drink and were totally relaxed. We were, therefore, off guard and completely honest in our remarks about one another.

The following day, six of us were called in to the director's office and told that we would have a week's leave and then spend the next ten days on an exercise in Pittsburgh, Pennsylvania, designed to test our ability to operate successfully under cover as though we were foreign agents engaged in a mission of industrial sabotage or intelligence gathering. We were advised that we could assume any cover we wished so long as it was in the private sector, that any letterheads, calling cards or letters of introduction we wished to have would be prepared for us. So that we would not be totally alone, we were divided into two teams. The team leaders could establish message drops so that they could communicate once with each other. Members of each team were told to remain in touch according to the elaborate rules of undercover work that we had learned at the camp. We were warned that if caught by the FBI—the agency charged with counter-intelligence surveillance—we were under no conditions to reveal our link to the OSS. We would demand to speak to counsel. A telephone number in Washington was given to each of us to call. Counsel, at the other end of the phone, had been appointed by the agency to handle these matters directly with the head of the FBI. It was not explained to us what might happen to us at the hands of that agency before we were to be allowed to speak to counsel. It has to be remembered that this was wartime and that the FBI was expected to be on full alert. We were also told that at the end of the exercise we would be expected to return to Washington, where we would explain to the OSS, the FBI, and the executives from the companies given us to penetrate, just what we had learned, and how we would carry out what we had been sent to do if it was espionage, or what secret documents we had been able to obtain from company files, if the object was intelligence gathering. We were also told that in the last class, one man, an aeronautical engineer, had managed to return from Baltimore with the blueprints of a new Navy bomber still in the planning stage. Naturally, the primary purpose of the exercise was not only to test what we had learned in camp, but for the government to judge how well manufacturers doing classified work for the armed forces were guarding their secrets and how well the FBI was protecting them from any indiscretions or outright theft of documents. It was pointed out to us that management changes and FBI shakeups had resulted from the

Baltimore episode. The seriousness of what we were being asked to do was unmistakable.

On my team of three, I had a professor of Romance languages at the University of North Carolina and a former Czech master mechanic from Massachusetts. The other team was headed by a former major league baseball player. The companies my team was given to infiltrate were U.S. Steel, Westinghouse, Mesta Machine Works and Jones & Laughlin Steel, all companies engaged in very important work for the war effort. The three of us spent a whole day together deciding on our cover. The professor chose Westinghouse, the mechanic chose Jones & Laughlin, because he knew the steel business and he thought he would have a better opportunity here to get a temporary position, pending clearance by the labor authorities. This left me U.S. Steel and Mesta. Each of us decided, as a result of what we had learned in training, that we would appear to come as close as possible for purposes of cover, to what we had been doing before joining the OSS. The professor wrote himself a magnificent series of letters from the university explaining that he was engaged in an important study involving hours of work lost under wartime conditions as a result of labor problems, a very reasonable activity, since we both had decided managements would generally be more receptive to labor problem questions and neither one of us was an engineer. He had been trained to handle men who would be engaged in the European theater of war in intelligence gathering. The mechanic and I were to be sent overseas in a parachute drop. Our role was more sabotage than intelligence gathering. The mechanic needed no letters other than letters of recommendation as to his technical ability from supposed employers in New England, and a bona fide medical reason for moving his supposed family to Pittsburgh. My own cover was to be a study organized by the Columbia Law School to examine insurance coverage in areas of steel plants where industrial accidents were most likely to occur. I am ashamed to say that I had the OSS prepare letters outlining the purpose of the study, which I then signed as dean of the law school and as professor of labor law and insurance law. I figured perhaps this way I would be taken to plant areas where accidents were most likely to occur and then figure out how to get there and what charges to sue to cause major damage. As I look back on this whole episode, I am flabbergasted at my own temerity.

The baseball player and I agreed on how we would communicate, and if both gave the all-clear signal, where we would meet during our stay in Pittsburgh to report any FBI activity which would help each of us decide how long we could stay in the city without risk of getting caught. I also arranged how within my team we would be able to remain in touch with a minimum of risk, each to the others. I then went home to get out of uniform and get back into civilian clothes.

My mother was appalled when I told her I had to get my civilian suits out of storage. I think she thought I had somehow been expelled from the service and was fleeing to Mexico. I had to tell her I was being given a vacation leave and was spending it in the Caribbean, where the wearing of uniforms was not necessary or even advisable. She produced my civilian clothes without much enthusiasm.

And so I started off for Pittsburgh. In those days one went by train. Without my uniform, I felt like an outcast already. This feeling was very much heightened when I went into the dining car for lunch. The dining car steward seated me at a table for four. Already seated were a rather formidable middle-aged woman and an equally middle-aged couple. I sat opposite the single woman who looked at me with immediate dislike. As she turned to the other man opposite her she said, "I really dislike being forced to eat with a man who should be in the armed forces and has managed to keep out of the war. Do you feel the same way?"

"Our sons are fighting in the Pacific. I feel exactly the way you do. The draft should take everybody."

I wanted to be far away. I thought all three of them would get up and ask to be seated elsewhere. They probably would have except that the car was full. It was not a pleasant lunch. I felt like telling them that I *was* in the service and engaged on a perilous mission. Obviously to them, tanned and very fit as I was, it must have been galling that I was a civilian.

The next two days I spent at the University of Pittsburgh library learning all I could about making steel. I had called the senior partner of the law firm that represented U.S. Steel. He invited me to call on him, and when I explained my mission, he called the chairman of the company to assure him that I obviously was a New York lawyer and that he would vouch for my credibility. He also called the head of the Pittsburgh FBI to give him the same assurances. This man asked to speak to me and told me to call at FBI headquarters so that an agent could review my documentation. We set a time for me to come in to the FBI two days later. In the meantime, counsel arranged for me a preliminary meeting with the head of personnel at the company. This is as far as I was able to get at U.S. Steel. At Mesta, I had better luck. This was a family business. The family had come originally from Germany and were very concerned about meeting all the rules. But they were engineers and liked to discuss how they avoided wartime accidents. Our meeting was helpful, but inconclusive. Although they showed me engineering drawings, I came away with little except an understanding of what was being built and where.

When I met with the professor, I was delighted to learn what he had been able to accomplish. He had been given to study the detailed drawings on the firing mechanism of the 16-inch guns for the Navy and had managed to put a set of drawings in his briefcase. I suggested that he go back to Washington as quickly as possible. He unfortunately waited too long. As he was about to leave his room at the William Penn Hotel, there was a knock at the door. There were two FBI agents with drawn revolvers. They took him into custody, took him out to a country house owned by the agency, grilled him for hours. The agent in charge finally admitted that his story seemed sound, but he decided to check with the president of the university by phone. Obviously, Gordon Gray did not know the professor under his assumed name. What followed was a series of threats and physical abuse which the professor had never had to endure before. Three days later, when I saw him in Washington, he was still visibly shaken.

I had great difficulty finding my mechanic. He had been given immediately a temporary position at Jones & Laughlin. Unfortunately for him, each section of the plant had differently colored identity badges. In his first lunch hour he had strayed into the open pit section where steel was poured, had been noticed as not belonging there. He panicked. A chase ensued, and he managed quite by chance to get through a door that opened on the street. He had jumped on a passing trolley car, made it back to a poor man's hotel near the train station, and had barricaded himself in his room. When I found him, he had all the furniture piled against the door and had not eaten for two days. When they dropped him later in occupied Czechoslovakia, I doubt if he lasted very long.

My friend, Mike, the ballplayer, met me for dinner as scheduled. I told him of the success of the professor and that my own meeting with the FBI agent had now been postponed. As I later found out, the postponement was due to the interrogation of the professor. Mike's group had had only very limited success. Each of us, however, learned firsthand how difficult operating outside the law could be.

When I returned to Washington I was told that I would shortly be leaving for Scotland to take my parachute training and then be dropped into the Vereors, a mountainous region in Eastern France, as a member of the Jedburghs, the men in OSS who were the real heroes of the war, operating behind the German lines in occupied France, carrying out sabotage operations with the French Resistance under control from London.

I was to pick up my orders at the old Q Building near where the Watergate complex is now located. I was told to be there at 9 o'clock one Thursday evening with my duffle bags to pick up my orders. The plane would leave for Scotland that night. I had just one week to say goodbye to my family. But I could tell no one where I was going, or what I would be doing.

The author and his friend and fellow naval officer, Norman "Ike" Livermore, visit an Air Corps installation to discuss air support.

The author, ready for landing in Sicily with the U.S 45th Division, where his role was to provide close naval air support to his battalion.

The author and his battalion seized the German airfield in Sicily shortly after landing.

At an award dinner with Admiral Kirk after Sicily, members of the naval air support team received medals of commendation.

The author's battalion capturing a German flag in Sicily. They were fortunate that, right before their landing, an elite German panzer division was moved to face the U.S. 1st, 3rd, and 9th Divisions, instead of their 45th Division, leaving them to face mainly Italian forces.

IV

BEHIND THE LINES IN CHINA

HERE ARE TIMES WHEN a man will consciously make a decision that will change his entire life. This is what happened to me in the Q Building that night. I must have paced up and down the second floor of that old building at least twenty times. I remembered the French I had met at Oran and Algiers a few months before, the shopkeepers, the French officers I had been introduced to by my friend Alex de Pourtales, the American liaison officer to the French in Oran. More than that, I remembered his comments to me. He was, like me, a Franco-American, who nevertheless couldn't tell on which side of the war the French he had to deal with had aligned themselves. Had the patriotic French gone off to join de Gaulle in London, and were those who stayed in French territory largely secret sympathizers with the Germans? How could one tell them apart? Alex told me he was unable to do so. But if he made a mistake, his life would not be at stake. Mine would. Should I take the chance which might never come again to try to change my orders, or was it my duty to go East that night because the orders waiting for me were behind the door marked, "Europe?" It wasn't the jump that bothered me; it was what I might find after I was dropped into France. I had been well trained during the course of the last four months in OSS camps and was sufficiently conditioned that being back in combat did not bother me; it was the fear that once there, I could be betrayed by my own people, by the French whose country I had made my own in 1939.

As I paced up and down the long corridor, I noticed doors to a number of offices. One marked "Far East" had a light on, so someone must still be working there. It was then that I made my decision to try to go West instead of East. I knocked on the door.

A voice said, "Come in." I opened the door. There was a naval lieutenant working at a desk. He had on a green eyeshade, and on the desk

I go West instead of East— Burma instead of China

and scattered on the floor were what turned out to be officers' resumes and background materials.

"I'm sorry to disturb you," I said. "I saw your light on and I just wondered if you might be looking for a naval officer to send to China."

"Who sent you?" he asked.

"I am on my way to Scotland in an hour or two. I am here to pick up my orders. In Scotland, I do my jump training and will then be parachuted into France. Frankly, I'd rather go to China, if you can use me."

"Do you know what I have been doing since 2 o'clock this afternoon? I've been sitting here trying to find an officer with the right background to be the American liaison officer on General Wingate's staff. This has the highest priority from Roosevelt himself, and I can take anyone if only I can find the officer I need. Have you had combat experience?"

I told him I had.

"Then go across the hall and bring me your travel orders and your Navy jacket."

"Wait a minute. Who is Wingate and where is he going?"

"He is commanding officer of a British army and he is on his way to retake Burma."

I did what I was told. He read my record, told me to stay in his office, and disappeared across the way. When he came back, he told me to come back the next morning. He would have my new orders cut by then and would tell me what to do.

That is how I went West instead of East.

My whole life was changed. It was just that simple. At least that evening. The next morning I was informed that I was to go by air to San Francisco and then by air again to India, but by noon the itinerary was changed to a train to Los Angeles. I had been bounced off my flight by a more senior officer. At 5 o'clock I was in a sealed car of a train bound for the West Coast—sealed because it carried engineers for the B-29s to come and OSS personnel bound for the Far East.

I looked around me as the train was pulling out. There were 29 men and seven women in the car, civilians and officers both. There were two rather attractive women, one very tall whose name was Julia Child, one short named Rosamond Frame.

Three years later I would marry Rosamond Frame.

But at that moment what interested me was to organize a bridge game to while away the three days' journey to the West Coast. The girls and I found a Navy lieutenant to make the fourth.

In Los Angeles my orders were changed again because I was bumped off my flight to the Orient by someone with an even higher priority. So, instead I found myself headed across the Pacific on the former luxury liner, *Mariposa*. Through some unexplainable good luck, I even found myself sharing one of the few private sun deck staterooms with a senior Army courier. By this time, I had begun to realize that I was not exactly in charge of my destiny. I was feeling like a pawn on a vast chessboard, headed east to do whatever I was told whenever I arrived at my destination. I wondered whether Wingate would wait for me, but I didn't give it very serious thought.

To tell you the truth, I was having a very good time. On the train trip across to Los Angeles, in between bridge hands, the four of us had told each other who we were, where we came from, and what we thought we were going to do in the Far East. Julia and Rosamond had been in the OSS almost since its inception. Julia had joined because she came from California and wanted adventure, and Rosamond because she had been born in Peking, grew up there, spoke eleven Chinese dialects perfectly and dreamed of going back there to help her country get rid of the hated Japanese. She had been working in the research branch of the OSS following and commenting on events in China. Since my cabin was always empty during the day, she spent the month at sea teaching me, or at least trying to teach me, the rudiments of spoken Mandarin Chinese. A paratrooper friend of mine from Boston who was also on the ship studied along with me, pronouncing that great language with an unmistakable Boston Irish accent. When one of us made a mistake, it was fifty pushups a throw, but Jim, who made more mistakes than I, could do them on one arm.

One of the more amusing adventures of this trip across the Pacific was the attempt by Jim Ward and me to tap into the liquor which the ship was carrying for Indian potentates. The ship's officers in a moment of frankness had told us that the ship had taken aboard at Wilmington, the port of Los Angeles, several thousand cases of premium Scotch whiskey destined for the princes of India, gifts of the British government. I told Jim of what had happened to my Great Great Uncle, Commodore Gaston de Saint Phalle, at the time of the Mexican War when sailors tapped the case of tequila containing his body. Jim suggested that perhaps we were more worthy of access to the merchandise than the princes, who, after all, were contributing nothing to the war effort while we were clearly going out to protect them against the Japanese invaders.

It was an easy matter to persuade a crewman to let us into the holds in return for a share of the loot. I still recall with amusement the sight of Ward and me, wearing only our undershorts, lifting cases in these huge holds to get at the five thousand cases of wines and scotch. I have never run across more cases of Kellogg's corn flakes, ketchup, tinned goods of all kinds. Knowing that the ship would be carrying several thousand troops, the dock master had cleverly put the wines and liquors on the bottom of the hold, with many layers of canned goods on top. In the Tropics, holds of steel ships become exceedingly hot. It must have been at times 110 degrees in the hold. We tried to make an enormous hole, but the more crates we took out, the higher the wall we created around the hole and the more difficult the job became. We found cases and cases of Coca-Cola, but the more warm Coke we drank, the hotter we became. At the end of ten days, we were no further along than when we had started and we finally had to abandon the operation.

The ship was said to be followed by enemy submarines, so we only stopped twice during the month's voyage: once in Tahiti, where no one was allowed ashore, once in Perth, Australia, where we stayed for three days, and I almost missed my ship. In Tahiti, we could smell the scent of flowers from the shore, see the girls in their *pareos* on the beach, and hear the music of ukuleles. Perth, then a city of some 350,000 people, was an Australian frontier town which might have served as a set for cowboy movies. I remember standing on a small hill in the center of the city looking down the main street which was not even paved. There were horses tethered to posts along the street and a handful of tired motorcars. There were bars on either side, and in the late afternoon, one could see men being thrown out on the street through the swinging doors. I found one bar which looked more benign than the rest. Inside were many young girls and a handful of men, either too young or too old to have been taken into the Army and sent to the far-flung outposts of the British Empire. I have never met more boisterous or friendlier people in my life. Early Americans must have been very like the Australians of the wartime period: direct, uncomplicated, friendly, generous to a fault. I sat with a young teenager and his two sisters. They insisted within the hour that I accompany them to a rose-covered cottage they had by the sea. Off we went, in an old battered pickup truck. I thought I would never be able to get back to my ship. There was not enough they could do for me. As it was, the *Mariposa* was just getting underway when I returned to the dock and I had to get a pilot boat to take me out.

We arrived in Bombay in April 1944. Wingate had marched into

*Behind
the Lines
in China*

Wingate
loses. I am
ordered to
Chennault
in China.

Burma with his small expeditionary force. His force had been ambushed. He had been killed. Instead of going to Burma, I was given orders to go into China to report to General Chennault. There were evidently serious political questions remaining to be resolved between the Army under General Stillwell, the Air Force under General Chennault, the naval units under Navy Commodore Miles and the OSS unit which until then had been directed by Miles. I was told that General Donovan, director of the Office of Strategic Services, had had Miles recalled to Washington where control of the OSS group in China was taken away from him. This meant that the naval units under Commodore Miles would continue to work with Chiang's intelligence services and that the OSS would operate independently under personnel yet to be appointed on projects yet to be developed. Miles and his executive officer were on their way back to China when I arrived in Bombay. Sadly, I left Rosamond, who was headed for Delhi until she could go to China. Although her orders were for her to go there, the American ambassador to China, not wanting his wife to accompany him, had declared China off limits as too dangerous for any American women.

As luck would have it, I found myself on the same train as Commodore Miles going from Bombay to Calcutta. It was customary, since I was a naval officer, for my orders to be turned over to Miles' executive officer, who was in charge of all naval officers on the train. I found Miles intelligent and charming. We played bridge for the three days it took the train to cross India. Miles did not seem angry at what had happened in Washington, except to say out loud each time we passed an Air Force base, "There goes the Royal American Air Force." Arriving in Calcutta, we had become more than just acquaintances. But when he saw my OSS orders, he turned to his executive officer and said, "Get this man off the train." I never saw the commodore again. He was, indeed, a very strange man, working hand in glove with Chinese General Tai Li, chief of Chiang Kai-shek's intelligence bureau and one of the most hated and feared men in China. I didn't care. I expected to be reporting to Chennault, who was a legendary and much beloved figure in China. My only concern was how I would function as a naval officer and whether the Navy would pay me, given Commodore Miles' attitude towards the OSS and its personnel.

The Office of Strategic Services (OSS) had a big operation in Calcutta from which vast quantities of material was shipped to different operational units throughout Southeast Asia. Like all OSS headquarters, it seemed to me to be full of people carrying on liaison activities with field operations all over, always frantic, people tripping over one another, filled with incoming and outgoing officers trying to get out of Calcutta as promptly as possible. With Wingate's operation no lon- ger active, OSS Washington confirmed that I should report to General Chennault in Kunming, China, but it took a week to prepare my orders that would take me out of Calcutta and on to China. Finally, orders were typed and signed and I would be on my way by air over the "Hump," as the Himalayan Mountains between Calcutta and Kunming were called. I couldn't wait to get away. There are people who enjoyed being assigned to headquarters. I was not one of them.

Calcutta in 1944 was a place of wealth and of despair. I went to lunch one day at the American consulate with three young consular officers. As we left the building, we saw a number of natives lying on the pavement, the bones of their emaciated bodies etched through the thin cloth of their cotton robes, their eyes staring out of death's head sockets, their lips pulled tight. "They'll be dead by the time we get back from lunch," said one of the young men. "I'll bet you on it," said another. I didn't want very much to go out with them. It was one thing to kill an enemy in combat who would otherwise kill you. Betting on the survival for a few hours of another human being reflected an acceptance of death and disease which I wasn't prepared for. It seemed to me that everywhere I looked in Calcutta, people were dying of starvation, of cholera, which had reached epidemic proportions in the city, and of malaria. The Ganges was always filled with dead bodies bloated beyond recognition. Yet the well-dressed English and the rich Indians were at the horse races every weekend, and otherwise living and eating well in this sea of misery. One night I was taken to a famous French nightclub with rooms upstairs. The girls wore jewelry and evening dress. Several I had seen in boxes at the racetrack the previous Saturday. Now they were here to make one forget how brief life could be. I couldn't wait to get out of Calcutta.

Beyond Calcutta and its millions of miserable human beings lay Assam and its tea plantations, and beyond that the Himalayas and China. "Flying the Hump" it was called in those days. It took approximately three and one half hours to fly across from Calcutta to Kunming if the plane didn't get lost or the winds weren't too bad. The plane used was the reliable DC-3. But the winds above the mountains would change direction as you changed altitude. As a result, a pilot might find himself straying off course very easily. Also, instruments were nowhere near what they are today. From time to time, a plane would disappear or the passengers asked to bail out because of lack of fuel. The planes themselves were remarkably reliable. Indeed, DC-3s are still today flying in mountainous regions of the world, where airfields have short runways nestled between mountains. Douglas has never made a better plane.

On the other end of the Hump lay Kunming, capital of the Yunnan Province in southwestern China, as depressing a place in China—and in a very different way—as Calcutta was in India. Kunming was barren, cloud-covered most of the time, and totally lacking in any kind of cultural activity. It was solely a wartime supply base. Its only advantage lay in its location and in the fact that it was reasonably safe from Japanese attack. It was a supply base for the armies of General Stillwell, whose purpose was to prevent any Japanese attack from Burma. There were various dreary army training camps in the area, where by agreement with Chiang, the Americans were only allowed to train Chinese officers below the rank of major. General Stillwell resembled an American frontiersman of the French and Indian War days, with a mind to match. He was thin, bald, scrawny, tough and prided himself on being able to march twenty-four hours a day, if need be. The officers around him matched his style. Worse yet, Stillwell openly disliked the generalissimo. He would refer to him as "Peanut." Chiang on his part was interested principally in having his junior officers trained. In the field the Chinese armies were a disaster. Since Chinese field grade officers had not been trained by the Americans, they were only able to tell their men to "climb the hill" or "come down again." The younger American-trained officers could only suffer horrendous casualties from the machine guns and mortars of well-entrenched Japanese, never being able to use the modern tactics they had been taught. In the meantime, American journalists wrote articles lauding General Stillwell's fortitude in the face of adversity. The general would have made an excellent drill sergeant in the prewar Philippines. He was neither a politician nor a strategist. In defense of General Stillwell, it should be pointed out, however, that his operation satisfied America's desire to show the Chinese that it appreciated their efforts against the Japanese. To President Roosevelt, who understood military strategy perfectly, Stillwell's activities counted for little in the war. Supplying him with modern weapons was not a priority, particularly when the military was short of weapons and there were heavy demands everywhere.

General Chennault was someone else again. Half Cherokee Indian and a tough disciplinarian, he had been hired by Chiang at the outbreak of the Sino-Japanese conflict in 1937 as an advisor to the Chinese government. Chennault had given up his active commission and at the request of the Chinese had, in 1939, hired a number of ex-pilots from the Army, Navy and Marine Corps at a minimum salary of $1000 per month to become mercenaries in the service of the Chinese government. This was the now famous AVG (American Volunteer Group). The pilots in this group had all for one reason or another left or been cashiered from the American Peacetime Officer Corps. They were a daring, ruthless, rootless, aggressive group of men willing to fight and die far away from home if the money was there and nobody asked too many questions. The AVG, like the French Foreign Legion, was made up of men whose pasts were better left unknown. To the Chinese, they were heroes. *Behind the Lines in China*

My friend, Paul Frillman, with whom I spent so much time in China, had been hired by Chennault to make sure his flyers turned up in China on schedule and were fit to fly. Paul had gone to China after graduating from college in Minnesota and completing his studies to be a Lutheran missionary. He had learned Mandarin in Peking before the Japanese invasion. He was a man of action rather than a man of God, and when Chennault proposed to him that there were souls to be saved, as well as men to be delivered to AVG headquarters in China, he accepted. Paul was a serious man, but he had great energy and a good sense of humor. He would later regale us endlessly with his stories of the trip across the Pacific by ship with his devil-may-care pilots and their wives or mistresses. One of his funniest took place in Singapore where they were to stop over for a ten-day period en route. Without notifying Frillman of their intentions, the pilots decided that the way to the hearts of English damsels from Singapore was through the lure of Hollywood. One of the group was selected as a movie producer, suitable ads were taken in the local press to let the public know that there was to be a beauty contest to determine Miss Singapore, who would then be offered a motion picture contract. Other members of the group acted as secretaries to the producer, advance men, advertising and publicity agents for the studio, or Hollywood agents. The idea took Singapore by storm. This was not surprising, as in 1939 there were not too many activities of that sort to excite the hostesses of the city. In any case, the response was beyond expectations. There was a cocktail party at the government house, dinners every night for the Hollywood group, and our heroes enjoyed a week of bedding the beautiful girls of Singapore (and their mothers) under promise that their relationship with the producer would assure the prize. According to Frillman, he managed to get his men out of the city just before the local press discovered the ruse.

Frillman confided to me that he was never so relieved as when he had finally delivered his group to the general at the end of the journey. He thereupon took up his duties as chaplain to the AVG and chief of staff to the president of the company, Claire B. Chennault. I have often wondered how Chennault managed to keep control of his AVG pilots without having to send more of them home. I suppose the answer is: Where would an unemployed American fighter pilot banished from the services go in the depression years before the war?

When war with the Japanese broke out in December 1941, Chennault was immediately given a commission as a major-general in the American Air Force and the AVG became the United States 14th Air Force. The past was forgotten, the high salaries also, and the pilots became commissioned officers in the United States Air Force. The planes were replaced with new Curtiss P-40s. These were not the best airplanes in the U.S. arsenal, but they were very rugged, needed little maintenance, and could use the less than satisfactory dirt runways scattered around China. Because of the background of the original pilots, a certain leeway was allowed in military discipline. The planes' noses were painted with tiger sharks' jaws. Chennault had long since become a genuine hero to the Chinese. This was now extended to the whole of the 14th Air Force. China being China, however, the country's local press everywhere continued to report the bravery of Chinese pilots in the shark's-head planes and asked why American pilots did not join the battle against the Japanese which the Chinese had fought alone for so long. It was a frustrating experience.

The officer B.O.Q. (Bachelor Officers Quarters) in Kunming was located right on the air base in an unprepossessing building just like all other buildings on the base. They resembled Hollywood's idea of a prisoner of war camp in Germany. Each room had two bunks in it, two bureaus, a desk and a chair. At the end of the single story building were located the latrine and showers. There were no trees on the grounds; there was no color anywhere. As if to maintain the monochromatic air of the place, the sky almost always was overcast. After settling in and introducing myself to the pilot who would be my roommate and who had turned out to be the younger brother of a girl I used to date in Newport, Rhode Island, I stopped by to introduce myself to some of the pilots in adjoining rooms. The pattern was the same. If a pilot weren't flying, he would be in his bunk reading a comic book and waiting to go on a mission later in the day. The pilots knew nothing of the country they flew over each day. They simply kept track of their missions to know how soon they would be entitled to be rotated home. They couldn't learn the language. It was too hard. There was nothing for them to do in Kunming except drink bad liquor in the few bars or to make casual love to the Chinese women they found there. On the base at least, there were movies. The pilots were risking their lives each day for a cause they knew little about in a country where there was no one to exchange ideas with except each other.

When I went in to see the general the next morning at 9 o'clock with my orders and my Navy jacket, I wondered what I would ever find to do in this depressing country. The general didn't wait long to tell me. He sat behind a big desk and cut an imposing figure. His secretary was a beautiful Eurasian from India. It was evident that her duties went beyond taking dictation.

"I am delighted to see you," he said. "Your record indicates you are a man who likes initiative. I have in mind an interesting project for you. I want the Yangtze River closed to Japanese commercial shipping traffic. It is too far for my planes to go there except occasionally, and they have to be over enemy country for too long a time. I will give you my chaplain, Major Frillman, who is an Air Corps major. I can get my hands on a Navy Lieutenant Commander Shoemaker and Major Leonard Clark of the Army, the explorer of Hainan Island, who ought to be useful if you get into any kind of skirmish. Of course, I can only take you to Kweilin several hundred miles east of here, but you fellows can buy trucks to take you the rest of the way from there. As far as supplies, equipment, guns and ammunition . . ."

"Excuse me, General, I wonder if you might turn to the wall map behind you and tell me just where the Yangtze is on the map and where you want us to carry out this mission against the Japanese."

I don't think it had ever occurred to Chennault that I would not know the country or speak the language. He showed me where he wanted us to go on the opposite end of that enormous country, to a promontory along the river halfway between Shanghai and Nanking. It was only later that I was to discover that Japanese heavy cruisers patrolled this stretch of the river on a regular basis. I saw that it was quite at the other end of China and that Kweilin, heavily circled in red on the map, was less than halfway there.

"I will look forward to meeting Major Frillman, General. I know Commander Shoemaker because we were together in the invasion of Sicily."

I met Frillman that evening. It seemed to me that I had known him forever. He laughed a great deal, had amusing stories to tell and quite evidently had a special rapport with the general. At the end of a long lifeline and beyond, this seemed to me to be a capital asset, indeed. Shoemaker joined us for dinner. We were delighted to see each other and at the thought of going off on a new adventure together. Shoe was particularly happy to be extricated from the Miles group. He said it was a vast bureaucracy and thoroughly under the control of the Chinese Secret Service and its infamous General Tai Li. To Frillman, Chennault was at least as well known in the country as generalissimo Chiang Kai-shek. "I will take care of our passports tomorrow," he said. "We will need a passport from Chiang for official reasons. But I will prepare one for Chennault to give us, complete with pictures and all the red ribbons I can find. In this country, the more chops and the more ribbons you have on a document which identifies you, the higher the rank of the official who gave it to you and your own standing. In much of the area we are going in, Chiang's passport will be the kiss of death. But the general's chop is good everywhere. You'd better get rid of those naval uniforms," he added. "You don't want to look like Miles' men where we are going."

The next day we met Clark. He was fortyish, square, very much the soldier's soldier and totally devoid of any sense of humor. The Chinese to him were Chinks, people to whom you gave orders and by whom you expected to be obeyed. I think we all three had the same reaction: How will a man of such limited sensitivity be able to function in a strange and generally hostile environment, unable to speak the language, and at the mercy of interpreters? Still he had explored Hainan where no foreigner had been before.

Preparations took the better part of a week. Chennault had given us two DC-3s to fill with what we needed to take. Clark took charge of the military equipment and had friends to help him at one of the Army training units. Shoemaker, a born scavenger, secured what he could from the Navy. I took the three weathermen who were assigned—all trained as radiomen—to get what we might need in way of communications equipment. Frillman was overall in charge. Since he knew everything and everybody, we would not have accomplished anything without him.

We left Kunming with high hopes and great expectations. Even Frillman was delighted to be escaping life at headquarters. When we arrived at Kweilin, our problems started. It had been decided that we would go north from there by train at least as far as Changsha to the northeast. There it would be easier to find trucks, because this was the end of the railroad line that was still functioning regularly.

In normal times the run from Kweilin to Changsha would take overnight. In our case it took two days. It seemed to me that the entire population of Kweilin was at the station: men, women, children, dogs and innumerable bundles wrapped in blankets and tied with rope. We were taken to the pullman car emblazoned in French with the words, "Compagnie Internationale des Wagons Lits Europeens." This car had evidently come from the old Shanghai Express. I remembered the film with Marlene Dietrich and Erich von Stroheim, and expected to see them come aboard. Shoe and I had one compartment, Frillman and Clark the other. As soon as the train started, we repaired to the dining car. This was living, particularly after Shoe produced dry martinis. We wondered what would happen at the first tunnel. It seemed as if every person in the station had secured a place on top of the cars. We toasted each other with a bottle of wine that night and went to bed happy.

The next morning we realized what it meant to have spent the night on a Chinese rather than a French train. Shoemaker and I had been bitten all through the night. Our mattresses were full of bedbugs. China is always full of surprises, we thought, and most are not pleasant. Twice that day the train was strafed by a single Japanese plane. In each case, the train stopped and everyone inside or on top of the train scurried for cover. It took a long time to get everyone back on board. By the time the train reached Changsha, we thought we had already covered half of China.

The next few months saw us edging our way north, trying not to lose our supplies and to keep our ultimate mission in mind. It was December when we at last reached the Yangtze. It was there that we discovered that Japanese cruisers were patrolling up and down the river. With the small amount of military equipment at our disposal, there was evidently little we could do, particularly since there were few Chinese troops in that region. It was then that we decided that we would divide East China, including the whole coastal region, into four sections, with each one of us taking on the responsibility for one section. This would enable us to concentrate our efforts to place agents in the Japanese-held coastal cities, retrieve information from there for transmittal to 14th Air Force Headquarters in Kunming, and organize a system to save any pilots downed in our respective areas. Our idea was enthusiastically approved by Chennault. We were proposing to cover roughly the eastern half of the country. He desperately needed to get good information on

To East China to close the Yangtze to Japanese river traffic ship and troop movements to substitute for what the Chinese government was giving him, almost all useless. We then journeyed down to Wutu in Kiangsi Province, the headquarters of the commanding general of the 3rd war zone, which included all of East China. There we would figure out with General Ku Chu-tung just what steps we should take to put our plan into effect.

General Ku Chu-tung's position in China during these war years was exceedingly important. He controlled roughly half the country. Generalissimo Chiang Kai-shek had been pushed westward by the Japanese. His headquarters was located in Chungking, a large provincial

city in the center of a rich agricultural area of western China, but of little strategic importance. Methods of transport in China from west to east were undeveloped. There were no railroads to speak of, the rivers in the west were not really navigable, the roads unpaved and in a poor state of repair. Marauding former military units become brigand forces accountable to no one roamed the countryside holding travelers and truck transporters up for ransom, if not the outright seizure of their goods. To understand the situation, compare China during the war years to the period of the Hundred Years War from the 14th to the 15th Centuries in Medieval France before the defeat of the English by Joan of Arc. General Ku was like the Duke of Burgundy in that period, an independent military and political warlord, with nominal fealty to the generalissimo, but in reality quite independent. Chiang needed him but would have liked to replace him with some other general he could better control. Each of the other so-called "free" areas of China, except in the remote Communist-held regions in the north of the country, were similarly controlled by other warlords, none of them interested in fighting the Japanese, with whom they carried on commercial activities, all of them busily building up their strength for the post-war negotiations with Chiang and ultimately the war with the Communists to determine who would control the country. It is interesting to note that when the Nationalists subsequently fled to Formosa in 1949, Chiang's defense minister at the time was this same General Ku, who fled with him. General Ku would then become the first Defense Minister of the new China Nationalist Taiwan, as Formosa would be renamed. Under these conditions, it was not surprising that U.S. government officials and the press had so much difficulty in understanding what was really happening in China and that U.S. military leaders in the country did not know to whom to turn to expel the Japanese occupiers of so much of the country, including all the important cities in eastern China. We were having the same trouble in China during World War II that we would later have in Vietnam: how to identify friend from foe. Even men like Frillman and John Birch, who knew China well and spoke the language fluently, found it difficult to follow what was happening from day to day.

Kiansi, where we were, was than a very backward part of China. Wutu was a small village in the province, hardly the kind of place where one would expect to find the general commanding roughly half of free China. General Ku installed us in a small temple by the river and promptly invited us for dinner. At this dinner we were surprised to learn from him that recently, for the third time in as many months, he had intercepted an agent of the generalissimo and General Tai Li who had been sent to assassinate him. We were also surprised to dine on coastal delicacies, which must have come from the Japanese-occupied part of China. General Ku was evidently working for both sides.

Even Frillman had trouble understanding just how best to establish a working relationship with General Ku. Ku himself was being paid by Chiang a rice allowance in the national currency for an army of three million men. We doubted if he had one-fifth of that. The balance of his rice allowance he simply kept for himself and sold in the market place. When he raised taxes, which he frequently did, he simply reported to the local newspapers that the central government of Chiang had forced him to do so by raising his contribution to the war effort. As a result, in this and other war areas, Chiang's popularity diminished each day. Nor did the local warlord's popularity increase. Everyone realized that he did not fight and that he was being paid by the Japanese to remain quiet. Under these circumstances, it was difficult to determine what we should do. We questioned Chennault. He approved our plan of dividing up the area into four sections with one of us responsible in each. He urged us to multiply our efforts to send agents to the Japanese-held cities of the coast and to continue our efforts to rescue his pilots when they were shot down in enemy territory. In both these occupations, we had been quite successful already. Our intelligence reports from agents we had been able to send to the occupied cities were very useful to Chennault's headquarters. Ship movements, troop movements, cargo manifests, were all sent back to Chennault by us daily by radio. In addition, the Chinese who worked for us were frequently able to rescue pilots and get them to us.

For Shoemaker, Clark, and for me, working with the Chinese involved all sorts of cultural difficulties. Unlike the French, the Chinese are perhaps the most curious people in the world. When we first arrived in Wutu, we would find every morning groups of Chinese looking into the windows of the small temple which General Ku had turned over to us. They were extremely curious to watch us shave, because in China this is unnecessary. If we went anywhere, we would be endlessly plied with personal questions. It was only later that I learned the purpose was to ascertain one's status and hence the amount of "face" that one was entitled to receive. Status was also very important to the interpreters who worked for us because their standing came from ours. I was pleased that in time I could understand what my interpreter was saying. I caught one once threatening a Chinese provincial general with a bombing raid on his headquarters by the 14th Air Force if he wouldn't do what I had asked him to do. The interpreter wanted the general to know that he was working for a most important man. Rosamond later told me that when she was about fourteen and rode in the summertime to Pei-ta-ho at the shore near Peking, the riding attendants would ask her: "How much does your mother earn as president of Yenching University? Will you marry an important American? Are you a virgin? Are young girls drowned at birth in the United States or sold as in China?" All questions of how much "face" to grant.

Sometimes "face" created problems which could be easily avoided. When I first came to China, I generally carried at all times when traveling a revolver in a shoulder holster. Then I realized how foolish this was. Obviously, if someone wished to do away with me, it would not be difficult, particularly since I often traveled alone or with an interpreter. It meant that if I stayed overnight in a hotel, I would be awakened in the middle of the night by the local police who would demand a passport and ask all sorts of questions as to why I was there, where I was going, who I was going to meet, or what I was doing. The police felt they had to take account of me because I was armed, and "face" required that they pay attention to me. When I gave up carrying a weapon, I was no longer worthy of their interest, and I was no longer disturbed in the middle of the night.

From time to time, my friends in the coastal areas and I would hear on the radio that an American pilot had been shot down or had engine trouble or run out of fuel on a particularly long mission. We would then try to locate him and have him brought in. We saved a number of pilots this way. It was always interesting. They thought what we were doing was far more dangerous than their work. It was very much of a mutual respect society.

"How can you live like this, Thibaut, far from everybody, with nobody to talk to? How can you eat this chow?"

For every pilot I saved, I would know I could count on a great evening with his buddies if ever I returned to his base. They had no more idea of what China was like than a UFO pilot from Mars might have of the United States if he landed at Scarsdale, New York one dark night. In many cases, they became very much interested in the country and in the daily lives of the people they met on their way back to their base. To the Chinese, these men were true heroes, not like the warlords who robbed them.

"So this is what China is really like." They could never have imagined it.

The relationships among pilots were interesting. There were the former AVG pilots, and then there were the others—the pilots who had come in just before, or since, the outbreak of war after Pearl Harbor.

The AVG pilots had a particular loyalty to each other and to General Chennault. He, in return, would try to favor his AVG group on promotions. But he was really an American Indian tribal leader, not the general commanding a military force in a democratic country.

I had occasion to witness this characteristic of Chennault on one of my trips back to Kunming to get supplies.

One of the AVG pilots had brought his young wife along when he joined. He had been a Marine Corps pilot and somehow had gotten into some sort of trouble and had either been given his discharge or had resigned his commission realizing that he would never be promoted. It makes no difference. I had met him several times. He was nice enough. He was also an exceedingly able pilot, and the others respected him for that. He liked to drink more than he should. When he did, his friends made a point of leaving him alone. He could be very nasty when drunk. He and his wife suffered each other. The bloom had long since faded in their marriage, if in fact it had ever existed. She was very blonde, with still a good figure, although she had put on a little weight since arriving in China. She kept herself looking well, tried to exercise when she could. The other pilots found her very attractive. They envied her husband. Above all, they envied the fact that he had his woman with him when they did not. Any one of them would have happily traded places with him. Now 28 years old, she had been just over 22 when her husband had met her at a dance in Omaha, Nebraska in early 1938.

Chennault must have met her at an officers' party in Kunming on some Saturday night. He danced with her that night, asked to see her again, wanted to have her. Obviously, Chennault could have had any Eurasian single woman he wanted, but there were few of these in China, and they would be in Chungking, the capital. In Chennault's world there was a simple answer. He called in the captain.

"I want your wife," he said. "I'll tell you what I'll do. You let me take her up to Dannang for a long weekend, and I'll rotate you back home within the month. You've been out here since the beginning of the war. I'll have no trouble sending you home."

"General, you have my life at your disposal. My wife you can't have."

Hincks didn't really care about his wife that much, but he came from Alabama and he wasn't about to let the general have her. A man's wife is under his protection, and he will certainly not permit an intrusion, no matter what their relationship is.

"Very well, then. We'll see about that."

Hincks went back and told his friends in the squadron what had happened. They kidded him, but any one of them would have reacted the same way.

The next morning the postings were put up in the mess hall. Hincks was sent alone to bomb the shipping at Taipei. The other pilots on duty were sent in pairs to other parts of China proper.

"The old man is dead serious," the pilots thought. "He's going to kill Hincks."

That evening just before dusk, Hincks came back, his plane wobbling in with holes in the fuselage. Hincks was dead tired, had too much to drink and went to bed early.

All that week, the routine was repeated. Hincks was sent out alone on some bombing or strafing mission without anyone to assist him.

On Friday, the general called him in again.

"The offer still stands. What about it?"

"General, you can have my life, but as I told you before, you cannot have my wife."

"Then I'll kill you."

Not surprisingly, Hank's wife Carol was told what had happened. Her first reaction was to be outraged. Then she was in turn proud of her husband, and then angry at the situation in which she now found herself that she should be a pawn. She would have liked to have shown Ken that she appreciated what he had done, but she didn't know how. She hated China more than he did. She didn't have friends because most other pilots' wives had returned to the States and she was very lonely. The thought of going home was very appealing.

"What the hell," she thought, "only three days . . ."

The following week, the same postings were made. At midweek, the general called Hincks in again.

"I'm sending you down to Mountbatten's headquarters in Ceylon for a week. It will bring you to your senses to see how pleasant life can be outside of this God-forsaken place."

While her husband was gone, Carol went to the general.

"Keep my husband in Candy, Ceylon, and I'll go with you to the spa for the long weekend," she said. "But as soon as we get back here, send us to the States."

When Hincks returned from Sri Lanka, his friends in the squadron told him what had happened. He had a great deal to drink at the bar of the Mess, then went home and beat his wife unmercifully. The next day he was transferred back to the States, but he did not take his wife with him. None of the men in the squadron ever spoke to Carol again, and I was later told that she ended up in a whorehouse in Chungking.

When the four of us had decided to split up and each take a portion of East China to work in, I drew the southern portion of the coastal area, including Fukien and Kwangtung Provinces and south from there to the Indochina border, an area of some fifteen hundred miles occupied by some three hundred thousand Japanese troops. It was quite a project for one officer, one enlisted man, some Chinese radio operators and one interpreter.

I established my base on the Min River between Foochow, a large city on the coast, and Nanping where Chi'en Tu, the general in command of an army group, had his headquarters. I was to maintain liaison with this general, who was responsible in turn to General Ku. Chi'en Tu was a mathematician, a scholar and an artist rather than a military man. He spent his days practicing calligraphy in painting as the Chinese do, with one continuous brush stroke. His sources of information were sometimes helpful, but not always pertinent. He liked to tell me, for example, that a group of American Navy officers and men would be coming down the Min River in a few days and that they were carrying so many machine guns, so many rifles and what their supplies consisted of. I would always pass this on to the American Navy officer in command. He would not realize that in China everyone passed on information to everyone else. I think the general assumed that the Americans

We divide East China into four pieces.

were playing the same game as the Chinese. Perhaps they thought we were vying for position as to which group of Americans would control China after the war. They were not far wrong—my Navy guests would never tell me where they were going or what they hoped to accomplish. They worked for Commodore Miles and General Tai Li. So to some extent they were an enemy, curious as this may sound.

What amused me most was how on every American or Chinese holiday all Americans, no matter whom they were working with on the China side, would always express greetings in the name of General Chennault. He was the one authentic hero to the Chinese, no matter where I went in the country.

As soon as I could, I went on down to Foochow, the provincial capital and a big trading city from which many of the overseas Chinese had originated. There I met two remarkable men who became my friends, the mayor of Foochow and General Li, a Christian divisional commander, who commanded the army protecting the city. I used to enjoy going to his headquarters and watching his troops marching to the strains of "Onward Christian Soldiers."

Shortly after I arrived, we received news that the Japanese would be attacking the city. The mayor was ordered to evacuate the entire population—350,000 people—so that the Japanese would find nothing to eat or to take when they arrived. You can imagine what was involved in putting this order into effect. Nevertheless, within a week's time, this modern city was totally evacuated.

I had met at the Foochow Golf Club the local head of the British MI-6, whose activities for the British were similar to mine. When the city was emptied, he moved into the British consulate. He suggested that I move into the American consulate across the street. Both consuls and their staffs had left. I did so. For a few days we both enjoyed the comforts of good beds and comfortable surroundings. We would get in his jeep or mine and tour this huge empty city by day or go to the golf course and try to play on a course which was no longer mowed. We had found enough food in the consulate to last for several weeks. We had also established suitable reserves of water. Moreover, there were regular drops of mail at the golf course. It was amusing to follow *Time* magazine's stories of the battle for Foochow. One week the Japanese would surround the city and perhaps advance in various sections, only to be repulsed by the Chinese with great loss of life the following week. There were even tactical maps of the battle by one R. M. Chapin of *Time*. It amused us to think that Teddy White, the *Time* correspondent in Chungking, was being fed this material by Chiang's press officers and reporting it verbatim.

Then after two weeks, we realized we could no longer stay in the city. The problem began each night after dark with the dreadful cries of dogs and cats killing each other out of a desperate lack of either food or water. Then when we tried to traverse the city, we started finding our way blocked by thousands of ravenous dogs and cats operating in giant packs. It became clear to us that we would end up being attacked and eaten ourselves. It was not the Japanese who drove us out of Foochow but the abandoned domestic animals of the city.

The Japanese did eventually come. General Chi'en in Nanping had been told when and where they would land. But he had purposely not advised General Li, his subordinate divisional commander. With no information, Li had been unable to organize a defense of the city. After Li was forced to regroup his troops, he was seized by Chi'en's men, accused of collaboration with the enemy and executed. It did not pay to be a Christian general in this part of China during the war! It did not make any difference that Chiang himself was a Methodist. In this part of China, he had little authority. I never did use his passport.

The war was going badly at this point. Chennault told me to come back and report. I took my radioman and we took the long way back to Kweilin by bus and by borrowed truck. Chennault was upset and angry. He was losing pilots and had difficulty getting replacements.

He was also concerned that the Japanese would try to come up the old French railroad line which went from Lao-Kay in French Indochina to Kunming. This line, when built in the 1880s shortly after Indochina had become a French protectorate, was a masterpiece of engineering. Interestingly enough, it was the Belgians (that little country of nine million people), the French, and the Germans who had done most of the engineering work in the Far East: the Belgians had built the railroads in China; the French had built docks, railroads and roads in Indochina and Shanghai; the Germans had built docks and shipping facilities in much of China. The money for these railroads had come from the United States, but the engineering work had been done by these other countries. Much later, on my return to the law, I would play a role in trying to keep the American investments in Chinese railroads from falling into the hands of the Communists. But now Chennault's concern was quite different. Would the Japanese be able to use the roadbed to come north and take Kunming? Would Stillwell be able to bring his troops back from Burma in time to protect the city? Without

Kunming, the whole of China would be lost. So over a three-week period I went, with a small group of Chinese soldiers, to reconnoiter the railroad route. It was difficult going. The provincial troops were a badly led rabble, but as agents of destruction, they had done a commendable job. How this French railroad was ever built sixty years earlier, I will never know. The river was a torrent flowing in a ravine for much of the distance between Kunming and the Indochina border. The railroad in many places had been cut out from its narrow bed on the face of the cliff. There were tunnels every few miles which had now been blocked. There was no reason to go all the way to Lao-Kay. The Chinese provincial troops had effectively dynamited the roadbed and restored the cliff face to its original sheer drop. They had also blown the cliffs above the entrances and exits to the tunnels so that they couldn't be used again. The Japanese engineers would have to start from scratch if they were to rebuild the line. Kunming was safe from attack by land. The air raids on the base, however, would soon begin. I was to spend Christmas eve of 1944 in a slit trench outside the B.O.Q. barracks in the midst of a Japanese air raid on Kunming.

Clark came back to Kunming in October. He had little good news to report from his area. The Chinese were not fighting there either, and the Japanese were now moving inland. Clark would have been cut off had he not returned. Chennault called the two of us in and told us to go to New Delhi for a month and get some rest. I was down to 140 pounds and Clark had recurring dysentery. We gladly went. I sent a message to Rosamond in New Delhi that I was arriving.

New Delhi was a city that had been laid out by the British as the capital of an empire designed to last a thousand years, with broad avenues and imposing buildings surrounded by parks. The city was full of military headquarters and staffs, in addition to the creaky British and Indian administration of a vast territory whose most important strategic areas had been seized or cut off by the enemy. It was like the trunk of a huge tree whose living branches had been cut off and burned. This did not bother anyone at headquarters. Every group issued memoranda to field headquarters elsewhere or maintained staffs of liaison officers to exchange bulletins with each other, few of which had any importance to the war effort. Above all was Mountbatten, the viceroy surrounded by both British and American general staffs. The younger officers played polo with the princes. The war was far away. To me, Rosamond was more attractive than ever. Since it didn't look as if she would get to China, she had rented a small house in town with two other American

Behind the Lines in China

New Delhi, India— engaged to marry

122

OSS girls, had bought a horse and was having a very good time in a city where there were a hundred men for every woman. Almost every weekend she spent at the Jaharaja of Jaipur's palace near Delhi where the most attractive visiting officers were invited. I felt as if I had suddenly returned to the sophisticated colonial world of Kipling.

At the end of a week of dinners, parties and balls, I went to the old red fort in old Delhi and arranged with the guardian of the palace to serve me a dinner for two late at night in the gardens. His repertoire was limited and the palace grounds were closed at night, but we arrived at an understanding. He would provide fish and chips; dinner would be served on a card table with two chairs; he would procure the ice (a difficult feat in Delhi at the time); and I would bring the champagne.

I told Rosamond that I was taking her that night to a very special party; she was to wear a long white evening dress, have her hair done that afternoon and procure a car from one of her English chums. We would leave at 11 o'clock. Everything worked out as planned. It was a beautiful moonlit night; I had a ring and the bottle of champagne. At midnight in the gardens of the palace, with a full moon shining, I went down on one knee, proposed and was accepted.

A few days later, I was selected, quite by chance, to take an extraordinary journey.

The war in the Soviet Union had been going quite as badly as the war in China, but, of course, the stakes were very much higher. The Russians depended on American supplies of tanks and trucks being shipped to them via Iran, and hence by road. If the Germans took Stalingrad—and it certainly looked as if they would—then the supply lines from the United States would be cut. It was important to find another supply line from the south, because Murmansk in the north was difficult to use in the winter and unsatisfactory at the best of times.

I have observed both in government and in large corporate enterprises that there are times when suggestions are made at the top (and later nobody remembers who really made them), but thereafter they take on a life of their own because it suits the private ends of someone further down in the chain of command. That is certainly what must have happened in the Iran-Contra affair when the interests of the United States became embroiled with the needs of the Israelis, some Iranian politicians, Saudi entrepreneurs and U.S. officers determined to supply Central American guerillas in the face of Congressional rulings to the contrary. "Will somebody not rid me of this man?" said Henry II to his courtiers in 12th century England, speaking of Thomas à Becket. Courtiers did, and "Murder in the Cathedral" duly took place. Was an order given, or was a wish merely expressed signifying kingly frustration?

Behind the Lines in China

Finding a route to the USSR through Afghanistan

I never did find out whether President Roosevelt had really decided that someone should be sent out to find an alternative route to the Soviet Union through Kashmir, Gilgit and Afghanistan. I doubt it very much. Suffice it to say that by the time this thought had filtered down to the OSS command in India, it had become a high priority project sanctioned by the president himself and demanding the utmost secrecy. Such highly confidential projects are apt to be badly thought through because they become set before someone with good practical common sense can determine whether it can be accomplished. The very difficulty of the project inspires those who will benefit most by any success achieved. In the case of this project, a look at any reasonable atlas would have been convincing evidence of the folly of the task. But who can question further down the chain of command an order given by the commander in chief? I was certainly not going to question an opportunity for an adventure such as this.

The plot was simple. I was to go up to Srinagar in Kashmir by train. There I would locate an English outfitter of mountain expeditions by the name of Corbin. I was to tell him a group of friends and I intended to take a pack trip to the Himalayas to hunt snow leopard. We would leave as soon as he could get the equipment together. Mr. Corbin had not had the opportunity to organize a hunting expedition since the outbreak of war in 1939. He was openly salivating at the thought that he could get back into business. He informed me that for a group of four, we would need some 37 horses and 17 bearers, one of whom would be in charge of men and supplies during the trip. We should expect to be gone some three to four weeks. I did what I was told as quietly and unobtrusively as I could. Mr. Corbin was enthusiastic and extremely helpful. With the money I promised him he was practically prepared to guarantee me a snow leopard. Had I demanded an "abominable snowman," I think he would have promised that as well.

When I returned to New Delhi, I was told that since this was, after all, British territory, there should be an English officer on the expedition. Headquarters had just the man in mind, a British Air Force wing commander with a record of 37 planes shot down, who had been sent to India for fear that if he remained in England, he would risk the destruction not only of himself, but many of his pilots on some ill-advised sortie. His frayed nerves were now reported to be in good shape. An expedition on land would be just the challenge he would need to

124

restore him to good health. It wasn't my idea to take a nerve-shattered British officer with me, but, obviously, I was not to argue. To complete the roster, the British suggested that we should take along two Russian-speaking interpreters. They had chosen two Russian women who had married two Frenchmen. The French had gone off to war and been captured in the debacle of 1940. The two wives had been under house arrest ever since. Sending them with us would solve a problem for the British surveillance squad.

The wing commander turned out to be a delightful individual. He had graduated from Oxford and spoke fluent French, having made frequent peacetime trips to the continent. Our two interpreters turned out to be so delighted to be allowed out of their house arrest that they would have gone anywhere and done anything. They were in their late twenties, daughters of White Russians who had escaped after 1917. They spoke fluent French and were very good-looking. We quickly decided that French would be a part of our cover. We set off by train in high spirits to meet up with Mr. Corbin and organize our pack trip. When we arrived in Srinagar, the British for some reason made no effort to invite us to their club. We were very excited about our trip and gave it little thought. We didn't want anyone prying into our mission.

The British are the only people who really understand the art of living comfortably wherever you find yourself. The Americans and the Germans consider it macho to be uncomfortable. The French plan only for food and wine and ignore lodging and bathing.

Our crew of bearers was divided into two. One group would leave before dawn so as to prepare the next night's camp. When we would come into camp around five in the evening (night comes early in those high mountains), there would be a large fire going with water boiling for the baths. In each tent there would be a rubber folding bath next to the bunk, a change of clothes would have been laid out on the rubber mattress, and the Sikh who was our major duomo would ask each of us whether we wanted our whiskey before, during, or after the bath. I shall never forget our trip to Gilgit in Tibet. After that, it became harder to travel. When we reached the tongue of Afghanistan, which separated that country from China, it became more obvious than ever to us that no supplies would get through to the Russians by this route. The pass on one side of the ravine was at 19,000 feet. We had to turn back the way we had come. When we returned to Srinagar, the British members of the local club entertained us at dinner and apologized for not having invited us earlier. They had heard the girls speak Russian and our conversations together in French and were very doubtful about who we were and what we were planning to do.

We decided before returning to Delhi that we were entitled to a rest. After all, it had been a grueling and dangerous trip. For three U.S. dollars a day we rented a houseboat on the lake for a week. It came with food and a staff of four, including an excellent cook. I hate to think what this would cost today. It had two large bedrooms, a dining room, a bath, and a large pine-paneled living room. The weather was beautiful, the mountains awesome in the background with Nanga Parbat rising spectacularly to 26,000 feet. The war was very far away. The four of us knew we would never see each other again. I think for each one of us that week in the Vale of Kashmir would be the experience of a lifetime, and we made sure that it was. Today, some sixty years later, I sometimes dream that I am back on that lake, without a care in the world.

It was difficult to return to China. Poor Clark had come down with typhus the day we arrived in Delhi. He was better now and ready to go back, but he had hardly had the vacation he was looking forward to.

In China, a new American ambassador, Pat Hurley, had been appointed to replace Gauss, the previous ambassador, and Gauss's decision to ban American women from China had now been reversed. When I returned to Kunming, I found that the OSS in Washington had sent a large detachment to Kunming and another to Chungking. None of these people knew anything about China or its politics, but they seemed to have unlimited financial resources. In Kunming there was now equipment of all sorts. There were also colonels, lieutenant colonels, and a vast headquarters staff, including American women as researchers and secretaries. It was only a question of time before Kunming would be like New Delhi. I would now report to an OSS colonel in Kunming rather than directly to General Chennault.

OSS had also rented a big house on the outskirts of town where transient officers could stay. It was in charge of a tough paratrooper colonel who would have been more at home in the jungles of Burma than running a "guesthouse" for visiting officers back from the field. But I was happy to meet there two old friends from New York, Jacques de Sibour, a Frenchman who was supposedly on his way to Indochina, and Ilya Tolstoy, grandson of the great Russian novelist who was there with small American groups of Army officers who were proposing to enter Russia through Mongolia on horseback. My roommate here was Farnsworth Loomis, the doctor on this team of roughriders. He had been born in Tuxedo Park the same month as me a few doors away. Ilya had somehow persuaded President Roosevelt, whom he knew, that his group of American horsemen could be of inestimable value to the Russians by going across western China and Mongolia into Siberia. Like my trip through Afghanistan, this ride to Siberia would never result in anything, but its appeal to a president who could not walk was understandable. Like his father, who did so much for the American cause in World War II through his scientific achievements, Farney would later be a famous microbiologist.

I was told that a dispute on military strategy was going on at the highest levels of the government in Washington. Admiral King, chief of naval operations, wanted to take Formosa and then go on to China before making the all-out attack on Japan proper. There were some thirteen usable harbors in Formosa. The Navy wanted two Formosans (Taiwanese to the Chinese) to be recruited from each of the designated harbors where American troops would land, given a six-month contract to take care of their families in their absence, trained, and delivered to a U.S. submarine which would meet them at a point off the coast of China between Kwangtung and Fukien Provinces. The Taiwanese would go ashore with Navy frogmen two or three days before the landing to reconnoiter the town. They would then be able to guide the assault troops after the landing. I only wished we had had this advantage in Sicily!

This was a high-priority project, and I was ordered to immediately return to the headquarters of the 3rd war area and figure out how to find the needed Formosans. There were supposed to be refugees from Formosa somewhere in that area. So back I went. When I arrived in Kweilin, I was given a truck, new radio equipment and two Chinese radiomen who supposedly had been security-cleared. I had also found the weather radioman who had been with me earlier. We set off together in a jeep followed by the truck operated by two Chinese drivers who had come with it. The Chinese radiomen had insisted, at the last moment, on bringing their wives. So we were nine. The truck was old; the tires were in very bad shape. We carried two fifty-gallon tanks of extra fuel. The road across the mountains was in very bad condition, and while there were now no Japanese in the area, it was thought to be infested with bandits. These were generally Chinese soldiers who with their officers had left their army units and were carrying on their own military operations against the local populations. The war in the Pacific by now had improved. MacArthur was on his way to retake the Philippines, but in China there had been no improvement. The central government's hold on the country, tenuous at best, seemed to be slipping further each week. It was a very difficult environment for an American group to operate in, particularly since it was impossible to know who was a friend or who was not. The trip was a nightmare which I shall never forget. I remember being at the wheel of the truck going around a sharp corner in the road with a sheer drop of two thousand feet on one side and a wall of rock on the other. As I turned the wheel to take the corner, the steering cable snapped. By luck we turned into the wall rather than the void. Our two mechanics managed to patch the cable in a few hours and we went on. It was some days, however, before I stopped having nightmares about the incident. All the bridges in the area had been blown up by the Chinese army. This meant steep descents down to the river, a crossing on a temporary wooden trestle, and a steep rise on the other side. At the approach to one of these ravines, the truck stopped. We put large chocks under the wheel. Our mechanics started to fix the engine. I was in the jeep reconnoitering the bridge when all of a sudden the truck jumped the chocks and plunged down the steep incline to the bridge. It gathered speed, went off the road, and landed in the river with the radiomen, their wives, and all the equipment. Sven Linquist, my weatherman, and I immediately plunged into the river to get our people out of the truck. Miraculously no one was killed, but both women had broken legs and one of the radiomen had a broken arm. I tried to remember what I had learned about setting bones. I set the broken legs, put on splints, and then did the same for the arm. The mechanics had gone off to try to find a sampan. By dusk we had the whole team loaded on the sampan with the equipment we had been able to save and were headed down the river. Fortunately, there was a sizeable town a few miles further along with a hospital. I saw the doctor the next day after he had had a chance to examine the broken limbs. He had been trained in France, so we could converse easily. There was no real damage done. I also had a chance that night to call General Ku and ask him to send a company of men to get the truck out, get it repaired and get it to headquarters. The next day Sven and I drove down to Ku's headquarters in the jeep.

General Ku was not helpful. "The coast is very dangerous," he said. "You must not go. I cannot be responsible for you there." I remembered my experiences earlier with him and let the matter drop. I simply moved my headquarters further east. There I set up our radio equipment, communicated with Chungking and Kunming and was put in touch with the Taiwanese underground. We went to the coast, selected the men, and paid their families with a bonus and subsistence for their needs for a year while the men were away. I then notified Kunming I was ready to deliver them to the coast. When all this was done, I received word that Washington had now abandoned the project to take Formosa. Admiral King had been overruled. The United States would go north not via Formosa and China, but to Iwo Jima, and then directly on to Japan.

Behind the Lines in China

No one had bothered to tell me of this change in plans. This was not surprising. The change involved a very basic change in Allied policy. The more conservative Admiral King had always been in favor of taking Formosa and then the principal ports along the coast of China before attacking Japan itself. MacArthur, the Marine Corps and younger flag officers in the Navy—the aviators and submariners—thought the war could be won more quickly and at less cost in men and materials by going up the island chain. Their view had won out. Formosa would have been a major attack on some eighteen harbors around the island and a difficult campaign, for a questionable strategic result. It turned out to be a very wise decision. It also gave me an opportunity to establish a new relationship with a Chinese group along the coast who were willing to fight the Japanese, unlike Chiang Kai-shek or the Chinese warlords who wanted to save their troops for eventual control of China after the war with Japan was won.

There are two events which stand out most clearly in my mind from this "Formosa" project.

Not wanting General Ku to be aware of my activities, I had moved my headquarters as soon as I could to the outskirts of a large city much nearer the coast in an area that was known to have many refugees from Formosa. Because it was not far from the Japanese-held ports on the coast, I decided it would be safer not to live in town. Because the Chinese are so superstitious about the dead, I thought it would be an ingenious idea to have my house built in the middle of the large cemetery a few miles outside the city. On the theory that the town might itself be safer if it did not house an American, the town fathers agreed and a small one-bedroom house with a primitive outdoor privy, as was usual then in China, was built for me. For further protection, the house was surrounded by a six-foot bamboo fence with sharpened tops. In addition, I had my platoon of Chinese soldiers furnished by General Ku equipped with German helmets and odd-looking rifles. I had thought earlier when I had a similar platoon furnished by General Ku when I was in Nanking on the Min River above Foochow that one of them must be the cook. Not at all. They took turns, one man every nine days. The food never changed. It was rice and tea for breakfast, lunch and dinner,

Headquartered in a Chinese cemetery

accompanied by fish, frog, pork, chicken, or whatever might be available. The Chinese are very much like the French. Everyone cooks and knows how to cook. If the foreigner does not try to eat Western food, he will eat well. More importantly, he will avoid getting dysentery.

One evening just before dark, a jeep pulled up to my cemetery and a Greek-American paratrooper and his interpreter came in. He carried a forty-five in a shoulder holster, a tommy gun over his shoulder and a sleeping bag. "Mind if I bunk with you, captain?" he said. He had been sent down to the coast on a mission by the OSS detachment but was reluctant to tell me what it was about, and after my experiences with the Tai Li Navy men, who were so secretive when they stopped by my house in Nanping, I didn't want to ask.

"I am going into town for dinner, but my men will feed you here. I'll take your interpreter to town with me when I go. He can get a bed in town. No one will touch your jeep. You can have the bunk under the window in the bedroom."

Around midnight on the edge of town as I was driving home, I noticed a man's body hanging from a lamppost. He had been shot several times and was not a pretty sight. Arriving at the cemetery, I saw that one side of my house had been blown out and the fencing was down. It was the side where the window had been in my bedroom. When I went in, the guard was there as usual, my guest fast asleep in his bunk, mine destroyed. My guest woke up as I entered.

"Nice friends you have here. Some character got over your fence and lobbed a grenade into your bed. I caught him with a .45 bullet just as he was climbing back over the fence, and finished him off among the tombstones. I figured you would want people to know what happened to him, so I took him in the jeep and strung him up to the nearest lamppost I could find."

Good luck again! Had I not been in town that night—and these invitations to town were not frequent—I wouldn't be here today.

The other event was more spectacular. The mayor of the city came over one day to tell me that the city had been able to obtain a recent American motion picture and that there would be a big first-night showing. He would like me to attend as his guest. All the notables of the city would be there. The film turned out to be Cecil B. de Mille's movie on Nero's feeding of the Christians to the lions. It was called *The Sign of the Cross*. It featured Loretta Young as the young Christian heroine. It was filled with chariot races and a great deal of blood and gore. It was a real 1936 Hollywood extravaganza featuring Nero as a Roman monster.

As the Christians were fed to the lions in the Coliseum, all the women in the audience crawled under the seats shouting "Aya! Aya!" The men laughed, which in Chinese indicates acute embarrassment. The next day the mayor and some of the elders came out to see me.

"We wondered why you had come all the way over to China. But now that we see what life is like in America we understand it better. We are very sorry for you living in a country like that."

So much for the effect of American films in "civilized" countries. When I think of the picture of uninterrupted violence and gunplay that Hollywood films continue to portray as life in America to audiences all over the world, I am not surprised at the growth of a counter-culture in the Islamic world. American moviegoers have by now been conditioned to constant violence from Hollywood. Even youngsters in America who make up the bulk of the motion picture watchers are used to this type of presentation and look for it. The effect abroad, however, is catastrophic. We have conditioned people all over the world to think of Americans as gangsters or cowboys, as a society dedicated to violence. It is perhaps just as well that we do not see ourselves as others see us: respected and feared but disliked. We constantly speak of our love of liberty and democracy. But we are even to our friends regarded as arrogant people who don't listen to others, and to our enemies as bullies. That Americans, who are the soul of generosity, would have earned this reputation abroad, is recognition both of the persuasive power of Hollywood and that a bad reputation is always more popular than a good.

During the course of the Formosan effort, I learned that there was a group of former pirates on the coast who detested the Japanese and would welcome working with the Americans. It appeared that a couple of years earlier the Japanese had raided the group's enclave while the men were away, raped the women and then killed women and children. The question was how to get to these men and under what aegis. Discrete checks with General Ku and some provincial sources indicated that the group's leader was a young man named Li Jen who was part of a very large family or tribe amounting to some eighteen thousand people all told, and that the head of the family was a former Hong Kong banker who had escaped the Japanese and was now living in a remote village far up in the mountains. I decided I would set out to find him, obtain an introduction to his nephew on the coast and with this proper family introduction, go meet Li Jen and see how we might work together against the Japanese. Since he was reputed to have 15,000 men and 10 seagoing junks, it seemed like a worthwhile plan. If we could put

It takes Chinese pirates to fight.

131

our small OSS radios on the junks and establish communication with the U.S. submarine headquarters, we could develop a most useful information network for the Navy. The problem was that the OSS radios had only very limited range. It would be necessary to place Sven somewhere up in the mountains where he would be able to serve as a relay from the junks to Kunming. I discussed this with Sven. It was decided that I would drop him off in a mountain village and then strike out on my own to find banker Li. Since Sven spoke only a few words of Mandarin Chinese and the mountain people spoke only Hakah, the mountain language, it would be a lonely time for him, but he agreed to do it. He must have sometimes wondered how he and his three other weathermen, experts in radio, had ever come to end up in the wilds instead of filing weather reports at some airbase in the interior. We checked with Kunming. Our project was approved. I don't think anyone realized what was involved. To the people of headquarters, life in the areas of China where I had been operating was a great unknown. How could they know? They knew nothing of China. But money and perseverance manage to solve many problems. From OSS I had not only Chinese currency, dollars, gold coins, but also safety pins and medical products in profusion. Travel in the interior was necessarily an adventure. There were no roads through the mountains, only tortuous paths to be used only by men on foot or horseback. The mountains were filled with bandits. It is interesting that in China at the time I would often have to ask directions. If I asked how far the next town was, the answer always was, "Are you coming or going there?" Distance in China was measured by the time it would take a person to get there by foot, so obviously it will take longer, and the distance therefore will be greater if the destination is uphill rather than down.

Our route through the mountains made for a magnificent trip. We tried to avoid any kind of main pathway, preferring to take circuitous routes. All of our bearers of radio equipment were women. When the rice harvest had been picked, the farmers sent their wives and daughters out on the road to work as baggage carriers, while they went to the teahouses to drink and exchange gossip. Each of our bearers carried a bag of unpolished rice and some dried meats. They stopped only for tea. At night they slept on the hard ground. They could carry forty pounds all day if necessary. They laughed all the time. They thought it was a wonderful holiday to be away from home. I would explain to them that after the war I would bring them to New York where they could wear a fancy uniform and be porters at Pennsylvania Station. They could not understand why American farmers did not send their wives out as porters when the harvest was in. When I explained that women in America went to beauty parlors in the afternoon, they didn't believe me. If this was a vacation, I thought to myself, what must life at home be like? I think what they really enjoyed was to have the chance to spend time with other women. They talked all day long.

I left Sven in the mountain village. I had rented him a little house, found a farmer to supply him with rice, pork, eggs and tea. We put his radio equipment together, tested it, and then I was off. As I disappeared over the hill, there he stood: 6´3˝ of lonely 19-year-old left in a remote mountain village in the heart of China.

At last I arrived at my own destination, a walled town with narrow streets and small doorways leading to inner courtyards. We stopped at the designated house. I knocked at the door. It was opened by a young girl in her twenties speaking perfect English and wearing a fashionable silk dress from Hong Kong. So it was that I met this delightful banker from Hong Kong and his charming family in this desolate little town in the mountains. I stayed several days with them. They lived very well, indeed. Tea in the afternoon was served with Huntley & Palmer biscuits from the original English box; meals were Western style. They had brought their cook from Hong Kong, as well as the rest of the servants. The two daughters had gone to the Couvent des Oiseaux in Paris and wore the latest fashions. When the girls and I spoke together, it was in French. It was bewildering to find this oasis of civilization in a remote village high up in the mountains of southeastern China. My host was an erudite and very sophisticated individual. He seemed to be very much up to date on the international news, which he received by radio. He told me couriers from all over China reached him several times a week. In addition, he had sources of information, it seemed, throughout China. While the warlords and even Chiang were playing the political and military games of prior centuries, here was an Oxford-trained banker using his mind and his information to keep constantly abreast of what was going on in the world. I don't know how he managed it, but there were even recent American, English and French magazines in his library. We talked at length about his larger family and the relationships of individuals within it. He exercised extraordinary power as the head of the tribe. He prepared for me a passport with his chop and the usual red ribbons. But before he would let me go on my way, he insisted on first sending his couriers to warn his nephew of my arrival and to get back from him the assurances he sought that I would be well received. One morning he told me, "You may go now, but when you get near the coast, you will travel only by night. My guide will accompany you."

It is difficult to people in the West to understand the role of family in China and much of Asia. For centuries, the family has been the central unit around which all society gravitates. Governments come and go. The family continues. Governments will take your money one way or another if they realize you are rich. You must never leave a will, or the government will confiscate what you have. Trust individuals but never a government official. The family may consist of several thousand members, as was the case of this sophisticated banker. A Chinese family is like a clan in Scotland, or a tribe among the Indians of North America. If a member of the family achieves material success, he will go back to his village and build a school so that others may be educated as he was. If he goes abroad and finds a job, he will try to persuade others in the family to join him. It was said in China that the Chinese who came to work in the United States to build our railroads all came from one small area in the Kwangtung Province. It makes no difference what government is in power at home. Those who are outside the country send money home each month to the family. The system is the result of centuries of upheaval, of famines, wars, disasters of all sorts. In China, this concept of family goes along with respect for age. The head of the family is entitled to great respect. Everyone knows who he is. If he makes a demand, it will be obeyed. When he dies, members will come to worship at his tomb, and it will never be desecrated. That had been one reason why I had chosen to live in a Chinese cemetery.

I would be very sad to leave this very happy household to continue my journey.

It was obviously going to be important for me to be extremely sensitive to the relationships between the members of this family or tribe. What value would this Hong Kong banker's passport and introduction be to a pirate chieftain who must be only a distant relative? Would he recognize the instructions that were now being given to him to work with Americans and specifically with me? How could I build a relationship with this man that would enable me to get help for what I was trying to accomplish?

After three nights of travel, we arrived early one morning at a little port village on the coast. I was taken to a small inn and put in a room to sleep. "They will come for you tonight," I was told. That night around 11 o'clock a group of men came for me. I was guided over endless paths between salt marshes where every half mile or so a guard would spring up and request identification. Finally, at dawn we arrived at our destination, a walled town at the end of a promontory stretching out into the sea. We were at the tip of a long peninsula separating Fukien from Kwangtung, a village whose houses had walls four feet thick. This would be my home for several months to come.

My house was in the middle of the village, next to Li's. The village itself was dark and medieval. The walls of my house were easily over four feet thick. There were small windows looking out to sea, but a teak floor. Lunch was a communal affair with Li and his captains; evenings I ate alone. We lived on fresh fish which the fishermen along the coast brought in. It would often happen to me that as the guest of honor, I would be given the eye of the fish. Only the head of a big fish would be served. The body of the fish, if it were large, would be left to the women to eat.

My hosts had indeed operated as pirates in the prewar days, stopping coastal steamers operating between Shanghai and Canton or Hong Kong. The house where I lived was beautifully furnished with furniture and furnishings found in coastal vessels that had been stopped, searched and stripped of all valuables.

The group was obviously operating totally outside the law. They were practicing piracy; they were also making salt, which in China was a government monopoly and, therefore, forbidden. In addition, like the Capone gang in Chicago, they were selling protection to the fishermen and their villages along the coast.

Two of their principal bases were the islands of Quemoy and Matsu. Years later, when I listened to Kennedy and Nixon holding their television debate prior to the 1960 election, I was reminded of my visits to those little islands. Who could ever have imagined that these insignificant bits of land would have been featured in a political debate on television in the United States between two candidates for the Presidency?

It is very difficult to understand how in one Chinese family, no matter how large, can be found at the same time a Hong Kong banker who is the symbol of propriety and a man who makes his living through piracy. Loyalties and responsibilities in the Far East, I concluded, are very difficult for others to understand. Perhaps the answer has to lie in the extraordinary capacity of the Chinese to maintain a civilization for over nine thousand years, longer by far than any other civilization. Korea goes back five thousand years, Egypt the same; but China is unique. It means that survival becomes the first criterion if civilized behavior is to endure. In the part of China where I now was, slavery was still practiced. Unwanted daughters would be sold as soon as a buyer could be found and worked until the end of their days or sold again if they grew to be pretty enough. After survival came family loyalty. I have been to areas in China which were extremely poor. There in the middle of the rice paddies, I would find a college, or a hospital, which would have been built and endowed by a family member who would have succeeded in Singapore, or Brunei or Indonesia or even the United States. In Communist China today, the overseas Chinese send some five billion dollars a year back to look after family members. This is the biggest source of hard currency the government has. The Chinese send far more than any other country. For a family to survive over centuries, it is not enough to function as a cohesive unit. It is also necessary to avoid taking a political risk. The Chinese will not side with one faction lest the other faction win and one's life or one's business is lost as a result. Dynasties and governments come and go; care must be exercised not to declare oneself so as not to make a mistake. Mao's "let a thousand flowers bloom" campaign was orchestrated to make the population think the government was in favor of relaxation of its revolutionary principles. He thought that way he could force people to declare themselves for or against his government. Again, the Cultural Revolution represented an attempt by the government to purify the revolution by allowing young toughs to terrorize the population into denouncing any neighbors not in favor of Mao's ideas. Neither of Mao's methods worked, even though he created untold suffering to individuals and families in the process. The tyrant comes and goes, but the family survives.

I found my pirates easy to work with. I had brought a box of limpets with me, explosives in the shape of a half-ball with magnets all around the edges. You put them against the side of a ship with a time fuse to detonate the charge at a set time hours or days later. The pirates thought these were wonderful weapons. They took them to Shanghai, Amoy, Foochow and other Japanese-held ports and placed them a few feet below the water line on Japanese vessels. I taught them how to insert the time fuse and which to use. I also taught them how to use the radios. We placed one of these on each of their junks. They learned how to send simple messages which Sven Lindquist from his mountain village could pick up and send on to Kunming. I sailed in their junks with them.

When I left, Li Jen called his men together. With his knife he cut both our wrists and rubbed them together. "We are now brothers," he said. "When you are in trouble again, come and find me and I will help you." Then he told his men, "This American has helped us against our enemies. He is our friend. Now we will show him Chinese hospitality." With that, as many men as the ships would carry boarded the junks and we set sail. There was a large city some miles away. When we arrived, the shore batteries opened fire. The junks sailed into the harbor. The men piled ashore with their guns. Li demanded to see the proprietor of the principal inn. "We will be three hundred for dinner tonight," he said. "I want a banquet because I am giving a farewell party for our honored guest from a foreign land. I want plenty of wine, music and women. If you value your life, you will accommodate us well."

I will never forget that night or the next day. The innkeeper did as he was told. The pirates each with his fedora on the back of his head as was the trademark of the group showed up with their guns. As the night wore on the party became exceedingly rough. Guns were fired in all directions, even through the windows and into the upper floors of the inn. There were toasts drunk all night. I have imagined what the sack of Cartagena by pirates must have been like in the 17th century. But this must have been the equivalent. I was delighted when we all went back aboard the junks and set sail the following day.

True to his word several years later, in Saigon, in the middle of the night Li Jen's emissary would knock on my hotel door to bring me back to China so that he could help me.

It was time to go back and get Sven. I went back to the village where I had left him. I found that he was no longer alone. There was a young Chinese girl living in his house with him, cooking for him and washing his clothes. He still spoke only a few words of the local dialect, but he seemed content. I asked him what had happened. He told me that after I had left him alone, the villagers had felt very sorry for him. The local innkeeper had agreed to give a dinner for him and everyone in the village chipped in. The elder of the village had come to take him to the inn. He could not speak to them at dinner nor they to him since neither understood the other's language. That did not matter. Sven understood that the villagers were extending the hand of friendship to him. The elder gave a little talk and Sven had sense enough to realize he should say something, too. He got up and, not knowing what to say, recited the Lord's Prayer slowly and with feeling, and then sat down again. As I listened to Sven's story, it reminded me of a New York friend who had been sent on a mission to Outer Mongolia and, knowing that no one could understand him, delivered with great emphasis a campaign

speech he had once given on behalf of William Travers Jerome when he
had run for the governorship of New York many years earlier.

Since the dinner had gone so well, the elder decided to give another.
Everyone was asked again to contribute and the excess was used to buy
from a local farmer a young 12-year-old girl. They offered the girl to
Sven at dinner. The girl had half-guided him, half-carried him home.
The next morning he had awakened with the young girl lying beside
him. She took good care of him, washed his clothes and fed him.

For me this presented a very delicate problem. If I left the young
girl behind, we would have angered the village elders by rejecting a gift.
The young girl would be taken outside the village walls and stoned to
death, for no one else would have her. I decided that I would have to

A dowry to
prevent a
young girl
from being
stoned to
death

find her a husband by offering a suitable dowry. It was a delicate matter to explain to the elder that American custom made it impossible to
bring home a young girl to whom one was not married. After several
hours of discussion—for such matters are not to be decided quickly in
China—we agreed on the amount of the dowry and, at the elder's suggestion, I promised to officiate at a suitable marriage ceremony. I had
a small copy of a New Testament which would do for this purpose. I
surmised that if she were married in accordance with a foreign rite, this
would give her added protection and status in the village. All went according to plan. The ceremony was held in the village square. The elder
had found a young farmer whose father was delighted to receive the
dowry. The bride arrived in a painted sedan chair. I had put on my dress
uniform and a tie. I recited those portions of the Christian rite, including Psalms and Gospel which appeared pertinent, and pronounced
the young couple man and wife. There were libations and rice cakes
afterwards. Sven and I kissed the bride. I wondered only how I would
enter this expenditure for the dowry in my expense account. Little did
I know the complication which would ensue. You can expose a young
Swede from Minneapolis to enemy shellfire. But God help you if you
jeopardize his morals.

Sven had done an excellent job with the radio equipment I had left
with him in the mountains. Operating twice a day in the early morning
and the evening, he was relaying information received from the OSS
suitcase radios I had installed on the pirate junks back to Kunming and
thence to Manila and on to the U.S. submarines operating near the
Chinese coast. At its best the system enabled the submarines to receive
information within twenty minutes of the time it was broadcast from
the junks. Since much of the Japanese cargo fleet had by this time been

sunk, the enemy was using small coastal steamers to move their cargos, staying as close to shore as possible. Information from the Chinese junks was, therefore, very useful to the subs.

Fate sometimes plays odd tricks. When we returned to Kunming, Sven wrote to his mother in St. Paul, Minnesota, to tell her of his adventures in China when his officer had left him in the mountains alone with his radio equipment. Naturally, the story of the young girl given to him by the villagers was not omitted from his story. His mother immediately wrote to her Congressman, objecting to the manner in which her son had been treated. It was not the danger or even the risk of death that concerned her. It was that he was being subjected to a life of depravity. The Congressman in turn passed her letter on to one of the two senators from Minnesota whose office contacted the Office of Far Eastern Operations at OSS headquarters. When I returned to the United States, I was made to prepare a suitable explanation and to call on the senator's office with my explanation. Wartime conditions in China were indeed a far cry from life in Minnesota.

There remained for me one last task in China before coming home. Had it succeeded it would certainly have been an extraordinary adventure. That it did not succeed probably saved my life.

On my way back to Kweilin in my jeep to take the plane to Kunming, I stopped off for the night at a German monastery near the main road. For once I was wearing my Air Force shirt and tie. As I pulled up in front of the monastery, I could see monks scurrying away like beetles in a kitchen when one turns on the light at night. I was surprised because in China monks would generally make an effort to greet a stranger. When I came to the door, the abbot was there to meet me.

"Come in, my son. It is the duty of my religion and my order to receive guests and to greet them honorably. But today it is difficult for us to do so. We are Catholic monks, but we are also German. We have just heard on the radio that our country has unconditionally surrendered. It is difficult for us to receive an American officer on a day like this."

"Father, I did not know. I have come from the interior and have had no world news in several weeks. If you will allow me, I will come back another day."

"My son, you will stay. We must learn that we are men of the Church first, and you will teach us that nationalism, like pride, is a sin. But you must understand that we are very sad as we think of what our loved ones face today."

He sat me next to him at the evening meal. He spoke to his monks.

"This is a very sad day for us because we are Germans," he said. "The Lord has sent us a stranger in the uniform of those who will occupy our land. It is a warning to us that we must put aside earthly preoccupations and receive this stranger as a guest and as a friend."

Theirs was a very natural human response. I would have preferred to be almost anywhere else that day.

Arriving at Kunming, I found the place very much changed. Bureaucracy was everywhere. At OSS headquarters, colonels were tripping over each other to issue orders to other colonels. The old personal relationships had disappeared. I felt that I was once again in New Delhi. Planes were landing every few minutes at the airfield with additional materiel which was no longer needed. The colonels and the staff sergeants bulged out of their neat new uniforms. There was military gridlock everywhere. The only element of initiative left was in dreaming up schemes for others to do.

"Saint Phalle, get yourself naval insignia, and go over to the Navy and pick up a year's pay. You've also been promoted to lieutenant commander, so you must pass a physical and be sworn in."

"How do you feel?" the doctor said.

"Fine," I said.

"Congratulations. You pass."

No eye tests, no urine analysis, no nothing. Examinations in the field were special. I move, therefore, I am alive—and pass. The Navy in China was entitled to per diem, the Army and Air Force not. When I left Navy headquarters, I felt rich: pay and eighteen months of per diem, and nowhere to spend it.

That night I dined with Nicoll Smith and a group of other officers who had just returned from the Thailand border. Nic was an extraordinary bon vivant and raconteur. He had written a famous adventure book entitled "Burma Road" after the famous roadway which was to cross the Himalayas from India to Kunming, across successive mountain ranges and deep ravines. The book was only called that because Americans admired the challenge of the road. It was a fascinating collection of stories of the Far East written by a latter-day Somerset Maugham. Nic had been sent to the border between Burma, China and Thailand to lead a group of Free Thais supplied and trained by the OSS. Between forays, he had taught his Thai officers how to play poker. Like all Orientals, the Thais adored gambling. Nic taught me as much as any man how one could judge luck, ride it when it was with you, and stop taking risks when it was against you.

The officers at OSS were obviously frustrated that I had returned from the field. I would be debriefed and sent out again. Field officers should not be left at headquarters. At this final stage of the war, the OSS force at headquarters was obviously swollen beyond reason. But, unfortunately, there were too few officers with any field experience.

The war in the Pacific was now going very well. With the loss of the Philippines, Japan now found itself cut off from its services of supply in Burma, Malaysia and Indochina. Roosevelt's strategy had proven correct. Unlike Europe, where men like Churchill had views on strategy quite different from those of the president of the United States, there was no other power in the Pacific to dispute Allied hegemony after Japan was defeated. To Churchill, as well as to Stalin, the only question in Europe was whose armies would be located where on the day of Germany's unconditional surrender. Here, Churchill was right, and Roosevelt, as later events would show, was clearly wrong. Churchill wanted to take Yugoslavia and come up in a sweep through Rumania and Hungary to keep the Russians from turning the smaller countries on the fringes of the Soviet Union into satellite states following the surrender of Germany. The decisions made by the Allies at Yalta made it certain that the Cold War would follow the end of the conflict in Europe. There was, however, no such problem in the Far East since the Soviet Union had taken no part in the war in the Pacific. I could not know that I would eventually play a small role in the terrible error made by the U.S. military and political leaders in the Far East a few months later to let the Russian Communists participate in the final strategy of the war against Japan.

Intelligence sources had advised the OSS command in China that the Japanese intended to seize all French officers in Indochina and place them in detention camps to prevent any attempt by the French military there to support Allied activity in that area against the Japanese troops left behind after the bulk of their forces had been withdrawn to defend the Japanese homeland. It was deemed important to send an emissary to warn General Alessandri, commander of French forces in the Tonkin area of Northern Indochina, of Japanese intentions. The problem was who should go and how would he get there? I was a natural choice. It was decided that I should go down to Nanning in South China and from there proceed by sampan and eventually on foot to the Tonkin, Indochina border, where I would be taken to General Alessandri and give him a personal report of Japanese intentions. I would outline to him how American forces would try to support French and Vietnamese attempts to fight the Japanese and eventually recapture control over the country. It was an innovative program. The only problem was that between Nanning and the Indochina frontier there was only unexplored country with no roads. It was decided that I would explore the area by air with a sketchpad to see just how far I would be able to proceed by river transportation. This was important in case it would eventually be advisable to send military equipment and supplies to some base to be established near the border. The aerial reconnaissance was to be done in a P-51. I would sit on the pilot's lap with a pen and sketchpad. You can imagine that flying upside down in a fighter plane at just above stalling speed is not the best manner to make a topographic map. I quickly learned how inaccurate existing maps of the area were, however. There was one place where the river I was planning to go up disappeared under a mountain, only to reappear several miles further downstream. For some unexplained reason this did not seem to be of major concern in Kunming, and I left for Nanning, where Major Glass, a retired oil company executive was directed to receive me at his home, find me an interpreter, a Chinese guide who would be somewhat familiar with the area I would have to go through, a river sampan and whatever supplies I needed. Two outboard motors were sent on by air.

Major Glass was a cultured and charming individual who did all he could to help me. He had a very nice house on the river at Nanning. He was very kind to receive me as his guest. Together we made precise and elaborate plans for my trip. Everything appeared to be in order. I was to leave the next morning, when sitting on Glass's terrace having breakfast, I suddenly felt myself keeling over in a faint. I woke up at the military hospital in Kunming several days later, not knowing what had happened to me or how I had been flown there. I think I probably owe my life to Glass's prompt use of the wireless and the availability of a plane to come and get me out. I have often wondered since how that expedition might have turned out. Would I have been able to get as far as Langson on the Indochina border? Would I have reached Alessandri before the Japanese took him into custody? Would he have been receptive to the U.S. government's proposal? If he had been, what would have been my role from then on? I suspect that here again Lady Luck played an important role. There were too many reasons why this plan should not have succeeded, and if it did, why the ultimate consequences might have been disastrous.

As it was, I was told I had a bad case of cerebral malaria and that I should expect frequent recurrences, because the disease was incurable. Again, luckily for me, the disease only came back once, the following year. It shows up in blood tests but that is all—I have had no further after-effects.

When I was able to leave the hospital, my military masters decided it was time to send me home. They gave me a week's leave in Chungking to spend with my fiancée, who had by now arrived in China.

Chungking was in a ferment. Patrick Hurley, the American ambassador, was a Chocktaw Indian given to war whoops at formal state dinners. The Chiang government was beginning to focus on the civil war with the Communists which was sure to follow the defeat of the Japanese. Through Rosamond, who spent most of her time explaining what was happening to the American journalists, I met Teddy White. The three of us had lunch or dinner together every day. I, too, was fascinated with what I learned. The world that I had just come from—medieval China—bore no resemblance to what was being discussed in Chungking. It was understandable that correspondents like Teddy White felt as strongly as they did about Generalissimo Chiang, his Vassar-trained wife, and her brother, T.V. Soong, the Minister of Foreign Affairs, and her brother-in-law, H. H. Kung, Minister of Finance. It was an open secret that the finance minister enabled his family and friends to convert Chinese money into dollars at 20 to 1, the official rate, so that they could bring it back to China on the black market at anywhere from 300 to 600 to 1. On a recurring round-trip basis it was easy to see how great fortunes could be easily replenished. Teddy and his friends had become adults in Depression days. They were great admirers of Roosevelt, who had given Americans hope in the darkest days of the Depression. They were politically to the left, idealists, and appalled at the degree of corruption they found in China. I found in Teddy and his friends much the same outlook as I had observed with Herbert Matthews and his fellow-correspondents from the *New York Times* when I worked for the Sulzbergers while I was in law school. White was finding in China what Matthews would later find in Cuba: a regime totally corrupt. To both these men and their friends, any alternative would appear preferable. It was only a short step for them to say that the opposition was agricultural reformers rather than authoritarian Communists who would quickly establish in both countries a ruthless dictatorship of the left. Rosamond and the other children of Christian missionaries in China held the same political point of view as White. Indeed, Birch, who later became a hero to the right in the United States because he was killed by the

143

Communists as the war ended, was the son of missionaries and held the same political views as Rosamond on Chiang, for the same reasons of idealism. I was to find again the same reaction from Maryknoll monks and nuns in the Guatemala, Salvador and Nicaragua of the 1980s. In this regard, Americans are noticeably more naive than Europeans. In the United States, we have always tended to judge foreign politics and foreigners in terms of black and white. We accept a Mayor Daley or a Governor Curley but preach revolution against a Chiang or a Battista.

On my return to Kunming, I was asked by my friend, Commander Sam Savage of the Miles Group, if I wished to return with him to the United States. He had found two pilots from the 14th Air Force who had completed their term of duty in China. More importantly, together

we were able to obtain permission from General Chennault to fly back in an ancient DC-3, which was going to be scrapped for parts if it remained in Kunming. Together with Chennault's Eurasian secretary, a motorcycle and all our gear, we left Kunming for the United States in June of 1945.

It was a most unusual trip home. Through Chennault and naval headquarters, Sam and I had been able to obtain orders taking us back to the United States via Karachi, Cairo, Baghdad, Bucharest, Tel Aviv, Rome, Capri, Nice, Paris and London. Our orders had been approved by Eisenhower headquarters with copies directed to the commanding officers of each of these sectors. The only refusals had come from the Russian commander who controlled Rumania, and the British commander in Baghdad. Our voyage was certainly a remarkable opportunity, and we enjoyed every minute of it. Our plane, with its Chinese and American markings in bold colors on either side of the fuselage, created a stunning effect wherever we landed in both the Middle East and in Europe. We even managed to spend a day in Baghdad, after all, on the grounds that we were low on fuel and had to land.

You cannot imagine what Baghdad in 1945 was like. It was the capital of Mesopotamia, a country the British had put together after World War I out of an amalgam of disparate tribal entities: Kurds in the northeast, Shiites in the southeast, Arabs in the Western half of the country, both Sunni and Shiite. Baghdad itself was a large city full of dirt roads, with few cars. It resembled what Kansas City must have looked like around 1910. But it had one of the most beautiful mosques in the world. We spent our time there while the plane was being serviced, in the company of British officers who were not going to let us out of their sight. This was British controlled territory and they didn't want Yanks interfering! There were minarets everywhere. One could imagine a bygone world of harems and flying carpets. But it was dusty and reeked of vanished civilizations.

Although the return voyage took a month in all, we only spent a few days in each city. We would have prolonged the trip if it hadn't been for our two pilots, one of whom came from Alabama, the other from Mississippi. They did not like Rome, Capri, the Riviera or Paris because the girls didn't speak English, and they didn't care for wine. When we arrived in Glasgow for the last leg across the Atlantic, however, they solemnly declared that the plane would have to have its engines overhauled before we could go any further.

I retain extraordinary memories of that trip home: the noise, smells, and desperate attempts to forget the war in Cairo, the miles of shattered tanks between Cairo and Tripoli, the cafes of Tel Aviv with 800-piece orchestras of refugees, and women, each of whom claimed to have been rescued from camps by General Eisenhower himself; the auctioning of women guests at Air Force weekend dances in Rome; the simple unspoiled, untouched beauty of Capri; the joy in Nice at greeting four American officers; the poverty of the French in Paris; the calm assurance of London after so much suffering in the war; the drabness of Glasgow.

The greatest joy for me was to find so many members of my family again in Paris. My Uncle Alexandre, as was reported so well in *Is Paris for Burning*, had been the leader of the Resistance in Paris. He was the same as I had always remembered him: optimistic, outgoing, full of plans and ideas for the future. I had dinner with my cousin, Jacques, his brother-in-law, Fernand de Drouas, and a young Frenchman named Valery Giscard d'Estaing, who was in love with Jacques' sister, Thérèse. On the way back after dinner, I remember the three of them discussing what each one would do now that the war was over. Fernand wanted to be a banker, Jacques a politician, but Valery announced to the others' amusement that he was going to be president of France. He certainly had single-mindedness of purpose! He would later tell Alexandre that he was not rich enough to give his daughter enough of a dowry to enable Valery to pursue his political goals. So he married an heiress to the Schneider fortune instead of my lovely cousin and eventually became president.

Paris, the City of Light, was certainly dark in those days. When I was not dining with the family, Sam and I visited the nightclubs in search of excitement. After two years in China with no one to talk to or go out with in the evenings, we had a great desire to dance, to drink and to meet pretty girls. One night at the Sphinx, which was the principal nightclub in Paris at the time, I met a beautiful young girl. Much later in the night I walked her home. I would have guessed she was seventeen. She was lovely to look at, tall and willowy, with long hair falling down over her shoulders. She was also a good dancer and spoke simply but well. She lived in a garret on the fourth floor of an old house. She asked me to come in and, of course, I did so. Her bed was under the window looking out on the adjoining rooftops. It was a night of full moon. As I took her hand in my hands in the moonlight and caressed her hair, I felt a wig coming off in my hands. Her head was almost bald. Some patriotic French teenagers at the end of the war in May had seized her for going out with a German and shaved her head. She was very upset that I would have seen what had happened to her and cried bitterly, but for me the moment had passed and I could do little to comfort her. She was too young to have been treated badly by a gang of young toughs who had never fought for their country.

That moment in the garret will remain in my mind forever.

The old DC-3 did not fail us. From Glasgow to an airport near the famous golf course of St. Andrews on the coast, on to Iceland and Greenland and then Labrador. We landed at Idlewild Airport in New York, and we left our two pilots to go on to Alabama, where they would leave the plane.

It had been just a month since we started our trip home, but China already seemed very far away.

*The author and fellow OSS officers in Kunming, China wait to
go out to select war zones, in undercover operations.*

*The author's fiancée Rosamond Frame was featured in an
OSS book on agency heroines of World War II. Born in
Beijing, she spoke all eleven Chinese dialects.*

Kunming street scene. The woman in the second rickshaw is the Chinese artist who did the beautiful scrolls referred to on page 153.

The author with his "staff" in China. The young man at the author's left was installed alone in a remote mountain village with the unit's radio, to avoid Japanese pursuit.

The trip home from China via India, Egypt, the Holy Land, Iraq, Italy, the French Riviera, Paris, London, Glasgow, Iceland, Greenland and Newfoundland, was made in a DC-3 called the "China Express" that was declared by General Chennault to be no longer fit for service.

V

REASSIGNMENT TO THE OSS
AND THE END OF WAR

IKE A GREAT MANY OTHER Americans coming back from the war, being home after a few days was an enormous letdown. My experiences in China had been dangerous sometimes, difficult much of the time, but rarely routine. I found on my return home that if I went out to dinner, I was asked where I had been. Then, as soon as I started talking about China, I would be interrupted and

It is difficult to adjust to being home. told what was happening there. No one was interested in what *I* had to say. They wanted to tell me of their own wartime sacrifices. They were sick of the war and of hearing about it. But it was too much a part of me. I desperately wanted to find somebody to talk to who would want to share with me what I had been through and allow me to purge myself, so to speak, of these experiences once and for all so that I, too, might concentrate on my own future.

The war in Europe was over. Not so in the Pacific, but I felt I had served my time there, and might not have to go back again.

My father had remarried during my absence. This I knew, because he had written to tell me. I now met my stepmother and my half-sister, Brigitte. My stepmother was as different from my own mother is it was possible to be. She was Chilean, and a well-known writer and poet in her own country. Her writer's name was Maria-Luisa Bombal. She had written two successful novels: *House of Mist* and *The Shrouded Woman.* Both novels were short, very poetic, emotional, and reflective. In a country like the United States, where action counted for everything, they seemed strangely out of place. Curiously enough, Maria-Luisa wrote in French rather than Spanish. My father had translated her novels into English for her. It was obvious to me that they were very fond of each other. Intellectually, they communicated easily and constantly. For my father, it was obviously difficult to have another child. He had satisfied his feeling of responsibility to my sister and to me by pointing out to us when we were still very young that children chose their parents in heaven. It was a novel theory. For my stepmother, having a child was also an unnecessary complication in a poet's life. I felt immediately sorry for Brigitte. If it was really her choice, she was not well advised. My father loved her and talked to her as though she were an adult. But childhood is very precious, and she had very little of it. My father's business affairs had not much improved. He was constantly urging Maria-Luisa to write more. On top of this, my brother-in-law had volunteered for the Army and was still somewhere near the front in Europe, sending home a very small allotment. So my sister lived with my father. She, too, had a small child to look after.

My mother was still working. She had moved out of her apartment when I left for China and taken one room in an apartment hotel. She and a friend had taken a job in a war plant on the West Side of Manhattan making electronic gear. She had done a good job and enjoyed feeling that she was part of the national effort to win the war. My father and Maria-Luisa were far above the din of battle, but my mother as usual wanted to be where the action was and to feel part of it.

In the midst of this rather dismal domestic scene, I was delighted, shortly after my return, to receive a call from my friend, Bob Johnson, whom I had first met at the Quonset ACI school and seen again in Los Angeles as we were both waiting to go to China. I had rendered Bob an enormous service when we met again in Kunming, China, and he was anxious to do something for me. He was currently president of the Roosevelt Raceway on Long Island and invited me to bring a friend to dine with him at the track. He sent a big black limousine for us. At the track he had a glass-enclosed living room and dining room looking out at the trotters. We were served cocktails and an excellent dinner. My date, a lovely young stage director and actress, was suitably impressed. She sat next to Bob at dinner. Before each race a steward would bring the scratches, followed by another steward who would make recommendations. Whether it was a lucky night or consistent horses, I don't know, but Anne won six out of eight races following our host's recommendations. I didn't dare have her try her luck again. On the way home, I told her the story of what I had been able to do for Bob Johnson.

Bob Johnson and I were both in Kunming at the time, he waiting to get orders for home, I waiting to go back to the field. To understand the situation, I must fill in more background on Bob. In today's world of Wall Street, he would either be masterminding LBOs or outfoxing the arbitrageurs. In the late 1920s, Bob Johnson was what was known as a "plunger," a man who took risks in the market, a kind of Jesse Livermore, the dean of them all, a man who would be a multimillionaire one day and borrowing money from his friends to get to Cannes the next. When he had money, Bob was the most generous man in the world. He loved people, and parties, and beautiful women. He wanted everyone around him to have as good a time as he was having. I never saw him angry, or mean, or nasty to anyone. I liked him very much. Despite our age differences—he was well over fifty, I was twenty-five—we were good friends.

In one of his down periods following the stock market crash of 1929, Bob had met in Palm Beach and married a very wealthy widow from New York whose real first name was Beulah. She was too wise to allow Bob to manage her money but loved seeing him happy and enjoyed party-giving as much as he did. She was too fat, drank a good deal, laughed a lot, and was older than him. Bob needed a success. If Wall Street temporarily wouldn't give it to him, the war would. Bob Johnson, as soon as war broke out in 1941, set about getting a Navy commission. Inducted as a lieutenant commander, he then volunteered for overseas service, and in due course chose to go to China, believing it to be a theater of war where Beulah would be unable to follow. The route to the Far East took him through Los Angeles. He had friends in the movie colony there and was soon seen dining at Ciro's and other fashionable nightspots with various young starlets who were waiting to succeed in the movie capital. While there, Bob fell in love with a young starlet. By the time his orders were ready to take him to Kunming, he had no desire to go there. Once in China, he constantly worried about how to get back to his young love in Hollywood. When I ran into him he was on his way home, but what was he to do about Beulah? This was the problem he now brought to me as we saw each other in Kunming. Bob was there on his way home. I was there to pick up equipment to take back to the coast. By chance, my mother had sent me a copy of Somerset Maugham's *The Razor's Edge*. It was not the best book ever written, but it gave me the answer to Bob's problem. I made him read it. He would have to pretend to be Larry, find his salvation at the feet of an Indian philosopher. I prepared a letter for him to send to Beulah, telling her of the furlough he had been given in India, where he had met this extraordinary man who had suddenly given meaning to his life, teaching him his philosophy of care for others and complete abnegation of oneself. "My dear Beulah," said the letter, "I cannot wait to go back to India and sit at the feet of this extraordinary philosopher, who has opened my eyes to the true meaning of this world and what we must do in this life to earn our reward in the hereafter. His rules are not easy for me. He requires of his followers that they take vows of poverty and absolute chastity. I recommend, my dear Beulah, that you cancel any plans you may have had to meet me in California on my return to the States, because I will not be coming back. Make plans instead to spend the winter in Acapulco with your friends. I will write you from time to time from the Himalayas, where I shall be continuing to live a very different life. I will pray that the Lord bring you the same intense joy that I am feeling as I write you these words, knowing that this sacrifice that I am now making must render me more fit to share in my Master's spiritual life." *Reassignment to the OSS and the End of War*

It was a great letter, and Bob and I were both deeply moved as we read it over. I had never met Beulah, but I had the distinct impression that it would have the desired effect. Bob signed the letter and sent it off to New York. At the same time he wrote to Los Angeles to notify his love that she need wait no longer. He would soon be arriving in Beverly Hills.

A few days later, I introduced Bob to a wonderfully talented Chinese painter friend of mine who had painted for me four beautiful scrolls which I was planning to give to Rosamond as an engagement present. They depicted a famous Chinese love story of a warrior who had to win a battle to earn from her father, the emperor, the right to her hand in marriage. In her studio the artist had a large scroll of a lovely young woman surrounded by her handmaidens who were preparing her for her lord's return home after a long journey.

"I want you to buy this scroll, Bob," I said. "I will explain to you later what you must do with it."

I think he thought I would ask him to give it to us as a wedding present. My idea was quite different.

"Knowing you, Bob, and your desire to be part of the social scene, you will sooner or later surely make the tabloids in Hollywood in the company of your young love. With the world as it is, someone is sure to send the photo on to Beulah in Acapulco. You will have made a fool of her in front of her friends with your stories of sitting in poverty and chastity at the feet of an Indian guru. She will be very angry and will most likely take the next plane for Los Angeles, where she will hire Jerry Giesler, the great matrimonial lawyer, to divorce you and leave you

153

without a penny. This scroll is your anchor to windward, as we say in the Navy. If the script as I have outlined it to you should occur, I want you to call Beulah, arrange to meet her by yourself, give her the scroll which by then you will have had beautifully framed in gold bamboo, and tell her that you had done all this on purpose because, after spending two years in the Chinese jungle fighting the Japanese at knife-point and living like an animal, you felt you were not ready to take up again your life with a tender and sophisticated woman of the world like Beulah; you needed to go through a period of acclimatization to American civilized behavior before going back to her. Admit that you have done her a great wrong, tell her to punish you with the harshest of divorce terms, and then tell her that because of your great love and admiration for her, you want her to have this beautiful painting which you purchased in China especially for her."

I felt like saying, "Give her the painting and run," but I knew that Bob would handle the whole affair with extraordinary charm, and the quality of the painting would take care of the rest.

Events ensued exactly as I had thought they would. I think within the first week of Bob's stay in Beverly Hills, the social press had already featured his photograph as a naval war hero just returned from two years of warfare behind the lines in China. The caption pointed out that the pretty young girl in evening dress beside him was the girl "he had had to leave behind when he went off to serve his country." Beulah left Acapulco, rushed to Los Angeles, and hired Giesler. Bob called on her at her hotel, and Beulah was so moved by his gift that in the divorce she left him enough money to make a new start in Wall Street.

Beulah built a very modern house for herself in Southampton, Long Island, and in the foyer, facing as you entered, with curved mirrors on either side, hung the painting we had bought together in China.

In Japanese the same ideograph means both "disaster" and "opportunity." It all depends on using imagination, as Bob did.

When I went down to the Office of Strategic Services headquarters to be debriefed, I was advised that I was going to be sent out to Los Angeles. The OSS had taken over a boys' school on Catalina Island off the coast to train officers and men who were coming back from operations behind the lines in Europe. These officers would, after two weeks of training, be sent out to the Far East. My duties would not be onerous. This extraordinarily beautiful island, a favorite weekend paradise before the war, was now off-limits to civilian visitors. The OSS had air-sea rescue vessels for the purpose of landing exercises, motorboats to go back and forth to the mainland, and the latest radio equipment. I would be expected to spend two months there, teach Chinese history, geography, and culture, handle the landing exercises, and teach knife fighting. My duties would be light. I would be expected to be out on the island Tuesdays, Wednesdays and Thursdays, but free to spend from Thursday evening to Tuesday morning at 6:00 a.m. on shore if I wanted to. I would be expected to get my health back as quickly as possible so that I could be sent back to China. At the end of two months, I would be going back there to take command of the small American group attached to the Chinese Communist headquarters in North China. *Reassignment to the OSS and the End of War*

I had one last exercise to do before leaving Washington. I accompanied General Magruder of the OSS command to meet with the Joint Chiefs and explain what the intelligence reports that my team had gathered in China revealed about Japanese troop strength in Manchuria. For months information coming back from the sources which Frillman, Shoemaker, Clark, myself and others had placed in various island cities of China indicated that the Japanese order of battle had changed, as the American forces in the western Pacific moved towards Japan. It was quite evident to us that the armies, which the Japanese had sent to Manchuria when they had taken that part of China long before World War II and which protected the northern plain of Japan against the Russians, had long since been removed, although very quietly, so as not to leave the Soviet border totally undefended. I did my best to get this message across without success. General Magruder did his best to support what I was saying. Nevertheless, we both had the distinct feeling that our military leaders, faced with the overwhelming difficulty of invading Japan proper, were ready to invite the Soviet armies to move into Manchuria to prevent any Japanese troops that might still be there from ever getting back to the mainland. Looking back, I believe this was one of the great errors of World War II. I learned with consternation several weeks later that the Soviet Union had declared war on Japan and that its armies were even then occupying Manchuria and the coastline facing Japan. There was no fighting to speak of. As our intelligence reports had indicated, the Japanese forces had been withdrawn. There might never have been a war in Korea if American policy-makers had not urged the Russians to join the war in the Pacific. Failure to keep the Soviets out of the Far East

The Japanese who had occupied Manchuria already for many years had established many factories there, with products shipped to Japanese consumers. The Russians now took everything that could be moved, including entire factories, for shipment to the Soviet Union.

My time in southern California went a long way toward making me forget Washington, policy decisions, even the war itself. Los Angeles in 1945 was a very different city from what it is today. At the end of the war, Los Angeles was still a small city. There were essentially two groups of people active there: the professionals as we used to call them, the doctors, the lawyers, the real-estate people, the land-grant owners— solid, rich, very middle-class, very comfortable. They were kind to me, received me in their homes, made me feel that if I chose to come back to Los Angeles after the war, I would be welcomed. The daughter of one well-known doctor, Nancy, who subsequently married Ronald Reagan, was one of the girls I frequently took out to dinner. The other part of the city—and it was still a separate area—was Hollywood. That world and the other were quite separate. As the summer wore on, I found that this world offered much more excitement. I met some great directors like Ford, whom I greatly admired; I went to studio parties; I felt the strange pulse of a society totally unreal, focused on very different goals, its leaders living by rules not evident in other communities. There were people from every background, every country, those who were creative, others who lived off them—but constant movement, constant effort, constant change. It made no difference who one had been, only who one thought one was and what part one could play successfully. To a young naval officer playing a very different role three full days a week, Hollywood's irreality was very appealing. There were good people and scoundrels such as I had never run across before. There was a cynicism about women—sex was the price they paid to get a part; great wealth but also despair; there was glamour, and passion, and unexpected generosity, which remained largely unnoticed, or at least unreported. The press, like everywhere else, focused on the contradictions in a person's life, on the striving for power and for fame, no matter how fleeting, and on the scandal of the moment.

It was not easy to be on hand Tuesday morning by 6:00 a.m. in Catalina Island. There was a late boat at 4:00 a.m., if I remember correctly. Once there, I lived on a very different stage, although a stage it was.

The teaching staff were all officers and enlisted men who had served in various parts of the Far East or who were experts at map-making, bomb assembly, small boat handling or underwater demolition. We were experts supposedly, but our mission was to teach other experts, many of whom knew more than we did, or had experienced at any rate some extraordinary adventures in the European theater of war. We looked forward every other week to the new group coming in, wondering how they would differ from those who had just been through the course. I used to volunteer to pick up the new contingent, if only to see how the pecking order would be established and whether I would be able quickly to recognize the one who would turn out to be the leader of the group. The new class didn't know each other. Their work behind the lines in Europe had given them a self-confidence, but also a desire for privacy, no need for self-expression, an inner reserve which was quite apparent in most of these men. The most remarkable officer in any group of men during that summer was an individual who, even on that trip over to Catalina for the first time, was immediately recognized by the other men in his group as the one who would lead them. It was uncanny because I realized it myself, and later that night when I discussed this particular group with my colleagues, I was unable to put my finger on why I had recognized his strength of character and qualities of leadership or why the others appeared spontaneously to depend on a man they had only just met. I suppose it may have been a quality in his eyes when I first spoke to him. His eyes were unusually clear, deep blue in color. He looked right at you when he spoke. He spoke very quietly but with great authority. Every gesture reflected a magnificently coordinated body. He was evidently quite used to command. He was a born leader. Every once in a while one runs across people like that, but not frequently. There are not many of them. Dean Witter, whom I would meet much later in my life, had this same quality. This officer (whom I will leave unnamed, since I don't know what he may have done after the war was over) also had a good sense of humor. I decided to find out who he was as soon as possible. This was not as easy as it sounds, because each member of the group adopted any first name he wished, and it was no one's business to find out who they really were, where they were going or what they would be expected to accomplish. It was only much later that I was able to find out about this man's remarkable career. He was then a Marine Corps major. He had volunteered in the Spanish Civil War and had served there on the loyalist side with such distinction that the German officers advising Franco had carefully made note of him. When the war broke out between the United States and Germany in 1941, he had volunteered to be sent into southwestern France where there were still a large number of Spaniards who had fought on the Republican side. He probably had maintained contact with many of their leaders. Suffice it to say that within a short period of time, he had gathered around him several thousand of these men and with the aid of massive parachute drops, had put together a not insignificant force of men who were ideally suited to guerilla fighting against the Germans in the Pyrenees region. With a bit of effort, the Germans recognized their leader as the officer they had previously run across in Spain and sent an entire German division to that region to capture him. Surrounded in a mountain village, the Germans notified him that if he didn't surrender, villages in the entire region would see the men shot and the women and children taken to Germany for slave labor. He had then walked out of the village and surrendered. Tortured and sent to Buchenwald, he was expected to be shot from one day to the next. By miracle, he had been freed by the American troops and had promptly volunteered for service in the Far East.

It is worth recounting what he did at Catalina with some of the men in this particular class. It was the practice during the second week of their stay on Catalina to select a small group of these men, generally four to six, and take them out by air-sea rescue ship to one of the outlying islands or to the California shore some miles away. They would be given a rubber boat when still some miles off the coast, told to get ashore, bury the boat in the sand and avoid detection for three days, during which time they were to live off the land. On the third night, they were to find the rubber boat again, inflate it, and row out to sea where they would be met at a prearranged point. In all instances, they were given a designated task to perform while on shore.

The performance of this group in training exercises had been so satisfying that it was decided to send the major and some three of his classmates to San Clemente Island where there was a final staging area for the B-29 crews destined to bring an end to the war in the Pacific. The island, as you can imagine, was very heavily guarded. It was with considerable unease that we took the four at night in the air-sea rescue boat to within ten miles of the island and saw them take off for the shore. Three nights later we picked them up right on schedule. What they had done almost led to the closing of the Catalina training class.

The major and his three men reached shore safely without being detected, buried the boat and their wet gear in the sand, and set off on foot towards the commanding general's house. Again, they managed to avoid the heavily guarded area around the house. They found in the drive the general's command car. Without turning on the ignition, they managed to get the command car down the hill and into a sheltered area with limited visibility. There, they took it apart, and buried it. The next day, when the general requested his vehicle, it could not be found.

You can imagine the consequences in a heavily guarded island, where nothing of any size could be removed without everyone's knowledge. But no matter how much hell was raised by the commanding general, his command car was not found. The following night, at a time when guards must have been doubled everywhere, the men entered the house and removed and buried the living room furniture. No one knows how they managed to do all this. There were frantic calls to Washington. The naval captain in charge at Catalina, queried, denied that he had sent anyone to San Clemente.

I have often wondered what might have happened to this remarkable officer. Did he die somewhere on Iwo Jima? If not, how was he ever able to readjust to civilian life? Like my friend Bob Clark from China days, is the major wandering around the world to this day carrying on impossible military tasks?

The war in the Pacific ended while I was still at Catalina. I was ordered back to Washington then, to the headquarters of the OSS, to serve my time in the Navy until I could earn enough points to obtain my discharge. The OSS had no excuse anymore to send anyone out to the Communist headquarters in China. With the end of the war in the Pacific we had lost all our leverage over Chiang Kai-shek.

It seemed very strange to be back in Washington. I was given an appointment on General Donovan's staff, but there was very little for me to do. One day, one of Donovan's senior aides asked me to prepare for the General a study which might be useful for him to leave for the succeeding organization. It was quickly obvious in Washington that even though World War II was over, it would be followed by another kind of conflict between the United States and the Soviet Union, requiring that intelligence and secret operations in foreign countries be continued.

It seemed to me that from an agent's point of view—the man out in the field by himself obtaining the information which would be essential for the country, or perhaps taking on a particularly dangerous sabotage operation such as the destruction of a nuclear-supply plant—the essential focus should be that mysterious element of luck about which I often speak in this book. If your life depends upon another's ability not to get caught, how can you find out if that man is lucky or not? This, I thought, was the basic question. If you are going to have an organization that sends agents into the field, it must determine in advance whether such men and women have had a record of luck. They may be brilliant, courageous, dedicated, but if they are not lucky, they will be caught.

The essence of such a study, in my mind, was therefore how to determine whether a particular individual was relatively lucky, or not. The first sentence of the first paragraph of my proposed outline read:

"If your life depends upon another man's, you had better make very sure that that man was born lucky."

The outline of the book—because I never reached further than the outline—gave out under various chapter headings how one could determine whether any individual has luck on his side or not. I submitted my outline to the general via the senior aide who had presented the problem to me. A few days later, I received a brief note from the general stating that the OSS was a serious organization and that my idea for the book was not acceptable.

Two years later, I read a book by the famous French resistance fighter, surnamed Camus. The first sentence of the first paragraph read as mine had. I bought the book and sent it to General Donovan at his New York apartment, along with my original proposal and his answer. He was kind enough to call me, and we then became good friends. He was an extraordinary man about whom I will write more later. He had all the qualities and faults of many of my Irish friends: great generosity, a terrible temper, a poetic streak, flair for public speaking, great courage, very little patience.

At this time I was living in Washington with my law school friend, John Graham, who, with his wife, had rented a house in Georgetown. John, like me, was waiting for his discharge from the Navy. His wartime experience had left him a very different man. After his graduation from Harvard, he had been everything his father, a very successful New York commercial banker, had hoped for: editor of the *Crimson*, Harvard's daily newspaper, member of the Porcellian Club, married to the daughter of a Boston Harvard Overseer from Beacon Hill just after graduation, a shy and gracious girl. In law school John was considered by his classmates to be typical of the ultra-conservative moneyed class. He was liked but made fun of by the rest of the students. Then the war came. John had been sent as a Navy liaison officer to Recife in Brazil, the capital in the northeast of one of the poorest sections of the country. Horrified by what he had seen in the way of abject poverty, and frequent famine, John had changed his political views entirely. When he came home, he found he could no longer relate either to his father or to his in-laws. His wife didn't understand what had happened to him. His former style of living had become anathema to him. The marriage was breaking up. While I was living with them, John met a very different

Reassignment to the OSS and the End of War

A guide for the OSS successor organization

young woman from Hamilton, just outside of Boston, who was work- ing in Washington and who, unlike him, had veered sharply to the left while in college. They would marry and John became headmaster of a small liberal boarding school in New York State, until the trustees of the school, who wanted their students to achieve material success, de- cided after a year not to renew his contract.

My friend, John Bainbridge, had, early in the war, married a wom- an from a well-known family from Baltimore who had had a remark- able career. She had traveled all over the Far East, including China and Tibet. She had driven an ambulance for the French military prior to the defeat of the French in 1940. Marriage to her was her retirement, whereas John, after leaving the Navy, was only beginning his active life. The marriage could not succeed and didn't.

One day, as I was sitting in my office, the *Army-Navy Journal* came across my desk. There in black and white was the magic formula I was waiting for: anyone who had been caught behind the lines for a period of eighteen months or more could obtain an immediate discharge. I immediately called the Bureau of Naval Personnel and volunteered to be the first one out under this new regulation. After some hesitation, BuPers agreed that I qualified. By 9:00 o'clock the next morning, I had obtained my honorable discharge. By the time the troopship arrived in New York bearing Rosamond and Julie McWilliams (now Julia Child), I was there to meet them—as a civilian. They both looked tired and bedraggled. I picked up a phone on the pier, called Elizabeth Arden and took both of them there for a thorough beauty treatment as fast as I could.

Everyone in Washington seemed to know the war was coming to an end. All of a sudden there was an urge to party, to enjoy life, to love and be loved. I had not been oblivious to this. I had met some very attractive women in Washington, including a young woman from Philadelphia's Main Line who shared an apartment with the girl my friend, John Graham, liked so well. We tried to avoid interfering with each other's private life insofar as it was possible to do so. What would I now do with Rosamond coming home? I had asked her to stop off in Peking on the way home and try to find us a place where we could live in Peking. She had done so brilliantly buying a small temple in the Western Hills outside the city. In addition, she had found and spoken to an American lawyer, well known in Peking and Shanghai before the war, who had told her he would be willing at 70 years of age to retire and prepare me for taking over his practice in China when we took up residence there. But was this what I now wanted to do? I had met and fallen in love with Rosamond in the Far East. Would our feelings for each other be the same in New York or Washington when the war was over and we were adjusting to a very different life? Rosamond with her charm, and her verve and enthusiasm for life, had appeared to me to be at home anywhere, including war-time New Delhi, as a weekend guest of Indian Maharajahs and the British Raj in its declining days of Empire. We came from totally different cultures, she from the intellectual world of American missionary professors and educators in China, I from a sophisticated though impecunious Society background in New York and Paris. Was I now ready for any kind of marriage relationship? We didn't really know each other. We had shared ideas together, made love on a liner cruising the Pacific, in Bombay, New Delhi and the capital of China, but we knew little of each other's day-to-day habits, desires, reactions or idiosyncrasies. Would I like her American friends? Would she relate to mine? How would my parents, my French family, react to my wish to marry a young woman who came from a culture so different from mine? If we married, where would we find a place to live in New York where no new apartments had been built for five years? If I went back to the law, how would I support her? These were all difficult questions for the two of us to resolve. I knew she loved China and wanted to go back there. But would we be able to go there now that the country faced civil war, and what future would there be there for foreigners if the Communists won?

Through all these periods of hesitation we had been very happy to find each other again. Rosamond had not changed. Her joyousness and enthusiasm were the same. The qualities and faults that I had discovered in her and loved—her probity, her openness, her charm, her intelligence, and her simplicity—were all there.

I had really wanted to put off making any decision for a while. Yet here I was, plunging into a marriage with a woman I loved but barely knew in a world which was foreign to her and a great adjustment to me.

My old friends had been no help to me. I think they had decided long ago that after the war I would marry the daughter of a well-established New York or Philadelphia family and escape the difficulties of my own family's dysfunctionalities by becoming part of my new wife's family. My friend, Ike Livermore, who had married the granddaughter of J. P. Morgan, hoped I would marry one of her younger sisters. But how would the man I had now become be able to share life with an unsophisticated and unworldly young girl?

Rosamond and I talked a great deal now of what our future togeth- er would be like. She told me one evening: "If in your heart of hearts you do not really want me no matter what the difficulties we might face, then I will stay in Washington. One of the young men I grew up with in China is now in the State Department where he will have a success- ful career. He wants to marry me. He called me and proposed marriage to me when I came home. If you are not altogether sure about us, you must tell me so." It was true that all Rosamond's Chinese missionary friends were joining the State Department in the hope of being sent back to China. *Reassignment to the OSS and the End of War*

What could I say except what I felt, that I loved her and wanted her to be my wife, that we would face the future together, that together we would be able to surmount any problems which life might send us. It was time to move ahead.

My father had found Rosamond intelligent and charming. My grandmother Auchincloss loved her. My uncles loved her because she spoke perfect French. My mother, of course, was another matter. She would have wanted me to marry a young heiress from Long Island whose father would be in a position to help me in my chosen profes- sion and give us an apartment in Manhattan where we could entertain properly.

Rosamond had a wonderful aunt who was one of the heads of the Presbyterian Church. Rosamond's mother had died of cancer in Boston several years earlier, just as she was about to be appointed president of Mt. Holyoke College, so her aunt, who was an elder of the Presbyterian Church, would host the wedding. Aunt Margaret was a great lady by anyone's standard. Although I am sure she had reservations about her niece marrying a French Catholic, she never let on. She was quite in- sistent that Rosamond should become a Catholic and agree to bring up the children in that faith. She had found my mother more difficult to swallow, but she pointed out that if it was up to her as Rosamond's aunt to organize the wedding, she planned to do it exactly as she thought it should be done. I liked Aunt Margaret. She was direct, unflappable and determined to do whatever her niece wanted.

The night before the wedding Rosamond and I took my mother out to dinner. Rosamond had taken a room in my mother's hotel so as to get a good rest before the wedding. We had a cheerful dinner, cocktails

163

and good wine. Afterwards I left the two of them at the hotel on 60th Street and went home. My mother had asked Rosamond to stop off to have a nightcap with her.

Perhaps because she had had a drink she didn't need, my mother then said to her:

"I don't want you to marry my son. Go back to China or Washington. If you marry him, you will destroy his career before it has even begun. He has no money, nor do you. He needs to marry someone who will be helpful to him, who knows the sophisticated world of New York—not a missionary's daughter from China."

I only found out later as we were on our honeymoon that my fiancée had spent the night in tears and had almost gone away the next morning. But it was our wedding day and custom forbade my seeing her until we would meet again in church.

On January 12, 1946, in the Lady's Chapel of the New York Cathedral, Rosamond and I were married. The reception was held in the ballroom of the Savoy Plaza Hotel in Manhattan. Some three hundred people came to the reception: diplomats, missionaries, personal friends, a few generals and admirals, the lawyers I had worked for, friends of my parents, French relatives. It was a great party. We hated to leave.

*On Catalina Island, California, where
the author taught officers on their way
from Europe to the Far East*

*The author and his wife, Rosamond, on their
wedding day, January of 1946*

VI

BACK TO CIVILIAN LIFE

HEN WE CAME BACK from our honeymoon in Florida, I was faced with making a decision as to my career. I was not sure what I really wanted to do. I had been fortunate during the war in many ways. Trained by the Navy and its Air Combat Intelligence Service, I had been to Panama and Central America, then with an Army battalion on the landings in Sicily, then with the Office of Strategic Services trained in intelligence and sabotage, then as an Intelligence and Sabotage Specialist for General Chennault of the Air Force in East China. I had experienced combat, felt fear, suffered depression bred from loneliness, met and served military commanders in all three services, engaged in diplomacy, learned that I could handle unusual and demanding situations in different parts of the world. I was a lawyer but had yet to prove that I was qualified to be one. I had blown bridges but didn't know how to build one. I had learned much about human nature but not how to advise clients or solve their legal problems. Was I really meant to be a lawyer at all?

It is at times like this that one should not make a quick decision. However, I was given an opportunity shortly after my marriage to move to Washington and take a job that would make up for my inexperience as a lawyer.

Because of my experiences in China, I was asked through a friend to go down to Washington for a meeting with Tommy Corcoran, who had been the chief architect of much of President Roosevelt's revolutionary social programs of the Depression years. I knew that his firm, Corcoran and Rowe, represented important clients that dealt with the U.S. government, including the government of China and the Soong family—a very rich and powerful family in China, which included among its members H. H. Kung, the finance minister, and Madame Chiang Kai-shek.

I went down to Washington for my appointment with Corcoran,

Decisions, decisions

166

met his partner and was offered a job as a lawyer. When I returned to New York and told Rosamond, she told me that I should not accept the job offered because it would mean that I would be working for the Chi- ang government and she considered he was nothing more than a war- lord engaged in looting the country. Rosamond had known Chiang and his lieutenants in Chungking. She had never before put any pressure on me at any time. That one interview had convinced me that Corcoran was a remarkable man. Indeed, he had certainly proven it: the National Recovery Administration, the Securities and Exchange Commission, and many other legislative acts of the New Deal had been the result of his handiwork. He worked constantly, never took a day off, was a difficult taskmaster. But I had known others in my brief legal career. That did not bother me. I knew how much I would have to learn. It was obvious that he would be a remarkable guide to the mastery of my profession.

His partner, Bill Rowe, also had many qualifications, not the least of which was that he was legal and financial advisor to a street-smart young Texan who had political aspirations (and an ambitious wife) by the name of Lyndon B. Johnson, later president of the United States.

Corcoran had a young man named Bill Youngman, who was his legal assistant. One day, sometime after I had turned down the job I had been offered in Washington, Tommy Corcoran called Bill Youngman into his office and said to him:

"Bill, how much money would you like to have in ten years?"

It was "Bill" and "Mr. Corcoran."

"Mr. Corcoran, I have worked for you for several years. I work everyday, most evenings and often on weekends. I don't even have time to go shopping with my wife on Saturdays. How would I know how much money I would like to have in ten years?"

"Bill, if you will do exactly what I want you to do, you will have ten million dollars in ten years.

"The insurance business in the Far East has always been in the hands of the British. I propose to take it all away from them, particularly in China, which is the largest market by far in that part of the world. But we must move fast before they realize what is happening. Now the insurance business has nothing to do with insurance, which people who run insurance companies don't understand. The insurance business is nothing neither more nor less than the management of other people's money—the premiums paid for their insurance coverage. The risk is handled by independent experts called actuaries whom all insurance companies use.

"If you accept my proposition, I want you to leave tomorrow morning, Bill. You will go to Manila in the Philippines where you will find an old man named C. V. Starr, who used to be in the insurance business in the Far East before the war. He knows the insurance business well and had an excellent reputation there before the war. You will offer him $100,000 per year as chairman of a new insurance business that you will form in the United States. You will be president of the company. It will be a Delaware corporation which you will have formed before you leave. He can hire all the technical personnel he needs, but as president you will invest the premiums. We will offer long-term policies in China with the full premium payable in advance. I believe our representation of the government of China will make it possible to convert the premiums received into dollars at the official rate. We should be able to pay losses whenever incurred in Chinese currency. Since the value of the local currency can only continue to decline, you don't have to be a genius to see that the new insurance company must make a great deal of money. Before you leave tomorrow morning, I want you to form the company. It will be called American International Group."

Bill naturally accepted Corcoran's offer. In ten years, he would be able to retire with his ten million dollars.

The money Corcoran had offered me was not very great, but I was very tempted to accept his offer and move to Washington with my bride. I had reason to believe he would not have made me the offer he did unless he had wanted me to undertake the task he subsequently gave to Bill Youngman.

Should I have insisted that I take the job with Corcoran, I would certainly have enjoyed working with him. It would also have been my ticket to going back to China. When I married Rosamond, we both had the idea that we would go back to China as soon as possible.

My wife's concerns about Chiang were not mine. I have never been concerned either then, or since, with the morals of my clients. What I do myself is one thing. But I do not consider that I have any right to tell anyone else what to do or to judge what he does. It is hard enough to apply a code to one's own behavior. I admired what my French godmother had done to protect her own soul—I would not have had the fortitude to do what she did—but what right do we have to judge the conduct of others?

Obviously, Chiang thought the ends he was striving for—saving the country from the Communists—justified the means—getting all the money possible to pay for troops to carry on the war, win it, and stay in power. Roosevelt himself had often claimed that the ends he sought justified the means he used. He had certainly proven that, when he had thought up the land-lease program to give the British old American destroyers with which they would be able to defend their convoys against German submarines.

Taking such a job—even though I was unprepared as a lawyer—would have enabled me to put to good use all that I had learned during the war: how to handle different countries, how to create an industry where this industry had disappeared because of the war, how to work well with leaders from another country—China—with whom I had worked well during the war.

This job would have enabled me to leapfrog successfully into a world of power in a place—Washington, D.C.—where people with initiative could succeed even though they lacked a thorough grounding in their chosen profession.

I might even in due course have persuaded my bride that more could be accomplished from inside than from outside the Chinese leadership. She was looking at the decision as an expression of her anti-Chiang political views and not as an opportunity for her husband's future and consequently hers.

In any event, I chose not to go to Washington and work for Corcoran. I would instead go back to the law. We would be very poor but we would not have compromised. I would learn my trade as a lawyer. We would evidently postpone putting to the test what I had learned over four years of war. But it was a very difficult decision and I am quite sure now that it was not the right one. Rosamond might temporarily not have approved. But she would have loved living in Washington and would have functioned very well in the post-war environment there.

Anyone reading this book might say: "That Thibaut de Saint Phalle. He might, had he taken the chance, been publisher of the *New York Times*, or chairman of American International Group, or president of some large American company after he left Becton, Dickinson, if he hadn't muffed all his opportunities."

I remember a conversation I had many years later with my friend, Senator Gene McCarthy of Minnesota, when he was running for the presidency in 1968. The pope had recently declared that even a Catholic layman might be elected to the papacy. "Thank God, Thibaut," McCarthy had said to me, "the presidency does not have to be a dead end."

So I went back to the law in New York, to Chadbourne, Wallace, Parke & Whiteside, the firm I had left four years earlier to serve my country in the United States Navy. At the same time, we took over from my father a small apartment he had lived in on East 19th Street in Manhattan.

Rosamond told me one day that although her mother's salary as president of the women's division of Yenching University had been 37 U.S. dollars per month, there were never fewer than fourteen servants in the house. If her mother had not given at least three dinner parties a week, the cook would have given notice because it would have been a reflection on her cooking. If Rosamond returned from a party, she was expected to leave her clothes on the floor so that her Amah could pick them up in the morning while Rosamond was still asleep, and wash and press them. "I have never learned to cook," she said, "not even a boiled egg." We had to learn from each other the hard way. Ros had never lived in New York and had few friends there. She found the people rude after the politeness of the Chinese.

We found that most of our friends were other lawyers or people we had met and liked during our wartime experience. That is apt to happen in New York because it is so big. Lawyers socialize with other lawyers, doctors with doctors, architects with other architects. We used to say to each other, "Why don't we know more psychiatrists or writers or journalists?" Teddy White, of course, was a close friend from China days when he was senior journalist from *Time* magazine there. And through him we came to know writers and publishers. We also had a good many friends who were working at the United Nations in one capacity or another.

Nine months almost to the day, our eldest son was born. He arrived at the New York LeRoy Sanatorium, ushered in by the doctor who many years earlier had brought me into the world. Just to make matters a little more complicated, I received the visit of an uncle, Dom Bernard de Chabannes, a tonsured French Benedictine monk from the abbey where my godmother had become a nun many years earlier. Bernard demanded to see both wife and baby. In his black cloak and with his tonsured head he created a sensation in the hospital. As he blessed the infant in his blue bassinet, various grandmothers observing theirs asked him for his blessing. It was quite a sight to see the good monk walking down the hall facing the baskets and making the sign of the cross on Jews and Christians, black and white, alike. He fascinated my wife, Rosamond, who had never met a monk before. She asked him one day what he thought was the worst sin. "My dear Rosamond," he said, "because I am away from the monastery a good deal, the abbot as a punishment sends me for two weeks to Marseilles to hear confessions before Easter. In Marseilles, they live on garlic and, after eight hours in the confession box, I am left reeling. I don't know really of any sin except calumny. To say derogatory things about someone else I think is unpardonable, but sometimes even murder can be understood if not condoned." Ros loved him.

Bernard used to walk all over New York. He essentially spoke no English, but his appearance made up for it. The police who were not then in cars but dealing with traffic would hold up traffic for him to cross. Whenever he entered a restaurant, the meal was on the house. He was dumbfounded. "People in New York must feel very guilty," he would say to me. "They follow me around the streets as though I were the Pied Piper."

It was interesting to me to observe what happens to a man who has spent all his life in a monastery and yet is a person of extraordinary integrity, of great initiative, a sense of humor, and remarkable candor. Like a child, Bernard had no understanding of the rules by which we govern ourselves. Were people following him in the street because he was a man of God or because he was tonsured and dressed differently from others? Did the police stop traffic out of respect for a man of God or because as Catholic Irish they wanted others to defer to him? Two events occurred which particularly endeared Bernard to me.

He had been sent to the United States by the French de Gaulle government to indicate that despite the war, French culture was not dead. Bernard was an artist and had reproduced in his monastery French religious paintings from the 13th century when monasteries were producing beautiful illustrated manuscripts on parchment. Bernard had taught the monks how to recreate this same beautiful work in the 20th century. In particular, he had designed and reproduced a series of Christmas cards based upon paintings from the 19th century and a family Bible which followed all the sacraments of the Church and contained beautiful illustrations of baptism, confession, marriage, with appropriate illustrated pages for names and dates. One of my aunts, learning of his visit, had asked him to bring along as his secretary her son, who, though barely nineteen, had been a tank crewman in Marshall Leclerc's Army in Italy. Despite his year of war, this young man was extremely unsophisticated and very much in awe of Père Bernard.

After two weeks in the United States, Bernard decided that he should visit French Canada where there might be greater interest in his religious wares from the monastery. He asked me to find him a car and to teach him how to drive. I bought the car and taught him to drive as well as I could. He then called me in the office one morning to tell me that since the mayor of New York's name was O'Dwyer, he must be Irish, hence Catholic. "Would you please call him, Thibaut, tell him I wish to go to French Canada on the Lord's work and ask him to issue me a driver's license?" I could have told him it was not usual for a casual tourist from abroad to call the mayor of New York and ask for a driver's license. But I didn't. I told him instead that he would have to take a test. "But I wish to leave tomorrow," he said. I put down the phone and thought about it. It was a Saturday when few people worked. If Bernard doesn't have any reluctance about calling the mayor of a city of 7 million people about his personal need for a driver's license, why should I?, I reflected. I called City Hall, asked for the mayor's secretary, identified myself as one who had worked for the mayor's election, and a few minutes later was able to tell Bernard that if he would get himself to my office, I would take him to City Hall for his test. My last sight of him in the city's test vehicle was his heading up one of the small one-way streets near City Hall going the wrong way. When I returned home at lunchtime fearing the worst, there was Bernard packing to go.

"How did you ever get your license?" I asked.

"He was a nice young man," said Bernard. "I showed him my work and gave him a set of my cards. He told me that anyone who could do such beautiful work had a right to kill himself if he chose, and issued the license. He was Jewish, but Jewish people love artistic beauty even if they cannot understand our religion."

The next day Bernard and his secretary left for Quebec. Two days later I found in my mail a summons from the State of Connecticut accusing Bernard of doing ninety miles per hour on the Merritt Parkway. To my surprise he made it to Canada.

While in Quebec, Bernard and my young cousin were well received and entertained every evening. It was then that Bernard decided his young secretary should marry. He would pick the young lady from among the families they met in Quebec. Much later we had feedback from the young man's mother in France that Bernard had tried to sell her son in marriage to several young girls of good family in Quebec. She was outraged. But Bernard had simple views regarding marriage. He considered himself quite able to judge whether the marriage would turn out to be a success. After all, in France marriages were frequently "arranged." If the girl was Catholic and the parents well established, there was no need for a long courtship or getting to know one another. These were simply recent customs of no importance.

I followed Bernard's career thereafter to the extent I could. He developed tuberculosis and was sent to Davos, Switzerland to recuperate. There he had learned to ski—robes and all. Then he had gone to Spain to study Spanish religious art. On his return he had sent a letter to General Franco, the Spanish dictator, demanding that he allow people to view the magnificent paintings in the monasteries of Spain, which had been closed to the public since the Civil War. "How can you call yourself a Catholic," said Bernard's letter peremptorily, "when you refuse to allow a Catholic nation to see these beautiful works of art?" Franco had directed his Spanish ambassador to France to call the French Foreign Minister to find out who was this rude monk who ventured to preach to El Caudillo and have him punished by his abbot.

Bernard was sent back to Marseilles churches to listen to confessions, but the monasteries in Spain reopened.

A few years later, after Rosamond had her cancer operation, I took her to France to visit the shrine at Lourdes. On the way we stopped at Dourgne to visit Père Bernard at his monastery. He was as ebullient and full of ideas as ever. "The problem with this modern life, Thibaut," he confided to me, "is that leaders in government and industry—individuals who are responsible for what our world will become—have no time for reflection. I have found an old abandoned monastery on a mountaintop in the Pyrenees, which is ideal for what I have in mind. Beauty brings us closer to God. The site there is beautiful enough to take care of this. But beautiful music is also soothing to the soul and encourages meditation and clear thinking. The National Radio Agency in France has agreed to design and build there the equipment I need. I am engaged in rebuilding the monastery myself even if it takes me twenty more years working alone. Then I will invite business leaders to visit. I want no one to spend less than ten days nor more than three weeks. There will be silence. Only I will speak or read aloud and then only at meals."

"If there is no talking, how will you handle the wives?"

"If a man wishes to bring his wife, she will be welcome, but the same rules will apply. If they wish to talk, they should go outside on the mountain."

Bernard would complete his hideaway in the mountains. He lived to see his dreams come true. I was to see him again before he died. His success is reported further on in this story.

* * *

The news from China continued to be bad. Paul Frillman had become consul general in Mukden, Manchuria, in despair as he watched the Russians taking away everything they could, moving whole factories to the Soviet Union. Paul saw no hope for China. He thought that sooner or later the Communists would win because the Chiang government was both inept and corrupt. For expressing his views Paul would later in the McCarthy era lose his job, quite undeservedly so.

Our friend, Major Clark, had had a very different experience. At the end of the war, Clark had decided to become an explorer again. He had managed to persuade *Life* magazine to give him a sizeable advance to prove that what the Air Corps pilots flying the Hump had claimed was true: that there was in Western China in the Himalayan chain a mountain going up to 33,000 feet, far higher than Mt. Everest. Clark set out in 1946 to find this mountain. In Lanchow, the focal point for caravan routes going to Tibet and Mongolia, he had met a White Russian woman named Natasha we had all known in Kunming. She might have had a last name but if so, no one knew it. She spoke Chinese, Japanese, French, German, Russian and any number of Chinese dialects. She was tall and very beautiful with the high cheekbones and dark eyes one so often finds in Russian women. Her father had been a senior Russian officer who had fled to Manchuria when the White Russian armies were defeated by the Communists in 1922. She worked for the Americans in Kunming as a translator. There were many rumors about her loyalties. But she was attractive, brilliant and extremely knowledgeable. At the end of the war she had gone to Hong Kong and married an American businessman who drank too much. It was never clear what she was doing in Lanchow or for whom she was working there. Clark fell in love with her and she accompanied him on the rest of his journey. I remember seeing photographs in *Life* of Clark's mountain and his engineer's triangulations. I didn't pay much attention. Some months later, I received a phone call from Duncan Lee, a former Donovan lawyer who had spent time in China with OSS towards the end of my stay there. The call was from Hong Kong. It told a terrible story. Clark was in prison in Canton. He needed an American lawyer desperately. He had been accused of murder and feared that if he was left in prison until the Communists arrived—and they were close to Canton—they would obtain secrets from his operations in China which the United States government would not wish to have revealed. The following day, newspapers around the world were filled with the story of an American OSS secret agent about to be taken by the Communists.

Later, when he returned to New York, Duncan told me what had happened. Clark had called Natasha from Western China and told her he would be coming to Canton. She immediately invited him to stay at her house, which was one of the finest in the city built many years before the war and completely renovated. She was planning a dinner Friday night for her husband's birthday. There would be a friend of theirs from England spending the weekend. Duncan Lee had gone to the dinner and noticed that there was a good deal of tension between Clark and Natasha's husband. Evidently, he had been told of the affair. There were too few foreigners in China at the time not to have every instance of untoward behavior reported back. There had been a long cocktail hour, much wine at dinner, and a good deal of drinking after dinner. When the guests had left around midnight, the host had already been helped up to his bed. The Englishman stayed in the library having a nightcap with Clark and Natasha, then he too went upstairs to the bedroom he shared with Clark. Some time thereafter Clark came to bed. A few minutes later, Natasha came into the room and got into bed with Clark. The Englishman woke up saying as might be expected, "Old chap, you simply cannot do that, in the man's own house." Clark, who had always been trigger-happy as we had learned to our sorrow when we were together in Kiangsi, pulled out his revolver from under his pillow and killed the Englishman with one shot. The sound of the shot awakened the host, who entered the room. Before he could say anything, Clark shot and killed him also. Natasha and Clark then took the bodies downstairs and placed them in the living room as though there had been a terrible row between the two men who had then killed each other. It was Natasha who realized first how difficult it would be to explain the shootings. She persuaded Clark that she would have to shoot him as well if there was to be any chance of saving him from a murder charge. He finally agreed, and she shot him through the shoulder near where the other two bodies lay. She then left him lying unconscious and ran across the street to wake Duncan Lee and bring him over. Clark was taken to a hospital where as soon as he was well enough, he was accused of murder by the Chinese police. The American consul was unsympathetic. It was then that Natasha reached the American press to explain that Clark was an American agent who must be saved from the Communists who were at the gates of Canton. I suppose under the political conditions then existing in Canton, the police were really little concerned with keeping an American under arrest. Clark eventually was released just before the city was occupied, was taken to Hong Kong and flown home. I heard from him a year later when he wrote to say that he had offered his military assistance to the Israelis in the first Arab War. He never did serve with the Israeli army. They had refused to appoint him a brigadier. The Arabs would, and he confessed that he had served with them. I'm afraid Major Clark would be a problem wherever he ended up. He had courage but very little judgment. Natasha moved to the United States where she opened an antiques gallery on Cape Cod.

What happened to Duncan Lee was more disturbing. People in the OSS knew that Duncan's Canadian wife was a Communist. Those of us who knew Duncan and liked him as an individual thought of him as a gossip who exercised no particular authority in the Agency. When he was later accused of being a Communist spy, we paid little attention. When this was shown to have been true much later on, it was hard for us to imagine that he could ever have given the Russians useful information. He was never prosecuted and ended his days in Canada.

From time to time our little apartment on East 19th Street received other visitors from the Far East. One of our frequent callers was Margaret Mead, the famous anthropologist, who was a close friend. Margaret was as intense as she was intelligent. As soon as the baby had been brought home, she asked to come for cocktails. Then she disappeared in the baby's room, shut the door and remained there for almost an hour. Worried that something might have happened, I finally looked in on her. She was sitting there with the baby on her lap, tears rolling down her face. Neither Ros nor I could figure out what was wrong. We brought her out to the living room, gave her a stiff drink, and she eventually relaxed. It wasn't that she didn't like the child. "That child is so beautiful and so happy," she said. "Now as it grows you will fill it full of 'don'ts,' of silly regulations and rules that don't matter. You will make the child self-conscious and afraid to do whatever it was meant to do as an individual. Why don't we urge a child towards self-expression instead of filling it with our own prejudices?" It was some time before Margaret was fully relaxed. I had the feeling that in her own life Margaret Mead must have felt restrained at times. But she was a lovely and brilliant human being.

* * *

One morning in my office I received a phone call from a man who identified himself as my cousin, Jacques de Saint Phalle, whom I had last seen at the Benedictine Monastery in Dourgne in southwestern France when my godmother, Genevieve, had taken her final vows to become a Benedictine nun. I had been ten years old at the time and Jacques was only a year older. He wore his head tonsured as a monk at that time, and everyone in the family had expected him to remain in the monastery for the rest of his life. Instead, he had sought the abbot one day and told him what he really wanted to do was to be an airplane pilot, not to earn his wings after death as a monk.

So Jacques was allowed to leave the monastery and volunteered for the French Air Force as a pilot trainee. Three years later when the war broke out he still only had experienced a few hours in a Piper Cub and had not yet soloed. To escape from France, Jacques sought the help of a young female de Grammont cousin who knew well the Pyrenees Mountains between France and Spain. As a way of serving her country, she was acting as a guide for young Frenchmen who wanted to serve in the French forces under General de Gaulle. Jacques eventually reached a safe house in Pamplona, Spain, where British agents picked him up and through various devious means eventually landed him in England. Jacques much later was to give me an account of this trip. It was not easy. Not only was it necessary to avoid German patrols on the French side of the Spanish border, but he had to overcome the very much more difficult problem of avoiding capture by the Spanish secret police and German agents operating in northern Spain. The Franco regime at the time, while technically at peace with the Allies, was under the control of the Nazis, particularly in the north where the final battles of the Civil War in Spain had been fought. The mountains were still filled with Republican sympathizers and ex-soldiers. How had this 19-year-old cousin managed to survive her life as a cross-frontier guide in these dangerous mountains? Her luck was to run out later in life.

Some years later she had fallen in love with a kin of the French Rothschilds and married him against her family's wishes. He was handsome, very rich and very much in love with her. They had had one child,

177

a girl. One day while going down a playground slide the child hit her head at the bottom, suffered a concussion, and went into a coma from which she never recovered. The parents brought in specialists from all over the world, to no avail. When the child died, several years later, still in a coma, the parents divorced. They had suffered so much together fighting to save the child, they needed to separate and find a new life to forget the trauma they had been through. They remained good friends, but each went his own way. She was left with the chateau they had shared. She never remarried.

When we stayed with her over a weekend at her chateau some forty years after she had taken Jacques over the Pyrenees, she was there alone with the memories of her adventurous youth and of the young men she had led over the mountains. She remembered Jacques well. She pulled out of a desk drawer in the library an old photo of Jacques as a young man in dungarees and a torn sweater which she must have taken during their trip. She was drinking brandy as she showed it to me that Saturday afternoon. I wondered how many other photographs of young men might be in that drawer. But when I mentioned her to Jacques a few weeks later, it was quite evident he remembered her well. They had after all shared together a very dangerous experience during several weeks.

The first visit Jacques made when he eventually reached London in 1942 was to find the Air Force officer on General de Gaulle's staff who was gathering up French pilots who had served in the armed forces. The British did not need French pilots, but the Russians did. Jacques was quickly enlisted for service in the Groupe Normandie-Niemen which was headed for the Soviet Union to fly fighter-cover for what remained of the Soviet bomber force after three years of the German onslaught. Few questions were being asked, and Jacques did not reveal that he had never even flown a Piper Cub alone. I don't remember now how officers and men had managed to reach Moscow. Jacques's story always begins where the French unit of one hundred and twenty pilots and accompanying mechanics and other service units arrived at their base camp somewhere outside of Moscow. The enlisted men had been appalled to find that class distinctions in the Soviet armed forces were even greater than in France. The pilots worried about what kind of planes they would be given to fly. The Russian fighter pilots were on one side of the field with their planes, the French on the other. It was then that Jacques went to his colonel to tell him that his qualifications as a pilot fell far short of the mark. The colonel pulled his personnel sheet out of a file.

"It says here you are a pilot. It is only Thursday. On Monday morning we fly fighter-cover for the Russians. You have four days to learn how to fly if you don't already know. Dismissed."

Jacques took up the problem with the other pilots. "Don't worry," they said. "In four days you will either learn, or kill yourself in the process."

The planes were small, very light, and very fast, made of pressed wood. Jacques managed to get his plane into the air but landing it was quite another matter. By the time he attempted to land, both sides of the field had been alerted and everyone had turned out to see what would happen. Jacques came in fast, pancaked the plane, smashed it, but came out of it bruised yet alive. He went up to apologize to the colonel who was standing by.

"That was not so bad," the colonel said. "I never expected you to make it alive."

"You have until Monday to learn," he added.

Monday morning the colonel risked his own life to ask Jacques to fly as his wingman. They took off, met up with the bombers and soon thereafter were pounced upon by German Messerschmidts. Jacques was immediately shot down, parachuted out of his plane, and woke up on the ground with a Russian farmer standing over him with a pitchfork at his throat.

"I opened my jacket to show the French and Russian flags joined at the words, 'This is a French friend of the Soviet Union' sewn into the lining. I prayed the farmer could read."

He could. Jacques was carried to the farm, cared for and eventually sent on his way back to the base. By the time he reached it some six weeks later, he spoke sufficient Russian to carry on a conversation. The French at the base thought he had been killed and were delighted to see him again. Out of the first sixty pilots in the group, he was one of the few to survive that first year. Out of a total of one hundred and twenty in all who served in the Soviet Union as pilots of the Normandie-Niemen Group, he was one of eight who survived the war. All eight were taken to Moscow, decorated by Joseph Stalin himself as Heroes of the Soviet Union, and given their airplanes. These were promptly confiscated when they flew them back to France.

Immediately after the war, Jacques joined Air France as a civilian pilot. Now he was being sent to the United States to learn to fly the Lockheed Constellation which would become for many years the mainstay of the Air France fleet of aircraft. Jacques had married a young French movie actress at the end of the war, not at all the kind of girl a

179

French country nobleman was expected to bring home. Lili would have made a remarkable wife for any man. She was beautiful in a wholesome yet provocative way, with regular features accentuated, very big eyes, sculptured nose, full lips, high cheekbones and a body to satisfy Spanish tastes. She said what she thought always. She woke up singing in the morning and everything in life interested her. She loved the excitement of the United States after the pallid atmosphere of Europe in its after-war resuscitation. She liked Americans and they liked her. She was attractive, earthy, full of fun. We loved her—which is just as well, because she would spend a year and a half living with us while she went twice a week to a famous gynecologist who treated couples who appeared incapable of having children. The specialist had discovered early that the failure didn't lie with Jacques but with Lili. After eighteen months of tests, he produced a pill which supposedly would do the trick, and Lili went back to France, pregnant and much relieved. If she had not been able to have children, her mother, Jeanne, must have thought, Jacques will have the marriage annulled and find another wife. Lili would eventually take three of the famous specialists' pills and give birth to three children, the eldest named Rosamond after my wife, who had asked her to stay with us during this whole period. Shortly after Lili went home, we received a call from her mother, Jeanne, simply announcing that she was coming to the United States to take care of our second son. This was her way of expressing her thanks for what we had done for her daughter. It served to cement the already very close relationship we had established with Jacques and Lili. Jeanne was an interesting woman in her own right: an enthusiastic but hardly successful actress. Married and divorced from a businessman from Monte Carlo, she had decided to make her mark in automobile racing, a sport in which few women participated at the time and hence were the more renowned for it. Jeanne had special clothes for the purpose designed in Paris, crafted not only for utility but to highlight her woman's figure. She must have cut quite a swathe in the auto rally circuit. She once told me that she had twice won a prize: first in a winter rally starting from Murmansk in the Soviet Union and later from somewhere in Norway.

Jeanne and Lili became very much part of my family. To Jeanne, who had broken all the rules to live the kind of adventurous life she wanted, the marriage of her daughter, Lili, to a marquis was the greatest thing that could ever have happened. She then and there decided that she would devote the rest of her life to her daughter's happiness and success. It was not to be an easy task. France is not a class society as

Britain is. Nevertheless, there is in France enormous respect for social position, considered more important than money, and, of course, for historical tradition. It was inconceivable to Jeanne, despite her own accomplishments, that her daughter would marry the oldest son of an old family. Jacques was perfectly happy to remain in the French Air Force. But not Lili. She wanted Jacques out of the French Air Force as soon as possible and into a job that would enable him to take his place in the world to which he belonged. She couldn't understand how his father could have left him to be brought up in a French monastery. She was horrified that the father, after his wife died, had married the boys' nurse, had not paid his debts and had been forced into exile in French Africa. To her a nobleman should always behave like a nobleman. It was a given. *Noblesse oblige*, I think they called it. She fully intended that her husband should be the best at anything he did and should restore the family name as she saw it to its resplendent earlier standing. Jacques was, in her eyes, the leading noble of that part of France. Fine. She would give a magnificent lunch in the chateau and invite all the country squires of the Nievre and Allier to attend. She knew that they would know who she was and would come ready to judge, since she was not to the manor born. Never mind. She would show them. So Lili called her friends in the cinema world in Paris, the extras, the starlets who hadn't yet quite made it, the wardrobe women and prop men, in sum those who made the movie business work. She told them of her problem. They rented trucks and brought period furniture down. They emptied the wardrobes to find 18th century costumes. Those who could cook, cooked. When the lunch was given, there were forty seated at the big oak table in the dining room and a footman behind every chair, complete with wig and dressed in 18th century livery. A cousin in Epernay was importuned to send several cases of champagne. The event was a resounding success. Jacques accepted the grateful expressions of the guests as though he lived that way every day of his life. Jeanne had been the chief cook. She had paid for the "help's" trip from Paris, presents to honor the occasion, and all else. She was so very proud of her daughter! As for Lili, she took it all as a great joke, but was very proud nonetheless that she had been able to carry it off. This was what life was all about! To give her husband the social standing that had been denied him, to have a good time, and to put it over on those women whom she was sure had come prepared to dislike her. Lili was the genuine modern woman, ready to take on anything and anybody and to make a success of whatever she undertook to do.

The two women next took on the problem of the chateau. It was desperately in need of care, having been well nigh abandoned in the mid-nineteenth century. The system they developed was simple. Every friend from Monaco and the surrounding area was invited to help. The work crew included the Prince of Monaco's chauffeur, who appeared with one of the Prince's cars, a cook at the leading hotel, carpenters, masons and plumbers from Monaco to Menton, various friends from Paris. Everyone was given a bed for the summer and all the food he or she could eat in exchange for a summer in the country, work, work, work, and a good time. The roof was repaired, bathrooms installed in smaller bedrooms and in tower stairways, curtains were made and hung, the garden was planted, the hedges cut, garages built. Slowly, the old house responded. Everyone was given prizes by Lili for his or her accomplishments. Lists began to form for the following summer's festivities. And Jeanne was everywhere, giving advice, praising particular accomplishments, talking to the farmers to find out if they might be interested in selling farmland adjacent to the chateau. While all this was going on, Jacques went off to learn to fly Constellations in the United States for his new employer, Air France. There were always pilots not on duty spending the weekends at Montgoublin, and there were always good-looking young actresses out of work to keep them happy. Word began to spread among the senior pilots of the line that Jacques was a young man with a future. Not that he needed recommendations from the standpoint of proficiency. Jacques was a born aviator and had sufficiently proven it in the Soviet Union. But he was not one to market himself to his superiors. Lili and Jeanne handled this for him very well.

Whenever I happened to be in France, I would plan to spend weekends in Montgoublin. It was a happy place, full of laughter, practical jokes, accomplishment, simple gaiety. After all those years of destruction, it was pleasing to participate in the rebuilding of an old castle. We were all young, had boundless energy, were full of ideas and plans for the future, a desire for living life to its fullest. In today's world it is difficult to imagine why such simple pleasures as eating well, drinking good wine, working with one's hands, exchanging confidences, and laughing together could bring us such a feeling of satisfaction and happiness.

One day Lili decided that since Jacques had been personally decorated by Joseph Stalin, the undisputed ruler of Russia, as a hero of the Soviet Union, it would be fitting for her to invite the chiefs of the Soviet Air Force to a weekend party at her husband's chateau. She called the Soviet Embassy in Paris and wrote to the chief of staff of the Air

Force in Moscow through the air attaché, inviting them to fly to Mont-goublin's nearest airport in their own Soviet Air Force planes. One can imagine the effect on the French Foreign Office in the middle of the Berlin Air Lift. Nevertheless, she succeeded. The Soviets were delighted. It was a very successful weekend in the French countryside with a great deal of excellent Russian vodka brought by the guests in their fighter aircraft. As many of Jacques's friends from the Normandie-Niemen attended who could. It created quite a stir but did no harm. Critical editorials in the conservative press of the region only served to highlight that French pilots had been heroes in the war.

To help fund the cost of rehabilitating the chateau, Jeanne came from time to time to the United States and took jobs looking after children. When she could, she came to stay with us. The old chateau in three years recovered much of its former appearance. The farm was then repaired, fences put up, cattle and land acquired—land which to a Frenchman is wealth personified. Slowly the fields around the chateau which had been sold over the centuries were reacquired. In this Jeanne was the negotiator. She was tough, able, and would pay in any currency. The dour farmers of the region were no match for her. In fact, they rather admired her. And she had her friendly bankers, one in Lausanne and one in Monte Carlo, who would have stolen for her, if necessary. They extended loans and kept invested her small amount of capital.

About this time I was invited to a big black tie party at Elsa Scaparelli's apartment in Paris. Around four o'clock in the morning, a Russian prince whom I knew dressed in white tie and covered with medals came up to me.

"There is a time in every party where all of a sudden conversation seems to become muted. It seems to happen between three and four o'clock in the morning. At that time I like to wander into the kitchen and make a little vodka. Would you like to join me?"

We went into the kitchen. He found a bottle of pure grain alcohol on a high shelf, some orange liqueur, tea, and in a few minutes had produced a very clear form of vodka which had the rawness of the alcohol taken out by the touch of liqueur and the tea leaves which were allowed into the alcohol for a few seconds as it was brought to a boil.

The following weekend at Montgoublin it was raining Friday and Saturday. By the end of the day on Saturday, the need for a new diversion was clear. "At a time like this, I generally make up some vodka," I suggested. It was the beginning of a great party for the six of us spending the weekend together, and I was grateful to the Russian prince. I forget his name now. He was one of those who were listed in the Paris phone book under his first name. No one had given him a last name in Imperial Russia!

One would have thought that a marriage such as Lili's and Jacques' would have been close to the ideal. The wife who had made this marriage to this man her role in life, waiting for him impatiently to come home when he was absent; or the husband given a chance to spend his days flying, which is the only job he ever wanted to do; three beautiful children.

What is it in human nature that makes one willing to risk everything one has been given? Jacques was extremely good looking. Despite his responsibilities as a senior pilot for Air France, he had that unsophisticated boyish look that made women wish to cuddle him. The hostesses at Air France were not averse to mothering their pilot. After a time Lili became exceedingly upset. She knew what was happening because Jacques never attempted to hide what he did. She complained to my uncle in Paris who considered himself, and was considered by others, to be the senior member of the family although he didn't have the title marquis. My uncle agreed to speak to Jacques, who went up to Paris for a heart-to-heart talk. Jacques's defense was simple. "I love my wife, but I am going to be fifty soon. Why does she object if I make love to another woman from time to time in a casual way?" His attitude was very French. But even in the Latin countries such difficulties in the rules affecting the sexes are no longer acceptable. Lili nagged, and one day Jacques took a leave of absence and went to Madagascar with a particularly attractive Air France hostess. Times at Montgoublin became grim. Lili took up writing a book on the life of a great grandfather of Jacques who had been the finest horseman in France. Her friends spent as much time visiting her as we could. But she was sad. The joy and the enthusiasm that had been so much a part of her nature were gone. Then one day she learned that he was going to be coming back. She went up to Paris, found a specialist who in two weeks promised to make her svelte again, and told everyone her man was coming home and she would never nag him again. A week later I had a call from Jeanne. The doctor's injections had poisoned Lili. She was in the intensive care unit of a leading hospital, but they didn't seem to think she would recover. When Jacques returned, he might find his wife already in a coma. A message was sent to Air France, Jacques did rush back but had only a few minutes with Lili before she lapsed into a coma. Three days later she was dead. What a stupid, senseless way to end a life so full of promise. I took the plane and went to Montgoublin for the funeral. It was one of the saddest days of my life, not made any easier by Jeanne who was totally distraught and telling everyone who would listen that it was all Jacques's fault, that he had effectively murdered his wife. Jacques was like a cornered animal, totally at a loss without the wife who had in reality been his guide and his compass, as well as the mother of their children. As generous as Jeanne had been to those who loved and helped Lili, I knew she would never allow Jacques to forget what he had done. She did not hesitate even that day to tell the children that their father had killed their mother. Jeanne the generous became destructive in her grief and so it was the end of all that she had so forcefully and loyally tried to do for her daughter. I knew that Jeanne's condemnation of Jacques would never end—and it didn't.

Back to Civilian Life

* * *

One of our best friends in New York in this early period of my marriage was Ina Telberg, a first-generation American of Russian descent. Ina had come into our lives with my marriage. She had been an old wartime friend of my wife in Washington, D.C. and now lived in New York. She and Rosamond were quite dissimilar. Ina was 35 when I first met her. She was not beautiful. She had the large eyes and high cheekbones of her Mongol ancestry, but her face was interesting rather than beautiful. She was decisive, authoritarian, remarkably intelligent, well-read, disciplined, gregarious, always ready to party or spend an evening in talk. People might say "she should have been a man." She was also passionate.

An American heroine of Russian origin

Ina lived in an apartment on the Lower East Side of New York. It was furnished with heavy dark furniture, icons on the walls, red velvet draperies, objects in brass. There was a piano in a corner and books, books everywhere. Ina had a doctorate in psychology, had taught at Ohio State and had been secretary of the Policy Planning Board at the State Department during World War II. No one asked her what she was doing in New York after the war. We only knew she had not returned to her tenured position at Ohio State, preferring to be a simultaneous interpreter at the new United Nations in New York where she made a good salary translating Russian into French or Russian into English and vice versa. She had many friends, diplomats, bankers, lawyers or other interpreters like her who constituted the international community in the New York of the '50s.

For some reason, Ina preferred as her lovers corporate lawyers who were partners in the downtown major law firms. It used to amuse us. At her parties there would always be one man who quietly stood out in the cacophony of languages all around. He would be the lawyer of the moment, waiting for the crowd to leave so that he could have Ina to himself. He was always dressed in a dark suit, was good looking in a wholesome American way, and appeared ill at ease among the cosmopolitan crowd at the party.

In the late 1940s early '50s, a battle was going on in the United States among intellectuals and the public generally about what should be the foreign policy of the United States toward the Soviet Union. This was the time of the Alger Hiss—Whittaker Chambers controversy. The press was very much in favor of Alger Hiss, the former high official of the State Department who had played a leading role at the Yalta summit conference between Stalin, Winston Churchill and Franklin Roosevelt at which the broad outlines of the post-war world were agreed upon. Churchill's views had lost out to Roosevelt's determination to reach an accord with Stalin. The press, as usual, tended to favor any type of agreement with the Soviet Union. Through lack of knowledge about what had been going on in Russia, great admiration for the role played by the Russian army in defeating Hitler, and intense lobbying by the radio, television and entertainment industry in which Jewish executives with roots in Russia and Poland predominated, the public was reluctant to see in the Soviet Union the enemy to come. There were good reasons for this: the United States was again at peace after five years of war in both Europe and against Japan; veterans were rebuilding their lives; the domestic economy was booming; there was little desire to get involved again with problems abroad. This was a period when we turned inward—to rebuild our own lives and develop our own country for peacetime prosperity.

In my case, as in Ina's, our understanding of the world was quite different from that of our compatriots. I had, in late 1945, been taken by the leadership of the Office of Strategic Services to explain to the Joint Chiefs of Staff that we should not let the Russians into Manchuria in a belated declaration of war against Japan because my intelligence gathering indicated that the Japanese forces there had long since been moved back to Japan to defend the homeland. Then in 1948 I had been involved with organizing throughout France the elimination of Communist sympathizers in the event of any attempt by Stalin to try to take over the country. Scions of old families in France were only too ready to play this role and take revenge for what had been done to their ancestors during the French Revolution some two hundred years earlier. This was the time when the French Socialist leader, Jules Moch, with the same quiet but brutal directness used later by John Paul II regarding Russian intervention in Poland, had notified the Stalin regime that any attempt at a Communist takeover of France would result in the forceful elimination of known Communist sympathizers throughout the country. Nothing was said in the media. But the Russian threat quietly subsided.

In 1948, an extraordinary event took place, which began to lift the veil over what was happening in the Soviet Union. In that year there appeared a book by a former Soviet official named Victor Kravchenko entitled *I Chose Freedom*, which described in detail the ruthless repression by the Stalin regime of its own people. The result was endless discussion in the press and by intellectuals in the United States both in favor of and against the revelations by the author. The reply of the Russian regime was immediate: a lawsuit was brought in Paris against Kravchenko and his American publisher alleging libel against the Soviet Union. After prolonged discussion at the State Department, the United States Central Intelligence Agency decided to take control of the litigation on behalf of author and publisher.

Who best to handle the matter on behalf of the Agency than Ina Telberg who was not only a Russian by birth but a former professor of psychology quite familiar with Russian thinking.

The Soviet regime had chosen wisely in bringing its libel action in France. The French Communist Party largely controlled the press in France. Many members of the French government were openly members of the Party, regardless of the American Marshall Plan which was rebuilding the nation economically. These men clearly favored the prosecution. No one knew how the French judiciary would react since here too there were many Communist members or sympathizers.

Ina took leave from her duties at the United Nations. She made several undercover trips to Russia to check out the facts and with Kravchenko's help to determine whether persons he knew might be willing to support the facts reported in his book. At the same time the CIA mounted a detailed security system to protect the author during the trial in Paris. The Agency, working very closely with the French Surete was determined to ensure that Ina and the Russian witnesses as well not encounter foul play. The stakes were very high. If the libel action failed, the world would begin to appreciate and understand what was happening in the Soviet Union. If the lawsuit succeeded, Kravchenko's reputation in the West would be destroyed, his life at great risk of an assassin's bullet, and other Russians of similar courage unlikely to engage in any attacks on the Stalinist regime.

As preparations for the trial continued, Kravchenko himself began to lose heart. He had sacrificed his family, the threats on his own life were continual. Many of his friends and colleagues had deserted him. The pressures on Ina were unremitting. She had not only to prepare the defense with French and American lawyers, she had to maintain the faltering morale of her client.

Obviously, she would have to be in Paris for the duration of the trial. Not to feel entirely alone she told her current lover that he might accompany her to Paris during the trial. When she told us about this, I indicated to her that probably the CIA would want her in some remote part of Paris where the French Surete's agents could best assure her safety. She had neglected to mention this probability to her Wall Street lawyer friend who had rather anticipated a pleasant stay at the Plaza Athene or the Lotti. It was not to be. Ina was put up with her lover in a small hotel in the 9th Arrondissement where the elevator had long since ceased to function and where there was only one bathroom and one toilet per floor. This didn't bother Ina. She had encountered far worse in her Russian visits but her lover's patience was sorely tried. The inevitable happened the first night. Having to use the facilities in the middle of the night the poor lawyer, quite naked, had gone down the hall, opened the door to the toilet and quickly locking it, failed to notice that there was a woman hotel guest already seated there. The next morning he left Ina for first class hotel accommodations elsewhere. Poor Ina. In her world physical comfort was but one aspect of a romantic interlude.

Eventually the libel action brought by the Soviet government failed. Kravchenko's thesis had been found correct in a French court of law. It was a remarkable achievement which unfortunately neither the U.S. government nor Ina could take official credit for. Ina had risked her life not only in Russia but throughout the trial in Paris. She now went back to the United Nations and her interpreter's job. The few of us who knew what she had done never spoke of it except to each other.

A few years later Senator Joseph McCarthy began his attacks on officials of the State Department, the entertainment industry and certain members of the press. Many of those we had known during the war in the Office of Strategic Services also came under attack. We became increasingly concerned about the role that Ina had played and in her visits to the Soviet Union on behalf of the U.S. Government and the CIA since the end of the war.

In 1953 we had a call from a mutual friend one day who reported that Ina had had a heart attack and had been hospitalized. I immediately called the hospital to be put on the list of visitors as soon as Ina was out of intensive care. A few days later I went to see her. She seemed unworried.

"They know what I did for them at the top of the Agency. They will never allow anything to happen to me."

The following day as I was working in my office, I received a phone call from a man who introduced himself as a partner in a New York investment banking firm. He said he wished urgently to speak to me. We made an appointment for the next day in my office.

My visitor was a man of about sixty years, impeccably dressed in a dark blue pinstriped suit which quietly advertised its London tailoring.

"What I have to discuss with you is quite confidential. I am here on behalf of the Central Intelligence Agency. Here are documents which will give you my credentials. For reasons you will clearly understand as we talk I have no written outline of what I wish to discuss with you but you have I am sure the means to ascertain my authority in this mission. I wish to know whatever you can tell me about a woman named Ina Telberg."

"She is a friend. I know a good bit about her wartime background. I know her to be a remarkably able woman who has rendered immense services to the United States government at great risk to herself. Why do you ask?"

"McCarthy is after her. Next Tuesday he will address the Congress of the United States alleging that she is a Soviet agent and has taken numerous trips to the Soviet Union to make periodic reports to her masters in the Kremlin. If she says she acted on behalf of the United States, we will have to say we have never heard of her."

I don't know what happened to me then. I knew the rules of the so-called Secret Service because I had served in it during my wartime experiences in China. But I was outraged that some part-time investment banker functionary would dare to say that the government of my country would casually abandon one who had served it with such distinction.

"Look, I don't know who you are or what you are doing here. But I do know what Ms. Telberg has done for our country. I have been to see her during these past few days and as her lawyer have carefully recorded on tape what she has done for this country of ours. The tape is in my office safe. There is a copy elsewhere in case you should attempt to seize it by a court order."

"I'll tell you what I will do" I added quickly. "I will give you until next Tuesday to persuade the senator that he should not go after Ina. If he does what you say he will do, I will call a press conference right here in my office and read the tape to them. She is at death's door in the hospital and cannot defend herself. But I can act for her."

"You know not even the president of the United States can stop Senator McCarthy."

"I don't care what you do or how it is accomplished. That is none of my business. But I have made clear to you what I will do if McCarthy ever goes after my client. This discussion is now over. I hope never to see you again."

I don't know what was said and done. I, of course, had never discussed the matter with Ina, was not authorized to represent her, or what I said. But Senator McCarthy never went after her.

I never told Ina Telberg that the government of the United States was going to deny all that she had done on its behalf. That would certainly have ended her life.

Ina recovered from her heart attack but the fire in her was gone. She was not ready to accept life as an invalid. She died quietly a few months later never knowing that her country had ever tried to turn its back on her.

VII

THE MAKING OF A
CORPORATE LAWYER

T LEAST IN THE MIDDLE OF the 20th century, when I started practicing law, lawyers who worked in the large New York firms—and I assume the same is true of Chicago and other important U.S. cities where a corporate lawyer normally deals with major corporations and banks—were insulated from much of the competitiveness among lawyers which existed outside of these firms. These firms generally needed no clients other than the ones they already had. There was little pressure to bring in new clients, since much of the business had been inherited from the last generation's partners. A young lawyer started by working for one or two partners, then acquired increased responsibility with respect to one or two of the corporate clients and then eventually became the lawyer responsible for those clients as former partners in charge retired or died. One got to know the corporate executives who managed those client companies, their qualities and their faults, their integrity or their greed. It was only natural to eventually begin to guide their decisions, which were business decisions rather than legal ones. This happened because a lawyer brought a historical perspective to given situations. He could often predict the consequences of a business decision more successfully than the client himself because he had observed the problem in other circumstances. He or the firm might have run across a similar situation for another corporate client. This experience would also enable him to explain to the client the consequences of the decision he was now facing. It was this knowledge that the client came to depend upon from his corporate attorney.

Back at Chadbourne, Wallace, Parke & Whiteside, the large New York law firm I had left to serve in the United States Navy during four years of war, I now had a small office of my own next to the one occupied by a friend who had only been taken by the war for a few months.

When I had left the firm in March 1942, Mel Goodman was working on a Federal Trade Commission antitrust case. When he left for the service two-and-a-half years later, the case had still not progressed very far. The only consolation for going into the Army was the thought that he would never have to deal with that case again. When he came back in 1946, he was put right back on the same case, which had not yet reached trial. In July 1947, the trial ended. The federal judge announced he would render his decision by the middle of August. On the 8th of August, he died. I have never seen a lawyer so crushed as poor Goodman. Five years of uninteresting work and now it would all have to start again. I was more fortunate. Corporation work was, in any event, more interesting. And in the summer of 1947, I had a lucky break. I had done work off and on for the Piper Aircraft Company. William Piper, the Founder and chairman of the company, had decided that every returning service-man would want to own a Piper Cub. In 1946, the company had done a large public offering, but Mr. Piper was a flying enthusiast rather than a businessman, and now a year later the company was in deep financial trouble. After a four-day board meeting and under intense pressure from the company's commercial bank and its investment bankers, Mr. Piper had been sent on an extended public relations tour, and a specialist in turning around companies in financial difficulty had been hired with a three-year contract to try to save the company. Unfortunately, all this had happened very quickly while the partner in charge of the account was in northern Ontario on a three-week fishing trip. In those days there were few phones in that part of Canada, and it was not expected that Lee Morey would call in. Bill Shriver, the newly appointed chief executive, was asked if he wanted a senior partner of the firm who knew little about the company to act as his legal adviser or a young man who knew the company, but little about the law, much less about creditors' rights or bankruptcy practice. Shriver decided knowledge of the company was more important. I met him. We liked each other immediately, and I left with him for Lockhaven, Pennsylvania the next day. For me, it was a wonderful opportunity. The company was, indeed, in poor condition. In going through Mr. Piper's desk drawer, I found contracts and purchase orders for millions of dollars. For awhile, I had to keep moving the company's bank accounts from bank to bank to make sure they weren't attached. In these situations time is essential. You have to estimate as accurately as possible how much is owed to whom, then separate the big creditors from the smaller ones. It is always the small creditors who will throw the company into bankruptcy because they are

The Making of a Corporate Lawyer

Saving Piper Aircraft

192

generally not sophisticated enough to know that this is the last thing that should be done if they are to be paid.

I watched Bill Shriver operate the company and slowly bring order out of the chaos which had existed prior to his coming. He knew exactly what to do, and in what order, because he had spent his entire life as a doctor of companies in financial trouble, starting with the Chrysler Corporation at the height of the Depression.

Bill was born in Baltimore in very humble circumstances. He had left school early to go to work and continued his education as he found the time to do so. He read voraciously and remembered everything he read. He had obtained a job at Chrysler and worked his way up from draftsman to junior engineer to project director. On the way he learned all he could about accounting. When the Depression hit the company, he was ready. Automobile companies don't manufacture very much themselves. They buy parts made to their specifications, and then assemble the parts to create a finished automobile. If they cannot pay their suppliers, this means they go out of business. In the early 1930s, Walter Chrysler, the chairman of Chrysler, had picked Bill Shriver for the important job of maintaining relations with Chrysler's suppliers, giving them only enough money to keep them operating. Bill had an extraordinary touch with people because he never tried to hide the facts as he saw them. The suppliers knew how short of cash Chrysler was. Because he didn't lie or make excuses, people trusted him. Above all, he never made a proposal to one creditor that he didn't make to all, so people knew he would never favor one creditor over another. Curiously enough, this rule is very hard to keep because there is always some good reason to give someone special consideration. Bill never did, and people knew it.

Needless to say, I learned a great deal from watching how Bill Shriver operated. He first divided up the creditors of Piper into three groups. The first, those who were owed only a small amount of money, he paid immediately in cash. The very large creditors whom he knew he would not be able to pay except over a long period of time, he left to one side. For the others he called a meeting of creditors. His behavior at such a meeting was interesting. He would start off by telling the assembled creditors that he understood first how angry they were that management had not told them how bad the situation was. "That is not my doing, gentlemen," he would say. "I wasn't the one who created this mess. I am here to solve it and meet our obligations to you. All I can tell you now is that I will not prefer any one of you over the others. It may

Bill Shriver teaches me his profession.

take awhile, but if you give me your confidence, you will all be paid. In a month, I will tell you just how much I can pay on account." Anger or threats were useless. Everyone was always treated alike.

What Bill specially looked forward to was the eventual meeting he would have with the commercial bank that had extended credit to management without supervising how the funds were used. He always took me with him for the meeting with the bank. "I have never seen such a poor banking relationship in my life," he would say to the credit officer. "I cannot understand how you could continue to extend credit when you should have known the company was simply getting further into difficulty. Never have I seen such a lack of elementary common sense on the part of a bank—and Lord knows, I have worked with many banks that got themselves into trouble by using poor judgment. You deserve not to have your loan repaid. This has been gross negligence, if I ever saw it."

By the time Bill Shriver was finished with the credit officer, he would have arranged to borrow several million dollars more on the promise that he would repay the loan within 18 months. All the loan officer wanted to make sure of was that Shriver would not express to the president or chairman of the bank the same sentiments regarding the prior loan that he had expressed to him.

With the money from the bank in hand, Bill was then ready to talk to the larger creditors.

"The only time to borrow money from a bank, Thibaut, is when you don't need it or you can't pay back the loan. In either case, if you play your cards right, they will beg you to take their money. But before going to the bank, I always try to figure out what I can sell to pay the loan back. Otherwise, you're not being fair. What bankers don't know is that a company in trouble can be made to generate a great deal of cash. When sales go down, receivables go down and inventories also. This frees up a lot of cash. It is the companies that are growing that always use up more money than management has planned for, not the companies in financial trouble."

How well I remembered Bill Shriver's words of wisdom when I became financial vice president and treasurer of Becton, Dickinson and Company and later had to borrow millions to save the chairman's investment in the Virgin Islands.

For the next year-and-a-half, I spent three days out of the week at the Piper Aircraft plant in Lockhaven, Pennsylvania. There was nothing to do in that town in the evening. You had to eat early, and if you wanted a drink you either had to mix your own cocktail or drink your whiskey straight. The best food in town was at the local diner. After supper we would go back to the plant and Bill would proceed to teach me his methods of accounting.

"Accountants are very strange people," he would tell me. "They always tell you where you've been, but never where you're going. Generally, the first thing I do when I come into one of these situations is to get rid of the accountants. It is not that the next firm will act any differently, but at least they won't try to give explanations for what they didn't do for prior management. Financials prepared by an accounting firm are not a working tool for management. What management needs to work with is the projected cash flow and what we managers call a 'Source and Applications of Funds statement.' Without these two tools, management is blind. Where are the funds coming from that are used in the business, and for what are they to be used? If you know this, you can run a business. If you don't, you can't. You must also carefully watch your receivables. When I come into a situation like this, I get a daily report on the receivables divided into 30, 60 and 90 days and make sure they are effectively policed. The cash flow is essential. For the rest it is just necessary to pick the right people, those who are willing to learn and will follow what you tell them to do. I always try to find such people in-house. They may not have gone to the right schools or wear the right clothes but that is not necessary to run a business. I don't worry that the men I choose wouldn't impress the directors in New York City or a vice president of a commercial bank which will lend me the money I need. But the men I pick will know how to produce a product of quality and to work with the men on the factory floor. Because they haven't come from the outside, they will know the men by their first names. The men will be proud that one of their own has been picked to run the plant. Don't ever forget to do this because as an outsider you must have the loyalty of the work force."

Bill Shriver did his best to avoid holding directors' meetings. He didn't admire boards of directors.

"When things are going well, it's fun to be on the board. The directors go up and collect their fees and tell the stockholders everything is going well. But they don't have a clue about what's going on and they don't understand the statements they are given unless someone like me is there to explain to them. You saw them when they hired me. It is 'Fireman, save my child!' But I can assure you six months later it is 'Well, that wasn't so hard' and a year later it is 'Any fool could have done it.' I don't mind. I do my job and then go back to my farm in Indiana until the next workout comes along. Human nature being what it is, Tom Dolan will come looking for me soon enough."

Bill Shriver and I were to spend ten years working together on the resurrection of "sick" companies. After Piper we worked together in many different kinds of businesses. He would operate the company; I would do the legal and financial side. We rebuilt an electronics company in the Midwest, a transportation company, automobile parts.

I loved working with Bill Shriver. He was always capable of reducing complex business problems to simple terms. We were talking one day of the Rockefeller family, and of all they then controlled in American industry. "Thibaut," Bill said to me, "Beware of the 'good' in business, because they have no loyalty. In any line of work, they are not helpful to have on your side. If you find a company that is in trouble because it has been managed by a crook, that is preferable. If you save his company, the dishonest man will appreciate that you have saved him from prison and reward you accordingly, but the good man who has gotten into trouble through his own ineptitude—probably because he inherited the business from his father and doesn't know how to run it—will feel he owes you nothing and will try to get rid of you as soon as possible so that he can ruin a good business a second time. Stay away from people like that."

I wish I had taken Bill Shriver's advice to heart. Twice I would fail to do so, and suffer as a result.

As a lawyer in the corporate department of the firm, I also did a good deal of work on securities issues, sometimes representing the company issuing shares, sometimes the underwriter bringing them to market. When I first started to work for Lee Morey, the partner who handled these issues of stock, I was simply given the name of the company, the person at the company from whom I would get the information I needed and the date on which I should submit the first draft of a complicated registration statement to be filed with the Securities and Exchange Commission, regulator of securities issues. Lee Morey never explained to me how to prepare a registration statement. He wanted me to learn on my own. When I had painfully finished the job, I would take it in to him. He would read it carefully in front of me, then tear it up and tell me to start over. I would then have to go to a more senior associate and get his advice before preparing a new draft. It was a painful process, but at the end of a year I would be able to dictate a registration statement that would satisfy my perfectionist boss the first time. It was a painful but effective way to learn. Many years later I would still be able to dictate in a remote Helsinki hotel room a complicated oil concession agreement which would satisfy my clients without change.

* * *

Tom Dolan was the senior partner of Arthur Young & Company, the well-known accounting firm. It was he who had recommended Bill Shriver to the Piper Aircraft board. Tom came from Toledo, Ohio, where he owned a chain of variety stores. He taught me another important lesson. Like Lee Morey, the senior partner at Chadbourne for whom I did a great deal of SEC work and whose father had been a steel worker in Gary, Indiana, Tom Dolan believed that he should contribute to my education. He was very much the same kind of man as Lee Morey and Bill Shriver: self-made, self-taught, very experienced in business, demanding of himself and of others, with little respect for investment or commercial bankers, men who managed money, or those who earned their livelihood through social or business contacts. Dolan was direct to a fault, meticulously honest, conscious of his own worth, critical of those he disdained, an implacable enemy of those he considered phony businessmen, a great friend of those willing to learn. I hope this same kind of pugnacious midwestern self-made businessman is still around. Tom Dolan, Bill Shriver and Lee Morey taught me a great deal about business and businessmen. They made a good deal of money, but money was not an end in itself. They were professionals in their line of work and very proud of it.

Tom Dolan taught me a lesson I will never forget. A large midwestern manufacturing company in Ohio wanted to acquire a wood veneer manufacturer in New Hampshire, a family-owned business which the heirs were willing to sell. Lee Morey had offered me the opportunity of negotiating the transaction. I thought I had done a brilliant job, negotiating Draconian conditions for our client, the purchaser, and a very attractive price with seller guarantees for future sales. I even told my wife what a great job I thought I had done. Then a few days after the closing, I had a call from Tom Dolan inviting me to lunch. He had a very different outlook on the transaction I had negotiated.

The law is knowing an acquisition must be fair.

"You did not handle the Blair matter very well," he said, "and I am disappointed in you. You forgot that after a merger or acquisition has taken place, the parties must continue to live together. A negotiator's job is not to make the toughest deal possible. He must negotiate a deal that is fair to both parties, not just his client. You have demonstrated an immaturity of which I no longer thought you capable. Don't ever forget what I have just told you. This is not a war but a marriage and should be treated with the same care."

I have never forgotten what Tom Dolan said to me that day. I would think of it again when I was to negotiate with Ferd Eberstadt the sales price and his fees for the first public offering of Becton, Dickinson shares in June 1962. Ferd was another from the same mold and I learned a great deal from him as well.

These were wonderful days at work. I worked very hard, spent many evenings in the office and many weekends preparing for the following Monday. But I was doing work which pleased me, and I was constantly learning from the lawyers, accountants and business clients with whom I spent my days.

One of the firm's clients was Howard Hughes, with whom I would spend a good amount of time in later years when my firm represented the Technicolor Corporation. Hughes' relationship with the Chadbourne firm came out of his acquisition of control over TWA, an airline that the firm had represented since its founding. One day Hughes and his Houston team of lawyers and businessmen had appeared in the office to discuss what to do in response to Pan American's special fares for Roman Catholic priests so they could come to Rome for a Marian year celebration. Gerald Brophy, the attorney representing TWA, needed to find a practicing attorney in the office on a Saturday who might be helpful. I was brought into the conference room.

"Are you a Catholic?" Howard Hughes asked from the head of the conference table.

"Yes, I am."

"My friends and I are going out to lunch. It is one o'clock. By the time we get back I would like to have from you a program for TWA to use this summer to encourage Catholics to go to Rome for the Marian year. If you're a Catholic, you ought to be able to tell us what we should do. Don't make it complicated or long. Maximum five pages."

That was my introduction to Hughes. No questions, no words of greeting. Just rapid commands.

I spent the next hour-and-a-half designing a program which would give parish priests a free trip to Rome if accompanying ten or more of their parishioners. If twenty or more, they would get additional perks. It was not a brilliant job, but by the time I had located a secretary to work Saturday afternoon and draw up the plan, I had only one idea: to leave the finished product in the conference room and get out of there.

I did not wait for comments.

The next day Gerald Brophy apologized for Hughes' behavior. Apparently he was satisfied, because with a few changes TWA adopted the program. It was several years before I met Hughes again—and again under special circumstances. I always felt he might have been a great man. He had wealth, determination, initiative, and concentration. Yet somehow everything he touched, or bought, or interfered with, turned out to be a disaster. He was a loner, utterly unable to understand people or select those who could help him. He was always frightened of people—and as a result frequently selected inappropriate advisers.

* * *

It was at this time that I began to work with my Uncle Andre, the youngest of my father's six brothers.

Learning
from "the
uncles"

He was in many ways the most dynamic of the uncles. By the time Andre had reached the age of 16, the other uncles had become well established in the United States, so he didn't have to experience the lonesome apprenticeship which his older brothers had been forced to go through in a strange country. The family in the post World War I period had become well established both in Europe and the United States. Francois had become a vice president of the Baldwin Locomotive Works, my father was a highly respected stockbroker, and Alexandre was head of the family banking and brokerage firm in Paris which even had offices on the French ships going back and forth from New York to France. Claude had left the French Foreign Service to represent his brothers' investment banking operations in Poland and Germany. There was too much work to do for young Andre to start from scratch. The new world was no longer new, and we were very much, as a family, a successful part of it. So Andre was taken under his brothers' wings, so to speak, and became a combination of international banker and stockbroker. There was no Glass-Steagall Act in the 1920s to keep commercial banks from acting as brokers and underwriters. Andre learned the deal business and loved it. When the Depression wiped out the family business, however, in 1930, he became a stockbroker. Nearer my age than my father's, we became close friends. When I came back from the war and started practicing law again, Andre asked me to be his lawyer. Like Mr. Piper, who thought that everyone returning from the war would set out to own a Piper Cub, Andre was convinced that every returning serviceman would need a home and that, in view of the dearth of housing, the business to be in was factory-built quality housing. Andre found a man with the necessary qualifications in the home building industry and they founded together Anchorage Homes. Andre brought out a public issue, the funds of which were used to build a brand new factory in Westfield, Massachusetts, near Springfield. It was a great venture, and Andre threw himself into it with all his customary energy, investing his money and that of his clients. He also went to Washington and obtained a loan from the Reconstruction Finance Corporation, which still had funds for such projects deemed by the government to be in the public interest. He also set up a marketing program and hired my first cousin's husband, Steve King, to run it. People returning from the war were desperate for housing. Anchorage Homes offered quality houses at fair prices. The orders rolled in. Unfortunately, no one had realized that in shifting production from wartime needs, there would be delays of all sorts in making delivery. There were also other problems. Prefabricated housing was a new industry which came up against antiquated regulations on zoning, specifications, and labor laws. Local contractors, even though they were to build the houses, were unfamiliar with this new industry and didn't know whether to be for or against it. Labor unions in the building trades thought that they would be hurt and fought the industry before local zoning boards. Delays of all sorts began to plague the management's efforts to meet deadlines. Because of inability to synchronize parts deliveries, houses, even where permitted, could not be delivered on time. Buyers would have made sizeable down payments, which had gone into the production process. Customers and their banks became increasingly concerned. I began to spend long evenings in the office trying to learn about the bankruptcy laws and in particular how a small company in trouble might be able to make use of Chapter 11 of the bankruptcy code in order to keep its creditors at bay while it could sort out its problems. The key to keeping the corporation in business was to obtain additional funds from the government.

Approval of this eventually came down to hiring the head of the government agency to run the business at a very substantial salary. This was not acceptable to the company's directors who felt they were being subjected to unfair treatment, not to say a bribe. The company then had to be put in Chapter 11. Andre's fortitude throughout this whole unfortunate episode was remarkable. All his own money had gone into the project. He lost it with the money of his friends and clients who had backed him. Perhaps the one who suffered the most was Steve King, who as the marketing manager for the company had made all the arrangements for the buyers to obtain bank loans. He had to face each of his customers to tell them they would never get the house for which they had purchased a lot. His only consolation was that the bank that had agreed to put up all the loan funds was so impressed with the manner in which he had handled his irate customers that it offered him a job. In due course he became president of the bank.

The hearings before the federal bankruptcy judge in Massachusetts taught me a great deal about bankruptcy law procedure. Andre and I shared a room at the local hotel during the hearings. I would stay awake all night worrying what I would do in court the next day. Andre slept like a baby. When the final defeat came, he simply turned to me and said, "You did all you could. Now I'll have to go back to New York and start again."

They were fighters, these uncles. So was my father. I did not find out until much later that my father had promised to repay his clients after the New York office of the family investment bank had gone under during the Depression. Over the years, little by little and one by one, he had paid off his creditors, living a terrible life of penury in the process.

Alexandre was not only my uncle. He was also my close friend. After the end of World War II, he created a private bank in Paris on a side street next to the American Embassy. The Communist press in Paris used to say that this was how the American government sent money to the French government after the war—through adjoining basements. In time Alexandre asked me to be a director of his bank. I enjoyed it, although I found too many petty jealousies among board members. It was a wonderful opportunity to learn how private banking operated in France—in relationship to private industry and with the all-pervasive and controlling government bureaucracy. France has not changed that much since the 17th century when Cardinal Richelieu ran the country with an iron hand, under a weak King Louis XIII.

Andre did not take long to find another venture in which he could put all his energy and talent. This time he founded an airline, California Eastern Airways, with three men who had been Air Force pilots during the war. These three men were totally different in character. To make them function as a team they had agreed that on any major decision there had to be unanimity. On occasion they would spend three days in a hotel room until a decision had been reached agreeable to all. Andre was their banker and later president of the company. Their idea was to inaugurate low-cost service from New York to the West Coast, a route controlled by the big airlines who charged high fares for the privilege. Since the route was controlled by the Civil Aeronautics Board, the new company had to issue a ticket which would take you to cities along the way until you reached Los Angeles or San Francisco, even though in fact you flew direct. The traveler didn't care, but this was a technical violation of CAB rules, even though it gave the delighted passenger a $99 fare instead of several hundred dollars. The big airlines tried hard to put the firm out of business, but the Congress and the public loved the company and kept it alive for a long time.

Andre did three other things of interest during his life: he became very close to John Kennedy in his attempts to reinvigorate the Democratic party; he became a leader in the Moral Rearmament group; and he eventually lost his life believing in the medical treatments of a certain Dr. Max Jacobson whom he met through the Kennedys. Jacobson was one of the first to treat his patients with amphetamines, which he did by injection without telling them what his potions contained. Most of his patients were actors who obviously have to work under great stress. It gave them the capacity to work endless hours. Jacobson used to say, "What is the use of living 90 years half alive? Better to live only 60 but to full capacity."

As he was coming out of the cold waters of a lake in New Hampshire one July, Andre at the age of 60 had a massive heart attack and died. He was a fine human being, father of Niki, the well-known artist and sculptress. He had followed Jacobson's ideas only too well. They had cost him his life.

* * *

The full story of Dr. Max Jacobson should now be told. I met him originally through a friend of mine who was a roommate and very close friend of Jack Kennedy. He had heard from Andre that I was counsel to a large medical instruments company which was also heavily involved in biochemical research and that I had many friends in the medical department of the Brookhaven National Laboratory. It was explained to me that Dr. Jacobson was close to the Kennedy family, that they believed in his work, and that while the connection should not be discussed, they would appreciate it if Dr. Jacobson's research could be brought to the attention of the medical establishment. As a result I went to see Dr. Jacobson. The doctor, like many others, had his offices on the ground floor of an apartment building in a very good location on the East Side of Manhattan. Jacobson had the look of an old-time Viennese psychoanalyst. He was tall, stooped, grey-haired, had a German accent and the eyes either of a madman or a genius. On his desk was the famous Mark Shaw photograph of the president walking with

The Making of a Corporate Lawyer

Dr. Jacobson's amphetamine therapy

his small daughter at Hyannisport with a very nice dedication by the president. Jacobson gave me a series of papers he had prepared on his work and told me he would be most happy to go to Brookhaven to visit Dr. Hughes in charge of the Medical Department whenever it would be appropriate. He also asked me to speak to the Research Department of the medical company of which I was a director and counsel. I told him I had heard a great deal about him from Andre. It was then that he made his remark to me about living a shorter life but one of constant activity. He explained to me that he himself went without sleep two or three nights a week because it was at night that he took care of his muscular-dystrophy patients. One late evening a very handsome woman had been brought in to get treatment. She was in a wheelchair. "I told her to get out of that chair and walk towards me, that she could do it if she put her mind to it, that she needn't be afraid of falling because I would catch her if she did. She did get out of that chair. I have been taking care of her ever since. There on the mantle is a picture of my wife. She no longer needs a wheelchair."

The Making of a Corporate Lawyer

It was clear to me that whatever one might be inclined to think or say about Dr. Jacobson, he believed in his power to help his patients. I did arrange for him to go down to Brookhaven to meet the doctors there. Subsequently, I received a call from two of my friends on the medical staff simply advising me not to become his patient. As doctors, they would not tell me more. The medical company decided not to meet with him because he had not published any of his findings.

The desire in all of us to find answers, or as we get older, to believe in a doctor's power to enable us to have more energy or physical stamina, will often lead us to trouble. Andre refused to believe the Brookhaven caution. He went on seeing Jacobson until his sudden death and persuaded me to do the same, even though I should certainly have known better. In my own defense, I can only explain it by saying that ever since 1952, every once in a while I would feel my blood pressure go down into the 50s and be so tired that sometimes I would be physically unable even to drive a car. I had been examined by all sorts of specialists in internal medicine, but many years would still have to pass before the correct diagnosis was found. Perhaps, I thought, Dr. Jacobson's remedies would help me. So I, too, agreed to be his patient. It was an extraordinary experience on each visit. I would go, be taken into one of his examination rooms, and lie down in my undershorts on an examination table. Dr. Jacobson would come in with Eddie Fisher, Alan Jay Lerner, Truman Capote, or whomever else among his literary or show business patients might be "on duty" for the afternoon if his nurse were not there. Fisher was frequently on hand. He was married to Elizabeth Taylor at the time, and I could only guess was frequently in need of Dr. Jacobson's remedies in order to meet his marital duties. Jacobson would direct him to put certain liquids and powders into a Waring blender and turn on the power. Then the doctor would fill a syringe with this mixture and proceed to give me an injection. He would vary the dosage, because at times I would almost become unconscious. But the effect was extraordinary. Although I felt temporarily light-headed, I could then go back to the office and spend countless hours in difficult meetings or half the night preparing complicated documents. I had no idea at the time that he was injecting his patients with various doses of amphetamines. I can certainly understand today why writers and actors would find his ministrations helpful, because stress on such people is very great as is their need for stamina.

One evening when I went to see Jacobson, I learned that his wife had died. We sat in his office and talked for a long time, or rather I listened to him reminisce because he needed desperately to give expression to his feelings. It was then that he told me of his first visit to Palm Beach and his subsequent medical calls to the White House and the president's apartment at the Hotel Carlyle in New York. It was shortly before Christmas. The president had planned a State visit to Canada first, then to Paris to see de Gaulle, then to a meeting with Nikita Kruschev, secretary of the Communist Party of the Soviet Union. The president wanted to take his wife, Jacqueline, on the trip, but she was too depressed to go. He had then asked Jacobson to go down to Palm Beach to his father's house where she was and see if he could help her depression. According to Jacobson, when he arrived in Palm Beach to see her, she had remained alone in her room already for several days, refusing to come down even for meals. He went up by himself. Minutes later she had come down where the family was waiting and seemed to be her normal self. According to the doctor, he visited her in Washington from time to time thereafter. But after his first visit, she resumed her regular activities as First Lady, and much to her husband's delight, accompanied him on his difficult journey to Canada and Europe. The Canadian press reported that the couple seemed to be on their second honeymoon. Jacqueline Kennedy, as might be expected, bewitched the General in Paris. It was obvious that Dr. Jacobson was extremely proud of his unsung role in reducing the president's burden on this difficult trip.

The last note to Max's story is perhaps the saddest one. I had a woman client in Paris born in Corsica whom I believe was the youngest lawyer ever admitted to the Paris bar. I had helped her at one time obtain a divorce from the American she had married, a handsome playboy called McVitty. Micheline was much admired by the Corsican community in Paris and represented clients having problems with customs or transport, areas controlled by the Corsicans. She was intellectual, dynamic, very attractive physically, and created a stir in Parisian social circles. One day I saw her again on a plane bound for the United States. She was on her way to marry Alan Jay Lerner, the composer of "My Fair Lady." The marriage must have been a stormy one. In any event, Alan Lerner became a patient of Dr. Max. Micheline heard about it and brought suit against the doctor, alleging that his remedies had deprived her of her husband's love and physical attentions. Since he was famed for achieving the opposite, the doctor's friends thought this was, indeed, a low blow. In time, as complaints against Dr. Jacobson and his "special" remedies increased, he was indicted and his license to practice medicine taken away. Had he performed a helpful service? We live in a world in which experimental drugs are constantly being developed and used despite efforts of the Food and Drug Administration to control abuse. Cigarettes have now been proven addictive. Jacobson's use of amphetamines are only precursors of a growing trend in our society to abuse our health to maintain a schedule of work and play which does not allow for adequate rest.

It was through Andre that I renewed my interest in the airline business beyond what I did as a young lawyer at Chadbourne. In addition to TWA and North American Aviation, the firm was corporate counsel to Eastern Airlines headed by the legendary Colonel Eddie Rickenbacker, the hero of the Lafayette Escadrille in World War I and the founder of the airline, with the support of the Rockefeller brothers. By the end of World War II, Rickenbacker was in his seventies, but no one would have had the temerity to suggest that he retire. There were numerous vice presidents at the airline whom I knew well because I handled its legal work, but all decisions were taken by the colonel and he never consulted anyone. Men who run companies in that style end up having no worthwhile assistants since they don't listen, don't teach, and take no advice. The result is that the company becomes badly managed, eventually falls into the hands of incompetent successors, and is taken over. Eastern was a fine airline, but it had no management depth. It couldn't

The Making of a Corporate Lawyer

have had with one man running it for so long. The same also became true of Pan American. Both companies have long since disappeared.

* * *

It was also through André that I became involved a second time with Tommy Corcoran in Washington.

I have always felt that if you are in any kind of a jam, it is a good idea to turn the problem over to a lawyer. I don't mean your every kind of contract, trade or corporate lawyer, but one who has been a negotiator or who has appeared before judges and juries. That kind of a lawyer, you will find, is generally also a born actor. In the OSS in World War II, General William Donovan—"Wild Bill" as he was known in World War I when he was commander of the New York National Guard Division and a much-decorated hero—was such a man. He was often briefed on a case on the way to the courtroom because he had been too busy to prepare much in advance. Once in court, he became the consummate trial lawyer, the actor in a courtroom scene. It was no wonder there were so many such lawyers in the OSS. They naturally gravitated to one of their kind. Among them was a friend of mine who handled a remarkable saga for Tommy Corcoran, about whom I have spoken earlier. He was as Irish as Corcoran—or Donovan for that matter—and a man always ready for a new challenge. In the OSS in World War II, he had operated behind the lines in Europe with remarkable efficiency. He was intelligent, ruthless, and utterly fearless. After the war he had gone back into the private practice of law but he craved more excitement than that. To his friends, he was rather a gentle and witty person who enjoyed good company, a good bottle of wine and a dinner to match, and especially good conversation. He could quote Yeats by the hour and whole passages from *Ulysses* if given half the chance. He was a born actor. But it was Tommy Corcoran who gave him the part of a lifetime. At 31, footloose after six years in the service of his country, he was ready when the call came.

Tommy
Corcoran
fights the
Chinese
Communists
—for himself.

I don't remember now who recommended Jim to Corcoran. It may have been Donovan himself, because Donovan would be very much involved in the matter as a lawyer and would be handling the case with British counsel of equal repute all the way to the Privy Council. But let me backtrack a minute. It is 1949. The Chinese Communists have defeated Chiang Kai-shek. All planes belonging to China National Airways Corporation, the government airline, have been used to carry the favored few, their belongings, and the treasures of China's museums to

Taiwan, new seat of Chiang's government fleeing the Chinese mainland. After completing their runs to Taiwan, the planes were ordered to
Hong Kong to escape seizure by the Communists. The new government
of China, under Mao Tse-tung, had immediately notified the British
government that, as the de facto government of China, its claim to
the planes should be recognized. However, an American corporation,
through the State Department, notified the British government that
the planes were American, duly registered as such, and certificated by
the Civil Aeronautics Administration. The British government notified
the parties, with immense relief, that the planes were to remain on the
ground at the Hong Kong airport until a British court had determined
who had the better claim to the planes. Tommy Corcoran had anticipated the British action and had long since prepared his case. Donovan was directed to handle the U.S. claim that the planes belonged to
an American corporation, based in Delaware, and not to the Chiang
government. There was, therefore, no question of Chinese national
government ownership. What had happened was that Corcoran, sensing the overthrow of Chiang, had created a Delaware corporation to
hold the registration certificates of all the planes belonging to CNAC,
the Chinese national airline. H. H. Kung, Chiang Kai-shek's Minister
of Finance, and his brother-in-law had made this possible. Corcoran,
however, was the only shareholder of the corporation which now owned
the aircraft. Since all the planes were from American manufacturers,
this had not been difficult—and Corcoran was there to help with the
Washington bureaucracy. When the Chinese Communist government
requested the British government to return the fleet to China, Corcoran
advised the government that these were American planes belonging to
a U.S. corporation owned by Americans and that the company's pilots
would be on hand to take the planes away as soon as the government
granted permission. It was then that the British government, not wanting any problem with the United States or with China, decided to let
British courts decide the issue.

"The job I want you to do is a very simple one," Tommy Corcoran
told my friend, Jim. "The legal proceedings may take several years. In
the meantime, several hundred U.S. planes will be parked on the far
side of the field in Hong Kong waiting for the case to get to the Privy
Council and be decided. Until that happens, the planes are safe. Once
the decision is rendered, all hell will break loose. If the decision is in
favor of China, you will make sure that those planes are destroyed on
the ground. If the decision is in our favor, you will make sure that they

are protected until they can be flown away. Your only problem is that people in Hong Kong are Chinese and you will have to distinguish the good from the bad. Your experience in the OSS behind the lines will help you here because your life will depend on your ability to give our trust to the right individuals. The British, who are a very small minority in their own colony, will be quite unable to give you any help, and you will have to take great care that they do not find out what you are doing or they will put you in prison for many years, if they don't hang you instead. I will explain to you exactly what you will do."

"Your program sounds almost impossible to me. The local government won't help me. I will have to rely on Chinese whom I won't be able to distinguish. I can't get control of the airfield. It sounds like a tall order."

"Nonsense," said Corcoran. "You are both a lawyer and an Irishman. It only requires acting one part in the daytime and another at night. And we have Chinese friends on both sides of the border who will help you get started. During the day you will be an American playboy with too much money to spend. God knows, there are enough of these around the Riviera that you can copy. You will have unlimited funds, a beautiful house staffed with Chinese servants, a Rolls Royce, a box at the race track next to the governor's, the most beautiful women in Hong Kong at your feet, a life of indolence and gaiety. I want you to be seen every day at the races, to be seemingly inebriated, always to be accompanied by a beautiful girl. I want you to be avoided by the ladies of the Church as a lecher, by government officials as a wastrel, by the police as an incompetent alcoholic. I want you seen at every party, not admired but tolerated and reinvited, a man whose friends are as deplorable as he is."

"At night you will play a different role. I have acquired a property on the far side of the island where at 2 a.m. each morning you will take charge of the men who are to accomplish your mission. No one will question your return to your mansion in town early in the morning. You will have been out on some debauch and will be expected to sleep until noon. Before you leave, I will present to you the officer in charge of this gang of cutthroats you will be working with, although when you see him again he will not look as he does in Washington. He will help coordinate with you the shipment of arms, the location of depots, the communications and cutouts, the payment system to be used, and all the other practices of your trade. From your daytime world there will be one other who will help you. This will be one of your apparent mistresses who will have links to the police and to the Hong Kong government. But all of us will operate entirely on a 'need to know' basis. I want you at night to be focusing on what I have hired you to do and nothing else. You will receive word when the final decision is near, and at that time I want every agent of the Chinese Communist apparatus to be quietly eliminated. How you do it will be your job, but I want it done. You will have during the night created a system of intelligence which will have identified for you all those who must disappear. There will be no attack from across the border. The British army will see to that, but you must accept constant infiltration. I would think if you have two thousand of the right men at your disposal, properly trained and equipped, you could get the job done. After all, the work will be done quietly, Chinese district by Chinese district, over a period of several days, so that the authorities are as unaware as possible of the reasons why so many are suddenly murdered in the Chinese sections of Hong Kong. Please use some ingenuity in your work so that this is seen as some war between local Chinese Tongs. Bear in mind that your efforts will not have gone unnoticed by the enemy and that he will also know when to strike. It will be a short and bloody war that you must win. When you have won it, make sure your men are ashore or on fishing boats at the edge of the airfield to protect the planes or destroy them with machine gun and mortar fire, depending upon whether we win or lose the case."

It took two years before the decision was rendered. The Privy Council had ruled that the American corporation, not the Chinese government, was entitled to the aircraft. A few days before the decision was announced, pitched battles took place in every Chinese section of Hong Kong and in the area near the airfield. Several thousand persons were killed or simply disappeared, yet there were few complaints to the police. In this dark world of intrigue outside the law, there is no appeal to the forces of order. Nobody bothered to ask Jim at a dinner party or at the races whether he had noticed the strange events in the bay or on the other side of town because they knew he was unaware of what was happening in the native world around him. A few weeks later, the events went unnoticed in the round of farewell parties following Jim's decision to close his mansion and return to the States at the behest of his "mother," a rich New York matron. Word was given out that she was demanding an accounting of his expenditures abroad.

The tale should end there, but it doesn't. I had a call from my friend a few weeks later asking me whether I would like to help him dispose of airplanes belonging to CNAC. There was no mention of Corcoran or of the Chinese government. It was only later that I found out that H. H. Kung had asked for his planes and been reminded that the lawsuit had been won by Bill Donovan in the Privy Council on the premise that the planes were not the property of the Chinese government but of an American corporation owned and controlled by U. S. citizens.

There are times when it pays not to ask too many questions. I assume the proceeds were used by Corcoran to finance the war against the Communists in other parts of the world. My job was to find buyers. Through Andre, I was able to find buyers for two of the Constellations, and the commission paid for a great vacation in France and a private school for my oldest son.

One last word about Tommy Corcoran. Talk about the cross-currents in American life: Here was the man who had been the architect of the social programs of Franklin Roosevelt's New Deal which required government supervision of broad aspects of our economic life and much tighter government regulation of business. Yet at the same time he was a fighter against world Communism, the ultimate central planning system. Is it possible to reconcile the two faces of this same man? Ollie North would have been a hero to Corcoran; Ronald Reagan as well. Was it the godlessness of Communism that affected men like Corcoran? Was it a fierce sense of independence of mind coming from his Irish cultural heritage? The world awaits a study of this extraordinary man.

* * *

If a
beautiful
young
woman
saves a
man's life,
is she not
entitled to
a reward?

I suppose what I liked most working for a large law firm with big clients was the variety of work that I had to do even within the corporate law department to which I was attached.

In many ways the most interesting lawyer in the Chadbourne office was George Whiteside, who was the firm's number one litigator and one of the four "name" partners. He was then in his sixties, tall and white-haired with a delightful manner and a voice which varied from coaxing soft to that of a drill sergeant. I had had no occasion to work for him, although his secretary, who was the wife of the mayor of New York, was a political friend of mine.

Then, one day, I had a call from a French woman who asked to see me on a matter of great urgency. Her story, which took place on the Riviera at the height of World War II, was a most interesting one.

When she came to see me, she was still under thirty, very striking, and the kind of woman that one would instinctively wish to protect.

She was the daughter of a French admiral. She had had occasion in 1938 when she was only 16 to meet at a charity gathering in the south of France a very wealthy American expatriate who had been taken to France as a child, educated there, and lived all his life in a beautiful villa not far from Menton. Married and divorced several times, he fell in love with this young girl. Determined to have her, he went to Toulon and proposed to her father that he persuade his daughter to come and live with him. In exchange, he would provide for her until she was of marriageable age, and more importantly, he would deposit a large sum of money in the admiral's name in a designated Swiss bank account. The negotiation was concluded, the young lady delivered to her "protector" and the American's part of the bargain would probably have been kept, had the war not intervened. You will remember that from 1940 to 1942, France was divided by the German occupiers into two zones, with the south governed by the French from Vichy—with certain rights to citizens and foreigners not at war with The Reich to pursue their activities normally. Then, when the United States entered the war, all this changed. It was of particular concern to the American because he had some Jewish blood and he was afraid that if the Germans found this out, he would be sent to one of the Polish death camps and marked for extermination. He, therefore, asked his mistress to hide him in the cellars of the villa among the rare vintages of wine, and she did so. When the German Gestapo officers eventually came looking for him, she told them that he had left for Lisbon and supposedly for the United States some time earlier. Despite the worst threats to her own life, she did not divulge his presence and looked after him until the Germans left the area. When he could reenter his luxurious apartments, he told her, "My dear, you have saved my life. I am a rich man and I wish to reward you suitably for what you have done at the risk of your own life." He thereupon, over a candlelight supper, gave the young woman a check drawn in dollars on the Chase Bank in Paris in the amount of $250,000. Some days later, he raised the subject again, declared that after all to a man that wealthy his life should be considered to be worth more than $250,000. He thereupon gave her a second check drawn on the same bank for $350,000. In those days, either sum represented a fortune in France. It was not clear whether she had been meant to return or tear up the smaller, earlier, check. In 1947, two years after the end of the war in Europe, she had taken both checks to Paris to cash them at the bank, whereupon she discovered that her "protector" had stopped payment on them just three days earlier.

The Making of a Corporate Lawyer

Like all such stories, this one reached the French press. The young woman sought advice from friends in Paris as to how she might recover the money and was advised to come and see me in New York. Now the law in New York on the validity of gifts or bequests to a mistress had been made by my firm in defending the interests of the wives and legitimate heirs of the Patino family, whose mining interests we represented. The children of Antenor Patino had adjusted easily to great wealth. They lived in Paris, sent their children to good schools, but there was no pressure on anyone to work and the temptations of life in the fast lane on the Riviera, St. Moritz and Paris were great for those new to great wealth. The men of the family lived extravagantly, traveled frequently between Europe and the United States and indulged in mistresses. The inevitable then happened. A generation passed and a son died leaving both wife and mistress. The mistress demanded protection of the New York courts for her years of faithful service and attention. George Whiteside, it can be said, made the law in New York on the subject. He so carefully argued the case for the sanctity of marriage that the judges of the Court of Appeals had ruled that bequests to a mistress were payments for immoral behavior and therefore would not be recognized by the courts of New York. Now when I went to him with my tale of how this young French girl had been treated, he thought carefully about what could be done to recover from the estate of the American who had abandoned her in France after she had saved his life and then died a New York resident. George Whiteside was then in his early 80s, still a magnificent trial lawyer, highly respected by both judges and members of the trial bar. "I probably have one good case left in me, Thibaut," he said. "It will be very difficult, but I think we can manage to find a distinction with prior cases because she was forced into the relationship against her will through an infamous bargain and, after all, saved his life at the risk of ending her days in a German army brothel. I believe we can recreate for the courts what she faced and secure their sympathy. Hatred of the Nazis and the methods of the Gestapo are strong. It will be a great challenge."

The thought of participating in such a case with a great trial lawyer presenting evidence to establish the factual base and earning a portion of the eventual payment if we won was heady stuff for a young lawyer, and I went home to tell my wife that perhaps in two or three years our days of hard work and poverty would be over. Unfortunately, all this was not to be. The firm's senior partner, an elder of the Presbyterian Church and a man of stern moral principles, had the potential defendant's background carefully researched and discerned that some of his wealth had come from mining companies the firm represented. This was enough for him to obtain support from a majority of the firm's other partners that we could not accept the case because of a conflict of interest. I had to advise my "client" that I could not help her. She sought other counsel, who perhaps neglected to focus the presentation as we had planned to do, and the case was lost under the Patino precedent. When two years later I read of the Court of Appeals' ruling in *Time* magazine, I thought again of how unjust the law can sometimes be, and the importance of presenting a case in terms that a judge can understand and relate to. Professor Michael's definition of fact was certainly proven to me that day. The unfortunate French woman did not even get a settlement for her claim.

Nevertheless, as far as I was personally concerned, there was an extraordinary denouement to this story which brought me a very substantial amount of money and a series of clients over several years.

*　*　*

I had done some legal work for a family in the textile business in the north of France. Roubaix, Lille, Tourcoing had been great industrial centers in the north since the start of the industrial revolution in France in the mid-nineteenth century. It is a flat region of slag heaps, factories, and endless rows of small houses interspersed with Catholic churches. As one factory owner told me one day: "We work constantly up here because we cannot bear to look out of the window." Before the advent of cottons and synthetics, men's suits were made of wool and this was the basic material used in these textile plants. After World War II, this family had come to the conclusion that it was only a question of time before the Russians would sweep across Western Europe. Good managers of small family businesses should therefore promptly establish a stake in the New World. The head of the clan who was also the chairman of the mills came to the United States and studied the economies of each Latin American country before deciding that Colombia probably had the best future. I had done the financial and legal planning for the venture. Eventually, a French nephew moved to Colombia and built a large textile plant. Today that plant produces in woven cloth many times what had been produced in northern France using the most recent and efficient Sulzer machines that can change the pattern of the weave automatically and as frequently as desired.

A telephone call came to me from Paris one day from the president of a French insurance company, the CARR, who said he had serious problems with an insurance group in the United States, and that I had been recommended to him as a lawyer well versed in international legal and financial matters. He proposed to come and see me as soon as I could receive him. This was the start of many years of litigation with Stewart Hopps and the Rhode Island Insurance Company. Several months after I had been retained as the attorney for the French insurance company, the president, Raymond Schmit, asked me if I had ever wondered how he came to retain me.

"I have a director from the north of France on my board. When I was discussing with the board what we might have to do in the United States to get out of our very serious problems with the Hopps companies and that we would need a very capable lawyer, he spoke up and said there was only one lawyer in the United States for us, a man of such integrity that he had turned down, because of the moral considerations involved, the opportunity to make a huge fee out of representing a woman who had been the mistress of a very rich American expatriate."

Strange are the ways of the world!

I am sure I shall never run across a more complicated legal problem than the Rhode Island Insurance Company or a more engaging criminal personality than Stewart Hopps. To understand the sequence of events, it is necessary to go back a little into history.

For many years Stewart Hopps was the agent in the United States of a well-known British insurance company called the Pearl. For any number of reasons, Britain for centuries had dominated the insurance business. We are all familiar with Lloyd's of London and its famous bell which tolled disasters at sea. Britain had the international trade, the ships which moved goods, the financial strength, the court system, and the standards of integrity which made the insurance business naturally gravitate to London. The essence of the insurance business is that individual risks are shared, particularly when fire, natural disasters, or product liability is concerned. This is done by initially insuring the risk and then by obtaining reinsurance so as not to keep the entire risk in house. Reinsurance can be placed with insurance companies all over the world. The companies participate in the reinsurance without seeing the actual reinsurance policy until they receive a copy many months later. Like many professions controlled by the British, insurance is based on mutual trust.

Stewart Hopps was the highest paid business executive in the United States when World War II broke out. He had a storybook apartment in New York and a large renovated Pennsylvania Dutch house in eastern Pennsylvania. He collected works of art and had even staged a party at his property in the Pocono Mountains where he had hired Barnum and Bailey's Circus to entertain his guests. Unfortunately, with the advent of war, taxes took away most of his income and the insurance business, which depended upon civilian trade, became a casualty of war.

It was then that Hopps was approached by Lowell Birrell, a corporate lawyer turned financier.

"With your knowledge of the insurance business and my knowledge of corporate law, our capacity to make money together will be limited only by our willingness to work," Birrell said to Hopps.

The two decided to team up. They formed at Hopps's instigation a series of insurance brokerage agencies which, guided by Birrell, were incorporated in states like Kentucky, Rhode Island, Utah and Nevada, where the insurance commissioners were more lax than elsewhere.

At first they restricted their activities to the United States. Their plan was relatively foolproof. They had managed, through various concealed entities, to buy control of an old and respected insurance company called The Rhode Island Insurance Company based in Providence, Rhode Island. The Hopps-Birrell brokerage companies, acting as brokers for a fee, then placed insurance with The Rhode Island. As they acquired other insurance companies, using the assets of The Rhode Island for that purpose, they then reinsured the policies issued by The Rhode Island, again using the Nevada, Kentucky or Utah brokerage firms to place the reinsurance. For placing the reinsurance within the group of controlled companies, the brokerage companies controlled by Hopps would get the reinsurance commission. Eventually, Hopps-Birrell had control of several insurance companies based in the United States. This meant many reinsurance commissions. The insurance company left with the ultimate risk on the policy might have received only 15 percent of the premium. The rest went via commissions into the pockets of these two entrepreneurs.

It was not for nothing that they had selected a company based in Rhode Island as the key insurance company in their empire. That state, the smallest in the United States, has tended to be controlled by one political party, the Democratic Party, and therefore be subject to political abuse within that part of the regulatory system under state, rather than federal control like the insurance business. Furthermore, one of the state's former senators had recently been appointed by the president of the United States as attorney general of the United States. Men like

Hopps and Birrell would not hesitate to use this appointment to indicate that they had particularly powerful connections with the executive branch of the federal government.

This was not all.

Not content with taking money in commissions on insurance placed, they would seek out companies desperately in need of money to avoid bankruptcy. They would then offer to have their captive insurance companies subscribe to bonds in such a company. For their efforts Hopps and Birrell would get options on large amounts of common stock. All this meant that if the company was saved, they made a large gain on the value of their options. If the infusion of capital failed, it was the captive insurance companies that would incur the loss.

All this goes to show that the depredations in such companies as Enron at the beginning of the 21st century represent nothing new in outrageous human behavior. But in every instance it takes executive ability, legal talent, and the connivance of bankers.

You can imagine what it meant to me as a young lawyer to be given such a challenge. I knew that if I turned over the matter to the senior partners in the firm, it would mean that the case would be turned over to one of the senior corporate partners to manage with a junior partner to assist and me to prepare appropriate legal documents. So I decided to do it all on my own. The firm gave me its approval. My client didn't care. He knew he was way over his head in dealing with Hopps and Birrell. He wanted to have an American to hold responsible if things didn't work out. It was sufficient for his purposes that his board in Paris had said that I should be retained as counsel.

The reason which had caused the president of the French company to come to the United States in such haste was that the Rhode Island Insurance Company had asked for the appointment of a receiver in the state court. The French insurance company, my client, was not only due large sums on policies in the process of reinsurance, but as manager of The Rhode Island's reinsurance in Europe it had placed reinsurance with Swiss, Portuguese, British, Spanish, German and Italian insurance companies, each of whom owed The Rhode Island for losses and in turn was owed on retrocession of premiums earned from the insured. It was a very complicated situation.

The first step to take was obviously to get an accounting firm familiar with the insurance business and having no relationship with Hopps, Birrell or anyone connected with them. It was the kind of financial puzzle I enjoyed. I selected the firm and it immediately went to work to try to balance the accounts owed back and forth by and to my clients. I then went to Providence, Rhode Island to meet with the receiver and his counsel. It was an interesting exercise. The receiver, as might be surmised, was a lawyer with good political connections in the state. He had named as counsel two sets of lawyers: the leading corporate law firm in the state, a Republican firm with good connections with the business community, and a well-known political firm connected with the state Democratic organization.

I was advised by the receiver that he intended fully to collect what was owed by my client and the European reinsurers. For their claims, they would have to share with other creditors of the Rhode Island Insurance Company. The receiver pointed out to me that the attorney general of the state would head a group of officials on a trip to Paris to lay claim to what was owed. He also referred to the fact that the attorney general of the United States had been a senator from Rhode Island and therefore could be expected to use his good offices to press the receiver's claim with the French government. The delegation would be accompanied to Paris by Stewart Hopps, who knew the Rhode Island company well and would act as adviser to the delegation.

Hopps was always clever enough never to appear as a shareholder of any company he was engaged in looting, nor as a director or officer. He was always just an adviser to the board. This meant if anything happened, others would bear the consequences.

We did not make progress in the negotiations. A meeting was called to take place in Paris—in the spring, of course. Now in those days—1948—one went to Paris in a Lockheed Constellation or a Boeing, both propeller-driven planes which had to refuel once or twice along the way. My clients, our accountants and I flew on Air France; the Rhode Island delegation on TWA. Both groups were forced to land twice, spending a night in Iceland where we sat and faced each other in a small airport filled with other stranded passengers. The most interesting member of the receiver's group was the attorney general of Rhode Island, a blind man. He had been a steel worker, was injured and lost the sight of both eyes in an accident and was put in a home for injured workers. There he met and eventually married the volunteer who came to read to him. She helped him to get a college education by correspondence. He then ran for the Rhode Island legislature, was elected, and in due course became Speaker. He was then named probate judge of Rhode Island which is an office, curiously enough, that does not require a legal degree. From there, with his political connections he became attorney general of the state, having picked up his law degree during his term as probate judge. Because he was blind, he had an uncanny ability to follow the most intricate financial transactions described in any meeting, even though he, of course, could not read and could not make any notes during the discussions.

It was most difficult to negotiate with a blind man. He sat there all day long, looking like a steel worker dressed in a business suit, with ashes from an ever-lit cigar strewn over his waistcoat and this extraordinary memory for figures. He could recall a detailed financial statement summary three days later without losing one figure. At the end of four days we were in accord on the totals: what was due to my client, the French company, the CARR, by The Rhode Island, and what was due by the CARR to The Rhode Island. The figures were not in our favor; the CARR was a debtor, not a creditor. The receiver then announced that unless he was paid forthwith, he would bring in the U.S. attorney general to force the French government to take action against my client. I curtly notified the receiver that if he did so, I would go to the French government and ask that it intervene in The Rhode Island action alleging fraud by the American insurance company and the insurance commissioner of the state for permitting the fraud. I pointed out that Mr. Hopps had come to Europe in 1947 in a chartered Constellation to show the Europeans who were just recovering from the war how powerful the Rhode Island company was when, in truth, it had already been barred by the insurance commissioners of the states of New York, Indiana and California. I added that if the attorney general wanted this kind of publicity for his state, and for the Democratic Party which controlled it, this was what he would get—with names highlighted. It was a thoroughly unpleasant end to four days of discussion. I went back to my hotel to find that evening that I had a call from Stewart Hopps who asked me to dine with him.

"You realize, of course, Thibaut, that none of us want to create a cause célèbre, much less an international incident involving the United States and French governments. I believe the attorney general was trying to put additional pressure on your clients when he should not have. I am always in favor of compromise when it is possible to give credence to the other fellow's point of view. I would suggest we leave matters as they are. On my return to the United States, I will try to persuade the lawyers to hold up any action in the courts pending our examination of more basic questions."

I remembered Tom Dolan's words of wisdom. It was obviously to everyone's advantage not to reach a position that would make it impossible to reach a compromise.

That suited me just fine because I was aware of CARR's responsibility to the European reinsurers with whom it had placed Rhode Island's business, and I didn't know whether these companies were debtors or creditors. Also, I did not know enough insurance law or the facts of the situation to know what liability, if any, the CARR owed to the reinsurers. So the next day I advised President Schmit that it might be worthwhile to get the reinsurers together and perhaps have me represent all the reinsuring firms so that, if possible, I could negotiate an offset between creditors and debtors. This, of course, cannot legally be done in receivership where there is no common ownership. But it was worth a try if there were some companies that owed money and others that were owed. Schmit understood exactly what I was talking about when I explained it to him and saw the value in attempting the offset.

"You have no idea what trouble you will have," he pointed out to me. "Imagine putting the Swiss, the Germans, the English, the Italians, Spanish and Portuguese all in one room and expect to negotiate a joint effort. It will be a Tower of Babel with similar results. But, of course, insurance being based on trust, it is essential that I get out of this ugly business without causing these other companies to lose money regardless of my potential legal liability to them. If you could accomplish the offset, you would be doing me an enormous favor and earning yourself a good additional fee as well, because I would undertake to have CARR pay it to you. I will have to go to each of the company presidents and explain your idea to them. Send me a memorandum as soon as you get home. It won't be easy because the Latins will claim that they are owed more than the books show and the Swiss will think that the Latins have doctored the books in their favor. The idea, however, is a good one."

Eventually each of the companies sent a representative to meet with me in New York prior to meeting with counsel for the receiver. The Swiss and the Germans who owed money wanted to pay what they owed and be done with the receiver. The Latins were owed money and didn't understand why they would not get paid. The president of the Swiss company who had insisted on coming himself was constantly engaging in monologues which either bored or annoyed the Italians, the Portuguese and the Spaniards, who all too frequently walked out of the discussions. Each had to review the documents which their colleagues were planning to submit. I thought on several occasions that the task was impossible. But finally each one agreed to the principle of offset, although the Swiss representative kept saying that what I was doing was highly irregular and would not stand up if this were a Swiss court. I kept pointing out to him that whatever I could get the receiver to agree to would become the ruling of the Rhode Island Court because the court would have to approve every agreement made by the receiver. It was a slow and very painful process only made possible by the desire of those who were owed money to get what was due them through use of the offset process. Then when all was done, I next had the problem of making sure that the individual executives didn't discuss the offset agreement with receiver's counsel. It was essential to success that I be able to speak for all. The receiver's counsel who understood what I was trying to do was in the meantime sending claim letters and demands of all sorts to obtain what was owed by the Swiss and the Germans. I was anxious to send all these foreign executives home as soon as possible so that I could negotiate my transaction with the receiver's counsel and get their agreement to submit the offset to the receiver and, after his approval, to the court. Since the overall balance was very much in the receiver's favor and he was anxious to obtain the money, I knew I had a good chance if I didn't lose control of my flock. This is what finally worked out.

Hopps was helpful because he was not anxious to have any more come out about the affairs of The Rhode Island than was necessary.

I had been surprised during that first visit to Paris with the receiver to notice that Hopps' wife was accompanying her husband. I could not understand how a man of his evident refinement could have married a woman who was so evidently beneath him in temperament, education and culture. Also, she acted more like his secretary than wife. Later he told me the story. It involved a meeting late one afternoon in Stewart Hopps' luxurious apartment in the Carlyle Hotel in New York City. She had just finished taking dictation for the day. It was shortly after The Rhode Island had gone into receivership. His secretary had asked him if she could review with him an important personal problem the next day. He had agreed. The next morning she said to him:

"Mr. Hopps, I have been working for you for ten years. I know everything you've done and I have carefully and fully recorded it as only a capable secretary can do. I have ascertained that a wife cannot be made to testify against her husband. I wish to marry you."

"How much time do I have to consider this delightful proposal of marriage?"

"I would like to have your reply by tomorrow morning because if the answer is 'no,' there is much that I have to do. If your answer is 'yes,' I plan to accompany you to Paris with the receiver. Time is important because it is fitting that a young bride be well-dressed if she is to accompany her successful husband on an important trip to Paris."

"I had little choice in the matter, Thibaut. We were married two days later, and I brought that terrible woman back to my suite at the Carlyle as my bride. It was embarrassing, but unavoidable. That is why you saw her in Paris with me."

I must say I enjoyed the occasional discussions with Stewart Hopps. He was undoubtedly a scoundrel, but a brilliant and charming man as well, lover of the arts, and women, and good living. He was also an excellent dinner companion. Can any man be thoroughly bad who so enjoys the good life? One day I asked him how he had ever been able to get other men—with supposedly unblemished reputations—to serve as officers and directors of the insurance companies he was about to empty of their assets.

"Easy," he told me. "Over the course of a lifetime, most men have committed an act of stupidity or of folly which they regret but cannot change. Other men are born gamblers, or lechers, or are money-mad. I detect in other men the faults that are in me and I use them to my advantage. Ask me about any individual if it interests you, and I will tell you why that man is doing what I want him to. You want to know about the chairman of the board. He is a pillar of his community in Rhode Island, is involved with every charity. But he has four daughters to marry and a wife who spends far more money than he earns. I opened an account for him outside the country which I keep supplied with funds. Another of our directors loves too well the horses at Narragansett. He found himself owing the Mafia a great deal of money which he had no ability to pay. He came to me for help one day. I made him sign a promissory note which pledged everything he had. Then after giving him a terrible tongue lashing, I tore up the note in front of him and told him, 'Pay me back when you can.' That man would walk through hell for me. One director is the treasurer of a large steel company. He has taken money from his company. I found out about it. He knows that I can end his career if I want to, but I protect him. One other has to gamble, and I make it possible for him to go to Havana when he wants to, knowing his losses will be covered. You may wonder why so much of my activity is now in Cuba. The government and insurance company regulators in that country are compliant if they are taken care of. I hold board meetings there and fly in the directors by private plane with a week at the

Hotel Nacional following the board meeting. The gambling is there; the women are beautiful and willing; all expenses are paid. Do you wonder that board meetings go smoothly? It is only unfortunate that our president spends all his time in the bar. That I must do something about. But he is my link to the politicians in Havana and they would not like it if he was removed."

It was then that I learned how Hopps and Birrell had, not content with milking insurance companies in the United States, extended their operations abroad. With the end of World War II, the world of international business had opened up for Hopps and Birrell. They had then retained the services of an international tax lawyer who had left one of the major New York firms. Together they added an international dimension to what they were already doing so successfully in the United States. Hopps told me much later that he had once attended a meeting in New York in the boardroom of the law firm where their new adviser had been a partner. Hopps, Birrell and the adviser with two of his assistants were present. On the table in front of each of the twenty-two chairs were stacks of corporate papers of each of the twenty-two corporations in various and far-off financial centers such as Panama, Jersey, Guernsey, Tangier, Switzerland, Lichstenstein and Luxembourg, where earnings might be accumulated in secret and free of United States taxation.

"Tell me again how much of an increase of capital you need in The Rhode Island," the lawyer had said addressing Birrell.

"One hundred million dollars will do it nicely."

"Then this is what I propose we do."

The lawyer then went around the room followed by his legal assistants specifying what each company would issue in the way of bonds, notes, subordinated debentures, preferred stock and common stock. He even had, to show his versatility, issues of options and warrants to the principals, including, of course, a generous participation for himself.

"There it is," he said. "If it meets with your approval, I will go ahead and have these steps taken. It will take a few days because, of course, we have to have the documents translated into the relevant languages of French, German and Spanish and pay the various documentary and filing fees. But in a week it will all be accomplished, and I will have a bound set for your files—along with my bill for fees and expenses," he had added with a smile.

A year later there was a falling out between Hopps and the shareholders of his international operations. One of the principal minority shareholders, who had invested many millions in Hopps's foreign insurance empire, asked me one day to represent him. He had heard about how the CARR had been able to extricate itself from its problems with Hopps. He had also heard that that foreign reinsurers were very pleased with the final outcome of their negotiations with the receiver of the Rhode Island Insurance Company. Would I be willing to bring a shareholders' suit against the directors of the parent U. S. company if they were unwilling to force Hopps and Birrell to put back the money that they had taken out through their control of the foreign insurance operations which were headquartered in Cuba? He was willing to put up a $50,000 retainer and had the funds needed to meet the expenses of the accountants, the lawyers in Havana, and the depositions which might have to be taken for months in Rhode Island and elsewhere, particularly in Havana. The Chadbourne firm agreed to accept the case—and, of course, the retainer—and once again to allow me to handle the matter on my own. I accepted the challenge, and began proceedings against the parent company in Cuba, as well as its American officers and directors. But I wanted to sue the individuals as well as the companies in an American court.

In the New England states, curiously, in certain instances one can begin a lawsuit by filing a writ of attachment which successfully ties up all of a defendant's assets. Having failed to get satisfactory answers either from the officers or directors of the parent U. S. company, and not having succeeded in enlisting the support of the insurance regulators in Havana despite giving them detailed written evidence of misappropriation of insurance company funds, I finally resolved to take action in a U. S. Federal District Court. I made an appointment with the federal judge in Providence and went to see him after sending him a sixty-page memorandum reciting endless instances of international corporate looting.

"What do you want me to do?" asked the judge.

"I want you to issue writs of attachment against the officers and directors of this company in the amount of 30 million dollars."

The judge bowed his head before speaking again.

"Do you think there is that much money in the State of Rhode Island?" he asked. After some discussion he granted what I had requested. I returned to New York elated because it was in the discretion of the judge to grant or refuse what I had asked. Quite evidently, he was satisfied that I had a good case even though he could hardly believe what was explained in the memorandum. How could supposedly responsible business executives behave this way? How could public officials participate in such a massive fraud? The question now was to find the assets to levy on. Hopps, of course, had no assets in the State of Rhode Island. Birrell, to avoid this and other problems, flew off to Brazil, where he was safe from extradition. But we found others, the American directors of the company, and this was important because they would put pressure on the principals. The chairman of the board lived in Rhode Island and was well known both in business and society there.

In the last days of the Cuban regime preceding Castro, I spent a good deal of time in Havana trying to trace what might have happened to all these premiums on worldwide insurance policies. It was a difficult pattern to trace because neither the Cuban regulators appointed by President Battista nor the local banks would cooperate. By the time Castro took over the government of Cuba, we had made very little progress of a kind which I would be able to use in the U. S. District Court in Rhode Island.

With Castro's takeover, this litigation came to an end.

Since that time I have had many business dealings in different countries of Latin America. There is a very different business culture in those countries. Anyone undertaking to do business there should expect surprises which cannot be anticipated. One unfortunately finds corruption in government in every country. But where the middle class is as weak as it is in so much of Latin America, very often government tries to prevent any business action being taken which will improve the economy unless local interests are protected. That is why it is so important to have a local partner with good political connections, if investing abroad.

* * *

My work for Sperry continued to be interesting and challenging as I gradually took on more responsibility in the Chadbourne firm. I learned to work well with John Sanderson, the financial vice president, who was the man most responsible for growth and diversification at the company. He was a brilliant man and very easy to work with once he had decided that you could handle responsibility. Furthermore, he was very direct and one always knew where one stood with him. I liked that.

At the end of the war Sperry found itself a very large military technology company, with its principal client, the U. S. government, no longer interested in purchasing its military products. It had then to redirect its engineering skills to other activities. Agricultural machinery represented to him an attractive opportunity for Sperry. Sanderson had sensed that the post-war demands for more food production presented a market where Sperry engineering skills could play a major role. He used me to make acquisitions in this area. The companies he found to acquire were located, of all places, around Lancaster, Pennsylvania, home of the Amish who were still riding in horse-drawn wagons and didn't use any farm machinery. The first company he sent me to acquire was a small Amish engineering company making simple hay balers and other rather unsophisticated farm implements. As a careful lawyer, I asked to review all the corporate documents. There were none, I was told. The secretary of the company was a nice Amish woman with a bonnet and downcast eyes. She carefully explained to me that the Amish made no use of government facilities: they filed no records, didn't send their children to public schools, paid no taxes, did not serve in the military in times of war, never used the courts, minded their own affairs. If there were any differences between members of the community, these were settled by the pastor because God had given him the capability of making such decisions wisely. If one was aware of our Lord's urging that one should "render unto Caesar what is Caesar's and unto God what is God's," one realized that among the Amish there was not much for Caesar but a great deal for God. How would I ever be able to prepare a proper "Opinion of Counsel" that Sperry had properly obtained title to all the assets of the Dellinger Manufacturing Company? I realized I would need the help of a competent local attorney and rest my opinion on his.

"No problem," the lawyer said. "I know everyone in the county and everything that has been done here since I was a boy. More importantly, I know whose word is good, and whose isn't. We will talk to the pastor. Then you and I will design an opinion letter that will satisfy your client," the lawyer said. It was done his way. He opined that Pennsylvania law had been fully satisfied and I based our firm's opinion on his.

This was only the beginning of my visits to Lancaster. There was another farm machinery company there which had developed some really interesting automatic hay balers. The company belonged to a Mennonite group, who were quite different in many ways from the Amish, although their background was similar and their respect for their "man of God" identical.

A Mennonite parishioner had died two years earlier. As he lay close to death, he had sent for the pastor, a remarkable man who was a bishop of the Mennonite faith. The bishop was asked to dispose of the company at the parishioner's death. He was advised to whom within the family of the dying man proceeds should be distributed. The bishop was temporarily at a loss on how to sell the business, but he consulted two of his friends, the local Cadillac dealer and the town barber. "Why don't the three of us buy it?" they said to the bishop.

They asked for advice from a local bank and a friend of theirs in real estate who became a fourth partner. The four agreed upon a figure which the bank was willing to support through a partial loan of the amount. The transaction was completed and the proceeds of the sale duly distributed to the kin of the deceased. The four partners then decided, wisely as it turned out, that if they were going to manage a business, they had best have an accountant working with them. So they found a young man in Lancaster named Paul Lyet and offered him a ten-percent share in the business if he would act as its accountant and guide them in how to run the business they had just purchased.

"Sell it," said Paul. "None of us know anything about this business."

That is where Sperry entered the picture. In six months, the business bought for $100,000 was sold to Sperry for $1,600,000 and lifetime annual employment contracts for the four major partners at $75–$100,000 each. Paul Lyet was the real negotiator. The others signed the papers and were paid their share of the proceeds. Paul eventually ran the business and built it from nothing to sales of 4 billion dollars, ending his days as chairman of the Sperry Corporation, a task which he handled, as everything he ever did, with consummate skill.

My relationship with the bishop was one of the more memorable incidents in my life. As Sperry grew, it was constantly in need of money. I handled bond issue after bond issue: $50,000,000 here, $100,000,000 there. Shortly after the New Holland Machine Company transaction was completed, I was working on a Sperry bond issue when I received a visit from the bishop.

The bishop had a great flair for marketing himself. He had designed his own clerical garb. It was grey, with a pink bib, and a shawl collar buttoning very low, so as to accentuate his fine figure. Before coming to New York, he would always go down to the Conestoga National Bank in Lancaster and get some shiny new silver dollars, which he would use to tip porters, bellhops and doormen.

"You have no idea what an effect this has on the service I get in New York, my boy. I think I must be as well known in New York as President Truman himself."

The bishop, as far as I was concerned, earned every penny he was paid under his lifetime contract, through one phone call he made during the Korean War. I was in Lancaster one day trying to figure out with management how we could get some steel to keep the plant going. The bishop volunteered to help. He picked up a phone, gave his title, and asked for the president of a big Midwestern steel company who was famous for his irascible personality and his refusal to talk to anyone he might consider his inferior.

"I am a bishop and run a small farm implement company in Lancaster, Pennsylvania," announced the bishop, "and I wondered if the good Lord might let you see your way clear to sending me a little steel to keep our employees busy."

The next day the freight cars loaded with steel scrap started rolling in. The bishop had fully earned his keep.

"Young man," he said, "I want you to solve a small problem for me. I have received a notice from the company that the prospectus you are preparing with the Securities and Exchange Commission will have to report the salary of $80,000 per year which I am receiving even though New Holland is only a subsidiary of Sperry. You can see that my parishioners might not understand why their bishop is receiving that kind of salary and might wonder what I am doing to earn it, and why I am not spending the time looking after their religious affairs instead. I want you to call the Securities and Exchange Commission or whoever and explain to them that as a man of God, I must not be asked to reveal this information."

"Bishop," I told him, "the lawyers I know at the SEC do not really know men of God since they have few dealings with them. They will laugh at your request. You will have to decide to reveal the information, to give away the money you receive, or give up the office you hold, subject to being reinstated but only if the company should so decide, after the registration is completed, to take you back at the same salary."

The bishop was indeed a man of God. But that didn't interfere with his enjoyment of the good life, or the respect from his fellow men to which he believed himself entitled. He chose to resign his position at the company and was effectively reappointed after the underwriting had been completed.

Paul Lyet was a remarkable American business executive. He had taken a great wartime engineering company and converted it into an equally successful peacetime business by adding farm machinery and other activities. The farm machinery business that Paul Lyet built for Sperry had added $4 billion to the yearly sales figure. Unfortunately, his successors after Paul retired proceeded to demolish what he had accomplished. The farm machinery business was sold to Ford which could not make a success of it. In due course, the rest of Sperry was sold to other firms, and this great company, as so often happens in American business, disappeared.

* * *

By 1950, I had already spent four post-war years with the Chadbourne firm. I had become very good at what I did, enjoyed the work immensely, but wondered when I would be invited to be a partner. The rule in the large firms of the period was that at the end of five years if one was not asked to be a partner, the firm would try to place the lawyer with a client as house counselor in an executive capacity.

If the client were a large corporation, this would mean a large increase in salary and a job with a good future. I had been fortunate in working for a number of partners whose responsibility in the firm was growing. I was anxious to make more money because it was now clear that we would never be able to go back to China. One great friend in the firm, Frank Moon, had already left to become general counsel of W. R. Grace, the big chemical firm, and I was beginning to get soundings from headhunters as to possible opportunities outside of the law firm. Dick Keresey, who had been working at the Cravath law firm, had gone off to Houston to be an associate counsel of Standard Oil of New Jersey, the oil colossus. Bainbridge was writing laws for African countries; Tuohy was at the Long Island Lighting Company; Benecke was running the family firm. Where was I? What should I do? We now had two children with another one expected. We had recently moved to an apartment that met our needs, but the two older boys were reaching school age and schools in New York were expensive.

Even though Stan Dunn and Lee Morey had become personal friends, I did not feel I could say to them that if I were not soon to be made a partner, I would leave the firm. Looking back on it, I realize I probably should have done this.

It was at this point in my career in late 1950 that I was offered a partnership in a much smaller firm where I would be the corporate partner.

When I told Stan Dunn and Lee Morey of my decision, they said: "Thibaut, why didn't you talk to us? We were planning to make you a partner in January."

Another fork in the road and path not taken.

What would have happened had I stayed at the Chadbourne firm? I would probably in time have become one of the senior partners, remained a lawyer, but not have engaged in the many other activities which I would have a chance to do by maintaining my freedom of choice and my independence.

*The author, in 1954, was a partner in
charge of corporate law matters at
Lewis & MacDonald (New York) and
Ten Eyck & Saint Phalle (Paris).*

VIII

PARTNER IN A SMALL LAW FIRM

*I*T *HAD ALWAYS BEEN VERY* difficult for me to go to school. And camp was the same problem. When I was sent to the Adirondack Camp in New York State in the summer of 1930, I had promptly developed 104 degrees of temperature and waited for my parents to come and get me and take me home. Of course, the worst experience was being sent to a boarding school in Normandy in 1928, the year we moved to France. In the first place, I knew no Latin and no Greek and the students in my class were well into these subjects. They were studying the history of the Roman Empire, having completed the course on Greece and the Eastern Mediterranean. In math, they were also well ahead of what an American boy of ten had studied. I promptly developed a temperature and was sent to the infirmary. There I simply packed my bag and sat on the side of the highway waiting to be taken by the first motorist towards Paris and home. This happened twice. The second time the headmaster called my father and told him he didn't think I would amount to very much, so not to bother to bring me back. My mother, in order to save me from my father's wrath, declared that I was physically unwell and had my appendix removed. During World War II, the school would serve as a headquarters for the German army defending the coast of Normandy. At one point, there had been question of my being parachuted onto the grounds for the purpose of destroying the building and those in it at the start of the Allied invasion of 1944. How I would have enjoyed that assignment!

In the years when I was practicing law, an odd parallel to this sensitivity took the shape of getting the flu whenever I had a change of jobs or careers to consider because some other firm or a headhunter had made me an interesting offer. It got so that whenever I developed some winter infection and came home with a fever, my wife would put me to bed and then sitting on the edge would ask me, "Who offered you a job today?" It became a kind of macabre family joke. While there generally

Responsibility as a lawyer is now mine.

231

were interesting decisions to make, I was always being affected by this need to look for new challenges and particularly new opportunities to learn. These kinds of decisions were at once very frightening but also very exciting. But once the decision was made, I never looked back on it.

When I had the choice of remaining or leaving the Chadbourne firm, the same phenomenon occurred. It was indeed a challenge because the firm that had made me a proposal to join as a partner was small but had excellent corporate clients. The senior partner had been a remarkably able single practitioner lawyer during the days when the law was still simple enough so that a man could handle all branches of it on his own. Unfortunately, George Lewis was now gradually losing his memory. Would I be able to have myself accepted by the firm's corporate clients while George was still able to function reasonably effectively? Would I know enough to handle the complicated corporate reorganizations that sometimes should be made? When I came to join the firm, we would be only three partners, with one other, George's son, who had been brought up in a lawyer's household, loved the law, had a real affinity for it, and was in his last year of law school having spent five years as a businessman first. Pete Lewis and I quickly became the best of friends. He was extremely intelligent, cynical as his father was, aggressive when he thought a client had been wronged, fun-loving and very hardworking at the same time. The third partner was the "nay-sayer" that one must have in every firm. He had started in one of the big firms as a male secretary to the senior partner. He had put himself through law school at night. Then he became an expert in real-estate law and all kinds of litigation. He was the rock on which the firm functioned. But he always had to be shown that what was proposed had legal or business justification for it. Every firm should have a partner like Charlie MacDonald. In our case—Pete Lewis and mine—Charlie's insistence that we justify what we proposed to do kept us from making innumerable errors.

George Lewis, our senior partner, had a remarkable middle-aged Irish-American secretary who had been with him many years and used language almost as colorful as that of her employer. I have often wondered why it is that so many highly devout Irish Catholics use such earthy language. It is like a small child using words that have no meaning to the speaker. Helen had never married and had little respect for men's intelligence or morals. One day I discovered in some Latin translation the writings of St. Jerome, one of the best known of the early Catholic philosophers. After ascertaining that St. Jerome was accepted by the Irish church, I obtained an old woodcut of him, had it nicely framed and gave it to Helen for Christmas. Below the picture, I had set forth one of the saint's sayings:

"I find it difficult to accept that God created cockroaches and vipers, hyenas, scorpions and other such animals. But for God to have created woman makes me almost doubt His godliness."

She didn't think it appropriate. But I never saw whether she hung it in her apartment. Nevertheless, we were good friends. She had organized a buzzer that rang in my office so that if George Lewis was taking a call on some particularly complicated corporate matter, she could send me a signal. I would then find some reason to run into Lewis' office and participate in the discussion. Together we managed to keep matters in hand until in time, with his son's help, we managed to add top lawyers from other firms as tax and other specialists who would join the firm as partners.

After I had been with the firm two or three years, I went through a period of discouragement. There was so much to do in New York and frequent trips to our Paris office did not simplify things. That was one trouble with business clients. When they want to talk to you, you have to be available. And time differences can be a terrible nuisance. But I loved what I was doing. The long hours did not bother me, and I found I was beginning to manage well keeping various balls in the air at the same time. I felt as if I was constantly on a stage, even though at times the actor seemed to have forgotten his script.

On one of these hurried trips to Europe by air, I had come back on the Boeing Stratocruiser from London, sitting next to a charming man who identified himself as chairman of a Canadian company called Canadian Javelin. As we flew over Newfoundland, he kept looking out of the porthole and commenting on what should have been happening on the ground below. This went on for many minutes as the plane sped over the province. It seemed almost as though his company controlled everything in the province. Then we began to talk about other matters. He said he had just been to Germany on an important business matter. He had had a bad marriage and had divorced his wife. He had a six-year-old daughter whom he wanted to educate in France so that they could travel there together. He wanted to marry again so that his daughter would have a mother. He had found the ideal woman whom his daughter also loved, but she was Catholic. We talked to the Church and the difficulty of obtaining an annulment. The time went quickly as we talked. It was obvious that he loved his little girl very much. I told

233

him I, too, had a small daughter. He told me to buy stock in his company and it would pay for her schooling.

When I arrived in New York, I called my father and asked if he knew about the company.

"The chairman has gone to Germany to raise money because the company is close to bankruptcy. They have spent all the money they have raised. If the chairman is successful, the company will be saved. But no one knows what happened in Germany." I thought of my new friend's love for his little girl. Such a man would not give bad advice to someone who wanted to send his own daughter to a private school. So I took a few dollars and bought a little stock in Thérèse's name. The stock went up enough to give her some school money later on, but I for once had sense enough to sell the shares when the chairman asked me to represent him in problems with the SEC. He may have loved his daughter, but he had clearly cut corners on his obligation to his stockholders.

Many years later I was asked by one of the big Canadian mining companies to try to obtain from the Panamanian dictator, General Omar Torrijos, the copper mining concession in Panama which had been granted to Canadian Javelin but was in default. I met with the general with a very special introduction which would enable us to converse privately and with no one else present except his secretary. I made my presentation, pointing out, of course, that I understood the concession holder to be in default. The general politely listened.

"I know the concession is in default. I also know of the company's problems in the United States and Canada. But when the chairman of Canadian Javelin came in to see me seeking the concession, unlike every other American company that wants something in Panama, he came without any American lawyers. Furthermore, after we had agreed on the terms, he said, 'General, why don't you have your people draw up the agreement? I would trust you to put down on paper exactly what we have agreed to and no more.' I can assure you he was the first American to treat me that way. That man may be guilty of questionable practices elsewhere, but I would never do anything to hurt him."

It is an interesting vignette which American businessmen dealing in the Third World might take note of.

One of our clients was John Jacob Astor, scion of the famous New York and Newport clan. Although Jack had a great deal of money, he was often in trouble. The newspapers were always ready to report on what he had done, almost done, or failed to do. Like members of the Saudi Royal family today, no matter how distantly related to the king,

Jack was newsworthy and the news generally involved women. I remember once being in Belgium negotiating a loan for a client when I received a frantic phone call from Pete Lewis in New York telling me that Jack Astor had had a heart attack at sea while on a North Cape cruise. I was to find the best heart specialist in Europe and meet the ship when it landed in Copenhagen, Denmark. I had to finish my meetings in Brussels before I could go anywhere. I did find out that the leading heart specialist was a Dane. I called him and made arrangements for him to meet the ship, get Jack to a hospital, and arrange to meet me at the plane when I arrived. Two days later when I arrived in Copenhagen, I found a delicate press problem. My first shock came with the specialist, a fine doctor and human being who assured me that my client had had no heart attack. He had simply eaten too well and had had too much alcohol. In the meantime, it appeared that there was a medical convention in Copenhagen. A friend of Astor's had gone to the convention dinner, made a fool of himself by declaring that doctors in Denmark were allowing his stricken friend to die, and had himself arrested for causing a disturbance. The press had, of course, picked up the story. From attacking the medical profession, Astor's friend went on to the judicial system for imprisoning and fining him. Astor had his small daughter and an English nurse with him on the ship. But he also had a young starlet he had embarked with in New York, and that was more serious because he was in the middle of a divorce action. There was also a question of money. Luckily, one of the companies I had represented in the United States was Danish. I went to see the president the first morning after my arrival. When I arrived in his office, he was sitting reading a newspaper with six-inch headlines across the top. The Andrea Doria, flagship of the Italian lines, had been rammed off Nantucket and had sunk.

Partner in a Small Law Firm

"We have about 30 percent of the insurance on that vessel," he said.

I did not stay very long, just long enough to have him tell me that he was advancing me $20,000 and would be happy to give me more if I needed it. I had no idea how long I might have to stay in Copenhagen to straighten things out. How does one handle a heart attack case that wasn't when the press is around constantly? But first I had to do something about the young lady who wasn't supposed to be there. I went to see her at the hotel, was given her assurance that she wouldn't go near the child. She would have been delighted to go home or go on to Paris, but Astor had taken her passport. I did not look forward to seeing him. He had been put in an intensive care unit of the very good hospital in

Elsinore far from Copenhagen. The press couldn't reach him and the hospital wouldn't talk. That much the heart specialist had been able to accomplish for me. I felt like an utter fool and ashamed of my client and that he was an American. When I went to Elsinore to see Jack, he seemed physically quite well but in a terrible mood. He had learned about the Andrea Doria. "I shall never sail on a ship again," he said.

"There is a train that goes to Paris, and you can catch a plane back home from there," I suggested. "Or you can go by plane from here to London and then on to New York."

"Charter a train for me from here to Paris. I'm too sick to go anywhere by air, and I don't want to see anyone, particularly the press."

I'd never chartered a whole train before, and I certainly saw no reason to do so for anyone who was just pretending that he'd had a heart attack. But at the request of my partners in New York, I did get Astor a private railroad car to take him and the girl, the child and the nanny, to Paris, arranging for them to get on at a station outside of Copenhagen. The worst of it was that he was so nasty to the young starlet. She didn't want to stay, but he wouldn't give her back her passport and made her move to a pension in Elsinore where she would come read to him while he was in the hospital.

The problems with Jack Astor never seemed to end. I was glad he was not my direct responsibility. A short time later, while still not fully divorced, he married another woman and took her on a honeymoon to Europe. On the way over, at the captain's table, one of our more famous New York trial lawyers gave her his business card and suggested to her that if she were unhappy, she should come and see him. She did so on her return from France, and he promptly brought suit against our client for divorce. We claimed she couldn't get a divorce because Astor was still married. The judge, to everyone's surprise, decided there was no technical reason why a man couldn't find himself married to two women at the same time and be obliged to support both of them, regardless of any intent not to commit bigamy. My contribution was to find the chauffeur who had driven the married couple around France. He made a marvelous witness and had no need of coaching. He simply said he had never seen a woman be so nasty to a man. He could not imagine that a married woman could treat her husband in this manner. The judge gave the plaintiff wife $75 a week alimony. The great lawyer who represented her wrote a book referring to this as one of his finest cases. To me the case was only interesting because there was a pitched battle one night in our office when a detective hired by one of the wives' lawyers tried to break into the office safe and was repulsed by the detective Pete Lewis had hired on another case who was there writing up his report. Judging by the broken chairs and books lying on the floor the next morning, it must have been an exciting row.

Odd questions would be put to one as a lawyer from time to time. On one occasion, I might have made a great deal of money. A man I knew in Hollywood as a producer of films for the new medium of television wanted to do a series on postwar Paris and the Europe of the Cold War. He needed a title. Remembering those extraordinary French train whistles as the train departs, I told him there was only one title to use—"The Orient Express." The title enabled him to stage whatever story he wanted, but the show always started at the railroad station in Paris, the Gare de l'Est, with the whistle blowing its mournful sound and the train taking off towards the east. I should have asked for a royalty on the idea. It was a great success.

There were good times and bad times in all the travel I was obliged to take in my legal practice. I had recently had to take responsibility for my sister. Alix had never been very strong. She had a remarkable mind, very much like my father, but the practical problems of this world were quite beyond her. She had married essentially to escape the problem of coping with my mother's constant demands and irresponsible behavior. But she had married a man who had been abandoned as a child when both his parents had died in Mexico in an automobile accident. The parents' money had been turned over to an uncle in trust for the boy. The uncle used the money to buy a beautiful property in Carmel, New York, and supply the lifestyle such a property demanded. The boy grew up on the streets of New York with little schooling and few opportunities. When he was old enough he went to Wall Street instead of to college and learned about financial deals while reading every newspaper, article and book he could lay his hands on. He met my sister at a party and fell in love with her. But he had never learned to control his temper and when he became upset, he would be apt to throw things. The effect of this on my sister's fragile temperament was overwhelming. Gradually, as she could not handle these outbursts, her mind took refuge in slipping into a world where she couldn't be reached. She then had to be periodically hospitalized. Since she was very religious, I decided to get her out of the mental hospital where she was and put her in a convalescent home in Belgium where she might gradually find her balance again. Through a cousin I found such an establishment run by an order of nuns. I then took her out of where she was, had a friend meet her at the airport and take her over to Paris, while I took an earlier plane the same night and met her the next morning at the airport to drive her to Belgium. It worked as planned. But it took her a year to find herself again, and when she had relapses from time to time, I would get calls from the doctor to come and take her home. Whenever I had to go to Paris on business, I would always block off two days so that I could go up to see her. If I left Paris by car at the end of the business day, I would go through Roubaix at about four o'clock in the morning and reach the hospital in time to meet with the doctor and then breakfast with my sister and stay with her through lunch. There were no autoroutes in France in those days. In order to keep from falling asleep, I would make up a story. As time progressed the story grew. I became more and more interested in it and began to look forward to those terrible all-night drives so that I could pick up the thread again. I hope it is now ready to put down on paper. What fascinates me is that after a thirty-year period, the concluding chapter is now quite different. Today it strikes me as a much more satisfying story. It is a simple plot. A businessman who goes to France frequently decides one day to effect his own disappearance for a variety of reasons. Part One explains how he does it, because in the Europe of today, it is not easy. Part Two reviews how his family, his friends and his enemies explain what might have happened, and in so doing, explain the kind of person they think he was. Part Three is the story of how one person figures out what must have happened and finds him. Part Four reveals what he then decides to do: to abandon his new life and return to the problems of the old or maintain his new existence. When I was young, he didn't go back. Now that I am wiser, he does.

So much of my time in Europe involved explaining Americans to Europeans or vice versa. It seemed to me that being both American and French, I had been given a particularly interesting niche to fill and I enjoyed it immensely.

I have always had a tendency to transform what started out as a purely business relationship into one between friends. That is probably why I became as involved as I did in the sometimes stormy relationship between my client, Ernie Byfield, and his beautiful "friend," Vala.

Ernie was the son of a man who had made a substantial fortune in real estate—particularly hotels—in Chicago. He also owned hotels in Los Angeles, New York and Miami. As a result, Ernie had moved with his family from hotel to hotel as a child and, when I first met him, was living on a permanent basis in a Manhattan hotel suite. Ernie had a very engaging personality. He was in charge of advertising for the family hotel chain and took other accounts as well. He was not an intellectual, but as in the case of many advertising executives, he loved people and had a keen sense of decor and great appreciation of the theater, both in London and New York. When I first met him, he was planning to redecorate the family hotels in Chicago in the style of Beau Brummel and Brighton during the 18th century. I found that idea for Chicago appealing and, in fact, it worked out very well if one ignored the expense involved in Ernie's frequent visits to London and Brighton and his insistence on authenticity. This led to stormy meetings with Chicago and New York hotel managements and boards of directors, where I served as his legal adviser.

It was at or about this time that Ernie met Vala and fell head over heels in love with her. He insisted that I meet her, and the three of us had dinner. She was indeed very beautiful. She always wore black, which fitted her doll-like features, her beautiful figure and her Russian accent. She always wore a small hat and a veil, beyond which one noticed immediately enormous eyes with varying colors from light to deep blue and violet. She treated Ernie with a scolding kind of affection. To him, she was a European princess. When we were together, we always conversed in French.

Vala wants a son.

One day Ernie called me to say he was going to get married. Since he was forty, this did not seem strange, but I asked him why after all these years as a bachelor he had decided to marry Vala. "I am tired of living in hotels," he said. I pointed out that this did not seem a valid reason, since he could well afford to buy and decorate a Park Avenue apartment. "True," he said, "but Vala is very important to me because she has a way of captivating my corporate clients with her beauty, her sophistication and her charm." Again, I pointed out this was no real reason to propose marriage. "Thibaut, you don't understand. I want to have children while I am still young enough to enjoy them." It is here that I made a singular mistake. "Ernie," I said, "are you sure that Vala is still young enough to have children?" He assured me that she was, that he had introduced her to his doctor, and that the doctor had no reservations. "In that case," I said, "I congratulate you, because I believe Vala will make you very happy."

At about 3:00 a.m. that night, the phone rang by my bed. My sleepy "Hello" was followed by a stream of invective at the other end for at least five minutes expressed in French, Spanish and, for all I knew, Russian. "How would you dare tell him I might not be able to have children?" That was the gist of her message. I could only murmur my apologies based on a profound lack of medical knowledge, together with an invitation to lunch at my club the next day so that I could apologize directly in a more tangible way. My invitation was accepted.

Lunch was delightful and informative. Vala did not seem in the least angry. She told me she and her family had escaped from Russia when she was six years old and gone to live in France. At seventeen, she had married a young, handsome Frenchman. "He would come home for lunch just to make love to me," she told me. "Then again before dinner and at night. He could not have enough of me. It was two years of intense physical love and great happiness," she said, "but unfortunately, he was poor, and so I had to leave him. My next husband was very different. He was a Spanish diplomat, sent to Tokyo as ambassador by Franco. We were very happy there. He treated me with great courtesy, taught me the role of a diplomat's wife, and I became a celebrated hostess. But he was much older than I and soon retired. So I left him. My third husband was a brute, a self-made millionaire in pharmaceuticals from Mexico. We lived in Mexico City, Paris and New York, and for the first time in my life, I had an opportunity to dress well, buy beautiful things, and travel as much as I wanted to. He was very generous with me, bought me extravagant jewels like the necklace I have on and this large diamond I am wearing on my finger. I even managed to save $250,000 a year on the money he gave me for groceries. But I could not talk to him because he had no conversation and he bored me very much. So I divorced him. Now I have Ernie."

"I have had physical love with my first husband, courtesy, intellectual discourse, and friendship with my second, money with my third, but I have never had a child and now I shall have one with Ernie. You are right," she added, "I am unfortunately too old to have children. So I am marrying one. I shall make Ernie a very good wife. He needs to be taken care of, clothed properly, live well. I shall protect him because he doesn't understand how difficult life can be. He shall be my son."

It was a revelation, and I immediately realized she would do for my friend exactly what she said. He would be much better off being the child than having a child.

Imagine my consternation when the day before the engagement was to be announced, Ernie telephoned me to say that Vala had called it off. "She says she won't marry me, because I don't love her anymore," he said.

I could see what was coming.

"What has she asked you to do, Ernie?"

"She wants me to draw a new will and to put all my money in a trust for her, so that the trustee can make up the difference if I fail to give her $60,000 a year to spend on herself."

"What are you going to do?"

"She has hired a lawyer at Coudert Brothers, the well-known international law firm, and wants us to meet him there at 10 o'clock tomorrow morning so that he can draw up papers for me to sign and so prove to her that I really love her. The lawyer agreed to act as my trustee, to make sure I meet my commitment.

Had I been right when we had had lunch or was she going to treat my client as she had her Mexican husband?

We spent the next week at Coudert Brothers while I fought against all three of them to save my client's money. At the end, half of Ernie's fortune was placed in trust. Her lawyer was not the trustee; I was. This same lawyer was killed three weeks later when an angry woman involved in a divorce action where he represented the husband hit him on the back of his head with the heel of her shoe. The law is sometimes a dangerous avocation!

Ernie and Vala were married in a simple Russian Orthodox ceremony complete with candle-bearers. They seemed very much in love. As a wife, she turned out to be everything she had told me she would be.

She did not bother me as trustee to any great extent except that she did call me from Milan on their honeymoon to ask me to tell Ernie he had to wear white tie and tails to go to the opening night at the La Scala Opera.

Unfortunately, two years later Vala developed an incurable cancer and died.

* * *

As a result of the work I had done for the CARR and its president, Raymond Schmit, in the matter of the Rhode Island and Stewart Hopps, Schmit and I had become good friends. One day he called me up to say, "Thibaut, come as quickly as you can and be sure you have a letter of introduction to General Eisenhower. I will explain the whole story to you when you get here."

It was a complicated story, but interesting for an insurance company. Schmit's idea was that with all the American servicemen stationed in Europe, it should be possible to sell them automobiles at a special price, and since the cars were to be sold on credit, they would have to have an insurance policy. Since most of the GIs were stationed in Germany, the cars should be German and the German policy should be issued by a German company with CARR handling the reinsurance. Consent of the United States high command outside of Paris should be obtained first to make sure the financing company and its rates would have been cleared and approved. I had come with a letter to the chief of staff from George Allen, a close friend of President Truman, so all went smoothly at SHAEF. Schmit and I then went to Cologne to meet with the head of the Nordstern Insurance Company, a Mr. Schnell, who was not only president of this large insurance company, but also the mayor of the city and in charge of its reconstruction, including restoration of its remarkable cathedral which had been badly damaged by Allied bombing. Mr. Schnell could only see me at seven in the morning. He was over 65, worked from seven in the morning until eleven o'clock every night, but took weekends off so that he could spend time with his friend, Konrad Adenauer, and plan for the rebuilding of Germany on a new premise of a close relationship with France. I liked Schnell immediately. He was direct, efficient, intelligent, and dedicated to what he was doing. As his executives came in while we were talking about the prospective finance company, they stood in front of him as though at attention. He would tell them what he wanted them to do. They would bark out, "*Jawohl,* Herr Schnell," then turn on their heels and walk out. I told him that this was not the way the day would be started in an American company. We would have a management meeting, coffee and then a discussion.

"I haven't time for all that. With three full-time jobs, it is up to me to figure out what I want done, to call in the person who will do it and order it done before something unexpected comes up to take all my time for the rest of the day. My love is the cathedral. That is where I want to spend as much of the day as possible, talking to the masons, looking at old photographs, making sure the work gets done the way it should be. The rest I do is unimportant, but this cathedral is German and Catholic culture at its finest and must stand again." A great human being, Herr Schnell.

He sent us on to Volkswagen in Hanover, seven miles from the Soviet forces in East Germany. That, too, was a miracle of German determination to rebuild. Buses brought in workers from 100 miles away, north, south and west. We lunched with the head of international sales. He had been the youngest colonel on the German general staff, was captured by the Soviets and spent time in a Russian prison camp. He was famous for having organized a hunger strike among the German officer prisoners until the Russians gave them back control over their men in the prison camps. He had only just been released, but had immediately set out to organize Volkswagen internationally as though he were planning a military offensive. In short order we had together reviewed in detail what we needed. Volkswagen would supply the cars wherever we needed them at a fixed price and handle a portion of the financing. This was the beginning of United Installment Sales, which eventually financed the sale of thousands of cars to American servicemen in Europe. It was extremely complicated because the men kept being moved around, both in Europe and back to the United States, and the security instruments on the cars had to be filed anew as the cars changed locations. I had earlier spent six months preparing all the security documents for use by farmers buying New Holland farm machinery on credit to match the individual requirements of each of the then 48 states. But this, from country to country, was worse. Every once in a while, I would repossess an Austin Healey and eventually had one in Paris and one in Bellport, to the delight of the children. Schmit's original idea was to build an insurance business on automobiles all over the world. But the financing business quickly outpaced the volume of insurance. Eventually the finance business had to be sold, but before the sale was concluded, I had two rather strange experiences.

Western Europe after the war passed through a period not seen since the Middle Ages. The war and postwar period had brought out the best in certain people, like Schnell and the colonel who would rather die of starvation than lose control of his men. The period brought to the surface of the power structure in other instances the very worst in human beings. In prewar Europe it had been relatively easy to check up on people, to ascertain their backgrounds and reputation for integrity. In postwar Europe, this became difficult, if not impossible. People appeared out of nowhere claiming background, experience and talents that could not be verified. All this was occurring at a time when a silent war was being carried on, on the one hand, between the Soviet Union and the Communist parties of each European country and, on the other, with the United States and those Europeans who wanted to rebuild a new Europe on the moral integrity of the old. I have talked about the fear of certain industrialists like my textile-industry friends in the north of France that nothing would stop the Russians if they chose to move west. On the other hand, here was Volkswagen seven miles from the Soviet forces in East Germany building the largest auto plant in

Europe. Some men were strong and insisted on building a new Europe. Others were weak and talked only of fleeing. Still others had much to hide of their wartime behavior. Still others were active agents of the Soviet effort to take over Western Europe before it could effectively be rebuilt. Among the more positive was a French Socialist leader named Jules Moch, who understood better than most what the Communist Party in France was trying to do to prevent the moral and physical rebirth of France. In 1948, he had boldly, as interior minister, issued a blunt warning to the Communist Party in France that it would not be allowed to take over the country. It was very much feared at that time that this might happen and that the Soviet forces would support such a move. Each department of France was quietly organized by Moch to make sure that this didn't happen. Lists were prepared of the French Communists in each region who on D-Day would have to be rounded up and executed. This was to be a war in the dark, without prisoners. His message was given out and accepted. Nothing fortunately happened. I was very proud of having played a small part in this effort with some of my cousins and the support of our embassy in Paris.

It is hard not to look back on that postwar period in Europe without some nostalgia. The role of the United States in seeking to rebuild shattered economies was exemplary. There were also remarkable business leaders in Britain, France and Germany who, ignoring the past, sought to recreate a very different future for their countries. I like to include my friend, Raymond Schmit, among them. He built his insurance company in Paris using enormous flair and imagination. He had succeeded, after the war, in having his company insure most of the great art collections owned by individuals and museums throughout continental Europe. In a period when art theft was an almost daily occurrence, he had organized two groups of "special forces" to recover stolen art objects. One was made up of Corsican or Sicilian mafia operatives, the other a group of former SS commandos. Relying on the premise that stolen art objects can only be sold to the concern that insured them because under the law a thief cannot transfer title to art, he would try to ascertain who had committed the theft, settle on a price, and then at a prearranged meeting to recover the stolen pieces, have his contact men there to seize both art and thieves for delivery to the police. One night this had resulted in a pitched battle in the Black Forest which had almost cost the life of one of Schmit's executives.

During this period Raymond Schmit asked me one day to come to

France as quickly as possible, since he had found a bank interested in purchasing the CARR at a very high price and wanted me to meet its president. Shortly thereafter, we met for lunch at Laserre in Paris. Later I told Schmit, "This man is not French. He speaks with the shade of an accent. He has the head of a Slav. Check him out." That afternoon I arranged to meet the head of the CIA in Paris, whom I knew. The CIA had no record on this man. I then checked with its French counterpart. The same answer was in due course given me. Three months later, I had a call from Schmit in the middle of the night. The previous evening the bank president had been arrested for using a false name, which in France is punishable by several years in prison. Eventually, the story came out: the bank belonged to the Soviet government. More interesting was why the Soviets wanted control of CARR. The answer was that in its reinsurance business, the CARR reinsured a Soviet-owned insurance company in London called Baltica which insured the cargoes of Soviet ships all over the world. As I have explained, it is only many months later that a reinsurer learns just what he has insured. But the "bordereaux" have to be accurate then or the cargoes are not insured. I examined the "bordereaux" in the CARR office in Paris. No one paid attention to these, but they spelled out in detail where Russian arms were being shipped. I came back, called Allan Dulles, whom I knew, and went down to see him in Washington. "If the company is for sale, let me buy it for the CIA," I said to him. To my great surprise, there was little interest. Perhaps he had other and better ways of finding out the information which I was offering him, but I doubt it. This was an incredible opportunity to have an accurate report of Soviet shipments all over the world with no one being the wiser.

Later Schmit called to say that he had met a Belgian financier in Brussels who was keenly interested in buying the finance company we had created to finance the sale of Volkswagens to American servicemen.

"Have you checked him out carefully?"

"He is closely connected with the second largest bank in Belgium and they speak very highly of him. He owns a bank in Tangiers and finances export transactions all over Europe."

I didn't like what I heard. Tangiers always reminded me of Hopps and the Rhode Island. But I said nothing. My own checks with the bank in question revealed that they financed his operations in Tangiers. The bank knew, however, little of his past. Schmit sensed that I was

Partner in a Small Law Firm

unimpressed and promised to have him come to New York and meet with me. Two weeks later, I heard from the Belgian who told me he was in town, staying at the Biltmore. I had no time for him during the week, so I invited him to come out by train Sunday morning and lunch with me in Bellport. He was delighted to do so.

He arrived on schedule, and I met him at the train. We sat in the library talking until lunchtime. Rosamond was not too happy to see him because weekends were the time we spent together as a family. The Belgian was neither warm nor particularly friendly. As we talked, he was all business. I didn't like him and wondered why Schmit had sent him.

At the time we had a friend of one of my French relatives in Paris who worked for us. She was a woman in her late forties who had been a show girl in Paris just before and during the war, had made enough money after the war selling art to the Americans coming to Paris, but apparently had lost the money at the racetrack and found it helpful to rent her apartment in Paris and come to work for us for a year. She was earthy, said what she thought, spoke French to the children and cooked magnificently. She had promised to cook a hare country-style for the Belgian.

We sat down at the table. Louise came through the swinging kitchen door carrying the hare, took one look at the Belgian and dropped the plate on the floor. Without saying a word, she vanished back into the kitchen so quickly that I don't think my guest had time to see who Louise was. I made my apologies, somehow we got through the meal, and after coffee, we talked some more before I took him to the train. I was anxious to get back and find out the reason why Louise had had such a shock when she saw him. When I came home, the house was in an uproar.

"I will not stay one more minute in this house," Louise told me emphatically. "I wish to leave tonight. You can send me a check if you want tomorrow."

She was so angry and upset that it took me some time to get her to tell me the story, which had taken place in Paris during the early days of the war. Louise evidently was living with a Frenchman who was in the business of acquiring and selling black market items: American cigarettes, Scotch whiskey, lingerie. The business, as you can imagine, was controlled by the Italian Mafia and the Gestapo. Apparently, the Belgian was working for the Gestapo as an informer, a courier, and a bird of prey living off the crumbs allowed to fall by that sinister organization. Whenever he came to Paris, he always had a beautiful young girl with him whom he would mercilessly beat if she did anything to displease him. Louise, who would not have allowed any man to treat her that way, disliked the Belgian intensely. Furthermore, each time he came he was accompanied by a different girl. Finally, one of them broke down and confessed to Louise that she had Jewish blood and that she was therefore at his mercy. If she did not do whatever he wanted, he would simply denounce her to his employers and she would be sent to a German army brothel or to Buchenwald. That was evidently the fate that had overtaken her predecessors. Louise hated this man so much that she eventually left her Frenchman over it. Now she was seeing this monster for the first time since 1943 in my house.

I was as angry as she was. The next morning, I called a detective friend of mine who was both Jewish and Irish and asked him to have the Belgian's room searched. He called me back before the day was out to tell me that he had found in the room four suitcases full of jewelry, furs and pornographic literature. The FBI was quietly informed and I hope took care of the matter. At any rate, I never saw the Belgian again. I called Schmit and told him the story. I was surprised that he was not as angry as I was.

Adventures in post-war Europe or with Europeans always seemed to involve the unexpected. But the practice of law in the United States was equally an opportunity to constantly learn about human nature.

George Lewis for years had represented the Bon Ami Company. It manufactured a standby cleaning product which housewives swore by before the age of synthetic cleansers. The chairman of the company was an 86-year-old young man, with the energy and wrath of an 18th century Scottish preacher. He was a match for old George. One day, Eversley Childs called me up and said that he was being harassed by the Securities and Exchange Commission because he had sold some of the shares of Bon Ami held in his children's and grandchildren's trusts. Since he controlled the company, it was not permissible to do this without first filing a registration statement covering the stock to be sold.

"What right do those damn bureaucrats have to tell me what I can do with property that I have given my children? It is my property and I guess I can do what I want with it under the 14th Amendment. Thibaut, I want you to go down to Washington and tell those monkeys to mind their own business. That damned Act is unconstitutional anyway."

Eversley Childs was not a man to fool with even though he was only five feet tall and very old. He was famous because at the last stock-holders' meeting of Bon Ami, a strike-suit lawyer from Chicago had asked him whether the company had a retirement plan.

"Of course not. People in this company are paid to work, not to go to Florida and play golf on the shareholders' money." This was before the days of golden parachutes.

"I thought if there was a retirement plan, you might take advantage of it."

"Young man, you come out in the hall after the meeting and I will beat you to a pulp," said Eversley amidst the plaudits of the shareholders present.

I did not know what to do. Obviously, something was required. I called the general counsel of the commission in Washington and made an early morning appointment to come down and see him.

"Before I explain to you why I wanted to see you," I said, "I would like to put to you a hypothetical question which might have been put to you when you were practicing law in New York before coming down to the SEC. Suppose a client who had been acting in violation of the rules of the commission by selling control stock told you to go down to Washington and tell those so-and-so's to stop interfering with the disposal of his own property, how would you have handled such a situation?"

Luckily, he burst out laughing.

"I think I know what you want to talk to me about," he said.

With his help we concocted a solution that gave the SEC what it wanted while preserving my relationship with my client. Childs received a nasty letter, but I gave the commission my assurance that so long as we were his and the company's counsel, there would be no further violations of its rules.

Our relations as a firm with Howard Hughes raised some interesting questions. Among the firm's corporate clients in the 1950s, the Technicolor Corporation became particularly interesting because, as the great pioneers of the film industry vanished from the scene, motion pictures came increasingly to rely on the clarity of the film and the beauty of the picture portrayed. This meant that every director and producer wanted his best pictures to be filmed in this new medium. Howard Hughes, during this period of his life, had become less interested in aerodynamics and more in the shapes of beautiful women, starting with Rosalyn Russell. All his films which featured his love of the moment naturally had to be in Technicolor. Hughes insisted in discussing whatever his plans were with Pete Lewis and with me, which meant that we would have to go out to Beverly Hills to see him, generally on short notice. He always stayed at the Bel Air Hotel, but he was so concerned with assassination that he would never spend two nights in the same suite. The routine was always the same. We would get a call around midnight at the Bel Air that a car would meet us at a given time to take us to Hughes. We would be driven around the city, then taken to some dark street where a black Cadillac would be parked, its shades drawn, and showing no sign of life. We would have to identify ourselves to the chauffeur, and then get in the back seat with Hughes. He would tell us what he wanted. It generally concerned his insistence that some girl of his get a part in a Technicolor production. We would then get back in our car and return to the hotel. He was totally unconcerned with the fees charged. I could never understand either his fear of bodily harm or this necessity for secrecy.

One day George Lewis called me into his office and closed the door so that even his secretary would not hear what he wanted to tell me. "Thibaut, I have been advised that the government wants you to go to Indochina. I am going to receive a call from John Foster Dulles, our undersecretary of state. I told them I would never consider letting you go unless Dulles called me personally. I have always wanted to tell that man a thing or two, so now I will have that chance."

Two days later Dulles called. Lewis called me into his office to hear the conversation:

"Mr. Dulles," he said, "you have been senior partner in the most prestigious firm in New York City. I am a poor old-fashioned practitioner operating on my own with very little help. But I knew that sooner or later, Mr. Dulles, you would feel constrained to call on me for help. Now what, Mr. Dulles, can I do to assist you?"

There was more of the same and it went on for half an hour. I tried to signal to George that he was gambling with my life. My urgings were to no avail. It was a great opportunity and he was going to play it to the hilt. At the end, he said that very regretfully he would let me go if it might help Mr. Dulles and the U. S. government.

"You have at last done something helpful for me and this firm," George Lewis said. "If you ever come back from this trip, I will be surprised." Fortunately, he didn't mean half of what he said. I think he was actually quite proud of me. But he would never admit it.

Partner in a Small Law Firm

To date, I had never regretted having left the economic advantages of working in a large law firm. I was working just as hard as before, but the work was varied and I felt I was independent. I loved every minute of what I was doing. Every morning, whether in New York or in Paris, I would look forward to what the day might bring in the way of new challenges. I was beginning to be confident that whatever the problem, I would be able to handle it.

Now I would face a new and perilous adventure in a very different environment.

IX

FOREIGN ADVENTURES

*A*T *LEWIS & MCDONALD (NY)* and Ten Eyck & Saint Phalle (Paris) our work was cut out for us. The New York firm represented a number of important corporations in the United States. We started with four partners and soon acquired another three, along with a number of associate lawyers who thought a small but growing firm offered an opportunity not available elsewhere. Taxes and international taxes in particular had represented for us a chance to establish a niche in this particular field of law. Ken Lidstone, a part-time professor of international taxation at the Harvard Law School, filled this need admirably. At Harvard, Ken dealt with international tax policies. In particular, he lectured on the development of tax systems for countries which had only recently become independent. He had become very close to those members of the government of Egypt who were charged with developing a modern tax system for that country. The Egyptian government at the time was anxious to increase agricultural production. It looked to the United States for financial assistance in building the dam at Aswan on the Nile which would assure adequate water supplies for increased production. Building this dam had become a most important project for the new Nasser government.

As our firm grew, I found my own role changing. I was taking on more responsibility, generally, for matters in both New York and Paris, and I was in charge of all corporate and international legal matters.

I even drafted a corporate tax code for Saudi Arabia. It was a challenge: Arabic is a language which hasn't changed much since the 9th century and is devoid of accounting terms so dear to Americans. To solve this problem, I did the draft in English, then had an Egyptian lawyer put it in Arabic, then another lawyer translate it back into English. The result made no sense. We ended up having to give the English phrases in parentheses throughout and provide that the English would

A growing international law practice

prevail in the event of conflicting interpretation. It was a poor way of writing legislation. But perhaps our Supreme Court could do the same for tax legislation in the United States to make our own poor legislative drafting understandable.

One evening Ken received a call from his friend, the Egyptian Foreign Minister, telling him that he was having increasing difficulty making the United States understand the urgent necessity of getting funds so that work on the dam could begin. Secretary Dulles was not well, and the State Department was being run by Herbert Hoover, Jr., his deputy secretary.

"I am charged by President Nasser to ask you to go to Washington, see Secretary Hoover and tell him that if the United States will not help us in financing the Aswan dam, we will be obliged to nationalize the Suez Canal and get the funds we need from the imposition of new tolls."

I was at a dinner party that night when Ken's call had come in. All five partners were so close that we had no hesitancy in calling each other at any hour. Depending upon what the problem was, one or another of us might be the one called. In this case, Ken called me because the problem was international. I told him that I thought if someone asked that a matter be handled in this unusual manner, it was our duty as Americans to deliver the message as requested—no more, no less—and to report back the answer in the same manner.

Ken went to Washington the next morning. His standing at Harvard warranted a prompt appointment with the deputy secretary of state. He delivered the message as requested and listened to a diatribe full of expletives. The gist was that the threat to nationalize the canal was an empty threat, that the Egyptians had no technological capabilities, that they would never be able to steer even a small vessel through the canal, and so on. Lidstone pointed out that he had been asked to deliver the answer and that he would be embarrassed to repeat the message as given.

"Tell them exactly what I have said," said Herbert Hoover, Jr.

One more telephone call late at night. It seemed to me, and I told Ken, that if he had told the secretary that he had been asked by the Egyptian government to deliver the American reply as given to him and the secretary had told him to do so, then he should comply. The next morning Ken called Cairo. There was a dead silence on the other end of the telephone line. Then the foreign secretary spoke:

"We would have nationalized the canal in a year, hoping that there would be a change of American policy in the interim. Now we will do it in three months."

Sometimes the messenger is an unexpected one. We were convinced that the Egyptians meant exactly what they said. And it happened that way. They promptly nationalized the canal. The consequences were predictable. The French and the British attacked Egypt, as did the Israelis. Eisenhower then intervened. He made it clear to the French and the British that they would have to withdraw their troops. MacMillan, the British prime minister, lost his job. The Egyptians nationalized the canal successfully. Whether the brutal attack by the Soviet Union on Hungary a few weeks later was linked to this because Stalin saw an inability on the part of the Western European Allies and the United States to agree on policy is debatable. There has, to my knowledge, never been an accounting of Deputy Secretary Hoover's behavior on this matter in any journal. Since then, of course, Abdel Nasser is gone and the Egyptians have become our friends and close allies.

Even back in the 1950s and 1960s, there was a need for the United States to exercise its power with extraordinary sensitivity. Herbert Hoover, Jr.'s behavior was, of course, an extreme example of what should not have been done. But there have been many other instances. We sometimes forget that other countries, particularly the Europeans, judge the United States quite differently from the way they regard each other. We are held to a different and much higher standard justified in the eyes of others by good actions taken by us in the past.

Generally, for about two weeks every other month I was in the Paris office where we had a partner and an associate on a full-time basis. The office was located at 16 Place Vendome on the second floor, overlooking that beautiful square with the Ritz on the other side and Morgan Bank next door. There was a boardroom next to my office with an 18th century painted ceiling and the furniture of Louis XIV's study at Versailles surrounding a magnificent light oak rectangular board table. My client, Edouard Le Roux, had his office on one side of the magnificent boardroom. I had one on the other side. In the back were secretaries' offices and an apartment. I was fortunate since Edouard was my client that I did not have to pay rent.

The boardroom is where I used to hold my acquisitions negotiations when representing an American company. The chairman of one client told me one day: "Thibaut, it would be an insult to Louis XIV's furnishings not to overpay you for any negotiations concluded in that beautiful room." Edouard Le Roux had impeccable good taste.

Foreign
Adventures

How to
make a
fortune
in France
between
wars

It was shortly before this time that I had met Edouard Le Roux and became his counsel. I don't believe his name was originally spelled this way. His family had been poor peasants in Normandy and he had all the characteristics of the Norman peasant, along with unusual intelligence: shrewd, suspicious, cunning, determined, acquisitive, patient, observant. He had come to Paris very young, educated himself by reading and watching others. He had obtained a job as a runner for a Paris securities broker. As he made his rounds of other brokerage houses, he observed, gathered information, and reported back to his employers accurate information about the activities and deals being arranged by competitors. He soon became indispensable to his employers. Since he was also deferential, young, good looking, presentable, and appealing to women, he soon found himself included in activities outside of office hours, when there were friends to be made and business transactions to be discussed. It was only a question of time before a junior partnership was his. Then he laid the basis for his eventual very substantial fortune. Paris in the 1930s was a study in contrasts. There was great wealth being made in banking and the securities markets, while poverty was rife and social pressures were growing rapidly. In 1936, the Popular Front Party of Leon Blum had come to power, labor unrest was a constant, and the "German" problem was becoming a greater threat each day, particularly after the Allies had kept France from preventing the seizure of the Rhineland by Adolf Hitler, who had become chancellor of the Reich in 1933. France felt its social, governmental and military fabric disintegrating. It was under these circumstances that Edouard had made his move for a real business coup which would make him a rich man. Like all such transactions, it was not complicated. It was solely based on accommodating greed. As Balzac had once pointed out: "Behind every great fortune lies a great crime."

Edouard had observed that control of the great French "Compagnie des Wagons-Lits," the European equivalent to Pullman sleeping cars in the United States, had been obtained by a certain Captain Soames, an Englishman who had won a Victoria Cross in the Coldstream Guards in World War I. Soames had subsequently married one after the other three very rich young women in London and had used their fortunes in a series of investments that had not worked out. His latest was the "Compagnie des Wagons-Lits." Edouard ascertained that Soames had borrowed most of the money from Barclays Bank in London. Through friends in the bank's management, he found out the price at which the bank would sell the shares to repay the loan. Armed with this information he had put together a group of French investors to buy control of the firm through a forced sale of Soames' position. They first went short on the Bourse until the stock had been driven down below the sales point set by the bank. When the bank sold out Soames, they arranged to pick up his stock. Soames, financially wiped out, put a bullet through his head. Edouard then approached Pierre Laval, a French politician from Normandy with ambitions to become prime minister. In exchange for financial and political support, Laval promised to nationalize the company if he succeeded in becoming prime minister. The Le Roux group arranged to give Laval substantial financial support, and he was duly elected prime minister of France. Laval then nationalized the company, as he had promised to do, and Edouard made a great fortune as a result. He was also successful in marrying Thérèse Fabre, the daughter of one of the great fortunes of France. The Fabre family controlled several shipping lines, including the Chargeurs Reunis. Knowing Le Roux's reputation in business, the Fabre family would, for a long time, not see him. This meant little to him. He had become a success in business and very wealthy. He bought a large property adjoining J. P. Morgan's estate on Long Island and divided his time between New York and Paris. He was convinced that war was coming and that France would lose.

When the war came, Edouard's friends were on the side of Vichy. They believed that France lost the war because Leon Blum had destroyed the French work ethic and moral values. Edouard himself had moved to the United States in 1939 and settled into his beautiful property in Glen Cove, Long Island. Shortly after he bought the house, Junius Morgan, who owned a sand bar in front of the property, built some inexpensive summer cottages there and sold them to New Yorkers pining for an escape on water. Two years later, a fall hurricane uprooted the houses. As soon as the storm hit, Edouard had his butler bring up some excellent French champagne. As the houses slid into the sea, the family sat in the library sipping champagne and watching the houses on the sand bar disappear.

Why would Edouard Le Roux have wanted the legal advice of a young lawyer who then had little sophistication in international finance? I have often wondered about this and after his death asked Thérèse one day. She explained it this way: "Edouard has done so many things he should never have done that he no longer knows the difference between right and wrong. He needs a guide, particularly in Wall Street. You were that guide, Thibaut."

One day Edouard came into my office in New York and told me: "I don't trust paper money anymore. Every government is copying old gold coins—the British the gold sovereign of 1913, the French Napoleon III's Louis d'Or, because they know that if they used today's date, everyone would think there was copper added to the gold. I want my own coinage: and the gold content certified by the British Assay Office. Can I sell these in the United States under American law?"

"This is not a question I get every day, that a man wishes to have his own gold currency. Give me a few days and I will give you the answer."

Three days later, after an examination of the federal statutes, I would tell him to go ahead. We then spent an interesting winter afternoon in my office designing the face of the coin.

In those early days, with a wife and three little children to support, money was scarce. Edouard Le Roux was generous to me in many small ways.

There was not a shred of emotional attachment in Edouard Le Roux, neither to his native land, France, nor to his adoptive country, the United States, nor to his wife or children. He was objective in business, cynical about the businessmen he knew, distrustful of all politicians on both sides of the ocean. He considered the men he dealt with in business to be like him, ready to take advantage of him if they could. In France he bought politicians when he needed to. His French lawyer was like him: ruthless, unforgiving, cynical.

With his wife and two children I never saw him affectionate or understanding. On the contrary, he had taught his children to be the same as him. I used to wonder how it was possible to be so cynical about human nature as he was. Edouard was right out of a Dickens novel.

He hated for me to send him bills for the legal work I did for him. But from time to time he would give me purchase and sales slips, for shares he said he had bought for me—so that I could report the gains on my tax returns. He also made a cottage available to us on the grounds of his Long Island estate, to use on weekends. His son often came on a Saturday or Sunday to have dinner with us. I think the young man was glad to get away from the confining atmosphere of his parents' house. There were never other children there.

I met a number of Edouard's French associates: the Consul of Monaco, bankers from Tangiers and from Switzerland, various French government ministers.

Le Roux had two good friends with whom he invested: Bobby Lehman, the head of Lehman Brothers, and Andre Meyer of Lazard

Freres in New York. Unfortunately, whenever I found him an unusual corporate acquisition, he would discuss the transaction with one or both of these financiers. I never was quite sure that they weren't buying along with him if the deal was special. The greatest transaction I brought him was a gold company founded in 1880, the oldest company still listed on the New York Stock Exchange. I pleaded with him to buy thirty percent of the stock before sharing the idea with his investment banker friends. I carefully explained to him that since 1880 probably 30 percent of the shares had been lost in some attic. Edouard never understood that he could therefore acquire control for a very reasonable investment. He would have made an additional fortune and realized his great dream: to control a company listed on the New York Stock Exchange.

During winter afternoons when I was in Paris, with our venerable Chinese houseboy lighting the fire in my office and the great view of the square outside under lights, I used to wonder why I spent so little time in Paris and so much in New York.

Barent Ten Eyck, who was our resident partner in Paris, was a delightful, cultured human being, a born pianist and raconteur. His wife was demanding, assertive and very physical. One day she asked me to stop by for cocktails where she took me aside out of Barry's hearing and said to me: "Your client Edouard fascinates me. I am quite mad for him. Can't you send Barry for a few days to New York?" I was flabbergasted. Le Roux was then 68. In my world, men went after women, not the other way around. I didn't know what to say. But Le Roux had a sixth sense on such matters and undoubtedly took care of the matter.

Many years later, when I went to Geneva to teach in 1971, I ran across Edouard and Thérèse Le Roux again. They had moved to Switzerland for tax reasons and had a beautiful apartment there facing the lake. Edouard by now had an advanced case of the gout and was almost blind. Thérèse was the perfect French wife to the end. When he died, she became a remarkable person in her own right.

Anyone who has spent time in France knows that France is a country run by women. The Frenchman may strut, and be faithful to his mistress rather than to his wife, but it is the woman of the house who educates the children, manages the day-to-day finances, and makes the important decisions. In any French restaurant or grocery, it is the wife who stands by the cash register while the husband cooks or serves the customers. In many households the husband gives his paycheck to his wife each week.

When Edouard died, Thérèse became a Fabre again. Remarkably

intelligent, conservative, honest and direct to a fault, a patron of the arts, she decided to use her husband's fortune to mark a new beginning in her own life. With her standing in French society, her relations in the academic, cultural and art world of Paris, New York and Geneva, she was ready. Her first venture was to leave for Cambodia, settle herself in the best hotel and begin to explore the magic of Angkor Vat and the art of the Khmer civilization. Phnom Penh is a small place, and foreigners came to Cambodia few in number. In no time at all, Thérèse had met Prince Sihanouk, the ruler of the country, and often went to tea at the palace to tell him what she was discovering about the cultural history of his country. After a few weeks, he said to her one day: "It is silly of you to stay in a suite at the hotel. Why don't you come and live in the palace. I will fix you an apartment and you will be free to come and go as you please. It will be more comfortable for you here." So Thérèse moved over to the palace. She was there having tea with the prince the day that President Nixon sent the American ambassador to tell Sihanouk that he had to be out of Cambodia within 24 hours because United States military forces were invading the country. Thérèse, who had an American passport but was very much opposed to the war in Vietnam, evidently told the ambassador in no uncertain terms what she thought of the American policy and the unjustified removal of Cambodia's ruler. One will recall that Sihanouk fled and no country in the area wanted to take him, for fear of American retaliation. Thérèse went back to Geneva and undertook to find him asylum.

Some years earlier, she had been introduced to Josef Broz, or Tito as he was known in Yugoslavia. He had invited her to Brioni one summer and there she had met Chou En-lai, now prime minister under Mao Tse-tung in the People's Republic of China.

I wanted to learn as much from Thérèse as I could about her quiet summer in Brioni visiting Tito and his beautiful wife who had given up a dancer's career for this enigmatic guerilla leader. Tito had recreated a different Yugoslavia out of the chaos of a world conflict, a revolution and a fierce civil war. He had always fascinated me. I vividly remembered one Sunday in 1956 reading in the *New York Times* about the break between Yugoslavia and the Soviet Union. Stalin had been reported in the paper to have exclaimed when the news of Tito's defection was brought to him: "Who in hell does that man think he is?" Only if Tito were not Yugoslav but a Russian could such a remark be understood. Some months later I read an account by a British intelligence agent based in Yugoslavia during the war which seemed to provide the an-

258

swer. Churchill evidently wanted to find out as much as possible about this leader of the Communist guerilla fighters as a possible prelude to abandoning Mihailovich, the Serbian leader who did not seem able to arouse popular support for those willing to fight the Allies behind the German and Italian lines. The agent had managed to get to the village where Josef Broz (Tito) had lived as a child. He had tried to find those who might still remember him: the village priest, the schoolteacher, the postman, in addition to possible family members. All had disappeared. All that was known was that Broz had been a radical youth who had fought in Spain on the Republican side in a unit commanded by a very young Russian colonel known for his intelligence and ruthlessness. Was it possible that Josef Broz had been made to exchange identities with this colonel in the Soviet Union after the fall of Madrid only then to vanish in Siberia or before Beria's firing squad? There is evidence that some of those who knew Broz as a boy from the village were taken to the Soviet Union. Could they not have instructed the young Russian colonel all that Broz might have known about his parents, the village gossip, even his intonation of voice, before they in turn were made to vanish? It is hard to believe that everyone who knew Joseph Broz as a youth could have been made to disappear.

Thérèse now wrote to Chou suggesting that he invite her friend, Prince Sihanouk, to take refuge in Beijing since the Americans had forced him to flee his country.

When Sihanouk arrived in Beijing, Chou showed him the letter he had received from Thérèse Le Roux. Sihanouk then told Chou what an extraordinarily cultured woman Thérèse was. Chou suggested that Sihanouk invite her to China. When she received Sihanouk's invitation, she curtly replied that if the Chinese prime minister wished her to come to China, he should extend the invitation himself. Shortly thereafter, the Chinese ambassador to Paris sent an aide to Geneva to extend the invitation on behalf of his government, forwarding a letter from Chou asking Mme. Le Roux if she wished to bring anyone with her and what she would like to see during her stay. She replied that she understood Chou was a very cultured man. She wished to learn about Chinese art and culture and in order to learn more about Chinese medicine, she proposed to be accompanied by her friend and doctor from Geneva, Dr. Claude Paquet. "Could she also have a brief meeting with Chairman Mao, about whose ideas she had read so much?" She was advised that she would be in Chairman Mao's box for the May Day Parade and that Chou himself would accompany her on an artistic tour of China.

Foreign Adventures

Foreign
Adventures

On May
Day in Paris
one gives
lilies of the
valley.

With her special sensitivity Thérèse Le Roux soon realized that despite the rhetoric in Communist countries about the role of women, there was little role for the prime minister's wife. On May Day, she bought lilies of the valley and sent them to Mme. Chou En-lai with a note that in France on the first of May, it was customary to send lilies of the valley to someone one loved. Because Chou En-lai had been so kind to her, she wanted to express her affection for his wife. Needless to say, the gesture was not lost on Chou En-lai. Before leaving China, Thérèse was invited to speak of her impressions on Chinese television. She said that she was a French capitalist and disapproved thoroughly of Communism, but she said she had found in China an extraordinary cultural inheritance and very friendly people who obviously had a civilization with which few could compare. In this way, Thérèse made many friends in China. Because she said what she thought simply and without malice, she earned the respect of those she came in contact with, regardless of their own political persuasions.

What an ambassador Thérèse Le Roux might have made! I was extremely fond of her.

* * *

One day in the New York office, I received a phone call from Ted Voorhees, a Philadelphia cousin by marriage who was head of the bar association there.

"I have a complicated problem, Thibaut. With your international connections and your office in Paris, you may be able to help me. If I don't find the answer, our firm is going to lose its principal client. I need someone with a knowledge of French law, good connections with the French police, and enough sensitivity to counsel a woman distraught by the disappearance of her children."

The story was an unusual one. The client was the wealthiest privately owned coal company in Pennsylvania. The owner's daughter had married a young man who had held many different jobs in the United States and had even lived for a period of time in Paris. He had been a journalist, a gallery owner, an antiques dealer, a would-be writer of fiction. According to my cousin, Ted Voorhees, the couple, who had two children, had recently found it more and more difficult to maintain any stability in their marriage, and the wife had at last reached the point where she thought divorce was the only solution. Although his firm did not generally take marital cases, they had agreed to represent the wife. Negotiations had been proceeding when suddenly the husband disappeared with the children, having picked them up at school without returning them home. While the lawyers had been negotiating the last difficult question of visitation rights, the husband, believing he would lose those rights, had gone to Washington and obtained a new passport for himself which included the children. It seemed obvious that he must have taken the children abroad, but where?

"You must find those children and bring them home. They are probably somewhere in France, since that is where the young man lived for a time and he knows many people in Paris. Get a first-class detective on the case. Let me know how much expense money you will need. Get started right away. They must be brought back," Voorhees added with particular emphasis.

It was an interesting challenge, but I wasn't sure just where to start. Obviously, the first thing to do if the children really were in France was to find the right detective, but how? This was a different world—it had nothing to do with the law as I practiced it. I would have to tap into my old OSS connections, but again, who here could help me? My partners would be of no assistance. This was something I had to work out strictly on my own.

Finally, I hired, by phone, a wonderful old Russian who came highly recommended and supposedly knew his way around the world in Paris where information is sought, bought and sold.

My friend in Philadelphia kept putting the pressure on me for action.

"The children love their mother and, if given a chance, they will come running to her," he told me. "You have only to find the children, and they will immediately leave the father and come to her. You should have her with you. I will deliver to your flight from New York to Paris not only the mother but the grandmother."

I figured that if our quarry had worked as a newspaperman in Paris, he would surely have a way of checking on arrivals by plane from New York. So I decided that we would fly to London, change planes there and then go on to Paris. For the first time at Idlewild—now Kennedy—Airport, I met my two charges. The mother was dour, but the grandmother gave me the impression of a woman who would face anything if necessary.

"I hope there is not going to be any shooting," the grandmother said to me. "But I am ready for anything. You have only to tell me what you want me to do." I noticed that she was carrying a Bible as well as her pocketbook.

"I am afraid my problem is going to be to find the children," I said. "I have no idea whether they are in France at all. It is rather like finding a needle in a haystack. I'm afraid that I shall have to carry out the search by myself. In the meantime, you both are to stay out of the way because you cannot help me. Because the good hotels may be watched, I have put you up in a French voyager's hotel near the Gare du Nord railroad station. You will be safe, but it won't be the Ritz. My secretary or I will keep in close touch with you from day to day."

I had brought my wife to the airport to reassure the ladies that I was not an abductor myself. It did not seem to comfort them very much because on the flight I noticed the grandmother was reading snatches from the Bible to her daughter.

"What in God's name am I going to do with these women while I search?" I thought to myself.

Once in Paris, the ladies were the least of my problems. I was not impressed with what my Russian had accomplished, which was nothing. Through a French lawyer friend I found a French police inspector whom I immediately hired with instructions to get a team together and go through every arrival card since the day when the quarry was supposed to have left Philadelphia with the children. Imagine what a job it was to review a week of arrivals in Paris from all over the world! And suppose he had landed elsewhere first.

While this was going on, I went to a meeting I had arranged from New York with a leading French trial lawyer, who was also Edouard's French lawyer. He was a friend of the current minister of justice and certainly knew his way around the courts. In those days, French lawyers received their clients at home in the mornings, wearing a dressing gown. I went to see him in his magnificent Paris apartment.

"Mr. de Saint Phalle," the famous lawyer told me, "there isn't anything of a legal nature that I cannot accomplish in France, but what you are proposing is not only illegal, but if you are caught at it, you may be subject not only to disbarment but to spending up to twenty years in prison. I must advise you, my American friend, that under French law, the husband has just as much right to the children as the wife. What you call a kidnapping is not a kidnapping under French law. The father came to France with the children. He has a right to have the children with him. As a matter of fact, you tell me the children's photographs are even on his passport. If you try to take the children away from him while he is in France, not even I will be able to help you. You will be put in prison and it will be years before you can get out."

The problem was definitely becoming much more complicated. I hadn't counted on operating outside the law. But first I had to find the children. In that, I became lucky. The following day I had a call from my French police inspector. He had found the card. The address in France given on it was in a Paris suburb. I called the wife, my client, at her hotel. She identified the address as belonging to a French professor friend of her husband. What to do next? That very evening we had a council of war in my office on the Place Vendome—my secretary, the inspector, the Russian sleuth, and me. Who should call the professor? What should he say? How would we avoid letting the father know that we were on to him? It was not a good proposition, but something had to be done quickly before the children were taken elsewhere, perhaps out of reach. Finally, I called the professor and said I was a friend of the children's father and that a mutual friend had seen him on the plane with the children and that they were staying in Paris. How could I reach him? It was hard. I had to identify myself, which fortunately I could do using the name of another friend of his in Paris whose name had been given to me by the wife. He wasn't there, I was told. He had stayed with them for a few days but had now gone to Paris with the children. She gave me the address of the apartment where they could be found. It was time to act.

From the days when I was visiting my sister in Courtrai, Belgium, I had learned how to cross the frontier between France and Belgium, avoiding customs by passing through Roubaix in the middle of the night. I had my secretary, Miss Hess, telephone the legal officer at the U.S. Embassy the next morning who told her if two children appeared at the embassy without a passport, they would be given a "laissez passer," but only to return to the United States. If I could get them to Belgium, the battle was won!

First thing next morning I rented two cars—one was a Peugeot, looking like any other Peugeot—which would be the getaway car. The other was a high speed Citroen which would be parked on the outskirts of Paris at the beginning of the main highway to the north. There I would switch cars and head for the border. Once over the border I would drive to Brussels. I did not want the ladies with me, but I realized I had to have them. They seemed ready for anything and promised to do only what they were told. The Russian had been sent to watch the apartment house, the address of which I had been given. The inspector would follow us in his own car and guide us to the outskirts of Paris. The problem was to get the children out of the apartment house. It was a long vigil. I hadn't thought of a way to force them out. I assumed he would not want to keep the children in the house all day. I certainly would not have been able to if they were mine.

But by five p.m. we had not seen him. Again I made a call. This time I was advised they had borrowed a car and left the apartment. Destination unknown, but probably the Chateaux de la Loire."

My secretary and I went back to the office after returning the getaway cars to the agency. I was dead tired. Where would a man take two children? What would I do under the same circumstances? It was Friday. Where would one go for a spring weekend in the Loire valley?

"We have to be able to identify the place. Where would you go?" I asked my secretary. Then I realized she wouldn't think like an American father.

"Never mind. Take the Michelin and call every hotel in the region. Sooner or later we must find him if he is there."

Around eleven o'clock we had located them. They were at the inn in the park of the Chateau de Chambord, one of the finest of the "Chateaux de la Loire." I immediately called the inspector to come over. I rented a car, this time a big Mercedes, and called the ladies to hop into a cab and meet us at the office. I told them to also bring an overnight bag. I had no idea what might happen. We left about 1:30 a.m. The two ladies, the police inspector, my secretary, Miss Hess, and me. Each of us was lost in his own thoughts. It was Friday night. I had hoped to spend the weekend at an old mill in the Eure where the food was good and I could sleep well under the spell of water passing over the wheel. Instead, here I was, headed for another adventure which might turn out as badly as the last.

Our plan of action was set as we drove to Chambord. We would arrive just before dawn. I would place the ladies behind large oaks near the entrance to the inn. Miss Hess and I would do likewise. At breakfast time the police inspector would come forth, show his badge to the manager and tell him he wanted to check the papers of an American who was staying there with two little children. Our expectation was that when the manager went up to fetch the father, the children would come down with him and go out to play while he talked to the inspector. I would then signal to the mother to come out from behind the tree at which point the delighted children would naturally run to her; Miss Hess and I would come forward in the car and all would jump in for the drive back to Paris. I had some doubts about what my cousin Voorhees had told me, particularly since I had come to know the wife who was not an especially warm person, but I had never met the husband and at this point I had to rely on what I had been told.

Everything worked out according to the script, everything that is, except the finale. When their mother dashed out from behind her tree, the children took one look at her and fled inside hanging on to their father's legs as though they were being chased by a bear. For the first time in twelve years, I heard Miss Hess let out a French curse. Then the father came out of the inn and he and his wife exchanged some harsh words. There was nothing the rest of us could do. It was like being at a play where at the big love scene suddenly hate rages. To top it all off, at just that moment an American tourist bus pulled up in front of the inn, disgorging middle-aged men and women who immediately took the side of one or the other of the quarreling spouses. It was horrible, but it gave me an opportunity to seek out the grandmother who had advanced from her tree and was staring in consternation at the scene in front of the inn.

"There is only one thing to do to save the situation," I told her. "You must stay here for the weekend or go somewhere else with your daughter, son-in-law, and the children. You must go too because I want to be sure your daughter shares a room with you. I don't want your son-in-law to have any excuse to spend the night with your daughter, because that would be the end of her divorce action. You must all come back to Paris Monday morning, and I will then figure out what the next move should be."

"But he will murder us in our beds if we do that."

"If you love your daughter and your grandchildren, you'll take that chance. He doesn't look like a murderer to me and the children obviously love him. I will give you a number where you will call me tonight and tomorrow night. Obviously, your son-in-law doesn't have much money. I want you to pay the bills. Have him choose a first-class hotel and insist on good meals and wine. I want you to relax and forget bygones for a few hours. Concentrate on giving the children a first-class tour of the chateau country. I think I can rely on you. Make sure your daughter is pleasant all weekend long. Now go talk to her while I try to sell your son-in-law on the idea."

She did as she was told. I took the husband, Henry, aside and tried to talk to him. He was a nice man, obviously terrified of his wife and very fond of his children. "They wouldn't give me any visitation rights," he said, "so I took the children."

"That was a mistake. I'll do what I can to straighten that out. But this is the children's holiday. France is so beautiful in the spring. The weekend is on grandmother. Why don't you just show everybody a good time and get back to Paris Monday morning. You obviously know where to take them in the Loire Valley. On Monday, I will have reserved rooms for all of you at the Vendome across the street from my office and we can all see where things stand then."

What happened next was worse. Henry had only a French two-horsepower Citroen. In order for him to take grandmother, mother and the two children, I had to leave him my big car and take his small Citroen. On the way back to Paris all I could think of was that he would dump mother and grandmother in some forest and take off with my car across the border somewhere. How would I explain what I had done to my lawyer client?

Miss Hess, the inspector and I drove back to Paris in the little car. On the way I thought it best at least to have a really good lunch. In the middle of the lunch, the inspector, well into his bottle of wine, turned to me:

"You know, it pained me very much to see those two children torn between two selfish parents. I learned a great deal today. Like all Frenchmen, I have a mistress and I don't pay enough attention to my kids. I'm going home, saying goodbye to my mistress, and looking after my wife and children from now on."

Miss Hess obviously did not believe him. But I was glad to see something good come out of this sad venture. I left the inspector at his car, drove Miss Hess home and set off in my own car for the mill and sleep, sleep, sleep. It wasn't that easy to rest. Grandmother called me just as I had finished dinner to tell me things were going very badly. I repeated that getting through the weekend as I had told her was her only chance, but I wasn't very sure about what might happen before Monday.

On Monday morning I went to the office. Around ten they called to say they were at the Vendome. I asked Henry to come to see me to discuss the next step. Hesitantly, he agreed to come and I sent Miss Hess to pick up the children and take them to her apartment.

"Henry, the children are gone. Your wife and her mother will go back to New York tonight on TWA with the children. I want you to go back with them. The children need you with them, but in a divorce you will lose them. My advice to you is to go back—all of you. Your wife loves you in her own way. She has money and can help you do what you want. Don't punish the children."

266

He insisted on talking to his lawyer. I spoke to him, too. Understandably, he didn't want to lose his fee and it was difficult to make him understand that that was not the issue here. The day was a long one and even longer for Miss Hess, who found the children swinging outward to the street on her lace curtains. I took everybody to the airport three hours in advance, gave them drinks and dinner and saw them all with great relief onto the plane.

I flew back myself the next day and sent a huge bill to my client. He asked me what I had done. When I explained and pointed out what I had risked, he had it paid promptly, but it took grandmother to explain to her husband what we had accomplished together. Until recently I received Christmas cards from her. She was a great lady. I am happy to say that when I checked several years later, the couple was still together.

Most of my time at the Paris office was spent on corporate matters resulting from acquisitions previously negotiated on behalf of American companies in France or elsewhere in Europe or in negotiating new acquisitions, but there was always enough of a variety of other business to keep one learning about the foibles of human nature. From time to time the American Embassy would ask us to handle a matter of some sensitivity. Once I was asked to rescue from a French prison an American of Italian origin who had staged the St. Valentine's Day Massacre in gangland Chicago in the '20s. The man was not allowed back in the United States. But still he was an American. The French didn't know what to do with him and only wanted to make sure he would go back to Italy and never come back to France. The charge against him was that he had illegally brought jewels into the country. After I arranged for him to go back to Italy and the French charges were dismissed, he asked me if there was anything he could do for me. I told him if he wished he could send my secretary, Miss Hess, a jewel, since that seemed to be his business. I was somewhat surprised that he never did, because generally the Mafia is very punctilious about paying those who have saved them from prison.

Through Barry Ten Eyck we were involved in a strange case for Stavros Niarchos, the Greek shipping magnate. In the '50s and '60s, the easiest way to make money in Europe was to own the Société des Bains de Mer which controlled the gambling casino and much else in Monte Carlo. Since Monaco was also the center for society's activities in the south of France, it was a foregone conclusion that the two richest men in Europe would get into a dispute as to which of them would control the corporation that in turn owned the principal leisure activities on the

The Greeks
fight it out.

coast. After much wrangling, a compromise was finally reached and appropriate documents signed, only to find shortly thereafter that Onassis' signature had vanished from the documents executed by him. Barry had thus been called in to get the courts to clear up the matter once and for all. It was the kind of case that people with too much money and too little to do could enjoy discussing on their yachts and in restaurants overlooking the Mediterranean on a warm summer night. Barry handled the matter successfully and enjoyed every minute of it.

While Ten Eyck was trying to reestablish peace between the Greeks, I was finding myself spending increasing amounts of my time on assignments in other parts of Europe. After the kidnapping case, I had gone down for two weeks to rest in Spain.

In those days Spain was very poor and had few tourists, because in Socialist Europe after World War II Spain under Generalissimo Franco was considered to be a Fascist dictatorship—which of course it was—and hence anathema. Because it had escaped World War II, it had suffered none of that war's destruction and loss of life. But it had never recovered from the terrible Civil War of 1933–37. It was now a military dictatorship under Franco, with few human rights and labor unions without authority.

I stayed at the Hotel Ritz in Madrid where for a few dollars a night I was getting a suite in one of the best hotels in Europe, with impeccable service and excellent food.

After a few days visiting the Prado Museum, I had decided to take a train to Malaga in southern Spain to explore the beaches at Torremolinos. The concierge asked me whether I was planning to go at the beginning or end of the month.

"Why do you ask?"

"Because the trains are apt to be late, and the Generalissimo expects his minister of transportation to report to him at the end of the month on whether the trains ran on time—so at the end of the month the trains leave an hour early."

I found a little hotel on the beach at Torremolinos. The owner despaired of tourists ever coming to the area. Before I left he offered to sell me his hotel and a half-mile of beautiful beach for $10,000, so he could go back to Italy and participate in the economic boom just beginning there. Like a fool I didn't accept. When I went back to Torremolinos a few years later, the beach was covered with hotels and that piece of land was worth at least ten million U.S. dollars!

Spain has always appealed to me as one of the most fascinating parts of Europe. Whenever I could, I continued to visit. In 1958, the generalissimo decided to try to revitalize the Spanish economy which had been so somnolent under his rule. To do so, he called upon the Opus Dei, a group of conservative Catholic activists including businessmen and Spain's leading economists.

The Opus Dei had been formed by a devout Spanish priest in 1928 and grew very quickly throughout the Spanish-speaking world. Its members, mostly businessmen and government officials, led communal lives and had taken vows of celibacy and poverty. In Franco's Spain where the Catholic Church was extremely powerful, members of the Opus Dei were ready to take power and quickly did so. When I was asked in 1960 to advise a Japanese company to bid on the acquisition of the leading steel company in Spain which had been losing money for years, I was advised by the American ambassador to Spain, a friend, to get Opus Dei to help in deciding on the choice of a Spanish partner. The law then required that every foreign investor have a 50 percent Spanish partner. At that time the prime minister and the ministers of the economy, foreign affairs and treasury were all members of the Opus Dei.

Imagine my consternation when I returned to New York to meet with my Japanese clients to tell them that they had only to follow my instructions to win the bid. At my description of the Opus Dei and its position of power, their eyes glazed. They paid my fee in full and chose a Spanish tobacco company as their partner. The bid was won by a Japanese competitor which chose the Spanish partner I had recommended. My hopes to have a valid excuse for frequent business visits to Bilbao where the Spanish steel industry was headquartered were dashed.

Fortunately, other clients interested in investing in Spain made it necessary for me to learn proper Spanish once again. So I signed up in 1969 for a month's intensive course of study in Barcelona to learn to speak, write and read Spanish perfectly.

Barcelona was a city much disliked by the Franco regime because it had been the capital of the anti-Franco Republican regime during the Civil War. There were even special taxes payable if a foreign firm chose Barcelona in place of Madrid as a city in which to invest.

Barcelona was originally a Carthaginian city settled by Lebanese traders in Roman times. It was from there that Hannibal set out to conquer Rome in the fourth century B.C.

It was during my stay in Barcelona that the American astronauts landed on the moon. With great difficulty I managed to rent a television set to view this great event. When I turned on the set, the announcer said he was taking the viewers to Castel Gondolfo, the pope's summer place, to get the pontiff's reaction to the news. We next saw Pope Paul VI looking through his telescope. When asked for his reaction, the pope said that while it was indeed a great achievement, it would have been better for the Americans to give money to the poor. The announcer then said that since this was an American achievement, he would take the viewers to ask the Americans what they thought. The camera moved to London and focused on a young girl lying prone in dirty fatigues at the foot of Nelson's monument on Trafalgar Square. Asked for her opinion on the moon landing, she said:

"I guess it's great, but I would rather have a good f_ _ _."

Unperturbed, the television reporter told his viewers that this young American girl thought it was a remarkable feat but that in her opinion there were other worthwhile things to do.

I never did see pictures of the landing on the moon. So much for news of the day in a Spanish theocracy.

After the death of Franco in 1975, the country was ruled by his carefully chosen successor, King Juan Carlos. Many thought he too would rule as a dictator aided by the army. He chose not to do so but to be chief of state under a parliamentary system. It has worked very well.

Today, Spain is in a unique position of being at once the political and economic key to both Latin America and the Islamic world.

President Reagan was very aware of the importance of Spain. He would send me in 1982 to travel all over the country lecturing on the importance for Spain to remain a member of NATO. Spain has since been a faithful ally of our country.

Elsewhere in this book I have commented on the importance of Spain to our relations with the Arab (Moslem) world. We must not forget that for over 700 years—from 711 when the Moors first came ashore to the fall of Granada in 1490—southern Spain and the cities of Granada and Cordoba were the centers of civilization in a Europe laid waste by feudalism and constant wars.

Personally, I am addicted to Spain, its history, culture, its art and even its music. Others may prefer the Dutch or Italian masters or the French Impressionists. But no artist can compare, in my view, to Goya, Velasquez or El Greco.

In 1957, on a late fall day, all of a sudden the personal world I had constructed became unhinged. I had a telephone call that day from a doctor in Bellport, Long Island where we had bought a house, so that the children could be raised in the country rather than in New York City. Rosamond had consulted the doctor because she had a mole high on her chest which appeared to be growing. The doctor reported that it was cancerous and that a specialist should be called in immediately. Through our good friends in the medical department of the Brookhaven National Laboratory, we met with Dr. Pack, who had been coroner of Hackensack County in northern New Jersey and was the founder and head of the Pack Medical Group in New York City. In those days cancer research was in its infancy. Ten years later, when I became a trustee of the Cancer Research Institute, only relative progress had been made. Today, the situation is very different, particularly where melanomas or breast cancers are concerned. Pack recommended drastic surgery before the cancer could spread further. After the operation he advised that if it didn't come back within three years, remission would be complete.

Foreign Adventures

After the operation we went down to Bermuda at the invitation of a new friend and client of mine, Jean-Jacques Martinat, who was responsible for designing most of the great perfumes as an independent advisor to the industry. He had one laboratory in New York above a theater on West 44th Street, and one in Bermuda in the basement of the perfume factory which he had built and designed for a Bermuda family he knew. The owner of the perfume factory, a Mrs. Scott, was a thirty-five year-old charming and handsome woman who had never married because she felt it necessary to look after her 85-year-old father who had been Speaker of the Bermuda House of Commons for over a generation. Martinat was the smallest Frenchman I have ever seen but the kindest, and he obviously knew the perfume business. That February in Bermuda, it rained almost every day. We hardly noticed the weather. Each day we drove to the factory and among the retorts and the colored vials we spent the day designing and bottling fragrances. Liqueurs are made just as perfumes are. We made green and yellow Chartreuse, distilled plum, peach and other brandies, learned the art of making perfume and the role of the lowly whale in making the fragrance linger on the skin. Before we left, Mrs. Scott confessed that she had fallen in love in Italy the previous summer and was willing to sell the perfume factory. I could understand her feelings. The British have always had a particular liking for Italy and the Italians. It is like the feeling of Americans toward the Chinese, a feeling which Rosamond and I knew so well. So we stayed an extra week while I prepared certified statements with her accountant and drew up a sales contract with her lawyers. Martinat and I would be equal partners. I would be responsible for law and finance, he

Buying the perfume faƈtory in Bermuda

for operations. We would make not only perfumes but also liqueurs. I was confident that I could market the liqueurs through my friends, the Kriendlers, who owned "21," the most famous restaurant in New York. I knew them and I knew they would be delighted to have a private label for their own liqueurs. As near as I could make out, the factory should earn from 50 percent to 75 percent of its capital each year, and it could be sheltered through a Bermuda corporation. I thought once again that wealth was around the corner. But once again this was not to be. Mrs. Scott's father, in order to prevent her from going to Italy to live happily ever after, had the Bermuda House of Commons declare the perfume factory a national monument, which as a result could only be sold to English subjects. Poor Mrs. Scott. She remained in Bermuda to take care of that terrible old man, while Dr. Martinat and I returned to New York. I learned, however, that a lesson learned is never forgotten. I could do calculations in pounds, shillings and pence as quickly as Mrs. Scott's accountant, but I didn't tell him I had learned all this years ago when I was in school in Bermuda during the Depression years.

I also learned something about the English when their interests are at stake. At about this same time I had become American counsel to Hambros Bank in London. The bank, because of its standing in international affairs, had become adviser to the British government in the development of its trade with the United States after the end of World War II. Sales of British china, woolens, and automobiles were all financed through Hambros after the war with the British government standing behind as guarantor against losses. This made the effort very worthwhile for the banking institution while assuring the government that British exports to the United States would receive appropriate attention. I became the U.S. adviser and counsel to the bank.

My work at the Hambros Bank was one of the most interesting and pleasant of my legal career, probably because of my admiration and respect for Olaf Hambro, its chairman. Olaf ruled the firm as an absolute dictator. While the other partners had desks outside his office in a great room shared by all, Olaf's office, while small, was his alone. When his partner, Charles, came in he stood in front of Olaf's desk to receive his instructions. Charles would not even be asked to sit down, even though he was a governor of the Bank of England. One day when I had given Olaf verbally the results of a lengthy report which I had been preparing on Hambros management of British export companies in the United States—each one, from motor cars to Wedgewood china, a loss operation—he called in Sir Charles who stood before him. "Charles," he said,

"I've always had the impression that you were an utter idiot. Thibaut's report has now proved it." I then knew that when Charles succeeded Olaf as chairman, my days as adviser to the bank would surely end.

When Rosamond and I came to London, Olaf would lend us his flat at the foot of St. James Street in the apartment house next to the Queen Mother's palace looking out on Hyde Park. He had a cook and a valet there who would immediately unpack me, press my suits and shine my shoes to a mirror-like polish. Only then would the cook be allowed to unpack Rosamond's bags. "Why can't we go to London more often?" she would say, appreciative of the two servants who were there to take care of us.

One day Olaf said to me, "In the United States, Thibaut, you have no bankers. In my bank, if my managing directors or their deputies don't lose money on a bad loan from time to time, I replace them. If you don't take risks, you don't make money. The essence of a good banker is to know when to take a risk and when not to." He then told me the story of his grandfather Hambro who had been chairman in Queen Victoria's day.

"One wintry Friday morning in the 1860s my grandfather was sitting in this office when his elderly secretary came in to tell him that a man was outside asking to see him. 'His collar is very dirty,' she said. 'What's more he has not shaved, he smells badly and on top of that he's a foreigner,' she added. 'Should I call the guard?' 'No, I'll see him.' My grandfather received him very politely. He asked him what he wanted, and was told he needed three million pounds sterling 'That is a great deal of money,' my grandfather said, 'and when will you need my answer?' 'I must have your answer by tomorrow morning.' 'And if I give you the money, what will you do with it?' 'I will be able to pay my troops who have not been paid in three months.' 'What will they do then?' 'They will throw the Austrians out of Italy,' was the reply. 'My dear sir, you are tired. I will send my carriage to take you to a comfortable house which we own. There you can bathe and refresh yourself. You will come back tomorrow at 11 o'clock and I will give you my answer.' My grandfather then sent telegrams—there were no telephones then—to all his correspondents on the continent. The next morning at 11 he arranged for the man to get his money. The man was Count Cavour, the Italian leader who created modern Italy and put the House of Savoy on the throne. He paid his troops and they in turn beat the Austrians. The result was the creation of the kingdom of Italy. We were always bankers for the Scandinavian countries, but as a result of my grandfather's decision, we have ever since been bankers for the government of Italy—even during the brief period after the war in 1945 when there was a Communist government. We have made a hundred times what we risked losing then. My grandfather was a banker."

But Olaf was a wily old fox. What he didn't tell me then, and I learned only later, was that the Bank of England had guaranteed Hambros against loss on its U.S. operations. It was too important to continue sales of British goods in the American market to earn needed dollars. Hambros was taking no risk here because it supplied an essential financial service, which quite obviously the government did not wish revealed.

Men like Olaf are no longer in charge of British merchant banks. The banks have become much larger, bureaucratized. The system has changed, as have methods of banking. Was it better then? I believe so. But then the same is true not only of merchant banking but of law, medicine and science. Only now are we beginning to see a return to entrepreneurship and individual initiative. Let's hope it will last. If this book is a hymn to anything, it is to the glorification of individual initiative, rather than the deadliness of group decision-making. Man was made to exercise his extraordinary faculties with full freedom of individual expression, not to meet established criteria or accommodate conformity. This can be true even of our government leaders. Two of our most successful presidents in the 20th century were undoubtedly Franklin Roosevelt and Ronald Reagan. Neither was recognized for his intellectual capacity. Both were pragmatic politicians very well aware of the psychology of the public and what it meant to be an American. Each in his own way was an entrepreneur.

My years spent as a legal adviser to Hambros taught me a lesson I should have learned as a child from my grandmother—that the inability of the English and the French to understand each other is enough to test the sweetness of a saint. In the late summer afternoons my cousins and I would study the Bible with my grandmother. This Bible was in two huge illustrated picture albums, one for the Old and one for the New Testament, published from woodcuts at the beginning of the 19th century. As she explained the simplicity of Catholic dogma, as illustrated in the New Testament, she would speak in an uncharacteristically acid tone about English Protestantism adopted to suit Henry VIII's proclivity for marrying his mistresses. These outbursts of a saintly woman who herself had an English grandmother troubled my cousins and me, even though we were only children. While she immediately caught herself,

Foreign Adventures

Why aren't the English like the French?

the reference to "perfidious Albion," as Great Britain was known to her detractors, could not be erased from our minds. Loyalties in England, I discovered later, are quite unlike loyalties in France. During the war, I never ran across abuses of enlisted men anywhere as I saw in the British army. Even before the Revolution, France was not a class society. And the abuses of the Industrial Revolution, bad as they were, were as nothing compared to those of 19th century Britain. To the French, the English are devious, never reveal their sentiments, loyal only when it suits their interests, fair-weather friends. To the English, the French are unpredictable and unreliable. They spend their lives eating, drinking, and womanizing. Above all, they are highly emotional romanticists, unable to understand rudimentary self-interest. It is hard to pinpoint where this lack of mutual understanding comes from, but it is very deep. I remember well, from my days of teaching at the Management Center in Geneva, that in any group of senior executives, from twenty different countries or so, there were only two groups that you could not mix in a seminar without quickly creating tension: one was the French and the English; the other the Russians and the Israelis. Between Germans and French, no problem; between Israelis and Arabs, no problem either. Why between the French and the English? After careful reflection, I believe the basic lack of understanding comes from the fact that the English are historically Scandinavians, whereas the French are Latins. Harold was a Dane; and the Normans were descendants of the Scandinavians who had seized areas of the French coast and settled there. They were "sea" people, not "land" people and their French "culture" was only a veneer. All I know is my own experience. My friend, Bill Shriver, who helped me write the report for Hambros, was in London one day to review files at the bank and found an entry written by one of the partners, saying, "It is necessary to have Thibaut come over for several days to report because it always takes a period of time to understand what he is trying to tell us."

My experience with the English managing directors of Hambros was a revelation. It made me realize that, although by discipline and thought processes, I was an American, nevertheless, in terms of both emotion and logic I was thoroughly French.

I would be sitting in my office in mid-town Manhattan with thirty corporate financings, mergers or reorganizations facing me, when a cable would come from Hambros asking me if I could manage to be in London two days later. I would switch my calendar around and cable back that I would arrive three days hence. The car would have been sent to fetch me and when I arrived at the Savoy—owned by Hambros—I would find a note from Sir Charles saying, "So nice to know that you are in London, Thibaut. Do come to lunch tomorrow. We are having some foreign bankers and the American ambassador. If you are free, perhaps you might come a little earlier, say 11 o'clock. Greatly looking forward to seeing you." It would then be 11 o'clock the previous morning and I would have rushed over unnecessarily. Politeness, tops; consideration, negligible.

The discussions, when we did get together, always approached the subject at hand very indirectly. It might even take a day or two to come to any conclusions which might guide me on my return to New York. There would be many persons to be involved in the decision-making process if Olaf was not there to take charge, and it gave me the opportunity to study loyalties among the ruling class in England. The foremost loyalty of course is to one's father, then to one's friends at Eton or Harrow, then those at Oxford or Cambridge, then in descending degree: mother, wife, sisters, other well-bred Englishmen, other English, and finally foreigners. Relationships with brothers always seemed special in England because of the rule, totally absent in any other country that I know of, that the eldest receives all of the inheritance including land and social position, while other children are left pretty much to strike out on their own. I have always thought that it was this rule of primogeniture which was responsible for creating the empire on which the sun never set. Younger sons, after receiving the same excellent education, were sent out in the army, the navy, the church, or colonial service abroad. Human mortality being unaware of the system, younger brothers, married to new blood, might inherit the title and position of the deceased elder brother. In this way, new ideas, experience and bloodlines were brought into the power structure. The system was unfair but certainly beneficial for the country.

When Olaf died, the person I most closely worked with was Harry Sporborg, the only partner who was not a member of the Hambro family. He had been a well-known solicitor whose principal client was a family which controlled the steel business in England. The company chairman, late in life, had taken up flying and with his wife had perished in the channel on his way to the continent. Harry, as executor and trustee, took charge of the business. Shortly thereafter, he was invited by Hambros to join the firm as a partner. He was an excellent addition. As Olaf would say: "He is eminently sound." This was a particular British accolade. A man might be brilliant, but if he was not sound, one should beware of him. Next to Godliness, came soundness. I think of Jimmy Carter who was reputed to be brilliant but was certainly not sound.

One of my most memorable experiences with Hambros occurred when I invited Harry and his wife to be my guests at the Travelers Ball in Paris. Some years earlier, I had been prevailed upon by one of my partners to become a member of the Travelers in Paris. Situated in a rococo house built by a German princeling for his mistress in the 1870s, it was conveniently located on the Champs Elysees. It has one of the most beautiful marble staircases in Paris and a solid silver bathtub at one end of the dining room. In immediate post World War II Paris it had convenient bedrooms at a time when these were scarce. It was truly a replica of men's clubs in London with strict rules to exclude women except for the ball held each June.

Harry and I had lunch together on the day of the ball. Not knowing what would happen, I had decided to take him to a small restaurant not far from my office in the Place Vendome, Chez Bosc, in the Rue Duphot. I often ate there with a banker friend from Morgan's because the food was good and it was a quiet place to talk. Mme. Bosc, the owner, was well over six feet tall, always dressed in black, and carried her white hair in a tight bun. What was most remarkable about her was the size of her hands. She could bring "deux couverts" and a bottle of wine easily in those enormous "paws." We often used to joke about what Mme. Bosc might do in an alley on a dark night. Harry took one look at her as we entered the restaurant, turned pale, showed his embarrassment, and I thought for a moment he was going to ask to be taken elsewhere. She looked at him without a sign of recognition that I could notice.

Sitting in my office after lunch, Harry told me the story of Mme. Bosc: "During the war," he said, "I was based in the New Forest, which you will remember from *Robin Hood* is that dense forest area near Nottingham. There I was in charge of all British intelligence operations on the continent. Part of my job was to arrange the escape routes for British and Allied flyers shot down over Europe. Our best agent in Paris was Mme. Bosc. One evening shortly after curfew three German Gestapo officers banged on the door of the restaurant where we just had lunch. There was a colonel, a major, and a young lieutenant. Mme. Bosc told them she was not allowed to serve anyone after curfew, that she had little food left, and would they come back the next day. They insisted. The colonel made it clear he made the rules in Paris. He was hungry, and she had best let them come in if she valued her liberty. So she let them in, gave them a table and promised bread, soup, and eggs.

Mme. Bosc turns down a decoration.

She was worried because in the medieval cellars under her restaurant three English escapees were hidden behind a locked door. When the colonel asked for wine, she said, 'You will have to select what you want.' The lieutenant was sent down, followed shortly thereafter by Mme. Bosc who strangled him with those hands you saw. When he didn't return, the major was sent down, and he met the same fate. Then she did the same to the colonel, taking him quietly from behind as he sat there. Then she fetched the flyers and they buried the bodies in the cellar. The Germans never found out what had happened to the three men because they never traced them to the restaurant. At the end of the war, I was sent to Paris to confer the Cross of Mary and George on Mme. Bosc. I walked over from the embassy with the decoration and arrived at the restaurant in the late afternoon. Mme. Bosc was alone, putting out place settings for dinner. It was dark outside the restaurant and she had on that same black dress. 'You cannot come in, Monsieur,' she said. I explained that I had been sent by Her Majesty the Queen to confer a great honor upon her because of the services she had rendered British airmen during the war. 'Keep your medal, Monsieur. I don't like the English. I only disliked the Germans more because they were occupying my country. Now go away, and don't come back.' That was my experience with Mme. Bosc until today."

All those who were taken to Paris as children in the 1920s remember with nostalgia the hotel where they stayed at the time. To me it had been the Vendome because my father's office had been where IBM is today and we conveniently stayed at the hotel above. To Harry, it was the Hotel des Saint Peres on the Left Bank where I had often stayed when Rosamond and I went to Paris on holiday in the 1940s. Then, unlike today, it was small and run-down, but both management and guests seemed to have that special rapport which comes from experiencing an adventure together. For those who stayed there, it was a time filled with memories.

It was then that Harry told me how much he liked the Hotel des Saint Peres. "I tried the Ritz once, across from your office. But the doorman kept asking me which Latin American country I came from. He couldn't believe an Englishman would be able to afford the Ritz. I didn't feel welcomed there." Harry Sporborg, that same afternoon that we were discussing Mme. Bosc, quite unwittingly helped me understand an event which occurred during the war and which helps explain the difference between the English and the French that I have alluded to. Just before the war had broken out in Europe, I had met and become a friend of a Frenchman who was slightly older than I. He went back and forth frequently between Paris and New York and was equally at home in both cities. Well-born, well educated, with a successful future ahead of him, he had been caught up in the war in its earliest days and fought bravely in the French army. Demobilized, he had become, under the name of Charlot, one of the few key operatives in the Resistance in France. His group's specialty was blowing up German ammunition trains, a particularly dangerous occupation. He had become a legend because of his daredevil tactics. He had what the French call *panache*. It gave other operatives a feeling that somehow the country would still recover its self-respect. Then one night the Germans, having been advised in advance of an operation which he had organized, seized Charlot and executed him, after the most terrible torture, to make him reveal the names of his associates and his connections with his sources of supply in England. Charlot never gave any information and no one seemed to know who had denounced him to the enemy. Harry knew, and from him I now found out without revealing my interest. "Yes," he said, "I knew the work Charlot was doing. He was a very brave young man indeed. But he was taking too many risks and in my view jeopardizing the networks I was trying to create. So I let the Germans know where to find him."

I have often wondered if the French would have done the same to an English agent of theirs operating in English territory. Certainly the Russians treated Burgess and McLean quite differently.

X

A GIFT OF PROPHECY

I HAD FIRST RUN ACROSS Mrs. Mackensen back in the early '50s when, as a young corporate lawyer, I became adviser and counsel to the scion of a family that controlled the Sherman Hotel in Chicago, as well as the Ambassadors East and West. The first was a large convention hotel *par excellence;* the other two were sophisticated and residential. My client, who was more interested in decorating than making money, did not care for Pat Hoy, the general manager of the combined hotel operation and this feeling was heartily reciprocated. My task was therefore to act as a mediator, prevent my client from redecorating the Ambassador East yearly and try to keep directors' meetings focused on results rather than architectural redesign. This required more visits to Chicago than I liked and dinners with Pat Hoy, the general manager, where the discussion inevitably centered on Chicago politics and the art of booking lucrative conventions into the Sherman Hotel. Pat was the typical successful manager of a major convention hotel, shrewd, unflappable, ambitious, politically very astute, and a master showman. In Chicago, a city known for the savvy of its politicians, Pat was recognized as a master of the art.

The hand doesn't lie.

To please Pat, I had agreed to attend the final lunch of one such convention which several businesswomen—largely from the Midwest—had been attending. The principal speaker was a woman well known to the participants and much admired as someone who had an uncanny gift of prophecy.

I was surprised by how young the speaker was. I would have guessed she was no more than 35, with an attractive personality, and an unusually well-modulated speaking voice. She told a number of stories about her work, carefully pointing out—which appealed to the women who were listening to her—that she had been given the gift of looking into the future by our Lord, and therefore she tried to treat it with great responsibility and care.

It was later when she was answering questions after her talk that she suddenly riveted the attention of her listeners. One member of the audience had asked her what seemed to be a rather inane question:

"Do you ever find that in reading someone's future you see in that person's hand something so terrible that you simply don't want to divulge what you are seeing?"

She answered the question by telling a story which remains clearly in my mind even today, some fifty years later.

"I was speaking to an audience much like yours. In fact, it was in this same hotel not so very long ago. When I had finished speaking and lunch was over, a young woman came up to me and said: 'I really need to speak to you. Do you think you could take a few minutes to give me a reading?' She seemed so charming and so distraught that I told her that while I make it a rule never to do this because I need to relax after a luncheon talk in order to be rested and have a clear head before giving anyone a reading, I would nevertheless make an exception for her. If she wanted to, she could come up to my room in a half hour and I would spend a few minutes with her.

"She arrived in my room promptly. Since I had no table and no special lamp to light up her hand, she sat on the bed and I used the night table light holding her right hand in mine and trying to make her relax. I assumed her hand would reveal to me why she was so anxious to see me.

"You will understand now why your question was so prescient and why it is sometimes so difficult to speak of what the hand tells you. 'I'm sorry, my dear, but I cannot read your hand because it tells me that two months ago you died and yet here you are very much alive.'

"The young woman then told me a most remarkable story:

" 'My husband and I live outside of Chicago in Winnetka. We haven't been married more than a few years and are very much in love. We had hoped for some time that we would have a first child. A year ago, I, at last, became pregnant, but when the baby was due, all sorts of problems arose. My husband had been born at home and he had insisted that his child be born in the same house which we had inherited from his parents. My doctor had agreed to this even though during the pregnancy, it became obvious that I would have a difficult time delivering the baby. When the time came and I went into labor, every imaginable difficulty occurred and the baby was stillborn. Worse yet, I lost a great deal of blood and was on the verge of going into a coma. It was around nine at night. What I do remember was that the doctor took my husband aside and I could hear him whisper: "I don't believe your wife will make it through the night but if she does, we may be able to save her."

" 'Now our house is on a corner and I could see the street lamp's glow through the window. Because I loved my husband and wanted so to live, I determined that come what may, I would keep looking at that light in order to last out the night. Several times I felt myself doze off, but out of sheer determination I managed to keep my focus on that light. When the doctor came back early in the morning, he said to my husband: "I don't know why or how, but your wife has lasted through the night and she will be saved." '

"There are times like that where the hand shows what should happen, but the event doesn't occur. In time this young woman's hand will change. We must always remember that our Lord has given us a free will. When we exercise it, the future course of our life may change and the hand will reflect such a change. That is why the gift I have been given is so delicate. It is a great gift and I hope and trust that I have used it wisely."

When she had finished giving this answer, there was a hush over the ballroom where she had been speaking. The mistress of ceremonies took over and the lunch ended.

Some months later, I thought of Mrs. Mackensen again. I had always tried to stick to corporate law because I never liked to get involved in peoples' personal problems. Above all, I tried my best to avoid women as clients. However, from time to time I have found myself acting as a divorce adviser for friends who should never have become husband and wife. In addition, I have twice broken my own rule about representing a woman. Both times I regretted my decision.

I had a friend in New York named Elisa Daggs who was a brilliant career woman. She had been an artist and from sketching in watercolors, had become a fashion designer. From there, she was hired by Conde Nast to be the fashion designer and an executive at *Vogue* magazine. Her business life was a success. She was acclaimed and much admired in that difficult world of fashion. She had many friends and was very much in demand on the New York cocktail and dinner circuit. Her private life, however, was difficult. Her former husband was an unsuccessful artist. They had divorced some years earlier. The child born of the marriage had remained in the mother's custody, but had her father's personality. Mother and daughter quarreled incessantly. I had been asked to find a family in France where the daughter could live while she studied fashion design in Paris. That, too, had turned out badly. Their oldest son had fallen in love with the girl, failed his university entrance exams, and the young girl had had to come back hastily to New York. Unfortunately, the daughter was only 16 and too young to move out on her own. I could sense new troubles ahead between mother and daughter.

To be helpful, I thought of Mrs. Mackensen. Since she lived in New York, it was no great feat to get her number from Pat Hoy. I passed it on to Elisa and suggested she call for an appointment. I then put the matter out of my mind congratulating myself on having done a friend a favor.

A few days later, my phone rang in the middle of the night.

"You bastard, how could you do such a thing to me?" It was the voice of Elisa and she was obviously very unhappy.

"What happened?" I asked sleepily.

"I went to see that woman of yours," she said. "Do you know what she told me? That Patsevitch (the publisher of *Vogue*) would call me in next Tuesday and fire me."

I didn't know what to say, particularly at four o'clock in the morning.

"What else did she tell you?"

"She said two weeks later, he would call me up, apologize, and offer me a bigger job at the magazine at twice the salary."

"And you called me up in the middle of the night to complain?"

"She said I wouldn't take the job. But I would become editor in chief of *Modern Bride* shortly after that."

"Elisa, it's 4 o'clock in the morning. It sounds like a great future to me. Now let me get some sleep."

It happened just as Mr. Mackensen had predicted. For my pains, I ended up writing two articles for *Modern Bride*—one with Pat Lawford on what qualities one should look for in a wife, the other on how to start a wine cellar with $50. You can see all this took place some years ago. The same wine cellar today would cost $5,000.

The episode reinforced my admiration for Mrs. Mackensen. It also persuaded me to be much more careful in making recommendations to friends in trouble. How many times I have made recommendations to friends and acquaintances that I have regretted later.

It wasn't so long after the episode with Elisa that I found myself again in touch with Mrs. Mackensen. This time, however, it wasn't to help a friend. It was because I myself seemed to have a difficult problem to which I couldn't find a solution.

I was happy with the choice I had made in leaving the Chadbourne firm. I liked the independence that being a partner in a small firm gave me. There was a large enough base of substantial corporate clients who had been represented by George Lewis for many years to lead me to believe that—even though we might eventually lose one or two who might prefer over time to be represented by a much larger firm with a greater diversity of legal talent—by that time, through my own efforts, I would have become counsel to new corporate clients who would more than replace those lost. I was increasingly confident in my own ability to attract legal business. We had plenty of work to do. I also felt that having an office in Paris would prove very helpful, as American corporations were increasingly finding that their business was becoming more international. The demands of international trade required that American corporations establish factories abroad rather than simply distribute their products there. I sensed early that there might be a particular role for me to play here as a corporate lawyer able to think globally instead of just as an American. With this in mind, we had already brought in as partners in New York two highly competent tax attorneys experienced in international tax matters.

In a way my problem was a race against time. Would old George lose corporate clients faster than I could persuade them that I was able to meet their needs or replace them with new clients whom I would have brought into the firm?

It was in this connection that one February day when I had become discouraged I determined that I too would call on Mrs. Mackensen. I neither gave her my name nor explained the reason why I wanted an appointment. She had a small apartment in mid-Manhattan. In the middle of her living room a card table, two dining room chairs and a desk lamp had been arranged. Mrs. Mackensen did not waste time in preliminary conversation.

"I want you to sit right here," she said, pointing to one of the chairs, "and lay your right arm with the hand face up across the card table. Relax, because I will be talking to you for an hour or two."

I did as I was told. With a marker to separate the lines and the lamp head bent low over my hand, she started talking.

"I am not sure whether you are a lawyer or a psychiatrist," she said. "But the reason you came to see me, you can forget about. The man you are so concerned about is your partner, and you are afraid clients will leave because he may make a mistake. But you shouldn't be concerned because he will die in November of this year."

It was then mid-March. George Lewis had a heart attack and died on November 12.

"You have another much more immediate problem. You have a partner in Paris. And he has just fathered a child to one of your clients there. That could turn out to be serious. I would advise you to do something about it."

She was right. On my next trip to Paris, I learned the story over a great dinner and a good bottle of the owner's best Burgundy at our favorite bistro in the Les Halles area. My French partner didn't appear concerned. Nor was he about to marry the lady. Because of my American partners, however, he and I decided it was more important to remain friends than to have a professional relationship. So we wound up the partnership and I lost a wonderful place to stay in the center of Paris in the little square behind the rue de Rivoli where we had both office and residence.

Mrs. Mackensen talked on for a full two hours. On the past, she was remarkable and absolutely correct.

"You are part French," she said. "Your father was born in France of an old noble family and came to the United States with no money to make his career here. He became a very wealthy man but lost everything in the Depression. You put yourself through school, college and graduate school by earning scholarships and working on the side. You had a remarkable war career ending with intelligence and guerilla operations in the coastal region of China. There you met a young woman, a daughter of missionaries, whom you married after the war. You have had three children by her—two boys and a girl. But your marriage will end—whether by death or divorce I am not sure. I see you marrying again but not any person you know today. That marriage will not last, and I see you marrying again for a last time. I also think in time you will occupy an important position in the American government at some part of your life. You will also spend several years on an island somewhere in the Caribbean where you will exercise considerable executive and even political responsibility."

I sat there entranced. There was no way she could have learned anything about me. Mine had been a cold call.

I noticed, however, that as she delved into the future, her predictions were much less specific. After she had finished what she wanted to tell me, I asked her why that was.

"The past is very clear in a person's hand," she said. "And the gaps in what I see will be told me subconsciously by the person I am talking

A Gift of Prophecy

Hearing my own future

285

to. It is this gift of transmission of thought that is truly the gift I have been given. It has nothing to do with me. I am simply a conduit. As I tell you something from the past that I see in your hand, it will trigger your thought processes of recall. I will sense these and pass them on to you. The events, which have made an impression on you, are those I will be made aware of by you and thus be able to pick up in my subconscious. For the future, I am affected by what you hope to do or accomplish as much as what your hand tells me. The further I peer into the future, the less you can tell me because your own desires and goals will change and these will affect the choices you make." She laughed. "People do not realize how often they face a fork in the pathway of their lives. And choice inevitably leads to further choice so that often their original intent will have disappeared. St. Thomas Aquinas once said: 'We never solve our problems. We simply adjust to them.' It is the same way with each of us. We make a conscious decision: to change jobs, to marry or not to marry, to go or not on a given trip, and this decision entails a great many other decisions which will very likely change the direction of our lives. In your case, you have been faced almost constantly with choices you might have made. Your hand is covered with cut-offs, although the direction you wished to follow is quite clear. Your right hand will change considerably in the future as you exercise your freedom of choice. We can exercise it for material success, or for God's or human love, or for other aims, and our lives will forever be changed accordingly. Because of this ability I have been given to respond to thought transference, I am particularly made aware of the likely choices that the person I am talking to may make. I have told you perhaps where you were meant to go, but you may not get there, or not get there directly because of the endless choices you will make in your life."

"But my children," I said. "You have described them perfectly, not only in number and in age, but in personality and character."

"I cannot tell you what will happen to them. It is your analysis of them that is being transmitted to me by you, and what you would wish them to be. To see their future, I would have to be giving them a reading. One cannot see the future through an intermediary."

It was a remarkable experience. Since then, as choices have presented themselves, I have wondered whether these are changes in the road which will be eventually reflected in the lines of my right hand or whether I am more through good fortune than reasoning following in the course that Mrs. Mackensen related to me so many years ago.

A year or so after my visit to Mrs. Mackensen, I began to develop some Latin American business clients in addition to the French firms for which I did international legal work, both in France and in the United States. It had begun through the efforts of the head of an important French family-held textile firm to find a country in the Western Hemisphere where he could establish a factory that would be safe from the Russians if they should sweep across Europe, thus enabling the family to rebuild its fortunes in the New World. As a result of this first exploratory trip throughout the Latin-American region and the ultimate negotiations for this client who had decided to establish the plant in Pereira, Colombia, I began to advise other companies in South America.

A Gift of Prophecy

I decided that I had better learn Spanish again. I had learned it in Panama when stationed there at the start of World War II, but had long since forgotten it. So I set out to find someone with whom I could practice my conversational Spanish for an hour or so a week after work. I was lucky enough to find a very nice and very cultured Mexican woman temporarily down on her luck who was willing to listen patiently to my halting speech in her language and gradually add to my vocabulary. Carmen was ideal for the task. She had been Mexico's public relations consultant in New York. In a change of administration she had lost her highly paid position and was giving lessons to persons like me, pending a turn in her tides of fortune. As we conversed and exchanged ideas, we became friends.

Carmen's passion in life was psychics. The worse her financial situation became, the more she sought out fortunetellers who might tell her when her own situation might change. At our sessions of Spanish, we often talked about what some astrologer or palmist might have said to her the previous week. Each week, it seemed, she checked with the Mexican Consulate or the United Nations to see if some need for her talents might not be opening up. I felt very sorry for her. So, of course, one evening I told her about Mrs. Mackensen in my schoolboy Spanish. Her switch to English and her entreaties were immediate. So I gave her the phone number before I left. It was a Thursday. When I came back to her apartment the following Tuesday afternoon for another lesson, there were suitcases strewn all about her one-room studio.

"Tell me what has happened," I said, sensing that my Spanish lessons were probably at an end.

"You cannot imagine what has happened, Thibaut. I did what you told me and called your Mrs. Mackensen. It was extraordinary. She understood my problem without my having to tell her anything. 'You are either from Mexico or Costa Rica,' she told me. But that she could tell from my accent. 'But,' she continued, 'you are very depressed, and you should not be, because tomorrow morning you will have a call from your sister, who will tell you she is in New York for a few days. She will invite you for lunch at the Plaza, and you will go. There she will tell you, 'Carmen, you look tired and depressed. Pack your bags and come back with me to spend the summer at our hacienda. It will do you good and you can come back in September refreshed and with a new and different outlook.'"

"I can see you have accepted your sister's invitation to go to Mexico for the summer," I said. "What else did Mrs. Mackensen tell you?"

"It is very detailed but very complicated," Carmen told me. "She said that coming back in the plane from Mexico City, I would feel this swelling in my throat; that I would come back to the studio on a Saturday evening with the swelling getting larger and larger; that I would be panicked and try to reach the doctor all day Sunday, sure that I had a tumor and would die. The doctor would see me Monday morning and operate on Tuesday, but the tumor would not be what I thought and would be benign. She told me I would, a few months later, leave New York and go to Washington to work for the O.A.S.; that I would marry a diplomat down there and go and live in South America."

"Carmen, except for the operation, that sounds wonderful. You will forget your Thibaut and his need for Spanish and look forward to your days as a great diplomat's lady."

"No, Thibaut, I will not forget you. But your Mrs. Mackensen may be as wrong as all the others. I'm sure we can start our lessons together in the fall. But the rest will do me good, and I look forward to being back in Mexico with my family and friends—and waited on, as they do so well in Mexico," she added.

And so Carmen left. I did not hear from her if she returned in September and didn't try to reach her, having other matters on my mind. Then one day—I think it was in November—Carmen called me and asked me if I would take her to lunch. I told her, of course, that I would be delighted. I asked her to come down to my office the following day at noon, and that I would take her to my club which was upstairs in the same building.

She arrived looking very chic in a dark suit with a little hat with a veil, and Hermes scarf wrapped high around her neck.

When she sat down, the scarf slipped and all I could see was an ugly red scar which disfigured her neck from ear to ear. As I looked at her as we were speaking, it was all I could do not to focus eyes on that terrible wound. I tried to make light of it, but when a woman's physical beauty has been so badly harmed, what can one say that will be believed? The story was just as Mrs. Mackensen had predicted. Nor had Carmen's finances improved, even though her sister had met the medical expenses involved.

"Come, Carmen. We will have a drink and a good lunch. You are my friend, and I will help you out with a loan, which I can afford, and when things turn around, as they will, you can pay me back. You are alive and well. The rest is unimportant."

I did not see Carmen again after our lunch together. I had felt so sorry for her that when we went down to the office after lunch, I gave her a check for twice the amount I had planned. Three days later, I received a nice note from her, then silence. It was only a year or so later that a Latin-American friend from Washington told me that she had been given a job at the O.A.S. and had moved down there, but she had not stayed there very long, since she had married a diplomat from one of the South American countries, a member of the O.A.S., and had gone back with him. She did not repay my loan, but then, I really hadn't expected her to. One must always expect such loans to turn out to be gifts.

So ends my story of Mrs. Mackensen, begun with a lunch in Chicago and ended with a lunch at my club in New York.

I later heard from someone who had tried to find her that Mrs. Mackensen had disappeared. She had become blind. The great gift that God had given her had been taken away. Like all such persons she was very religious. One can only hope that somehow she was rewarded when her gift was taken away.

Should one believe that there are people who can see into the future? Is thought transference as possible as Mrs. Mackensen had indicated to me, and as these three true stories that I have just recounted appear to verify? I don't know, but I am willing to accept what I have seen.

My mother once told me a similar story: She and my father were driving down to Palm Beach for a stay with friends in the winter of 1927. In those days, one had to drive all the way on Route 1. It was an arduous trip, going through every town and city along the way. One morning, as they were driving through St. Augustine, just below Jacksonville in northern Florida, my father had suddenly turned very pale. He told my mother: "Marie, there is something very evil here. Let's drive through and get out of the area as quickly as possible." As soon as they were through the city, he regained his calm.

A Gift of Prophecy

The following year, they had been invited on a bird shoot at a castle near Toledo in Spain. As they left Toledo, my father had turned to my mother, who was again driving, and said to her: "You will come to a crossroads a little way from here, turn right and come to high gates. There is a long drive up to the castle. There our host will put us, I think,

My father meets his past.

in a room I remember well, although I don't know why." My father then gave a detailed description of the castle they were going to and the bed-room in question. Their host who was there to greet them showed them to that very room. In the course of the next few days, my father had a chance to ask his host if anyone in his family had ever gone to Florida.

"Yes," the Duke had replied. "I had an ancestor far back at the start of the 17th century who accompanied Ponce de Leon in his discovery of Florida. My ancestor was killed in a battle with the Indians of the region near a little town called St. Augustine."

My father was always convinced after that that in a previous re-incarnation, he had been that man. I did not believe him, but having studied the religion of the Cathars in Southwestern France, I used to tell him jokingly that he hadn't made much progress on the path to perfection in those three hundred years if he had gone from being a Spanish Duke to a French-American stockbroker. He didn't think my comment amusing.

The fact of the matter is that any normally sensitive person will run across events in his or her life which have been predicted but cannot be understood. It may be due to thought transference as Mrs. Mack-ensen said. It may be simply due to karma, in the Japanese sense, that events occur in one's life because they are ordained from above. My wife, Mariana, was warned she would come into my life. My own ex-perience with Bobby Kennedy spoken of in another part of this story is but another instance of the same phenomenon. I am quite incapable of understanding why such events happen. But I have seen enough to accept that they do occur.

XI

INDOCHINA—1950–54

*I*N *1950, AT THE START* of the Korean War, General William Donovan, director of the Office of Strategic Services during World War II, made a speech at the Naval War College on strategy in the Pacific. He spoke of the advisability of involving Chiang Kai-shek and the Chinese troops in Taiwan to assist the United States if the Communists on the mainland should decide to intervene in Korea. "You must get hold of one of the officers who worked for the OSS in China," he said. "He knows the coast of China like the back of his hand and could organize any landings there you might want to orchestrate. This man should be brought back into active service."

Colonies are no longer possible.

The following week I received a visit from two admirals who asked me to come back into the Navy. It was two months too late to order me back. My appointment as a lieutenant commander USNR had expired, and they could not call me back except in a time of general mobilization. I had respectively declined. I thought this was the end of the matter. I was wrong.

The State Department a few weeks later invited me to come down to Washington to discuss my availability to undertake a mission to Indochina. John Foster Dulles, the secretary of state, and others in the Department of State saw the Korean War as a vast Communist conspiracy to extend this alien philosophy to other parts of the Far East. This so-called "domino theory" was popular in Washington at the time. The British were taking bold steps to prevent Malaysia from becoming Communist. Could the Americans play a helpful role in keeping Ho Chi Min and the Communists from taking over Indochina? William Bullitt, former ambassador to the Soviet Union, was spoken of as able to play such a role. Someone else had suggested me because of my experience during the war in China.

The State Department had decided that there was a high likelihood that the French would lose the war in Indochina. The day of colonial empires was over. Countries wanted their freedom. This should not mean, however, that they need adopt this alien philosophy of Communism. The United States could play a role here if it was careful and worked with the French and not against them in helping a new national government in Indochina get rid of this foreign Communist-led independence movement. In hindsight, it seems obvious that this project could not succeed. But in the immediate post-war years, with American confidence in its ideas and its power very high, it did not appear as far-fetched as it might today. Are we not today similarly trying to convince ourselves that we can effectively bring about liberation and democracy in poorer and less-developed countries in different parts of the world?

Substitute "Moslem fundamentalism" for Communism and the parallel is frightening. It is difficult for the United States to learn that we cannot save the world from its own illusions.

The plan decided upon by Secretary of State John Foster Dulles envisioned that it might be possible to turn a French colonial war into a struggle between those Vietnamese who believed in democracy and the Communists. Vietnamese "irregulars" trained by Americans would play a leading role. The Americans selected would have had guerilla warfare experience in the Far East during the war. They would train the Vietnamese, particularly the so-called "Montagnards"—the Meos, the Nungs, the White and Black Thais and other mountain tribes—in jungle warfare tactics. These Vietnamese troops led by Americans would then be turned over to the French high command who would fit these irregular units into their military field strategy.

It was a complicated plan because it would involve a treaty to be negotiated between France, the United States and the Vietnamese government of Bao Dai, to be followed by the establishment by the Americans of a training camp somewhere in Indochina where the Vietnamese would be trained and, finally, the establishment of areas of responsibility between the French military and the "irregulars"—Vietnamese trained and led by American military officers. I had been selected because I had the Far Eastern military experience which was needed. The American ambassador to France would oversee the operation from Paris and Lieutenant Colonel Richard Stillwell, temporarily attached by the Pentagon to the CIA, would supervise the American military activities. He was an experienced military officer from years of combat experience during World War II.

The French had installed Bao Dai as emperor in Indochina. Unfortunately, although he was the head of the royal family of Annam, his appeal to the Vietnamese was very limited. His links were to France; his advisers were Vietnamese who had served in the French banks in Hanoi and Saigon. It was not that Bao Dai under other circumstances might not have managed to create a love for himself among his countrymen since he was extraordinarily brave, a world-class hunter, and descended from kings who had ruled large parts of the country for many generations. Additionally, many of his advisers were honest and able men.

Malaysia during this same period of time was being saved by the British government from a Communist takeover, through a combination of the use of force and an accommodation to the country's nationalist aspirations. Would the same policy serve in Indochina? During my days on the border between China and the Tonkin Provinces of Indochina in 1945, I had had communications with Vietnamese nationalist leaders, including Ho Chi Minh, a man of ability and integrity. When the war ended, the British at first wouldn't allow the French back. Then when the French did come back, the government had one set of ideas, the military another. Slowly, but irrevocably, relations between the French and the Vietnamese had worsened until military action seemed the only solution. To the French civilians who returned after six years of war and deprivation in Europe, it seemed like an opportunity to pick up again the good life they had led in Indochina before 1939, growing and sending to France the produce of an essentially rich country. But the Chinese, who had settled in the country as merchants, had now become the go-betweens among the French businessmen and the Vietnamese farmers who produced the rice, rubber and other products for export. The native population was hardworking, but not politically aggressive. Who would have thought that such a people would fight for forty years to establish their nation and in the process defeat the French, the Chinese in their midst and, of course, the Americans, at an incredible cost in lives and in property? One can only be filled with respect for a population, which endured so much for the sake of freedom.

There are times when it is much better not to know what is going to happen. The fall of 1950, when I began to go down to Washington to be briefed on the situation in Indochina, was one of those times. The material which I was given to read by the State Department was either hopelessly out of date, irrelevant or taken from the *Illustrated Daily News* or from French magazines commenting on life in the colony. It was totally useless information with which to brief a man who was supposedly being sent out to negotiate a treaty between France, the government of Indochina headed by Bao Dai, and the United States. I secured what pertinent information I could get and returned to New York, where I called General Donovan and asked if I could come down to see him in his office.

When I met with him, I gently pointed out that in a certain way he was responsible for the position in which I found myself, because of his speech at the war college. I also explained to him that after considering Bill Bullitt, former ambassador to Moscow, for this job, they had decided to send me even though I knew little of diplomacy and had operated in the Far East strictly as a military officer. Donovan told me that in his office he had voluminous OSS files on various countries, including Indochina, and would be glad to arrange with his librarian for me to work there and brief myself on who was trustworthy and who was not in that country, but on one condition: that I was not to reveal what was in the library and what I had learned to anyone in the State Department. It was a most unusual request. I explained to him that I had been called to Washington by John Foster Dulles to go on this mission, and that I would appreciate it if he would call Mr. Dulles and tell him his condition. To my surprise, he immediately asked his secretary to get Dulles on the phone and proceeded to tell him the condition he had put to me. This did not seem to cause Dulles any problem. I spent the next week in General Donovan's air-conditioned library in one corner of his law office studying records and making copious notes. It was a curious exercise. Information about Japanese agents who had been assigned to Indochina during the war was reasonably detailed, but there was little about French or Vietnamese collaboration, about the political or economic conditions within the country, or about the personalities of the French or the Vietnamese who occupied positions of authority in the country. I was really no farther along than when I had started. The agency data in Washington was also of little help. It was as though Indochina had disappeared off the political map from 1940 to 1944. The State Department didn't seem to be concerned. Their stock answer to my questions was always: "You'll find all that out when you get to Saigon." The department did insist, however, that I spend several days in Paris to be briefed by the French government and its intelligence services. The embassy in Paris was notified of my coming.

It seemed to me that my wife was the only person who appeared to take my mission seriously. With her background of having been in China during the war and her knowledge of my activities there, she hastened to the world's most renowned department store for sportsmen—Abercrombie & Fitch. There, as was the custom in those days, she was greeted by a man dressed in a tailcoat who sent her to the gun department.

"I want to get my husband a bulletproof vest," she said to the startled employee who greeted her.

"He is going hunting with a few friends?"

"No. He is about to go on a very dangerous mission for our government."

A few days later a twenty-five pound bulletproof vest was delivered to our apartment. I was made to swear that I would take it with me and wear it on any trips into the countryside. This was long before lightweight composite materials had been developed. When I arrived in Paris, I stayed at the Hotel Meurice. I have often wondered what the chambermaid did when she found my bulletproof vest in the wastepaper basket. I have stayed clear of that hotel ever since. A week later, however, when I found myself with three companions underneath a Citroen pinned down by machine gun fire, I thought what a fool I had been to break my promise. And I even had worn the damn thing getting on and off the plane to Paris because I was only allowed forty pounds in my suitcases!

The American chief of mission in Paris in 1950, who subsequently became one of the United States' most respected ambassadors to the Soviet Union, was "Chip" Bohlen. He accompanied me on my visits to the French foreign office, explained much better than I would ever have been able to do just what my mission to Indochina was intended to accomplish, and made it possible for me to get the detailed briefing that I needed to get from the French government. I had learned during the war in China what a mistake it is to send on a mission to a given country a person whose father or grandfather was a national of that country. My friend in the OSS in China, who was half-Chinese but an American citizen, had a very difficult time in China because the Chinese did not accept that he was an American. I had a similar problem throughout my involvement in Indochina. This is, unfortunately, a mistake which the American government makes all too frequently. They will send an Italian-American as ambassador to Rome, an Irish-American to Dublin, a German-American to Bonn, and an Afro-American to black Africa. This policy, popular with the nominee and the press in the United States, makes the envoy's job much more difficult than it need be because it leads the government of the country to which he is sent to think that it can more easily be made to respond to American pressure through the ambassador. That was certainly the case with me.

Because my father was French and my family well known in France, in many ways my acting on behalf of the American government could be regarded in the French Foreign Ministries as some sort of disloyalty to France—if not treason.

Representatives of the American government abroad should always epitomize the qualities and talents that make foreigners look up to the United States: a professional degree from one of our major universities, a directness, a generosity of spirit, an appreciation of foreign culture, a capability of speaking the native language, a successful non-governmental career. Joe Rodgers was a great ambassador to France in Reagan's second term because he seemed to the French to be the typical "good" American: direct, open-minded, successful in his business, willing to learn, appreciative of French culture, humorous and humble about not being able to converse well in the language. My job was particularly delicate because my mission was more military than diplomatic, and I represented a country that was quite openly against the reimposition of colonial rule in Indochina.

The trip to Indochina in the days when travel was by Lockheed Constellation was a long one, via Rome, Beirut and Karachi. When I got there, I was met at the plane by the deputy head of mission, Ed Gullion, and taken to his house. Gullion, who later was to be Kennedy's controversial ambassador to the Belgian Congo as it sought to become the independent country of Zaire, was even then a most interesting human being. He was violently anti-French, said exactly what he thought, was brilliant but very cynical, looked more like a movie actor than a diplomat. Only later did I discover why he felt so strongly about France. His father was the only senior American officer during World War I to have been cashiered by the Army at the request of the French military. The boy was brought up in Kansas, well aware of what had happened to his father, and he never forgave the French. It was a great error to have sent such a man to Indochina or later to Zaire.

The American ambassador, on the other hand, who had come from being American ambassador to Lebanon, understood the French problem in Indochina, since Lebanon was a country temporarily turned over to France, as a mandate from the United Nations, until it should be declared ready for independence. He remained non-partisan and objective, and while sympathetic to the aspirations of the Vietnamese to rule their own country, he was respected by the French as an able diplomat. He was as helpful to me as it was possible to be, even lending me the embassy plane when it became important to look at possible sites for the training of the Vietnamese irregulars which were to constitute this special guerilla force. He was too careful a diplomat to tell me what he thought of my mission. Secretary Dulles had, of course, fully briefed him, as had Ambassador Bohlen in Paris. Of the French political or military establishment, he was careful never to criticize or comment on personalities.

Saigon, the capital of Indochina, was in December 1950 a remarkably beautiful city. Not for nothing was it called the "Paris of the East." It had, shade trees lining the streets, and parks like those of southern French cities, a famous riding club with pagodas, tennis courts, restaurants, and just outside the city an excellent golf course. Because of periodic attacks against the French, the road to the golf course was opened every morning shortly after dawn by a 35-ton Sherman tank. Prominently displayed on the walls of the dressing rooms were signs advising the members to be sure to get off the course before dusk because otherwise their safety could not be guaranteed. In 1946, there had been the sad episode of two American officers failing to pay attention to these words of caution and getting shot while playing. One was killed; the other, my friend Joseph Coolidge, barely escaped with his life.

It is hard today to imagine what Saigon was like at the end of 1950. The war in Indochina was not going well. There was no front as such. Grenades were thrown over walls into dinner parties and there were bomb explosions in the streets, plantations attacked and destroyed at night; there were sects trying to create a "third force" to replace both French and Vietminh with Vietnamese leaders bent on dictatorial powers. The country, one could see, was gradually falling into chaos where order could no longer be imposed by civil or military means. Rumors of new insurrections were constant. One didn't know whom one could trust. The maitre d' hotel, the bar man, the taxi driver, the concierge, anyone could be the source of death in the night. To understand Saigon in 1950, you have to reread Graham Greene's *The Quiet American.* That was certainly not what I hoped to be.

What fascinated me, as one who had just arrived, was the casual manner in which the threat of violent death at any moment was accepted by the French population. I had arrived with several letters of introduction to the social community and was quickly adopted by the French businessmen who did not really understand what I was doing there. To their wives it was sufficient that I had come from Paris and had news to impart. One president of a local French exporting concern asked me whether I had come to attend the annual stockholders' meeting. With the business community, politics were far away and there was a social life to lead, with tennis, golf and swimming or riding in the daytime and dinner parties every evening. Receptions and dinners were formal and very French. The women wore long dresses, the men jackets and ties. One was not aware that there was a war going on unless during the evening a hand grenade was tossed over the garden wall where a dinner was being given. At any time in the evening one might hear an explosion followed by the sound of racing police or military cars and then the mournful whistle of the ambulances if people had been hurt. There were three distinct cities in Saigon of the period; the Vietnamese city on the outskirts of town where lights went out by nine o'clock at night, the French city which closed down around midnight and the Chinese city—Cholen—which went on until morning with the residents and any tourists who were there shopping, carrying on business, eating extraordinarily good Chinese food, or gambling at the city's casino which covered one square block and where you could play any game you wished, even one invented for the night. The Chinese love to gamble; I have never quite understood why. In a recent trip to the Far East where there were large Chinese colonies, I made up my mind to find out what in the Chinese temperament made people want to gamble. Curiously, the answer was always the same:

China is an agricultural country, I was told. From time immemorial the Chinese farmer has always worked very long hours in his rice paddy, generally seeing only his family or neighbors from the adjoining farm. He remembers having been taken as a small boy to the festivities of the New Year celebration each year with his father: ten days of eating, drinking, talking to friends one hasn't seen since the prior year, and spending time at the gaming tables. At the end of the celebrations, the Chinese farmer goes back to his farm, generally much poorer than when he came. He doesn't really care whether he wins or he loses, because there is not much to buy anyway if he should win. What he remembers is not that he lost money that he had no use for, but that he saw and exchanged ideas with other men, had a woman or two, drank too much and ate well. Gambling is forever associated in his mind with the few days of joy he has each year.

I did not see very much of the Vietnamese except those who were the managers of French banks. These men had been educated in Paris. Their way of looking at life was French. Yet they were not accepted as equals by the French community.

The Chinese were different. They were forever asking questions, probing questions, which sought to find out how relations between the French and the Americans might be changing, so that they might profit from it. One night I was invited to meet with the Chinese head of the Indochina gambling syndicate in Cholen. His office, most luxuriously appointed *1950–1954* with black silk walls and red and gold lacquer furniture, was located two floors below the casino. There were guards in all the hallways. We sat facing each other while we drank tea. It was very late at night.

"I am told that you have been sent from America to arrange for the withdrawal of the French from Indochina," he said. "What is of interest to me is when the French will withdraw. We will have to make arrangements. And I don't want to be taken by surprise." Of course, I was not able to explain to him that my mission was very different.

I constantly had the impression that the Chinese knew everything that was going on in the city. They controlled the liquor, prostitution, the opium trade and the gambling. They were active in the ports. They were the middlemen between the French exporters of agricultural products and the Vietnamese farmers. They were everywhere, and at the same time, nowhere. It was difficult to find out just what they controlled or who worked for them.

The French intelligence community was another quite separate world. The Americans had a man there at the time, who was attached to the French "Deuxieme Bureau," the French intelligence service. His name was Tom McKay, a former investment banker who had later joined the CIA and was station chief in Saigon. He spoke very good French and put me in touch with his French counterparts. There was one Frenchman in particular whom I immediately liked. He was forthright, extremely knowledgeable and a magnificent storyteller. He would tell me endless stories about Frenchmen sent to remote rubber plantations in the interior of the country. The women of the village would fight among themselves to see which one would be chosen to cook for the plantation manager. If she had a daughter, she would mix love potions out of the most extraordinary materials—herbs, roots, tiger parts, menstrual fluids of the daughter—all of which would be added to the Frenchman's food until he could not do without the girl and brought her to the plantation house as its mistress. There were other stories about the use of tiger whiskers cut very fine so they could not be noticed in food. It might take several months, but eventually the victim would gradually waste away and die. The French Intelligence Service in Saigon had broken the primitive codes used by the Chinese on the other side of the border who supplied arms to the Vietcong fighting the French.

One day the head of this service came to find me and gave me the translation of a message to Ho Chi Minh from the Chinese military command in Nanning, in south China. It apprised him that the Chinese would have to cut the shipments of weapons for an extended time. They had to arm their divisions for action in Korea because they intended to attack MacArthur's forces if he crossed the Yalu River. I took this message to the ambassador, and he forwarded it marked "Urgent—Top Secret" to the State Department for transmittal to MacArthur's command in Korea. We knew the message went through. MacArthur evidently did not believe it, and the consequences became history. I was quite certain that the message from Nanning was authentic. MacArthur was in many ways a great man. But he always reminded me of Colonel Rickenbacker, founder of Eastern Airlines, who would never listen to anyone's advice and was consequently surrounded by second-raters.

The Americans of this period in Saigon were much like the Americans I have run across in other Embassies around the world. There were too many of them, and they didn't mix with the interesting French, the Vietnamese or the Chinese. Because too few of them spoke French, they tended to remain cloistered with each other and consequently did not participate in the life of the city or find out what was really going on. Neither the American Embassy nor the CIA had anyone working the native bazaars for information. As in Iran much later, this meant that no one in the embassy knew what the political sentiments of the local Vietnamese population were.

The French military officers in Saigon kept themselves quite apart from the life of the city. Because my cousin, Christian, Jacques' older brother, had been killed in an ambush by the Vietcong in the center of the country, I was accepted by the military as one who was capable of understanding the position of the French officers who were carrying on a miserable war far from home, with little support or understanding from the public in France, which had little sympathy for a colonial war in the Far East. It took almost a year for Jacques to find his captain brother's coffin when it was sent home for a burial. The Communist stevedores in Marseilles had refused to unload the ship. The dead had disappeared. Jacques found the casket much later in a military warehouse. It was a lonely task, all right, to serve with that French expeditionary force.

It seemed to me that everyone in Indochina was simply wanting for something to happen. It was quite evident that the current situation could not last. The old colonial regime, appealing as it was to the

French, could not be reestablished. The French in the know were busily converting their local currency, the "piastre," into francs or better yet into dollars. Traffic in the currency was a constant reminder of lack of confidence in the future.

The entire Far East, I was convinced, was undergoing a period of great change. I was not concerned about the so-called "domino theory" that so troubled the American State Department. It did not make sense to me that the Chinese Communist regime would spread throughout Southeast Asia. I had never met a Chinese who was not an entrepreneur. How would it be desirable for the Communist regime in China to force a people as cultured as the Chinese to submit blindly to a regime like that in the Soviet Union? How would such a regime ever be able to extend its control to Indochina? The Indochinese had always disliked and feared the Chinese. After all, it was to protect themselves against the Chinese that the Annamite kings in the 1880s had called on the French for help.

After a few days of briefing by the U. S. Embassy staff, the ambassador took me over to introduce me to the French high commissioner, M. Pignon, at his palace. Imagine a Socialist of the MRP party as high commissioner and so representative of the imperial grandeur of France! Pignon was short, with many bad teeth, almost bald, with far too much girth to act in any kingly capacity. He could have been a small-town postmaster, one of those men who stop for a beer on the way home, bowl on Saturday nights, and avoid church on Sunday. He hated his role, gloried in never wearing a tie, wore unpressed khakis and an open shirt, yet whenever he went anywhere, it was in a big car filled with civil and military aides, always accompanied by a motorcycle escort. He was so genuine that I liked him. Who could ever have chosen such a man to play such a role? As head of the French Civilian administration in Indochina, he exercised enormous power. To the Vietnamese nationalists, he had the power that General MacArthur had in post-war Japan. Naturally, he was despised by the military. Yet he was very correct in his relations with them.

He took great pains to introduce me to the French military command in Indochina and explained my mission, asking that I be given a military officer who would be my liaison with the high command in organizing the military part of my mission. With the help of the American ambassador, Pignon would approach the Vietnamese authorities and the emperor's principal advisors to set the groundwork for the proposed treaty of mutual assistance between France, the United

Indochina
1950–1954

In Saigon
there were
multiple
agendas.

States and the government of Indochina. It was agreed that a French paratrooper colonel would be assigned to work with me, that he would accompany me insofar as possible on my trips to the field to organize a training camp for the irregular forces which were to be trained by American officers experienced in jungle warfare, and that he would act as liaison officer for the mission with the French high command. The officer designated turned out to be a knowledgeable and highly qualified person with whom I immediately established a good relationship.

Our work with the French military was on two levels, as it tends to be in any country where covert operations have to be organized and then blended into the regular Army units operating in the field. If the operation was to be successful, it was absolutely necessary that its commanding officer be a man with a vast knowledge of the country, its various ethnic groups, their loyalties and their needs.

In enlisting such a person, I was very fortunate. Through French friends in Saigon, I was introduced to a Colonel Carbonnel, a French officer who had resided in Indochina for many years, and who had all the qualifications I was hoping to find in a proposed leader of irregular forces in Indochina. Colonel Carbonnel during 1945 had held out almost single-handedly against the Japanese in the mountains of Tonkin and Laos after the French army officers had been ordered to barracks and disarmed by the Japanese army. He spoke numerous native dialects and was liked and trusted by the mountain people. Like many of the French military one met in Morocco, Algeria, Lebanon and Indochina, he had studied the culture of the country as a young man in Paris, then came out to Hanoi in the Tonkin where he had immediately become a part of that fascinating but little known culture of Annam. He was always French and a foreigner, but if there was a problem to be solved or a local dispute to be settled, it was he that people turned to. The military sent him to settle disputes in far-off parts of the country, where he learned the customs and dialects of the tribes. His understanding became his passport to restless and warring tribesmen. Had he been a native he would have been a leader of men or a judge. He was that very rare representative of a colonial occupying power, operating much as those extraordinary British "residents" who represented so ably the British government in various parts of India in colonial days. He understood the country far better in many ways than the Vietnamese intellectuals trained in French universities who went back to Vietnam and became its nationalist leaders pledged to an alien Communist philosophy which had roots mainly among the workers and dispossessed of the cities. Had there been a few more Carbonnels in the Indochina of 1950, and far fewer generals from France who had never served in the colonies, how different might have been developments there. Carbonnel was a soldier's soldier, one who would be able to work closely and effectively with the young American officers I would hope to send to Indochina to select and train mountain tribespeople and then lead them in the field. *Indochina 1950–1954*

I am very proud that the program that I had planned with Carbonnel to create a force of "irregulars" from minority groups would later become the "green berets," the American Special Forces of the later war in Vietnam.

Unfortunately, Carbonnel could meet with us, and make recommendations, and show me the route to follow, but he did not make the decisions. It was the French high command that decided where I should go to find the training camp to be established. Their recommendation: a distant circular valley surrounded by mountains where there was a village called Dien Bien Phu.

The ambassador loaned me his plane so the paratrooper colonel and I could pay a visit to this remote area. We landed to find delegations of Black and White Thais waiting to greet us. As I climbed down the plane's ladder—there were no airport facilities—I turned to the colonel and said, "What are they (the High Command) trying to do to us?" The small valley, surrounded by high mountains, was totally indefensible.

"I agree with you. What I don't understand is why they would want to do this."

When I arrived back in Saigon, I went to see High Commissioner Pignon and complained to him that I thought the French high command was trying to sabotage the American effort by recommending that we establish our training camp in an area impossible to defend. He did not seem surprised, but immediately set up a meeting with the general staff in his office. The colonel and I sat on one side of the table. General Salan, who was later to command the French army in Algeria and was then in command in Indochina, General Navarre, his chief of operations, and the secretary of the general staff, Pierre Messmer, sat on the other side. The high commissioner, as usual, didn't waste any words:

"M. de Saint Phalle has come to me with a strong accusation against you, gentlemen. He wants to know why you recommended that he establish the training camp for the American training of irregular forces in Dien Bien Phu, which he considers indefensible. He also tells me that the French officer you have appointed to work with him agrees. This is a serious charge. What have you to say?"

Salan defended Navarre. Navarre explained that because of its remoteness and the hostility of the native populations in the mountains, the enemy would not venture into the area. Four years later, Navarre's hypothesis would be proven thoroughly wrong. Could it be that he really believed what he was saying? With hindsight, I have to believe this, although at the time both the colonel and I saw in the general's recommendations a desire to locate the American-trained irregular force base camp in an area where it would be overwhelmed by Vietcong attack.

There was an interesting side note to this very serious confrontation with the French high command. At one point in the discussion, Messmer interrupted to say something in support of Salan. Pignon turned on him:

"Messmer, you have nothing to say. You are only a clerk here, to record the conclusions which will be reached."

Little did any of us know then that Pierre Messmer would eventually become prime minister of France.

The conclusion to our meeting was a decision to try to locate the training camp off the coast, where in case of need it could be serviced by U. S. submarines. With that in mind, I flew up a few days later to Haiphong, the port south of Hanoi in the north of the country from where we could explore the islands off the coast of Tonkin Province. This area became famous much later in the time of president Johnson and the Tonkin Resolution adopted by the U. S. Congress. In those days, the area north of Haiphong all the way to Moncay on the frontier

with China constituted the Baie d'Along, one of the most beautiful coastlines in the world with islands rising out of a very deep and clear sea—mostly uninhabited islands largely serving fishermen, pirates and smugglers.

Haiphong is the port of Hanoi. In Hanoi, the capital of Tonkin Province, I met the governor of the province and the military commander. Together we went to Haiphong, which is not only a big port but also the principal naval base, where we were received by the naval commander and taken to a lunch at the house of the French civilian advisor to the local Vietnamese authorities in charge of the coastal region from Haiphong to the Chinese border. He had a big house in a part of the city overlooking the sea. It was a clear and beautiful day. I was greatly looking forward to the trip ahead—two weeks in a converted infantry landing craft which would enable us to visit each of the sizeable islands along the coast even if we had to land on a beach. We were to be accompanied by a company of French naval commandos who would assure the vessel's safety because no one seemed to know just what we might find. This was not an area where coastal vessels ventured, and there was no way of knowing to what extent, if any, certain of the islands might be occupied by garrisons put in place by the Chinese Communist government in the same way as they were rumored to have occupied the Spratly Islands further off the coast toward the Philippines.

Even though I was on a military mission, I was to be accompanied by a representative of the Indochinese civilian administration. Bernard was an interesting man. He was tall, very thin and unusually strong. He was thirty-five. He had been in the French colonial administration since before the war and had a most unusual record in the Resistance. When the Germans had defeated the French in the summer of 1940, he was in Marseilles as a junior official waiting to be sent either to Indochina or to Morocco. When the war ended for France, there was little to do in Marseilles in the colonial office. Bernard joined the Resistance and was trained as a saboteur and a gunman. One day he received orders to go to the house of the Vichy-designated mayor of Marseilles who was known to be an active collaborator with the Gestapo and the German military authorities and to gun him down American gangland fashion. He was told that how he did it was his own decision but to do it quickly, because coming events in North Africa made it essential that this man, with his hold over the dock workers and his relationships with certain elements in the French navy based in Toulon and Marseilles, be eliminated promptly. Bernard had waited until the following Sunday. He had then entered the man's apartment with a passkey after bribing the concierge and had gunned him down, with his wife, and their two children as they were having their Sunday lunch. He had escaped into the hills on the coast near Marseilles, but someone had given him away to the Germans. He was captured, taken to Buchenwald, tortured repeatedly, and when the Americans found him at the end of the war, he weighed about eighty pounds. It had taken well over a year of rest, exercise and sheer determination to get him back to approximately normal. Then they had sent him to Indochina. It was a harrowing story. But it was difficult to communicate with him. As a result of what he had done and what had been done to him, he was an observer rather than a participant in life. He had no great interest in what we were doing on this trip, and were it not for the commanding officer of the commandos who was brimming with enthusiasm for the venture, I would not have enjoyed that week as much as I did. The weather was perfect, the sea a deep, deep blue, the islands had very few beaches. They came up out of the deep as though suddenly thrust upward by a volcano. We saw no ships but frequently small junks with faded colored sails, seemingly headed from nowhere and going in no particular direction. We did find an island that seemed to have what I was looking for, a commanding height for radio communication, an abrupt coastline to bring a submarine near shore, no beaches for a hostile landing. I was pleased with what we had found. It seemed to be what I needed as a training area where no one would try to interfere.

When I arrived back in Saigon, I notified the ambassador that I had found the ideal location and was ready to proceed as soon as the treaty was signed. I met with Commissioner Pignon and gave him the same report. I also advised the high command and the colonel, and I worked out a system of supply for the island.

M. Pignon, the high commissioner, had been having trouble persuading the Vietnamese authorities that they should cooperate with the French military. He decided the best way out of the impasse was to send his deputy up to Dalat with me to call directly on the emperor. The American ambassador agreed. M. Garnier and I left the next day for Dalat. I was glad to get out of Saigon for a few days. The high commissioner's residence in Dalat was a fourteen-room mansion, an exact duplicate of the French Embassy in Belgrade and was deemed to be one of the finest embassy buildings anywhere. It was located not far from the royal palace in a park of pine trees and small ponds. We had twelve servants for the two of us. Garnier was a professional diplomat. He had been ambassador to Czechoslovakia, was urbane, witty and not surprised by anything. He could not understand why the French government didn't simply turn the country over to the inhabitants and allow him to return to Europe. He didn't understand why the American government wanted to get involved, and he certainly didn't see why I was being sent around to set up guerrilla operations when I should be practicing law in a civilized place like New York, where he hoped someday to be sent. With the emperor he was at his diplomatic best, even though he obviously felt as though he was playing a part in a Viennese operetta. My own role was minimal. I was there to offer technical explanations of the American role, and to make clear that the Vietnamese "irregulars," as I called them, would serve under American officers, especially trained for such a role. The "irregulars" in turn would operate under overall French military command. I did have a chance to go on a night tiger hunt with His Majesty. I would have gladly spent a month in Dalat. The weather was perfect. It was very hot during the day, but at several thousand feet of altitude, the nights were cool and refreshing. With fourteen-foot ceilings in the commissioner's house, I certainly did not long to be back in my apartment in New York City.

Bao Dai was very much intrigued with the idea of training Vietnamese irregulars, even though they would be serving with the French army. He knew the back country well, was admired by the mountain tribes as a hunter, and I think saw the advantage of balancing out the intellectual nationalists from the cities with his own corps of mountain troops loyal to him. He gave his consent to the project quite enthusiastically, and the required treaty was duly signed in Saigon by the American ambassador on our return.

Bao Dai was a brilliant man, very well educated, with the political sense of his forebears. But he did not belong in the industrial world of today. Worse, he did not like to work more than an hour or two a day, and delegated too many of the chores of his office to subordinates trained by the French who had no links to the Vietnamese politicians. Bao Dai was brave, an interesting conversationalist, a womanizer, and a big game hunter of great repute. In Dalat, he was free to exercise his pleasures. One day while I was with him, in his Jeep, we ran across three large tigers stretched out on the macadam road, warming themselves in the sun. It was all we could do to get them to move. I went hunting with Bao Dai at night lying in a tree overlooking a tethered goat in a clearing some yards away. There were other perks to being emperor. His empress remained in Hue, the ancient capital of Annam. Every year in the spring, the emperor held a contest in Paris from where the stewardesses who would serve on his aircraft would be selected. It was a good job for a year for an adventurous girl, and the perks were substantial. Bao Dai was also quite fearless. While I was in Indochina, he had gone up to Hanoi where the leadership of the Vietcong—his Communist nationalist enemies—was located, and had walked alone on foot at the head of a political parade traversing the city, where anyone could have shot him. He would have been successful as a French medieval king. In a restless Asian country determined to be free of its colonial past, he was simply an anachronism.

It was not my role to pass on these observations of a state of affairs which must have been quite obvious to the American ambassador. The treaty I had come to participate in was duly signed in Saigon. It was then referred to Paris for French ratification. There it evidently raised a negative reaction. It was one thing to agree to a proposal of military aid from the secretary of state of the United States, as explained in more detail by the American ambassador to France. It was quite another to implement a formal agreement entered into by the three governments, American, French and Vietnamese. Faced with putting the program agreed upon into effect, the French government in Paris balked. We were advised in Saigon only that a new general had been appointed to head the French military effort in Indochina, that he was a hero of World War II, General de Lattre de Tassigny, soon to be a marshal, and that the French minister of overseas territories, M. Letourneau, would accompany him to Saigon to reorganize the military and civilian effort to win the war in Indochina. It obviously meant that the French government had decided that control over the country would be reestablished by force. I was asked to remain in Saigon to see what would happen, but it seemed obvious that there would not be a role for the United States in such a changed policy.

As though by fortuitous reaction, the efforts of the Vietcong military forces in the Saigon area immediately took on ominous proportions. Few secrets can be kept in any country and, clearly, the new French policy was quickly known. My apartment in the Majestic looked out on the river and the narrow open area beyond the far bank before it vanished into the jungle. At night this area, too, went over to the "enemy." I could sit on my small terrace and watch the puffs from the mortars and hear the sound of machine-gun fire in that area as French positions were probed in the darkness. I sat there many nights, watching, waiting for something to happen, wanting to go home, where people knew what they were doing and were not engaged in the shadowboxing of a war that could not be won.

One night about 1 a.m., the doorbell rang. I did not know whether to answer it. No one had been announced by the desk, but the clerk on duty was probably asleep. I had already found his post unoccupied many times when I came home from a dinner party.

The man at the door was quite evidently Chinese, dressed in the remnants of a khaki uniform which could have come from any country's storehouse. I had never seen him before. I asked him to come in. He did not speak English, and his French was about on a par with my Mandarin. He pulled out a soiled envelope from his jacket pocket and handed it to me, standing by the door as I read it. It was very much to the point. It came from the pirate leader I had worked with in Kwangtung Province. It was written in poor English, and it took me a little while to get the message he was trying to give me. He had heard I was in Indo-china because of the reconnoitering trip I had taken up the coast which clearly had been reported to him in detail. He had assumed that if I was back in Asia, it must be that I was in some kind of trouble again. Since we were made blood brothers before I left China, it was his pleasure and his duty to help me again. I was to leave with his messenger and follow him to China so that we could meet, and I could tell him what needed to be done. He had no problems with the Communist authorities. Their power was negligible in the coastal areas of south China. My friend had taken the precaution of rounding up a few wealthy landlords, executing them publicly, and sending photographs and explanations to the Party in Beijing to authenticate his groups' ideological support for Mao. Black, white or red, authority is the same, the message clearly said. "I continue to run my area as before. You will be safe here, and I will help you as I have before." I wasn't sure what I wanted to do. Obviously, if our message to the State Department for MacArthur was correct—and I was sure that it was—then this was too great an opportunity to miss. There was only one narrow-gauge rail line and no roads from south China to Hanoi for the Chinese Communists to supply arms to the Communists in Vietnam. If through my Chinese friends, with supplies sent in by U.S. submarines, the rail line could be destroyed, it would be very difficult for the Chinese Communists to rebuild, given the difficulty of the terrain. This would put additional pressure on the Chinese in supplying the Vietcong even partially and might even take their attention away from what they planned to do in South Korea. It would certainly help me to maintain my relations with men like Carbonnel and the head of the "Deuxieme Bureau," who understood much better than the French colonial office in Paris what needed to be done to keep Indochina from going over to the Communists.

I turned to the messenger and somehow made him understand in a combination of French and Mandarin that he should find himself a place to stay and come back to see me in a week, by which time I would either go with him or have a message to take back to his commander. The next day I reported to the ambassador what had occurred. I figured that since my mission had been diplomatic, as well as military, this was the least I owed him. He immediately saw the possible importance of what I was talking about and sent a message back to Washington for me over his signature. It also reported to McKay and the "Deuxieme Bureau" on what I hoped to do, whether or not the rest of my mission failed. They were enthusiastic.

In the next day or two, Saigon became transformed. Whenever a high-level visitor arrived from Paris, it was the custom for the military command and the high commissioner to dress in full regalia and go to the Ton Son Hut airport preceded and followed by squads of uniformed men on motorcycles and accompanied by the full diplomatic corps. The French do this magnificently, almost as well as the British. The occasion this time was special. Word had preceded him that de Lattre had shown in occupied Germany that he was not only a commander of troops, but an extraordinary showman as well, one who believed in expressing the prerequisites of power so that they could be understood by all. The fact that the minister of overseas territories was accompanying him made it all the more important to demonstrate to the Vietnamese the significance of this event.

In the midst of these events, I received the visit at my hotel of a Colonel Richard Stillwell whom I had met in Washington, and whom I had been told would be in overall charge of the training and use of the Vietnamese irregulars once the treaty was approved and went into effect. When I came to know Dick Stillwell better, I would have bet my last dollar that he would someday be Army chief of staff and perhaps even head of the Joint Chiefs; he had just that much capability. At any rate, he was my kind of American officer: intelligent, quick to evaluate the facts and make decisions, highly organized, a born patriot, direct to a fault, cultured, ready to take risks, objective, and with a sensitivity and a droll sense of humor that I hadn't expected to find in a man who had graduated from West Point and spent his entire life in the Army. When I learned in Indochina that he had been assigned to the CIA on detached duty, it was obvious to me that he was being trained for a higher command where knowledge of intelligence and irregular operations behind the lines would be highly useful. It was no wonder that he would eventually become a four-star general in command of American troops in South Korea.

Dick didn't waste any time in explaining to me what had happened in Paris. There would be no U. S. participation in the conflict in Indochina getting the Vietnamese mountain people to cooperate with the French if we couldn't quickly find a way to neutralize what General de Lattre was about to do.

"It is a disaster. That man has no idea what jungle warfare is like. It is one thing to wage war with tanks on the plains of Germany. It is quite another to fight a dirty war in the bush when you can't recognize friend from foe and no prisoners are taken. Unless we can get our irregulars in action, the French will lose this war. You and I have no time to waste. Have you ever flown a plane?"

I had to admit that outside of a commercial license equivalence in a Link trainer in Panama and lessons when I went to the Piper aircraft factory, I had no accredited hours in the air.

"Never mind. Tomorrow morning as soon as the airport opens, we are going to Hanoi. You will be the co-pilot. We have to get off before de Lattre gets back. He is due to return tomorrow morning from an inspection tour. I have arranged for you to meet with the commanding general in Hanoi. Hopefully, he will not be replaced and you will be able to convince him that our American program is sound. Since you have already met him and he knows what we are planning, we may have a chance. I will pick you up here at five thirty. The general will be expecting you before noon."

At 5:30 in the morning we were on the way to the airport. There were delays in taking off. When I saw the C-46 on the side of the runway, I realized why. The plane had large Chinese nationalist markings on it and otherwise no identification. Stillwell was at the controls. I sat in the co-pilot's seat. As we finally headed down the runway, I realized that the diplomatic corps was in attendance at our departure, and we passed de Lattre's plane shortly after the takeoff. It couldn't possibly have been a worse exhibition of what not to do in a foreign country in a time of war.

Stillwell did not seem unduly disturbed. "That was unfortunate but couldn't be helped. We really had no choice. Hopefully, in the excitement of de Lattre's arrival, our departure will not be especially noticed. After I leave you, I have to go on. I will send the ambassador's plane back for you this afternoon. I will be in touch with you to find out what happened. In my view, this problem, if it can be solved, will have to be solved in Washington and Paris, not here. In any event, we will meet up there, as soon as you return."

On the flight I briefed him on what I had done and how I hoped that Carbonnel would play a key role on the French side. I also told him about the messenger from China who was to come back for instructions. That excited him greatly and he gave me precise instructions on what I was to tell this man before he went back to China. He was noncommittal about the rest, but I could see that he was following closely what I had to say and converting my comments into future action. It was an odd trip, flying an empty plane from Saigon to Hanoi, with Chinese markings on the fuselage on a mission to persuade one French general in the north to ignore what would surely be instructions from his commanding general in the south.

My meeting in Hanoi was pleasant, but I thought unproductive. The general listened to my explanations, appeared to agree with me, but stated that if contrary instructions came to him from de Lattre he would, of course, have to obey them.

When I returned to the airport in the afternoon, the embassy plane was there waiting, but it had been surrounded by French troops. It took some frantic calls to Garnier and the embassy to get it released in order to fly back to Saigon. It was clear to me that our morning's departure had been well noted, that de Lattre was indeed taking charge, and that our U. S. mission was dead, at least in Indochina.

There was nothing further for me to do. I spent a few days saying goodbye to the friends I had made. Carbonnel was ordered back to France; Pignon was blamed for having dealt with the Americans; the civil administration was totally subjugated to the European general staff officers who had accompanied General de Lattre from Germany. It was with a great sadness that I once more went to the airport to get in the Air France Constellation back to Paris.

Before leaving Saigon, I had had a second visit in the night from the messenger from China. I sat with him on the floor with the French naval chart I had brought back from our trip up the coast toward Moncay. I marked the island which we would use as a drop and the place which would serve as a cache for arms, detonators and plastic explosives. It was as good a location to make pickups from junks based in China as to deposit food and supplies for a training camp. We then agreed on telephone and message codes from Hanoi or Haiphong, from Hong Kong, and from McKay's people in Saigon who had their own method of sending messages to China. Then I wrote a letter to my friend and explained how essential it was to blow that rail line. Remembering what his men had done in Shanghai, Canton and Amoy during the war against Japanese ships with limpets, blowing up ammunition trains headed for the Indochinese border would be child's play.

As I waited to go through the formalities of departure, I thought about the little that had been accomplished on this trip, but it was clear that this was not to be the end of the effort to save the situation in Indochina. How could this mission have been handled differently? It seemed evident to me once again that events in one country were decided by people in power somewhere else, operating without knowledge of the local conditions, under assumptions that were erroneous. My mus- ings were interrupted by the cacophony of French voices accompanying Minister Letourneau who, as it turned out, was on my same Air France flight to Paris.

The next morning in the washroom of the Constellation we hap- pened by chance to be shaving at the same moment somewhere over the Middle East. I asked him why he had sent Marshal de Lattre de Tassigny to Indochina to win a war that couldn't be won.

"Mr. de Saint Phalle, I have been in the French Chamber of Depu- ties for thirty years. When there is something to do that can be done, I try to make sure that it is done in my name so that I can get the credit for it. When something that I am responsible for is bound to fail, I try to get someone whose shoulders are broad enough to take it over. Then the failure is his, not mine. De Lattre is such a man. You are right, of course, his policy will fail. He knows nothing of Indochina. It would have been better for him to continue being in charge of the French sector of Germany. But he is a hero in France and will bear the respon- sibility lightly. As for me, no one will blame me, and I will probably be prime minister in due course."

"M. Letourneau," I replied, "if the porthole in this washroom were bigger, I would surely pitch you out over the desert below. In my view, you are a disgrace to France, because you have taken away the one chance that Indochina might be saved."

I felt very much better for having said that. But it didn't bother the minister one bit. He went on shaving, looking at himself in the mirror and seeing the face of a prime minister. He was right, of course, on his analysis of General de Lattre's eventual failure in Indochina.

It was some 45 years later that I learned how little was known in France of Secretary Dulles' effort to try to help the French in Indo- china.

It was May 1995, and President Clinton had selected the 50th an- niversary date of the ending of World War II in Europe to invite a few key military heroes from each of the allied nations to come to the White House for ceremonies celebrating the end of the conflict in Europe.

France had sent three of its military leaders: General Boissieux, brother-in-law of Charles de Gaulle, who had been with him at Ram- bouillet in 1954 awaiting word that Paris had been freed; General Massu, commanding general of French forces in Germany in 1968 when France was threatened with civil insurrection; and Colonel Philippe Peschaud, formerly General Leclerc's chief of staff and currently president of the foundation established to honor Marshal Leclerc, killed in an airplane accident in 1947.

My close friend, Michel Le Goc, had invited my wife, Mariana, and me to attend a dinner which he was giving for the three French heroes. It was what Michel called a *dîner de famille,* a setting for reminiscences of a time in which each one of us had played a part. The only other participants were Jacqueline Grapin, our hostess and Michel's wife, and two young journalists, friends of the Le Gocs.

While the champagne was served, I talked with General Boissieux who confirmed a story I had heard long ago from my Uncle Alexandre de Saint Phalle who had been one of the leaders of the Resistance in Paris. Alexandre had worked his way through the German lines to get to Rambouillet, having heard that General de Gaulle was there and would want to get to Paris before the Americans in order to accept the surrender of the city on behalf of France. When Alexandre arrived in Rambouillet forest to greet the general—and he was the first of four emissaries, including the Communist Resistance Group and two American liaison officers—de Gaulle looked at him and said, "Alors, Saint Phalle, en retard comme d'habitude,"—"So, Saint Phalle, late as usual"—hardly the warm greeting one would expect for someone who had risked his life to get there.

Obviously, in de Gaulle's memory of military history, this was a reference to our ancestor Marshal Grouchy who is considered to have caused the loss of the battle of Waterloo by getting there with fresh troops a day after it had taken place.

It wasn't only my uncle who suffered from General de Gaulle's abrasiveness. In 1969, when the situation in Paris had turned ugly and de Gaulle had left a hastily called cabinet meeting at which Pompidou had recommended that the government resign, de Gaulle had gone to meet with Massu at French military headquarters in Freiburg, Germany. Remembering Massu's opposition to de Gaulle's policies in Algeria in 1958, de Gaulle's greeting to Massu was a curt: "So, Massu, still as pigheaded?" "Still Gaullist, General," supposedly Massu had replied.

"If I need you, Massu, how long will it take you to get underway?" "A quarter of an hour, General." "Very well then, I can now return to Paris."

And back de Gaulle went to Paris to tell the Ministers the government would not resign and the police should be prepared to restore order with force if need be. Truly, Massu had saved France at that time, despite his personal empathy for the French military in Algeria who had opposed de Gaulle's policies there.

At dinner the conversation turned to the role that Marshal Leclerc had played in Indochina. General Massu, Colonel Peschaud, and Michel had all served with him there. All three of the French guests believed that had Leclerc not been killed in a tragic air accident, he might have brought peace to Indochina because he had established a relationship of trust with the Indochinese leader, Ho Chi Minh, whom he regarded more as a nationalist than a Communist.

Leclerc would not have wanted France to lose Indochina, but he felt that as a result of the fall of France in 1940 and the Japanese occupation, it would no longer be possible to reestablish the French colonial system within the country. He thought it preferable to keep the solid French economic and cultural relationship with Indochina by letting the country become independent over a short interim period rather than carry on a prolonged war which would only result in a permanent loss of a relationship which had existed since 1880.

I learned for the first time that night at dinner how d'Argenlieu, the admiral sent by de Gaulle to take back Indochina after World War II, had differed with Leclerc on the approach to take. Leclerc had been asked by the government to succeed d'Argenlieu as high commissioner in Indochina. Leclerc had to then go to de Gaulle asking him what he should do since both he and d'Argenlieu had been close associates of de Gaulle in the liberation of France. I did not know until then that de Gaulle had refused to make a decision between the two men and their divergent points of view, preferring to leave the decision to the politicians. As a result, Leclerc had gone back to Morocco as commander of French forces in North Africa. Events would show that the politicians had made the wrong decision.

It is curious how frequently history repeats itself in one country as in another. The mistake made by French politicians in 1946 regarding Indochina was no different from the mistake in the same country made by American politicians in 1960. In law schools and business schools one learns the importance of careful and unemotional analysis. In both these instances, the wrong answer was arrived at through emotional bias: the French, because after a military defeat in part caused by a succession of weak governments and social missteps, they wanted to again find a place in the new political world which they had lost by default in the old; the Americans because the Kennedy administration in 1960 succumbed to the entreaties of Cardinal Spellman and others in the

Catholic Church who thought that four million Catholics in Vietnam would be murdered if the Communists were not defeated. It was curious that in each case between two noted military figures called on to advise on the decision to take, one was correct and the other was wrong. Leclerc was right, d'Argenlieu wrong. Fifteen years later it was General Wainwright who made the correct analysis and told Eisenhower to avoid entanglement in Vietnam at all costs. It was General Taylor, an equally renowned paratrooper commander, who told Kennedy the American military could win the war easily in what was now Vietnam. Having served for so long in French Africa, Leclerc understood human nature and the aspirations of colonial peoples; d'Argenlieu and later de Lattre were renowned military commanders but lacked the political or historical judgment required to deal with the national aspirations of an Asian country.

At dinner, which was like a family affair, filled with discourses and reminiscences about events at various times and in various places around the world, someone, I think it was Massu, raised the question of why the United States had not taken any action to help the French in Indochina. Michel asked me for my comments. They were extremely surprised by what I had to tell them, and grateful to learn that Americans had tried to help.

Baie d'Along, on the Indochina coast, in 1950. On one of the largest islands, the author found an ideal location for a center where Vietnamese mountain tribes could be trained to fight under American officers against Vietnamese Communists.

XII

LAW, POLITICS AND THE CHURCH

T THE END OF DECEMBER 1950 I arrived back from Indochina and was immediately summoned to Washington for
a thorough debriefing on what I had seen, done and learned.
Debriefing is an American phenomenon which probably grew out of
World War II. It is very popular in the State Department. The returnee

is closeted with a variety of government officials in a small conference

*Debriefing
is dear to
our State
Department.*
room either in the State Department or in a hotel while they listen to
his presentation and then they ply him with questions that may or may
not seem to him to be relevant. The procedure may go on for hours or
even days. The questioners never reveal how policy decisions may be
affected, and the person questioned is rarely given the impression that
what he has done is significant or important or helpful. At the end, he
is politely thanked, and he leaves with a feeling of frustration as though
he had served as a punch bowl on a hot day, left empty after the guests
have served themselves.

I was to make many trips to Washington after the first debriefing
as the U.S. government officials in charge of Indochina policy debated
what to do to reverse the decision of the French government to carry
on the war without American participation. The ideas proposed were
innovative, if not successful.

It was clear that General de Lattre had quickly taken over French
policy in Indochina. His policy would be based on the imposition of
a military solution looking to the reestablishment of French colonial
domination. If the American government was going to effect a change
in French policy, the best way to do it, in the view of the State Department, was to persuade the general that he should change it. For this
purpose an American of stature would have to be found who might
be able to reason with the general. The ideal candidate for such a role
quickly surfaced. It would be Henry Cabot Lodge, Republican Brah-
min, ex-governor of Massachusetts, ex-American aide to General de

Lattre de Tassigny in the final days of World War II in Germany. Governor Lodge's French, while good, was not sufficiently fluent to prepare a persuasive document using the proper French prose. It would have to withstand examination by Foreign Office officials, as well as the general and his military and civilian staff. I was called on to prepare a first draft. It would have been hard to make the case I wanted to make in English. In French, it was impossible for me to do it correctly. French is a language of nuances. By the time the State Department linguists had fussed over it and the governor had added his own brand of native witticisms, it had become unrecognizable to me. The general's reply gave me much amusement.

"Dear Henry," it said, "you could not possibly have written such a letter, because as I remember our discussions in Germany your French was perfect and you would not have made the errors revealed in this letter." The rest of the letter was an appreciation of his interest in French policy in Indochina and a turndown of the expressed offers of assistance. Could it have been Garnier's sense of humor showing through? I ascertained that my Dalat friend was now in charge of the general's secretariat in Saigon, and chuckled to myself. One had to maintain a sense of humor when everyone else seemed to have lost his or hers. The State Department officials showed no amusement at seeing their stratagem fail.

The next diplomatic maneuver was more innovative. The new prime minister in France was George Bidault of the MRP, a Catholic Socialist party. The State Department now thought of appealing to him through the pope, who might persuade him, as a Catholic, to reverse General de Lattre's policy. Now there were approximately three million Catholics located in the north of Vietnam, principally in the Tonkin Province. If the Communists were to win, they might very well kill the Catholics or at the very least enslave them. It seemed reasonable to think that the pope, in order to save the Catholics of North Vietnam, might urge the French prime minister to replace General de Lattre and restore the policy favored by the American government, turning the conflict into a battle between the forces of democracy and the Communists rather than a colonial war. The proposal would certainly appear today to be complicated and far fetched, but the State Department was convinced that the French faced disaster if de Lattre was not removed. I was consulted on the plan, but was, to my regret, not invited to the audience with the pope in Rome at which the matter was to be discussed. The report of the visit given me by Dick Stillwell was not a surprise. Pius

XII refused to intervene. "The purpose of life on earth," he told the American officials who came to call on him, "is to get to heaven. The surest way to get to heaven is through martyrdom." He would not interfere with Bidault to save the Catholics in the Tonkin Province.

This seemed like a strange message coming from a pontiff who had done so much at the end of the war to save the Germans from Soviet revenge regardless of whether their leaders were Nazis who had participated in the genocide of the Jews.

In today's world it is not easy for a pontiff to engage in international politics.

It is often difficult for ordinary men, myself certainly included, to understand how churchmen look out upon the world. I remember a Jesuit priest assigned to the United Nations in New York who particularly incensed my stepmother. She was convinced that he was a Communist using his position at the U.N. to destroy private property and private enterprise in Latin America which she held dear. At one time, she wrote a long letter about this priest to Pope Paul VI asking that the Holy Father remove him, if only to save the Church in her own country of Chile. The pope's reply arrived in due course. It pointed out that, indeed, the ways of God were sometimes not easily understood, that she should look upon Father Arrupe as a man engaged in the Lord's work and not criticize him even though she might neither understand nor appreciate him. It did not mollify her to receive such a message. Paul VI, however, was considered very special in my family. When he had been young Bishop Montini in Milan at the end of the war, he had spent a night in a convent in central Italy where my Uncle Claude was spending a few days with my godmother, his sister, who lay dying of tuberculosis. The bishop had told Claude, after praying with Genevieve all one night just before she died, that he had passed those hours with a saint. After such a pronouncement Bishop Montini could do no wrong in my family.

There wasn't much that could be done in Indochina after the attempt to enlist the pope's aid failed except to watch what was happening with a feeling of helplessness. When Eisenhower came into office he had extricated the United States from the war in Korea by declaring the war had been won. As an experienced general and strategic planner, he understood the limits of military power and the importance of not spreading that power in too many directions. He had sent General Ridgeway, the commander of the U.N. forces in Korea, to Indochina to judge whether the French could be aided. Ridgeway had recommended avoiding interfering in Indochina at any cost. It is interesting that some years later President Kennedy sent General Maxwell Taylor to make the same type of evaluation. Taylor's analysis was the opposite of Ridgeway's. Here were two distinguished paratrooper generals, one the commanding officer of the 82nd Airborne, the other commanding officer of the 101st and hero of Bastogne. Yet one, Ridgeway, understood the situation in Indochina correctly; Taylor misread it completely. Ridgeway would have been sent to Vietnam a second time instead of Taylor except that he was suffering from cancer. The world might have been quite a different place had he been able to report back, because there was no reason why he would have changed his earlier opinion. Ridgeway was a real "thinking" general, capable of understanding all aspects of a conflict; Taylor was not.

There was not much more to show for my own mission to Saigon. My anti-government Chinese friends in China had been supplied for a time; they had repeatedly blown the railroad line to keep Chinese Communist supplies and arms from reaching the Vietminh fighting the French. Then the French had inexplicably complained to the American government that they had no conflict with the Chinese—even though the Chinese Communists were continuously supplying the Communist Vietminh forces in Indochina. The American government then cut off the supplies of explosives to my friends. I still went down to Washington from time to time to participate in discussions as to whether anything could be done to defeat the Communists in Indochina. When Dien Bien Phu was surrounded, there was again some interest in helping. It was reported that Vice President Richard Nixon had even considered using the atom bomb to relieve pressure on the French. The French abandoned the battle for Indochina in 1954. After that, I had no contact with any Vietnamese except that Ngo Dinh Diem, when he was living in New Jersey as a guest of the Catholic archbishop of New York, Cardinal Spellman, used to come and lunch with me from time to time. He was a good man, religious, honest, persuasive, but he was also timid and not a leader of men. With Eisenhower in the White House, he could get nowhere. It took the election of John Kennedy and his brother Robert's interest in foreign affairs to bring the whole Vietnam situation back into the American focus. Diem was forever asking whether I could arrange for him to address a joint session of Congress believing mistakenly that I might have strong connections with the administration in regard to its policy on Indochina! With Kennedys in office the administration's policy had changed. Cardinal Spellman, a dedicated anti-Communist churchman, would certainly have recommended Ngo Dinh Diem to the Kennedys as a man of integrity who might coalesce the country against the Communists. It always seemed to me that Cardinal Spellman, because of his strong anti-Communist sentiments, must bear some of the responsibility for our unfortunate policy in Vietnam, as well as General Taylor, whose recommendation was also so unfortunate.

One of the traits of Jack Kennedy that I greatly admired was his objectivity. Despite his constant physical pain, relieved only by a great sense of humor, he was a very serious man constantly questioning what he was being told by his advisors and determined to get the best advice possible.

Indochina—or Vietnam as it was now referred to—was a case in point.

After he became president, Jack Kennedy had begun to send military advisors to Vietnam to aid the Saigon government so it could defend itself against the Communists based in the north and headquartered in Hanoi. Under McNamara as defense secretary, these advisors had rapidly increased in number until the Americans appeared to be directing the civil war in that country. Some members of Congress, led by Senator Wayne Morse of Oregon, a former dean of the Oregon Law School and a prominent Democratic liberal, began to make speeches on the floor attacking the president and predicting that the United States would sooner or later be dragged into the conflict if it didn't stop sending advisors to Vietnam. According to several Democratic senator friends, Kennedy had called the senator over to the White House one fall day and took him out onto the lawn so that they might not be heard. He then told the senator that he had in fact sent a special emissary out to Vietnam to judge for himself what was occurring there and that he should return home with a firm recommendation. The president had told Morse that the recommendation would probably be to get out, that if it were so, he intended to call the senator over to the White House and give him credit for the change in policy which he would then announce.

It was November 1963, just before the president took his political swing through the west which would bring him to Dallas.

It was only later, when Wayne Morse was running for re-election in Oregon in 1964 with little chance of success because the AFL-CIO was campaigning against him as a result of his stand against the Vietnam War, that he found out who the emissary was. During the Oregon campaign John Kenneth Galbraith came out to his camp in the mountains for dinner and told him. McCarthy, Pell and other sena-torial friends who served on the Foreign Relations Committee found no way of having the Galbraith report made public because a personal emissary's findings are personal to the president who sent him and must not be publicly revealed. Wayne Morse was defeated and the ill-ad-vised war went forward under what President Johnson assumed was a renewed mandate to continue the war as a result of his election in 1964. Galbraith's report would have given Kennedy on his return from Dallas the excuse to terminate U.S. involvement in Vietnam.

As with individuals, nations are subject to periods of good or bad luck. What might have happened had this report reached the president earlier? Clearly, it would have been the end of American involvement in the affairs of that unfortunate country.

In the United States, the Catholic Church has frequently played a political role, sometimes wisely, sometimes not, but probably nowhere to the extent thought by some. It has depended upon the character of those in the Church who have held power. In Boston, Cardinal O'Connell was one kind of churchman. In New York, Cardinal Spell-man was quite another.

I had met Cardinal Spellman at the Hoguet's in New York when I was still in law school. He was charming as a person, but reflected, I thought, a single-mindedness of purpose and a determination which struck me even then as frightening. The same was true of the Monsi-gnors and priests he had brought into the chancery of the New York archdiocese. They were able, ambitious, dedicated people one would have expected to find in Wall Street rather than in the Church. Many had already been trained in law or in finance.

The Catholic archbishop of New York occupies a special place in the political life of the country. By the very nature of his office, the prel-ate has to be a public figure and a politician as well as a priest. He must deal with the Irish, the Italians, the Hispanics who constitute the over-whelming majority of his flock, and now African-Americans who want their own native chants and liturgy, as well as homosexuals who want to remain in the Church while violating its clearly expressed teachings. He must of necessity be a fundraiser extraordinaire. If he has time he must also be a teacher and a priest. Cardinal Hayes, who preceded Spellman, managed to keep the balance between all these demanding functions. Cardinal Spellman will have to be judged by others.

In a real sense the role of a churchman is a constant attempt to win the hearts and minds of men. Some do it by threats, some by persuasion. When I was fourteen I had told my French grandmother one day that I had lost my faith in God because the Church had too many rules and I didn't see that many of them made any sense. She hadn't appeared very upset by what I told her but arranged for me to go and see a simple parish priest whom she sometimes visited in order to understand her religion better. This priest was an old man with a most serene face. I saw him at the parish house of a small church in a workingman's district. He was very kind. He explained to me that any large religious organization had to have rules which everyone could follow. The rules were primarily designed for persons with little background or education who might be most in need of such rules of conduct. It didn't mean that one had to follow them. One could apply one's own intelligence and discard some as meaningless, but one should always realize that these rules had been adopted over the centuries by very wise men and that one ignored their guidance at one's peril. "Each one of us," he said, "has to, if he can, abide by the rules which he feels he can accept. I do not believe that other rules of conduct and other religions are not equally going to help us get to heaven. A love of God and a determination to do good rather than evil is sufficient. We all know in our hearts what is right, although many times we bend a bit to do what we want to." What he said was so true, and so simple, that I went home refreshed and happy with my faith once again.

One of Cardinal Spellman's convictions was that he didn't like the French. My Aunt Jacqueline's exposure to these sentiments came about as a result of an attempt on her part to help a young French relative, Georges de la Grandiere, distribute in the United States an extraordinary film he had just produced in France. The film, *Mr. Vincent,* had won many prizes in Europe. Georges had had a remarkable war record in the French resistance, and after the war he had decided that he would devote his energies to making sure that such horrors would never reoccur. He would turn men's minds to helping rather than killing one another. He had been asked by the French government of General de Gaulle to give talks on his wartime experience around the country. He took the occasion at the end of his talks to tell people that he proposed to make a film about the life of St. Vincent de Paul who had been kidnapped, sold into slavery and served twenty years as a galley slave. After he had saved his captain in a terrible Mediterranean storm, he had been returned to France and freed. He had then become the king's almoner to the poor and founded the Order of Charity that still bears his name to take care of the poor and homeless. Shortly after his death Vincent had been canonized. Georges had kept track of the donations he had received from listeners as subscriptions to stock in the company he had used to make the film and had repaid them many fold out of the film's profits from distribution. But the Legion of Decency in the United States, at the Cardinal's request, had given the film a "C" rating making it unfit for Catholics in the United States to see it. "A Saint should not be represented as a galley slave," was the reason given. My aunt was outraged. Through Mrs. Hoguet she arranged to see the Cardinal, who informed her that "the French are unworthy of being Catholics." So much for "the eldest daughter of the Church," as an earlier pope had labeled France.

Law, Politics, and the Church

In many ways an organized religious group has to be managed, like a business. If there were no administrators in the Church and no money raisers, who would build the churches or monasteries where the Franciscans and the Benedictines pray? Who would build the great universities where the Jesuits teach or the Dominicans preach? A universal church has to speak through many persons, some are ministers, some are pastors, some need to exercise power, and others cater to the poor and the weak. There are many like Peter who renounced Christ three times and Thomas who would not believe what he couldn't see.

The Church is also a business.

One day I received an inquiry from a lawyer in Rome asking me what I knew about a new order of the Knights of Malta supposedly headquartered in New York City. I do not know why I was called except that during the period of the Crusades to free Jerusalem and long thereafter the Saint Phalles as Crusaders had been active in the Order and had served as Knight Commanders at Rhodes, at Acre, which is now in Israel, and at Bodrum in Turkey. The knights were a military as well as a monastic order. When the Order was founded after the capture of Jerusalem in 1087 during the first Crusade, its purpose was to care for the sick and the pilgrims who would come to the Holy Land. The Knights of the Order of the Hospital later became known as Knights of Rhodes when they moved there after the fall of Jerusalem sometime around 1308. They moved to Malta and became known as Knights of Malta after Rhodes was captured by the Turks in 1523. The Knights have always been an order recognized by and under the protection of the pope. The order maintains diplomatic relations with the countries of Europe whose ambassadors to the Vatican generally also function as ambassadors to the order. Ever since Malta surrendered to Napoleon in 1798, the order has maintained its headquarters in Rome across the plaza from the Vatican. The order has become largely ceremonial, a kind of semi-monastic association of European noblemen dedicated to

pious works and support of religious hospitals. On ceremonial occasions the Knights are still entitled to wear their full-length black capes with a white "Maltese" cross sewn over the left breast. My uncle, Jean d'Ormesson, was for many years ambassador in Rome to the Vatican and to the Order of the Knights of Malta. To become a Knight of Malta one must have sixteen quarters of nobility in his ascendancy and must take a vow of chastity.

I reported back that there was indeed an Order of the Knights of Malta recently formed in New York by Cardinal Spellman. Leading Catholic men in the United States had become members, paid annual dues, and held an annual white-tie dinner in New York City at which the Cardinal spoke. As it turned out, the purpose was political rather than religious. It had been created by three conservative prelates, Cardinal Spellman and two Italian cardinals, Ruffino and Ottaviani, as an effort to counter the decision of recent popes to enlarge the College of Cardinals by naming additional prelates from the developing countries. It was felt by the three founders of the American Order of the Knights that such an organization with political and economic standing within the Catholic laity in the United States would encourage the Vatican hierarchy and especially the pope to adopt a conservative posture in the selection of new cardinals and in the development of Vatican policy. The plan was to take control of the Order of Knights of Malta in Rome and use it as a conservative political lay group within the church. The method used was to threaten to have the order dissolved by the pope if it refused to become a conservative order within the Church. In due course, after many threats and counter defenses, a compromise was reached: the Knights of Malta headquartered in Rome would continue as before in their charitable activities, but nothing would be said about the new Order of Knights based in New York and under protection of its Cardinal Archbishop. The initiation fee for the American Knights of Cardinal Spellman was a minimum of $10,000 and a $5,000 annual donation was expected. The Knights would meet annually in New York for dinner when they would wear their robes and hear the Cardinal speak. They would be told that their donations were used to support the founding hospital in Rome. Belonging to the Knights and wearing the magnificent cape from the Middle Ages quickly became the apogee of the Catholic layman's charitable relations to his church. What had brought about the request to me from the lawyer in Rome was that a

326

Texas Knight, complete with ten-gallon hat and cowboy boots, turned up at the grand master's house in front of the Vatican. "I've come to see how you've spent all this money we've been giving you," he said to the startled grand master, an octogenarian, after he had been received more out of curiosity than deference. The grand master listened to him quietly, asked a few questions, and sent a letter to a friend in New York to find out what was going on. The friend then asked me to look into the question. I am sure the Texan would have been highly surprised if he had been told of the rules of the order and the requirement of chastity.

In the Catholic Church in the United States, there has always been a great philosophical divide between what I would call the conservative Irish members of the hierarchy, those more liberal, the Jesuit Order, and the monks and nuns who work with the poor or in the developing countries of Central and South America. These, like their counterparts—the worker-priest of Europe—are apt to be much more sensitive to injustice between rich and poor. They see an important role for the Church in taking the part of the downtrodden against the wealthy who, in their view, are not doing enough to educate the poor, to assure their care when sick, and to give them an opportunity to own their own land. This cleavage within the Church in the United States has recently grown so deep that the night when he died, Pope John Paul I was apparently busily trying to find the answer to the two major problems facing his ministry: how to reestablish his control over the Jesuit Order, and what to do about the Church in the United States. Paul VI had done nothing about either problem. Under John Paul II the American question remains as intractable as ever. Mario Cuomo, when he was governor of New York, had even found it necessary to debate in public the accusation of a New York bishop that as a Catholic he was "in serious risk of going to hell" because of his support of abortion rights. Little has changed in sixty-five years.

"I'm a good Catholic," Governor Al Smith of New York, in the privacy of his Albany Office, had reminded a ranking Roman Catholic clergyman as they debated a proposed constitutional amendment on child labor laws. "I'm bound to obey the Holy Father, and I'm bound to obey you in all matters of faith and morals," he told the prelate. "But there's nothing in the law of the Church that says I have to obey the Church in matters that are economic, social or political. No, Father. That's not part of the Church to tell me that. Anytime you come to me on matters of faith or morals where I've been wrong, you can be sure I'll go along with you, but this belongs to me. This is the governor of the state of New York's duty, and it belongs to me. It doesn't belong to anybody else."

The issue was children. The governor was arguing for a federal child labor law. Leading Catholic clergymen were warning that such a government regulation would violate the sanctity of the family.

* * *

One day I received a telephone call from a man who gave his name as Nicolas Reisini. He identified himself on the phone as the distributor of U.S. films in different parts of the world and told me that my name had been given to him by the Technicolor Corporation as one who could handle complicated international transactions quietly and expeditiously. I made a date to see him. I asked my partner Pete Lewis who represented Technicolor in the firm to join us. Nick Reisini turned out to be a character right out of the motion pictures he distributed: short, swarthy, "sharply" dressed in shark skin from a tailor who made clothes for Hollywood personalities rather than Saville Row Englishmen. He was cultured. He dropped names, insisted on pointing out to us that he had originally been a Greek diplomat and had been in the shipping business before deciding that there was a better future in film distribution. He had a company in London, one in Tokyo, one in Paris, and one in New York. He purported to be the largest foreign distributor of American films in the world. He had a house in each city where his company had an office. He would need legal, tax, and probably financial advice in carrying on his international operations. He did not talk about Tangiers or Monte Carlo, but there was something about our discussion that made me want to check further into his background. I called a friend of mine in the FBI in Washington who told me he would check him out and call me back. As a result of the call, I went down to Washington to be briefed in person. The story made little sense. It gave Reisini's background, birth dates and place of birth, activity as a diplomat and other pertinent data. It then stated that he had been stopped at the border on his return from Mexico one day and arrested as a war criminal who had worked for the Japanese in the Far East during World War II. He had supposedly organized an intelligence operation for them in the islands of Southeast Asia, during the war, that had resulted in attacks on American ships and in the death of numerous Americans. It was a nasty story. There had been hearings in Washington. Later the charges had been dropped, largely because of the intercession of two men, one of whom was the chairman of the Pru-

328

dential Life Insurance Company, the largest insurance company in the United States, the other Cardinal Spellman, archbishop of New York. The charges were quite specific. They stated that far from being Greek, Reisini was born in Harbin, China, of Russian parents who had escaped from the Soviet Union. The children of many such persons had worked for the Soviet government or the Japanese government in Manchuria, as had their parents, in many cases simply in order to survive. Such persons, because they were stateless, otherwise faced imprisonment at the hands of the Chinese.

I was flabbergasted by what I had heard. My partners, though concerned, took the position that since the government had not won its case, our client had committed no crime and that since we had never been asked to represent him other than in a normal attorney-client relationship, there was no reason why we should not continue to act as his attorneys. Reluctantly, I agreed. His work was interesting and challenging, particularly since the distribution of films abroad can be extremely risky business and very capital intensive if you want to be sure of getting the best films.

One day Nick asked me to go to Europe for him. He told me his large house in Paris was at my disposal. It was across the street from UNESCO on the Avenue Kleber. I decided to test the charge against Nick in my own manner. He was anxious to explain to me what he wanted me to do for him in Paris and had agreed to take me to the airport so that we would have a chance to talk while waiting for the plane. I suggested that my wife, Rosamond, accompany us. Rosamond had been born in Peking, was a concert pianist, and spoke all eleven Chinese dialects. I told her while I checked in she was to go into the cocktail lounge with Nick and while sipping her drink to suddenly start talking to him in Harbin dialect. She did so. He immediately answered her in the same dialect. Then he stopped and asked her why she had done this. "I understand you were out there as a child," she said. At that point I joined them. I could never be sure whether the rest of the charges were true or false, but it seemed evident that Reisini was indeed born in Harbin.

When I arrived in Paris, Reisini's car and chauffeur were at the airport. The house was almost as large as the UNESCO headquarters on the other side of the avenue. It was staffed with some twelve servants. All spoke to one another in Russian. The majordomo installed me in a magnificent apartment on the third floor, consisting of a bedroom, bath, dressing room, and library-sitting room. There were telephones everywhere with frequently blinking lights indicating their almost constant use. The service was impeccable, the food excellent, the servants entirely at my disposal. I noticed however, that whenever they conversed together, it was always in Russian. Had Nick been a former Japanese agent? Was he now a Russian or Chinese agent? What could be happening here?

It was incredibly hot in Paris at that time of the year and the heat that summer was worse than usual. I had promised Reisini that I would carry with me some materials for him which I would deliver to a messenger who would meet me at the railroad platform in Heidelberg, Germany as the express train destined for Prague rolled into the station around two in the morning. The messenger would identify himself through a series of passwords, and I would then turn over the package to him and take the return express coming through Heidelberg headed for Paris twenty minutes later. I shall not forget that trip. My first-class ticket was for the lead coach. The engine was a coal burner. The windows were open, as the coach was not air-conditioned. Whenever we came to a tunnel black smoke filled the car. The Czech government officials who were on the train all seemed to be very fat and accompanied by equally corpulent women. As soon as the train left the station, both men and women peeled off most of their clothes. It was a terrible journey. I was very much relieved to see the last of those Czechs at Heidelberg. There was no trouble giving my parcel to the German who was destined to get it, but unfortunately the train in the other direction was an hour late. There were two French generals from the occupying forces pacing up and down the quay. One turned to the other and said, "These Germans, they can't even run their trains on time." Considering that in those days about all that did run on time in France were the trains, it was an amusing remark. The trip back was uneventful. But I was puzzled. Nick had explained to me that what he was giving me were confidential accounting statements on his European operations that he didn't want the French tax authorities to know about and therefore did not wish to send by post. Were they something more? I do not know.

But I continued to represent him.

Nick told me one day that he had bought a house in Tuxedo Park, New York. I asked him why.

"In the United States, it is always very important, Thibaut, to be properly introduced. I invest a great deal in many stocks. My broker, a partner in a firm I use, is a leading member of the Tuxedo Park community and will arrange for me to become a member of the Tuxedo Club. I very much want my wife to be accepted there and for my boy to attend the Tuxedo Park School. It will be important for him later on. Also I have bought a controlling interest in a communications company. The president lives in Tuxedo and has an imposing communication antenna through which he can communicate anywhere. It will be very useful to me because it will permit me to communicate directly all over the world.

Somewhat later, I had a call from Nick one day asking me if I would go down to Wall Street with him the next day for a meeting with his bank. On the way down in his car, he explained to me that he owed the bank a great deal of money and that it might be difficult for him to come up with an installment due if the bank wouldn't extend the payment date.

"I can make one call, Thibaut, and three million dollars will be immediately transferred to my account. But I am not sure I want to make that call."

Knowing what I did about Nicolas Reisini and surmising the rest, the thought went through my mind: Is the call to be made to Moscow, to Beijing, or to the Vatican? Just who controls this man? After all, three million dollars in 1953 was the equivalent of thirty million dollars today.

I couldn't bluntly put the question to him. Instead I found a way of speaking about the Prudential Insurance Company as a possible source of funds since it was the largest insurance company in the United States. Did he know the chairman?

"That man is only interested in money. Even though he is now very rich, he always wants more."

We also talked about religion and whether he believed in God at a difficult time like this.

"Thibaut, religion is too often manipulated by people who use it to get their own earthly purposes. When I first came to New York, I arranged to call on Cardinal Spellman. I asked him if I could contribute to his charities. He is fond of children and had a foundation established in Rome to help the orphans. I have given much to it."

I was scarcely any further along, although I understood better what might have secured for him earlier support at the immigration hearings.

Almost thirty years later I was in Tuxedo Park for my younger daughter's wedding. She was not yet born when I was Nicolas Reisini's lawyer. It was a warm and beautiful day. We were on the lawn in front of the house on the lake where the bride's mother lives. On the opposite shore was a very big house with a boat dock in front and a tall antenna up on the hill behind it. One of the bridesmaids asked whose house it was. Its windows were all boarded up.

"That's Nicolas Reisini's house," someone answered. "He went to prison for eight years for stealing a great deal of money from a bank."

I couldn't help it. I asked what happened to him.

"He died in prison of a heart attack half way through his term."

Had Nick failed to make a call that would have saved him? To whom would his plea have been addressed? Had he been turned down at the other end? Was this whole story a myth?

I have my own ideas about what might have happened. But of course we will now never know. A man like this man takes his secrets to the grave with him. I prefer to think that the government's allegations were true. It does not shock me to believe that a Russian-born Manchurian of uncertain parentage, belonging to no country and faced with an uncertain future, might owe no loyalty except to those who would pay him and only for so long as payments were forthcoming. Conversely, in that world, the employee's pay ceases when he can't or won't any longer deliver what is asked of him. It is a harsh world.

Being an unabashed romantic, I like the idea that a foreign agent would have the initiative to hide out in of all places the confines of Tuxedo Park where no one would ever think of finding a person who would be engaged in nefarious activities against the United States.

After all, I was born there.

XIII

HAITI

O N A NOVEMBER DAY IN 1952, I returned from a long day at the office feeling as though the blood had all of a sudden drained out of my body. I told Rosamond how I felt, took to my bed and waited for a doctor. On examining me, John Frame reported that my diastolic blood pressure was 55, that I should immediately try to go off somewhere and rest for at least a month. Obviously, we couldn't go as a family: two children were in school, and we had no one to take care of the youngest. It was then that I thought of Emerson Cook.

I had met Emerson through my new partner in Paris, Sam Mercer. Sam, who spoke perfect French, had graduated first in his class at Yale Law School, gone to work for the large New York law firm which represented the French government after the war, but preferred to live in Paris, and so joined me there. Sam had gone with Emerson on various trips to Haiti to discuss with the Haitian government Emerson's possible services in connection with various matters, including a World Bank loan for the Artibonite Valley water development, restructure of the National Bank's loans with New York banks, and the establishment of new air routes between Haiti and Florida. Emerson had acted as lead investment banker on the initial public offering of Mackey Air Lines, a regional Florida air carrier. So I called Emerson Cook that evening.

An unscheduled visit to Florida

Emerson was delighted. "Thibaut, come down tomorrow. I will get you a poolside room at Spellman Prentice's new motel, La Coquille, where you will be my guest. When you are rested, after a few days, we will have Mackey fly us to Andros Island. There is a new resort just opened down there, because the bone fishing is supposed to be spectacular. The ex-governor of the Bahamas is in charge of the resort. At this time of the year, it will be almost empty. I'll bring Shirley and we'll have a great time. After a week there we'll go on to Haiti and you can help me negotiate the loans which I had mentioned to the government on a last visit with your friend, Mercer."

So I left Florida the next morning, after a few hurried phone calls to my partners. The scenario started out just as Emerson Cook had explained it. I met Shirley, his wife, for the first time. She was much younger than Emerson, a good painter of the outdoors, enthusiastic about the trip to Andros and Haiti. We made our plans, and four days later, the three of us were in Andros, where the bone fishing turned out to be spectacular. It was almost too good to last. The food was excellent, as were the wines. There were only a handful of guests. His lordship the governor and his wife were sophisticated and excellent conversationalists. In short, this was heaven. My guilt feelings were cured by John Frame's admonition. It was all too good to last.

After the third day of fishing, Emerson took on a funny look and declared to us at dinner that he wanted to buy the fishing club. "The governor says it belongs to Axel Wenner-Gren, Thibaut, and he doesn't want to keep it. I can keep it filled with my friends from Palm Beach. Let's go to Nassau tomorrow. You're back in shape and can negotiate the transaction. We should be able to wrap it up in a couple of days and then go on to Haiti."

When Emerson Cook was in one of these moods, there was no arguing with him. Not for nothing had he been the youngest pilot in the Lafayette Escadrille in France in World War I, was now the only investment banker in Florida, and president of all the good social clubs in Palm Beach. He loved people, was everybody's friend, an incurable optimist, with no malice or hang-ups about anyone.

The next three days, I spent in Sir Stafford Sands' office in Nassau. The dean of "the Bay Street Pirates" had earned his reputation. He was suave, uncompromising, and persuasive. Flanked by three Swedes who showed no emotion whatsoever, it was a tough negotiation, as barren of opportunities to score as the financial statements before us. At the end of three days the agreements were prepared. It only remained for me to find out from Emerson whether he really wanted to pay that much for a fishing resort not easy to reach. Nevertheless, if he wanted to syndicate the deal, the papers were sufficiently precise to serve as the basis for a private syndication or even a public offering. In the meantime, I wondered what had happened to my vacation.

On Saturday, we received an invitation to come to lunch the following day at Dr. Wenner-Gren's island just off Nassau, where the Swede had designed and planted what were probably the world's most extraordinary tropical gardens with plants and flowers carefully gathered from everywhere. It was an unusual day for any number of reasons, beginning in the launch on the way to the island.

As the three of us were taken out, I chatted with a very pretty girl in her twenties who had evidently also been invited for lunch. To make polite conversation, I asked her what she thought of Nassau. "It is the ___hole of the world," she said. "I hate it. But I've seen nothing of it, because I was only here on my honeymoon when I was on my back the whole time in the hotel." I was not prepared for her comment on such a beautiful Sunday morning.

When we arrived at Wenner-Gren's we found the governor, many Swedes, and the whole English colony already on the terrace having drinks. Wenner-Gren was tall, distinguished, white-haired and extremely polite to his guests. Then just before lunch he turned to his Swedish friends, shouted to them in Swedish and immediately, as a group, they dashed down to the beach, took all their clothes off and ran naked into the water, servants hurrying after them with a mound of bath towels.

When they returned we were taken into lunch. The dining room was a large octagonal room with bay windows looking out to sea on two sides. Emerson and I found ourselves on either side of our hostess, a former opera singer from Kansas, whom Axel Wenner-Gren had met as she was on her way to Sweden some years earlier on a Swedish liner to sing at the opera. She must have been pretty then because she had regular features. Now she was heavy and her face was bloated from too much drinking. Obviously, this day she had had many martinis and had some difficulty speaking. However, on the top of her head was a glorious parrot, later identified for me as the most successful fundraiser for E-Bonds during the Korean War. The parrot had no difficulty expressing itself. When it disapproved of any of Mrs. Wenner-Gren's remarks to Emerson, who was trying to make reasonable conversation, it simply leaned out over her head and said in clear tones, "That's a crock of shit." I could see from his looks over to me that Emerson was having difficulty holding up his own end of the conversation with this constant distraction.

The parrot did all the talking.

Our fifth at the table—if you include the parrot—was the young girl from the launch to whom I had obviously been identified as Emerson's lawyer. "Can you take me to dinner tonight?" she whispered to me during lunch. "I will choose a restaurant where we can dine well. I will expect you to pick me up at my apartment at 8:30. Please wear a black tie. In Nassau one follows English manners, even on Sunday."

I took a nap that afternoon having explained to Emerson and Shirley my good fortune and looking forward to an exciting evening. Men—even those happily married, as I was—are romantics at heart and crave adventure.

My euphoria was short-lived. Milly wore a white satin evening dress with little on underneath. She looked bewitching. We went to an expensive restaurant with soft music. We danced. I held her close. As dinner ended she turned to me:

"I wanted to have dinner with you tonight because there are two important matters I want to discuss with you. I know you have been negotiating to buy Axel's fishing resort. I don't give a damn what you pay for it. As you may or may not know, my firm handles all the publicity for the resort. My fee is $150,000 a year. I want it put at $300,000 a year with a five-year contract and for that I will have the price your client pays reduced by 20 percent. It is a take-it-or-leave-it proposition. When you come back from Haiti, come to my office at 405 Park Avenue and let me have the answer. I get to work at 7:30 in the morning. Meet me there at 8:00. I'll give you a cup of coffee and a drink. That is my breakfast."

Her other question was equally direct. "As a lawyer," she said, "you must know, if a man dies in New York, leaving a portion of his estate to his mistress, whether the courts will recognize this legacy or declare it void against public policy."

So much for my romantic ideas.

The answer to this particular question, I unfortunately knew only too well. In early 1948, when I was still an associate lawyer at the well-known Wall Street firm of Chadbourne, Wallace, Parke & Whiteside, I had been asked to take the case of a French woman who had been abandoned by a wealthy American who had later died a New York resident. My firm was not allowed to represent her. We had created the law on the subject in the state of New York: a mistress could not inherit.

Now as I listened to this beautiful woman's request for guidance, I had no difficulty in telling her that she stood no chance whatever in having her bequest honored. "It would be best if he did not die a resident of New York or any similar state," I added.

And so my evening had not at all turned out as I had expected. The next morning I reported to Emerson what he would have to do if he wanted to buy the Andros resort. Emerson burst out laughing. "You know, Thibaut, I have done a great many things in my life I would not want to be asked about on judgment day. But I have never bought a

woman and I am not going to do it now." Emerson and Shirley thought
my romantic evening was a wonderful joke and they reminded me often
of it afterwards.

When I returned to New York I went as agreed to Milly's office at
8 a.m. She was having a cup of coffee and a scotch and soda. "Well," she
said. "What is the answer?" I gave her Emerson's reply just as he had
given it to me. She did not seem concerned. And I have no doubt that
when the resort was sold a year later, Milly arranged to have her contract
amended. The Millys of this world rarely fail to protect their interests, at
least while the beauty lasts and the drinking fails to take hold.

Our visit to Haiti was a very different story. Little was I to know
how much time I would spend there in the years immediately following
this first visit. In time, I traveled all over the island by car, by taxi, by bus
or horseback, by private plane. I even went on muleback to the top of
Christophe's Citadel filled with cannons and cannon balls. No one can
explain how they could have ever been brought there, so steep are the
sides of the mountain on which the Citadel is built. No one knows how
many Haitians lost their lives in trying to bring the cannons up there.
But we do know the Marines failed in trying to bring them down. After
the French, under Napoleon's brother-in-law, had failed to recapture
the country, for ten years there had been no diplomatic representation in
Haiti. Then in 1823, the emperor had invited diplomats from European
countries to return. He had brought them up to the top of the Citadel
and then, to show them how loyal his troops were, marched a company
of them off the walls of the parade ground on top of the Citadel.

Haiti is certainly one of the most beautiful lands I have ever seen.
In the days when it was a French colony a young man could go there for
a year or two and come back wealthy. I have seen parts of the country
where the topsoil is twelve feet thick. Unfortunately, man in his folly
has destroyed the richness of the soil by ruthlessly clearing the land
and cutting or burning trees for firewood. Haiti is a microcosm of what
happened to the forests of Spain when goats and sheep were allowed
to roam freely, to the spread of the deserts in north and central Africa
in the last century, and to the terrible climatic changes going on today
as a result of fires set in the Amazon valley by settlers from southern
Brazil determined to farm an irreplaceable global natural asset. In the
case of Brazil, the damage will be much greater than in Haiti because
the climate of the entire Western Hemisphere may be affected in per-
petuity. With population increases now causing a 100 percent rise in
only fifty years rather than six centuries, the demand for land will only

What a
place Haiti
muſt have
once been.

continue to increase. In Africa, denuding the land brought deserts and even less rain. In Brazil, it will cool the Gulf Stream, reduce rain, and cool the eastern United States and Western Europe. Once destroyed, it is quite impossible to renew a rainforest. Is there no way to explain that with population growth as it is and will continue to be, the world is a very small place indeed, where each one of us is increasingly responsible for the well-being of his neighbor? Under these circumstances, aren't religious worries about population control the equivalent of the 13th century discussions about angels dancing on the head of a pin? It is not wars that will control population growth in the future. It will be starvation brought about by systematic destruction of our environment at an accelerating pace. There is an extraordinary balance in nature. When one part of the ecological system is hurt, the whole of the system goes out of balance, with each part affecting the others. If the forest cover is destroyed, climatic change immediately results. In the tropics, this means fewer rains and more deserts, as in Africa. It means the earth will not retain its moisture, therefore washing away the topsoil in India and creating floods in Bangladesh. It also means gradual deterioration of the ozone layer in the atmosphere because the true cover which gives the earth its layer of protection from the sun has been depleted. This in turn will bring about a rise in the level of the oceans as the ice caps melt. It means, in due course, the end of cities located on the coasts as the water rises. Is this a folly which occurred eons ago and explains why every religion contains the story of Noah's ark and the great flood? Is this why, as you fly over certain parts of the Bahamas, you can see below the water roads which head out of the sand on the bottom only to disappear again a mile or so later? Is this where Atlantis was located rather than off the coast of Spain?

The answer should be self-evident: for every acre that is cleared, new trees and shrubs must be planted, so that the world's ozone layer can be protected.

Haiti has many lessons for us in today's world. As I came to know the Haitians by working with members of the government, business people, and any number of individuals all over the country, I developed a great liking for them. Why is it that these people, alone of all the African peoples in the Caribbean basin, have such an artistic sense? I am told that the Haitian people originally came from a mountainous region of Mali (where that other great tribe the Berbers of North Africa are thought to have originated). Their tribe had lost a civil war and been sold into slavery by the victors to the Arab traders on the coast. These in turn sold them to the French, who brought them to Haiti to work in the sugar plantations on the north coast. The fact is that the Haitians' artistic creativity, their religion, and their music are all quite different from that of the rest of the black populations of the Caribbean area. It is likely that their artistic sense came from their native religion, because religious rites are so frequently expressed in art. I have been fortunate to attend voodoo ceremonies in the interior of the country where the men play cards for copper coins while the women are led by music and the priest to go into trances, dance with abandon and drink fresh chicken blood. Their belief is that the body of a man can be poisoned and as a result brought to a state paralleling the dead so that the mind is destroyed and his soul thought to have left the body. Such poisoned men are then truly slaves. As you can imagine, the fear that the voodoo priest can and will turn a man into a zombie gives him enormous power in the community.

The economic plight of the people of Haiti has turned them toward both religious, artistic and musical expression to turn painful daily life into a promise of something better and towards a beauty of expression sadly lacking in daily life. In my escapades into the country at night many miles north of Port-au-Prince, my guide, who from his days as a Haitian driver for the Marine Corps, which occupied the country from 1916 to 1934, was known as "Little Shit." He was Emerson Cook's taxi driver, and as nice a human being as I had ever met. His knowledge of Haitian religion and mythology was vast, and he would tell me stories for hours on end in his own French patois as we took the road to the voodoo meetings. These have been forbidden by the government for years but still took place regularly in the remote countryside. Little Shit would stop the taxi frequently en route, stretch out with his ear on the pavement to try to catch the distant sound of drums. I would do the same and hear nothing, but he always found the way. He was extremely proud of his name, bestowed on him by the Marine Corps, but I doubt very much if he knew what it meant. He knew no English. His conversations with Emerson, whose French dated from the Lafayette Escadrille, were quite rudimentary.

It will surprise many people to know that the Haitians are the best-read people in the world if you compare books sold to the number of people who can read. I have had more interesting philosophical discussions late at night at friends' dinner parties in Port-au-Prince than anywhere else in the world.

At the time of this first visit to Haiti, the country was ruled by Presi-

339

dent Magloire, a black rather than a "colored" or "metisse," as the people of mixed blood are called in French. Magloire was a good president, certainly by Haitian standards. Good-looking, tall, and with an imposing presence, he loved to dance, and every Saturday night he would go up to the Cabane Choucoune Hotel above the city to dance with the elite of Port-au-Prince. It was an adventure to be on the dance floor with Haiti's ruler. Always in fear of being assassinated by his chief of police, who was reputed to be the richest man in Haiti, Magloire would dance the merengue surrounded by his bodyguards in shoulder holsters. These men were equally at ease on the dance floor, but one had the feeling that one false move and the dancers would all be mowed down on the Cabane dance floor. The floor was outside under a thatched roof. Below one could see the lights of Port-au-Prince far down in the valley. It was much cooler there than in the city. Haiti was a relatively happy place then. This was before Papa Doc and his gang of supporters, the Ton Ton Macoute, were not yet in evidence.

Emerson Cook's interest in Haiti was to help the government raise money abroad. The country had a conservative banker in charge of its Central Bank, a native who had been put in charge by the Marines for whom he had acted as a paymaster to the Haitian workers at the Marine bases. His knowledge of economics was not profound, but he was a sound banker who was careful not to borrow unless he saw the way for the government to pay back the loan. Emerson and I greatly enjoyed doing business with him. Above all, he had great integrity and was surprisingly uninterested in personal gain for himself. He was that rare person in public life: a true patriot.

Since the purpose of the visit was to discuss a loan from New York banks to the government to be funded through the Central Bank, my role was to study the banking system and to make recommendations as to how it might be improved, including making sure that the bank, acting as trustee and agent for the government's loan, would exercise its obligations on the loan free of government pressure. As a result, I had the opportunity to discuss the banking system with ministry of finance officials, to make recommendations on the banking laws and to draw new legislation on the control of the banking system and on the role of the Central Bank. At the same time, I rewrote the insurance law. The minister of finance at the time, Alexandre Dominique, had become a friend of Mercer's and quickly became a friend of mine as well.

Alexandre Dominique came from a poor family but had had an opportunity to get an American education. His family had had a butcher shop in Port-au-Prince. Alexandre studied economics. He was appointed by Magloire because of his personal integrity. Because of this, he was terrified that he would be pressured by other ministers not as honest to adopt financial projects in which they were personally interested. Obviously, this role involved great delicacy. If he did not respond to pressure, he risked being assassinated by those he turned down. If he did, he risked being sacked by the president whom he would not have advised honestly. On a subsequent visit, Alexandre confided to me that he had become convinced that his predecessor in office had been poisoned. The story in Port-au-Prince was that this elderly man had gone home to lunch and then to make love to his current mistress in whose arms he was supposed to have expired. But the body had been immediately taken away by the police and buried on the same day without the proper Catholic religious observance under the aegis of the Archbishop. Had he been poisoned, as Dominique was told? And if so, by whom? On orders of the president, the chief of police, or other members of the Cabinet? It was quite evident that if the story were true, Alexandre Dominique did not know how to escape the same fate. In a country as poor as Haiti, there were too many opportunities for government officials to request a bribe and too much pressure to accept payment, if only for the sake of physical survival. I did not look forward to the time when my friend might ask me for advice in a given situation of this kind.

A year or so later it happened. Dominique sent me a cable asking me whether I could come to Haiti immediately. I took the plane the same day for Port-au-Prince, arrived late at night and was taken to the Cabane Choucoune as usual. At 6 o'clock the next morning, a man stood in my room, calling through the mosquito netting, "Wake up, I need to talk to you." We sat on the edge of the bed, and the finance minister of Haiti handed me a piece of paper with a simple letterhead: "The White House." The letter contained only two paragraphs. It was addressed to the president of Haiti. The first paragraph contained a brief recommendation for an engineering firm in the Midwest I had never heard of which had applied for the contract to build a dam in the Artibonite Valley. The second paragraph read simply: "If you can afford to hire this firm, you cannot afford to do without them." The letter was signed simply, "Harry S. Truman." Alexandre Dominique was in a state. "The president has told me I must tell him what he should do by 9 o'clock this morning. The letter arrived three days ago and he is embarrassed it has not already been answered by courier."

"Alexandre," I said, "Have you spoken to the American ambassador?"

"Of course not. That would indicate I doubted the genuineness of the document and be seen as an insult to the president of the United States."

He was convinced it was genuine and indeed the signature was clearly either the president's or a good facsimile. Without waiting for my analysis, he went on. "Thibaut, you are my friend and I have always been able to talk to you freely. This is a twenty-five million dollar contract. If this firm does an unsatisfactory job, the president will replace me. But worse yet, the country cannot afford to lose such an amount of money on bad work, since, as you know, Haiti is a very poor country. Our government is filled with persons who do not approach public service as you and I do and are always looking for payments for anything they do on official business. But how could the United States president act in this manner? I have always admired and respected the United States. Why would the president of a rich country like that behave like a Haitian?"

"Alexandre," I replied, "there has to be an easy answer. President Truman is not about to recommend an incompetent firm to your government. I have, however, never heard of this firm—which doesn't necessarily mean anything. But anyone who reads a newspaper has seen the president's signature on public documents reproduced in the press. It is easy to reproduce a letterhead and a signature. I confess that I did it myself to serve my government during the war. Don't be so concerned. I will go back tomorrow, check it out quietly and send you a message, the text of which we will agree on in advance to let you know whether the firm is capable of doing the work and whether the signature is that of the president's. That is not difficult."

"You understand this, and I myself believe what you tell me, but President Magloire will not understand why your president would do such a thing to us even for a friend, and he feels he must answer the letter today."

I could not convince him to take additional time despite my offer to go with him to his meeting with Magloire. "That would never do," he said. "Obviously, he does not know I sent for you or showed you this letter, which has been sent to him in confidence by the president of the United States." There was nothing further I could do.

Later that day, Dominique came back to see me. He was all smiles. "What have you done?" I asked.

"We gave the firm a $250,000 contract for a preliminary study. If they do it well, we will know the firm is reliable and we will then give them the full contract."

"And if they do a poor job or none at all. Then what?"

"Then we will know that the president of the United States behaves as our politicians do."

I did not pursue the matter further because I was asked not to. The firm with the contract pocketed the money and was never heard from again.

This is perhaps an extreme case of what can happen when the normal safeguards of intergovernmental exchanges are ignored, but, unfortunately, I have seen real instances of senior government officials in various countries demanding favors—in some cases very substantial favors—in exchange for economic assistance. I have come to the conclusion that morality has nothing to do with economic well being. The worst instances I have run across were those of people who were very well off—political appointees—but their standard of living demanded constant replenishment of capital. Maintenance of social standing can often be the greatest temptation to corruption.

My legal work for the government of Haiti led to additional legal representation in that country. I received a visit one day in New York by a young woman who was a mining engineer. She was the granddaughter of two famed presidents of the Anaconda Copper Mining Company and had discovered somewhere in the interior of Haiti a large amethyst deposit. She brought some to the office with her because she had decided that the operation might be large enough to support a public offering. I think she had begun to be very frightened about want might happen to her in Haiti if she didn't have a well-financed American company to support her claims. She had built an airstrip in the area, had put together a makeshift army of guards, prospectors, engineers, who worked with her. She had built herself a house in the jungle, cleared the land and flew herself in and out of there in her own plane. What she wanted from me was help in getting the financing she needed. Unfortunately, before we could put the financing together, she was unexpectedly diagnosed with terminal cancer, and died very suddenly. So far as I know, her mining venture died with her, because I have not heard since that any mine has been developed in Haiti.

I had never met a woman mining engineer who flew herself to a hideout mine in a foreign country before that. Joanne was hard, very good-looking, very direct, very Irish and fun loving. She could be alternately coarse, crude or soft-spoken and cultured. She had once married a hopeless alcoholic whom she had met at a New York cocktail party, married in three days and taken down to her mine site, where he lived in an alcoholic state until he was able to escape several weeks later and fly back to New York. She should have been a man. She had all the acumen and drive of her Anaconda crusader grandfathers.

Another who became a friend and client was the scion of an old Swiss family named de Coppet who, along with a Harvard roommate, had inherited five million dollars when each of the two fathers had died their senior year. The two young men had decided that after gradua-

tion they would go down to Wall Street and make their fortunes. Unfortunately, this was 1929. In the Great Depression that followed, they promptly lost half of the fortune they had inherited. They then decided a change of air was called for and they started a freighter trip around the world. In due course, the freighter they were on stopped in Haiti. They liked what they found, and since they both spoke French fluently, they had no language problem. They took a suite at Oloffson Hotel on the bay in Port-au-Prince and settled in. Both being very fond of poker, they began regular poker games at the hotel. Marine Corps officers and local dignitaries would drop in to play. After a while, as often happens in faraway places where there is little to do in the tropical evenings, the game became a fixture. One night, when they had enjoyed a good deal of the local rum, they found themselves winning consistently. Finally, there were only four players left. Still, they won every hand. Then one of the remaining players, looking at the mound of chips in front of our two friends, said, "I will play one more hand, table stakes to the extent of the chips in front of you which are all the chips on the table." The young men did not need to win nor did they care to play high stakes with the local businessmen and government officials who could not afford to lose much. Nevertheless, they finally agreed to play a last hand … and won again.

The next day, while they were still in bed nursing a hangover, a group of men carrying files arrived at the hotel to deliver them to the young men. Upon examination, they found they had won the deeds to all of the former sugar properties east of Cape Haitian in the north of the country almost to the Dominican border. The man they had been playing with was the minister of finance. These were the properties that had been planted in sisal under a program sponsored by Eleanor Roosevelt and funded by the American government. When the war broke out, the American government bought all the sisal to make rope for the

344

U.S. Navy, and so the two young men became exceedingly rich. One, Waring Strebeigh, had returned to New York. His only duty was to negotiate the sale of the production once a year in Washington to its only customer, the U.S. government. The other, Andre de Coppet, remained in Haiti to handle the production and the delivery to the U.S. Navy. When I met Andre many years later, he was paying over 75 percent of the entire Haitian budget and besides that building roads, schools and housing for his workers in the northern part of the country. It was a story out of Somerset Maugham's *Tales of the South Seas*. Perhaps the exception was that Andre de Coppet was scrupulously honest. He liked and admired the Haitian people and did what he could to give employment to those willing to work. He gave his advice when asked, but he had been careful to stay away from local politics.

One Saturday morning when I was working at my desk in the office—one worked on Saturdays in the 1950s—I received a phone call from Port-au-Prince to tell me that a severe government crisis had occurred, that a Haitian senator had been sent to New York with all relevant papers which he would personally deliver to me that morning so that I could study them over the weekend, and that I should make an appointment with the New York surrogate—the judge in charge of the settlement of descendents' estates—as early as possible Monday morning. A few minutes later a very tall, handsome, well-dressed black man asked to see me. His name was Senator Loi. His story was startling: It concerned a former president of Haiti, Dumarsais Estime, who had during his term of office organized a World's Fair in Port-au-Prince. He was reputed in the country to have made some 100 million dollars out of the venture. While allowing a substantial discount for local exaggeration, the government was convinced that there was certainly enough money to finance a local coup d'etat. Estime's wife was very active politically in the country and was thought to be financing arms shipments to the opposition. The government wanted this stopped. A way had to be found to do this. The senator had been sent to the United States with all necessary powers, it was thought, to do so. His presence resulted from the fact that Dumarsais Estime had been found dead in his beautiful New York Central Park West apartment a few weeks earlier. This meant that his personal estate would be probated in New York City before the New York courts. Senator Loi had it on good authority that his wife had already petitioned the Surrogate that she be appointed Executrix of the estate on behalf of their three children. Because of its French background, Haiti uses the Napoleonic Code as the basis for its laws. In Haiti, as in France, an estate is left to the children of the deceased in equal shares. I could find no quarrel with what had been told to me and asked the senator what he wanted me to do. "It is simple," Loi said. "The president left three children, that is true. But he also left four illegitimate children, and as you know, under the Napoleonic Code illegitimate children are wards of the state. We want you to represent the state and ask that you be appointed executor. If not, there will be a revolution in Haiti."

We went together to see Judge Frankenhaler on Monday morning. Much to my surprise, he cut off his court proceedings and gave us as much of his time as we might need. He asked many questions, Loi gave him the answers he was looking for, and at the end of our session he appointed me executor of the estate of Dumarsais Estime to represent the four illegitimate children who were wards of the state. The task then began: to find without delay where the late president had hidden the supposed fortune that he had acquired during his term of office. I had a personal interest, because by agreement with the Haitian government approved by the surrogate, I was to receive 20 percent of all assets of the estate in addition to being reimbursed by the government for all costs incurred.

Our first job was to make sure that the widow be under constant surveillance whenever she was not in Haiti. This was not easy, as her husband had left her a palatial apartment in Paris as well as the one in New York. I had both immediately put under seal. I then hired a police inspector in Harlem who took a leave of absence and worked directly for the Haitian government under my direction. A Paris colleague did the same there. It turned out quickly that several million dollars of jewelry had been purchased in Paris a year before the president's death. Since madame always traveled with a bodyguard and a jewelry case which never left her side, that could explain this purchase. We also quickly found leads to bank accounts in New York, Paris, Geneva, Tangiers, and Saigon, but the sums were not as expected. False leads came everyday from Port-au-Prince. It was a lengthy and discouraging process.

Then, a sudden lead seemed to be promising. Estime's doctor who treated him for malaria in New York was a specialist in tropical diseases living in Brooklyn. He had evidently been treating the president just prior to his death. Mme Estime went to his house in Brooklyn frequently with her bodyguard and her famous attaché case. I secured a court order for a search of the house, served it on the doctor and on madame's lawyers as required by the order, and one fine spring day

346

lawyers and court attendants proceeded to search the premises. When we arrived at the attic we found a Louis Vuitton French trunk with the initials "D.E." on the side. This is it, we decided. A locksmith was found, the trunk was opened and we all peered inside expecting to find stock certificates and currencies. Alas, there was only dirty laundry! We could surmise that whatever had been there had somehow been withdrawn despite the order of the court, but that promising lead had failed. Was the Haitian government's action sufficient to prevent the purchase of arms to finance a coup within the country? I shall never know. At any rate there was no coup, and in time the search for further assets was abandoned. There was little reward to show for the exercise, but as *opéra bouffe*, it was surely a classic.

As I have said before, I like the Haitians and I believe they have been dealt a bad hand by the United States. They suffered occupation by the Marines from 1916 to 1934, hardly an opportunity for the absorption of American culture. Then the country served as a laboratory for the more outlandish agricultural ideas of Henry Wallace and Eleanor Roosevelt. Thereafter, the United Nations doctors, in curing the yaws, that syphilis-like disease that killed the young, substituted perhaps a worse disease—hunger from the overpopulation that ensued. In the 1950s when I first went to Haiti there was as yet none of the population pressure which is so great today, the eventual and foreordained result of the curing of yaws. During the Clinton administration, the United States government again sent troops to Haiti on a supposed peacekeeping mission to restore democracy. It did little to solve the economic problems which make it impossible for democracy to flourish there.

The United States is constantly holding out to the populations and governments of developing nations the promise of economic wealth if they will but adopt democratic institutions similar to those in the United States. Yet we always fail to realize that in a country where there is no middle class, democracy is but a sham, or at most a cover for political abuse. Haiti is a country of remarkably hard working and cultured people who cannot possibly subsist in a small area where the topsoil has disappeared because of years of devastation. It is a Catholic country where the Church encourages population growth and democracy must remain a myth.

But Haiti is one of the few countries in the world where I have traveled in utter safety by myself in the remotest country districts among people that have hardly enough to eat themselves. I have been given food and shelter when there was little of either. I have felt perfectly safe.

Haiti

We are no friend to poor countries.

347

Haiti   True, in their history, the Haitians have been guilty of terrible acts of violence against their own people, but if you study what they did to the French at the time of the Revolution, you will be surprised how few acts of vengeance there were, compared to how Frenchmen behaved toward Frenchmen at the time of their own Revolution, which incidentally occurred at the same time. Toussaint L'Ouverture, the Haitian hero of the Revolution, was a self-educated man of great moderation. Haiti has always been a battleground between the blacks and the coloreds. The mistake of the French was to get caught in the middle and risk being considered as the enemy by both sides. Haiti today is a country where the respect for authority is still strong, although authority has been so often abused recently. It is also a country where the Catholic Church is both heeded and respected, although it is a foreign church whose priests and monks come from abroad.

In the 1950s when I was there, prejudice in the United States was a day-to-day problem. A Haitian president, cabinet member or ambassador headed for Paris, New York or Washington, would have to pass through Miami, because that was the only airplane terminus from Port-au-Prince. There he would have to spend the night in a tenth-rate hotel, because the good hotels did not accept blacks. He would then make the morning flight to New York, check into the Waldorf-Astoria and take a suite on the *Ile de France* or the *Liberté* on his way to Paris.

Today, as Haitian refugees in their leaky boats make their way to Florida, there is a new and perhaps worse prejudice facing them when they arrive. The Latinos don't want to see them come, because unlike the early Cuban refugees, they are poor and uneducated. African-Americans dislike and fear them because they see their own chance for a job being lost to strangers from yet another country. They have seen the Cubans, and now the Haitians and the Nicaraguans and the Salvadorans—many black and poor—being helped by church groups to settle in south Florida and find jobs, and they say, "What about us? Why isn't someone helping us?" It is a very valid argument to them. Are we to discriminate against those born in Florida because they have had a chance to get an American education? We still cling in the United States to the principle that an American—be he white, black or Asian—has got to make it on his own like everyone else. The African-Americans who succeed leave the ghettos for the white man's world when they can without further thought for their former neighbors. The Latin Americans and the Haitians come from a quite different culture. They survive—as did the Cubans earlier—because they help each other. The most discouraging social phenomenon in Florida recently is to see the blacks in their townships loot and destroy each other's property to signify their deep feeling of abandonment. The Haitians and others who have survived political and economic repression at home and the perils of the journey are quite different. They know if they are to survive it must be because of their capacity for hard work individually and together as a family and community. How do we pass on this concept to the African-Americans of our American ghettos when so often the family consists of a single mother and no father to help support numerous children? Why aren't anti-abortion activists demanding more government support for needy families with children to feed? Morality is fine but does little to control the world's population explosion.

There are many Haitian taxi drivers in New York. Many live in Brooklyn and their children attend Catholic schools there. The schools are strict. If the children can't keep up, they are sent to public schools. I recently had a Haitian cab driver tell me that he had nine children and all nine had graduated from college in the United States. He too lived in Brooklyn. One has to admire what the Haitians who have come to the United States have accomplished.

Haiti

*Emperor Christophe's impregnable fortress in Haiti. No
one knows how many men died in building it, but U.S.
Marines were unable to bring down its cannon.*

XIV

A TOUCH OF POLITICS

*M*UCH HAS BEEN SAID in this book about the role that luck plays in a person's life—good luck or bad luck—because they alternate. No one is forever lucky or unlucky. As I look back, I have been probably more fortunate than most. How can one prepare oneself for a stroke of good luck so as to be sure to take advantage of it when it comes? Conversely, how can one avoid consequences of a period of bad luck when it, too, comes? I suppose Napoleon's comment is as good as any ever made on the subject: apprized in the field that the members of the governing Directorate in Paris, jealous of his accomplishments in winning victories on the field of battle against the Austrians, had denigrated his accomplishments by ascribing them to luck, he merely said, *La chance est aussi un talent*—Luck is also a talent. This says it all: hard work, preparation, skill, knowledge, training, will enable you to take advantage of luck when it comes.

Politics is a lure for the unwary.

An experience we had in Bellport, Long Island, led me to think of this question once again. We had moved there in 1954, hesitantly, not at all sure that this was the answer as to how to avoid bringing up three healthy children in the New York City environment where the public schools taught you little and the private schools taught you that you should go through life as someone special, different from others. The simple answer was to move to suburbia, but the thought of having to be disciplined enough to catch the same train each morning and return in the dead of night in winter was abhorrent to me. I went to Bellport, Long Island, originally to sail—on those weekends in the spring and fall that beckoned one to get out of the city. I had a great friend who had a sailboat out there. In college, Uncle Willie, as he was known to the children, weighed well over two hundred pounds and had a twenty-eight inch waist. For that he was sought after by the Yale freshman football coach until, reluctantly, he agreed to play, and promptly broke the varsity quarterback's leg as he sacked him. After that, he was left alone.

Willie, like Ferdinand the bull, was a most peaceful man. He liked to sail, tell stories to the children, drive fast European cars, and spend his time drinking beer with friends. The twenty-eight inch waist had long since succumbed to lager. My boys loved him, so I would take one or the other to sail with Willie off Bellport whenever the chance arose. That was how we discovered this lovely village of the 1820s, when Bellport, New Bedford and Nantucket had all been centers of the whaling trade. In the 1950s, long after the cut to the sea had filled with sand, it had become a village where the scientists from the nearby Brookhaven National Laboratory lived. They had bought the old houses for amounts even they could afford, fixed them up, and turned the gardens over to their wives, so that the effect was that of an English village, with a village green, a proper village church, and flowers everywhere.

Bellport had appealed to us as a place to raise our children. So we first rented a house for the summer, and eventually moved out for year-round living, first renting, and then buying our own house. Because my hours at the law firm were so long—I had reached the point where I had three secretaries who worked eight-hour shifts—I had rented a small but attractive apartment in a private house on East 85th Street near 5th Avenue in New York where I stayed during the week. My thought was to work hard during the week and take long weekends with my family in the country. It didn't work out that way except in the summer.

I had found my brief venture in city politics after the war fascinating and absorbing. But one day my wife told me: "You can either be a serious lawyer or a politician, but not both. Since you are not independently wealthy, you'd better stick to the law." It was good advice.

In Washington, however, I expanded my political relationships. My friendship with Claiborne Pell, senator from Rhode Island, had always been very close, going back to our time at the Bovee School together when we had both been eight years old. I had done legal work for him from time to time and our families knew each other well. I also knew Hubert Humphrey, Frank Church and Gene McCarthy well. In 1960, I had suggested to Frank Church that he move to New Jersey to become president of Fairleigh Dickinson University. This would have given him an excellent base from which to run for the Senate from that state and eventually from that position, to make his run for the presidency. In my view had he done so, he would have been the Democratic candidate in place of Jimmy Carter in 1976. I know he thought about it a long time before deciding that he could not leave his position as the leading Democrat in the state of Idaho. I was with Gene McCarthy in the

Senate the day he decided to run for the presidency against Lyndon Johnson. These three senators, along with Bill Fullbright of Arkansas, had all been on the Senate Foreign Relations Committee. They had served the country well.

At Bellport, our neighbors and friends, the scientists from Brookhaven National Laboratory, came from many countries. The chief engineer who built the cyclotron was Dutch. There were German mathematicians, Italian biochemists, and a Greek doctor, whom no one respected, but who discovered L-dopa. Brookhaven was unusual in that it was run for the government by a group of seven universities headed by the University of Rochester. Because it was not a government agency, the rules were more liberal than would have been true otherwise. Scientists from Europe with leftist leanings could work there. Sometimes even Soviet scientists came, and the Brookhaven people attended meetings in the Soviet Union. Among our friends were mathematicians, physicists, botanists, doctors, biologists, zoologists, engineers, chemists, and others interested in the peaceful uses of the atom.

Quite often we would go to dinners given by the director, a physicist who was at once an academic, a researcher, and an efficient administrator. At these dinners, as likely as not, Rosamond would be seated next to a middle-aged man who had no dinner-table conversation, no social graces and the physical appearance of a truck driver who had sat in his cab too long. She would complain on the way home that, try as hard as she could, she was unable to coax any conversational interest out of this man. I asked the director about him.

"That man is one of the two or three in the United States who has done more than any other scientist for our understanding of the atom," he said.

"My wife thinks he has the manners of a truck driver."

"He was a truck driver," my friend replied. "Let me tell you his story, because it is an unusual one. He is not a Ph.D. or even a college graduate. And he has not been able to extend our knowledge after his extraordinary discoveries of ten years ago. He was driving a truck when he met Dr. Oppenheimer. It was shortly after the end of the war. Dr. Oppenheimer was on his way to Los Alamos. Paying no attention to the gas gauge, he ran out of gas on that stretch of desert road in Arizona that they warn you not to cross unless your gas tank is full. When the car stopped, he sat by the side of the road waiting for some motorist to come by and help. In due course, a large long-distance truck came along and offered to take Oppenheimer to the next gas station. As he sat in

353

the cab, Oppenheimer saw that the floor was littered with copies of the *Journal of Atomic Physics.* He picked up a copy, looked at the driver, and started asking him questions. He soon realized that the driver was fully familiar with the subject."

"What are you doing driving a truck when you have this knowledge of physics?" he asked.

"Simple. I made a girl pregnant in high school. I am a Catholic. So I married her. We now have three children and I drive a truck to make a living and support my family. But the only thing that interests me is physics. And so when I can, I read whatever I can find on the subject."

"Obviously, you know the subject. If you should ever decide to get into atomic physics, come and see me and I'll give you a job."

"Oppenheimer gave him his card. The next year, the truck driver showed up in Washington. Eventually, he came to us and has been here ever since. He is certainly a genius in the field."

Wasn't this a story of luck?

My partner, Pete Lewis, was having marital problems at the time. He had married a beautiful Czech girl from the coal-mining district of Hazelton, Pennsylvania, who had come to New York to work for the investment-banking firm of Hayden Stone where she worked on mergers and acquisitions. Trudy appeared to be a professionally tough Wall Street executive, whereas in fact she was a highly moral Catholic girl who dreamed only of getting married, moving to the suburbs and raising many children. Pete didn't want children. He wanted his beautiful wife to be a clotheshorse to match the wives of his New York Jewish real-estate development clients. He bought her the most expensive and fashionable dresses to wear, but she hated the wives of Pete's clients who were just as hard-boiled as Trudy appeared to be. Pete's refusal to have children had affected Trudy to the point that she could forgive him nothing. He, on the other hand, making frequent trips to Hollywood on Technicolor business, was certain to seek in relationships with other women the kindness and solace his wife wouldn't give him. It was a terrible situation as I was very fond of both of them and could do nothing to help.

One day as I was about to leave for a short two-week trip to our Paris office, Ten Eyck & Saint Phalle, Pete Lewis came into my office. "You're leaving for Paris next week Thibaut. If Ros is not going to be using the apartment while you're gone, would you mind if a friend of mine from California spent a few days. I see her when I go out to Beverly

Hills. Now she has agreed to come east and take in some theater. You wouldn't mind, would you?"

This was a moment I dreaded would happen. Pete was my partner and my friend. He was also godfather to my daughter and a friend to us. I couldn't refuse, but I couldn't discuss it at home either, because Rosamond would certainly have told me to say no. It was March and I was quite sure Rosamond would not be coming in.

A Touch of Politics

"Of course you can. I'll leave you the keys on my way to the airport."

I arrived back on a Sunday afternoon and called home on arrival. Something was decidedly wrong. The children were enthusiastic and loquacious as usual, but Rosamond was distinctly frosty. The next day I found Pete Lewis extremely upset.

"What happened?" I asked.

It took a while to get the story out of him. He was wild about a girl from California, a young movie actress he had met out there on one of his trips. Everything had turned out as he had hoped. She seemed to be as fond of him as he was of her. She loved the apartment and settled in. The day before she was to leave to go back to the coast, on a Saturday morning, he had taken her down to Bergdorf and bought her the most beautiful mink coat he could find, spending some $35,000. Sunday he had driven her out to the country to play golf. When they returned, all was as it should be in the apartment, but the coat was gone. She accused him of sending it back to Bergdorf's after he had had his way with her. She had gone back to California angry and deceived. He accused me of having a light-fingered cleaning lady. I feared the worst.

A $35,000 mink in the incinerator

When I went to Bellport on Friday as usual, I was not met at the station. That evening I learned the truth. Rosamond had come in to see a friend on Sunday. A determined woman, she had assumed it was *my* friend to whom the coat belonged. She had taken the new fur coat down to the basement and put it in the incinerator.

I had to explain to her what had happened. But there was no way to retrieve a $35,000 mink coat—nor a love affair ended on a sour note, nor the lingering effects of misplaced suspicions.

I never loaned out the apartment again.

During this period of my life in New York, I spent a good deal of time in politics. It was not something for which I had any particular vocation. I like people, and the feeling is generally reciprocated. But I am a very private person. The glad-handedness and sophistry of the

A
Touch of
Politics

Taking
power
from
Tammany
Hall

political world leaves me uncomfortable. For some reason I have never been able to remember off-color stories, not even when they are humorous. And the endless chitchat of politicians can be extremely boring. But in the post-war period, those who had spent time in the armed services were led by what they had experienced during the war to take more than a passing interest in political affairs. I had been asked to join the American Veterans Committee in New York by a colleague who was active in it. I was immediately turned off by the attempts of radical leftists in the organization to take it over and dropped out quickly. But I spent more time with two close friends who, disgusted with the way Tammany Hall ran the city of New York, had decided to take over control of the Democratic Party in Manhattan. Somehow or other our experience during the war had convinced us that this was not an impossible undertaking, particularly after meeting Carmine de Sarpio, Bert Stand, and others of the district leaders. My particular political friends were Courtlandt Nicoll, descended from the family that was given an original land grant covering half of Long Island, Joe Broderick, son of a highly-respected supervisor of banking in New York State, and Arnold Fein, a lawyer who later became a much admired judge of the appellate division of the Supreme Court. There were some twelve of us, as I remember, on the original board of directors of our organization, The Fair Deal Democratic Party, as I recall. Joe Broderick, the youngest partner until then admitted as a member of the firm of Sullivan & Cromwell, was our leader.

The first difficulty in electing a district leader in Manhattan was to get on the ballot. Judges of the Supreme Court in the county of New York were elected after designation by Tammany Hall. Since the Democratic Party controlled the county and was in turn controlled by the district leaders appointed by the Tammany Hall organization, it was clear that any petitions filed to have placed on the ballot new candidates not approved by the organization would be invalidated for one reason or another. Getting control of the districts was not an objective for the faint-hearted. But under Joe's leadership and with the help of lawyers who were members of our group, we eventually did get control of all the district leaderships in Manhattan by replacing the Tammany nominees.

Did this mean New York had become better managed as a result of our efforts? In many ways, yes. But to an extent that I would never have expected at the time I joined the group that replaced the old Tammany organization, I have come to have an appreciation of the machine politics that then controlled our larger cities. There were certainly ample rewards to politicians under the old system. But there was a quid pro quo carefully observed. Cities in America were always areas to which immigrants naturally gravitated, just as they later became the areas to which the blacks coming from the south in search of jobs, or now the Hispanics, have tended to migrate. The machine tried to find jobs and in return demanded and received the vote. But these were not votes that would affect key areas of foreign and domestic policy outside, perhaps, labor issues. On those issues the big-city machines were willing to follow the guidance of the national leaders of the party. It must be remembered that most of the men who ran these organizations were the sons or grandsons of immigrants, if not immigrants themselves. They were dedicated Americans and perfectly willing to put national interests first on the broader issues, if not too many questions were asked about bids and contract awards for municipal services. Roosevelt, for one, understood such men as Carmine deSapio and Mayor Daley perfectly. They would follow his lead on national and international issues: he would not concern himself or the party with municipal contracts—and the electorate poor would be helped by the machine politicians to get jobs or food baskets for their elderly. Democratic votes in favor of aid to England before the United States entered World War II would never have been forthcoming were it not for the machine politicians who ran the big cities. It is interesting to note that Roosevelt's stab in the back speech about Mussolini's attack on France after it had already lost the war to Germany in 1940 cost him the New York county vote in 1944, which went to Wendell Wilkie. Not even the Tammany machine could protect the White House on this speech which every Italian in the city took to heart as a personal rebuke. That it was amply merited had nothing to do with the political reaction of Italian voters who were determined to punish Roosevelt for his speech against Mussolini.

Politics left some fond memories: serving motion papers on Bert Stand in his district headquarters in a darkened street in lower Manhattan in the middle of the night, where "the boys" were sitting around a table playing poker and I wondered if I would be allowed to leave quietly, or those 3 a.m. dinners with Arnold Fein and his wife of belly lox and bagels on the lower East Side after a night of campaigning. The political tapestry of New York City is endlessly changing and constantly stimulating. The problems are particular to large cities where immigrants tend to congregate. Ethnic pressures continue to grow. The city needs its wards and its ward politics if it is to take care of its poor and its elderly. Business leaders turned politicians will not do that. The leadership must be "born" within and come from below, not superimposed from on top. The ties that are important are religious, ethnic, national—nothing else counts.

It is a world to which few of the elite are ever admitted.

Ten years after the founding of this local Democratic group headed by Joe Broderick, we decided to hold a tenth anniversary dinner to celebrate our political accomplishments starting from nothing. The dinner was a black-tie affair attended by the mayor of New York, the District Attorney, and the Democratic senator from New York, and Mrs. Eleanor Roosevelt. I had never seen our directors at a black-tie affair—borrowed or not (generally we met in slacks and a sports shirt)—and I must say, they looked more distinguished than expected. Joe himself was not there. A year or so earlier, he had called a board meeting of the Fair Deal Democratic Party. We expected that he would announce his engagement to one of the handsome women on the board. Instead, he told us he had decided to give up the law and politics to become a Dominican monk. We were dumbfounded. He had intelligence, integrity, great presence, perseverance, and understanding—in short, all the qualities which make for a great lawyer or political figure. What would the Church do with such a man? There were Cardinals who were monks. Or would he be a theologian, a great teacher of modern Church doctrine? I had suggested to the board that we send a telegram to the director of the seminary in Canada where Joe was still being prepared for the priesthood asking if he could attend the dinner which was, after all, in his honor since he had founded the organization.

The answer was read at the dinner: "Since Brother Broderick has only been studying at the Seminary for just over a year, we do not feel he is ready to come out into the world just yet, and hence he must decline the invitation you have extended to him." When the telegram was read at the dinner, there was dead silence. It was an extraordinary moment, as each of the important political figures who were our guests were made to realize how the Church considered that one who had made such a success in temporal life might still, despite a full year of study in theology, not be ready even to attend a dinner in his honor. It had a very sobering effect on the assembled guests.

Through Courtlandt Nicoll and his and my friend, Maurice Rosenblatt, I became involved at this same time with the National Committee for an Effective Congress (NCEC), whose treasurer I became until I left for Switzerland in 1971. The idea behind the Committee's creation was a simple one: it should be possible to help finance candidates for Congress regardless of party who were intelligent, honest, and far-seeing. This would mean they would not have to depend for their election on PACs or other organizations which frown on candidates who think independently, preferring to give money to those who will do as they are told.

While the committee was dedicated to working with candidates irrespective of party affiliation, in practice the persons we supported tended to be liberal rather than conservative, because we believed that there was an effective role for government to play in planning for the country's economic growth and in protecting the elderly and the less fortunate of our citizens. It was an interesting group containing such intellectuals as Barbara Tuchman and Henry Steele Commager, businessmen and lawyers like Sidney Scheuer and Tom Finletter.

It was during a period when intellectuals and people with ideas tended to be from left of center rather than from the right. Many years later, because the ideas of the left became redundant and sterile, there was a reawakening of conservative thinking at the same time in both England and the United States, but this was not so in the 1950s and 1960s. Men like Taft and Goldwater were highly regarded by some in the Republican Party but were hardly intellectual giants. Furthermore, these men were considered by most to be out step with the new responsibilities which the United States had undertaken abroad in the aftermath of the war. The focus of intellectual discontent and action centered on attempts to get rid of Senator Joe McCarthy. It is hard to understand now, several generations later, the fear and hatred that that man inspired both in his aims and his methods. There was, in his view, a vast Communist conspiracy in the United States determined to turn over the country to the ruthless Communist regime of the Soviet Union headed by Joseph Stalin. It is true, of course, that there were Communist sympathizers close to the seats of power—men like Hess in the United States and Burgess and McLean in England, but in an attempt to unmask them, McCarthy denounced many people who had no connection with the Soviet Union. Many of my friends in the OSS like Ina Telberg, Paul Frillman, and John Davies, who had rendered enormous services to the country, had found themselves under attack. As McCarthy became more shrill in his vituperations against the liberal establishment, he began to polarize the country between those who favored his activities like Representative, later Vice President, Nixon in California, and the Democratic leaders of the Senate, friends like Bill Fullbright who was chairman of the Foreign Relations Committee, Frank Church of Idaho, McCarthy of Minnesota, Claiborne Pell of Rhode Island.

What was happening had come home to me in a very personal way when I took my three children to the Catholic Church in Bellport one Sunday to hear the priest in his sermon announce that there was an antireligious Communist conspiracy gaining strength in the country, that with President Eisenhower sick, parishioners should write to their Congressmen demanding that a senior committee of key senators be appointed to guide the country in this hour of crisis. His candidates: Senators Homer Capeheart of Indiana, William Jenner of Illinois and, of course, McCarthy of Wisconsin, were of extreme conservative views. Next week, he said he would point out who were the leaders of this Communist conspiracy. My children, on the way home, kept asking me who were these unidentified monsters who would sell out our country to Stalin. The next Sunday we were told it was the National Committee for an Effective Congress. I wanted to invite our priest for lunch so that we could show him a fine Catholic family of his parish and identify my link to the Committee so that he could ask any question he wanted. My wife persuaded me not to do so for fear that the children, who understood none of this, might be attacked as Communists in school. Passions are easily stirred in a small community like Bellport.

Here was the Church in politics once again.

What had caused this particular problem was an attack by Mc-Carthy on the Army of the United States and a decision by the leaders in Congress to force hearings on the issue. A few of us at NCEC played a key role in urging the hearings and in making sure that the Democrats played a passive role, leaving the conservative Republicans to judge for themselves the type of man McCarthy was. This is what happened. Senator Flanders of Vermont, an outstanding Republican, made a speech demanding the hearings. With others I worked all one night on the speech which launched the hearings. A pixie-like lawyer from Boston named Welch defended the Army in such a way that Mc-Carthy revealed himself for what he was, a bully who would use every form of lie, deceit, and innuendo to attack innocent people. The result was censure by the Senate at the urging of its chairman, Senator Arthur Watkins of Utah, a conservative Republican who was thoroughly disgusted by what the hearings had revealed.

This was the end of McCarthyism. It would not have happened had the Democrats not refrained from making it a non-partisan investigation. Here NCEC played its finest role in helping rid the country of a very dangerous man. I was proud of having played a role in this effort.

When my close friend from the days when we were in the same class as eight-year-olds at the Bovee School in Manhattan, Claiborne Pell, decided in 1960 to run for the Senate from Rhode Island, Jack Kennedy, who was having a poll made by my friend, Lou Harris, to analyze his chances for the presidency, offered to have Lou Harris examine at the same time Pell's chances in Rhode Island. When the survey was completed, it indicated Pell had little chance. But owing to a split in the Democratic organization, Pell, an economic conservative, won the nomination and in the general election received even more votes in Rhode Island than Kennedy running on the same ticket for president. In state elections the voters are swayed by local rather than national concerns. This is one good reason for the indirect election of president or prime minister. The United States is the only developed country where the man in charge of policy for the country is elected directly. In most other countries, he is the leader of the political party that controls the legislature. The American system was devised as the result of fears on the part of the Founding Fathers that too powerful a government would result in political tyranny. The result is that we frequently have in the United States the executive branch in the hands of one party and the legislative controlled by the other resulting in a stalemate when little gets done.

I could never figure out why Church's predecessor as chairman of the Senate Foreign Relations Committee, Bill Fullbright, who had been president of the University of Arkansas, founder of the Fullbright scholarships, and a man of sense and sophistication, disliked the French so. One day in 1965, I went to see him to give him a copy of my book, *The Dollar Crisis*, and get his support against a proposal to take the United States off the gold standard. As I waited for him to get off the phone, I thought of the approach I would take.

"Senator," I said, " I have found the solution to your problems with de Gaulle and the pressure he is putting on us to pay our debts in gold. All we have to do is undo the Louisiana Purchase and our debt will be taken care of. As I thought about it, I realized that it would solve his problems with you as well because Arkansas was part of the Purchase and you would become French."

"What do you suppose de Gaulle would do with me?"

"Obviously, Senator, you would be the next ambassador to the United States."

Fullbright burst out laughing.

"Well, that would fix Johnson. He's always calling me over to the White House on some fool project having to do with his war in Vietnam. And I could save my roses from Mme. Alphand, whose dinner guests are always running over my rose bushes."

Mme. Alphand was famous with the press as a great ambassador's wife. But she had turned a friendly and very important senator into an enemy of France for something which she could easily have solved.

One day I received a phone call from a Mr. de Menil from Houston, Texas, who asked if he could invite me to lunch. I was then 39 and beginning to get calls from time to time from companies that were interested in hiring me away from the law. This happens frequently to successful New York corporate lawyers at this stage of their careers.

Mr. de Menil told me at lunch that I had been recommended to him by a headhunter in New York. He was looking for a general counsel for the Schlumberger Corporation, a large New York company listed on the Stock Exchange, which was controlled by his family. He pointed out to me that if I accepted the position, I would have to move to Houston and take up residence there although I would be spending part of my time in New York, part of my time in Paris, and a good deal of my time travelling, since Schlumberger was in many respects the leading oil services company and active all over the world with interests in many different areas. The oil services portion produced an enormous cash flow. The salary Mr. de Menil proposed to me was twice what I earned as a corporate lawyer. I reported all this to Rosamond, who told me to check out the costs of living in Houston.

"I suspect we cannot afford it," she said.

Women are much wiser than men in such matters. She was, of course, correct. Mr. de Menil expected his key executives to live as he did. The house would cost $250,000, the clubs $100,000 initiation for each of several. It became clear to me as we continued our discussion that while in due course my stock options would make me very rich, I would be working for the banks for some time in the interim. I turned down the challenge.

When I tell Texans the story, they cannot understand my decision. They say, "Look what it did for George Bush to move to Texas!"

XV

BECTON, DICKINSON

*P*RACTICING LAW IN *NEW YORK CITY* in the '50s and '60s was
hard work but it was also fun. As one became more and more
proficient in the profession, it was possible to spend less time on
the technical and more on the psychological. This was true especially
in personal relationships with clients, learning to understand better
their needs and desires, their willingness to take risks, their motivation.
As a business lawyer, what interested me most in acting as an advisor
and counsel to business executives and their companies was handling
mergers, acquisitions, or corporate restructuring for clients. To do any
work well I felt I had to understand a client almost as well as a client's
business. I had to have a close personal relationship with the chairman,
the president, and the key officers. In most cases, they became friends
as well as clients, men with whom I could happily discuss more than
just the legal questions about which they needed to consult me. I had
respect but little liking for lawyers who looked at corporate law only
as a problem to be solved analytically. What I enjoyed was the human
relationship. It was the human dimension of a given legal problem that
I found interesting. Even in corporate mergers, one had to be always
aware that after the difficult price negotiations, the parties would have
to continue to work closely together.

From
lawyer to
corporate
executive

In representing other than business clients, the human dimension
was, of course, even more important.

I am reminded in this connection of the tragic death of young Bill
Woodward. His parents, William and Elsie Woodward had been friends
of my parents. They were two highly admired people in the New York
business and social community. Bill Woodward who was the chairman
of the Central Hanover Bank had given me my first job in the summer
of 1937. His son William had married a young actress from the Midwest
who was unfamiliar with the social life on Long Island. The marriage
had not been a success, and there were rumors of an impending divorce.

One evening young Bill had gone to New York by himself. When he returned in the middle of the night to their home in Long Island, his wife,
thinking he was a burglar, had shot and killed him. The district attorney,
not believing her story that she thought he was a burglar, had had her
indicted. Now her mother-in-law Elsie Woodward had asked my firm
to represent her. I had sat in on the meeting to discuss the case.

"I don't care whether she is guilty or innocent of the murder of my
son," Mrs. Woodward had told us. "She is the mother of my grandchildren and I want her acquitted. You will send all your statements
to me. I am entirely at your disposal for any help you may need." Elsie
Woodward never told us whether she believed her daughter-in-law to
be guilty of the murder of her son and we never asked her. We knew our
role. She fulfilled hers. Although the two women were not close, and
had nothing in common, it was Mrs. Woodward's action at the trial
that resulted in her daughter-in-law's acquittal. Afterward I don't think
the two women ever saw each other. The children were brought up entirely by their grandmother. Years later, I would see Bill's wife skiing in
Gstaad. She eventually committed suicide.

The practice of law in a small firm requires close relationship of respect between the partners. When I joined the firm in 1950 as a partner
there were only two active partners left in what had in earlier years been
a much larger firm headed by William Travers Jerome the famous New
York district attorney who had prosecuted the murder of William Mc-
Kim White, the architect most responsible for the beautiful mansions
built in the city in the last years of the 19th century and the early years
of the 20th. We had in our safe file the entire transcript of the case along
with Jerome's margin notes showing how he would handle the trial. I
read them one weekend. I hope they have been preserved in some law
school as a record of how a brilliant prosecutor handles a difficult case.

The firm had grown slowly since my coming in 1948. Ken Lidstone, a professor of taxation at Harvard, then another tax partner, then
George Lewis, Jr. who became my close friend and godfather to my
daughter Thérèse, then Charlie Jaffin to help me on the corporate side,
then Ted Kheel and another labor law partner who brought us the *New
York Times* as a client. We knew each other well, respected each other
and enjoyed working together. Because the firm was small, each of us
knew what the others were working on and we were always ready to
lend a hand if need be. I enjoyed vicariously following what each of my
partners were involved in and made sure they were up to date on my
international merger negotiations.

Becton, Dickinson

364

On a given matter, I might represent an American company making an acquisition abroad or a foreign company seeking to expand in the United States. Businessmen in every foreign country had a different way of looking at dealing with Americans or making an acquisition in the United States. The Japanese were always seeking U.S. government approval for anything their companies might want to do in this country; the Europeans distrusted lawyers who wanted to make business decisions; the French were distrustful of Americans generally; the Germans were easy to work with. They knew what they wanted. I was always surprised when Americans whose business was to be acquired by Germans would tell me they would retain some shred of independence. This is not the way the German mind works. When Daimler acquired Chrysler, the American executives accepted orders or resigned. If an American company wanted to purchase a business in Europe, its lawyers would prepare a forty-page document requiring the foreign company and its executives to guarantee all aspects of its business. This would convince the foreign executives that the Americans distrusted them and make the negotiations more difficult. Why were American businessmen incapable of negotiating their own transactions? Europeans did not want lawyers to negotiate for them. They had difficulty understanding the role of lawyers, our tax system and American accounting regulations.

Today, all international business has been Americanized. American lawyers and accounting firms and investment bankers frequently represent both American and foreign firms involved in an international acquisition. American legal terminology and American accounting rules have now become the norm.

One of my first international acquisition clients was Becton, Dickinson and Company (B-D), a medical instruments firm in New Jersey created in 1897. The company made thermometers, hypodermic needles and syringes, blood-drawing equipment. In addition, it was gradually expanding its operations to take in chemical compounds used in diagnostics and surgical tools. It had grown rapidly after World War II. The company had made a first small acquisition in Brazil because Corning had a plant there and the glass manufactured there was therefore of sufficient quality to make hypodermic syringes where stock and barrel were freely interchangeable. The company believed it was now ready to expand to Europe. Its bank sent them to me for advice on negotiating an acquisition in France. The chairman, Fairleigh Dickinson, had made several trips there recently and had decided to acquire a small engineering firm there which already manufactured steel tubing of smaller dimensions. My wife and I were invited to accompany Dickinson and his wife Betty on a trip to France to meet the owners of the factory and negotiate the acquisition.

Going on a trip abroad by ship with a couple one had only just met is a strain at best. Neither Dickinson nor his wife spoke much French. They did not know France outside of Paris. In Paris, they knew only the restaurants where Americans went like the 'Tour d'Argent' and 'Laserre' and a few art galleries. They had met René Schmukler and Andre Vintraud, the two owners of the French factory at a technical seminar in Paris but did not know them well. These two men had come to France after the war and had established this small company to make medical stainless steel tubing. Schmukler had come from Hungary after the war. He was the engineer and head of the company; Vintraud, a Pole by birth and only recently in France, was in charge of marketing.

On those days a trip across the ocean on one of the big liners was a delightful experience. My wife was very outgoing and could relate to almost anyone. My job was to learn as much as I could about the company I had been asked to represent and to try to understand just why the owner wanted to buy a company in France and why this particular one, which had so little to recommend it. The food on board was excellent, the wives found much to talk about, and Dick and I had plenty of time to get to know each other. I learned that his father had founded the firm, that the father had only had one child (at the age of sixty), that he had been a brilliant engineer, that he distrusted everybody, that he had been persuaded during the depression to give $5,000 to start a small college in northern New Jersey where he lived and had set up his company, that he had sent his son to military school in North Carolina where he came from and then to Williams College only because his wife insisted upon it, that his whole life was his work. Dick had never engaged in sports. He was well read, his wife played golf, he had few friends, but loved going to France and enjoyed French food and wine.

In Paris we settled into two suites in what is today the Inter-continental Hotel on the rue de Castiglione with large bedrooms and sitting rooms facing the park.

Schmukler and Vintraud were invited by Dickinson to come to Paris to meet with us. They were to bring with them financial statements. To my surprise, the price had already been agreed upon. The American company's chief operating officer had already visited the plant and would fill me in on my return on any additional details I might need to complete the transaction. Dickinson, Schmukler and Vintraud all appeared to feel that the deal was already in place. Schmukler was to be president, Vintraud sales manager; there would be four directors: On the American side, Dickinson as president of B-D, Bob Burrows, the head of international operations, and Schmukler and Vintraud on the French side. For suggesting to Dickinson that since his company was making the acquisition he should control the board, I was designated as a fifth director. We had a great meal together with our wives and then the American group went back to the United States. All international transactions are different but I had never run across anything as cavalier as this one.

It was the start of a whole series of international transactions on behalf of B-D in France, Brazil, Puerto Rico, Panama, Ireland, Italy and even Monaco. On each of these Dick Dickinson handled none of the details of the transaction. The only problem was that no one else handled the details either. The company was apt to stumble into acquisitions that then had to be straightened out later. On the way home I asked Dickinson why he had wanted to buy a company in France and why this particular one. He had a ready answer. "The best nickel comes from Cuba, Thibaut. The French control it and that is why the French make the best stainless steel. We need the best steel for our needles. We will use many millions of feet of stainless steel tubing a year as we grow. This plant will be our initial test in France. The location near Grenoble is fine because electricity is plentiful. We will get our feet wet and learn from having an outpost here." I could not understand why he wanted to be in business in France with two refugees from Hungary and Poland.

Fortunately, I had an office in Paris. To satisfy Dickinson's desire to find out how big the European market for B-D products might be I had the office order a market study made. It was interesting because a market study in France was a new idea. Just finding a firm to do it was difficult. France in the '50s was still engaged in establishing a modern economy following the destruction of the war. Brilliantly, the French government had used its Marshall Aid funds on infrastructure to build dams, establish a proper electricity grid, and begin its nuclear plants. The Americans helped the British in developing nuclear capability but not the French, so France had to train its own nuclear engineers and build its own nuclear plants without American assistance. Because of this, the French are now far advanced over the British in nuclear engineering.

I found myself greatly enjoying my relationship with Dick Dickinson. He had a very broad interest in international affairs, was extremely well read in history and economics. In business, he was a conceptualizer, not a manager. His father had taken him to the plant at a very early age. He learned the business by observing what others were doing but he had never had the opportunity to learn by working his way up the ladder. When his father died while Dick was still in college, he had suddenly become president of the firm without any prior training for the job. He was never a hands-on manager, preferring to leave this to others and to sit in his office figuring out intellectually what trends might lie ahead to affect the company's business.

Later, when the government brought an anti-trust suit against the company, the government was sure all the president's files had been shredded because he could produce none. In fact, he never dictated any notes and had no business files.

I had never represented a family-owned business before. It was a completely novel experience where none of the usual rules applied. The president was accountable to no one because the company was his. There was no board of directors. The executives had no direct interest in the growth of the business because management owned no stock. The Becton family which had been a minority owner from the inception of the business raised no questions because the two founding partners had long ago decided to pay themselves a good salary and forget dividends. The company in earlier years had paid a huge fine as a so-called Section 102 (of the Internal Revenue Code) case where the governments imputed dividends to the owners for failure to pay them. The company was a business lawyer's answer to a prayer.

In addition to its own business, the company controlled a university—Fairleigh Dickinson University—with some 22,000 students in four separate campuses in northern New Jersey. This added responsibility had come about in a strange way.

During the 1929 Depression, a group of publicly-minded citizens in Rutherford, New Jersey had called on Dickinson's father, founder of the company, and prevailed upon him to give some $5,000 to found a small two-year college to meet the needs of a rapidly growing community. The father had given the money while complaining that it was a mistake since youngsters should be working in a plant rather than wasting their time learning what would be of no use to them later on. The college had been named after him and in a few years had become a large, thriving university.

As I came to know Dickinson better, I found him grateful for suggestions that I could give him in devising strategy for his company's interests abroad. It had very soon turned out that the acquisition in France needed new management. The company's product line was of inferior quality. If B-D were to sell the products of the French factory under its own name and brand, the factory would have to be completely re-equipped with American machinery and equipment. Under French law this meant getting the consent of the French government to a substantial increase in the shares of the French company and the use of such capital increase to import into France new American equipment, all of which Becton, Dickinson manufactured itself. It sounded easy but it wasn't. Various technical ministries of the French government had to be involved. Since the equipment was not purchased from outside firms, its fair value had to be determined. When I submitted detailed cost figures to the French Ministry of Commerce, a high official said to me one day: "I don't need all those statements. I merely weigh the equipment you plan to import, to determine its value." It took a good deal of effort to persuade the French government to agree to an independent appraisal of the value of the imported equipment and then a waiver of import duties. But I wanted the estimate of value to be accurate because of the minority shareholders. The lead ministry was the French ministry of Finance which had to give its final approval after other pertinent ministries had acted. I needed to get a waiver of import duties on the grounds that this equipment would result in the manufacture of goods which in large part would then be exported from France. Fortunately, I was able to demonstrate that the French company would be able to import a very sizeable amount of syringes from the B-D Brazilian plant, packaged with the French needles made in France, and then re-exported as French products. This finally ensured the approvals I wanted since the French trade balance with Brazil was heavily in deficit and the French government was delighted to allow imports from Brazil which could result in new French exports. It was a long negotiation but one that ended up very satisfactorily for my clients. This was just at the time in 1958 when Economic Minister Pinay saved the French currency with his borrowing from abroad, supported by France's gold stock. I remember one day sitting in the office of one of the Deputy Ministries of Finance. He turned to me and said, "It is quite extraordinary, the Swiss who are careful financiers are pouring money into our country." I felt like explaining to him that it was only French money that had flown to Switzerland earlier and was now coming home again.

Becton, Dickinson

369

Dick Dickinson loved to talk about international politics and economics. One day, on the train on the way to Grenoble, he turned to me and said:

"Thibaut, I am very much concerned about the value of our currency. You seem to know a good deal about this common market the Europeans are trying to put together and what it may eventually mean to our country. You helped us get our French project approved through using the Franco-Brazilian trade deficit. We are lending more and more dollars to rebuild Europe. I'm afraid in time they will not want our dollars and will instead expect us to import from them so that they can repay us what we have loaned. When we get back to the United States, I would like you to write a book on the subject of our balance of payments. At the university I have a very bright man in international finance. He is an Iranian, Nasrollah Fatemi, who was ambassador to the United Nations and is now head of our international finance department. I will introduce you to each other. The two of you will get along well."

This was typically Dick Dickinson. Like a great many very rich men who have not had to struggle for a living and have been free to spend time thinking of how to bring about solutions to problems others are not free to think about, he saw this question as one that we would enjoy working on together and which might someday result in a useful piece of work which the university could publish. Few of us can be head of a substantial company and in addition control a major university.

In the years to follow I would spend a good deal of time working with the president of the university. He was a remarkable man, combining educational skills with an unusual competence as an administrator and marketer while the other universities—including Harvard with a $19 billion endowment—were losing money every year and having to raise tuition constantly. FDU was making $1 million dollars a year while still paying comparative salaries to the teaching staff. His system was simple. He would tell me:

"Thibaut, I follow three simple rules. I have studied what Harvard does. Their classrooms are working only a half-hour per day. This is ridiculous. Education is the only business where the customer—the student—is totally ignored. At FDU our classrooms are functioning from 8:00 a.m. until midnight. If someone wishes to learn, classrooms should be open on *his* time.

"Secondly, I will not accept gifts for buildings—such givers like to give a building so that it can be named after the donor—unless the giver establishes a fund to carry the maintenance.

"Thirdly, I take advantage of my location in the New York metropolitan area by employing on my professional staff ambassadors to the United Nations—highly qualified men from developing countries—who may have lost their position because of a regime change in their own country. That is how we were able to get Ambassador Fatenie from Iran when the Shah lost his throne."

During that trip to France I had other matters on my mind. The French plant was on strike. The head of its local union was a woman, wife of the leader of the Communist Union which controlled all the union locals in Grenoble. On top of that, the American and French engineers were trying to work together to put the new American equipment in place. As if that were not enough, I now had to get M. Schmukler to resign his post as president so as to put a more qualified engineer in his place.

René Schmukler, the president of the French company, was not only a very secretive man and very hard on his employees, he was also an active Stalinist who once a month went to Budapest for a few days, ostensibly to see relatives. I had warned Dickinson that a French president has unlimited power in the company and cannot be removed except for cause. At that time in France being an active agent of a foreign country and a Communist would not be considered sufficient cause for dismissal. For an American parent to dismiss the French head of its subsidiary in France was particularly delicate. But we accomplished it on technical grounds while avoiding any mention of the political problem at issue. What had caused me to look into why the company's president made all these trips to Hungary was that one day at a board meeting in Paris, Schmukler, in losing his temper with Andre Vintraud, his fellow executive and director, had accused him of being "nothing but an imperialist and a saboteur"—a purely Stalinist turn of phrase. It was obvious that Schmukler was an active Communist.

One of the quirks of French company law is that a corporate board of directors has to include at least one employee from middle management and one from the workers. Both employee members of the board must be given all copies of financial data. I had made it a rule to have a special meeting with the head of the workers union to explain to her in detail what the figures meant and what we were trying to accomplish in bringing in new equipment to make the business grow. Now, to my surprise, she called me aside and told me that she had told her husband: "You can do what you want but my company will not join the strike." Since Schmukler had objected to my briefing the union, this gave me the key I needed to support his dismissal before a French labor tribunal.

Out of the relationship between French and American engineers I learned an interesting lesson. American engineers had designed and built the machinery and equipment now being installed in France. But the French engineers who had to use this equipment would come in to work on weekends on their own time to see how they might adapt them to better meet French conditions. They would say to me: "These are remarkable pieces of equipment but perhaps we are better process engineers than the Americans because in France we are constantly forced to adapt." This reminded me of what Speers, Hitler's Economic minister and productive genius, had said when during the war he made such an effort to get French foremen to come and work in German war plants: "These French foremen are the best anywhere."

When I returned to the United States, I met Nasrollah Fatemi and we became instant friends. We would be working together for many years collaborating on three books and several university courses together. He was a philosopher, a social scientist, a very religious person, and a true gentleman. He did not like the Shah and exiled himself because of him, but I think he would have been horrified if he had lived to see what has now happened to his country under the control of the mullahs. We started planning the book together and I undertook to give some courses for him in his MBA program at the university.

I found myself gradually undertaking more and more projects for Dick Dickinson and for the company. This did not mean I had any less to do for other clients. But it was variety that made the practice of law in those days so exciting. I sat in my office one morning and figured I was working at one time on some thirty-six different matters including those at the Paris office where I went four or five times a year. Fortunately, I had a marvelous secretary both in New York and in Paris. Thankfully, this was also before the fax machine and the invention of e-mail. Today such a schedule would be impossible because of the demands brought about by the new technologies. Some of the matters I was working on appear elsewhere as stories in this book. If living is learning, experiencing, and doing, my life was indeed very full. I loved my work, its variety and its demands.

It was through my work for Becton, Dickinson in France that I met Dr. Charles Merieux. The son of Pasteur's chief collaborator, Dr. Charles had created the Institut Merieux in Lyon and had become known all over the world for vaccines to treat various diseases. There was an obvious connection between Merieux's activities and B-D's work growing out of making injectables. So I was asked to put together a partnership program which became B-D Merieux in France. Dr. Charles' son Alain Merieux became its first head. Today, Alain has become not only president of Institut Merieux which itself owns the Institut Pasteur but the head of its extensive biochemical operations around the world as well as a very important political figure in France. We have been friends now for over thirty years. He and his father represent for me all that is great about France.

Becton, Dickinson

In order to make their vaccines, the Institut Merieux maintained a farm outside of Lyon where the company kept some three hundred horses. The reason: tetanus vaccines have to be grown in the bellies of horses before they can be extracted and used as human vaccines. Dr. Charles called me one day and asked me if I would come to Lyon for several weeks to go through all his books and records so that I might advise him how to reduce his tax burden. In addition to the fee I might ask of him, he promised to take me to dine in all the great restaurants around Lyon.

Dr. Merieux had never run his company to make money. What interested him was the role his company might play in the future of biochemistry in the treatment of disease. He constantly traveled all over the world lecturing and participating in conferences. At the end of two weeks with him, I told him I could save three million dollars in taxes each year for him if he would only create a company in Ireland and move his horses there. He would then take out the vaccines in Ireland rather than in France. I would arrange with the Irish government to give the new Irish company a ten-year tax holiday. The horses would be happy in Ireland since many racing stables already raised their horses there. Dr. Charles listened to me politely and then turned down my suggestion. "These are French horses, Thibaut. They would not be happy in Ireland." I pointed out to him that his horses were valued on his company's balance sheet at one franc and the vaccines in them were surely worth at least 30 million dollars. But I failed to persuade him.

French horses wouldn't like Ireland.

In return, the French government did him no favors. Dr. Charles called me one day in New York and asked me to come to see him in Lyon on an urgent matter. When I arrived there he told me he had received a phone call from a friend of his who was minister of health in the then French de Gaulle government.

"At a Cabinet meeting today, the government decided that something had to be done to make the State-controlled Rhone Poulenc

Company more profitable so that it might compete with large private chemical companies internationally. It wants Rhone Poulenc to acquire the Institut Merieux which is very profitable."

"But I don't want to sell my company."

"The Cabinet thought that might be your answer. I was directed to find our just how much of your business comes from French hospitals, the military, the French foreign assistance programs and to advise you that if you don't sell your company, the government will be forced to cancel all these contracts. You should accept the offer I am authorized to make to you. The government will be willing to let you continue to operate your company as before. I can probably negotiate that you can keep if you wish 45 percent of the shares."

I suggested to Dr. Charles that even though in France the government did control over 50 percent of gross national product there was still a way out. He could have a public offering of a minority stake in his company using a French bank close to the administration and keep control. He turned me down.

"I have two sons, Thibaut. The oldest, who will want to run the company if anything happens to me, likes to race sports cars and has no real interest in the business. The youngest, Alain your friend, thinks like me. If the government acquires a controlling interest in my business, they will put Alain in charge when I am too old. In this way, I lose control but I keep peace in my family which is far more important."

As I see in today's unforgiving global economy how business decisions are made I am often reminded of these two stories involving Dr. Charles and his approach to business. Global competition has changed the way business decisions are made today. It has unfortunately also changed the practice of law as well. The law is no longer a profession but a business and one too often controlled by the plaintiff bar. It is hard to think that these changes result in any good for anyone.

What Dr. Merieux would not do in Ireland, Becton, Dickinson was very interested in doing. I was asked to undertake negotiations with the government of Ireland to see if it would approve an investment by B-D to create a plant there to service the British market. It was worth doing because of the size of the market and that under the then system of dominion preferences it was possible to bring Irish products into both Great Britain and Canada duty-free. The Irish government had an interesting program in order to entice foreign companies to invest in Ireland. The company could get a ten-year tax holiday, reimbursement of training costs of Irish workers, a construction loan to build the plant, and a permit to import equipment duty free. A detailed presentation for approval had to be made to a special government body created for this purpose. To qualify, the investment had to be made in western Ireland where unemployment was particularly high. It was a good program remarkably well administered.

Becton, Dickinson

I set out for Ireland. After meeting with the foreign investment board in Dublin, I rented a car for two weeks and set out for the west of the country. A friend had told me that in order to make the country appear bigger the road were very narrow and winding. There were no hotels in western Ireland at the time outside of the few big towns. This gave me a chance to stay with farmers along the way. It was a wonderful way of absorbing the charm of the region. It seemed as if everyone I met had relatives in one part or another of the United States. I was received everywhere as a friend. But I found one big problem. Under the conference rate set by the British, it cost as much to send freight from Dublin to Liverpool as from Liverpool to Sydney, Australia. Since our products destined for England were not bulky, I had interest in avoiding the conference freight charges. So I went back to the east coast, met with the fishing industry who agreed to take B-D's Irish products across the Irish Sea at a reasonable price and found on the Boyne River north of Dublin, a farm which would satisfy our needs perfectly. I then went back to Dublin to sell the development board on my program.

Taking B-D to Ireland

The board accepted my reasons for putting the plant near Dublin rather than in the west of Ireland. The government was rather pleased that I would use means of transport to Britain through the fishing industry which needed government support.

I could now negotiate with the owner of the farm, a Mrs. McGalloway. I hired a solicitor to represent me. He carefully explained to me the "rules of the game" in Ireland. "Tell me your final price. I must know it, not because I will use it, but because it will enable me to make the appropriate initial offer to the owner's solicitor. You must not get involved in the negotiating process until much later. I will tell you when."

A few days later, the solicitor called me. "We are ready for the final negotiations now. We will meet at the pub and finalize the transaction. Here is what you have to do. We will have a first round of drinks to initiate the discussion. Then the owner will turn down your final offer as proposed by me with an explanation of her widowhood needs. You will counter with a new offer made only because she is such a wonderful person even though you may be risking dismissal for making it. Her lawyer will propose a second round to celebrate this new offer. She will

In Ireland, negotiations are in a pub.

turn down your proposal again while telling you how much she wanted to accept because she likes you so much. We will then have another round. Then you will propose your final price and she will accept it. We will then have a last round to confirm the transaction in the spirit of Irish-American friendship." He was right but it took several intermediate rounds of drinks. At the end of the evening, all parties felt they had had an excellent time.

In Italy people like to sing; in Ireland people like to talk and important events take place in a pub, generally over a drink—or several—and a few good stories.

In addition to France and now Ireland, B-D had a distribution unit in Panama, a plant in Puerto Rico, a manufacturing operation in Brazil, and a joint venture operation in Mexico. At the time, our Mexican partner was itself a family partnership whose manufacturing business for medical products we had bought. One of my jobs was to supervise the Mexican operation although we had an American employee who served there full-time. He was a good friend and whenever I went down there we would go on a hunting and fishing trip below Puerto Vallarta which was then a beautiful, unspoiled beach town on the west coast of Mexico.

One day our Mexican partner who was president of the joint venture told me that he was under pressure from the Mexican government to have us hire a Mexican attorney who had particularly good relations with the government health establishment to represent us in Mexico. Our legal problems were very well handled by an old-line Mexican firm and I did not see any reason to change. "Have lunch with him anyway. He's a very distinguished man. He will take you to his club and you will enjoy meeting him."

The Mexican attorney was charming and very sophisticated. We had an excellent lunch and good conversation. At the end of lunch came the pitch: "The Mexican government feels that your company would be much better off if it had a lawyer in Mexico better able to deal with the medical establishment. Business in Mexico is not handled as in other countries. Here personal relationships are extremely important. If I were your counsel I could make sure your business grew substantially."

"What would you propose?"

"I would be happy to undertake this representation for you on the basis of a percentage of the sales of the company in each year. I believe five percent would be a fair figure."

376

This was before the Proxmire anti-corruption law was passed in the United States.

"I cannot make this decision for the company, but if it was mine to make I would decide to keep our present lawyers who have represented us well in Mexico for many years. But I will submit the matter to my president and see what he thinks."

Becton, Dickinson

We agreed to lunch again a few days later. In the meantime, I phoned Dick Dickinson. I explained the proposal to him and asked for his decision.

"You're in charge down there, Thibaut. You make the decision."

Never pay a bribe.

"I already told him, I would turn him down. If I make the decision, we will lose all our Mexican business since it is with government hospitals, state hospitals or the army."

"But that's an awful lot of money."

"Then you make the decision."

"No it is up to you. But we will lose a great deal of money."

I had lunch with the Mexican lawyer and told him that my president had left the matter to me and that I could not accept his proposal even though I had been delighted to meet him.

When I went back to our Mexican headquarters there was an urgent message from our head of sales. When he came up I told him I knew what he was going to tell me. "We've lost all our business." I then told him of my lunch and that Dickinson had left the decision to me. I told him he would lose his bonus for the year. He burst out laughing. "At last I won't have to make payments to the hospital administrators out of my pocket anymore. Word will have gotten around all over the city that you won't pay bribes."

We both agreed that since our products were the best on the market we would have all our sales back in six months. It worked out that way.

Some years later I was at the Stanford Business School in Palo Alto speaking to the dean who had been president of the Ford Motor Company. He was on his way to San Francisco to address a luncheon about the Anti-Corruption Act.

I told him that I thought Senator Proxmire had made a mistake by passing a criminal sanctions law and that I had told him so. The bill proposed by Senator Church would have required that companies paying bribes report this in their reports to the Securities and Exchange Commission and in their annual report to shareholders. That would have been quite sufficient. It would certainly have simplified my life had I been able to tell the Mexican attorney at lunch that I would have to publicize in B-D's annual report the payments made to him and why they were made.

Some of B-D's ventures abroad worked out well, others continued to have problems. None of the company's executives enjoyed going abroad. To them it was a waste of time better spent at home in their customary activities. This was particularly true of the engineers who were often required to spend time overseas making sure the company's highly sophisticated equipment was working as it should. In Brazil the problems were not technical but financial. Brazilian currency was constantly declining in value as inflation continued to increase each month. If you exported from Brazil the government kept the hard currency earned and gave you the Cruzeiro equivalent only several months later when it had even further declined in value. Whenever I went down to Brazil the president of the company there would say to me, "I have great news for you, Thibaut. We are making more and selling less. The value of our inventories is increasing constantly." That is not what I wanted to hear. "You are simply telling me you need me to send more money so that you can build more inventory. That is not my idea of an economic investment."

In France Mr. Schmukler called me one day to tell me the company had on hand hundreds of thousands of feet of plastic medical tubing that had been rejected because of not being of sufficient quality and what should they do with all this inventory? It was just at the time of the hula-hoop craze. This gave me an idea. I called my cousin Jacques in Paris who was a marketing genius and asked him what to do. He called me back to tell me we should get Brigitte Bardot, the very popular French actress to go up the Champs Elysees at night rolling one of our hula hoops and followed by the press. If I would pay for the cost of bringing her current lover from Brussels for a concert, she would do this. Jacques would have *Paris Match* do a special feature article on her hula-hoop run up the Avenue. So I told Schmukler to convert his medical tubing into hula-hoops. The day after *Paris Match* came out with the issue our French subsidiary received orders for all the hoops we had on hand and much more besides. So much for the power of marketing even in France. Two weeks later I received a letter from my old governess retired in Ghent, Belgium asking me how I could ever have been written up in a story involving a movie actress and hula-hoops. "What did I do wrong in bringing you up that you would end up like this," she asked. I wrote to her immediately to reassure her that her efforts had really not been entirely wasted, despite appearances to the contrary.

Less amusing was my effort to create a Research Center for Becton, Dickinson in Monte Carlo. It came about in an effort to find a place in confiscatory tax Europe where researchers would be able to work free of taxation and in a climatic paradise. Monaco seemed to be the ideal place, particularly since there was a hospital there with enough extra land on which we might build the necessary laboratory facilities. The head of the hospital was enthusiastic when I spoke to him. At the time, the Prince of Monaco's business manager was an American named Ted Dale. He became enthusiastic at the thought of turning Monaco known only for its casino and yacht club into a medical research center known all over Europe. We reached an agreement to be signed at the palace.

I invited Dick and Betty Dickinson to come to Monte Carlo for the signing and secured a suite for them for several days at the leading hotel.

My timing could not have been worse. The night they arrived we had had a festive dinner. At ten o'clock I took them back to their hotel. At a little after eleven o'clock General de Gaulle's envoy to the Principality of Monaco called the secretary of the government to inform him that if Mr. Dale was not dismissed the next day the French army would take over the principality. Apparently, Mr. Dale had been engaged in political activities in the Principality which were considered against French interests. It was do or die for this paradise of the rich.

By the time the Dickinsons woke up the next morning, the Principality was on full alert. Officers in handsome uniforms were at the entrance roads. Others were on motorcycles touring the city. There was great tension in the air. When I called my chairman he said to me, "What kind of an *opéra bouffe* is going on here, Thibaut? I have no time to be part of it. Get us out of here."

So ended our great opportunity to have working for us the brains of European research efforts in continental Europe.

It would take years before the mayor of Nice would manage to accomplish in Nice what I had tried to do in Monaco.

Today over two thousand companies from all over the world have their research centers in adjoining Sofia Persepolis just outside of Nice with special tax advantages extended by the French government. Sometimes it doesn't pay to be perceptive. But what an opportunity we missed. We would have had it all in Monte Carlo!

The next transaction with which I was entrusted by Becton-Dickinson was long-term borrowings from two insurance companies. B-D had never borrowed any money or issued any stock outside the family. The transaction was handled through an investment banking firm. The company's commercial bank had recommended using Ferdinand Eberstadt's small boutique investment banking firm as one which would not frighten a family-owned business. This was my introduction to Ferd Eberstadt, a second generation American of German origin, who had had a distinguished career during the war as head of the U.S. War Production Board. He had been a lawyer before that. He was intelligent, precise, demanding, arrogant, opinionated, but totally honest. I came to admire him greatly and in time we became very good friends. He met the clients, told them what he would do and how much it would cost them, what he would expect them to give his associates in the way of financial information. He proposed to negotiate a 20-year bond issue of $20 million dollars for the company. Since the company had never issued any long-term debt the terms might be onerous but these could be renegotiated in time once the parties had experienced a satisfactory relationship. He was fatherly, confident, and very clear about what he would do. The clients went back to New Jersey confident that the money would be forthcoming very shortly.

As in any financial transaction, the problem is always in the details. How many times had I gone through a business deal agreed to by two company presidents on a golf course and then turned it over to corporate counsel with the statement that all that remained for completion of the transaction was the simple mechanics of reducing the accord to paper. The investment banker, if he knows his business, can play a very important and useful role in making sure that the lender or investor gets the information he needs from the company and that the company gets from the lender or investor terms that do not inhibit the company. The two insurance companies selected by Eberstadt relied on him to get them the information they needed for their protection. B-D relied on him to get terms that would not unduly constrict the company in its future plans for growth. I found it a pleasure to work with Eberstadt on this transaction. I was particularly happy that the two lenders gave me a list of three law firms to represent them as counsel on the transaction and left it to me to decide which firm to choose to represent them. I had worked with one of the three before so this was an easy decision.

Some weeks after completion of this financing which gave Becton, Dickinson the money to finance the growth of its business, I received a phone call from Dick Dickinson inviting me to dinner. He talked at length about his plans for the company.

"It is time we ceased to be a private company. We are growing much too fast and we need to plan for becoming publicly owned. You have now been working with us for a number of years. Henry and I have gotten to know you and trust your judgment. You have established a good rapport with Art Sherwood who is the company's general manager. I would like you to leave the law, join the company as financial vice president and general counsel and prepare us for going public."

Becton, Dickinson

"No, Dick. Now you pay attention to my advice because I am on the outside. You pay me well for my advice and you know you can rely on my independent judgment. But if I join the company I will be an employee and to you nothing more than a servant because you own the company. You will pay no more attention to me than you do to everyone else who works for you. Besides you frequently talk of selling the company to a larger concern. If you do that, where would I be? As the first outsider to be brought in since 1897, I would be the first to be let go, and I would then have to rebuild my legal practice from scratch."

But at the end of the evening I had agreed to join the company as Dickinson wished, to be on the board as well, to receive the same pay as Sherwood, and to purchase along with Sherwood some 250,000 phases of company stock from him at $4 per share, paying 10 percent to him now and the balance out of the public offering of company shares whenever this should take place.

Proposal to join the company

So it was that I left the practice of law. When I told my law partners what I was doing I told them that, as general counsel of Becton, Dickinson I would be happy to give them any outside legal work that they were qualified to handle. I asked for nothing for my interest in the law firm because my new corporate salary would take care of my needs.

To my surprise, my partners wanted a share of my stock purchase. I told them no. The stock purchase was paid for by me, not the law firm. It had no value unless I gave it value through my efforts to come. Inasmuch as I was responsible for a substantial percent of the firm's law business and asked nothing for my capital interest in the law partnership, I thought their demands were very wrong. Although I continued for a time to give them Becton, Dickinson law business, the episode left me with a bad taste.

No matter what the circumstances, the first day after leaving one's profession of many years' standing in order to undertake a totally new job, is a wrenching experience. As I drove my car out to the company's plant in suburban New Jersey, stopping for a sandwich along the way, I said to myself, "What in God's name are you doing this for." I had left my beautiful mid-town office, my partners and my friends, and my secretary of so many years for a new life in an unknown place to work with people I did not really know and to handle business matters I might not be qualified for.

My new colleagues went out of their way to help me get acclimated but they were no more used to having an outsider in their midst than I was in being there. Every morning at 8:00 there was a staff meeting attended by the president of Becton, Dickinson, Dick Dickinson, Henry Becton, Art Sherwood, the head of manufacturing, the head of sales, and me. Others were invited as Sherwood decided. Art Sherwood ran the meetings. Dick didn't say much but everyone tried to figure out how he might want to decide any matter. There had never been anyone in charge of financial matters. I was merely part of the general manager's portfolio. There were no budgets and no cost figures for individual products. I discovered there were 7,800 individual products if one counted the different hubs on individual syringes added to satisfy doctor customers. To me, who had spent those years with Bill Shriver simplifying product lines, the lack of system and controls was staggering as was the total lack of coordination between manufacturing and sales. The company was an orchestra directed by the general manager as sole conductor with individual musicians playing their own instruments quite independently of each other. I listened, asked for information, and visited each of the thirty-five subsidiaries and divisions. I was learning. Everyone was anxious to explain to me what they were doing.

The accountant had been a member of the board of directors. This would not do and I took his place on the board. Before going public, we would have to have three years of financial statements audited by an independent accounting firm. To select the firm would be my decision. I was in no hurry to choose one until I had learned enough about how the financials were put together to avoid having the accountants bring me any surprises that I would not already have anticipated. Dickinson didn't care about financials. What interested him were the sales totals by product line. On the basis of sales figures he estimated what the profit by product line should be. Sherwood had recently attended the Advanced Management course at the Harvard Business School. He made the calculations of results and no one questioned them. The business was growing. That was the main thing. The company designed and built its own equipment. There was no pressure from either Becton or

Dickinson to reach any given financial targets since the only shareholders were family members. The directors asked no questions. The board
now consisted of Dickinson, Becton, Sherwood, the chairman who had
been sales manager and had left some years earlier to join Bristol Myers
as head of sales, and myself. It was a perfunctory board with no outside
member.

I was given the financial statements of prior years to analyze and
dissect. I was cursorily familiar with them because I had been given a
copy of the analysis made for the lending insurance companies by the
Eberstadt technicians. The more I looked at these documents now the
more concerned I became. The sales figures appeared to be accurate
and I knew that these were what interested Dickinson. Becton was the
treasurer of the Republican Party in New Jersey and the affairs of the
company did not interest him so long as he was receiving the same salary as Dickinson. I had been taught accounting at Columbia and in the
long evenings in Lockhaven, Pennsylvania, Bill Shriver and I would go
back to the Piper aircraft plant after dinner so he could teach me all he
knew about the practical side of business accounting. To him balance
sheets, profit and loss statements, and particularly cash flows were what
the movement within the blood stream might be to a doctor or melody
to a musician. I had learned in my international acquisition work how
managers hid profits from the tax inspectors in France and Italy but
this was different. B-D manufactured all of the highly sophisticated
equipment it used in the making of its hypodermic needles, syringes,
thermometers, surgeon's knives, vacutainers and other medical products, but there seemed to be little capital equipment on the books and I
could find no write-offs for product obsolescence. I was puzzled. By my
calculations, the problems had to be in the inventories and the capital
accounts of the parent company. If the figures were to be restated in
accordance with proper accounting principles the company would not
have earned what it told Eberstadt and the insurance companies it had
earned. I came to the realization that the company had to be clearly in
default under its recent insurance company borrowings. The company
had represented the accuracy of its financial statements and I knew now
they were clearly erroneous although I could not, without reconstruct-
ing the statements over several years, state what they should have been.
It was as if Sherwood had merely estimated what he thought the profits
should be in any year. How much of this Dickinson knew, I had no idea.
I spoke to Dickinson about it. He told me to call Ferd Eberstadt and go
down to Wall Street to discuss the matter with him.

When I had finished my presentation to Eberstadt he became as angry as anyone I have ever seen. For a good hour, and unable to interrupt him, he castigated me as if I were personally responsible for what I had found. I finally interrupted to tell him that it was not of my doing and that his own people, if they had done their work properly, would have found what I had.

"Get Dickinson in here tomorrow morning," he finally said as he dismissed me.

Dick would not go in alone. So the next day I had to listen to Ferd's vituperation all over again. "Sherwood must go. I want him out of there immediately. I will send young Dennerstein out to you tomorrow morning and he will stay as long as necessary to restate your financials as they should be. Then you will have to talk to the insurance companies."

I never did find out how much Dick Dickinson knew. So long as the company was a family business and had no public stockholders or any outside borrowings, it did not really make any difference.

Ferd and I both knew the mess was his responsibility as well as the company's, which was probably why he was so angry.

No one at the company knew the details of what had happened. Sherwood took a leave of absence. Eberstadt's people spent three weeks at the plant and prepared a detailed presentation for the insurance companies as though *they* had found the problem. They made the insurance companies feel that Eberstadt was continuing its active supervision of the company. Eberstadt told the insurers he personally would continue to oversee B-D operations and the company agreed to pay his firm a monthly fee for the balance of the year to pay for its supervision. Eberstadt also insisted that I countersign any check over $5,000.

So my role at the company changed. I had Sherwood's job as well as my own. Because all the insurance company funds had not yet been disbursed, I was able to take full control of the company's finances, focus on collecting the receivables, establish a lock-box system to hasten cash flow, establish budgetary controls. Each company or division president was required to give me his budget for the year. The first year they were wildly optimistic, the second year they were too pessimistic. It was like an artillery straddle in the military: first short, then long. The third year the budgets were reasonably accurate. I found myself now working the same never-ending hours that I had put in as a lawyer. But at least I now had a stock interest in the company which I had to make valuable.

As the company continued to grow, one of my problems was to

cut down on the number of products, which had reached 7,800 when I came. I told the sales people if anyone wanted a product that couldn't be produced in large runs, the price would have to be the actual cost. This allowed me to reduce the product line the first year from 7,800 to 350.

I was afraid that Dick Dickinson would sell the company before we had a chance to develop its real potential. While this was only the beginning of the period of corporate integration, Becton, Dickinson was an attractive target in a field that was sure to grow. Dick would not tell me when he had been approached by another company. One day he came to me to say that the McKinsey consulting firm was going to make a thorough study of our company. "Please give them all the assistance you can. They will have people working with our people for two months."

They were everywhere. Financial experts, marketing consultants, manufacturing specialists, research people. They made my life miserable with their questions. Finally the reason became clear. Dickinson had been approached by the Gillette Company in Boston to acquire our company. A price had been proposed and accepted subject to verification and analysis of value and future prospects for the company. I had not been consulted. I gave the consultants what I thought the results would be in the coming year and explained why I had written off all I could in the prior year in order to start with a clean slate on my watch. When the study was finished, the B-D board was given a copy. McKinsey did not think my projections could be supported and had advised Gillette to lower the purchase price. Gillette had done so. Dickinson had refused to renegotiate the price; the deal was ended.

The incident was a lesson for me. I realized that even though I had a very key role in the company and was consulted and my recommendations followed on most matters, the company might be sold at any time without my being aware of it. It was a very sobering experience.

When the McKinsey report was given to us, Dickinson had asked me whether I was confident of my projections. I told him that when I had worked on restructurings with Bill Shriver I had always made it a point to include in the monthly reports a safety factor which would mean that the annual audit figures would be better than expected. I had done so here and I expected the first audited figures by Ernst and Ernst, our newly appointed independent auditing form, would confirm a better than expected result. It worked out that way.

From then on my analysis was accepted. I had learned my lessons

My chairman wants to sell.

385

well from Bill Shriver. If you are running a company you have to concentrate on cash flows, not on profits as reported by auditors. The auditors of necessity look at what has happened, but not what is going to occur.

The next thing that happened to us was a full-scale audit by the IRS. We were vulnerable because of the expensing of capital expenditures for the manufacture of equipment in prior years. The IRS agent spent three months and went over with great care all of the company's financial records. At the end of that time he told me he would very much like to visit one of the company's principal plants. This gave me much concern but he was determined and I couldn't say no. So I sent him to the Rutherford, New Jersey plant. A week later he came back..

"I couldn't find any entries in the books for all that machinery and equipment I found in the plant."

I had visions of fines and perhaps imprisonment ahead for my chairman.

"Experimental. If you come back next year you will probably find everything changed."

"I thought you might say that, Thibaut. But I saw products manufactured, then packaged, labeled and addressed for shipment in a remarkable display of automation. This can't be experimental."

I was desperate.

"Look, this is a family business. I have only just come and I am here to make sure we are keeping books and records as they should be. You and I have worked closely for three months and I am quite sure that you don't want anything done that would close the doors on this business and terminate my employment. I have a suggestion for you. Go to your supervisor, explain to him what we have found and ask him to give you an additional month's period of time so that you and I can visit each of the company's subsidiaries and divisions and determine exactly what should be capitalized and what may be expensed. To date, the IRS has certainly benefited because it is only as a result of past expensing that I am now in a position to pay the income tax the company will pay this year."

"I don't think that will work, Thibaut, because there is no provision in the tax code which allows Uncle Sam to finance a company's growth. But let me see what I can do."

To my surprise, in two week's time he returned with the approval of his supervisor. It was a wonderful opportunity for me to visit all the various plants and ascertain for myself that financial records were being properly kept. I suspect what had happened at B-D in the past was not so different from other privately held businesses. I was, however, very grateful for the decision of the IRS. They could have closed down the company.

Slowly, the company began to be run as any business ought to be. We acquired other small businesses in complementary fields; we set up a research operation in the chemical and biochemical area. We were also approached from time to time by much larger corporations that wanted to buy the company. I now became involved in such negotiations, but I think Dick Dickinson was now focused on taking the company public.

This is not to say that there were not emergencies along the way to turning B-D into a publicly owned corporation. The principal distributor of B-D's products had been for many years a company based in Chicago, Illinois: American Hospital Supply Corporation. In 1960, the president of the company notified Dickinson that it would handle competing products. Dickinson then notified the distributor that if this happened he would feel obliged to cancel its special arrangement with the distributor, and he did so. Unfortunately, the president of the distributor had very powerful connections with Republican Senator Everett Dirksen of Illinois. The 1960 presidential election was so close, that if Illinois had gone for Nixon instead of for Kennedy, Nixon would have won the election. Senator Dirksen had been generally credited with persuading Nixon, the losing candidate, not to ask for a recount in Illinois despite every indication that there had been massive electoral fraud in the city of Chicago favoring the Democratic candidate. Indeed, Kennedy had secured a large enough majority in the city to more than balance the heavy turnout down state in favor of Nixon. The new president and his brother, the attorney general, were disposed to extend political favors to Senator Dirksen.

Without warning, and to our complete surprise, the government of the United States, through its Department of Justice, served B-D in early 1961 with a massive anti-trust complaint seeking an injunction against cancellation of the contract with American Hospital Supply Corporation and triple damages for any loss incurred. It was a very serious matter for B-D because American was the largest distributor of medical products in the nation and a far bigger corporation than Becton, Dickinson. Dick Dickinson became very concerned that if the anti-trust litigation was not settled quickly, the B-D's initial public offering might have to be delayed.

He asked me what I thought.

"I believe the government has a weak case. To win, it would have to stretch the anti-trust laws beyond their current application."

"This is too important a matter. I want the most prestigious anti-trust firm in the country to guide us in this lawsuit."

I called and made an appointment with the leading Wall Street firm Dick had selected. We were received by two senior partners, two middle partners and several associates in a pine-paneled boardroom. They proposed getting a delay in answering the complaint while they organized a massive undertaking to examine our files for any evidence of anti-trust violation on our part.

Now, my view of answering the question put by anyone in authority is to give the most complete answer possible going far beyond the question put, especially if the authority putting the question is looking for something that does not exist. In our meeting with the lawyers, Dickinson had been very much put off by their attitude. They seemed to think without looking at the facts that we were surely at fault.

When I had told him what I thought the legal charges would be for that first meeting and the request for $100,000 retainer, he seemed much more objective in his outlook.

"What would you do?"

"Simple. I think this action was taken to repay a very important political favor. I believe the government's case is very weak. But when the government goes after you, it has to be taken very, very seriously. What I would do, if you will let me, is to overwhelm the Department of Justice with the most detailed amount of data that is possible to lay our hands on whether pertinent or not. I want to hire a group of law students, explain what to watch out for, put them to work examining every shred of paper relating to sales of our products, and then hiring a bunch of trucks to take all this to Washington. We will want to take up so much of their time on a bad case that the Department of Justice will never bother us again. Settle this case, never. We want them to be so sick of Becton, Dickinson and Company that if you really wanted to violate the anti-trust laws in the future, you will be able to do so with impunity."

That is what we did. After four years, after repeated attempts on the part of the Department of Justice to get us to agree to settle the case on any kind of basis which would allow for the government to justify the filing of its anti-trust lawsuit, the Department of Justice simply agreed to discontinue. The political debt had long since been paid. The lawyers at the Department of Justice were delighted to see the case off the docket, and B-D had had no interest whatever in even discussing the matter. More important, our public offering had not been delayed.

The Eberstadt firm would of course be the underwriter. Our relationship with Ferd Eberstadt had by now long ago been re-established.

Becton, Dickinson

At the end of the first year after the insurance company loan disaster and the dismissal of Sherwood, Ferd had invited Dick and me to a lunch at his firm with his partners. I told Dick I proposed to bring Ferd a gift to reward him for his "help" in putting the company in good condition once again. Without telling Dickinson what I proposed to give him, I visited a taxidermist in New York and purchased a stuffed crow which I had beautifully packed in a Tiffany box. It was only when Ferd was about to open it at the lunch that I began to wonder whether he had a sense of humor.

Eberstadt opened the box slowly telling his partners how pleased he was that the company had re-established his earlier confidence in its future and how pleased he was with us. Then he opened the box and saw its contents. There was a dead silence.

"I suppose I deserve this."

"Ferd, you not only excoriated me once but again the next day with my boss. We thought fitting that you might now want to eat this lovely bird. But this was my doing and not Dick's."

Ferd gets a crow.

He laughed. From then on, the crow was on the buffet in his dining room. He used to tell this story to his luncheon guests and I think was really quite proud. Of course, he claimed it was due to his supervision of our finances without mentioning its high cost to the company.

When we were ready to go public I learned a great deal from Ferd Eberstadt. He had told me, not without some degree of self interest, that since we intended only to sell a small portion of the company stock to the public, we should set the price low enough so that all the buyers of the company's securities would make a great deal of money. "In that way, on your next financing the public will pay too high a price because they will only remember how much money they made on the first go-round." Ferd felt particularly angry at what had happened on the first sale of Ford stock when the underwriters had set the price too high and the sale had not been a success, causing angry Ford owner investors to consider switching to other auto brands. Ferd and I set the price. He wanted to go at $20. I wanted $28. We settled at $25.

The evening before the underwriting was to take place, a catastrophe occurred.

I was driving home to my house in Hohokus after a day in New

York with the underwriters when I heard over the radio that the president of one of our smaller subsidiaries in New Jersey had been arrested for selling tainted blood to Cuba. No sooner had I arrived home than my phone started ringing—first Dickinson, then John Simmons, the executive vice president of the company, then Eberstadt. They were all frantic. So was I, but I had to think of what could be done. The subsidiary in question was so small its business and financial statements did not have to be reported in the prospectus becoming effective at noon the next day. I had to make sure that even though the head of the sub had been indicted, no action would be taken against the parent company or its officers and directors. If I could get the district attorney of New York County to agree to take no action the public offering would be able to take place. I had a former law partner who was a close friend of Bob Morganthau, then the district attorney. I also knew Bob well from the days after the war when we had both been active in Democratic reform politics in New York City. I asked my partner to call Morgenthau at home so he would agree to see me first thing in the morning in his office. Then I asked Dickinson and Simmons to sit down with the president of the subsidiary and to make sure we had a detailed statement of just what happened so that we would be able to show that there had been no intent to cause harm. The important thing was to keep everyone in the know busy so that word would not get out until we had the facts. I don't recall exactly how it was accomplished, but by the time I had my meeting with the district attorney I had the full story and I was able to explain to him that there had been no intent to harm; the vials in question had not been destined for export but for in-house testing.

By 11:00 we had the clearance we needed from the authorities and Eberstadt was able to go ahead with the underwriting without having to reveal any of this. It had indeed been a very serious matter. Had there not been a solution and had the public offering had to be postponed it would probably never have taken place because in the world of pharmaceuticals, a company cannot allow the quality of its products to be questioned without the risk of irreparable damage.

With the underwriting of B-D stock in June 1962, I was able to sell twenty-five thousand shares and use the proceeds of $625,000 to pay the balance I owed Dick Dickinson for my four percent stake in the company along with the capital gains taxes I owed the state and federal governments. On paper, I was now a millionaire at 44 years of age. I had worked very hard for the company and had managed to make my friend and client Fairleigh Dickinson a very rich man. But I was deeply grateful to him for giving me the opportunity to achieve financial independence. I had certainly worked very hard for it. Now I would have to decide what to do with the rest of my life.

In the early days after the public offering of B-D stock, I had made it a point to meet with analysts from Wall Street whenever they came to the company's offices in New Jersey to talk about the company. They always wanted to know how much we spent on research although they had little understanding of the difference between research—the search for what might in time result in new products—and development—the engineering process by which existing or new products might be engineered to become economically justifiable. The Putnam Fund came out to see me quite frequently and I had made a real effort to explain the company to them. At the public offering, this fund had purchased a substantial amount of stock.

Some months later, I received a phone call from one of the vice presidents of the fund.

"You have been helpful to us and we have made a good deal of money out of our investment. So I thought it fair to tell you what we are going to do. We are going to let brokers know that we think the company's stock has gotten ahead of itself and that the price is no longer justified. For this reason, we have sold our position. We expect to buy it back a few months from now at a considerably reduced price after others have followed our lead."

I walked across to Dick Dickinson's office. He was outraged. "My father was right. Investment managers and bankers are nothing but scoundrels."

My own view was different. Firms that manage other people's money have a duty to make judgment calls in buying and selling their investments. I saw nothing wrong in what Putnam had done even though it could be looked upon as a deliberate act to reduce the value of our stock. But with over six thousand mutual funds now publicly traded and countless money managers it is hard to imagine that there are not constant efforts made today to manipulate the equity markets. The investment world is not for the uninitiated or the squeamish.

I had promised my wife Rosamond that if and when I had made enough money to ensure our own future and the education of our children, I would leave the law and business and join the State Department. She had always hoped that one day I would do this. She was made to be a diplomat's wife. She had extraordinary charm, loved people, spoke many languages, adored travel. Unfortunately, she did not live to see what we would be able to do, after B-D became a public company.

In early June 1960, I was struck with a terrible personal tragedy. Three years earlier, when we were living in Bellport, Long Island, and when I was still practicing law in New York during the week, my wife Rosamond had been diagnosed with a cancerous melanoma. We had had the best doctor we could find in New York perform the operation. He had assured us that if the cancer did not come back for three years, she could consider herself in remission. But then just as the three years were up, the cancer came back and this time it was all through her body. She died in August, 1960. Our three children, Fal, Pierre, and Thérèse, were then fourteen, twelve, and nine.

It had been a nightmare. Knowing what would happen to my wife, I sent the boys to camp and my daughter out west to a ranch with a friend. Rosamond had not wanted the children to observe the physical change which the cancer would cause her. But when they returned, they found their mother gone and their father trying desperately to figure out how to look after them and keep a full-time job besides.

The property in Hohokus consisted of a large English-style country house, nine acres of lawn and shade trees, a pool, tennis court and three-car garage. It seemed terribly empty when we came home. I had to find someone to care for the children as quickly as possible, but where? There was no one in my family I could call on for help. I was desperate. It would take me three years before I found the right person. In the meantime, I knew I did not want to continue to live in New Jersey. I needed to be back in New York City. My children would go to boarding school when they were ready. I would try to keep Thérèse with me as long as possible. I cannot tell you how many efforts I made to find help. I called friends. I advertised. I even called on my dentist. He sent me an older woman from Long Island who wanted to find a temporary job for her daughter who would take care of children while getting her divorce. Mother and daughter arrived in a Cadillac, mother in a Helen Hokinson hat, daughter in a diaphanous silk gown with little on underneath. I had sense enough not to hire her. Several young women I knew, including two in Paris, proposed marriage as a way of solving my parenting problem. I was not ready for any additional responsibilities.

I realized then that there was no way I could maintain the job I had at Becton, Dickinson, including the constant travel and still undertake the new responsibilities I would have in keeping my family together and taking care of three children. Dick Dickinson was totally oblivious to my new responsibilities. He decided to bring in John Simmons from running one of the smaller subsidiaries and make him executive vice president of the parent company. John would not have been my choice. He was an able executive but didn't seem to me to have the breadth of vision to be in charge of a rapidly expanding, internationally-oriented company. But he had been Dick's roommate in college and the two were close.

Becton, Dickinson

With Dickinson's consent, I had shifted my focus to completing the public offering of B-D stock and assuming not only the business but the legal preparations for this important step in the future of the company. This meant spending less time in global travel and a great deal more on the preparation of the legal and financial documentation.

I knew I wanted to get out of living in New Jersey as soon as possible. I would go back to being a lawyer and represent the company as its outside general counsel once again rather than as one of its key executives, responsible for law, finance, and international operations.

Since I couldn't leave New Jersey right away, I put the two younger children in the Tuxedo Park School during the week and the older one in Saddle River, where I could take him each morning. What really had me desperate was that it was impossible to find anyone who would help me as governess for the children while I remained in New Jersey.

My old law firm had merged with a larger firm. With Dick Dickenson's approval, I temporarily joined this firm as counsel and recouped my former legal secretary to help me organize the documentation we would need for the registration statement for the company. So some days I worked out of the New York law office, some days out of my office at B-D. And I continued with my teaching at Fairleigh Dickinson University on weekends.

It was a very complicated life, but is was probably better to keep busy. The children and I were equally lost by the death of their mother.

It was a very difficult time for all four of us. The children missed their mother. Their father could not replace their mother's love and care. I had no nice mature relative to call on for help. It would take me two more years to find a really competent person to serve as housekeeper and help me with the children. In Europe it would have been easy to find such a person. In the United States, with all our technology and pride in comfortable living, for a widower with no family to call on for help in such a situation, there is no easy answer.

Somehow or other I managed to get through this very difficult personal and business period. The children managed to do well in school and we spent evenings, weekends, and vacations together. B-D went public as scheduled. I found an apartment in New York and eventually a competent housekeeper. I joined Coudert Brothers as a senior partner and gradually shifted my responsibilities at B-D. I did not realize, pressed for action in so many directions at once, how many options I really had.

Not wanting to go back permanently to my old law firm, I called Alexis Coudert, the senior partner of Coudert Brothers, and proposed lunch. I told him my plans, that I would come to the firm with at least $250,000 of legal work, that I wished to be a senior partner with the same participation as he and other seniors, that I wanted only to do corporate law and hopefully some on the international side, but I had no interest whatsoever in being part of law firm management. It took only one meeting with the other senior partners and Dick's approval of the arrangement. I kept my directorship at the company and my link to Fairleigh Dickinson University. It seemed like a good solution to me, particularly since the Coudert firm had offices in Paris, London, Tokyo and Hong Kong which would be very helpful in my acting as general counsel for Becton, Dickinson in projecting its growth worldwide.

It was only after I had accepted going back to the law firm that business executive friends told me, "Thibaut, you were a member in very high standing of what we call 'the Business Executives Club.' Why didn't you tell us and we would have made sure you became CEO or CFO of another company with New York headquarters?" It had never occurred to me.

I probably should have taken a year's sabbatical from B-D on full salary—which I had certainly earned—to figure out exactly what I should do at this stage of my life and with my new responsibilities for my children.

XVI

BOBBY KENNEDY

D URING THE YEAR AFTER MY WIFE died in 1960, I did not want to go to parties or see anyone except family or particularly close friends. In any event, I was so busy in my personal life being both father and mother to my three small children, moving away from New Jersey, settling them in the right schools, that I had little time to do anything else. My business life, as I have explained, was also in the midst of great change. I felt confused, unsure of my future direction, able to concentrate only on what I knew I needed to do in both my business and personal life.

Friends tried hard to be helpful. I went to dinner parties from time to time, but only very gradually did I develop any interest in pursuing a relationship with any of the attractive women my friends would have arranged for me to meet. I was too unsure of myself, and it took a long time for me to want to get involved. I was also concerned about the effect this might have on the children. Some time later at a dinner in New York one night, I met a young woman whom I found fascinating. She was intelligent, beautiful, charming, with an easy flow of conversation. I began to take her out. We found we enjoyed doing things together. I invited her to the house. The children found her easy to talk to. They quite evidently liked her. We invited her to go skiing with us on winter weekends. She was so open and relaxed that it seemed to us that I had always known her. When I wasn't with her, I began to feel I wanted to be. She was quite a bit younger than I was, but she had already had a very full life. It had been both unusual and unusually interesting.

Gretchen—and I have not given her right name for reasons that will become clear—was born in Nazi Germany. Her father had been a professor, art historian and author of several books on European artists. He and his wife had had only one child, this daughter. The wife's mother was Jewish. This was in the late 1980s. Her husband knew that it would only be a question of time before his wife would be arrested and he would be forced out of his job at the university. He was determined to save his daughter, who was 16. So he had gone to Hamburg, found the captain of a German freighter in the South American Trade and made him the following proposition: the captain would marry the girl, take her on his next trip to Brazil, swear not to touch her, and once there divorce her. In return for this, he would be paid in advance the sum of $10,000 in German reichsmarks. The captain had accepted the proposition, kept his word, and his bride in name only had ended up in Rio de Janeiro, divorced and safe from the Nazis. Unfortunately, soon after, Brazil had followed the United States in declaring war on Germany. As a result, Gretchen had spent several months in a Brazilian internment camp. Father and daughter did not meet again until after the war ended in Europe in 1945.

The new German government, looking for a man of intellectual standing and no possible link to Nazism, appointed the father as ambassador to France. His wife having died in a concentration camp, his 20-year-old daughter became his official hostess at the German Embassy in Paris. There at an official dinner party she met an important American government official, C. D. Jackson, who had been chairman of *Life Magazine* before taking up government service in 1940. They began to see a great deal of each other. The relationship had turned into a love affair and a proposal of marriage. But Jackson was already married. Gretchen had reviewed the matter with her father. The German ambassador had reminded his daughter that she was a Roman Catholic, that she could not marry a divorced man and that if she proceeded to have an affair with a well-known senior American government official, he would feel constrained to leave his ambassadorial post. One can only commiserate with what must have been the difficult role played by the first post-war German ambassador in Paris. Gretchen, who was understandably very close to her father, terminated the relationship. In time, she came to the United States, became a citizen and was hired by the National Conference of Catholic bishops in the United States to run their Washington office. She very soon became as well known in New York and Washington as she had been in Paris. She had all the attributes for success: poise, beauty, intelligence, sophistication, friendliness and enthusiasm. She was also a very good listener.

One morning I had a call from Jack Kennedy's close friend and Harvard roommate, Charles Spaulding, who was also a good friend of mine.

"I want you to come to a quiet dinner with Bobby Kennedy," he said. "I think he wants to discuss what is happening in Europe."

The three of us had a lengthy dinner at the University Club in New York in a private dining room. It was quiet and we could talk freely. At the time, Bobby Kennedy was serving as his brother's attorney general. As the president had explained the appointment to the press, "What is the point of being president if you can't give a job to a brother in need?" But Bobby had turned out to be a very able, active—almost aggressive—attorney general, in particular going after gangsters in the labor movement. He was well organized, ruthless and worked well with the Congressional committee headed by Estes Kefauver. Jack Kennedy had the charm and the wit, but his brother, Robert, had the determination, the fearlessness, the organizing ability and the will to succeed.

Bobby Kennedy

After dinner, during which we had spent a good deal of time discussing what was happening in Britain, France, Germany and the rest of Europe, Bobby announced that in February of the following year, in 1964, he expected that his brother would appoint him secretary of state.

"The job of being secretary of state is an impossible one. Either he finds himself testifying endlessly before the Congress, or he is outside the country on some mission for the president. He can never get his work done, much less organize his department. Because the position is the most important in any administration, the president most often waits until late December to make the appointment. The new secretary comes into office not knowing the officials in his own department who will be working for him and they don't know his policy wishes. Then January comes and he no longer has any time to organize his team. I want to change all that. The Department of State is never properly operational because the secretary of state is never there to take it in hand, organize it efficiently or mold it to the image of what he wants it to be. I promise to make it work as it should. Here is how: I want to select ahead of time twelve highly motivated persons capable of handling key geographical sectors in key areas of particular concern to the United States. I want to choose those men now so that they will have a year to prepare themselves to take on their functions. During this period I will also expect them to spend time with me so they can learn what policies I will wish to pursue in their mission area and what we will hope to accomplish. In that year's time, they must learn from me and I must learn from them. After that it will be too late. My team must be in place, ready to start functioning effectively as a team because after my appointment, I will have only occasional time to meet with them."

An unusual proposal from an unusual man

Kennedy then asked me if I would be interested in the position of assistant secretary of state for European affairs after his appointment as secretary of state. I would have to learn everything I could about Europe in the interim and quietly get to know the current officials on the European desk at the department. I would also have to learn all I could about the political figures at the helm in the various countries of Europe and the policies of the political parties they represented. If I accepted the job, he would call on me to meet with him from time to time to discuss his views in light of what was currently happening in Europe and its relations with the United States. He spoke at length about France. He found the French difficult to deal with and had no sympathy for French colonialism either in Asia or North Africa. In this I already knew that both Kennedy brothers held strong views. The distrust was mutual. General de Gaulle had not gained a favorable impression of the president when they had met in Paris in 1961 just before the president's visit to Moscow. We spoke at length of my work in Indochina in an earlier administration. I had very much the impression that Bobby was a man of action rather than a political philosopher. I asked him if I could give him an answer by early March, a month away. "Of course," he said.

Bobby Kennedy's analysis of the State Department was certainly correct. How many times since 1963 has it been proven? With the demise of the Soviet Empire, the United States has undertaken today more, not fewer, military, economic, and political commitments abroad. Demands for U.S. intervention are constant in today's world. This puts an even greater burden on the secretary and his Department of State to function effectively.

It requires above all that key State Department employees be given training which today they do not receive. They are trained in languages while now working in a world where anyone of consequence anywhere speaks English. But they are not acquiring degrees in law, economics, or political or military strategy which would be useful to them in understanding and resolving the changes now going on in an increasingly complex world.

Consider the difference with the education and training of key military officers in anticipating global problems requiring U.S. intervention.

I remember one year not so long ago when I was invited, along with several others, to spend two days at the Army War College in Carlisle, Pennsylvania. We were given computers tied to a central panel. The entire staff of the War College was present for the discussions.

As civilian experts with broad international experience both in and out of government, we were there to give our views on a series of foreign policy problems which, in the opinion of the staff, might occur in the future and which might require a response by the United States. Each problem involved an international political or military confrontation somewhere overseas. Question: Was it in the interest of the United States to intervene? What action should be taken? Should such action be political, economic, military? Should there be an appeal to Allies, to the U.N., to NATO? It was a most interesting exercise. As individual members of a so-called group of experts, we did not in every case agree. *Bobby Kennedy*

It would appear advisable to have similar exercises for key employees of the State Department from time to time so they may similarly be trained to consider how the country should respond to serious international confrontations which may occur in the future.

I remember thinking what a wonderful opportunity it would be for me to play a role in the development of a recent American policy toward Europe working for a man as intelligent and dynamic as Robert Kennedy.

Gretchen spent all her weekdays in Washington. But we had dinner together in New York on the following Saturday. I told her of my conversation with Bobby Kennedy and the proposal he had made to me. She took it very seriously. I think the same thought was occurring to both of us: what if we should marry during the year and go down to Washington to live the following February? How would it be if the assistant secretary of state for European affairs were married to the daughter of the first ambassador of Germany to France after World War II. Would this be a problem?

"There is something I must confess to you, Thibaut," she said. "I am a Catholic from Bavaria and secretary general of the Conference of Catholic bishops in the United States. But I have a secret passion for astrology and take lessons from a master in New York whenever I can find the time. The Church calls this a sin, but I believe in it. One's future can be read in the stars because we are all part of a universal system designed by God. If you wish, I will work on your horoscope with my teacher and tell you whether or not you should accept Bobby Kennedy's proposal. It will probably take two or three weeks. I will need the exact time and location of your birth, at least to the minute, because the heavens rotate so quickly. I can get the information I need on the Kennedy brothers."

I gave her the information she had asked for on my own date, hour, and place of birth.

Three weeks later she called and told me she had the answer I needed. We met for dinner that evening. I was extremely curious to find out what she would tell me. You see, I too, while I would be unwilling to admit it, tended to believe that an astrological chart, if prepared by someone truly qualified, could predict what would happen.

"You told me, Thibaut, that you had to give your answer before the end of the month. I did not do your chart because the professor and I decided that we should do the president's first. Bobby can only be secretary of state if his brother appoints him next year. According to the president's chart, Bobby will never be appointed. Because we were not satisfied with what we found, we redid all the calculations. I can hardly myself believe what we found. You should decline the job offer, Thibaut, because Bobby Kennedy will never be secretary of state."

"Why?" I asked.

"Because the president's chart shows that he will be assassinated in November."

I was stunned. I think she was too. It was a depressing February evening for both of us.

I was in a taxi in New York City on November 22nd when the news came over the radio that the president had been shot in Dallas. I had turned down Bobby Kennedy's proposal. My brief romance with Gretchen had turned into a lasting friendship. She would soon marry an English don at Oxford who, like her, was a fine skier. She would move to England. I have not seen her since. I wonder if she is still finding the future in the movement of the heavens.

XVII

ST. CROIX

O NE *FRIDAY MORNING IN FEBRUARY* 1959, while I was sitting in my office in New York wishing I were somewhere warmer, I received a telephone call from my friend, Dick Dickinson. It was quite unexpected.

"Thibaut," he said, "why don't you drop what you are doing and come with me to the Virgin Islands for the weekend. I have been financing a hotel project down there in St. Croix and have just heard from the developer that it is completed. It will do you good to get some sun for a couple of days. Forget your hourly charges and come. I will have my chauffeur pick you up at two o'clock."

Another unusual challenge

When we arrived in St. Croix after changing planes in St. Thomas, we found that the Buccaneer Hotel where Dick always stayed was filled with tourists and we were obliged to share a room. It made no difference. The air was warm; so was the sea. The guests were tanned and very relaxed. There was native music on the terrace facing the sea. New York seemed very far away. After the second dry martini, it had disappeared from my consciousness.

At dinner Dick explained his development project to me. He had been coming to St. Croix and staying at this same hotel on the beach each February for several years. Some two years earlier a local entrepreneur, Robert Lodge, a former stockbroker from New York and Darien, Connecticut, had told him at a cocktail party of his plan to build a housing development on the east end of the island at Grapetree Bay, geared to the needs of young executives from all over the United States who had only short vacations but enjoyed sunshine, beach life and relaxation. The plan was similar to that which had been tried in Jamaica and had proved successful there. Besides a hotel, there would be thirty-five individually-owned cottages leased to the hotel for all but two weeks in the winter and one month in the summer. The homeowner would make only a small down payment on his house, the balance to be represented

Don't trust promoters.

by a mortgage to the hotel corporation. The principal would be amortized over twenty years with the interest and principal payments made on the mortgage out of lease payments from the hotel corporation due to the individual owners. The system would both save the expense to the hotel of building bedrooms for guests and allow the owners to pay for their houses over a long period of time. Dick Dickinson had agreed to finance the construction of the hotel and houses until completion of the project, when the hotel corporation would be in a position to take out a mortgage on the hotel, and the homeowners on their own houses. In theory the idea was excellent. In practice it meant Dickinson was taking an enormous risk. But I was not there as his lawyer and I did not want to ask too many questions out of fear of what the answers might be. What I did learn was that the monies had been advanced to Dick by his bank and that he had secured the bank's advances by a pledge of all his stock in his company.

At about 11 o'clock that Friday night after an excellent dinner and a brandy, Dickinson suggested that we drive to the east end of the island to look at the completed project.

"You will see how beautiful it is, with a long stretch of sandy beach in the foreground, the hotel and pool in the middle, and thirty-five villas in an arc around the hotel or directly on the beach."

It was ten miles on a dirt road to get to the east coast of the island. The moon was full that night. As we came around a last corner before the start of the property, my friend stopped the car and got out. He didn't say a word. Neither did I. Before us in the bright moonlight lay a scene of desolation. There was no hotel but only girders sticking out of the sand. A huge cistern was only half finished. There were only a handful of semi-finished houses. No houses had been completed. There were no roads linking the houses. Uncovered lumber was lying everywhere along with steel girders and joints. I will never forget the scene I saw that night.

Dick didn't say anything. We got back in the car and drove back to the hotel in silence. That night I slept badly and so did he.

The next morning, Dick told me, "Stay here and swim while I find out just what is going on." He had begun to realize the desperate situation in which he found himself. Later that afternoon he came back to the hotel accompanied by Robert Lodge, his wife and Bob's lawyer and his wife who was in real estate on the island. They all sat around in the bar drinking rum punches.

When we left for New York the following afternoon, it did not seem to me that any satisfactory explanations had been offered or decisions taken. But I was not about to get involved in something that did not concern me. The whole business smelled of real trouble. The last thing in the world I wanted was to get involved in a real mess in a Caribbean island, hundreds of miles away. This was particularly true because out of the conversations taking place around me, I had gathered that the overweight lawyer who seemed to be everybody's friend had been representing both Dickinson and Lodge in connection with the hotel project.

St. Croix

The following weekend I had spent the morning in Bellport, Long Island iceboating on Great South Bay near our house. At lunchtime I learned from my wife that Dickinson's wife had called to tell her that she felt her husband was about to have a nervous breakdown and that she was going to take him away for a month's cruise to South America. My wife's response: "Don't worry, Betty. Thibaut will go down there while you are away. He will straighten things out."

This was the start of four years of the most difficult problem I think I have ever had to face. It is one thing to make a serious business mistake. It is quite another to run away and let others try to unravel what had to appear to be a hopeless situation. Dickinson had majority control of a large and highly reputed medical instrument company which his father and another man had created seventy years earlier. His stock I discovered had been pledged to a major New York bank that had advanced the twenty million dollars which appeared to have been squandered by a dishonest promoter and untrustworthy lawyer in a major real-estate project which was totally unsupervised. As I dug deeper into the situation, it was even more difficult because all this had happened on a Caribbean island many miles away from my office or anyone I knew and could trust.

As I look back on it, it seemed to me I was almost as stupid in trying to get my client out of a hopeless situation as he had been in getting into it in the first place. It was particularly unrewarding to get involved in a difficult problem in a far off community where the locals, no matter how honest, will necessarily stick together to defend their own where an outsider is involved. It is a recognized sport in such a situation to defend other members of the community where a rich outsider has been fleeced. There is undoubted pride in taking advantage of a rich foreigner stupid enough to want to try to make money in a tropical paradise where local businessmen do not have the capital to develop properties on their own.

I should have just said no.

One should never get entangled in a situation where one doesn't know the locality, the people, what truly happened, the complete cast of characters and the reliability of each. Where everyone is a stranger, how can one find out whom to trust? New York was a jungle, but I had been operating there for many years. I knew the lawyers, the bankers, the businessmen; I knew how to check almost anybody; I knew both the honest and the dishonest, the knowledgeable on almost any matter. In an island community how could I ever find out where 20 million dollars had disappeared, much less how to find people who had not participated in taking it and would be willing to help me get it back?

Someone a year or two later wrote a book on the Virgin Island sport of taking advantage of the foreign investor. It was called *Don't Go Near The Water*. By the time I read it, I was ready to realize that it could well have been written, and probably was, about my own adventures in St. Croix.

My client was of little help to me. Before he left I had him tell me what he knew, leave me a general power of attorney, and tell his bank to let me have whatever money I needed up to $250,000 relying on the security of his shares on deposit. It was clear that he had no real friends on the island, including his lawyer, who also represented the man who had stolen his money. He didn't even know the persons who had bought the houses in the project. It was a most extreme case of tropical sun poisoning.

It was impossible for me to go down to St. Croix except on weekends because I was far too busy practicing law in New York during the week. In those days, there were no direct flights to the island. One had to go via St. Thomas and change planes, or via San Juan, Puerto Rico, and also change planes.

Not having my client with me made the job much more difficult even to get the facts. From my first few weekend visits I did discover a good bit of what had happened:

The lawyer tried to evade me even though I had been given a letter to him from Dickinson telling him to give me all pertinent information on the project and to help me in any way he could. (After all, he had been paid by Dickinson as his attorney.) The promoter told everyone on the island not to speak to me; the lawyer's wife had been not only Dickinson's real-estate broker, she was also the real-estate broker for the hotel corporation, the owners and the promoter; she had secured real-estate commissions from all even though their interests were quite different; the builder on the project had never built anything before;

404

he had run a weather station in Alaska for the U.S. government; the architect for the hotel and houses had no architectural degree; he had been in the advertising and interior decorating business in New York; the accountant had been doing the accounting for Dickinson, the hotel corporation, the law firm, the realtor, but he was little more than a local bookkeeper. The accountant and the builder were honest. The architect had only furnished the designs. He had never worked in the tropics before, and had furnished no detailed specifications of the hotel building or the cottages to be built.

St. Croix

The first time I had a chance to really evaluate the situation was Easter week. I had gone down there for the entire week in order to learn what I could. The timing was atrocious. Several of the house owners, having heard from the promoter that their houses were on their way to completion, had chosen to go down with wives and children to see for themselves what progress had been made. A few had almost completed houses, most only a hole in the ground. On Thursday of Easter week all power on the island went off, something which I was told generally happened at that time as the manager of the power station went "off island" to Puerto Rico for Easter. I found myself on Good Friday facing distraught homeowners demanding to see Dickinson whom the promoter had told them was the one responsible for all delays because he hadn't advanced the funds quickly enough. Now there is something about unshaven men who feel they have been defrauded that is unduly frightening. I told them who I was, that my client was in the same position as they were, that obviously both he and they had been lied to and taken advantage of. I promised them that no matter how bad the situation was I would treat all alike, but they would have to wait until I could ascertain what had happened. I asked them to appoint one of the owners to represent all of them. This they did, appointing the owner of a business in Indiana and Sterling Pile, who had been a classmate of mine at the Pomfret School many years earlier. This put the house owners on hold at least temporarily.

For several years in New York I had worked with a man named Bill Shriver, a so-called doctor of sick companies. Bill would be hired by boards of directors at the instance of banks or major creditors to try to save a business in difficulties caused by the dishonesty or incompetence of management. Bill would retain me to do the legal and financial side of the business while he handled operational problems. We were close friends and had successfully worked on a number of problem situations, starting with the Piper Aircraft Corporation in 1946 and going on to

Sending Bill Shriver down

other companies in other fields in different parts of the country. Bill was currently between salvage jobs. I called him for help. I retained him to go down to St. Croix for three months to recommend to me what we should do. I figured that, with his background and vast experience in the business world, his recommendations would be most helpful.

I called Dickinson's lawyer in St. Croix and explained to him that Dick had left me in full charge of extricating him from his disastrous venture on the island, that I was sending the lawyer a detailed letter from Dickinson telling him to follow any instructions, that he was to consider Shriver as my emissary and give him all the support he could since he would be coming down to evaluate the situation for me and prepare an action plan.

The lawyer retained an apartment for Bill Shriver and his wife on the side of the island furthest from the project and far from Christianstedt, the capital, where the lawyer had his office. It did not surprise me. Nor was I surprised when I received Shriver's evaluation of the lawyer and his wife. Bill was naturally disposed to be blunt. He thought the one should be disbarred and the other lose her real-estate license for having used the funds entrusted to her husband to buy other tracts of land on St. Croix and other islands for the promoter's own account. Bill's report was thorough, as complete as it could be under the circumstances since both lawyer and real-estate broker were not about to give out more information than they absolutely had to. Fortunately, on a small island in the tropics it is difficult to keep business matters secret. Bill loved playing the role of a typical Irish visitor who likes to sit in bars and tell stories. But he was a veritable ferret. As a friend of mine, supposedly interested in investment opportunities on the island and a good listener, he obtained a good deal of information at least as to where on the island the promoter had invested a substantial amount of the funds Dickinson had made available to him to build the project. When Bill Shriver had completed his report, he came back to New York and gave it to me, along with some helpful recommendations as to whom I might find to trust on the island, and whom to stay away from. Unfortunately, he had no recommendations on architects, builders, engineers, hotel operators, lawyers, accountants, and other professional people I would be very much in need of.

United States possessions, as might be expected, appeal as a base of operations to those who for one reason or another have failed at home. Sometimes it is due to divorce, bankruptcy, or commission of misdemeanors. Sometimes it is to get away from pressure, lead the easy life of

406

the tropics, or live in a place where the rum is cheap and girls seeking
sun and adventure plentiful. In such an environment the last thing one
should have to do is what lay ahead of me.

I took Bill's report, thanked him and paid him, told my partners
I would have to be spending a good bit of spring and summer in the
Virgin Islands, transferred funds on Dickinson's account to a local bank
and set off for St. Croix. My wife could not argue with me. She had put
me in the fix I was in to help Betty Dickinson with no knowledge of
what I might have to face. The children were more than delighted at the
thought of a summer on the beach.

The first thing I did on the island was hire another lawyer. From
Bill's report I had a good idea as to who was considered honest. This
may sound easy. But the most able lawyers from the mainland are unlikely to move to the Virgin Islands to practice their profession. On the
other hand, I did not need an Oliver Wendell Holmes. A knowledge of
local law and the criminal statutes, relationships with the local politicians, capacity to draw real-estate contracts, relations with local bankers
and businessmen, that is what I needed. I had to be properly introduced
on my own. It was quite clear that my client's standing in the community, as a result of the failure of the project which everyone knew he had
financed, had been severely affected. I would have to strike hard, and
quickly, if I was to make it clear to everyone that the Dickinson "come
and take my money" days were over and that new management was able,
tough and unforgiving.

It seems to me that in business it takes so much time and effort to
succeed and there are so many more enjoyable ways of spending one's
time that if one is going to do it, one should take charge quickly, be direct with everyone, and go after the problems in sequence, concentrating on the major ones and leaving the others until later.

I had already at an earlier meeting explained to those house owners
I had met on my first visit after Dickinson's departure that I would treat
all alike and would give them a detailed report of what I had found as
soon as possible. I now did that. All would be treated alike. The houses
would be built and delivered as agreed. But each house owner would
have to raise the funds necessary to complete his house or forego the
property. Any houses completed would have to be paid for with the
owner securing his own mortgage. The money I had would be used to
build the hotel, not the individual houses. If they did not all agree, then
I would abandon the project and, if they wished, they could go after my
client. If they did agree, I would somehow build the hotel which was

the one event which would give value to their property. Once built, the hotel would, if any owner wished, rent his property for cash so that he could pay off his mortgage through rental payments if he wished to. I would only deal with them through the two owners elected to represent the group. The owners had 30 days to accept or reject my proposition. If they did not like my proposition, I would try to help them sell their properties at no cost to them or buy out their investment for what they had advanced. Since their down payments had only been between $10,000 and $25,000, they could see that my proposition was a fair one. Without the hotel, no one would have anything of value.

I became immediately the most unpopular man on the island. Luckily, few of the owners could be there since they had no house to occupy.

Next I went to see the man who was supposed to be Dickinson's lawyer. I saw him alone. Our conversation was brief. I told him I was ready to take immediate steps to have him disbarred and demand reimbursement of all monies Dickinson had advanced to the project manager—his other client—along with all real-estate commissions received by his wife on project sales or real-estate investments made by the promoter. I wanted all his books and records on all transactions involving him, his wife and the promoter and all records relating to the project. Furthermore, I wanted all this within seven days. I suggested that he get the promoter to agree with this arrangement. I told him I wanted a meeting with the promoter and him so that all three of us clearly understood what I wanted and expected to get. I did not intend to press him for the return of the fees he had already received or the commissions his wife had been paid on sales to the home owners, but I wanted to have a full accounting from the promoter of Dickinson's advances and the return to the hotel corporation of any properties purchased by Lodge for his own account. All stockholders of the hotel corporation had to return their stock to Dickinson.

Fortunately, my client was in South America and couldn't intervene. I called his secretary at the office who knew her employer well, explained the situation to her in detail so that she could let me know if either the promoter or the St. Croix lawyer for Dickinson tried to reach him by phone through his office.

What a way to have to try to protect a friend and client! Fortunately, Dickinson didn't want to talk to either the lawyer or the promoter when they tried to reach him.

Slowly, the major bases were covered. A majority of the owners agreed to my proposal, and the others were either pressured by the majority to sign or sold back their properties to the hotel corporation for what they had paid as a down payment. Two of the owners understood what I was trying to do, were very helpful, and became good friends. This left the promoter's thefts and the problem of redesigning and building the hotel. There was also a new problem: I discovered in looking at the owners' deeds and the maps on file with the land office that no proper survey of the various real-estate interests had ever been done. Not only did the roads within the project not conform to anything on file, but boundaries of individual properties deeded did not conform either to the master plan or to each other. It was at this point that I realized I would have to go outside for legal help. A survey was essential.

At the time we had an office in Paris and I had just hired Denis Debost, a young Frenchman educated at the Harvard Law School who had had experience in land disputes in exotic places like Hawaii and Tahiti. I called him and told him I needed him in St. Croix for at least six months to clear up my land boundary problems and the job of finding and getting back the properties the promoter had bought with Dickinson's money outside the project. He was not happy to leave Paris but he immediately came and did a wonderful job. I could not have done what I was able to do without his help. We not only found that the promoter had bought properties elsewhere on the island, but in St. Martin, Martinique, and the French Riviera as well. In the course of the full year he spent on St. Croix, the young lawyer found himself being consulted by both locals and tourists who found that the titles to their properties might not conform. He became an expert on Danish and French real property law, including the old French royalist concept of *les pas du Roi* which gave all beaches to the king.

This left the problem of the hotel itself. In New York, the supposed architect, a delightful Chinese-born American, was now working in advertising and moonlighting as an interior decorator. Through him I found the original plans for the hotel with interior designs but there were no architectural drawings or detailed engineering plans. Because of the legal descriptions of the houses on either side of the hotel, it was quite obvious that no such hotel could ever be built as planned without taking away a big part of the cliff in the back of the proposed site for the hotel. This was a major problem. The project contractor and I were in a quandary. Neither house owner on either side was willing to sell his property. I would have to attack the cliff. This meant finding a talented engineer on the island. This was not an easy matter.

I finally located a former colonel in the Transportation Corps of

Sending
a lawyer
from
Paris to
St. Croix

the U.S. Army who had retired in St. Croix. He was my kind of man. Problems did not seem to faze him and he was continually "gung-ho" for action. He happily blew the cliff in back of the hotel so we could have the additional room we needed. He leased the biggest Caterpillar machine I'd ever seen and began to put roads where needed throughout the project area.

The only trouble was that he didn't always wait for detailed instructions and was not very good at observing property lines. When I complained that some roadways would have to be revised to conform with legal metes and bounds, his answer was always the same:

"Right—oh, Thibaut, just a bit of pick and shovel work, and I'll straighten it out."

I wondered frequently whether he did this on purpose in order to keep on using the expensive equipment we had leased. But eventually this part of the project was finished without too many complaints from the owners. I began to breathe again.

To build the hotel, there was a need for an engineer rather than an architect. Here I was lucky. The chief engineer of Dickinson's company agreed to spend the summer in St. Croix and help the contractor with proper engineering plans. He had supervised the building of all the company's plants both in the United States and elsewhere. His help was invaluable. His only problem was that he was a perfectionist on an island where fantasy was the norm.

The good work of our new legal team resulted in Dickinson's becoming certainly the largest landowner in St. Croix along with beach properties on other islands and even land on the Riviera. Gradually we sold the bulk of these properties. The proceeds went to pay for the building of the hotel and the houses we had taken back. It also enabled me to buy any land adjoining the hotel that I could get my hands on.

My most fortunate land transaction was with the Hess Oil Company which was purchased for several million dollars, a property on the south coast of the island that Robert Lodge, the promoter, had originally bought for very little. I had seized this property along with his other real-estate holdings. Hess wanted the property to process Venezuelan crude somewhere in the Caribbean and was willing to build a major refinery and port facilities in St. Croix. I enjoyed dealing with Hess. I named a very high price. It was accepted. Leon Hess did not even want to have a lawyer represent him. He said he had checked my reputation and would rely on me to draw proper contracts. I had to insist that he have the company's counsel review the documentation and give an opinion as counsel to the company. Leon Hess was a real gentleman and a pleasure to do business with.

These sales of property were very welcome indeed because they gave me the funds with which to finish the hotel. It also made me realize that if I was ever to get back the $20,000,000 that Dickinson had lost, it would not be out of hotel earnings but from establishing a real-estate office in the hotel when completed and first buying and then reselling all the property I could buy near the hotel that hadn't already been sold to the homeowners within the project.

For this purpose, I found a bright young woman who had some real-estate experience in the States and hired her for the real-estate office. I needed to proceed quickly before too many people on the island realized that the hotel was truly going to be finished and ready to open to the public. Quietly and slowly I purchased for the hotel corporation any nearby properties that came on the market. There were two large properties on two beautiful beaches just beyond the project limits. Unfortunately, the furthest property, before I could negotiate the purchase, was bought by the government for a public park and picnic area, but I was more fortunate on the nearer property: Jack's Bay.

This property belonged to Alexis Lichine, a wine importer who had purchased one of Bordeaux's best vineyards right after the war when they were cheap, and then made arrangements with Claude Philippe, the banquet manager of the Waldorf-Astoria Hotel in New York, to launch his wines to the benefit of both. Neither of the two men, as could be expected, had any real confidence in the other's integrity or ability to maintain accurate records of their partnership's earnings. They soon had a falling out but not before they had bought the property in Jack's Bay.

Shortly before the hotel was to open I received a friendly call from Alexis Lichine who said to me:

"With your name you must be French. No one in New York or Paris would understand it if you didn't buy your wine from me."

"But Alexis, I never thought of asking you if I could be your lawyer in New York."

In the course of the conversation, I realized that the partners were not getting along and that one of them wished to sell. I then arranged for another real-estate broker to call Claude Philippe for an unnamed client who might be interested in buying. My price was satisfactory to him but not to Lichine.

I soon had another call from Alexis.

"Thibaut, I think I can buy out my partner at a fair price. What do you think?"

I had the real-estate agent find an excuse to call him for her client and tell him that she was unable to get the consent of the adjoining hotel owner to put a road through its property to reach Jack's Bay. This persuaded the two partners to agree to sell the property which easily doubled the land for sale within the hotel project. It was certainly the most beautiful piece of property in all of St. Croix.

One morning I woke up and told my wife: "Darling, the hotel is going to open in a month and then our problems will really start." I knew because I had been the lawyer for two big hotels in Chicago and had learned first-hand how impossible it is to ensure honest accounting in any hotel project, to say nothing of all the other pitfalls of running a hotel at the end of the island of St. Croix with 17 miles of dirt road to get there and no housing for the staff.

The hotel did open on schedule. That in itself was a minor miracle. Everyone who was anyone on the island showed up, including the magnificent wife of the owner of the *St. Croix Daily*. She was well over six feet, her figure in proportion. As she went through the receiving line, Sterling Pile said to me:

"The Queen of Sheba could not have been more stately."

It was a grand party. Dick Dickinson had never been on the east side of the island since we went there together on that first awful night. He told Sterling Pile:

"I don't see why Thibaut told me all this was so difficult. It looks great."

I felt like saying to him, "Here is your hotel; now you figure out what to do next."

Bill Shriver often used to point out to me when we were trying to save a company whose board of directors had given up on their own ability to save it, that he always fixed his fee ahead of time, generally both in cash and in stock, because otherwise he might never receive it, since the person who had retained his services in desperation might later conclude that someone else could have done the job as well or better. In Dickinson's case I hadn't done this, first because I had no idea what I would find when I went down to St. Croix and after that because I naively trusted him, since he had become my employer as financial vice president and general counsel of his company. I should have taken the time to follow Bill Shriver's sage advice and fix my fee for what I was doing for him in St. Croix. My work there had nothing to do with my work at the company. He was 20 million dollars in debt in St. Croix. If I didn't pay it off, he would still have to pay the debt and lose the company as well.

Sometimes one compounds one's own earlier mistake. When the hotel was finished, I should have had the sense to bow out and submit a bill for my work. But it had been too much of an effort to let go now. I was very proud of what had been accomplished and was too stupid now to wash my hands of it.

Both Claude Philippe and Alexis Lichine came to the opening festivities, each with a girl from New York who should not have been asked to come. I told the manager to give them each a bill for his stay and when Philippe would object to being charged because he was a hotel man, to tell them that the bill was in order because no true hotel executive would ever have brought such women to the opening ceremonies of a major hotel.

And so one set of problems was succeeded by another perhaps even more difficult. My manager was an American by the name of Burgess who had originally come to work on the hotel building as a common laborer. He had graduated from college, then gone to the islands, married a local black girl, and taken to drink. He worked very hard, was honest, took responsibility and knew every inch of the hotel by heart. I liked him. After watching him handle different jobs in the construction phase, I made him manager. He didn't fail me at the opening of the hotel.

There were two important matters now to be taken care of. The hotel was the newest and the biggest on the island. It needed a hotel association to market it. I arranged for my lawyer to create one. Then I persuaded other hotels to become part of the association and to elect me president so that I could go after the airlines to give St. Croix direct service instead of having to change planes either in Puerto Rico or in St. Thomas. We persuaded the local government to agree to renovate the airport if we secured the service and then brought an action in Washington on behalf of the association to get the service we needed. In due course, American Airlines started direct flights. It was a real boon for the island.

The problem of the roads was more difficult. I found that the roads leading to the Rockefeller Hotel on the west coast of St. Croix had been recently paved by the government in St. Thomas. I made an appointment to see the governor. He became angry when I asked him to do for the east end of the island what he had done for the west end. He flew

413

me all over the island of St. Croix in his governor's plane to look at the road situation, but I had little hope of getting him to change his mind any time soon.

Here my new relationship with Becton, Dickinson and Company became most helpful. In the course of my work there I had met a very helpful commercial banker in Nebraska, where the company had recently set up a plant. In talking to him on another matter shortly after my visit to the governor of the Virgin Islands, I mentioned my difficulty with roads in St. Croix.

"Don't you know, Thibaut, that your company is the largest employer in Nebraska?"

I had never been to Nebraska and was very much surprised. After all, our operation there was very small.

"The Virgin Islands are under the control of the Department of Interior. The secretary of interior is ex-Senator Seaton of Nebraska. He can, I am sure, solve your problem for you. I would consider it a privilege to introduce you to the secretary if you will let me. When would you like to see him?"

"I would assume it is more when will he be free to see me."

"Not at all. You don't understand politics. When can you go?" It was a Friday. We agreed to meet in Washington on the following Monday. My banker friend called back to say we had a ten o'clock appointment with the secretary Monday morning.

On Saturday, Burgess called me at home.

"I don't know what is happening, Thibaut. The road from Christiansted is crowded with Caterpillars. They are laying a new macadam road out to the east end."

As we walked in to Interior Secretary Seaton's plush office on Monday morning, I could hear him giving the governor hell to finish the new road as quickly as possible.

It was almost lunchtime when we left Seaton's office. At the phone on the corner the banker proposed to me that we try to have lunch at the White House.

"Ike comes from Nebraska. You might enjoy having lunch with him."

The president was away, but General Gruenther invited us to lunch with him at the White House. It appeared he also came from Nebraska. I had never known a state like that one. Apparently there everyone helps a fellow citizen if he can.

Much later in my life when I was living in Washington, I had a call one day from a former student of mine in Geneva who was head of international operations for Corning Glass. He wanted to come down and lunch with me in Washington. I immediately thought he would be asking for help at Corning. Not at all.

"I am going to retire from Corning this year, and I will now be able to do something exciting and new after so many years with the company. I have several choices. You successfully made the transition to private life. I want to discuss my options and get your advice. The governor of Nebraska has asked me to join his staff. He considers Nebraska to be a one-product state and wants us to diversify. It sounds exciting. What do you think?"

"Why you?" I asked.

"I was born in Nebraska."

"What else have you done for the state?"

It turned out he had gone to the University of Nebraska, had been quarterback for three years during which Nebraska was the number one football team in the country. They take football seriously in Nebraska. I advised him to accept the offer without delay.

Lack of rain on the east side of St. Croix was a major problem for the hotel. The clouds came from the east with the prevailing wind but mysteriously divided as they approached the land and then formed again and dropped all their rain on the west side of the island. How could we make sure that rain fell on the east side of the island?

By this time Dick Dickinson had financed a local airline bringing summer tourists to Martha's Vineyard where he had a house. I persuaded him to send a plane and pilot down to St. Croix in January so we could try seeding the clouds before the season began. The results were better than doing nothing but not worth the expense.

I then examined the weather records on the island through my friend the contractor who had run a weather station in Alaska. These went back 100 years. We discovered that before two bad hurricanes had hit the island in the 1830s, the east coast had had the rain rather than the west. The maps indicated a "Cotton Valley" on the east end. It was obvious that before these two terrible storms, this was the "wet" part of the island. I therefore bought and we planted at Grapetree Bay some three thousand palm trees and assorted bushes. The result: the rain clouds no longer skirted the east end. Grapetree became green again, at least until the terrible storm of 1993 which hung over the east end of the island and destroyed the hotel and many of the owners' cottages.

Nature in the tropics has its own way of avenging man's attempts to bring about change.

It is one thing to find management for a hotel in the Caribbean. It is quite another to make sure that tourists come, and to try to extend the tourism months so that the hotel doesn't remain only partially filled for nine months of the year. I tried to find hotel managers with experience in tropical islands. One was chased away by a murderous cook; another had a wife with a "penchant" for local houseboys; I tried a New England hotel chain which had to be let go because its manager would only serve the food he gave to his summer guests on Martha's Vineyard. Imagine featuring Block Island swordfish on a daily evening menu in the Virgin Islands.

Management is an ever-present problem on a tropical island. Because of the fact that the hotel used the owners' houses spread out over a half mile area along the beach, every problem was magnified a hundred times: how were the guests to be brought to the hotel for meals? Could they have meals in their rooms? How could we assure proper telephone service in the rooms? What activities were available to the guests in a hotel complex at the end of the island? What auto services should be provided to take guests to other parts of the island? What could be offered to keep the guests busy and happy, besides the beach, the food and the tennis courts?

Telephone communication between the rooms and the hotel had not been properly thought through and the system never worked properly. So I had it yanked out. In every room, in place of a phone, I put a nice, friendly memo advising the guests that in order to protect their privacy and the desire for rest that had brought them to the island, I had purposely had the phone system to the rooms disconnected. "If you are one of those people who cannot get away from a phone in order to have a period of relaxation, then you should be somewhere else." Somehow it worked. Before the phone system was removed, guests were constantly complaining about it and the lack of room service. But they seemed to accept that this had been done for their own protection. This was a great lesson for me: how to deny a normal requirement, and turn it into a blessing. Lack of phone service to the rooms became a point emphasized in our brochure. And we never had any further complaints about the phone service.

The distance of the rooms from the hotel was also a difficult problem. To help solve it I bought a number of Volkswagen buses, painted them gay colors with the hotel insignia on the sides and had them shuttle back and forth between the houses. Fortunately, I was also able to purchase two of the owners' cottages near the hotel. On this additional land, over the course of two summers I was able to build additional hotel rooms with balconies.

From my prior experiences as a corporate lawyer advising the Byfield family in connection with their large hotel holdings in Chicago, I had learned quite a bit about the difficulty of hotel accounting. Creative accounting in the hotel industry is not the problem that it is in the motion picture industry. The problem is simply padded bills, cash payments on the side to employees, and outright theft. The only way specialists in hotel auditing have managed to maintain some control is to determine with the hotel client what should be a reasonable take on each portion of the business broken down in various departments involving food, bar, and even hotel services like laundry. If the results do not match the estimates, you then know someone has been dipping into the till.

The problem was made particularly clear to me when I had to let one manager go. Shortly thereafter, I received a visit from the head of a firm which furnished the hotel with most of its food supplies. He came directly to the point of his visit.

"Do we give the 10 percent override to you or to the new manager?"

"Neither, because you have just lost the account."

It was difficult to do because his firm furnished staples to all the hotels on the island. And so it went. I realized that in giving the business to a competitor, sooner or later the same system would be reestablished. It is endemic in the business. It is also very hard to control because it is totally a cash business. It reminded me of the Generalissimo Chiang Kai-shek's payments to his warlord generals in so many *piculs* of rice for each man in the general's army. This always resulted in a massive creation of imaginary troops facing the Japanese enemy. In the hotel business, bonuses are paid on the basis of results compared to estimates in each hotel department. Standard hotel accounting is based on careful estimates. If they are not reached, it indicates payoffs are taking place.

I longed to be rid of this terrible albatross that seemed to be around my neck. But I realized I could not do so until I could persuade the bank to look only to the hotel corporation for repayment of the 20 million dollars loaned to Dickinson. This would enable the bank to return to him his shares of stock in Becton, Dickinson which had guaranteed his personal borrowings for St. Croix. To accomplish this I would have to invite down to St. Croix the vice president of the bank responsible for the loan and convince him that the hotel corporation could now pay down the loan almost in full, with a showing that there was enough land left for sale and a small enough loss in the hotel operations that Dickinson's personal guarantee would no longer be necessary. This would require a very complete accounting and careful future projections of hotel cash flows. Fortunately, in one transaction alone the Hess Oil Company had bought enough land from me to build a major refinery on the island and had given me over half the money to pay back the bank. I called the bank, set up a meeting for a month later with the vice president in charge of the account who would come to St. Croix and then mobilized local accountants and lawyers to prepare the necessary financial statements and supporting reports.

The banker was due to come down on a Monday for our presentation. Over the weekend Denis Debost and I were still working feverishly to complete the needed documentation. I will never forget that last Saturday night. We were working in an apartment I had rented in Christiansted, the capital, to be far away from the hotel while we worked on our written presentation and the technical opinions. It was a gorgeous tropical night. Not knowing that we would have to work, my lawyer friend had agreed to take a girl—daughter of the Buccaneer Hotel in St. Croix—out to dinner. She had arrived at the apartment dressed beautifully for a night on the town. I told her she would have to sit quietly until we finished and gave her a book to read. It was only seven o'clock and I figured she could be patient for a few hours.

Peggy's father was Scottish, from the highlands. He had served with distinction in the British army and had retired after the war in St. Croix setting up a small hotel. His wife was English and a gentlewoman. Peggy kept two horses on the property. She was gregarious, headstrong, and quite wild even at seventeen. Obviously, her genes were from the Scottish Highlands.

At nine o'clock Peggy interrupted our work by appearing in the living room where we were working amid a mass of papers strewn over tables and floors.

"You are not paying any attention to me and I will teach you how to do so."

She stood in the middle of the room in her summer cocktail dress. Slowly, and very sensuously, she started taking off her clothes one by one, until she stood in front of us quite naked. She was everything a seventeen-year-old girl should be. We watched, entranced.

"Denis, will you please take this young lady to her house, leave her and get back here as fast as you can."

I found out the next day what had happened later that same evening. Peggy had put on riding clothes, gone down to the stables for her horse and ridden up the hill to the main house bareback. She had cantered up the steps to the terrace dining area where guests were having their dinner and ridden through the tables scattering guests, dinners and waiters. Then she had ridden back to the beach and started up again at a full gallop for a repeat performance. Only this time she ended up at a full gallop through the kitchen effectively ending the dining service for that evening.

It was clear that this Highland spirit was more than a match for a quiet French Burgundian.

It turned out that, as hoped, the banker was satisfied with our presentation. Dickinson's stock was returned to him, the debt substantially reduced, and the hotel corporation's stock replaced as guarantee for his. My job was finished. His personal debt was extinguished. He would recover his 20 million dollars. His business would be saved.

A few weeks later I sat down quietly with Dickinson to discuss an issue I should long ago have raised: my compensation for two years of work and—if I might say so—a very fine result.

"The hotel operation is now in good shape. While it may never make a great deal of money, you now have several hundred acres of prime land which you can gradually sell because the hotel will render the land increasingly valuable. I've never asked you for any compensation for what I have done. But what I would like is a small 3.5-acre lot near the hotel. I have designed a house to put there so that the children and I can keep coming to St. Croix now that I will have no further responsibilities there. After all, it was the last summers with their mother that we spent there."

His only reply was: "That is a lot of land, Thibaut."

I don't know which poet it was, Ogden Nash, I think, who said, "The rich are different from thee and me." It certainly is true. I had to insist, but I did get my three and a half acres of land. I designed a dream house, put in two large cisterns, but never built the house. Years later, I sold the property for $61,000. I seldom went back to St. Croix. There were just too many memories attached. I had done my job, learned a good deal about myself and my own limitations and about the necessity of getting along with people of very different backgrounds and capabilities. I could and should have charged at least a million dollars for what I had accomplished.

Looking back, I am particularly proud of having briefly been a patron of the arts. One wintry February day in Paris I sat with a young French artist, a nephew of my secretary in Paris, who was working on paper napkins in a Paris café designing a series of murals which he would do for different walls in the hotel on the history, the arts and the sports of the island. In return for room, board and a small salary, the artist spent a year on the island. His work made the hotel famous. I even bought thousands of tiny Italian colored mosaic pieces to make a large mosaic design behind the swimming pool. My artist friend, Daniel Buren, subsequently became one of France's most successful artists and now sells his sculptures all over the world.

Man is a strange animal. To succeed, he must pace himself to his own mental, emotional and physical limitations. I discovered in my case what these were. I learned that in order to maintain my own balance and objectivity it was necessary from time to time to close myself in a totally different activity, into which I could plunge completely, and in that way regain my composure. In St. Croix, this consisted of buying a sailboat, and when things became unmanageable ashore, going off to the British Virgin Islands which were then a sailing paradise, unspoiled, and quite empty of tourists. I would leave around midnight with my wife and three children. We would sail all night. By six in the morning we would have reached the entrance to Sir Francis Drake Sound in the British Virgin Islands. It was then simply a matter of choice as to where to anchor during our stay. There were beautiful beaches, empty anchorages, and fantastic spear fishing. After three days I would return rested, refreshed and ready to face an angry world again. Looking back, I can see what a godsend it was to have owned a 48-foot ketch to enable me to escape when events on land seemed overwhelming.

I have often thought back on this strange period of time in St. Croix. I had made many mistakes. I don't expect I shall ever face a similar situation again. I also learned a great deal that helped me elsewhere, in different circumstances. I met individuals who for one reason or another were dishonest, greedy, immoral, or vicious. Somehow the tropics can bring out the worst in human nature. But I also met people from very different backgrounds, nationalities and races who were naturally honest, hard working, loyal and trustworthy. It is not easy to avoid the bad and recognize the good. One always faces surprises and compromises. But St. Croix was a wonderful laboratory in which to learn, and to test one's capacity for recognition of both good and evil. I learned much more respect for self-made men, because they have learned the meaning of loyalty and respect for others. I learned to be careful of those who were given responsibility too early, or were born wealthy, because they might be inconsiderate or disloyal either to those above or below. I learned the importance of friendships and that the supreme arrogance is to think that one can ever accomplish very much alone. I learned that we must all be responsible for our own actions. I learned both the importance of self-confidence and the folly of stretching it too far.

St. Croix

I still think a great deal of my friend, Dick Dickinson, and why he got into such difficulty and was not able to make his own way out. Dick was by no means a stupid man. The risks he took in St. Croix were the result of wanting to do something constructive, to make it possible for others to enjoy the island as he had had the opportunity to do. Often one runs across people who, because they are good and want to do good, lack the warning system which will prevent them from making major mistakes. Bill Shriver used to tell me, "Beware the good, Thibaut, because they have no sense of loyalty to those who work for them." Dick Dickinson had inherited his company from his father, a ruthless, aged, self-made man who had educated his son in a military school and warned him on his death-bed never to trust anybody. He never had to learn from the experience of others or to work with others to accomplish a common goal. Like many sons of very rich self-made men, he wanted to do well with his money, and instead, in due course, lost all that had been left him, including his company.

I learn a great deal, but no financial success.

The author's boat, Barnabas, *on St. Croix*

A view of Grapetree Bay, Dickinson's project in St. Croix

XVIII

MME. BEAUVOIS

O NE OF THE POST-WORLD WAR II pleasures was to cross the Atlantic on one of the great ocean liners. I could leave New York on Thursday and be in my office in Paris on Tuesday morning. It was a glorious opportunity to rest, be well cared for, enjoy the beauty of the ever-changing ocean, along with great food, and all the advantages of life at sea. Travel by plane, as people do today, is a very poor substitute for shipboard travel. What difference can it make that one saves two days two or three times a year? We keep trying to live faster and faster but at a tremendous cost in terms of enjoyment of life. In our endless quest to save time, have we not lost irreplaceable opportunities to enjoy life more?

The joy of travel by ship

In the '50s and '60s, I made it a point each year to take at least two round trips by sea from New York to Le Havre. Since I had an office in Paris, it was always possible to charge the expense either to the office or to a corporate client. This made it possible to ignore the cost, savor the voyage and enjoy the round trip and its adventure to the fullest. Believe me, I did so.

I never enjoyed the English ships. It seemed to me they had far too much wood in them. They creaked mercilessly in bad weather. They seemed to have highly rounded bottoms that caused the vessels to rock more than they should. Unlike the British ships, the *United States,* that extraordinary masterpiece of ship design, had a roll like a metronome over and back in a sharp movement maintained by stabilizers amidships. That ship combined speed, a cold beauty of interior appointments, and brilliant engineering. Traveling on the United States always reminded me of staying in America at a Marriott Hotel. There was beauty and elegance, but hardly any soul. It was just too efficient. Even the passengers always looked scrubbed. My favorites were the French ships. It has always seemed to me that American ocean liners had been designed by engineers and British ships by seamen, but French ships by interior decorators and artists. My favorite was the *Liberté*—the old German *Bremen* of pre-war years which had been beautifully redesigned and decorated by the French line after the war. She was fast but sought no transatlantic records; she was comfortable, with large state rooms designed to be sitting rooms during the day; the food was excellent, with the finest Russian caviar in round tins served at both lunch and dinner; and she carried a purser who made a very real effort to make sure that passengers who wanted to have a good time on board would have every opportunity to do so.

As soon as I boarded the ship, I would promptly set out to find the purser to make sure that I would be seated for lunch and dinner with a stimulating group. I knew most of the French Line pursers. They occupied a most important role on board. The purser would always know who would be interesting to talk to during the trip. Since people who traveled relatively frequently all knew him, it was not too difficult to make sure that meals were shared with passengers one would enjoy. Like a conductor studying a score, this man would have already examined the passenger list with care in order to plan his seating arrangements. After all, what can be more important to make a sea voyage pleasant than one's dining partners, and how well one eats?

There is a kind of rhythm to transatlantic shipboard travel. There is no pressure to wake up early. To lie in bed feeling the motion of the ship and knowing that the day's events will only be pleasant is sufficient to start the day with a feeling of euphoria—no demands on one's time, no business or personal crises, only good meals, good conversation, a massage, a movie in the afternoon, perhaps a swim, a walk in the sea air around the sundeck, dressing for dinner, dancing until late hours if one finds the right partner—a very satisfying day to look forward to.

My father, in the 1920s, when he had a bank and brokerage operation on both sides of the Atlantic, was the first to have a brokerage office on the ships of the French Line. He would select a young man from the office in Paris or New York who was bilingual and put him in charge of the shipboard office going back and forth across the Atlantic for a year. In those days American business leaders frequently went to Europe on business trips. On board ship they would visit my father's office, if only to study the tape and see how their stocks were doing. Some would spend a good part of the day there talking to other business leaders and exchanging investment ideas. A perceptive young broker could do well for himself meeting these men. He would often be invited to cocktails or dinner on board, particularly if the business executive had his wife or daughter with him. He would explain where to dine in Paris. He might even take his new friends to dinner while the ship was in port. Many of my father's brokers would receive offers at the end of the year on board ship and take a job with one of the companies whose chief executive he had met on board. Others met their wives that way. Still others had brief but meaningful love affairs on board.

Once I traveled with the famous motion picture actor Pat O'Brien, and the Catholic bishop of Erie, Pennsylvania. The three of us had met because we would show up for a massage every afternoon at 6:00 p.m., after the afternoon movie. When you are lying down being pummeled and kneaded, you are apt to talk to the man next to you who is undergoing the same treatment. The bishop was a big, outgoing individual, on board with his wife and seven children. I knew that sooner or later Pat O'Brien would be able to stand it no longer and would ask him how a Catholic bishop of Erie, Pennsylvania could have a wife and seven children. The bishop explained that he was a bishop of the Ruthenian Church and that many centuries earlier the pope, upon Ruthenia's acceptance of Catholicism in place of the Orthodox faith, had agreed that their priests would be allowed to marry. As a good Irish Catholic, Pat found this difficult to accept. It was amusing to see how narrow the Catholic faith can be in Ireland. Whenever I met the bishop on deck or in the lounge, he would mention how strange it was to him that O'Brien would question his marriage.

I remember one very special crossing from Le Havre to New York. My friend, the purser, had arranged for me to sit at a most interesting French table. We were six in all: Maurice Drouon, the author, Alain Decaux, another famous author, both members of the Academie Francaise, the widow of a Lazard partner in Paris named Natalie Beauvois, and two French women journalists whose names I have now forgotten. They were friends of Sartre and Simone de Beauvoir and ardent feminists. One was young and danced well.

Maurice Drouon was working on his six-volume history of the Valois kings to be entitled *Les Rois Maudits*. He had some six author-collaborators, four men and two women as I recall, and had assigned each one a famous figure of the period. The group would meet rather frequently for an evening of discussion at Drouon's house in Paris. French history of the period of the second half of the 14th century was singularly complicated, with the start of the Hundred Years War with England, the incompetence of a series of kings starting with the seizure of the assets of the Knights Templar in 1314 and the attempts of both the

425

English and the Burgundians to control the policy of the French king. As a result, for over one hundred years, France was in chaos. Drouon's idea of assigning each of six historians to look at the life of one individual who played a major role in the life of the period was a brilliant one because each historian in the course of his or her research became an ardent partisan of the character to whom he or she had been assigned. As a result, Drouon told us his evening meetings with the historians became like reconstructions of history, involving all of the key figures of the period. During our meals on board ship we felt that we were reliving with him an incredible tale of historical analysis involving war, kidnapping, substitution of children at baptisms, rapes, even murders of princes and kings. When we weren't listening to Drouon, we would be entertained by Decaux who had just published a very well-received book of famous historical mysteries including that of "the man in the iron mask," Louis XIV's supposed brother. It made the trip a most interesting one. We had many spirited and entertaining discussions—we all offered to play motion picture roles in Drouon's novel when it would be turned over to Hollywood.

Natalie Beauvois was a very active participant in our discussions at lunch and dinner. She lived in Gex, that small semi-autonomous part of France just outside of Geneva on a property that had belonged to Voltaire and had been his residence in the 18th century. She was a French woman in her early 50s who had been married in the late 1920s in Paris to a young partner of the investment-banking firm of Lazard Freres. Because of her husband's growing reputation at the bank, she had traveled with him all over Europe and the United States in the period just prior to the Depression. Then in 1931 he had died suddenly of a heart attack, and his young widow had spent more and more time in Gex and less in Paris. In 1939 with the beginning of hostilities, she had given up going to Paris altogether.

In the 1950s, I made occasional trips to Geneva on behalf of various law clients. I promised Natalie I would try to spend a Saturday evening with her in Gex the next time I found myself in Geneva. It was November before I went back to Geneva—a cold, damp November, and the kind of day in Geneva that seems to last through the winter. As soon as I could get away from my bank meetings, I called Natalie. She told me she had a brisk fire going in the library and would be delighted to put me up if I could stay overnight. I borrowed a car from my hosts and was soon on my way.

Gex is 20 minutes from Geneva, nestled against the mountains that make up the true boundary between France and Switzerland. From here, Voltaire had given advice to Louis XV of France, Catherine the Great of Russia, the German emperor, and Maria Theresa of Austria. Natalie's house may have belonged to the French philosopher, but it was now little more than a remarkably comfortable farmhouse with a large library filled with books, a reception room, and several very comfortable bedrooms equipped with fireplaces. She was right. It was a wonderful place just to sit and talk on a cold November weekend. *Mme. Beauvois*

Because of her trips with her husband and her continued relations with Lazard and other European banking houses, we talked at length about the efforts of the United States to rebuild the European economies after the devastation of World War II, and whether governments were causing more harm than good in their constant interference with private initiatives. In the course of our discussions, it became clear to me that Natalie was extremely knowledgeable about the policies of the French government not only in France but also throughout Europe. I asked her why.

"I suppose in part, it is by way of atonement," she said.

During the course of the evening, and over a very good bottle of Chateau Lafite '47, I was able to get her to tell me the story. I have never been able to forget it. Let me recount it in Natalie's own words, as best as I remember them.

"During the war years, the Germans were concerned about this small section of Europe, not so much because it had any military significance, but because of Switzerland's position in the heart of Europe and because of the role it could play in financing wartime special operations, and, of course, intelligence activities. Geneva was important, not as Basel and Zurich were, but because everyone knew that if Hitler was ever to be defeated, the liberating armies would have to come through France, either from the west or from the south up the Rhone Valley. The area is very mountainous and easily infiltrated. The Germans did not want to waste front line troops here in occupational duties. A fearful story of murder

"The German occupation forces in this area were headed by a German colonel from Bavaria, who was in his early 60s, a nobleman from the border area with Austria who never had much sympathy for Hitler and the Nazis. He had fought in the First World War, had been awarded the Iron Cross. He loved music and was starved for human companionship. I forget how I met him, but he used to come to visit me occasionally on Sunday afternoons—perhaps because I had a piano and loved to play. I had a feeling that these visits were very important to him.

427

Since I was pretty well cut off from my French friends in Paris, I too enjoyed these visits. He was charming and very much a gentleman. If it hadn't been for the war, we might have become close friends or even lovers. As time wore on, I began to feel that there was something else involved. He told me once, 'This wretched war must finish sometime soon, then I will be able, I hope, to invite you to visit me at my small *schloss* in Germany, and I will take you to the summer music festival in Salzburg not far from where I live. My sisters would like you.'

"As you can imagine, Thibaut, I too was lonely. It was a terrible period which seemed to have no end. I was young then, and desperate to live and travel, and communicate again with friends in Europe and America. In 1944 a young man came to see me one day. He identified himself as working for the French Resistance in the Vercors region of France near Grenoble. He asked me if I would act as a message center for his group. He identified who would come, how they would identify themselves, and what help if any they might require. I was French and anxious to help my country, so I agreed. After that he came several times a month, generally in the middle of the night. Eventually we became lovers. He was 19, very good looking, had no conversation, but he knew how to make love, and that was sufficient. I desperately needed the physical release.

"One night he turned to me at my door as he was leaving and casually asked me when my German colonel might be coming next to see me. I should, of course, never have told him, but lovemaking can make a woman unwary. The following Sunday my colonel never showed up. A few days later his adjutant came and told me that the colonel's car had been attacked by a Resistance unit as it was going through the mountains near Chambery and the colonel had been killed. At that instant it was evident to me that my foolish remark had been the cause of his death.

"Some time after the war ended, in early 1946, I received a box of letters that the colonel had written to his sisters about his Sunday visits here during the war years. One of the sisters had written a note accompanying the package. The letter told how fond the colonel had become of me, that he wanted to declare his love for me, but couldn't because I was French and he was German. The letter went on to say: 'He hoped the war would end soon so that he might propose marriage to you and hopefully bring you back to Germany with him. He really loved you so very much. Here are the letters he wrote to us about you. Now that this terrible war is over, we very much hope, even if he is unable to bring you himself, that you will come to visit us.' I was devastated by this letter.

"Thibaut, I was sick to think of what unwittingly I had done. I felt the least I could do was to go out there and meet his sisters. That much I certainly owed him, although this was the last thing I wanted to do. From this letter they appeared to be lovely women, full of admiration for him, and for his sensitivity in not declaring his love for me while our countries were at war. You can imagine how I felt during that week that the sisters and I were together.

"When I came back here I immediately went to Paris and offered my services to the French Foreign Office where I have friends. I speak Russian and Hungarian as well as German. From time to time I am sent to the countries of Eastern Europe on sensitive missions where a woman can sometimes accomplish more than a man. I have seen enough of war. I would do anything to prevent the Russians from plunging Europe into a new conflict."

The next time I saw Natalie was in the fall of 1956. I had stopped off in Geneva for a few days to arrange financing for a corporate client of mine whom I was to meet in Holland to negotiate the acquisition of a Dutch medical company in Schertogenbosch. Natalie had made several visits on behalf of the French government to Hungary. She was very concerned that the Hungarians might revolt against the Russians thinking that they would get help from the western countries. She was depressed about what she thought would happen if the Europeans did not respond. I was very concerned about what might happen to her if she went back to Hungary. It was increasingly evident that the Russians would not tolerate for very long Hungarians striving for greater independence.

When a woman is determined to do something, there is not much that can be done to change her mind. The French government admired and respected the younger Hungarian leaders. But the French and the British were about to take military action in regard to the Suez Canal and intervention in Hungary was hardly one of their priorities. Nevertheless, Natalie assured me that if asked, she would certainly go. The risks did not concern her, expiation did. She felt, as I did, that Stalin would never allow the Hungarians to do what the Yugoslavs had done on declaring their independence from Russian domination.

I went on to my negotiations in Holland. For ten days my client and I could not get any outside news. In Schertogenbosch there were only Dutch newspapers. Headlines several inches high reported on the Anglo-French invasion of Egypt and the Soviet repression in Hungary. We could not get any news except by telephone through my Paris office. No one seemed to know what position the United States government would take. My client wanted to get back to the United States as quickly as possible. I tried calling Natalie but there was no answer.

It was only several months later that I found out through friends in the French Foreign Ministry that Natalie had indeed gone to Hungary and had disappeared during the fighting in Budapest. No one could ever tell me whether she might have ended her days in some Russian Gulag or lost her life in Budapest as reported by the ministry.

Europe in the 1950s was an area which is difficult for Americans of today to remember. It was a time of extraordinary change, of rebuilding in Britain, France, Italy, and Germany, with enormous economic aide from the United States. In the countries of eastern Europe in the hands of the Russians, it was a period of repression, subjugation, and economic despair. The Americans had given up eastern Europe to Stalin at Yalta. It would take another president, many years later, to reverse course.

As I look back at the 1950s and the reaction of the French to what was happening in the Soviet Union under Stalin, I can well understand what prompted Natalie Beauvois to volunteer to help the Hungarians reclaim their sovereignty. Occupied by the Germans since June 1940, the French had played only a limited role in the war against Germany after that date. When freedom came in 1945, all the old divisions within the population had returned: the military was sent to Indochina to try to reclaim their Asian empire; many of the intellectuals, some of whom were avowed Communists or existentialists like Sartre and Simone de Beauvoir who saw no future in the democratic system, while others preferred to live in the past, like Drouon and Decaux; the old families blamed the socialists for the fall of France; the civil servants who had ruled France for so long distrusted the private sector's capacity to restore the economic wealth of the country. There was a lack of confidence in the future among so many in the country.

To young Americans coming to France after the war, Paris was still the center of culture, beauty and the art of living. The best food in the world was in Paris. I remember well the visits I used to make at 4:00 a.m. with Julia Child to the Halles in Paris to shop for food and wine, followed by onion soup and a steak at the Pied de Cochon. But the French themselves were disheartened, depressed and unprepared for the emotional, economic and political rebirth that was now expected of them.

In 1950, a questionnaire was circulated in France by a well-known and highly reputed French public relations firm. The two major questions: Do you expect in your lifetime to be able to purchase an automobile? Sixty percent said no. Do you expect in your lifetime to own your own home or at least to have a modern bathroom where you live? Seventy-four percent answered no. Today France has more cars on the road than any other country in Western Europe and home ownership is very high, and no house is without modern plumbing. *Mme. Beauvois*

In the economic miracle that occurred, the French recovered both their spirits and their combativeness.

The French are great supporters of the United States, and always have been in moments of crisis. But in normal times, they think of Americans as uncultured, immature, and far too much concerned with violence, sex and making money. We, on the other hand, are still a very young country and very confident in our future. In this we are very much like Rome, to a French Athens.

The author at his house outside Paris with his three oldest children, Fal, Pierre and Thérèse. When Bishop Cauchon, who tried Joan of Arc in 1422, lived there, the house was already one hundred years old.

XIX

INVESTMENT BANKING

*W*HEN *I LEFT BECTON, DICKINSON* and went back to the law, even though I was now a senior partner of Coudert Brothers, the change had been difficult for me. If you have run a company and succeeded despite high risks—I was the first outsider brought into the business since its founding in 1897 and started as number three in the company, soon to be moved to number two after its chairman, Dick Dickinson—it is almost impossible to go back to being counsel instead of making the key business decisions. It was no longer my role to decide on strategy, make policy or take decisions. I was only an advisor. It was a role I no longer cared for. Dick Dickinson had quietly noticed this.

It was difficult to go back to law.

"You are not happy just being our lawyer, Thibaut. You have to find another role for yourself."

It was true that I missed the challenges of running a large and growing company. There was, however, really no reason for my being impatient for new challenges. I had one of the most beautiful apartments on Park Avenue and 55th Street in New York. It had a magnificent imposing entrance hall, papered in Chinese red and gold, a library, a dining room, living room and three large bedrooms each with a bath, kitchen and two maids' rooms. Through a decorator friend I had hired an Italian genius of *trompe l'oeil* to replicate the moldings in the main rooms of the apartment, highlighting them and also the fireplaces, so as to give my home the look of a Paris apartment, capitalizing on the high ceilings. Although the apartment faced west on Park Avenue, I even woke up to sunlight pouring into my bedroom as it bounced off Lever Brothers building across the street.

My two boys, Fal and Pierre, were at Portsmouth Priory School; my daughter, Thérèse, at Shipley outside of Philadelphia. They thought it was very exciting to have a home in the middle of the city where everything they enjoyed doing on vacation was near at hand.

I was a senior partner of one of the most prestigious law firms in New York with a substantial international practice and offices in Paris, London, Hong Kong, Tokyo and Washington, D.C. No one was putting any pressure on me to develop new clients. I was working on a new book on international controls over business with my friend, Nasrollah Fatemi. I was teaching a course on international business at Fairleigh Dickinson University in New Jersey. I went to the opera and concerts in New York, made at least two trips a year to Paris by ship. I had a lovely woman in Baltimore and as many as I wished in New York. Once a week I gave a lunch at home for partners and clients at my apartment. I was a member of the River Club, the Racquet and Tennis, and the Sky Club in Manhattan. I was also the owner of a 42-foot trimaran sailing sloop.

As for me, I had everything any man would want. But I was hungry for new problems to solve. I owned a wonderful house outside of Paris in a medieval village called Silly-Tilliard. The house had belonged in the 15th century to the infamous Bishop Cauchon, who tried and burned Joan of Arc at the stake. When he lived there, the house was already 100 years old. It was built in 1322. Whenever I went to Paris, I would spend a week out there making it more livable. There were passageways below the house which my boys and I converted into a wine cellar. Thérèse's French godmother and I designed a very special room and bath and guest room at the top of the house for her. I had even sent a young cousin to Portugal to buy lovely tiles to put in all the bathrooms, and carpets in the Aubusson style to put in the living and dining rooms. I did all this so that my children would get to know and love France, its beauty and its history as much as I did. I even took the children in the summer to Sancerre and to Burgundy so that we could buy casks of the best white and red wine—the best in the world—bringing the wines in bulk back to the house at Silly so that we could bottle it ourselves.

There is no accounting for taste. I had a friend nearby at Silly who owned a magnificent chateau. He always wore plus fours in the style of the '20s. One morning he came over to tell me that his chateau had burned to the ground during the night. He was happy.

"I have always wanted a California ranch house, Thibaut. Now I can build one there."

"Before you do that, Philippe, let me rent a truck and take the magnificent *pierre de taille* stones which supported your castle. I will be able to use them to build a heating system in my house that no one will notice was not done in the 14th century. My rule is that nothing can be added to the structure unless it is 14th century or older. Your chateau qualifies."

He was delighted to accommodate me. I was able to have a heating system without affecting the beauty of the house or its historical value.

Philippe subsequently married the daughter of the owner of Chateau Horut Brion in Bordeaux. She became a duchess and he co-owner of France's greatest wine.

I had everything any man would want. But I was frustrated for new problems to solve.

Why wasn't it enough to live the kind of life I then had in New York? I had even managed to set up separate trusts of $100,000 each for my mother and my father so that their own money problems would be solved.

I lived the life of a man of Florence in the 1500s. Why did I toss it all away through my impatience?

In part it was due to my accepting a woman client when I had been cautioned against doing so. But Alexis Coudert had promised me that he would do the legal work she required so that I could stick to my corporate and international activities. Then he went off to run the London office temporarily and I was left with the client and her legal problems. She was the widow of a highly-regarded investment banker, nephew of Bobby Lehman, head of Lehman Brothers. Philip Isles had married Elene in 1957. In 1960 he died suddenly of a heart attack while his wife was in the hospital giving birth to their second son. Philip had been married before and had three children. After his death, Elene felt that his executors had not treated her fairly and threatened suit against the executors and the children of the first marriage. I had promised to have a lawyer at Coudert make a thorough analysis of all the acts of the executors. This showed that they had, if anything, interpreted the will when possible in her favor. She was very well provided for. Philip not only was a painter himself, but had been a great collector of Impressionist art, all of which had been left to his widow.

Elene wouldn't accept our findings and asked me to bring suit. I refused and she left the firm. Three weeks later she came back and asked me to settle her claims as I wished. This was not difficult to do.

When you have solved all of a person's business or legal problems, you are entitled to think that that person, particularly if she is beautiful, intelligent, and rich, will then relax and enjoy all she has been given. Elene had worked at the United Nations. She spoke multiple languages. She was highly educated. I thought she would now be ready for happiness in a second marriage. In June 1965, we were married in New York with Bobby Lehman giving the bride away.

It should have been a very successful marriage. We went on a long honeymoon, first to London on the New France so that I could attend the inauguration ceremonies of the transfer of Lord North's property at Oxford to Fairleigh Dickinson University. Then we went to Paris for a few days at Silly to make sure my three children, along with Elene's two small ones, were properly behaving. When we got there, Elene said she would never come there again.

"There have been women staying here," she told me.

"Women. Can you imagine since 1322 how many have been here? Why, you came here for weekends yourself not so long ago." I did not want my beautiful historical house disparaged.

Elene went off to the Ritz for the weekend, saying she was bored. While she was gone, the children and I decided this was the time to put the wines in bottles.

Over the course of the evening we bottled some four hundred whites and reds. Elene's boys were in the upstairs bathtub naked as joy buds washing out the bottles. On the floor below, Thérèse and a girl-friend of hers were letting the corks simmer. In the garden, Fal, Pierre and I were pouring the wine into bottles and indulging generously as we went along. Every once in a while we would go upstairs so that the little boys and the two girls could also share in God's bounty.

Around midnight Elene came back saying she was bored at the Ritz.

"My babies! They've been drinking. How could you do this?" We were sorry to see her back.

After Silly, I took her to Venice and then on a cruise along the Dalmation Coast to Dubrovnik which I knew well from teaching there at international seminars. Every morning it was the same "What will we find to do today?"

I realized then that the path ahead would be a difficult one. I am probably not the easiest person to live with, but boredom or lack of ideas has never been a problem for me.

An investment bank in New York, Ladenburg, Thalmann and Company, sent me to Brazil as their counsel to buy a group of cattle banks. I leased a light plane and pilot in Rio de Janeiro and spent a month visiting all the branches of the bank in Minas Gerais and Matto Grosso. I then hired a young banker working for The Getulio Vargas Foundation in Rio de Janeiro—the leading economic think tank in Brazil—so that we could redo all the financials to reflect the wild inflation rate then existing in Brazil. I then returned to New York and recommended that my clients purchase the Brazilian bank. Shortly thereafter, Harry Lake, the senior partner, asked me to join the firm, along with a friend of mine who was counsel to Stavros Niarchos, the Greek shipping magnate.

Investment
Banking

We both accepted, on the promise that a year later we would be given control of the investment banking firm. Unfortunately, we discovered after joining the firm that Harry Lake was not in a position to deliver to us what he had promised. My friend Paul then had gone back to Niarchos as lawyer and business advisor and I joined Dean Witter & Company to become a partner and president of its foreign arm, Dean Witter International Finance Corporation.

Becoming
an
invveŝtment
banker

This was largely because I had become a good friend of Dean Witter, Jr. and he wanted the firm to expand internationally. He had already created a successful operation in New York and Chicago to give the firm an impressive national standing as the fourth largest in the industry and not merely a regional operation based in San Francisco. I realized that my employment represented a singular act of faith on the part of Dean Witter in the business acumen of his son. True, young Dean had created a resounding success in New York against entrenched firms, which had operated in New York for many years, but this did not mean that the same success might be achieved internationally.

Dean Witter, Sr., the founder of the firm, had become a living legend in California. He had come out of nowhere, put all his brothers and sisters through school and college, started as a simple soldier to become a major in the U.S. army in World War I, and eventually outdistanced all his competitors after starting a stock brokerage business in California by himself after the war. When I had gone out to meet with him for the first time, he had quickly pointed out to me that bringing me into the firm was not his idea but his son's. California in his opinion was large enough to meet his goals and he knew little and cared less about what was going on in New York, Chicago, or abroad. Dean Witter was a typical American of the West in the best sense of the word. Hardworking, dedicated, honest, frugal, strict. He had come from the north of the state, arid ranch country where he himself now owned an 8000-acre spread. He liked to fish and hunt, and to be with other men like himself. The world of society was inconceivable to him. He had been to France during the war. He had no desire to return. In politics he was a Republican. He thought little of Roosevelt's social policies. Men should be able to make their own way in the world. After all, he had done it and educated and cared for his siblings as well. If a man couldn't hack it, he was not worthy of being an American. Having said this, Dean entered into his son's dream with his usual drive.

"Thibaut, I have organized a lunch with Chairman Gianini and his president over at the Bank of America. He owns the banking business in California and might be helpful to you in what you are trying to do. I don't understand it but he will." I did not look forward to the lunch. Gianini would ask me all sorts of questions and I would not be able to explain what we might accomplish since I had no idea myself. This was not a good position to be in with my new employer expecting a clear and concise expose of my plans to the chairman of the world's leading commercial bank. My intuitions were justified. Dean Witter at the beginning of lunch turned to Gianini and said: "I wanted you to meet Thibaut because he is going to be heading our new international investment banking operation. Now I don't want you to think that we are going to be immediately actively competing with your world-wide banking operations, but simply that we are in this business and intend to be as successful as we have been in the domestic brokerage and the domestic investment banking business."

What could I say to our hosts about what we might accomplish? I didn't have the foggiest idea. What qualifications did I have just because I had been a successful financial lawyer and business executive? I thought the best thing to do was simply to say that, while I had no developed ideas, I would try to learn from what he and Dean Witter had already accomplished.

Dean had one suggestion which I perhaps should have acted upon but didn't. He called me up one day in New York shortly after I joined the firm to tell me he thought he could bring me the perfect number two man, none other then the former secretary of the treasury when Dwight Eisenhower was president of the United States.

I had turned Dean Witter's suggestion down for one very good reason: there was a friend of mine, Fernando Eleta, who was then foreign minister of Panama. He had recently come to New York as negotiator for Panama on the treaty which would eventually return the Panama Canal to Panama after so many years under American control. The former secretary of the treasury had been designated by the U.S. government as its leading U.S. negotiator. Fernando Eleta had told me one day in New York that the American had proposed that he would give in on one of the key disputed points in the treaty if Eleta would promise to support him on a business transaction in which he was interested. Eleta

438

was surprised by this and didn't know just what action he should take. Should he report this to the American secretary of state or ignore the matter and proceed as if nothing had happened? I did not want the possibility of anything like that occurring if the former secretary of the treasury should become a partner at Dean Witter & Co. and a member of our international investment banking team. It was fortunate. This same man was several years later indicted and sent to prison for tax fraud.

The first year of my activity went well, but more by luck than through any particular skill of my own. As I have often pointed out in this memoir: Napoleon was right in the rule he applied to choosing his marshals, that they be lucky. A businessman had called on me one day to say that he was the leading American expert on steel and other metal alloys which he manufactured at two small specialized mills in Ohio. He was an advisor to a steel company in Japan, as well as to a government concern in the Soviet Union. His business took him to Japan and to the Soviet Union at least once a month. He was too busy to invest the considerable profits that he was earning. I had been recommended to him as an investment advisor. Although brokerage was not the reason I had been hired by the firm, the brokerage fees earned by this account would be credited to my activity at the firm. I had also brought in a major domestic underwriting involving the sale of shares of the Pepsi Cola Company which a friend of mine had acquired through a merger of his company into Pepsico.

My new client, the expert on alloys, invited me one day to accompany him to Japan.

"We will stay at the Okura Hotel in Tokyo which I consider one of the finest hotels anywhere. It has by far the best Chinese restaurant in the world. I will be busy during the day but we will meet for dinner at night and this will give us plenty of time to discuss business matters. We will not be there more then a few days but of course you will be my guest."

I accepted. In investment banking, unlike the law, one doesn't have to worry about hours billable to the client. Time means nothing. It is only results that count. The first day in Tokyo, Bill had given me three years of financial statements of his Japanese client and had asked me to value its shares which were listed in that section of the Japanese Stock Exchange where the stocks of the smaller companies were traded. That night after an exquisite Chinese dinner we lay down on the floor of his suite with the client's financial statements spread out while I explained to him what I had found in my analysis of them: that the shares of the Japanese steel company were trading at little more than what the company was earning each year.

Now taxation had been my best subject in law school and since that time I had had numerous opportunities to judge how different countries taxed their business concerns. Each system gave its national businesses certain tax advantages in order to favor domestic companies in international competition. In Japan, because the country had few national resources of its own, the legislature had allowed businesses not to include in their taxable income earnings from sales abroad. The purpose, of course, was to encourage Japanese companies to export as much as possible. It was largely responsible for what became known as the Japanese post-war economic miracle. Bill could find no problem with my presentation. He promised to review the matter with the company's president the next day, and, if he found the analysis correct, ask him if we could buy shares of stock in the company on the open market.

The upshot to all this was that after approval by the company and the Ministry of International Trade, we were permitted to buy up to 20 percent of the company's stock. I then called Dean Witter in San Francisco and suggested to him that he invest in shares of this company a portion of discretionary accounts held by the firm. This was done. Within the year our shares were sold for a seven-fold profit.

This did not stop Dean Witter from asking me at the end of the year what I was going to do for the firm the following year.

This same client called me up a few months later to propose that I help him accomplish a very large international corporate takeover. It involved a well-known French industrial and mining company which was not well managed but had very substantial assets. Bill proposed to put together an American-Canadian consortium in which his company would participate, but he needed a substantial European partner who would be willing to put in the bulk of the money because his company and the Canadian firm he had selected were relatively small service-oriented businesses. Thyssen Steel was the obvious choice to me. At Bill's request I called the chairman of Thyssen and made an appointment for the two of us to see him in Düsseldorf. We figured an unfriendly takeover might cost approximately $200 million dollars, not much today but a great deal in 1967.

The chairman of Thyssen turned out to be the typical head of a big German business of the Nazi era: over seventy years old, tall, good-looking, snow-white hair, a commanding presence. In his large office on the 36th floor of the Thyssen building, he gave the impression of immense power.

My client left it to me to make the presentation. After I had ex- plained what we proposed to do in some detail and that Thyssen's participation would be $175 million U.S. dollars out of $200 million required for the takeover bid, the chairman turned to my client and said: "Now that you have explained this transaction to me, and I recognize that it may be of interest, why would I need you? I can do the operation on my own." Neither of us had expected this. I realized that Bill would not know how to respond and he looked over at me to answer. I was angry enough to forget just why we were there. The Frenchman in me took over.

Investment Banking

"Let me make it very clear," I said. "We took away from you Germans at the end of the war all your natural resources, which had come from outside Germany to feed your war machine. You cannot do this deal except under an American flag. You cannot do this transaction alone."

There was a dead silence in the room. My client admitted to me later that he thought we would be thrown out the window. After what seemed to us like an hour but was probably five minutes, the chairman said:

"I accept your reasoning. But $175 million is my capital budget for the year. However, there may be a solution: we control a bank in Switzerland which may be willing to fund such a transaction for my company. If you gentlemen will excuse me, I will place a call and see if that may be possible."

I knew what he was talking about, and I had carefully calculated why I could set Thyssen's share of the investment at such a high figure. Thyssen was thought, through I.G. Farben, to control UBS in Switzerland. But this had never been proven. The search for German assets in Switzerland had been abandoned in the Kennedy administration although it was not clear why this had happened.

He returned several minutes later. "There will be no problem. But I have a proposal to make to you. We control economic activities in the Saar Valley and there is a large plant there not in use which might suit our operation perfectly. Have you any objections?" We had none.

I thought this would turn out to be the finest operation of my life. That it didn't was because my client, after he returned to the United States, decided that running a large industrial consortium was not really what he should be doing. Much to my consternation, he abandoned the

My client wouldn't do it.

441

project. On his part, it was probably wise. What more did he need than his already successful business which gave him all the money he would ever be able to spend? It was for me a surprising lesson in forbearance. But why did he go so far in the first place?

The episode had taught me an additional lesson: that I could without fear handle any political or business proposal, regardless of who was involved. The lesson became very useful in other negotiations in the future.

It was, of course, an enormous psychological plus to know that I had behind me the power of a leading investment bank. If you are throwing your weight around, it helps to have this kind of economic standing at your back.

I had a great friend during this time of my life who controlled a company that I had hoped would one day call on me for a financing role. This was Charlie Englehard of Englehard Industries, a company that produced and dealt in all sorts of metals and metal products. One day I invited Charlie Englehard to lunch. He had just returned from a remarkable trip with Lyndon Johnson. Let me report it as Charlie told it to me:

"I suppose I was invited on the trip because I have been a close friend of Prime Minister Menzies of Australia. I had known President Johnson for ages and had been one of his strong supporters in New Jersey which led to his election as Jack Kennedy's vice president in 1960.

"The Vietnam War was on and not going well. The president, I think, wanted to talk to Menzies one-on-one quietly in order to further Australian support for the war. After I had called Menzies to tell him this was not to be considered as an official state visit, I went down to Washington to get on Air Force One with the president. I noticed when he came aboard that an aide had brought along a leather hat box which obviously contained a heavy object. I didn't feel I could ask the president what the box contained.

"After the trip had begun and halfway across the Pacific we were advised that Prime Minister Menzies, on a swim at a beach near his home in Sydney, had been attacked and killed by a shark.

"The president was of course deeply disturbed, but he had decided not to cancel the voyage and to go to Cam Ranh Bay in Vietnam instead. This airport was the port of entry where GIs began their service in Vietnam. When we arrived, the president announced that he wanted to address the troops.

"Unfortunately, no one told the president that the troops at the air-

Investment Banking

Charlie Englehard and the president

port that day were on their way home from Vietnam, not arriving. They were obviously more than anxious to get out of there. But the president made a great speech saying how much the country depended on them and how they would serve their country well in the difficult days ahead.

"It was obviously difficult for the president to be there at all. He pretty well knew that what the high command had been telling him was not altogether true. But he wanted to believe them because he had no idea how to get extricated from a war he now knew he should never have become engaged in.

"When we left Cam Ranh Bay, the president asked the pilot to send a message to Dean Rusk, the secretary of state in Washington, that he wished on the way home to go to Italy and call on the pope in Rome. At the time I didn't understand why this president of the United States would want to call on the pope, but I assumed it must have something to do with the war.

"Dean Rusk must have pointed out to the president that since 1929 an American president could not visit the pope without calling on the president of Italy first.

"One didn't tell this president what to do or how to do it.

" 'Get me Dean Rusk again,' he told the pilot.

" 'Who is our ambassador in Italy?' he asked Rusk.

" 'His name is Reinhart and he is doing an excellent job, Mr. President.'

" 'I want him out of there tomorrow morning. Call our ambassador in Madrid and tell him we will be landing there instead.'

"Angie Duke, the ambassador to Spain, was a friend of mine as well as Charlie's. The message was duly sent to him and he notified the Spanish foreign minister that some ten hours later at 4 o'clock in the morning, the two of them should be at the airport in Madrid to meet the president of the United States.

"After getting over his initial frustration and anger, the president had called Dean Rusk back and told him he would see the president of Italy first, though briefly, and to make arrangements for his call on the pope afterwards.

"But no one thought of calling off poor Angie Duke in Madrid.

"The president insisted on my coming with him to the Vatican. I carried the hat box.

"Thibaut, Jane has been after me for years to become a Catholic. I know that when I die, she will give all I own to the Church. But after

443

what happened on our visit to the pope, I think I owe the Church a good deal.

"President Johnson, when the two of us were introduced to the pope in his private audience chambers, told the pontiff he had brought him a gift and presented the hat box.

"It was a life size bronze bust of Lyndon B. Johnson."

Charlie Engelhard had a great sense of humor and told the story well. But even then, he was a very sick man. I never had a chance to do any work for his company.

During this period of my life I did a great deal of sailing. It took several forms. In the early '60s I had joined the New York Yacht Club sponsored by my friend, Dudley Johnson, with whom I sailed each year on the New York Yacht Club cruise. Dudley would always charter a yacht. I would be his spinnaker man. With Dudley this was an ungrateful job because he was a captain who very frequently made adjustments in his racing strategy. It was a good way to lose weight. I can't remember a year when I lost less than ten pounds over the three-week duration of the cruise. We never won, but we came close several times and we had a very good time, particularly on those rare occasions when the cruise went all the way to Maine.

On Dudley Johnson's cruises one always ate sparingly. When I went on yacht races with Bill Buckley, it was a very different story. Bill's wife, Patsy, would always order every meal for the duration of the race, properly packaged and labeled by meal and by day from the Café Chauverond, one of the best restaurants in New York City, and delivered to the yacht along with excellent wines to accompany every lunch and dinner. Then Patsy would give written instructions as to which member of the crew would be in charge of tidying after each meal.

Here again we would never win but we certainly ate well. With Bill Buckley it was always the conversation that made the cruise worthwhile. Bill's own wit was proverbial, but he always managed to have a racing crew on board with repartee to match his. The politics served up sometimes seemed extreme, but the discussions were always stimulating. I never cared whether we won or lost. It was always fun.

It had always been my dream to own a sailing yacht of my own. In 1963 my friend, Dean Witter, and I bought a 42-foot trimaran which would sleep twelve and had two queen-sized beds in the main cabin between the hall and the outriggers. After Dean had his first heart attack in 1967, the boat was mine to sail. I kept her first in Nassau at Lyford Key, then in Fort Lauderdale. In 1972, my two oldest sons and I even

444

sailed her from Fort Lauderdale all the way to St. Croix. She weighed 17 tons but one summer, along with a young lawyer who worked for me at Coudert Brothers and who had sailed in the Olympics, we clocked her at 23 knots while on a broad reach in a storm in the Bahamas. When she was docked in Fort Lauderdale, I would often go down with the three children on a Friday afternoon, shop for the weekend and set sail around midnight to be in the Bahamas by dawn. What wonderful adventures we had on her. It broke my heart to sell the boat in 1971. She was then in Granada. She had survived three hurricanes while I had owned her. I hope she is still afloat somewhere in the Caribbean today.

In business there are two kinds of effective leaders: those that are managers and those that are conceptualizers. I have never enjoyed being a manager. What I enjoy is to analyze opportunities or focus on solving a problem for clients. That is what I had done as a businessman and as a financial lawyer. That is what I enjoyed doing as an investment banker. At Dean Witter I had been asked to create a new business dimension internationally and manage it, while also doing what I loved, which was to find international opportunities for clients, and solve their international problems. I should have asked the firm to find me a manager for the day-to-day activities of the international operations of the firm.

Dean Witter, Jr. and I had become close friends as we worked together. But I was frustrated and dissatisfied because I hadn't created the organization the firm needed internationally. I had received proposals to join other firms. For a while I thought I had found the right opportunity with a smaller firm which had approached me. They were willing to have me as a "name" partner, had a small group of business clients, and several young active partners. My wife thought it would give me the base I was looking for and I accepted, provided I could also be allowed to teach at the Management Center in Geneva on a periodic basis. It should have been a good deal. The senior partner was an older man, an experienced investment banker, member of my wife's family, with junior partners young and very ambitious. The firm was called Stralem, Saint Phalle & Co. The combination should have been what I needed in the way of back-up support. It would have worked had I not had so many problems at home in my marriage.

I had much earlier discovered, as a corporate partner in a small law firm, that our success had been due in large part to our acceptance and appreciation of the diversity each of us represented. Our senior member in age was a real-estate specialist but was experienced in all areas of the law. He was the naysayer which every firm should have. We made

445

it a rule that any new firm project should have his approval because he would prevent other partners from taking on clients or cases they or we were not prepared to handle properly. I handled corporate matters in New York and international questions through our Paris office, but another partner was in charge of tax questions and a fourth of estate matters. We met whenever any partner requested a meeting. We respected and had confidence in each other's integrity and good sense. It was a wonderful relationship.

In marriage the same relationship has to exist if both spouses are to function to the full extent of their capacities and live together harmoniously. I had found throughout my second marriage that this had not been possible. The problems in my personal life were making it very difficult for me to function effectively in my business life. We had tried short separations. We had discussed divorce. I couldn't see any good answers. My wife liked to travel and was rarely at home. When she was home, she wanted to give and go to parties while I had a much more limited interest in the social life.

In a desperate move to save the marriage and not bring hurt to my small son and two small stepchildren, we considered in 1971 moving to Switzerland. The director of the Management School at the University of Geneva where I gave seminars on corporate mergers and acquisitions from time to time had been urging me to become a full-time professor there, with the right to take on clients independently so long as this did not interfere with my courses on international law, banking and finance.

I accepted his offer and my wife and I took up residence in Geneva in July 1971. It was an honest attempt on both our parts to see if we couldn't find happiness together by living in Europe.

The author with his wife Elene on the SS France *on their wedding trip in June of 1965. They were on their way to England for ceremonies at Wroxton Abbey, home of an Oxford College acquired by Fairleigh Dickinson University after negotiations conducted by the author.*

XX

FELICIA

O NE NEVER KNOWS WHEN adventure will beckon. Our inability to predict anything, it seems to me, is what gives flavor to one's life. "Man proposes, but God disposes." This is not what the Japanese choose to call "karma"—one's destiny, because that seems to imply predestination, a path which cannot be changed through one's own will. I prefer to think that we were given the freedom of will to affect our own fate. What we will do may be written in the stars. So be it. But I want to make my own decisions—right or wrong. It is easy to look back and see how differently one might have chosen. But how many of us, if we look back honestly at our own lives, might have to admit that we would have made the same decisions all over again? I had an opportunity to be parachuted into the Vercors in France during World War II, to become publisher of a leading American newspaper, to become president of a major corporation, to be an ambassador, to marry wealth and breeding. Yet I am not sure I would not have preferred again the other challenges I *did* choose. One must follow one's own path, anticipate the crossroads and, once a choice is made, never look back. Even today, I do not wish to think about what might happen to me tomorrow. You might say that at my age that is just as well. But I prefer to think that each day holds its own promise. Young Dean Witter and I became close friends as well as business associates. As often happens when the head of a family is a remarkably able and successful businessman, the burden to follow in his footsteps may force his oldest son into a profession that by temperament he should have avoided. Here the son should have been a doctor, an engineer or a scientist, but not a securities broker or an investment banker. My friend was not a people person or a salesman. He was a great shot, a fine fisherman, a man interested in technological change. He was badly miscast in the role of running a large brokerage house in New York where human relationships and sales ability count for everything.

448

Ferdinand Eberstadt, the investment banker and my close friend, used to say to me:

"Thibaut, there are perhaps three or four great minds in Wall Street. *Felicia* The rest succeed because they are astute salesmen. That is the key to success in the Street. These men do not read, participate in the great issues of the day, or push the country forward. But they certainly make a great deal of money."

My friend Dean, who appeared to be a confirmed New York divorced bachelor, finally married again, choosing a young woman of 27 who had already been married twice. He was determined to turn her into an experienced huntress. He took her to Africa every summer and to the family ranch in northern California in the fall. I warned him of what she might do to him if he was ever unfaithful, because I could see the light in her eye when she spoke of the game she had killed. I also knew my friend's reputation as a womanizer when he had been single. He could easily be "at risk."

A few weeks later I was in Europe on business. Coming home from Paris, I had reserved a first class seat on TWA. The plane had been held up in Rome and was two hours late. In those days, international flights left from Orly as Charles de Gaulle Airport had not yet been built. The passengers on our flight had been put in a waiting room where we either stared at each other from hard-backed benches or attempted to read. The undercurrent of frustration and anger was quite evident.

All of a sudden a young girl joined us carrying a miniature poodle in her arms. She was dressed in an expensive, close-fitting Mainbocher with a little fur collar and a fur hat to match. It seemed to me that our sad group might perhaps come to life. She was not only young but also very, very beautiful. All of a sudden, it seemed to me that French chivalry and shame for TWA's tardiness required some action on my part. I sat beside her and fetched her a glass of champagne from the bar.

Time went by quickly as we talked. She told me she was 22. She was married to an Italian Duke who had vast agricultural estates on the Po Valley. Each year he allowed her to come to the United States in the early spring to go to parties in New York and Palm Beach before heading for Mexico and a visit with her parents.

"My husband is wonderful to me. As an older man with great responsibilities to manage his estates, he feels that at the end of winter I should have a chance to go to the United States, enjoy parties with my friends and spend some time with my parents."

"It must be a lonely life for a young girl to go through an Italian winter in a humid castle far from the gaiety of Rome," I said.

Felicia

"He is very fond of my father and mother and always flies over to Mexico to see them and bring me back to Italy. By that time I am quite bored with my parties. Besides, in the summer, we always take a long trip to hunt in the Serengeti in Africa. He is an extraordinary shot and has taught me to shoot almost as well. I really enjoy these trips."

"Well, you do have quite a life for one so young: married to a handsome duke, living in a castle, parties in New York and Palm Beach, hunting in the Serengeti. And what do you like to do most?"

The young girl said, "I like to kill."

She turned her face close to mine, looked at me with those beautiful eyes and that face of the Virgin Mary and said simply: "I like to kill."

I had not expected anything like that and didn't quite know where to take the conversation from there.

When we at last boarded the plane, I found myself sitting next to a world-renowned French automobile designer who was on his way to Detroit.

"That young girl is the most beautiful woman I have ever seen. You were speaking to her. Do you know who she is? I would like to photograph her with my new designs."

"She is Mexican and married to an Italian," I said. I was not disposed to tell him more.

"If she's beautiful, she must be French."

"Don't be absurd. Of course, she must be French. With a face like that she would have to be."

"I will write her a note after we take off and she will confirm her nationality to you."

The French sometimes are impossibly arrogant.

As soon as we arrived in New York, I called my friend Dean and went over to have a quick drink with him. I told him my story and warned him once again.

Two years later, I found myself in Zurich for a meeting with some banks. At four o'clock in the morning, my phone rang. It was Dean.

"She did it," was all he said.

"How do you mean, she did it? What did she do and who is she? It is four o'clock in the morning and I have an early meeting at the bank. What are you talking about?"

"She did it. She shot him dead. You told me she would and I have never forgotten it. You told me Faith would do the same to me if I weren't careful. Don't you remember what you told me about that Mexican girl?"

I had almost forgotten. It shows what investment banking will do to the ability of a man to remember important matters.

When I came back to New York. I was given the full story. Felicia *Felicia* had been visiting her parents as usual in their hacienda in Mexico after her stay in New York and Palm Beach. The duke had arrived to spend a few days before taking her home to Italy. On a warm March day, mother, daughter and husband were sitting by the pool before lunch. As in many Mexican cattle ranches the pool is located in a garden area with the house in a U-shape surrounding it, with the bedrooms above on the second floor. As it was explained to me, Felicia had complained of a headache and had decided to take a rest before lunch was served. An hour or so later she came out of her room on the balcony and saw her husband making love to her mother by the side of the pool. Without saying anything, Felicia had quietly gone back into her room, taken a rifle out of the closet and with one shot from the balcony, killed her husband.

In Mexico, such crimes are deemed to be crimes of passion, to be quietly hushed up. The judicial authorities are not expected to take any action in these cases. This should have been what happened here. In addition, Felicia's father was one of the wealthiest and most respected men in Mexico. He would certainly want to make sure that his wife's infidelity not be revealed and become the subject of common gossip.

Unfortunately for Felicia, the duke was the holder of one of the oldest titles in Italy and a papal chamberlain. The family went to the Holy Father himself and demanded that the Papal Legate in Mexico be summoned to demand of the Mexican government an indictment and prosecution for murder of the unfortunate duke.

Now the Mexican government long ago nationalized the monasteries and convents of Mexico. But the Mexican people take their religion very seriously. They may have confused many of the saints with their former Indian Gods, but they are solid, practicing Catholics and expect a request from the pope in Rome to be obeyed.

Felicia was indicted, prosecuted for murder, and sentenced to many years in a Mexican prison. I do not know how long she served. I do not want to know. The thought of that beautiful face behind prison bars is almost too much to bear.

If there is any moral to this story, it is that my friend Dean never *My* suffered the same fate. He remained happily married, moved to Naples, *friend* Florida, and continued to hunt wild boar and wild turkeys with his *Dean* young wife in the Everglades until his death. *never* *forgot.*

XXI

FURTHER INTERNATIONAL
ADVENTURES

F IT HADN'T BEEN FOR my knowledge of Japan, I might never
have met Edgar Detweiler who later became my friend and my
client. Detweiler was one of those men to whom nothing in life
comes easily. It did not bother him a bit. The more difficult it became
to handle a problem, the more he enjoyed it. By profession he was a
mining engineer. Most of his life had been spent on mining projects in
Canada, South America and sub-Sahara Africa, areas where one could
confidently expect unexpectedly difficult problems to present themselves at any time.

I first met Ed in connection with a mining project involving iron
ore in Liberia. I had a great friend in New York, a corporation lawyer
who represented Stavros Niarchos, the Greek shipping mogul in all his
various worldwide activities which included many different businesses
organized and operating in very different parts of the world. Niarchos
had offices in London, Paris, Rome, Athens and Hong Kong, and a town
house in Manhattan, which served as a headquarters and communications center. My friend Paul kept his office there. A good deal of Greek
shipping money must have been invested in this mining venture. For
some reason Paul did not want to act as counsel on the project preferring to stay on the business side, as chairman of the board of the mining
company. He wanted independent counsel to represent the company.
He had asked me to serve as the company's lawyer. The corporation had
raised twelve million dollars in New York, Canada and even from Swiss
banks, but in the mining world, money disappears quickly and between
the problems of negotiating the concession, building camps and a railroad, and other necessary but preliminary steps, the money threatened
to run out long before production would be ready to start. It was clear
that large amounts of additional capital would be needed. The obvious
place to seek additional funds for a mining project at that time was in

An
African
mining
project

Japan. The company's board of directors deputized Detweiler, my friend Paul, a Japanese-American lawyer who knew everyone of consequence in Japan, and me to go there and seek the additional funds we needed.

I was greatly looking forward to meeting Detweiler. He had come to my attention at the time of the Revolution in the Congo when Patrick Lumumba had seized power. Detweiler had gone over from Belgium to meet with Lumumba accompanied by Lucien Lelievre, one of my former partners at Coudert Brothers whom I had recommended to the firm and who was in charge of our Belgian office. Detweiler had figured that with a new government taking over the country, it might be possible to renegotiate the copper concession there and he wanted to be the first on the scene to meet with Lumumba before the Belgians who held the Union Miniere concession could mobilize their forces. He and my ex-partner had chartered a plane in Brussels and set off for Kiniasha, capital of the Congo. When they arrived over the airport, they had found it closed to foreigners. This did not appear to alarm Detweiler. "We shall have to parachute," he told his startled companion. Fortunately, they were able to land safely, but Lumumba didn't stay alive long enough for them to accomplish their mission. As soon as I heard the story, I knew that our trip to Japan would be an entertaining one even if our mission should fail.

This was a time in Japan when the Japanese steel companies were taking over the world's steel business from companies in the United States and Europe. Their mills were the most modern, labor was still cheap, and the Japanese government, through its Ministry of International Trade (MITI), was ready to make sure that Japanese mills had all the raw materials they needed to meet production demands. The system was unusual to Westerners. The steel companies produced steel but neither purchased the raw materials they needed nor marketed the finished product. Marketing was entirely handled by the large Japanese trading companies under the sponsorship and at the direction of MITI which controlled both imports and exports. Our first port of call, therefore, on arriving in Tokyo, would be with that ministry.

We were well received.

"We are interested in negotiating with you," we were told, "because we will need vast quantities of additional iron ore, and the Swedes who control much of the African production are proving difficult partners. We will want your Japanese partner in the Liberian venture to be one or more trading companies, but we have not yet decided which one or whether there will be more than one. We do not want Mitsui or

Further International Adventures

453

Mitsubishi—they are already sufficiently involved in Africa. We do want you to meet with our third big trading company—Sumitomo—although we will probably not choose that company. Of the smaller trading companies, we will want you to meet with three of the largest. In due course, we will indicate to you the chief executives of the trading company or companies we want you to negotiate with. They will be well experienced in the type of technical problems which the production companies which will import the iron ore are likely to face. Our choice will ultimately depend upon our analysis of the ore in that part of Liberia. Some of our steel producing companies are better able to deal with quality problems than others. We will need core samples as soon as you can furnish them to us."

It was a surprising discussion. The Japanese government clearly intended to decide what company should be our partner under some sort of formula of division of markets between companies. It was also clear that the Japanese government intended to choose as our partner a concern that had the necessary technical expertise which might be required if the ore should turn out to have different or less favorable characteristics than expected. MITI went on to tell us to meet with all three of the major Japanese steel producers. We would subsequently be told which companies would become purchasers of the ore. To a Westerner, it seemed to be a surprising example of government intervention in business decisions. To an American it seemed to be a violation of all antitrust laws we were used to. The representatives of MITI explained only that since Japanese foreign exchange was limited, the government believed it necessary for it to intervene in the import and export process, as well as the production process.

Our meetings in Japan, though complicated, proceeded smoothly because the Japanese lawyer who had accompanied us from New York not only set up all our meetings and attended them with us, but was able later to explain to us what was occurring and what MITI had wanted to accomplish as a result of each of these meetings. We sometimes felt like puppets directed by the unseen hand of government bureaucrats who themselves never attended these meetings but were always well informed, both in advance and after the meetings had taken place. At one such meeting, I found myself face to face with the chairman of one trading company who had been commanding general of the Japanese army in Swatow, China during the war and who had tried to have me assassinated. I remembered him well because I had a poster with his face on it and had used it as a dartboard. He admitted he had been in

China during the war as a general, but was not inclined to discuss his activities and I did not press him. He gave me the impression that if he were ever asked again to take up arms against the United States, he would be happy to do so. His company had thirty-six offices scattered around the United States. I was pleased to find out that MITI did not plan to pick his company as our partner.

In due course, we were advised by MITI that our partners would be Kawasaki Steel and two of the "smaller" Japanese trading companies, even though the annual revenues of each was several billion dollars. The negotiations would take place in New York. The three Japanese concerns would choose a Japanese lawyer in New York who was fully familiar with both Japanese and American law and spoke fluent English. This last was very helpful because foreigners always like to make sure that any technical points are discussed in their own language as well as English.

So started fifteen months of negotiations. On the Japanese side there were 27 negotiators, nine from each of the three companies. On our side there were two, my friend the chairman and me. The discussions seemed interminable. They were frequently interrupted for weeks at a time to allow the Japanese participants to go to Liberia to check technical questions or to go back to Japan for consultation among themselves and their employers. In the meantime, Detweiler had to keep his company going in Liberia where there were endless problems of road building, camp employment, drilling, railroad design and building, all on a budget which was constantly being strained to the limit. Our chairman, Paul, had managed to get an additional 7 million dollars from one of the major Swiss banks, but not without unusual costs. Just before the final signing of the loan documentation late one afternoon in Paul's office, he and I were advised by the vice chairman of the Swiss bank who had negotiated the transaction that he had an aunt in the Swiss Engadine who would be very happy to receive a check for $300,000. Paul and I looked at each other, not believing what we had heard. We had, however, no choice. Without this loan the company would not have survived. We never did tell Detweiler about this unusual payment we had been forced to make.

I will never forget the last night of our negotiations with the Japanese. The meeting took place at the Harvard Club in New York City. It was 2:30 a.m. and the third night of endless discussions. Paul and I were both at the end of our patience trying to answer endless questions by 27 Japanese and their counsel who probably were as dispirited as we were but had endless patience. The Japanese lawyer suddenly turned to me after the group had come back to the meeting room following a break.

"Thibaut, I don't think we will have any more questions tomorrow. We are ready to take a vote on the deal."

Now in Japan it is neither the president nor the chairman of the company who signs a business agreement. It is the negotiators, who are middle-management executives. This meant that 27 persons had to sign. They might put their chops on the documents "up," meaning they agreed; "sideways" to indicate they took no responsibility; or "upside down" which meant against the deal. Thankfully, all gave their approval. I thought at this point we had, after 15 months, reached agreement. It was not to be.

The Japanese lawyer turned to me.

"We have one more serious problem, Thibaut. The presidents of the three Japanese companies will come to New York to sign the final accords which we have now approved. But we do not know of any hotels in New York which have suites suitable for leaders of Japanese industry."

He was serious. It was 2:30 a.m. in the morning and all of a sudden I did the unpardonable to an Asian.

"Why don't you just run your battleship up the East River and we will sign on the foredeck."

There was absolute silence in that room for what seemed like several minutes. I realized I'd better say something.

"I want to apologize for my outburst. It was not in order. But we have been at these discussions for fifteen months and it is 2:30 a.m. in the morning. Surely there are first-class hotels in New York suitable for your chief executives. We will find one together."

The room relaxed. The Japanese executives were housed at the Pierre Hotel on 5th Avenue in adjoining suites, and the signing took place in the ballroom of the River Club to which I belonged, with a party for the press and the Japanese business community. I learned one more lesson on the importance of "face." The Japanese later turned out to be excellent partners.

My own role in the matter ended with the signing of the agreements.

I did not hear from Detweiler for some time. I had moved to Switzerland and was teaching at the Management Center in Geneva when I had a visit from him one day. As usual, he was full of enthusiasm. We had lunch together in town at the Richemond as he revealed his current plans to me.

"I have solved the problem of the Middle East, Thibaut, and am go-

ing to need your help. It is the most exciting thing I have ever done and
I want to hold a place in it for you. I have just returned from a visit to
Nasser in Egypt. He has given us the go ahead if we agree to keep the
United Nations in the foreground."

The plan was typically Detweiler: "Full speed ahead and damn the
torpedoes." Over a long lunch, he explained his plan in detail and how
much he had accomplished to date. His idea was to create a new home
for the Palestinians on both sides of the Suez Canal which would be
internationalized, and both deepened and straightened to avoid the
problem of silting. The internationalized area would cover a mile on
either side of the canal. A German engineering firm would produce
very large machines which were capable of rapidly digging a new, much
enlarged canal in areas where the silting was presently taking place.
Detweiler's company had designed and was prepared to contract for
two- and four-bedroom, cinderblock air-conditioned houses, costing
thirty-five hundred dollars, to be built—by Palestinian and Arab contractors—in sufficient quantities to house all Palestinians willing to re-
settle. The gas currently flared by the Saudis and the Emirates would
supply all the power needed for heavy industry. Steel and other "dirty"
manufactured products would be produced there since there would be
no environmental concerns in the desert. Ease of transportation to and
from would enable new heavy industry to be established there since
power would be reliable and cheap. The area would become a center
for heavy machinery production and would easily be able to support
the immigrant Palestinian population. It was a grandiose and idealistic
program which in Detweiler's view would attract international capital,
including investment banks worldwide controlled by Jewish interests.

The government of Israel, for obvious reasons, was enthusiastic
about Detweiler's program, because it would allow for additional Jewish settlements in areas west of the Jordan currently not occupied by
Palestinians who would have resettled by the Suez Canal.

We agreed to meet in New York a few months later. Detweiler had
organized an impressive board of advisors, leaders of international business concerns and banks, to develop his program. "The cost is miniscule,
Thibaut, compared to the cost of the wars and the armaments race which
have marginalized the entire Middle East for so long. Everyone stands
to gain from this *economic* solution to an endless *political* problem."

Edgar was smart enough to understand that political problems
are much easier to solve if businessmen and governments can see an
economic benefit to bringing about a solution. Egypt had seen that

457

it would benefit from such economic development in the region. The question came down, as so often, to what would be the attitude of the American government. I was asked to sound out quietly some of my Democratic friends in the Senate. Detweiler and I went to Washington to talk to Senators Church and Pell, both of whom were key members of the Senate Foreign Relations Committee. We had economic feasibility reports, engineering studies prepared by the Germans, and written expressions of interest by investment bankers. We both felt we had very impressive documentation to support the project.

This was a period, after the departure in disgrace of president Nixon, when the United States had turned inward and had little interest in undertaking an active foreign policy. We needed to extricate ourselves from Vietnam. We were concerned about Cambodia and North Korea. The Soviet Union was as threatening as ever. Church was looking at the behavior of the international oil companies and the CIA. It was not a time when government sought a more active role anywhere. My friends in the Senate were rather more dubious than I had expected, but agreed to introduce us with a positive recommendation to the assistant secretary of state for Middle Eastern affairs, so that we might get his interest and support.

The meeting at the State Department was not a success. It quickly became clear to us that its principal focus was not on the Middle East, but rather on Asia and on Europe. This was, after all, the middle of the Cold War. Kissinger was in charge of American foreign policy as secretary of state.

To our surprise, the assistant secretary told us after listening to Detweiler's detailed presentation: "The Department of State has a program in place which will solve the Palestinian problem and doesn't need any new suggestions from the private sector, no matter how well-intentioned."

He went on to tell us that the State Department had decided to urge the Palestinians to move into Jordan where almost 50 percent of the population was Palestinian. I tried to point out to him that the Jordanian army had been trained admirably by the British and would probably easily repel any Palestinian effort to take over their country. It was of no interest to him.

"The Department of State does not make mistakes," he told us. Upon our return, I complained bitterly to my two senator friends, but they were not willing to take the matter further up the chain of command at State.

What we had predicted, in due course happened. The Palestinian army moved into Jordan, and was easily repelled by the Jordanian army. The Palestinians fled northward and into Lebanon, with the disastrous consequences that ensued to that unfortunate country, including a civil war, invasion by Israel and then by Syria, and the death of many Americans at the Lebanese Embassy compound.

Further International Adventures

Assistant Secretary Sisco left the State Department and was rewarded with the presidency of American University in Washington. His policy had not only turned into a disaster for the Palestinians, it had caused the occupation of Lebanon, first by the Israelis and then by Syria. No one in the U.S. government was held accountable.

The State Department rewards a terrible error.

Without American support, Detweiler's intriguing program for finding an economic solution to the problems of the Middle East was allowed to languish and eventually die. Could it have succeeded?

The world is more than ever in need of far-seeing leaders, men of stature and historical perspective, who also understand that to bring about political solutions to international problems, it is often necessary to show how economic benefits to the major participants will follow. We are still awaiting, both in the United States and in the Middle East, the type of political leader who will understand that the present situation between Israel and the Palestinians cannot be permitted to continue. The Palestinians are entitled to an independent state somewhere. Israel cannot be allowed to expand its settlements in Palestine territory. Land for peace, recognized by all other Arab nations, has to be the answer. Only then will Israel be safe and the Arab nations appeased.

For 50 years, ever since President Truman's decision to sponsor a Jewish state in Palestine, there has been endless turmoil in the Middle East. The state of Israel, established after several wars with neighboring Arab states, has still not been accepted by its neighbors. Its area is too small to defend. Its citizens are still determined to recreate the old Jewish state all the way to the Jordan River. In time it risks having Palestinian Arabs as a majority of its population. The American decision to force the Soviet Union to allow Jews to emigrate from Russia to Israel has only made the current problem worse. Detweiler's imaginative proposal to bring some new and dynamic thinking to an intractable problem had certainly been worth careful consideration by the United States government. Obviously, the longer the situation continues between Palestinians and the Jewish state the more intractable it becomes.

XXII

PROFESSOR IN SWITZERLAND

*I*N *JULY 1971, I* accepted an offer from the director of the Centre d' Etudes Industrielles (C.E.I.), the advanced management school affiliated with the University of Geneva, Switzerland, to become professor of international law, banking and finance and direct the seminars for heads of international businesses who might wish to attend. I had greatly enjoyed giving sessions there twice a year since 1969 on international mergers and acquisitions. By agreement with Bob Hawrylyshyn, the director of the center, I was permitted to do consulting work on the side and to spend time writing articles or books on international business questions. It was an opportunity that appealed to me. I still had much of my stock in Becton, Dickinson so that the pressure to keep on earning ordinary income was not as great as it had been. It was a chance to do what I enjoyed doing, in a city where I had friends, to ski in the winter, and to try to save my marriage, in a country which my wife enjoyed and where she had property and numerous friends. She was not excited about leaving New York, but she agreed to try it out. We exchanged our apartment in New York with friends for one in the fashionable Ruedes Granges and moved to Geneva. It should have been a move which would satisfy both of us. Instead, it meant that I would live in Geneva with two young stepchildren who now considered me as their father, our two very young children, and the governess. My wife, who enjoyed society much more than I did, would travel between London, Paris and New York. It might have worked had we been close. As it was, the move turned out not to be satisfactory to either of us. We were not communicating in Switzerland any better than we had been able to in New York, and marriage without the capacity to communicate is a void. In early 1979, my wife returned to New York, taking the children with her. She had never told me that she planned to do this. I was in Phoenix, Arizona at a board meeting when a New York friend

Becoming a
professor in
Switzerland

called me to say that he had seen my wife and children and that they were back in New York.

Geneva is a city where people invite you to dinner six months in advance. Perhaps because of its strong Calvinist roots, there is not much laughter—the leading families live in the Old Town near their Calvinist Cathedral and the leading private bankers are huddled below, next to one another. Among the old families, nothing much has changed since Calvin's day in the 18th century. The oldest son, one hopes, becomes a pastor or an educator; the second a lawyer; the third a businessman, doctor or a journalist; the fourth a banker. There is money because the Swiss are frugal and the old families intermarry. But Geneva is a serious city.

Geneva is also filled with foreigners living there because of the United Nations and various other international institutions. These live in a very separate world, having little to do with the normal life of the city. There are some 40,000 of such international civil servants. They bring in their own servants under special exemptions. Their children get free schooling. They pay no taxes in Switzerland. They do not much mix with the Swiss, preferring to see each other. To them, the Swiss have no interest in international politics. I remember once giving a cocktail party in Geneva, at which I had invited, in addition to some of my colleagues and their wives, and bankers and business friends, some U.N. ambassadors I knew. The next morning, a friend I had persuaded to act as my hostess received phone calls from Geneva friends asking her what happened to me that I had invited people from the U.N.? When I stop to think of it, it is probable that the same triage occurs also in New York, where the United Nations people tend largely to stick together.

Contrary to what people think, Switzerland is in many respects a thorough police state. Because of the role it plays, it understandably has to be. All hotel phones are tapped. So are the phones of foreigners. We had a friend who had moved from California some three years earlier. He had bought a property in the outskirts of Geneva. He still drove around in his large American car and had made no effort to obtain Geneva plates as the law required. One day three of his friends decided this had gone on long enough. One telephoned another and mentioned, "When do you suppose Ed is going to get Geneva plates for his Cadillac?" Within minutes, an inspector from the Geneva Motor Vehicle Bureau called the owner of the car to invite him to regularize his situation.

Every quarter, the Swiss government, ever anxious to keep its farmers happy, decides what the national economy can produce in the next quarter and sets the import controls on food products accordingly.

Switzerland is really three nations: the cantons where German is spoken, those that speak French and the Ticino area where people speak Italian. The German cantons control the federal government, but their representatives go out of their way to consult with the French and the Italians. It is a very workable system.

Swiss democracy is based on the premise that no one should have an advantage over another. In 1973, I had taken on a three-year lease of an apartment with a large terrace on the second floor of a house on the main avenue between central Geneva and the suburb where the Management Center was located. There was a bus stop in front. One spring day, I parked my car in front of the bus stop, ran up to the apartment where, from the terrace, I could see the housewives by their open windows across the street picking up their phones to tell the police there was a car parked in front of a bus stop. I had just enough time to dash down and tell the policeman that I had done this just to see how efficient the local officers were.

It does make perfect sense that the Swiss are so careful about how foreigners behave on Swiss territory. There are numerous foreign political figures out of office who have taken refuge in Switzerland. They are welcomed as refugees so long as they do not engage in politics. If they do, they are immediately asked to leave.

There was an attractive woman friend with whom I often dined. She had a job requiring that she spend an eight-hour day listening to phone calls in a post office building in the center of town. If she ever heard a conversation which was in a language she did not understand or one involving drugs, international politics, the commission of a crime, or even a corporate acquisition, she would tap her foot on a pedal and the recorded conversation would be passed upstairs for further analysis by experts in that field. People are rarely arrested. They are simply notified on the spot that they must leave. They are then accompanied to a plane or train and sent on their way. Language is not a problem. Almost every Swiss understands four languages: German, French, Italian and English.

A bank in Switzerland occupies a very special position. Tax evasion is not a crime in Switzerland. People from all over the world bring in money to be deposited in a Swiss bank in a numbered account. The only thing you must be sure of is that someone you trust has a power of attorney over the account in case anything happens to you. If you should die or simply disappear, only the person who has the power can take over the account. Every day there are instances of the difficulty this creates: Emperor Haile Selassie of Ethiopia, ex-President Ferdinand Marcos of the Philippines; ex-President Salinas of Mexico; the FLN in Algeria who could not locate the signatory of the money the Revolutionary Party had used when the party's funds had been deposited in a Swiss bank. *Professor in Switzerland*

The father of one of my good friends in Spain was dying at the Beau Rivage Hotel in Vevey a few years ago. He had gathered his children together, given my friend a power of attorney and the name of his bank. But when my friend went to the bank immediately after her father had died, she found his mistress had emptied his account an hour earlier. How many stories are there of fortunes acquired or lost in Swiss banks?

I greatly enjoyed my work at the University of Geneva. My colleagues came from different countries. There was an English economist, two Americans, a Dutch businessman, a Danish philosopher, a German, several Swiss, one of whom was a remarkable librarian whose family owned the sources of the Rhine River in central Switzerland. The director was from the Ukraine, his deputy Swiss. Klans Schwab was a German colleague of mine here before he left to inaugurate the World Economic Forum.

I greatly admired Klans Schwab and one of those on the faculty who supported his proposal that the Economic Forum be a part of the Management Center, but the director felt its focus would be too much on business strategy rather than on an educational experience.

As the Economic Forum grew, Klans Schwab would ask me each year to be one of the lecturers. I greatly enjoyed this. It gave me the opportunity outside of my regular work to meet key political figures as well as leaders of business corporations from around the world.

I remember two instances particularly.

The first took place in Daros one winter in 1973. The OPEC oil cartel had just voted a ten-fold increase in the price of oil. The Saudi Arabian oil minister, as one can imagine, was at Daros that year. He and I dined together one evening. I asked him since he had just spent a week with his father who was a sheepherder in the desert what his father thought of the position he occupied in the government. It was the kind of question one can only ask of a minister after a martini at a relaxed dinner with no other guests present.

"He is of course proud of me because I am a king's minister, but he believes I might be happier in the desert tending sheep as our family has always done," he said.

The second incident took place much later in 1979. A year earlier I had given a general review about the advantages for foreign industrial companies setting up research activities in the United States to take advantage of the new centers being created in certain states where there was a concentration of state-supported technological research activity going on in universities. I had specifically talked about North Carolina. The following year when Mariana and I arrived in Daros, we found an invitation to dinner from a Finnish group. At the dinner there were twenty-seven companies from Finland represented. All had within the year established individual research centers in that part of North Carolina known as the Research Triangle.

Sometimes, a message bears fruit.

We were a polyglot group but easy-going and always ready to pinch hit for a colleague. The programs at the Management Center were organized on a pyramid basis. At the bottom were the MBA students who spent a year, then came eight-week and four-week programs for middle managers who were to be promoted. At the top was an eight-day program for corporate chief executive officers. Other programs were functional: accounting, law, environment, research, production, business economics. I was in charge of the program for company chairmen and presidents and, on the functional side, business economics, banking and law. I designed the curriculum for these programs. This meant that I could not only design the program but invite the speakers, whether from the outside or within the school faculty.

The programs for company chairmen gave me the greatest challenge but were the most fun. There might be anywhere from forty to sixty students in any such seminar. They were there for eight days, but I would work them for long hours. I saw my role as acting as a catalyst more than as a teacher, hoping to develop stimulating discussions which would bring out the different ways in which companies were managed in different parts of the world as a result of differences in education, corporate goals, political backgrounds and cultural differences. My class was a laboratory of some of the best business minds in the world. I wanted to make sure that they would learn from each other as much as from me or other faculty members.

After awhile, I learned a great deal about how cultural differences affected the way in which multinational companies were governed. It is difficult to teach a Dutch chief executive very much that is new. He knows what he knows very well. He is reluctant to adopt new ideas. The American is very unsophisticated about international business. But he is apt to think Americans have the best managers, the best engineers, finance executives, marketing, research. The British are likely to be excellent at finance and marketing, but poor in production. The French will follow an idea to its logical conclusion but may not start with a correct assumption. The Japanese worked with one another every night for hours. They were always well prepared, but their ideas expressed in class were always those of the group, never the individual. *Professor in Switzerland*

One curious phenomenon which I noted from successive seminars with these chief executives was that there seemed to be two sets of nationals which, if they were represented in my seminar, the combination would unerringly result in a polarization of the entire group and create tension. One set was the French and the English; the other was the Russians and the Israelis. There was no problem between the French and Germans, who respected each other, or between Israelis and Arabs, who often lunched together. I had never realized before how strong anti-Semitism was in the Soviet Union. The problem between the French and British, I suppose, had always existed and was atavistic, steeped in historical tradition. Two sets of nations are always a problem.

For these seminars, I could select the speakers—I could choose from colleagues at the Management Center. I could also invite people from the outside. Otto von Hapsburg came several times to speak on the new Europe as he saw it. He was always a great success. I had Jacques Attali come to explain his brand of socialism after explaining to my class that it was important for them "to know the enemy." To show that French businessmen were able to exercise ingenuity, I invited my friend, Bernard Ginestet, owner of Chateau Margaux in Bordeaux, to tell us how he had obtained de Gaulle's permission to create a new type of business entity, a kind of corporate partnership called a *groupement d' intérêt économique*. I also had my friend Roberto Campos, former minister of planning and economic coordination of Brazil, who not only saved the Brazilian economy in the '70s, but also created the Central Bank, reformed the tax system and created a national housing program. Roberto, trained as a Jesuit, not only brought to his sessions a renowned intellect but was a great writer and a masterful storyteller besides.

My own role in these seminars was simple. I sent each of the members of the class a brief note before they came asking them to write down a brief paragraph stating the worst mistake and the best decision they had made for their company in the last five years. We did not discuss what they reported. But it was very helpful for me in making sure that the reasons for these successes and failures would be covered during our class discussions. It also gave me much insight into the human side of each executive. One French company chairman who had come to these seminars several times told me once: "I can't raise my prices while the French government makes me raise wages, so I don't know how to solve my problems at home. So I like to come to Geneva and learn about how others solve problems outside their own country." The head of the largest chemical concern in Britain told me, "the world thinks that we know how to market products, but that we can't properly make anything in Britain. So I ship from our German plant and give operating instructions on the package in German, as well as English." That way the customer thinks the product has been produced in Germany.

One time, I was forced by the center's director to take into the course a young man, only 35, who worked for Phillips in the Netherlands and was considered a young genius. During the week, I asked him why Phillips had insisted on his coming. His answer was interesting: "I was sent to Italy to run several electronic plants in the Milan area. My three predecessors had failed, but I had no choice. The first week I was there, the head of the union came to see me to tell me his men would strike all of our plants the following week. I was desperate. Out of my desperation, I called him in the next day and proposed to him that I cut the work day from eight hours to seven, allowing the work force to go on strike the last hour of the work day. After a week's thought, he agreed. Now we no longer have strikes. Each day the workers carry their placards around for the last hour saying, "Dutch, go home." Men stopped beating their wives. Their pay is safe; everybody is satisfied and we produce more in seven hours than we did before in eight. I am now considered a genius at Phillips, but I really did nothing."

Interesting that when the Jospin government in France insisted on a 35-hour workweek over the protests of all employers many years later, the same result ensued. Workers are producing more—not less.

My role in these seminars was a simple one. I had, for eight days, the most successful businessmen in the world. All I had to do was to stimulate an interesting discussion which would enable each of these executives to exchange ideas and learn from each other. I was the real beneficiary because I was learning from them all. I certainly enjoyed these seminars.

Teaching the MBA students was quite a different proposition. They

Professor in Switzerland

466

were there for a full year. All of them had been in business for about ten years and many were sent by the companies for which they worked. It was a real opportunity for the students to develop friendships which would last a lifetime. As professors, we come to know these students well. With them I could use the case study method, designing my own cases to make them truly multinational. I would try to have the cases reflect cultural differences.

At the Management Center, it was not the students who were graded. It was the professors. At the end of each seminar, the class was asked to fill out a questionnaire which graded each session for interest, presentation and value, together with a 1 to 5 grade for each speaker. The seminar was also graded overall. The seminar for senior executives was always particularly successful. Heads of companies from different parts of the world have little opportunity to know each other or exchange ideas. They were happy to get away from their normal careers and their telephones for a period of a week. Since we also spent a good deal of time on international politics, as well as corporate strategy, it was an opportunity to broaden one's understanding of political trends in different parts of the world.

One day the director of the center received the visit of the Canadian government official who was in charge of Canada's aid program to developing nations. He had an interesting proposal to make. "We want to avoid the mistakes that we and the Americans have made in the past in our programs," he said. "We are willing to put up $3 million if you will design and manage for us a pilot program which will include three weeks of learning at your center in Geneva, followed by six weeks in the country chosen for the program for two members of your faculty to work with companies to be selected within the country. In this way, we may be able to trigger management practices that may help the country make better headway in world markets. Since this is an experimental program, we would like you to choose a country which has been particularly averse to accepting Western political, economic and cultural ideas."

We spent three days discussing which developing country to choose. In many ways, the choice was clear. Algeria was proposed. Three weeks later, thirty-eight Algerians arrived at the Management Center. They were not a friendly-looking group. It was clear that they had been chosen for their leftist political learnings rather than their business acumen. The director spoke to them briefly, then proceeded to get me out of a course I was giving.

"Your French is better than mine, Thibaut. They are yours for three weeks."

I went into the classroom with some trepidation. They certainly were an unprepossessing lot of angry, bearded Moslems. I figured I'd better move fast before they realized I was an American.

"I come from a country that, when it became independent, behaved exactly as you are behaving here. We told the British, the French and the Dutch to stay away from North and South America. We did not want them going anywhere near the Western Hemisphere. We called this policy the "Monroe Doctrine," although we had no army and no navy to enforce this policy. I will make a deal with you. I will accept your political ideas provided you will go along with me in looking at my ideas on economics and trade. This way, you will learn what you came to find out about."

The spokesman for the group, after some discussion together in Arabic, agreed and we then proceeded to get along just fine. It was certainly, though, a constant battle to stay clear of politics, and I was glad to see them go. My colleagues who went with them to teach in Algeria had a rewarding but difficult time. Despite their French education, they were true Islamic revolutionists, determined to reshape the world to their liking.

Teaching finance and economics to the MBA students was stimulating in very different ways. Younger students that have been in business already for a number of years have minds that are sharp and quick. You have to be sure that you know your subject or you will lose them and if you lose them in one area, it will be hard to get them back in others. Economic theory is one thing; the practical side of corporate finance is quite another. From my time as a "doctor of sick companies," I had learned very important lessons which I enjoyed passing along to my class. Having majored in accounting, I would try to teach them to be very wary of accountants who tell you where you have been, but not where you are going. My favorite story was that of Rolls Royce, which went bankrupt while its auditors told the board of directors that the firm was still making money. If you are managing a company, you need to deal in terms of cash flow, not profits, and the source and application of funds must be the only bible to guide you. At the end of my sessions with the group, I would always divide them into teams and give them an acquisition case, with one team being the acquirer and the other the acquired. I had designed a complicated scenario, which included elements of policy, research, production, marketing and finance, then

I turned the groups loose to see how they might negotiate a deal. This was always a very popular exercise which took place over a full week at the end of the term. After the exercise was over, it also gave the group an excellent opportunity to discuss together why they had reached the conclusions they did and what they had learned from analyzing and negotiating an actual business transaction. *Professor in Switzerland*

Since that time, of course, accounting rules have become so flexible and porous that companies can report to their shareholders that they are making money when, in fact, the opposite is clearly true. In the so-called New Economy, a company like Amazon.com can use financial reporting of its investments to give a more positive picture to shareholders than warranted by the facts. When I was teaching in Geneva in the '70s, accounting rules were simpler. Then we dealt mainly with how it was possible in different jurisdictions, largely because of rules on taxation in a given country, to hide income so as not to pay increased amounts to the state or to make use of special national subsidies to get an advantage in international trade transactions.

Every year, as part of the curriculum for the MBA students, they would be taken on a trip to one or more of the countries behind the iron curtain, with a faculty adviser, so they might learn how a particular political and economic system worked. I had taken them in 1973 to visit Poland, Austria and Hungary.

The first of the sessions we had in Poland was with the secretary of the Communist Party. He had begun his exposé by stating that the government was on its sixth Five Year Plan. "Generally, if your first Five Year Plan doesn't succeed, you go on to a second one. Now we will see if the sixth works out any better than the fifth."

I thought this comment was so refreshing that I sought him out to see if we might lunch together. He was happy to do so.

At lunch, he said he wished to apologize for the Poles who had immigrated to the United States. Poles are elitist by nature.

"How can you say that? The Poles in the United States have made wonderful citizens. They work very hard, don't engage very much in politics, support their Church."

Poland, I discovered, was one of the most elitist countries in the world. This was true even under Communism.

He told me that just before World War II, he had gone to the University of Chicago on a fellowship. The first morning he was there, having very little money, he had gone to a diner in South Chicago to get a cup of coffee at the counter. There he overheard two black youths speaking Polish to each other. He was very much surprised since he had never heard of blacks in Poland.

"If you want to learn something in South Chicago," they said, "you go to the Catholic schools. The nuns who teach there are all from Poland."

That afternoon, we were taken by the authorities to visit a steel plant which they said had recently been furnished to them new by the Soviet Union. I had noticed that all the markings on the machinery bore Chinese characters. It could only mean one thing. This "new" plant had been sent to Poland by the Russians as one of the spoils from the Soviet occupation of Manchuria.

One of the students on this trip had been a Western symphony conductor in his native Japan. Aware that there was relatively little future for his talent in his home country, he had switched to banking and, after several years in Tokyo, his bank had sent him to Geneva to get his MBA. We had become friends because we both enjoyed the opera. The night before leaving on this particular trip, we had attended the opera together in Geneva. We went to the opera together during the next two weeks in Warsaw, Budapest, Vienna and finally New York, where I had had to go for a board meeting and my friend for a meeting of his bank. The best performance by far had been Tchaikovsky's *Eugene Onegin* in Warsaw. The first thing the Poles had done after the war had been to rebuild the old city. The second had been to build a new opera house. The opera in post-war days in Warsaw was the only time when a woman could dress up for a social occasion.

One day I received a phone call from my friend, Bill Witter, president of William D. Witter & Co. in New York and son of my former partner, Dean Witter. Bill had a very successful boutique money-management firm in New York. He and Jim Balog, chairman of his firm, wanted to find out whether I could organize for their international clients a one week seminar at the Center in Geneva which would focus on investment opportunities for American institutions in Europe where the firm's clients had done little investing up to that time. What were the exchange control and currency risks? The country rules on investing by foreigners? Were they welcome? Where were the exchanges? How were they run? What were the political risks? The economic and political situation in each country? It was agreed that, working with Jim, I would design a package for their clients for a one week program in Geneva ending with a grand dinner attended by their American clients and Swiss bankers from Geneva, Zurich, Basel and Lugano.

470

It was a challenging proposition. This was before the days when every U.S. investment banking and brokerage firm had multiple offices in Europe. As an educational institution there had to be a learning experience involved before my director at the Management Center would agree to let me undertake the program. The chairman of the Swiss Central Bank in Berne, whom I consulted, told me he would not participate, that the American institutions' clients of Bill's firm who together represented some 300 billion dollars of investments should please keep their dollars at home and certainly not bring them to Switzerland. The private bankers I contacted were enthusiastic.

In three weeks Balog and I had agreed on a detailed program which passed the educational test insisted upon by my director and satisfied Balog's clients. We agreed on a date, prepared detailed materials, agreed on lecturers both within and outside the Management Center, and prepared the international list to go to the Witter clients, the lecture staff, and the Swiss bankers who would attend the graduation dinner in the ballroom of the Richemond Hotel in Geneva. We had worked up together a very exciting program.

The affair turned out to be a smashing success. I was surprised to find how little American institutional investors knew about the opportunities of investing in the European securities markets. I was also surprised when, at the final dinner, bankers from the various Swiss cities came up to me and said, "Those from Zurich or Basel or Lugano are really very interesting people."

Switzerland has maintained its privacy—even from itself.

My personal life had been a lonely one after my family left. Fortunately, my friend, Adolf Lundin, persuaded me to join him in creating an oil company. He and his family were very kind to me. I also rented a small apartment in Gstaad for the weekends. Geneva in the winter is a depressing place. It doesn't snow, but it is generally very dark, with no sun for most of the winter months. As soon as one is twenty miles away from the lake, the sun comes out.

Adolf was a petroleum engineer and had served for a time as assistant director of the center, not so much to teach but to organize the work-study groups which were so much of the teaching process for the younger MBA students.

The Swedes are a remarkable people. A nation of only nine million people, it has one of the highest living standards in the world. Its business class is also one of the world's best educated. Because the country is small, Swedes learn other languages at an early age. To support their living standard, they know that they must succeed in international business. At the Management Center in Geneva year after year about *Professor in Switzerland* one-quarter of our students came from Sweden. They all spoke German, their second language, English, and most spoke French as well. After all, their king was a descendant of one of Napoleon's generals. Adolf himself spoke fluent German, English, Spanish, Italian. His mother's family had been Austrian, his grandfather the Austrian general charged with the occupation of the Crimea in the First World War.

When Adolf was first married, he and his new wife spent two years in Cali, Columbia, where he was a young mining and petroleum engineer. He then went to Geneva to become assistant director of the Management Center. It was there that I met him. We became fast friends.

Adolf called me one day at the Management Center to propose that we form an oil company together. He would handle operations, I would be the financial director.

"The oil companies are the biggest businesses in the world. How do you propose to compete with them?" I asked.

"It is because they are so big that they are inefficient. They are run by petroleum engineers, not businessmen. We will be able to compete successfully because we will be able to make decisions quickly, without having to get the consent of boards of directors and lawyers. In this day and age rapid decision-making is the key to success."

Launching an oil company The upshot was that we created an oil company. The capital was $250,000. Each of five owners put up $50,000. Adolf was the president. I was vice president and general counsel. The chief geophysicist of Shell Oil joined as chief geophysicist, as well as the geophysicist for Caltex, and an Egyptian oil lawyer by the name of Ahmed El Dib who had been practicing in Denver. We waited for Adolf to tell us what to do.

"The Allies at the end of the war took away from the Germans any sources of oil they had had. Germany has five large chemical companies that are desperate for feedstocks. Our job is to find new sources of oil in the Middle East and make these available to these German chemical companies. They will have given us the funding to produce the oil. You and I, Thibaut, will visit the German companies. If the first says no, we will try another."

Adolf called the chairman of BASF in Kassel for an appointment. He appeared surprised at the call but sent a car to pick us up in Frankfort and bring us to Kassel, headquarters of the company. He listened politely to Adolf's proposition.

"How much money do you want me to invest?"

"$20,000,000."

"And how much of the company will I own?"

"50 percent."

When he heard that the capital invested in the company was only $250,000, I thought the conversation was over. But Adolf said, "You don't have to put up the money until we produce the oil concessions. And you will have first call on all the oil produced." Put that way, it was a fair proposition. BASF desperately needed oil at a fair price. It would not have to put up any money unless we negotiated oil concessions to meet its needs. "So long as I don't have to put up any money until you find the oil, I will listen," he said.

We settled on visits to Egypt and Qatar after consulting our geophysicists. Ahmed was sent to Qatar to initiate negotiations. After long and complicated negotiations with the oil minister, we were finally able to secure a number of interesting blocks in the Persian Gulf belonging to Qatar. BASF then agreed to advance the funds needed to drill the initial wells. These were successful. As a result, our little company made, after taxes at the end of our first year of operation, a million dollars. Adolf said, "Drilling for oil is like shooting fish in a barrel."

To prepare ourselves for new capital requirements, we purchased control of a shell company listed on the Toronto Stock Exchange—that is, a company with many stockholders but no longer any viable business—and changed its name to Gulfstream Oil, the name of our little company in Geneva, which we then merged into the Canadian company. We now controlled a company with several thousand stockholders and a listing on the Toronto Stock Exchange. As I remember, we had paid 60 cents a share for our control stock.

When it was announced that we had negotiated a concession agreement with the government of Qatar, the stock had promptly gone to $12.00. At that point, we received a visit in Geneva of two partners of Casenove, an important British private banking group in London, seeking to make an important investment in our small company. We said no, but we would be willing to have the British bank invest with us on a *pari passu* basis in Texas. They put up $25 million for that purpose, and we put up the $1 million we had just earned. Each of the forty wells we drilled produced oil or gas.

In four months the forty wells in west Texas stopped producing. It would take them years to solve the problem and by that time we had long since lost our interest in the wells. Gulfstream stock went back down to 60 cents. We had lost our million dollars, the British

473

bank its $25 million. The oil business seemed all of a sudden much more complicated.

The following year our Qatar concession turned out to be the biggest gas field in the world. Gulfstream stock hit $12 again. We breathed a sigh of relief. But our optimism was short-lived because the government of Qatar decided at this point to nationalize our concessions. There was really no reason for such action. In the concession agreements, Adolf, Ahmed and I had negotiated, the government was entitled to 85 percent of the value of the oil produced after payment of cost of drilling, while we were receiving only 15 percent. It was a very fair arrangement. But business ethics in the Middle East are never predictable. The stock of Gulfstream went back to 60 cents.

Not to be outdone, we brought suit against the government of Qatar at the International Tribunal at The Hague for $200 million. After three years, we won the suit. But it would take many years before the government of Qatar would agree to give us back our concession. In the meantime, of course, they couldn't market the oil or gas in our concession area because we would have seized it and sold it for our own account.

Through all this, Adolf Lundin never lost his composure. He is the ultimate entrepreneur. When things were bad, he and his wife sold the apartment in Geneva and moved to a small house in the country. He is in business, of course, to make money, but he has always been much more interested in his love of the game than in its monetary consequences.

Unfortunately for me, when I left Geneva in 1976, I sold my shares in Gulfstream. Had I kept them for another ten years, I would have participated in the rise that occurred when the Qatar government finally recognized its error and restored our concessions.

In life one runs across three types of people: those who take advantage of opportunities, those who watch them, and those who don't see where opportunities might exist. It is the old story of the glass half-full, half-empty. To Adolf, the glass is always half-full. It never bothered him that in international business, and particularly in the oil and mining area, one continuously has to deal with corrupt and greedy government officials interested only in lining their own pockets. He did not make the rules but tried to profit from them. The early years that he and his wife had spent in Colombia had taught him that in business you accepted the world as it was and didn't waste time trying to change it.

Adolf and Eva, his wife, have been as close a couple as I have ever met. While he travels the world in search of oil or mining opportunities, she raises show horses on their farm in France just outside of Geneva. I have been at a dinner party there on a spring evening when she has left the table in the middle of dinner to foal a mare, returning for dessert as if nothing had happened. They ski together in the fall, swim in Sardinia in the summer and Mesquite in the winter. He shares his thoughts and plans only with her. She is the more practical of the two, but they are truly one. Of the five children, four work with Adolf and the fifth, a girl, works the farm with her mother when she is not climbing mountains with her Swiss husband. It is truly a united family. They have certainly been great friends to me in good times and bad. *Professor in Switzerland*

My work with Adolf and the oil company, in addition to my teaching obligations, kept me busy enough, but I missed my children, all five of whom were now in the United States. Under certain conditions, being an expatriate can be very pleasant. If you enjoy your work, have a good home life, have time to travel and have good friends in the country to which you have been sent, there is much to recommend it. But sooner or later we all want to be back in our home country, eating bacon and eggs and talking baseball to friends at home. Americans are fiercely gregarious; probably because in the country's early days neighbors were apt not to be close by, we have a need to talk to others, exchange ideas, engage together in sports or other activities. Life is so much less formal with us. We will call a friend at the last moment and invite him to dinner or for the weekend. Other countries are much more formal. Friends are not apt just to drop by. Trips are planned months in advance, not on the spur of the moment.

In 1975, I had given up my big apartment and moved to a small flat in the Old Town belonging to some friends. It was small, beautifully furnished and cozy. I spoke at length to the director of the Management Center and told him after four years in Geneva, I thought I needed to go home. My ideas were growing stale. I needed to be back in the United States, to spend more time with my children, to develop new ideas, to strike out in a new direction, even though I had no idea just what I wanted to do. I knew him pretty well. He agreed that that is what I should do. Above all I needed to get my divorce so that I could see my children on a regular basis and not only when my wife was willing to let me see them.

"There are days when I wake up and feel I just can't face a group of students anymore. I don't feel I have any new thoughts to share with them, and I know perfectly well that if I am not on the top of my form, I will lose control over my class. Worse yet, some days I don't even care."

On a trip to New York shortly thereafter, I took an actress friend of mine, Joan Fontaine, out to dinner. I told her during dinner that I was coming home, because I felt worn out and totally bereft of new ideas. I just couldn't face teaching anymore.

"Have you ever been to a bullfight, Thibaut?"

"Of course."

"Then you know it is not a battle between the matador and the bull. It is a fight between the matador and the crowd. The bullfighter, if he is any good, will have made his reputation very young, 18 or 19. By the time he is 25, he has made a good deal of money. He has all the women he wants. He is rich. Now he doesn't really want to fight anymore. He becomes more careful in the bullring. The crowd senses this, feels that he is frightened, and turns against him. The women take their shoes off and throw them into the ring. They want the bull to go after him. Now if he doesn't outdo his past performance with the bull, he is finished as a bullfighter.

"You are in the same fix, Thibaut. If your chief executive type students feel you are not in control and can't mesmerize them with your ideas and your presentation of them, they will be bored and complain about you.

"Let me tell you a story. When I was a young actress waiting for a part, I used to wander about the set. One day I saw a young girl, maybe four or five. It was late in the afternoon and she was very tired. She had trouble acting out a scene. Her mother was on the set screaming at her, 'Sparkle, Shirley, sparkle.' And the little girl fought back the tears.

"I've never forgotten that. You have to keep telling yourself: 'Sparkle, Thibaut, sparkle,' as I do whenever I have a cold and show up for a performance in the theater which may be a group from a dentist's convention which laughs when they shouldn't and I wish I was home in bed."

She was, of course, quite right. I went back to Geneva and until I could arrange to go home remembered to "sparkle." It is not easy to do.

In early 1976, I went back to New York to try to straighten out my personal life and to undertake a new career in the United States. I had no idea what it would turn out to be.

The author with his two youngest children, Marc and Diane, in Switzerland in 1972. In 2003, Diane was a research executive at a pharmaceutical company and Marc was a manager of two large private investment funds.

XXIII

EXPORT-IMPORT BANK OF
THE UNITED STATES

A
government
official in
Washington

T *HERE IS AN INCLINATION* on the part of the public to think that once a person is elected president of the United States, he or she will select the most qualified persons to serve in the new administration. This is, of course, not so. The new president realizes, if he thinks about it, that he was nominated by his party only because he was satisfactory to a majority within the party and would have a chance to win the election. The political system in a democracy is based on compromise as well as accommodation. This was perfectly satisfactory to the country's Founding Fathers. They wanted above all to guard against the tyranny of the kings because that is what they had left in Europe. The Constitution was designed to give limited power to both the president and the federal Legislature and to retain power in the states and in the people. This recipe for accommodation is thought to have worked reasonably well for over two hundred years.

I have explained in Chapter XIV how, when I returned from the war in 1946, some friends of mine in New York and I, anxious to do something in local politics in New York City where we lived, had succeeded in replacing the Tammany Hall political leadership.

I had never had any interest in national politics. From time to time, an international or national problem at the law firm might require my going to Washington. I was always glad to get back to New York. As far as I was concerned, the federal bureaucracy in Washington was made up of people who said 'no' without reason and were full of their own self-importance.

When I was working at Chadbourne, Wallace as a young lawyer after the war, I had had one depressing experience with the federal government. The firm was counsel for the Sperry Corporation. It was an excellent client. The company post-war was one of the great American corporations which had played an important role in the victory of the

478

Allies. Sperry had had more technology patents than any other company and had turned them over to the United States government for the duration of the war for one dollar.

Sometime in 1948 the chief financial officer of Sperry had called me and asked me to go down to Washington to get a re-assignment of our patent rights from the government. Not knowing whom to call, I had phoned the attorney general's office and set up a meeting for the following week. When I arrived for the meeting I had been surprised to find, sitting around a large table in a conference room, representatives from the State Department, the attorney general's office, the Patent Office, and various other agencies. When I had finished my little speech requesting return of my client's patents, while not forgetting to include a note of congratulation for my client's generosity toward the government, the functionary for the State Department asked:

"Mr. de Saint Phalle, what makes you think the war is over?"

"The war ended in May, 1945 in Europe and in 1946 in Asia. Surely you are not going to say Sperry is not entitled to get its patents back."

"A war is ended by a treaty of peace. Point out to us when the United States signed a peace treaty ending the war with Japan."

I was dumbfounded. No matter how much I tried to point out the inequities involved, the argument fell on deaf ears. Now, I have never had much patience. I advised the gentlemen that if my client hadn't received the re-assignment of its patents by the end of the month, I would be filing an action in the U.S. District Court against the United States of America to compel it to make the transfer.

The next morning the CFO of Sperry called me. I told him what I proposed to do. "What kind of a lawyer are you, Thibaut, if you can't even get our patents back three years after the end of the war?"

Our legal action had been duly filed and the patents were recovered. But I was not about to forget how I had been treated. Without the law, there would surely never be any justice. How many times have I recalled this incident when I started making trips to Russia after the demise of the Soviet Union in 1991?

I had run into another instance of legal abuse by the federal government in my earlier business career. In 1952, Axel Wenner-Gren, the Swedish financier, had asked me to find out why the State Department would not allow him to enter the United States. Again, I had gone down to Washington. The problem was traceable to an occurrence in 1938 when the deputy secretary of state had been sent on a mission to Berlin at the request of the U.S. government. When he arrived at Tem-

Export-Import Bank of the United States

To Washington wars are never over.

479

plehof Airport, Foreign Minister Ribbentrop and a military guard had been standing by the plane. But their presence had not been for him. He had been asked to wait. The foreign minister and the honor guard were for Wenner-Gren who was on the same plane. When the deputy secretary returned to Washington, a note was put in the files identifying Wenner-Gren as a German agent. Although it was well known that the Germans in their preparation for war were buying steel and armaments from Sweden, there was nothing in the files to back the substance of the claim that Wenner-Gren was a German agent. Yet whenever afterwards a request for a visa for Wenner-Gren had been made, it was always refused. I was never able to get Wenner-Gren his visa, even though during the war he rendered important services to the United States. Much later I had a similar experience when the French Foreign Office repeatedly refused to allow the French president to award me the Legion of Honor on the supposed pretext that I had been working for the Central Intelligence Agency in France. All this because in 1973 there had appeared in a French scandal newssheet a squib claiming that my role as a professor at the prestigious Management Center of the University of Geneva was only a cover, and that I was really a colonel in the Central Intelligence Agency, head of its operations in Europe. It would take the intervention of three French senior military officers to force the French Foreign Office to clear my name and allow the decoration to be awarded to me by President Chirac of France.

When I came back to the United States from my five years as a professor in Geneva, I had to consider whether I wished to return to law as a partner of Coudert Brothers in New York, go back into the business world, or continue to teach, but in an American university. Columbia University Law School had proposed a joint professorship with the School of Business. I held discussions at Harvard, MIT and Stanford regarding a professorship in international business. A former student in Geneva, head of a Fortune 500 company, asked me if I would become president of his company located near Hartford, Connecticut. I knew that I didn't want to teach law students. I also knew that I didn't wish to run a company. But I didn't know what I wanted to do. My personal life was at a crossroads. Three years earlier my wife had taken our two small children from our home in Geneva and returned to New York. She now told me I would not be allowed to see them unless I returned to her "on her terms." I knew this would be impossible for both of us.

I was now anxious to do something new, and different, in a new location.

Most men when they are going through a difficult emotional period of their lives will find understanding and encouragement from a woman they love and respect. But I was adrift here as well, and vulnerable to passing fancies which led nowhere.

After my past experiences with the federal government, the last thing I thought of was the possibility of moving to Washington and working for the U.S. government.

You can understand my surprise when a friend suggested that with my background and international experience I should consider a senior position with the United States government in the new administration. A drowning man will clutch at any straws. A few years earlier I would have dismissed this idea as utterly senseless. Now the thought of going to Washington did not seem so out of place. I was still counsel to my old law firm at Coudert Brothers and had an office and a secretary there. My former partners were anxious to help me re-establish myself as a lawyer there, but I knew this was not for me. Once you leave a profession, it is difficult to go back to it.

Jimmy Carter had been elected president in November 1976. To many people at the time this young governor of Georgia, a former submarine officer in the United States Navy, graduate of Annapolis, presented a fresh face in politics untouched by the Vietnam conflict or the scandal which had removed Nixon from the presidency. No one knew much about him, but friends of mine in New York who had supported him in the campaign persuaded me that he would need in his administration people like me who had had considerable experience in international affairs. I was invited down to Washington to meet the under-secretary of treasury for international affairs, who suggested that I apply for consideration as chairman of the Export-Import Bank of the United States. He was prepared to recommend me for that position. He also told me that unless there were political reasons for my not being given the appointment, he thought the decision was his to make. At the same time I was interviewed at the White House by the official in the new administration in charge of executive appointments, who suggested that I consider an appointment as ambassador to the OECD in Paris, a position which carried with it a lovely house in Paris and an official car and chauffeur. When I had been teaching at the Management Center in Geneva, I used to meet quite frequently in Paris with the economics section of the OECD. I knew the staff well. I also knew and admired the Dutch president of OECD. So I asked that I be considered for this position as well. I was told that for either position, in addition

481

to support from the senators I knew, I would have to be confirmed by the United States Senate. President Carter had decided that all senior appointments would have to be approved by a panel he had appointed headed by a woman from Princeton, New Jersey named Anne Martindale. This was no problem for me. Since returning from Europe, I had rented a small one bedroom gatehouse in Princeton and had made New Jersey my residence, even though I shared an apartment in New York with my second son. I did not know Anne Martindale but I called her and went to see her. She had evidently played an important role in President Carter's campaign in New Jersey. A former businesswoman endowed with both wealth and political acumen, I found her extremely knowledgeable about world affairs. She asked searching questions not only about my professional life and qualifications but about my personal life as well. I found out later that she had spoken personally to each of the persons I had mentioned to her as able to give information about my background and qualifications. Later, we became very good friends. She was to become ambassador to New Zealand in the Carter administration.

I learned that in the political world nothing takes place quickly. Two steps forward, one back. Two good friends, Senator Frank Church, the chairman of the Foreign Affairs Committee in the Senate, and Senator Clairborne Pell, a friend since childhood and also on the same Committee, sent impressive letters of recommendation to the president at the White House. Since I had played no role whatsoever in the Carter campaign, didn't know the president personally, and knew none of his campaign aids or key supporters from the state of Georgia, I felt at a considerable disadvantage. In due course, I learned that for the post of ambassador to the OECD where there had been originally five finalists, my dossier and that of Charles Saltzman had been sent to the president's desk for a final selection. Saltzman had Senators Javits of New York and Ribicoff of Connecticut in his corner. As it turned out, President Carter needed the support of the two key Jewish senators for a proposed new effort to achieve peace in the Mid-East, so Saltzman got the job. Still, I felt encouraged to have at least made it as far as the president's desk. My two senatorial supporters told me not to worry. I would get the bank position.

A few weeks later I received a phone call one morning from a man who identified himself as John Moore from Atlanta, Georgia. I did not know him.

"I have just been designated to be chairman of the Export-Import

Bank of the United States. I have before me your background file. I would very much like you to come down to Washington and spend a couple of days with me. Your resume is most impressive, and I hope to persuade you to be my vice chair."

I went down to meet with Moore. He had been a law partner in Atlanta of Griffin Bell, a leading lawyer in the city and the man chosen to be Carter's attorney general. In Bell's absence from Atlanta on a mission for the new president, John Moore had represented a close friend of the president's, a local banker who was under investigation for banking law violations. John Moore had handled the matter successfully. The president had been persuaded by his banker friend to make room for Moore in a key position in his administration, and so Treasury's recommendation had been ignored and John Moore named to the post that had been promised me—not a surprising development in the political world.

I met John Moore and liked him. I told him I did not want to be his number two because that involved being in charge of operations at the bank, but that I would be happy to serve as one of the five directors of the bank if he would allow me a role in strategic planning for the bank. This was agreeable to him. He would play the key political role. He would rely on my judgment and expertise to guide operations and strategy. In the four years we worked together, with one exception, I found working with John Moore an extremely pleasant relationship. While it was his responsibility to make the ultimate decision, he always listened.

The Export-Import Bank of the United States is in many ways a curious political institution. Like many such agencies of government it was started in 1934 by President Franklin Roosevelt. Its original purpose was to help finance the sale of American manufactured products to two friendly countries who could not afford to buy except on credit: Cuba and the Soviet Union. Curiously, by the time Jimmy Carter became president, Cuba and the Soviet Union were almost the only countries to whom the bank could no longer extend credit terms.

The bank was a so-called independent agency of the United States government. Its stock was wholly owned by the government. Each year the Congress funded its operations. The bank was not expected to make any money but its loans were expected to be repaid. It made loans to fund U.S. exports to foreign countries and was also authorized to guarantee loans made by U.S. commercial banks on export transactions. The bank was managed by a board of five persons, three from the majority party and two from the minority, each of whom was appointed by the president and then confirmed by the Senate. Although the original Ex-

Im Bank was an American initiative, other developed nations now had similar institutions to finance national exports.

In the spring of 1977, President Carter appointed me to the board of the bank and sent my nomination to the Senate. The same day that the *New York Times* reported my appointment, my wife called me early on that morning to congratulate me. The next morning, as I was on my way to an early tennis game at the River Club, I was served on the street with six lawsuits by my wife claiming that I had, five years earlier,

moved her and the children to Switzerland solely for the purpose of evading national, state and city taxes, and claiming damages in the millions of dollars. I could only assume that her purpose was that these allegations would convince the Banking Committee of the Senate to turn down my appointment. Since the chairman of that committee, Senator Proxmire, was known for his insistence on high ethical standards and the charges against me might be difficult to disprove, I was extremely concerned about how to handle the matter with the Senate committee. Fortunately, for the year in which we had moved to Switzerland, I had received a large refund from the Internal Revenue Service. The director of the Senate Banking Committee, with whom I discussed the matter, did not seem bothered about it.

"You have already explained to me about your marital difficulties," he said. "The subject is closed."

In due course I was confirmed without any problem.

Through a friend, I found a small house to rent in Georgetown. I was delighted to leave New York and my little place in Princeton, New Jersey. I was ready to settle into a new job and a new and different life. Washington is a place filled with transients. People are delighted to see you when you come and not dismayed when you leave. The "cliff dwellers" of Roosevelt's day are still there. They play golf at Burning Tree and Chevy Chase. They are the lawyers, the local bankers, the real-estate investors who have become wealthy from the growth of the city and especially its suburbs, since the end of World War II. When I had been in Washington at the end of the war, awaiting my discharge from the United States Navy, it was a sleepy city of some 250,000 people with little to recommend it outside of politics. Now it was an ever-expanding metropolis of over 3,000,000, a center for new technologies, and a cultural center as well, with opera, theater, and a first-class symphony orchestra. I was thirsty for change, new challenges, new friends, a different life.

The bank is located on Vermont Avenue across the park from the

White House. Jesse Jones, its first chairman, chose the location supposedly because from there he could keep an eye on anyone entering or
leaving the White House. A Texas banker, Jones distrusted the liberals
around President Roosevelt.

We were a diversified board of Ex-Im and I believe never once
arrived at a decision along political lines. In addition to John Moore
and me, we had an atomic engineer—useful because of the number of
atomic energy plants financed by the bank—a businesswoman from
Ohio and a commercial banker from Texas whose father-in-law had
given a great deal of money to the president's campaign. We soon became friends as well as colleagues.

I quickly developed a close friendship with Margaret Kahliff, one
of the two Republican directors of the bank. "Maggie," as she was
known to all, was the youngest of three children of a farm family from
Arkansas. The parents, who had little money, had been determined that
the three children would get a good education. The older brother had
become a remarkably successful business executive and made a great
deal of money. The second was Senator Dale Bumpers of Arkansas who
might well have become president of the United States.

Maggie had been a remarkably successful businesswoman in Ohio
while raising three children alone. By herself she had succeeded in creating a very good business distributing soft drinks in school vending
machines. Then she had sold the business, married again, and when
she became a widow, created a new successful business from what her
husband had left her.

The bank generally held board meetings twice a week on Tuesdays
and Thursdays. The staff was expected to attend. Other agencies of the
government, State Department, Treasury, Commerce, sent representatives if any loans to be approved were of particular interest to their
agency. Each proposed item of business was presented by the loan officer who had worked on the loan. The board members would then ask
questions. There would then be open discussion among the members
of the board followed by a vote. It was an excellent system because it
allowed any member of the staff and of interested sister agencies to express their views. It was responsible for the high morale within the bank.
I have often thought how helpful it would be to the judicial process if
decisions made by the Supreme Court would be arrived at after open
discussion by the justices before the Court rather than in chambers.
Wouldn't similar openness in the deliberations of the governors of the
Federal Reserve serve to teach the public how to judge better what was

*Export-Import
Bank of the
United States*

The Ex-Im
Bank is a
remarkable
institution.

485

happening in the economy? In Switzerland, the justices of the Appellate Court always deliberate in open court before voting on a particular case. Openness in a democracy ensures public participation.

One day John Moore had decided that the board of the bank should host a reception for foreign ambassadors whose countries were, after all, our clients. The five of us were there to shake hands with each of the foreign dignitaries. At one point I turned to Maggie and said, "Look at the face of the man next in line: the eyes are dead." She agreed. I had then asked the lawyers for the bank to keep a watchful eye on our guest. The next morning I had a visit from the FBI who brought five volumes of photographs of Russians so that I could identify who this was. I managed to pick out the person in question who was a KGB colonel just arrived from Moscow. He was sent back promptly to the Soviet Union.

I had learned during my activities with the OSS that people with "dead" eyes are those who have been guilty of assassinations or acts of torture. The eyes reflect the body's refusal to accept the validity of such acts.

John Moore, Maggie and I were determined to push American exports to the extent we could. One year, with just over three hundred employees, the bank did more financing than the World Bank with some 6,000 employees.

One time, Maggie had gone out to make a speech at Spokane about the bank's activities. There she had run across a man who had just exported several million dollars of agricultural machinery to Libya. When she came back and told me this, we resolved to go out together to meet this man. It was a great story:

The exporter had been an agricultural engineer in Arizona. One day he had had the good sense to understand that in a land where there was little water but many dams, water would move laterally across contour lines from the dammed waters above the dam.

He then moved to eastern Washington State and bought for very little all the acreage he could buy from the state or the county. He drilled wells throughout the area where, according to his calculations, there had to be water coming from the Grand Coulee Dam across the Columbia River to the west. Result: thousands of acres of new farmland in the desert and a fortune for himself. He was soon making $5,000 per acre in desert that produced nothing two years earlier.

It was then that he had been approached by Khadafi's agents to reproduce this miracle in Libya. He had gone to Libya and ascertained that it would be possible, in the south of the country, to do the same thing as he had done in eastern Washington with irrigation.

He came to Washington, D.C. and brought his contour maps of North Africa and the Middle East. We spent several days together reviewing his contour maps. Then he and I went to Egypt to meet with the new minister of agriculture. *Export–Import Bank of the United States*

When directors of the Export-Import Bank travel abroad, they are always well received both by officials of the country visited and by our own embassy officials, because the visit may represent financing of imports from the United States which the country needs. While at the bank, I had always tried to avoid going to Egypt. The American ambassador there—in a country where the United States was giving a billion dollars a year simply because it gave the same amount to Israel—was filled with his own self-importance and doing little to help the country. Now accompanied by my new friend, I realized I could help, because water in Egypt is far more important than oil. The agriculture minister was enthusiastic. "I am too new in my job to have created a bureaucracy yet, so I can make decisions."

Through friends, I obtained the subsoil studies which the American oil companies had made in the western desert of Egypt. According to my water expert, there was all the water in the world in Lake Chad not very far away. The oil company studies showed that that water went into the Mediterranean in Egypt. Therefore, drilling for water would be advantageous and the Egyptian desert could be made agriculturally productive. The Egyptian government, however, chose not to follow the ideas of their minister.

"It is better for us to import subsidized food from you under your P.L. 480 and sell you expensive oil than developing our own agricultural production," they told me.

At the bank, I found myself spending a good deal of time meeting with Congressional committees and individual members of Congress. This was the fascination of the job. I discovered that there were about 20 percent on the left that did not care to listen and about the same number on the right whose minds were similarly closed to any new ideas. But to the 60 percent in the middle, international politics and trade were matters of interest and concern. To these legislators it did not seem to matter whether one was a Democrat or a Republican. They talked to each other and shared many of the same ideas on public policy. It was only because the White House failed to explain its policies to the Congress, or sought to draw a political advantage from deliberate obfuscation, that so little was accomplished in terms of legislation, no matter who occupied the White House. I had been appointed as a Democrat. But

Export–Import Bank of the United States

I spent as much time talking to Republican members of Congress who might be willing to see me. My problem was never with the Congress but from within the administration. The advice always seemed to be: don't tell them anything. With those members of Congress with whom I had developed a close relationship, I would sometimes say in answer to a question, "Do you want the official line, or the facts?"

In the late '70s, a particular problem for the country was the sharp increase in the price of oil as a result of the policies of OPEC. The chairman of the Commerce Committee, which dealt with international trade issues, including energy, was Adlai Stevenson of Illinois, son of the famous presidential candidate with the same name who ran against Eisenhower in 1956 and later became Kennedy's ambassador to the United Nations. Adlai and I became close friends. I had great admiration for him. He suffered from the overhang of his father's talent and will, but in many ways he was a more thoughtful political figure. He had a particular dislike for James Schlesinger who was Carter's secretary of energy and had previously been both director of the Office of Management and Budget and secretary of defense. Now with the price of energy constantly rising, the administration's only policy appeared to be to urge the public to turn down thermostats in the winter and raise them in the summer. In the White House, for his February chats to the public, the president had even taken to wearing a sweater in the Oval Office. Schlesinger would not even answer Stevenson's phone calls to appear before his committee. I went to John Moore and suggested that we fund at Ex-Im the Canadian portion of a new pipeline to bring Canadian oil to the Midwest if the Canadian Export-Import Bank would finance a portion of the U.S. pipeline. Each country would benefit from an increase in exports. After obtaining the necessary approvals, I went to Canada to discuss the matter with its minister of energy who approved the project. Months later, nothing had happened on the American side. The Canadian minister called me to complain. "I have 34 employees and it sometimes takes me forever to move them, but nothing comes out of Washington." When I told him Schlesinger had over 30,000 in the Department of Energy, he was speechless. "No wonder you never get anything done."

Energy problems took up a great deal of my time. Atomic energy plants in Taiwan, South Korea and Romania, pipelines in Egypt, transmission lines in the Congo, these were huge projects involving many millions of dollars. They meant very large amounts in dollar value of American exports, to help balance the rising cost of imported oil. Our biggest problem at the bank was the Treasury Department and its policy favoring a weak dollar. The assistant secretary for international monetary affairs, Fred Bergsten, a remarkably intelligent man otherwise, was constantly talking down the value of the dollar on the theory that it would help exports. He did not seem able to grasp that in an increasingly global capitalist economy, the movement of capital was far more important than a temporary trade imbalance. It would take the new Reagan administration to reverse the mistaken monetary policies of the Carter administration built around a weak dollar. *Export-Impor Bank of the United States*

At the urging of friends in the Congress, and in order to help the Congress understand better the relationship between the value of the currency, trade and inflationary pressures, I set out to write a book on the subject. Oxford University Press agreed to publish it. I had previously written and published two books with Dr. Nasrollah Fatemi of Fairleigh Dickinson University, but with my government experience I now wanted to reach quite a different audience, not academic but made up of the people in government who had to understand the relationship between the value of the currency, inflationary tendencies, and the effect on international trade which was now becoming so important to the U.S. economy. It was a project which gave me enormous satisfaction because I realized that if I didn't understand thoroughly these relationships, I would never be able to explain them to those in government who had to know in order to legislate properly. Teaching, as always, is the only way to learn. In the course of trying to explain to others, I developed my own understanding of international economics. When Reagan came into office in 1980, and adopted many of the policies I had recommended in this book, I was then in 1982 able to bring out a new edition showing how the new monetary policies had proved what I had been trying to explain in the earlier edition. While the book, *Trade, Inflation and the Dollar*, did not have the wide circulation the publisher and I had hoped for, I like to think that it proved useful to two administrations and a good many members of Congress, as well as the academic establishment. I often think that the work might never have been started had we not had that terrible snowstorm in the winter of 1978, which cut off Georgetown from any road traffic for ten days and permitted me to sketch out the project in detail. A new book— on trade

I greatly enjoyed writing these books on international economics. It had always seemed to me that economists wrote to explain themselves

489

to other economists. At the bank, I was dealing with pragmatic members of Congress who had little patience with theories but a very real need for practical solutions to economic problems.

In the summer of 1978, an event occurred which completely changed my life. I had just spent the weekend in Bar Harbor, Maine visiting the Finletters, who were both close friends. He had been a senior partner of Coudert Brothers in New York and ambassador to Great Britain for the Marshall Plan. I had played tennis all weekend with the pro. I was now looking forward to taking my two younger children for two weeks to a ranch out west at the end of the following week. I had mentioned to my secretary on Monday in Washington that I seemed to see a small mark when I looked out of my right eye. I told her I didn't have time to see an ophthalmologist because I had too much to do before leaving.

She made an appointment for me anyway. The doctor gave me all sorts of tests, then told me to sit down.

"I don't want you even to go back to your office. You are within three millimeters of total blindness in that right eye. The retina is torn in all directions. If you are not operated on tomorrow morning, you will probably lose your sight in that eye."

"Who should operate?"

"There are only three eye surgeons I consider capable to do this operation. One is in Miami at the Bascom Palmer Eye Institute, one in Boston at Mass General, and one at Johns Hopkins in Baltimore."

He called Baltimore. The surgeon there had just returned from vacation and said he would operate on me the following morning if I were brought in that night. I was taking a friend out to dinner who was driving in from Middleburg, Virginia. I called her to tell her she would have to drive me to Baltimore instead.

The next morning the surgeon came in to see me at six o'clock. "I'd better check the other eye just to be sure," he said to me.

"My God, the other eye is worse. I'll do one tomorrow very early and the other next week. It is a six-hour operation. You'll be under heavy sedation until tomorrow."

I could only reflect that my secretary had saved my eyesight. If she had not made the appointment for me, I would have gone out west with the children. A few minutes on a horse and I would have become blind forever.

There I was for three weeks with bandages over both eyes. The surgeon thought the operations a success. Friends came to see me. My

490

next-door neighbor, a Jesuit priest who taught ethics at the George-town Hospital, said he was praying for me. A lovely divorcée by the name of Mariana Smith, whom I had met in New York a short while earlier at my friend Bill Witter's and then spent a weekend with at Bill's house in the country, came down to see me from New York. I had a nurse with a beautiful voice whom I couldn't see but who read to me. I was too drugged to even think of the future. After three weeks my nurse told me one morning that the doctor would probably send me a message that he now needed my bed for another patient. "He is a great surgeon, Thibaut, but he has no small talk or bedside manner. He has repaired your eye and now he has no further interest in you."

"What will happen to me? I cannot see."

"You don't have anyone at home? Call up whoever brought you here and tell that person to come and get you. I'd like to take you home with me, but I can't because I have to work."

It was frightening to have become so utterly helpless. I had many friends but nobody who could come to care for me at a moment's notice.

I called the friend who had brought me to the hospital. "There is a custom in China that if you see a dying man by the side of the road and take him to a hospital, you are then responsible for that person for the rest of his life."

She came to get me and took me back to her house in Middleburg. I couldn't see, was too weak to leave the bed, and wished I was at least back in my own home in Georgetown. So I called another pal from Washington and had her come pick me up and take me home. She was a capable business executive, but in trying to make me some dinner she filled the kitchen with smoke. I sent her home and crawled upstairs to my bed on hands and knees. I didn't think I'd ever get down again.

At that point I suddenly thought of that lovely Mariana who had come to see me at the hospital in Baltimore. I called her.

"How would you like to come and take care of a blind man?" I said to her.

"Would it be alright if I took the eight o'clock shuttle tomorrow morning?"

On the plane to Washington, Mariana had sat next to a nun who told her she was being sent to Baltimore as a specialist to work with people who had recently become blind. It seemed to Mariana more than a coincidence.

Export-Import Bank of the United States

Emerson's law of compensation works.

So Mariana came into my life and never went back to New York. That first afternoon she was with me my neighbor the Jesuit came to call on me. Mariana helped me down the stairs.

Export–Import Bank of the United States

"Dick, you remember calling me at the hospital and saying you were praying for me. Well, here is the answer to your prayers." Dick couldn't say very much about our housing arrangements after that. But it didn't make any difference. I soon came to the conclusion that I wanted her with me as long as she would stay.

Time in those waning days of summer passed quickly. I could not go to the bank except for an hour or so once or twice a week to meet with the other directors. Each day my secretary came over to review pending loan applications and take dictation. Father Dick with the remarkable prescience of Jesuits told me that John Paul I would be pope. Following John Paul's death, Dick predicted that we would have a Polish cardinal who would be elected pope to succeed him. My first grandson, Robert, was born in Philadelphia that summer. The weather was beautiful, Mariana kept the garden flowering. It was a time to sleep, rest a great deal, eat well, feel very grateful that my sight had been saved.

In early September, Mariana decided that we should go up to her fishing camp on Rangeley Lake in Maine while it was still warm enough to enjoy it

Already winter in Maine

By the time we arrived, it was mid-September and the nights were very cool. I was still able to do very little, going from my bed in one log cabin to the kitchen in another, to the lake shore to bathe in the cold water and then back to bed again. Mariana read to me in bed while sitting in a rocking chair by the big wood-burning stove in the kitchen. We talked endlessly, slowly getting to know each other. I was determined to do more each day to get my strength back. The goal was to climb the mountain across the lake on foot. If I could do it, I would have recovered enough strength to go home. Finally, after a month, I succeeded. Every morning we would get the weather report from atop Mt. Washington where it was already 30 degrees below zero. We realized it was time to return to Washington. I didn't like Rangeley in the fall, but being there had made me much stronger.

There was no phone or electricity on the island. There was only us, Mariana and me, with Mariana's launch to take us to the mainland once or twice a week to bring back mail and supplies.

I learned that the island, along with a bigger one further down the lake, had been bought by Mariana's great-grandfather while he was still at Yale in 1884. He had subsequently built camps on both islands. He

492

had became counsel for U.S. Steel, and spent his summers on the lake, writing books on the law and gardening. The island where we were had briefly gone out of the family. Mariana had repurchased it, and restored the cabins of the camp, after ridding the buildings of bats with a shotgun. She had then gone up each summer with her four children to teach them the outdoors and the simple life of the Maine woods. When the last child went away to school, she had at last left her husband and obtained her divorce. Peter was a nice man and an only child whom she had married at 18. *Export-Impor Bank of the United States*

It was in Maine that Mariana told me that after her divorce, in the difficult period of readjustment which followed many years of marriage, she had consulted, at a moment of discouragement, a psychic, who had told her she would move to Washington to take care of a blind man.

She never for a moment believed it would come about.

Life plays all sorts of games with us. We do what we were meant to do, despite our determination to the contrary.

During that Maine sojourn, I realized that I had fallen in love with a very strong woman. She was beautiful to look at and radiated an inner peace. I wanted to spend the rest of my life with her, but I couldn't marry Mariana. I was still married. Despite my trying to get a divorce for over five years in both Switzerland and New York, I was no further along than when I had first asked for one in 1972. We would have to be patient.

One morning in Rangeley we woke up to a light snowfall. "This is it, Mariana. We'd better get out of here quickly and go back to Washington before we are snowed in."

As a Catholic I had always been taught that the Lord never takes his eye off any one of us and that nothing can ever happen to us unless he wills it. I had had occasion to realize this many times during the war. Now I tried to understand what message he was trying to send me. He had taken my sight away but he had sent me a guardian angel. It was clear that I should alter my life. It is not wise to ignore such a message.

After a few weeks back in Washington, my eyesight, which had appeared to be improving, started to fade again. I called the surgeon who had operated on me and went back to Baltimore for an early morning appointment. In order not to risk being late, Mariana and I drove up the night before. We both were frightened and depressed. On the way up we didn't speak much. We bought a bottle of Absolut Vodka, ordered a sandwich sent to our motel room, got into bed and, to kill the fear that was in us for what Dr. Pierce might tell me the next day, quietly drank most of the bottle.

Dr. Pierce was a great surgeon but, as I said before, he had no bedside manner whatever.

"One of three things is going to happen, Mr. de Saint Phalle. Your eyes may stabilize at the level they are now. They may get worse and you will lose your sight in time, or they may get better. I cannot tell you what will happen because I do not know. The operation was a success but I cannot vouch for the future. Your age is against you. On the other hand, your physical condition is good. But there is no point in asking me what will happen."

"My friend Bill Witter has asked me to go scuba diving with him over Thanksgiving to do the Wall off Grand Turk Island. Should I go?"

"Mr. de Saint Phalle, you cannot see very well above the surface. I cannot see that it will hurt you to go below."

Whether it was the effect of the salt water on my eyes or pressure from the diving, or simply divine intervention, I do not know. But when I returned from the trip my eyesight gradually improved. I reported this to Dr. Pierce. He dismissed any possible effect of the trip saying, "There is no scientific rationale to believe that your trip could have had any effect on your eyesight."

Scientists live in a world that demands proof. Dr. Pierce is entitled to his opinion. But I have mine.

On a Sunday in 1979, the economic system in the West faced a new challenge. At the Annual Meeting of the International Monetary Fund and the World Bank taking place in Belgrade, Yugoslavia, the Saudis had indicated that the OPEC countries might have to consider getting paid for oil in a basket of currencies rather than in dollars as heretofore, because of a decline in the value of the dollar. Paul Volcker who had attended the meeting flew back to Washington for a night session with the president. By the time the meeting ended, he was named chairman of the Federal Reserve with the mandate to raise interest rates if need be but halt the dollar's decline. I was delighted to see the end of the Bergsten low dollar philosophy at Treasury. Chairman Volcker's tight money policy at the Federal Reserve would bring about a severe contraction in the U.S. economy and help assure the election of Ronald Reagan in the November 1980 elections. But he was certainly correct in taking the action he did. The current chairman of the Federal Reserve, Alan Greenspan, is following a very different policy, keeping interest rates lower than they ever have been in history.

At Ex-Im we redoubled our efforts to move American exports through our financing activities. We were finally allowed to do business with China. Then in early 1980 occurred the incident that almost cost the directors of the bank their jobs. We had arrived at the bank early one board day to find that John Moore had been directed by the White House to approve a loan for a regional airline in Australia controlled by Rupert Murdoch, the Australian press baron who had recently purchased control of the *New York Post*. We were told Mr. Murdoch had lunched with the president the previous day and the White House wanted the loan approved that day. Contrary to normal procedure, the loan officer's recommendation and supporting analysis had not been furnished the board in advance. The two Republican directors notified me in advance of the board meeting that without an Australian government guarantee they would certainly vote against the loan since the airline finances could not support it. At the board meeting the designated loan officer, David Peacock, always well prepared, found it difficult to support the position he took on the credit worthiness of the borrower. Three of the directors, including me, stated at the board meeting that unless the proposal was withdrawn, we would have to vote against it. The board meeting was then put on hold while the five of us withdrew to Moore's office to discuss the matter away from prying ears. It took many hours of discussion, some of it quite heated, before a proposal made by me was finally agreeable to all five directors. It would take away much of the prior risk in the loan. I had always taken great pride in the independence of the board. The loan as originally proposed could not be supported as anything but a payment for press support to a president running for office.

Export-Import Bank of the United States

The next day a front-page article in the *Washington Post* reported that the board of the Export-Import Bank had been pressured into making an indefensible loan on unusually favorable terms to an Australian airline controlled by Rupert Murdoch the newspaper publisher who had just purchased the *New York Post*. The story even reported that the publisher had, two days earlier, lunched with the president at the White House. The implication was clear: support by the newspaper for the president's re-election bid would depend upon the loan to the publisher's airline. The following week hearings were scheduled before the Senate Banking Committee. All five directors of the bank were called to testify, along with the loan officer who had recommended the transaction. The minutes of the board meeting were also subpoenaed. Naturally, each of us received phone calls from the press.

The Senate asks questions.

At the hearing, John Moore, to whom most of the senators questions were addressed, took the position that "yes, he had favored making the loan on the original terms recommended by the loan officer, but the rest of the board felt differently and, after discussion, the terms had been revised to meet the suggestions of Thibaut de Saint Phalle." As described by John Moore, the whole transaction became my proposal. It was a lesson in practical politics. Since Chairman Proxmire had always regarded me as reasonably apolitical, the furor died down and we returned to the bank with nothing else but a warning. In those days, relationships between the White House and the Congress were reasonably amicable.

We had a good board and enjoyed working together. Each of us also had an opportunity to do a good deal of travel on behalf of the bank. One day I was asked by the chairman of the board of the Bank of Israel to come to the bank's 25th anniversary and read a paper on the role of a central bank in a developing country. It was a great honor as he had invited the head of the Bank of International Settlements, the banker's bank, and banking officials from several other countries to address the meeting. Afterwards there was a formal luncheon attended by Menachem Begin, the prime minister of Israel, who had been head of the Irgun, the revolutionary group in pre-Israel Palestine after World War II. At the lunch I was asked unexpectedly to say a few words. Probably because I hadn't reflected on what I would say, I told how I had been in Jerusalem briefly at the end of World War II when my hotel had been partially blown up by a group which included the man who was now prime minister of Israel. When I sat down, I was immediately invited over to have dessert, sitting at the side of the prime minister.

"We don't do that any more," he said. I was rather ashamed of my remark.

I was invited to spend two weeks in Israel after the meeting. The first week I stayed in a kibbutz on the Lebanese border, guest of the former head of the Israeli Air Force in the war of 1967. Then I spent a week in Nablus in the Palestine area. On Thanksgiving Day, Dr. Herbert Stein, head of Nixon's Council of Economic Advisors, his wife and I were taken to a new Jewish settlement at Elon Moray near Nablus for a picnic Thanksgiving lunch. While at lunch, gunfire broke out.

Mrs. Stein said to me, "Thibaut, is it ours or theirs?"

"Mrs. Stein, it really makes no difference. If I were you, I would get under the vehicle that brought us here and hope that no one hits the gas tank."

I greatly enjoyed my week at the kibbutz. In these early Jewish settlements, everything was owned in common. There was no such thing as private property. The early settlers were real pioneers, very proud of again being residents of an ancient land.

In Jordan at the time, the American ambassador was a relatively interesting man whose wife spent all her time going across the bridge over the Jordan to shop in Jerusalem. I hoped to meet with the Palestinian community while I was there. So I called a friend in Jordan who was the Spanish ambassador there. He met me at the airport when I arrived and took me to a wonderful restaurant in the country where we had an excellent meal. When it was over, he asked for the check. *Export-Import Bank of the United States*

"Mr. Ambassador," said the proprietor, "There is no check for you. You Spaniards think of yourselves as Europeans. But to us Arabs you are Arabs. For 700 years we gave you civilization in Spain."

Through my friend I was able to spend two evenings dining in the homes of Palestinians. They were not at all downhearted about the Palestinians in the West Bank of the Jordan. "We are as intelligent as the Israelis. We are the bankers, the engineers and the businessmen all through the Middle East. Sooner or later our desires will have to be recognized to have a Palestinian country of our own. We are patient because we know it will happen."

It was a learning experience.

In 1979, I bought a house on the edge of Georgetown. We were lucky. It had a two-car garage and a nice garden. Mariana and I gave several dinner parties a month there. We had many friends in Washington. There were seldom fewer than 20 people at our dinners: directors of the Fed, members of Congress, social friends, journalists, commentators. We didn't take ourselves very seriously and our guests knew that when they came to visit us they could just be themselves. It was great fun. Buying a house in Georgetown

For me it was also therapeutic. For years I had been trying to get my divorce. My two youngest children were denied me. I wanted to marry Mariana. But I was getting nowhere.

After the election of Ronald Reagan in 1980, since the directors of the bank served at the pleasure of the president, all five of us handed in our resignations. The new chairman appointed by the president was Bill Draper, a venture capitalist from San Francisco and son of the four-star general who had served as ambassador to France for the Marshall Plan. He asked me to stay on as a director. I was very tempted to do so. Working at the bank had been a stimulating and rewarding experience.

The author and his wife Mariana on their wedding day (above) and at Mariana's 100 year old camp on Rangeley Lake in Maine (right), where the author was writing a book on the Federal Reserve. Mariana brought four children to the marriage, seen below in 2000 with spouses and grandchildren.

XXIV

WASHINGTON SEQUEL

I *NTERREGNUMS AFTER THE* election of a new president, particularly if he is of the other party, are always a fascinating period. Washington becomes crowded with new faces seeking positions in the new administration, while those who have held positions of power evaluate their options, prepare to leave town, or begin hibernation to the Washington think tanks.

One of the most interesting things that occurs is that the president-to-be appoints a person in whom he has great confidence to become the head of his transition team. They in turn name a highly-qualified person to represent the transition team in a detailed analysis of each department of government, with recommendations on the person or persons to be recommended to the president for appointment to be in charge of that department or agency under the new administration. I was delighted to get a call one day shortly after the election of Ronald Reagan in 1980 from my old wartime friend, Ike Livermore, to tell me that he would head the transition team in the Department of Energy. Ike stayed with us for several weeks at our house in Georgetown. He was gone all day and worked most evenings. I would have liked to have been able to spend more time with him. I understood the extent of his job because we had at the bank a similar group of designated experts who were constantly asking questions of the directors and staff about the operations of the bank and the condition of its loan portfolio. This practice of investigation and analysis by a transition team is a very good one. It gives new officials coming in an excellent grounding in what they will face after they are appointed and confirmed.

The so-called think tanks in Washington are a particularly interesting American phenomenon. The Brookings Institution was almost alone a few years ago as a group largely of liberal economists who studied and reported on the American economy and political strategies which were affecting it. Today in Washington, as well as elsewhere in the country,

Life during a change of presidents

there have sprung up numerous competitors, such as the American Enterprise Institute, Cato Institute, Heritage Foundation, Hudson Foundation, Atlantic Council, and the Georgetown Center for Strategic and International Studies. With the increase in wealth in the United States since the war and the creation of new Foundations with very substantial endowments, these study groups have grown both in size and in influence on the Washington political scene. They are an enormous source of information to successor administrations and to members and Committees of the U.S. Congress. It is an American phenomenon which has no real equivalent in other countries.

In the fall of 1981, I was approached by David Abshire, the president of the Center for Strategic and International Studies (CSIS), who asked me if I would be interested in joining his think tank to head up a group studying and reporting on international economics. CSIS, he explained to me, was an independent institution but affiliated with Georgetown University. The group I would head would advise business executives, as well as agencies of governments and members of the Congress. I would write articles and give symposiums. He agreed, if I was interested in the position, to raise a million dollar fund to endow a chair. At that time the prime interest rate was 20 percent. I figured that with $200,000 a year I could easily pay for my salary, secretary and travel. I frankly did not expect him to succeed. But a month later he advised me that Dr. Scholl in Chicago had agreed to fund such a chair and that I would be its first holder. So I reluctantly told Bill Draper, the bank's new chairman, that I would be leaving my job as a director of Ex-Im Bank. Unfortunately, I hadn't been told by Abshire that Georgetown University earned what it could on the principal of the chair and only passed on to CSIS five percent as its participation. So I had $50,000—not $200,000 from my chair.

A dinner in my honor was given to celebrate my coming to Georgetown. I was seated next to the Jesuit scholar who was the president of Georgetown University.

He turned to me during dinner and said,

"I don't understand, Thibaut, why we have to have a chair in international business. There are poor people and rich people in the world. The rich should give to the poor."

"That is why I am here, Father, to prevent that happening in quite the way you would propose."

Thus started a new adventure. After the very structured world of a government agency, I found myself among a group of thinkers who

500

were expected to create their own activity with a minimum of direction. The center included well-known writers, academics, former government officials, career military officers, journalists, economists, historians and lobbyists. There were few rules. One could have a business or do advisory work on the side. Every morning promptly at 8 o'clock, a small group of us would gather in David Abshire's office to discuss particular projects, who should be responsible for each, and where the funding was coming from. Abshire was the impresario, the chief fundraiser, and the man who made it all happen. He had had long experience as a former legislative aid in Congress, knew most leaders of the Congress from both parties, had been a consultant to successive presidents, and had extraordinary relationships with the heads of many of the country's largest corporations. I have never met anyone with the same capacity to raise money. He always managed to make business executives understand that without their advice and their financial support, the country risked further peril.

At the top of the Abshire chief executive support pyramid came what was known as the Kissinger Group. This consisted of the chief executive officers of fifty corporations from all over the world. They would meet twice a year, once in Washington and once in a foreign country. The member from that country would sponsor and organize with the help of CSIS the weeklong meeting in that country. Henry Kissinger would preside at each domestic or foreign meeting. Each of the members paid $50,000 per year to belong, giving CSIS a total of $1,500,000 in yearly "dues." In addition, the members naturally paid their travel and hotel expenses. When I joined the Center, I was given the responsibility for the Kissinger Group meetings as part of my "portfolio." It was not a role that I looked forward to. I had known Indochina well at an earlier time of my life. I disapproved of our war in Vietnam and the manner in which Kissinger as secretary of state had handled its extension to Cambodia and our extrication from that unhappy conflict.

The first Kissinger Group program in Washington for which I was responsible had gone well, but the second, in Brazil, had turned out to be much more complicated, largely because Secretary Kissinger had insisted that the group go to Brasilia even though such a side-trip was not on the original schedule and he hadn't bothered to tell me of his wish to change our program. It turned out that Kissinger had agreed to give a talk at the university there but, unknown to our group, had demanded a fee of $25,000 for his speech. Our whole group had been expected to attend the talk. The students, deeply offended that a foreigner had demanded such a fee for a speech when the university had so little money, threw eggs and tomatoes at Kissinger and the group as they arrived. Fortunately, I was not there. Roberto Campos, the chancellor of the university, a friend of very long standing whom I had often invited to speak at the Management Center in Geneva when I was teaching there, had warned of the students' reaction, and had taken me to his office, where we drank champagne and watched developments on his TV screen.

To make amends for Kissinger's fee on this unfortunate occasion, the next day I had to participate in a debate on campus with two Brazilian bankers on the theme, "Why the U.S. does so little to support the Brazilian economy."

I did have an opportunity to create a successful working group project while at CSIS between members of Congress and the business community. We had as participants ten Congressional leaders, ten heads of U.S. companies, two labor union leaders, and several academics. The project focused on strategies to ensure economic growth fifteen years later. We held a dinner meeting each month. At the end of a year, we put out a written report which then received wide distribution in the Congress and the business community. We had explored some interesting ideas, cleared up some misunderstandings, and outlined solutions that all concerned could agree to. Had I not had my bank experience, I would not have been able to get the support for this project from key members of Congress that I had come to know while at the bank.

My stay at CSIS gave me the opportunity to begin my research on my next book: a study on the Federal Reserve, how it operated and why the world economy depended upon the policies of the Fed to determine whether we would face world economic growth, inflation or, indeed, recession. This was a study which I had long planned. In order to get started I hired, at my own expense, a young lawyer with time on his hands, and sent him to the Library of Congress to make a list of all of the books or articles which had been written on the Federal Reserve since its origin in 1913. He came back a week later. "There is nothing," he said. I could not believe it. I went to see the director of the Joint Economic Committee of Congress who was a friend. "We have masses of material on the Fed," he said. We went down to the stacks to look, but we found nothing. He told me that he remembered a seven-volume work prepared by an economist at Catholic University. We couldn't find it. Much later, my friend called me up one day to say that on his way to work he had stopped at the Post Office, where he ran across the economist in question. I went to see him. The first volume consisted of Congressional hearings on how the Fed controlled inflation during the Korean War. I had long since obtained it from the Senate Finance Committee. The other six volumes were speeches by Representative Wright Patman attacking the Federal Reserve for not increasing the money supply fast enough.

It was then that I realized that I would have to do all my own research on this agency of government that, through its actions, determined whether the world economy would go through a period of inflation or recession.

I had run across the same problem in the '60s when I was writing my first book, *The Dollar Crisis*. The State Department and Treasury then claimed that much had been written on the subject, but we could find nothing in the files at either State or Treasury. Often in Washington officials talk of a problem at meetings and then assume that it has been carefully researched, but that almost never happens.

No wonder I called my book on the Fed when I gave it to the publisher, *The Federal Reserve—an Intentional Mystery*.

Both the president and the Congress pretend the Federal Reserve is independent. It suits them to do so. They wish to blame the Fed in periods of inflation and even more when recessions occur.

When the book was finally published in 1985, I dedicated it to the chairman of the Senate and the House Banking Committee and sent a copy to Senator Proxmire who chaired the Senate Banking Committee. I had gotten to know him well when I was with the bank. He received me with his staff.

"I won't read your book, Thibaut."

"You must read it. It is dedicated to you. We are going to have a terrible bank crisis because the savings and loan banks are making speculative loans and engaging in unsound or illegal lending. There will surely be a banking crisis. The head of the House Banking Committee may be involved himself in this. So it has to be you who stops it."

"Thibaut, you don't understand politics. No one in the Congress cares about economics or money and banking. We are not interested because we don't understand the subject and our constituents don't either, unless there is a terrible crisis. Remember what happened at the height of the Great Depression in 1934. The head of the largest bank in the world at that time, the Chase Bank, came down to see us and said the banking system is out of control. Now when the head of the largest bank in the world says something like that, we have to pay attention. We asked him what we should do. He said separate commercial banking from investment banking. So we passed the Glass-Steagall Act and then forgot about the banking problem. It was probably the wrong thing to do, and I suspect we will shortly do away with this piece of legislation. Of course, there will now be a bank crisis. When it comes, we will probably do the wrong thing again. But no one has any interest in the subject. You just don't understand politics."

He had certainly taught me politics when I was at the bank. I was the only director he would talk to. Because I had been an academic, he assumed I was honest, intelligent and objective. As a result, whenever we made a large loan to buyers of Boeing aircraft, I was the one called over to the Senate to explain why we had done it. He would thank me for my presentation. Then the next day there would be on the front page of the *Washington Post* an attack on the bank for making a large loan to help a big corporation which ought to finance its own sales. There was, of course, a constituency for helping to finance exports, but an attack on big business always played well to the Democratic voters in Wisconsin, the senator's home state.

I had written several articles on trade issues and given many talks on trade in briefing sessions to Congress, business and the press while I was at CSIS. When I undertook to write my study of the Federal Reserve, I had gone to David Abshire to explain to him what I wanted to do and why.

"It is a very interesting subject and someone should certainly do it. But I don't think it is something for CSIS to do. Our job is to brief heads of businesses, the administration and the Congress on problems that they need to be aware of because it will involve decision making in the next few months, not years. You must realize that the attention span of a member of the House can't exceed six months. The first six months of his-two year term he is figuring out where the bathroom is. The last six months he is running for office again. So he only has one year in which he can devote himself to legislation of interest to the electors who sent him to Washington. He couldn't care less about what the Federal Reserve does or doesn't do. You're doing well by helping our friends in government and business focus on short-term issues. We must always remind ourselves that we are not an academic institution. We deal with serious upcoming strategic problems which require answers, not what may affect the country or the world sometime at an indeterminate date in the future."

He was, of course, correct.

But in fairness to David Abshire, I didn't think I could do what he expected of me at CSIS and write a very time-consuming study of the Federal Reserve at the same time. So I regretfully gave up my chair at CSIS. I should probably have balanced both missions instead because CSIS gave me a wonderful base in both business and the political world.

If one gets an idea in one's head, as likely as not someone will come along to give it substance and hasten its execution. I had a great friend in Washington by the name of Struve Hensel who had been a partner of mine at Coudert Brothers in New York. Struve had made his mark in the McCarthy days when, as general counsel of the Defense Department, he had spearheaded the Senate hearings that condemned Senator McCarthy for his attacks on American citizens and institutions. It had so happened, although I didn't know Struve at the time, that I had worked one whole night on the speech which Senator Flanders of Vermont had given in the Senate the next day to defend the Defense Department and start the hearings against McCarthy. Struve was now retired from the law and living in Washington. He called me one day and told me that he had been serving as counsel to a leading law firm in Columbus, Ohio. The firm had wanted to expand its practice to the international field. They needed to find an experienced lawyer who might spearhead the operation, including the hiring of individual lawyers with international experience. This new international section of the law firm would operate out of Washington. He had recommended me. The job paid $100,000 a year and I would be permitted to continue to work on my book on the Federal Reserve. The senior partners of the firm with whom I spoke told me they did not expect me to bring in any business because they already had more than they could handle. I had told them I had been away from the law for so long that I no longer felt capable of handling complicated legal matters. But I accepted their proposal and somewhat regretfully left my perch in the safe haven of CSIS.

Looking back on it, I ascribe my decision to my continuing legal problems in getting my divorce so that I could marry again. Both Mariana's four and my three oldest children could not understand why this was so difficult, particularly since I wanted nothing except visitation rights with my children which had long since been agreed to. It would be 1983 before I finally secured my divorce.

My literary agent had insisted on auctioning the rights on my book on the Federal Reserve. When the book was finished, the law firm held a dinner at the Metropolitan Club in the pine-paneled Anderson room.

It was a festive occasion. Arthur Vorys, the senior partner, came in from Columbus, Ohio to preside. I sat him next to a lawyer friend from Paris who had flown in for the occasion. Vorys asked him what being a French lawyer in Paris was like.

"Any man in Paris who respects himself has a valet, a chauffeur and a lawyer," replied my friend.

"But that means a servant."

"Exactly. In France, a lawyer does not make decisions."

I think Arthur Vorys distrusted me from then on. But I fulfilled the role I had been assigned. We hired a brilliant international tax lawyer, a specialist on international acquisitions with a good Spanish and Latin American client list, a specialist on banking law who had been general counsel of Ex-Im Bank. My second son, who was one of the young partners at Davis, Polk and Wardwell in New York, called me periodically to ask me if the younger partners in the parent firm in Columbus had "gotten rid of you yet. We're all alike. We want to get rid of the older lawyers because they cost us points. The younger partners in Columbus don't care about creating an international practice in Washington D.C. They'll get rid of you, Dad."

Just as the new Washington firm was beginning to show a profit, it happened as he had suggested. What triggered it was that one of the leading partners in Columbus left the law to become president of Honda, U.S.A. in Marysville, Ohio. He had called me one day and said, "Do you know who I am, Thibaut? Honda is not like an American auto company. I am not like the executives of General Motors who never leave the head office in Detroit. I get to my office at 7 a.m., dictate to my secretary until 8; then from 8 to 4, I'm on the factory floor. At 4, I go back to my office, sign the mail, and prepare for the next day. The suppliers keep sending us parts only as we need them. We operate the way companies do in Japan, on a 'just in time' basis with our suppliers. You have no idea what it saves us to operate this way. We need far less cash than do American automobile companies."

I was not reluctant to be freed from the task of creating an international dimension for the firm. I had brought in two excellent corporate and bank lawyers who chose to remain with the firm: my friend who had been counsel to the Export-Import Bank, and an experienced former partner of a major New York firm who had been secretary of the Navy in the Carter administration. I was grateful to the firm for letting me finish and publish my book on the Federal Reserve. I could handle the Swiss bank work, my work with Adolf Lundin, and the work I was

Washington Sequel

Can you internationalize an Ohio firm?

doing with Bob Krieble from anywhere. For all this I did not need to be in a law firm. I would create a small consulting firm with my three clients as a base.

When my divorce was finally granted in 1983, I could at last marry Mariana. The judge who had the case called me one spring Saturday morning in Washington to tell me that the divorce decree would be signed that morning. I called him back to ask him if he would marry us that afternoon in Bill Witter's apartment in New York. After a moment's hesitation, he said "yes." I immediately called each of the children—Mariana's four and my oldest three—to tell them we would be married at five in New York with a dinner at the River Club to follow at seven. By some miracle, it had all worked out. At the reception and dinner at the River Club, we were some fifty family and friends.

Our honeymoon lasted only one day because on the following Monday morning I had to be in court to try the six lawsuits my wife had brought against me back in 1977. My wife appeared in court with three sets of lawyers. But at the end of the week, all her legal actions were dismissed. A year later, after she lost all her appeals, I was at last free. It had cost me several hundred thousand dollars in legal fees but, more importantly, a dozen years of unnecessary legal wranglings.

In 1979 I had purchased a house on Reservoir Street in Georgetown with a nice garden and a two-car garage. It could now be the start of a new life for Mariana and me.

Because I felt no need to have a large overhead, I had persuaded a group of friends who lived in Washington to act as board of advisors to my consulting firm on the understanding that if any one of us had a new client, we would share the work and the fees to be earned. There were two investment bankers, an Iranian Central Banker, two senior business executives, a physicist turned money manager, and a labor economist. There was no pressure on anyone to produce business. We met once a month to discuss client needs and who should participate in the work. It was the start of SPI Group, which by the year 2000 included forty former government or World Bank officials, a few diplomats and investment bankers and partners in other consulting firms. The group holds monthly meetings in Washington. There is a lunch and a speaker. Although I am now chairman emeritus, I look forward to attending these lunches whenever I am in Washington. We did a number of projects together for the Asian Development Bank in which our partner, the former deputy director of the Central Bank of Iran, played the lead role. Above all, the work was stimulating.

507

My principal activity during this period consisted of going to Switzerland twice a year to brief the Swiss bankers there on where to invest in the United States. The bank had three branches, one in Zurich, a second in Geneva, and a third in Lugano. They might just as well have been three separate banks. Bankers in Zurich are very Germanic, very cautious. "Who else agrees with you?" they might say as I recommended a particular U.S. company in which they should invest. In Geneva, bankers think as their French clients might. They don't mind losing money on an investment in IBM because the client will blame the loss on the vagaries of the market and not on this much-admired company, but they were reluctant to invest in a new untried technology because a loss here cannot be satisfactorily explained to the client. In Lugano, the attitude of the bankers was quite different. The clients in Lugano were businessmen from Milan—those 250,000 small entrepreneurial businesses that produce 50 percent of the gross national product of Italy. Here the clients understand the nature of business risk. They want to make money on their investments but they understand that to do so, one must be willing to take risks and to invest in new enterprises. The Italian, like the Chinese, is fundamentally a gambler. I found the same difference in attitude between investors in San Francisco and Los Angeles when I used to visit clients for Dean Witter and Company when I was a partner there in the 1960s. San Francisco until recently was old, third and fourth generation money—largely in the hands of the trust departments of banks, whereas in Los Angeles it was new money. There a client would come in with his wife. They had made money during the marriage and wanted to make investment decisions together, preferably in new ventures because that is how they had become wealthy. This was new money belonging to people who had become rich by taking risks. Like the Italians of Milan, they had confidence in their ability to succeed in business and in their own ability as investors.

Of the three very different business environments in Switzerland, it was to Lugano that I most enjoyed going. The head of the bank there was quite unlike other Swiss bankers I dealt with. His wife was Canadian from Calgary; his American clients were Texans; when he came to America on vacation with his wife and daughters, he would rent a fancy mobile home and explore the country dressed in cowboy boots and a Stetson.

My life was a full one. I was independent. I had enough to do. I enjoyed what I was doing. One day I had a call from a man who identified himself as the head of a group of Croats who wanted to have the United

States Congress recognize the right of Croatia to become independent from Yugoslavia. We met. He told me that in order to join his group there were three conditions: to have been born a Croat; to have come to the United States after 1946; to be worth at least ten million dollars today. There were thirty members of the group, all small manufacturers, mainly in plastic products such as bottle caps and closures. They were quite similar in their outlook to thousands of American owners of small businesses. They had come to the United States penniless after War World II, found a niche where money could be made, worked hard and saved. They were appalled by what Communism had done to Croatia. They wanted independence from Serbia and were determined to find American support for their cause. I told them that in my view, the initial steps had to be taken within Yugoslavia, not in the United States. They had two problems: one was to establish their independence from Serbia, the other to supplant the Communist regime in Croatia itself. When Croatia did become independent, I worked hard with this group and the new Croat ambassador to get support in the United States for a more democratic regime in Croatia. Unfortunately, this was only achieved after the Croatian president's death in 1998.

Washington Sequel

With three other members of our group I made several trips to Southeast Asia on behalf of the Asian Development Bank. The bank had sent many missions to the area headed by former diplomats and academics to try to help the various governments there accept the principle that economic development required access to private rather than government or international institution sources of capital, and that therefore local governments should treat foreign capital fairly from both a legal and a tax standpoint. The bank had decided to fund a new study, this time by experienced business executives. The study would cover nine countries. Hong Kong, Singapore and Taiwan, the bank thought, had established various rules which had encouraged investment by private capital. Would the experience of these three be helpful to the other six and in what way? What did Thailand, Indonesia, India, Pakistan, the Philippines, and Sri Lanka have to do to establish a climate in which private capital would be encouraged to invest so as to accelerate each country's economic development? It was a fascinating project. The six of us who worked on it had almost as much fun working together as we did in working with the government agencies, state and private banks, state and private businesses and the monetary authorities in each country. Our individual experiences were somewhat different. The problems varied in each country because the culture and historical experience in

Working for the Asian Development Bank

each had not been the same. Thailand, except for a fifty-year span when it was occupied by Burma, had had no colonial past. The Philippines had been under Spanish rule and American tutelage for long periods. India, Pakistan and Sri Lanka had been British colonies, with very different cultural and religious experience. Indonesia was a Moslem state but had a Hindu culture going back many centuries. Its economy was overwhelmingly in the hands of the Chinese minority.

It was as a result of my experience in working on this project that I made the decision, if ever I decided to retire, to write a detailed study examining how cultural differences had shaped economic development in different parts of the world.

Since there were six of us working together on this study, we could choose both the area of our focus, as well as which countries each one of us would work in. Most of my time was spent in India, Thailand, Indonesia and Pakistan. I had previously done a detailed analysis of Taiwan and Hong Kong, but Singapore was studied by others. Each of these three could now be ranked as developed countries. But each had achieved its developed status in a different manner. We saw little that could help the other six in their own development. Both culture and historical experience were too different.

In Thailand the society was run by a triumvirate of the banks, private businesses, and the military, with the king as the final arbiter. The king was much loved by his people. His prestige was sufficient to decide any matter which he found was important enough to warrant his intervention. Certain businesses belonged to the military: the airports, air traffic, meat distribution, for example. The military frequently appointed the prime minister, until too much corruption caused the king to replace the military with a civilian for a time. When scandals occurred, they were settled politely by the king. Thailand is a rich country with strong traditions, a rich culture and unfailing politeness.

Pakistan is a country which probably should never have been. It was created because the Moslems and the Hindus were unable to agree on having one country when India achieved its independence from Britain at the end of World War II. The Moslems are descendants of the fierce warrior stock of Genghis Kahn, who conquered all of central Asia in the 13th century. They brought peace but not culture to the lands they conquered. When the British controlled India, the north of Pakistan was the area of the Northwest Frontier where the local tribes were thought by the British to be helpful in protecting India from Russia to the north.

The British in India had suffered in three wars with Afghanistan and finally had solved the "Afghan problem" by dividing the Pashtun tribes in two, with part in Afghanistan and part within the Northwest Washington Frontier region of British India. This division of tribes was artificial. It Sequel never succeeded in maintaining anything but an artificial border between India and Afghanistan. Both the British in the south and east and the Russians in the north had been agreeable to maintaining Afghanistan as a buffer until recently. The agreement was destroyed when Soviet Russia invaded Afghanistan. Pakistan today is still two countries: the north the military tribal area; the south a trading society centered around Karachi. The glue that binds is the Moslem religion with all its negatives for modern economic development. Banks cannot charge interest on loans because the Moslem religion forbids it. Loans have to be structured another way which doesn't allow for the length of time over which the money is advanced. This makes any transaction endlessly complicated. Private banking and insurance do not exist. Pakistanis who are very hard-working people go abroad whenever they can to earn their living but then are discouraged from sending their money home for investment because of rules again imposed by the Moslem religion.

Pakistan had already had two wars with India. It lost both of them. As a result of one, the country already split in two, lost its eastern half which became the independent nation of Bangladesh. India and Pakistan are now at the brink of war over Kashmir where the population is largely Moslem, but the ruler historically came from India. The United Nations had effected a settlement of the dispute a few years ago, giving the northern third of the area to Pakistan and the southern two-thirds to India. It has not succeeded. Both countries continue to fight in the northern Himalayan area. Both nations now have the atomic bomb. It has now become a matter of such honor that neither country will yield. It is a recipe for disaster.

Superimposed upon the problems with India are severe structural, as well as religious, problems affecting Pakistan. Among the elite of that country there are great scientists, engineers, men with great experience in finance, traders, scholars, businessmen. But the social problems are enormous. The bulk of the population is poor, uneducated. There is massive corruption at all levels of society. Above all, a society in the north of the country famous for its military prowess, has now seen superimposed on it a religious hierarchy which, as in Iran to the west, has created a Moslem fundamentalism which threatens the country's survival from the inside. Since there is no proper educational system established by the state, education has fallen into the hands of the Moslem clerics, who have organized severe religious schools—the *madrassahs*, which are the only source of education for the poor. It is in these schools that Moslem extremism has flourished. This educational system has to be changed.

To the west and north of Pakistan is Afghanistan. When the Soviets attacked Afghanistan in 1982, the United States government told the CIA to help the Afghans defend their country. The U.S. missiles sent by the CIA were very helpful in winning the war for the Afghan tribes—the *mujahideen*—who fought the Russian invaders. Then when the Russians left, the CIA abandoned the country and "went home." The result was civil war and defeat of the northern tribes by the Pashtun in the south of the country, and the imposition of extremist Moslem rule by the Taliban self-designated clerics. These have now been aided by similar religious extremists from Egypt, Saudi Arabia, Pakistan, Yemen and the Sudan. We are paying an enormous price for our failure to remain involved in a country which we saved from Soviet occupation. We have now removed the Taliban from power. But it is not clear that we will have the determination to keep the country from falling again into the hands of warlords and chaos.

The most interesting country by far in our study was India. Here we found every conceivable trend in world civilization: three of the world's great religions took root here: Hindu, Buddhist, Moslem. The population in the last forty years has increased by more than the entire population of the United States. There are twenty-nine stock exchanges. Only slowly and painfully has the government relinquished its control over foreign investment, banking and insurance. Taxation is so ridiculously high that evasion is endemic. I was fascinated by one legal quirk: if a business wants to issue additional stock to meet its needs for more capital, it must sell its shares at their par value. This makes it almost impossible to raise capital through additional stock issues. I asked how this had come about. "The British gave us this law." The law had been adopted during the war because the British wanted Indian capital to go into British war bond issues rather than to Indian businesses. It made no sense, but it showed the deep respect in India for economic rules established by the British. Indeed, the British did much to establish the rule of law in India and a deep respect for the judicial system. In many ways we found that it was the judges in India who were most responsible for ensuring economic development in the country, by preventing wherever possible abuses by the state sector.

In Indonesia, we found a profoundly Hindu culture on which had been superimposed Moslem militancy. Until recently Indonesia was a Dutch colony. The Dutch had brought to Indonesia the Napoleonic Code under which notaries certify all legal documents, including rights to property and mortgages. When the Dutch had left precipitously, the crowds had sacked the offices of the notaries and destroyed all the documents they could find that recorded property ownership. As a result, it is not possible in Indonesia to get a mortgage since ownership cannot be proved. Credit is therefore very difficult to obtain. On top of this, the economic restrictions imposed by the Moslem religion and control of banking and insurance by the State has severely restricted economic development by the private sector. The Chinese minority, relying on a high savings rate and community resources both within and outside the country in Hong Kong and Singapore, has managed to control an ever-increasing portion of the economy. The result: fear of the Chinese throughout the government leadership. It was difficult in Indonesia to have much confidence in the country's economic future. On the one hand is the beauty of the country, the culture of its people. On the other, dictatorial power, corruption, cronyism, and religious intolerance constricting development of the economy.

Washington Sequel

Working with the Atlantic Council as a director and active participant was a particular pleasure for me. I had a strong link of friendship over many years with David Acheson, president of the council, and I had many friends on its board. I believed strongly in its leadership role in NATO and greatly enjoyed attending the annual NATO meetings as a council delegate. I had tried hard but without much success to make the Atlantic Council understand better the position of the French on European defense issues. It was a difficult role. The Atlantic Council had decided at one point to make a study of Franco-American relations for the State and Defense Departments. A high-level group of former ambassadors to France would play a leading role. I tried to suggest, but without success, that the problem came from the State Department and diplomats in the first place. It was true that the French Foreign Office had distrusted American policy initiatives ever since the end of World War II. In my view the way to solve this problem was to have French businessmen who knew the United States well participate along with American executives in the study. This suggestion was turned down. I was told the White House and the State Department would never be convinced of the value of the study if the French participated in it and if it did not rely on ex-ambassadors. The results of the study were predict-

The Atlantic Council and NATO

able: The French were at fault. They wanted NATO replaced by a European defense establishment; they had been ungrateful for American military protection all these years. The position of American diplomats reminded me of what Cardinal Spellman had one day told my aunt: "The French are not worthy of being Catholics." Fortunately, the French military had not the same envy problem as the Foreign Office had. They admired, respected and worked in close harmony with the Americans.

In June 1993, to celebrate our ten years of marriage, I took Mariana on a trip to southern Virginia to spend ten days relaxing and playing golf. We never arrived there. On a straight stretch of a four-lane highway, just as I was explaining to my wife that I was ready to reduce my activities to working with three clients only, a 17-year-old African-American girl on a visit north with her boyfriend came across the divider at high speed and hit us head-on. Our car came to a stop across the highway. We were then hit on the side by a large chicken truck. Our car was sent a hundred yards on its back as a result of this second collision. If it hadn't been that we were in a Mercedes, we would surely have been killed in the crash. My wife suffered a broken neck, I multiple contusions, curvature of the spine and a terrible effect on my immune system.

When an event like this occurs in one's life, one has to see it as a message that cannot be ignored. Our lives had been saved; Mariana in time would recover. But it was clear we needed to change our way of life. I would need to curtail my travel. Mariana's injury meant she should not winter in the north. We made the decision gradually to move to Florida.

At the time of the accident, I had already planned to work with only three clients: one was the Krieble Institute funded by my friend, Dr. Robert Krieble, founder of the Fortune 500 chemical company, Loctite, another was the group of oil and mining companies headed by Adolf Lundin, and the third was the investment advisory work I did for the Swiss banks. These activities were quite diverse. But all fitted my lifetime of international legal and financial experience. I would not need an office, nor partners or employees to work with me. I could be independent and using modern technology, function from wherever I chose. It has worked out well.

A year earlier my wife had warned me: "Thibaut, you love what you are doing, traveling around the world advising governments and businesses. But you are now seventy-two years old. Your former clients have long since retired. You have always done what you wanted, figuring that you could make whatever you needed to live comfortably. You never worried about money and have no funded retirement plan. You had better now focus on looking after us." It was very good advice.

One of the most difficult problems that any business or legal professional must eventually face is the loss of his office and his secretary. I had had at least one, and sometimes several, secretaries ever since 1941 when I graduated from law school. My office, whether I acted as a lawyer, a professor, a business executive, or a government official, was my sanctuary: the place where I could meditate, make decisions, plan ahead. I now had to fight depression because I had lost my secretary, the one person who made my business life function smoothly. I was like a refugee woman whose home and furniture have been taken from her. It took me a while to realize that all was not lost. We are appalling creatures of habit.

To my surprise, the Swiss banks didn't seem to care where I made my studies of the American economy and recommendations regarding their American investment strategy. I could prepare from anywhere my twice-yearly detailed reports that I sent them prior to my face-to-face visits. There was an additional bonus for the work that I did for the banks. It was most helpful to me in my own investment decisions. I was being paid by others to think clearly for myself.

The work that I did with the Lundin Group took on a new focus when Adolf had an opportunity to take over, from the United Nations, a copper mining project in Argentina. Ever since the end of World War II, Argentina was always the country that would find its bearings next year. It is a country that has everything: no ethnic or racial problems, a population immigrated largely from England, Germany and Italy, a rich soil, temperate climate. Yet its great natural wealth brought about its subsequent difficulties. The original settlers had created great wealth in developing a cattle industry. Argentine beef had become the standard of excellence. The Argentines sent their sons to school in Europe instead of at home. The children returned to play polo and live the good life in Buenos Aires. They became bankers and insurance company executives if they worked at all. They invested in Europe instead of in Argentina. Eventually the country fell into the hands of Peron, a socialist, and investment at home declined further as wealth left the country. No one bothered to develop the oil and mineral wealth of the country. As economic development declined further, Argentina reached the point by 1970 where no one wanted to invest in the country. Inflation had become endemic. The socialist government was corrupt and, worse, incapable. The military Junta which had taken over briefly was no better. Where other investors fled, Adolf saw an opportunity. He negotiated successfully to take over a very large copper project in the north of the country which the United Nations had earlier tried to help the Argentine government develop. It was called Alumbrera.

I became an early investor with Adolf in the project. It would eventually require many millions of dollars of investment, coming from the United States, Switzerland, Canada and Sweden. It turned out after several years of very hard work to be one of the most important copper deposits in the world. At that point, because the project would require that many hundreds of millions of dollars more be invested to bring the mine into operation, Adolf Lundin held a sales auction with the world's biggest mining companies and Alumbrera was sold to a major Australian company.

I had become a director of Alumbrera and with my options, as well as my initial investment, was able to make a very fair profit on the transaction. My bank clients and other Washington friends who invested along with me also did very well, including my friend and client, Bob Krieble. It pleased me greatly to have been able, through Alumbrera, to aid Bob in financing the considerable sums that he would spend each year to help spread democracy and an understanding of the American free-enterprise system throughout the former Soviet Empire.

My business relationship with Adolf Lundin in this way made it possible for me to satisfy my wife's injunction to me and to be in a position to devote my energies to working with Bob Krieble in the former Soviet Empire without undue material worries.

Washington Sequel

The author and his wife's home on Chincoteague Island, Virginia. The house was designed by the author and is surrounded on three sides by water.

The author with his close friend, Senator Claiborne Pell of Rhode Island, head of the Senate Foreign Relations Committee. They first met at school in New York when they were eight years old.

The author and his wife Mariana in South Korea, where he was sent by President Reagan to negotiate trade questions

The author in Beijing, for negotiations with the Chinese government on behalf of Burlington Northern Railroad

The French ambassador to Washington decorates the author with the French Legion of Honor, France's highest decoration.

At the Jockey Club in Paris for the French Legion of Honor award with French cousins and two French grandchildren

XXV

THE DREAM OF PÈRE BERNARD
DE CHABANNES

Whereas you have asked us dear Count Guifred, for the concession for the
Church of Saint Martin, in order to construct there a monastery for the remission of your sins and those of your parents, we grant your request in ced-
ing that this Church will not become a part of your lands. And we therefore
decree that from the present no prince, no marquis, no judge, no bishop, no
abbot shall serve any violence, invasion, or enslavement upon this monastery
or its dependents . . .

*T*HIS BOOK WOULD NOT BE complete without picking up again
the story of my very special kinsman, Père Bernard de Chabannes, a tonsured Benedictine monk who had come to see me
in New York in 1946 at the time of the birth of Fal, my oldest son.
He had told me then that he had found, high up in the Pyrenees, an old
abandoned monastery destroyed during the French Revolution, which
he intended to rebuild so that it might serve once again to bring men
back to God in a remarkably beautiful setting.

One man
rebuilds a
monastery.

I had heard rumors from time to time over the years when I queried members of the family in France that Bernard had indeed proceeded with his quest, but it was only some fifty years later that I had
occasion to check for myself. My wife, Mariana, and I were spending
the summer near Beziers in southern France. It was the region made
famous by that strange 14th century sect of the Cathars and that last
terrible crusade which brought about their extinction in a sea of flames.
What better time for me to visit that nearby Benedictine monastery
where as a young boy in 1928 I had witnessed the taking of vows by my
godmother, Genevieve. It was at once a return to roots, a pilgrimage to
those many in the family who had chosen monastic life, an opportunity
to expose to my new American Episcopalian wife the quiet and peace of

a Catholic convent, and a chance to satisfy my curiosity about whether
or not Bernard had attained his goal.

At the convent of Dourgne in Southern France, we spent a good
hour meeting with the nuns, now in their 80s and 90s, who had known
my godmother well when they were young novices together prior to
taking their final vows. They were like small birds, sitting in their par-
lour, full of laughter and stories, as though the passage of time had left
no marks on their existence. They remembered my godmother well but
in their cloistered life over so many years, they did not know that she
had become a Mother Superior in Italy and died there during World
War II.

We had brought with us my cousin, Jacques, who had grown up in
the monastery under the tutelage of Père Bernard and had then gone
out into the world to become a pilot. The two had not seen each other
since Jacques had left the monastery and had much to say to each other.
We took Bernard and Jacques for lunch in the village nearby. Everyone
there knew Père Bernard. He and Jacques talked all the way through
lunch about life at the monastery before Jacques left. It was very meaningful for both.

Bernard told us he had indeed rebuilt the monastery, working all by
himself over thirty-five years, and that there was now a small group of
monks and nuns making up his flock at the abbey he had restored. We
promised to pay him a visit the following year. He would be there.

The following year we came prepared for a climb. It was easy to leave
the car at the foot of the mountain. The village of Vernet, located in the
eastern Pyrenees an hours drive from Perpignan, was a thermal station
with plenty of parking area. We locked the car, put on our backpacks,
and started up the mountain on foot. We could see the monastery as we
started our walk. It appeared to be perched on a cliff. Although it was
June, the mountains in the background were still covered with snow. It
took us about three and a half hours to make the climb.

The dirt road leading to the abbey had obviously been kept in good
repair, but it was a steep climb. We had been asked in the village if we
intended to walk up or make use of the four-wheel-drive converted
military vehicle which was available to take up the many tourists who
visited the abbey each year. We had decided to walk. When we arrived, a
nun showed us to a small room furnished with only the bare necessities.
There were eight such rooms, all facing the valley below, each with two
beds, two chairs, a closet and a worktable. The floors and the white walls
were bare. Outside the windows, there was a sheer drop to the valley

several thousand feet below. And, to one side coming from the snowy peaks above, there was a torrent of water pouring down into the valley. The sound of all this water cascading down the mountain was pleasant to the ear. The view was spectacular.

The monastery looked as if it had been there forever.

Now, like all medieval monasteries, there was a sheltered cloister; it had flower beds and a lawn surrounded by low rosemary bushes on the inside and columns and a covered walk on the outside. The cloister was a place where one willingly engaged in prayer or meditation. The chapel was small, with white walls, the altar a simple native stone slab. On one side of the chapel was a dormitory for the monks and nuns and facing the valley were the eight rooms described above. Along the road leading up to the monastery in the rear were fields of vegetables and fruit trees.

The monastery was surrounded by a wall. The road up to it ended at a gate with great oak doors which we would learn were shut from 12:00 to 2:00 so that the monks and nuns could attend Mass, eat and rest in the middle of the day. Outside the gate was a small souvenir shop where one could purchase postcards of the abbey and religious articles.

We met Bernard in the garden before lunch. He was now almost ninety years old. Age did not seem to weigh heavily on his shoulders. He stood as straight as ever. He had certainly not lost the twinkle in his eyes. And he greeted Mariana as if he had always known her. "I gave your husband a good deal of trouble a few years ago in New York, but I was in a hurry and I needed his help."

"They spoil me here," he added. "There is little for me to do now that the abbey is finished. I have a room that is much more than the cell I am used to. I have a radio which allows me to follow world events through the BBC. I say my Mass in the late morning and walk for an hour every afternoon. I have my books and keep up my correspondence. I speak once a day at lunch or when friends like you come to visit. I no longer have responsibilities. I have allowed myself to be cared for."

It was true that the abbey appeared to run itself. The abbess who received us at lunch had only a small number of nuns in residence. Like all Benedictines, they spent much of the day either in prayer at the church or at work in the fields or gardens outside. There were a handful of monks (several of whom, by special papal dispensation, had been allowed by the pope to marry and live with their wives after both had taken special vows pledging their lives to the Church and the Benedictine Order).

Bernard ate very little. Halfway through the meal, he rose, spoke of me as an old friend and a kinsman and introduced my wife. Then he read from the Gospel of the Prodigal Son and spoke briefly of the joy of being reunited with a dear friend.

What surprised me most was that some fifty thousand people every year came to visit this monastery. They came for a few hours climbing the mountain on foot or taking the converted military vehicle which came up each morning and afternoon. Why was it that so many people from so many different countries would want to spend time during their vacation to visit a simple church and Benedictine abbey hidden away in the mountains of the Pyrenees? What were they seeking? Did they find what they were looking for and return refreshed to their daily lives? Had Bernard's work somehow struck a chord as he had hoped and was it this that had created a response in so many people?

We learned in the days that followed that except for those who had made arrangements to stay for a period of time, the pace of life in the monastery was in no way affected by these visits. People came, they participated in the day's religious services if they wished, then they went away again.

We found out that the original abbey had been built by the Count of Cerdagne toward the end of his life in the year 1091. According to local legend, this nobleman had not behaved well even by the standards of the time. He had made war against his neighbors, burned, pillaged and raped. Now he would atone for his sins in the simple monastic life of this mountain shrine. When he and his wife died, they were buried behind the church. During the Revolution, some six hundred years later, their bones had been dug up and scattered and the Abbey destroyed. Even in the quiet of the Pyrenees, people had yielded to long-suppressed passions to destroy. No one could now remember whether it had been due to hatred of the feudal system, long-suppressed anger at the Crusade against the Cathars, or still smoldering Protestant anti-Catholic feelings from the religious wars of the 17th century.

To me, it was enough that Bernard had proved himself an extraordinary man of action. He had had a dream of the good he might be able to do in a world too much dedicated to material gain. That he had spent so many years of his life on the side of a mountain peak rebuilding, all by himself, the church and all the monastic buildings of an abbey long destroyed was surprising enough. As he explained it to me now, he had persuaded a local builder in the valley to give him a diesel engine and an ancient wartime jeep. He would come down early in the morning, bring his materials to a site in the valley, attach steel, lumber and whatever else he needed to a steel line, then drive back to the top to start his diesel and haul his material to the top of the cliff. He built the walls, then the roofs, and then painfully laid the tiles, all by himself. One snowy day he had even rolled over the jeep in an icy skid. But he had finished the job and begun what he referred to as his mission to the world of achievers who had had no time for God.

In the summers, he did have some help from young volunteers from villages in the valley who would come up to camp at the mountain and help Bernard in his work.

How many of us can look back at the end of our lives and see that we have actually fulfilled the vision we had set for ourselves many years earlier? They say our reach must always exceed our grasp. In Bernard's case, he had the satisfaction of knowing that he had accomplished what he had set out to do. How many of us can truthfully say the same?

Bernard came from solid stock. The Chabannes family was one that had distinguished itself throughout French history. They had been marshals of France, kings' advisers, cardinals. Bernard's father had been a landowner in central France. A saintly man, he had had ten children of whom seven had become monks or nuns. It could clearly be said that there was a strong religious streak in that family, as well as a drive for achievement.

There were no business guests at the Abbey during the time we were there. They would come later in the spring and summer in small groups, by invitation.

On the second day of our stay, the abbess told us that on the coming weekend there would be a visit to the abbey by a number of regional church dignitaries. Did we want to help in the preparations? My wife, who was a great cook, said she would be happy to bake a cake. She was given 36 eggs and shown the kitchen. Unfortunately, the nuns helping her had to spend ten minutes out of every hour in silent prayer in the church.

This meant that every hour all cooking had to stop no matter what. My own role was simpler. I volunteered for the carpentry shop, much to my wife's amusement. In this unlikely role, and under the supervision of a young monk, I built both chairs and tables over several days. My wife was convinced that any chair I might build would bring to the floor some well-upholstered prelate. Fortunately, we were gone a day or two before the visit occurred.

Before leaving on Saturday we went to Bernard's cell. He had his books there, his work desk for his international correspondence, and his radio so that he could get the BBC news each day. We knelt before him. He blessed and embraced each of us. We knew we would never see him again.

We went back to the room to pick up our knapsacks, said goodbye to the abbess and headed back down the road on foot to the village below. We did not talk on the way down. We were lost in our own thoughts.

Before leaving, as he was blessing us, Bernard told us that the local bishop of Perpignan and his own abbot had told him that when he died he would be buried under the altar of the chapel he had so carefully rebuilt. This obviously meant a great deal to him.

It was not to be. A few days before his 90th birthday, Bernard had a massive heart attack. He was brought down by helicopter to a hospital, but afterwards was obliged to stay at the monastery in Dourgne, forbidden to return to his beloved mountain peak.

A few months later I received a brief note from his abbot:

"On Friday last, Père Bernard de Chabannes, *toujours debout* (still standing), went to join his brethren in the peace of the Lord."

Unless someday he is canonized, his remains will undoubtedly never be returned to lie in peace beneath the altar of his Chapel on the mountain.

In God's world it doesn't pay to have earthly aspirations, no matter how slight or how much merited.

Bernard had fulfilled his dream. He had early in life in his monastery reached the conclusion that the successful men of this world, the politicians, the businessmen, the bankers, had failed to understand that there was more to life than earthly success. He would try to make them see by rebuilding this shrine in the mountains to which they might come, that one could come closer to God through beauty and music and time for reflection.

That President Mitterand himself, hardly a man of principle, would have awarded him France's most important decoration, indicated that he was not unaware that my relative had struck a chord among the French of the 20th century.

There are not many saints in my story, but Bernard is certainly one of them.

I trust he will be there to intercede for me when I show up one day at the gates of heaven.

The author visits with Père Bernard, who was close to 90 years old, at the Benedictine Monastery in Dourgne, France.

A view of the monastery which Père Bernard rebuilt by himself over 35 years in the Pyrenees mountains.

XXVI

RUSSIA AND THE KRIEBLE FOUNDATION

I *FIRST CAME TO KNOW* Dr. Robert Krieble when, as chairman of the Loctite Corporation, he came to attend a seminar for chief executives of multinational companies which I had organized at the Management Center of the University Geneva in Switzerland. These seminars took place twice a year in the spring and the fall. They lasted eight days, which was about the length of time that chief executive officers could stand being away from their offices. I had the good fortune to think up the idea of choosing a company for each such session which had gone through a difficult period requiring the replacement of its chief executive. The first case we took was Volkswagen, the German auto manufacturer which in the prior year had lost some seventy million dollars. I had invited the new CEO to come to Geneva to speak to us. The previous afternoon, I had gathered my class of some forty-five CEO's from all over the world, given them five years of Volkswagen financial statements, divided them into five groups and told each group that it constituted the board of directors of Volkswagen. Should they move the company out of Germany where taxes and the cost of labor were very high, get out of the automobile business, or take some other drastic action? Each group would appoint one member who would then report to the new CEO of the company the following morning what his group thought Volkswagen's strategic policy should be. The new CEO would be flying in the next morning to spend the day with us. When I had taken him back to his Lear jet in the afternoon, I had asked him if he had enjoyed his day with us.

A student, friend, then partner in Russia

"I am the head of a large German company," he said. "The law requires that I have on my supervisory board a government representative from any province of Germany in which Volkswagen has a plant. Then I also must have a designee from each of Volkswagen's labor unions. It is true I have a few other chief executive officers of German companies on my board but they would not dream of giving me advice, any more than I would on any boards of German companies on which I serve. The chief executive officer of a German company is expected to know what he is doing. This meeting today, while very unusual, was extremely interesting for me, and I learned a great deal listening to the viewpoint of my peers. I would be happy to repeat the experience again."

The formula turned out to be a great success. Giving chief executives a chance to restructure the business of another company is like turning a group of children loose in a candy store. The exercise gave my class a respite from serious management problems. The seminar had received rave reviews and so I had no problem finding CEOs to attend later seminars.

Americans have a tendency to think that they know all there is to know about international operations. Few Americans attended my seminars in Switzerland. I had, therefore, been very glad to have an American like Bob Krieble attend, and I had spent time getting to know him there.

Afterwards, we kept up our relationship. Bob was a most interesting businessman with a broad knowledge of international operations, conservative Germanic in his desire to make all business decisions himself, simple in his tastes, very hard-working, dedicated to his business. He had married very young. With his wife and one secretary he had started his business of making chemical sealants. The company had been entirely financed from within, never going to the financial markets for additional capital. Bob was the son of a professor of chemistry at Yale. When the boy was only eleven his father had asked the president of Johns Hopkins how he should be educated. "Send him to us for five years, and we will see that he graduates from here with a Bachelor of Science, a Masters and a Ph.D." So it had come to pass. Bob Krieble received all three degrees before he became sixteen. He had then gone to work for General Electric. One day a chemist had sent GE a formula which could create a sealant which would bind metal to metal either permanently or for a predetermined period of time. When GE decided the product represented too small a market to be of interest, Bob tested it out with his father and then created Loctite Corporation on his own. The company turned out to be a great success. Becoming a Fortune 500 company listed on the New York Stock Exchange made Bob a very wealthy man, his closest collaborators millionaires.

One day Bob and I were having lunch in Washington as we did quite often. "I have just fired myself," he said. "I don't think anyone should be the president of a Fortune 500 company at the age of 70."

"What are you going to do, Bob?"

He looked at me. "I am going to destroy the Soviet Empire. They have the best-educated people in the world. If they could only communicate with each other, they would do away with the tyranny that has engulfed them. All they need are simple computer systems that are not even classified. I want to use my money to make this possible."

Unlike Père Bernard in the previous chapter, Bob Krieble held no religious beliefs. He was a scientist. If it couldn't be proven, it didn't exist. He had made a great deal of money and had sacrificed much in doing so: his children, family life, leisure time. But now at the end of his life, he too had a dream arrived at unemotionally as a man of reason would: free the Russian people from the tyranny of Communism. He admired Russian scientific achievements, their conquest of space, their stress on mathematics and physics in education, the powers of concentration exhibited in their mastery of chess. Bob was not a reader of Russian novels, an admirer of Russian music or ballet. But he was profoundly outraged that thugs like Lenin, Stalin and Beria would have prevented Russian capacity for free expression for 75 years. He was now determined to use the money he had accumulated to destroy these evil men in the Kremlin who were responsible. He would free the Russian people. It was a dream worthy of a great man.

He would destroy the Soviet Empire.

It was not so easy. At that time, not even the simplest computers could be exported to the Soviet Union. Through Pakistani friends of mine who exported American computers from Germany to Poland we managed to get some into the Soviet bloc.

With the advent of Mikael Gorbachev and the opening of the Soviet Union to American visitors, Bob saw a new way of getting across his message about the value of democratic ideals and of the free enterprise system. Through his friend Paul Weyrich and his relationships with other conservatives in the Congress, Bob organized visits to the Soviet Union by young Congressional staff members who had had considerable experience in U.S. election processes. When Boris Yeltsin decided to run for the presidency of Russia in 1991, it was the first time in the history of Russia that anyone had ever run for high office. These young electoral experts chosen by Paul and financed by Bob, went over to Moscow to explain to Yeltsin's campaign managers how you got out the vote, disseminated information about the candidate, and, most important of all, made sure that the opposition did not tamper with the ballot boxes. There were young men in the group who had good experience in this regard from Chicago and New Orleans. The upshot, of course, was that Boris Yeltsin became the first high official elected in Russia through any kind of democratic process.

The new president of Russia then sent a message to James Baker, President Bush's secretary of state, that he would like to come to the United States to meet with the American president.

Baker sent back a message that the president would not receive him. It must be remembered that, at that time, the Communist Party was still in control of the Soviet Union, and the Bush administration had established a close relationship with Mikael Gorbachev, the new head of the Communist Party.

The American president did not want to do anything which might jeopardize that relationship.

Yeltsin already had his bags packed. He turned to the man who had so successfully managed his campaign and said, "Shouldn't we get hold of that old man who was so helpful to you in explaining how to prepare for an election? He may tell us what to do."

Bob had received the phone call in the middle of the night. The next day he sent word back that the Congress would invite the new president of Russia to visit and if he accepted, the president of the United States would then have to see him. That is what happened. Yeltsin came, and was received by and addressed Congress. He also met with President George Bush and with Jim Baker. That meant that when Chairman Gorbachev a few months later was seized by the party conservatives who wanted to reinstate the old Communist Party apparatus, Yeltsin was able to count on Bush's support in holding out against them. Yeltsin's victory signified the end of the Soviet Union and its Eastern European Empire.

It might well be said that "the old man" had played a very key role in the destruction of the Soviet tyranny. Bob Krieble now decided that his Krieble Institute should go beyond explaining to the Russians how democracy worked and focus on economics as well as politics. He asked me to be in charge of organizing a group of businessmen who would be willing to make trips to Russia and throughout the former Soviet Empire to explain how the free enterprise system worked in the United States. I was fascinated by what we might be able to do in a country that for 75 years had only known one producer and one customer—the State.

My job was to prepare a series of lectures covering the various aspects of business including production, marketing, finance and research. Obviously, this represented a totally new concept to the Russians since during the Communist regime, it was only the State that designed and manufactured products.

It was an exciting assignment, and I felt thoroughly at home with preparing what I thought Russian businessmen would have to know if they were going to participate in the West's free enterprise system. But what a challenge! Russians had never had to be concerned with product quality, with marketing, budgets, product development, product life cycles, capital requirements, earnings projections or any of the other requirements of business as practiced in the Western democracies.

Russia and the Krieble Foundation

It was one thing after World War II to rebuild the economies of Europe and Japan when factories had been destroyed, but businessmen understood what it took to run a business. In Czechoslovakia and Hungary it was possible to find people who had participated before the war in an economy which recognized private property and private industry. But Russia! The Industrial Revolution which had transformed Western Europe, the United States and Japan had only briefly existed in Russia before the Bolshevik Revolution had destroyed all private property and private initiative. How would it be possible to reach people who had never known how the Western system of private enterprise functioned, where private property did not exist, where there was no judicial system to protect the individual against the excesses of the State, where no one understood product quality, or marketing, or research on finance? It was a staggering challenge made even greater by the sheer size of the Soviet Empire which stretched over eleven time zones and covered twenty percent of the earth's surface.

Upon careful reflection it seemed to me that I would have to limit my focus on what made the free enterprise system in the Western democracies function so effectively to one overriding characteristic. Bob might not altogether have approved, but I concluded it would have to be competition and the role of government in preventing anti-competitive behavior. For the Soviet Union there had been no competition. The State controlled all economic, as well as all political activity.

Our economic system is based on competition.

Once you decide that competition is the key, the rest is easy. It is competition that forces you to produce products of quality at an affordable price, to spend money on marketing, and on research. The need of competing businesses for finance creates competition among financial institutions.

My job for Bob was to prepare the course materials we would need, covering production questions, quality and cost, how to finance a company, how to market products, how to engage in research so as to be sure to maintain a flow of new products. My past business and legal activities and my teaching background made it possible for me to do this.

With the help of Bob and other directors of the Krieble Foundation, I prepared a list of heads of American companies who might be willing, at their own expense, to go to Russia and participate with us in these seminars. I wanted to find for each trip, if possible, a senior executive in production, in marketing, in research and in finance.

To Bob, comfort, luxurious accommodations, or good food were unnecessary. We flew coach, stayed in supposedly first-class hotels where there was often no heat, no hot water, and often only cabbage, stale bread and ersatz coffee for breakfast. No wonder vodka was such a staple of the Russian diet.

When we went to the cities in Russia, we would charter Russian jets. In most instances, we would have to land at very small air fields. Two miles away, the pilots would cut the engines and glide in. This terrified some of our speakers. But our Russian military pilots were accomplished flyers and never missed a runway.

Since none of the teaching staff spoke Russian or any of the languages of Eastern Europe, we had to have our talks interpreted. Sometimes there was simultaneous interpretation. But I much preferred having an interpreter beside me. We generally had the same women interpreters, who traveled with us wherever we went. Having my interpreter beside me was most important to me. She could tell—which I couldn't—whether her translation was reaching the audience or not, and could then quietly mention this to me so that I could, if necessary, explain my thought further. Speaking through an interpreter is very easy once you get the hang of it: using simple phrases wherever possible, stopping for a translation after each thought, letting the interpreter not fall behind, above all not confusing her in what you are trying to say. Most important, I always briefed my interpreter carefully before each session we would be doing together and went over any materials with her that I would be leaving with the students. After a while it became a game with my interpreter working as hard as I was in getting the message across.

The reaction of the audience varied with the location. In areas of Russia where there had been military or scientific installations, the audience was relatively sophisticated because people in that city would have been allowed to travel outside the Soviet bloc. On the other hand, in the agricultural centers like Voronezh where there were community farms, people were still Communists and largely uninterested in what we had to say. In Budapest, because the Russians had purposely allowed Hungary to experiment with Western methods such as trade banks and semi-private pharmaceutical companies, we did not have to explain very much. People understood what we were saying and were only anxious to have Western ideas come as soon as possible. Perhaps the most interesting area was Perm, center of the penitentiary centers—the Gulag—where spouses and children of those in prison or recently released were particularly interested in what we had to say. They knew better than anyone else how destructive the Communist system had been to the country's development.

When we arrived for our first lecture one morning in Rostov on the Don River, I was greeted by a man wearing a Polish military cap, a Chinese silk shirt with puff sleeves and military trousers with a red stripe down one side. He was the elected leader—for three years—of the region's Cossacks. He spoke little English, but he explained to me that whenever I might come again I should stay with him rather than at the hotel. Later he took me to the Cossack Museum in Rostov.

The Cossacks throughout Russian history had been farmers charged with the defense of the country against the Turks to the south. When Stalin came to power he had collectivized their farms in both the Rostov area and in the Ukraine. Despite this, when the Germans invaded, the Cossacks had played a major role in defending Stalingrad and South Russia against the invaders.

That night at dinner the Cossack mayor of Rostov told me he had ten brothers, of whom seven had died in World War II fighting against the Germans.

He told me an interesting story that evening. In the 14th century, the Poles had invaded southern Russia and seized vast territories inhabited by Cossack farmers. The Polish princes occupying the land had then come down to the area with their estate managers who were Jews.

"You haven't been paying the rents you should to your Russian landlords. From now on we will double the rents and you will pay them to our Jewish estate managers or lose your property."

As soon as the Russians had reconquered their lands, the Cossacks took their guns and their horses and took off for Warsaw to execute every Jewish estate manager they could lay their hands on. This was the origin he said of the pogroms which took place after that so frequently in Russia and, according to the mayor, was at the heart of feelings of hatred between Russians and Jews.

The response of the American business executives Bob or I spoke to was remarkable. Considering that many of these men were in their sixties, that they volunteered to give three weeks of their precious time to go to cities all over Russia, to teach for several hours a day, to live in very uncomfortable hotels often without heat or hot water, to eat atrocious food, and pay their own way, was truly extraordinary. They never complained. Some went back a second and third time. I don't believe businessmen from any other country would have done the same. It made me feel very proud of being an American. Bob himself went on all the trips four times a year, three cities each trip. We did all of the eastern bloc countries in addition to the former Soviet Union even including Albania. On most trips Bob's wife Nancy also came along. All told, our group must have lectured to some 80,000 persons during the course of these trips throughout the former Soviet Empire.

I had to explain how as new technologies were developed, one had to be prepared to reevaluate the value of one's products because the shelf life of a product was constantly being shortened. Technological change was a constant in today's competitive economy.

Russia has one of the finest educational systems in the world. A great many of our listeners were physicists or mathematicians. Although they had only very rudimentary notions of business accounting, they learned very quickly the importance of cash flows, budgetary procedures, and returns on capital.

What surprised me the most was that wherever we went in the former Soviet Union, the first question at the end of my talk always was: "Thibaut, in your country how did you solve ethnic problems?" This was obviously the biggest concern in Russian society but for some reason foreign observers there never seem to comment on this. There are hundreds of different races and ethnic strains in the former Soviet Union. There was even one republic in Siberia where the population was largely Jewish. Stalin had sent them there because he didn't trust the Jews. There are Chinese, Mongols, Tartars, Cossacks, Jews, Turks, Afghans, Uzbeks, Kazaks, Germans, Poles, Georgians to name only a few. The second question which always surprised me was the theme of fairness. "What is a fair profit in your capitalist system?" My answer to this was always linked to the concept of competition as the motivating force in capitalist society. "Charge whatever you think is fair because if you charge too much, others will go into competition with you and bring prices down. The role of government is simply to prevent monopolies from abusing their power and to make sure competition can subsist."

This was a very novel theory for the Russians. It was only in parts of the Soviet Empire that had experienced the capitalist system before the war, in Hungary, Poland and Czechoslovakia, that people still understood how our economic system in the West functioned.

Russia and the Krieble Foundation

There is nothing that brings people closer together than participation in a dangerous or uncomfortable exercise. That was certainly true of the Krieble Institute's trips to the former Soviet Union. On many of these trips we used charter jet aircraft piloted by former Soviet military personnel. Most airports in Russia are small, and very inadequately equipped. We were fortunate to have excellent military pilots. Still, every landing was an adventure. There is very little aviation fuel. We paid for fuel in dollars at an artificial rate of exchange. This ensured absolute priority for whatever fuel was available. Several times at airports in Siberia near the Chinese border we would find thousands of stranded Russian merchants who had been buying merchandise in Manchuria for resale in Russia. You can imagine the dearth of the simplest manufactured products in Russia if they think of shopping in Manchuria! These people would have been waiting for as much as two weeks for planes that never arrived because there was no fuel available. Passengers would be camping at the airport. There were no rooms and little food available. The dirt and the stench were indescribable. Yet the crowds would continue to wait patiently for planes which never seemed to come. The patience of the Russians cannot be overstated or understood by a Westerner. Where one has had very little chance to buy, acceptance of deprivation becomes the norm. In the cities we visited where there were no hotels with restaurants, no movie houses or music halls, or places to dine, or sports stadiums, there was little for young people to do in the evenings. A young man could take his girl for a walk but that was about it, and as for television there was only concert music or lectures—no news. Reading the great Russian classics and conversation, endless conversation, had become the only means of entertainment.

In America there is no conversation.

I remember an evening in Washington when one of my business friends whom I had taken on one of our trips invited me to dinner with two Russian women he had met there. One was a young girl who had married an American and now lived in Baltimore. The other was her 42-year-old mother. I asked the daughter how she liked life in the United States. "It is terrible," she said. "We get up early in the morning so my husband can go to his office in town at 8:00 a.m. He returns at 6:00 p.m. and turns on the television sports channel. If we have people for dinner, the men talk of baseball, the women of their children. There is no discussion." The mother echoed her daughter's remarks. "My husband was a general and paymaster of all military installations. We lived very well and had a large apartment in Moscow. Now that he is dead, I have a much smaller place. But a friend may call at midnight to ask 'are you awake and are you alone?' She will then come over and we will talk for several hours. There is no conversation in your country." I went home and reflected on that evening. In Russia, conversation is truly the opiate of the people.

We were in Moscow when the counter revolution to return the country to Communism took place in 1995. The Parliament—the Duma—had been sealed off by Yeltsin's army and police. My friend Ralph Hofstetter and I were dining with the deputy who was chairman of the Foreign Trade Committee of the Parliament. After dinner, around midnight, he asked if we would like to visit the Parliament and talk to some of the members who were holed up there. We took a taxi within a few blocks of there, walked through the police and military lines by showing his pass, crawled under the barbed wire and through the Parliamentary defense lines on the other side and through the gate of the building. All was dark inside because electricity had been cut off. The men who greeted us wore masks over their faces and carried submachine guns. We had to crawl up the stairs in the dark. On the third floor we were ushered into a room where we sat by candlelight for an hour or two with a group of deputies from Siberia who told us they had no particular affection for those who sought to overthrow the Yeltsin government. They were determined to remain in the Parliament only because they had been sent there by their constituents and would not yield to pressure.

Eventually we made our way back to the main gate the same way we had come. Our taxi was still waiting beyond the battle lines to return us to our hotel. The next morning the troops took over the Parliament building while helicopters fluttered overhead. The counter revolution was over. To the population of Moscow the turmoil had meant little. The foreigners in the city might try to flee, but to the Muscovites what could all this possibly mean to their daily lives?

One day when we were in Moscow, I received a phone call from a man who identified himself as staff officer and interpreter to the commanding general of the armored division south of Moscow. He told me the general and his colleague in charge of the armored division just north of Moscow would like to meet with me and any of the Krieble group who were in Moscow. Two days later the two generals and the staff officer joined my two friends and I at our hotel for lunch in a private dining room. I had been warned that the two generals might decide not to come in uniform because the strong feeling among the population of Moscow against the military as a result of the loss of the war in Afghanistan, but the two generals showed up at lunch in full dress uniforms covered with decorations. It was hard to tell who commanded in the north and who in the south. Both officers were very broad shouldered paratroopers with close-cropped hair and an inspiring physique. They were quite relaxed and explicit about why they had wished to meet with us. They were also very blunt.

"We are well aware of the American experience following the return of your troops after the Americans lost the war in Vietnam. Your military were very unpopular with the public which was only interested in quickly forgetting about an unsuccessful and unpopular war. The situation could have turned out to be very nasty. Your soldiers had been led into a situation that had not been properly planned, organized, or executed. Many of their comrades had disappeared or been killed in battle. They were angry and disheartened. They thought the people should have welcomed them home with open arms. They were not prepared for the way they were treated when they came home to America. It is the same thing in Russia. The two of us parachuted with our men over Kabul, the capital of Afghanistan. We were never told what we were meant to accomplish in that dreadful country or why we were there. Now we are back and reviled by the public and a government which will not even pay our salaries half the time. What we want to know from you is how the civilian authorities in your various states made it possible for your soldiers to be reintegrated in your civilian society. We know you accomplished this because there were no riots and no bloodshed in the United States after the war was lost. We must learn from those in your country who helped solve this problem because we must do the same here. If the bulk of our soldiers are not reinstated into the civilian society, there will be real trouble and perhaps even civil war."

"We also have another problem. We are very much concerned with the fate of our officers. They are intelligent, patriotic, superbly trained to defend the country, and now they have no role to play in this new Russian society, of which we have little knowledge. Will your Krieble group, which has been trying so effectively to aid our people to adjust to a more democratic society, help us? We know nothing about your so-called free enterprise system in which people are expected to survive and prosper on their own initiative. But if anybody can adjust it seems to us our officers should be able to, if what is expected of them can be explained to them. We don't want your military people to come over here and tell us. We want civilians like yourselves. Will you help us achieve these two goals? It has to be in your interest as well as ours."

It was obvious to us that these two senior officers were extremely concerned about both these matters. In the manner of military people, they were very direct in expressing their views. Fortunately, one of the business friends I had brought to the lunch had headed a civilian agency in his state of Louisiana, organized to help reintegrate retiring servicemen from Vietnam into civilian society. He explained carefully what had been done in his state. We also assured them that we would arrange to visit both their encampments on subsequent trips to Russia, to discuss before groups of officers the nature of how the political systems in the West functioned and what role military officers trained in physics, mathematics, or engineering might play in a competitive free enterprise open society.

It was a most unusual, open discussion. Here were two very senior military officers who for so long had been regarded as arch-enemies of the United States, but who were now faced with a very real problem which was in our interest just as much of theirs to resolve.

All three of us Americans who attended the lunch believed we had been given a rare opportunity to break into a closed society in a way which might give our country an opportunity to break down Cold War barriers. On returning to the United States I tried to enlist the Atlantic Council board of directors to take this on as a project, but unfortunately there was little interest. I believe this was a great mistake, because we could have cemented American relations with the Russian military elite who needed our assistance.

One ironic touch: at one point during the lunch I asked each of our two senior guests where in the Soviet Union he came from. One

said Kiev, the other Minsk. "But then you are not Russians anymore," I said, "since one is the capital of the Ukraine and the other the capital of Byelorussia." Both generals jumped up like corks out of a bottle, "What do you mean we are not Russians?" I realized then how artificial all these new barriers that have been created can turn out to be.

Bob Krieble had earlier funded the purchase of a former aristocrat's town house in the residential section of Moscow. He had donated the building to the Center for Liberal Conservative Policy a new democratic party headed by Arkady Murashev, President Yeltsin's former commander of the Moscow metropolitan police force, a parliamentary unit

538

of 180,000 men. Although very young, Arkady had played a leading role in Yeltsin's presidential campaign. He and his beautiful wife had spent time in the United States learning about politics in a democratic society. They both were intelligent, spoke good English, and were dedicated to creating a democratic society in Russia. Their integrity would make it difficult for them to exercise a position of power in the later days of the Yeltsin administration but, even so, they were highly recognized for their honesty. There were unfortunately few like them among Yeltsin's close advisors. Arkady is hard working, personable, ambitious. He will undoubtedly occupy a position of power when the Russian people finally decide to replace the current group of politicians interested only in their own power and wealth. He has the intellectual capacity to exercise great responsibility. He also has a sense of humor which will stand him in good stead until the day arrives when he again may be called upon to serve his country.

Russia and the Krieble Foundation

While Bob Krieble had asked me to run the business programs of the Krieble Institute in the former Soviet Union, his friend Paul Weyrich was in charge of the political programs. This meant I often traveled with Paul. Paul Weyrich by anyone's standards is a remarkable personality; highly intelligent, hard working, an arch-conservative in his political views with a terrible temper, very religious (Paul is a Deacon of the Antioch Rite of the Catholic Church, a sect midway between the Roman Catholic Church and the Russian Orthodox Church). As allowed in the Orthodox Church, Paul is married and has several children. His church is also recognized by the Church of Rome. This was made clear to me one day when two of my Catholic business executives and I attended the Mass with Paul at the Catholic Cathedral in Prague. Paul had excused himself and disappeared into the sacristy. "How would you like to take Holy Communion from Paul Weyrich, I asked my two businessmen?" When the priest came in followed by Paul dressed in his vestments, the priest announced to the congregation that he was highly honored to have Father Weyrich of Washington D.C. officiate with him at the Mass.

Paul Weyrich— a man of many talents

Later, Paul and I went to Vladivostok together. This was probably the most interesting of the trips I took for the Krieble Foundation. Vladivostok, the home base of the Soviet Far Eastern fleet and the nearest naval base to the United States, had occupied a very strategic location during the Cold War. In 1904, the Russian Tsarist fleet had been destroyed by the Japanese Navy at Tsushima, an event which the Soviet Navy was not about to forget. Vladivostok was a city totally under military control. To leave the city required a permit issued from Moscow, eleven time zones to the west. The same was true for anyone coming into the city. When we went in 1995, we were the first Americans ever allowed to visit the city since the Soviet Revolution. The first day of our conferences there we explained that we were not part of the CIA and indeed had no U.S. government sponsorship or connection whatsoever. By the third day we had established a warm relationship with our audience who naturally were full of questions regarding the United States, its policies, its economic system, the reasons for its wealth and power, its attitude toward Russia. On Saturday, I spent the whole afternoon small-boat sailing through the whole Russian Far East Fleet with two Russian seminar friends.

It was a cold and foggy afternoon. The cruisers and destroyers of the Russian Navy stood out, grey and forbidding, seemingly emptied of life, a grim reminder of a vanished world of military power. On Sunday Paul Weyrich had asked if I would like to attend religious services with him. When I came down to the lobby to meet him, I found him dressed in Russian Orthodox vestments with a toque to match. We took a taxi to the Orthodox cathedral. There little old ladies genuflected and tried to kiss his ring. The church, to my surprise, was filled with just as many young people as old. Everyone to my amazement knew and recited all the prayers of the service, proof that persecution in religion only strengthens one's faith. Prayers must have been carefully passed on orally from mother to children for 75 years since there had been no religious services during the Communist years!

The strength of religious fervor throughout Russia was one of the aspects of Russian society that surprised me the most. I had not expected to find faith that strong. In the United States the Church plays a very active political role in addition to its religious and educational activity. In Western Europe, church attendance has declined markedly. If in the West the Catholic and Episcopalian Churches are in decline, in the former Soviet Union, faith was like a fire that had been left smoldering for all that time and that now was allowed to burst into flame again. If anything is to help Russian society recover its equilibrium after the turmoil of the past eighty-five years, it may well be this religious faith.

My relationship with Paul Weyrich was a complicated one. He had favored my taking charge at the Krieble Institute of recruiting American executives to go to the former Soviet empire to explain the values of the American free enterprise system. But what interested him most in his relationship with the Krieble Institute was not so much bringing light to the former Communist darkness as making use of Bob Krieble's wealth and standing in the American business community, to restore what Paul considered the loss of moral integrity in the United States. As a churchman, a moralist, and a former conservative journalist, Paul was convinced that only a new dedication to conservative values would save the United States from moral decline. He wanted the Krieble Institute to operate out of his center in Washington rather than as an independent entity. While he respected my teaching ability, business experience and contacts, Paul preferred to see Bob's financial resources spent in pushing conservative causes at home. The success of the Gingrich "Contract with America" in 1994 had held out to Paul the possibility that the United States was at last headed for a rebirth of conservative values. What he wanted to do was to capitalize on this trend. Paul is a moral perfectionist, a Calvin, a Cromwell, a Savanarola. I admired him but I did not really like him. Life has taught me to be wary of extremists. In my view it is extremely dangerous to think that one is always right. It is perhaps a great strength. But where are we if not humble, if we have no sense of humor and have always to take ourselves seriously. If we were to succeed in creating an appreciation for democratic aspirations in Russia, and an understanding of the benefits of our free enterprise system, it was surely not to sell extremist positions, even if morally sound, to those who had only just escaped from Communist extremism.

Russia and the Krieble Foundation

In Iraq today, under American occupation, it seems to me there is much to be learned from the experience of successive American administrations in Russia under Presidents George Herbert Bush and Bill Clinton. But Iraq is far more serious. The current administration, it seems to me, would be very wise to call upon the expertise of Paul Weyrich—one of its own—who did so well in making it possible for the Krieble Institute to succeed in the former Soviet Union. Forget democracy, except as a goal. Paul had carefully selected some eighty well-educated young men from all over Russia and eastern Europe who were then trained for several weeks in the United States in our political and economic system. The were sent back to the cities where they came from equipped with fax machines to help organize the Krieble Institute seminars and to publicize what we wished to accomplish. Similarly, in Iraq, the administration might select, train, hire and send back young Iraquis who could then serve as a nucleus of representatives elected locally all over the country. As I explained in chapter XIV, a group of us proved the effectiveness of this in New York City after World War II.

Weyrich could help.

It may not be democratic but it worked. Paul understands this, as my friend Joe Broderick did. These locally designated persons would be in a position to replace the Iraqi governing group imposed on the country by our Defense Department as part of the occupying power. Certainly the political makeup of Iraq is no more complicated than that of our large cities in the United States today.

In Moscow in the 1990s, our embassy had even gone out of its way to tell the Russian government that we were in no way connected with the U.S. government or its agencies. It was, however, certainly true. I suppose the reason for this attitude at the American Embassy in Moscow went back to the refusal of the Bush administration to have any dealings with Boris Yeltsin even after he was elected president of Russia in the first free election that had ever taken placed anywhere in the former Soviet Union. When Bill Clinton became president, United States policy toward Russia was handled either by the president himself; by Vice President Al Gore who was given a special assignment to coordinate policy with Chernomyrdin, his counterpart in the Russian government, or by Deputy Secretary of State Talbott, a former *Time* journalist and editor who spoke fluent Russian and had been interested in Russian affairs since his days as a Yale student. It reminded me very much of how American policy towards China had been handled during World War II. American press representatives in China rarely left Chungking and had no idea what was happening in that vast country, being fed only what information the Chinese authorities chose to give them. The Chiang government in China didn't want American journalists going around China. But this was not true in Russia after Yeltsin's election. American journalists were free to travel in Russia. But they seemed very reluctant to do so, except perhaps to go to St. Petersburg which is one of the world's most beautiful cities. We did take one senior American journalist who asked to go on one of our trips to three cities of southern Russia but after a few days she was delighted to take a plane back to Moscow. If France had always meant Paris to the press, then certainly Russia meant Moscow to American government officials and journalists after the Soviet Union ceased to exist. It was of course true that travel in Russia was never easy but we chartered planes and wherever we went the groundwork for our teaching program would always have been planned by the Krieble Institute representative on the spot, the local officials, and the university if there was one in that locality. There was never any problem in meeting with the leading officials of the city or province. Often they relied on us to tell them what was happening not only outside of Russia but in Moscow as well. It must be remembered that Moscow was 11 time zones away from Vladivostok. There was little love lost between the Russian officials in Moscow and the leaders in other parts of Russia, many of whom were the same Communist officials who had run the provinces in the past and were determined insofar as possible to maintain their independence from the central authority. The Communist Party in Russia had published in the newspapers the Party controlled in Moscow a virulent attack on the Krieble Institute headlined "Agents of Influence." This turned out to be helpful to us in cities outside of Moscow where attacks by the Party in the Party press could only be helpful to our talks in favor of democracy and the establishment of a free enterprise system.

We made sure the Communist Party attack on Krieble was distributed to key members of Congress. It resulted in a formal motion passed by the Congress extolling the work Bob and the Krieble Institute were doing in the former Soviet Union. Bob deserved this Congressional accolade. The entire Krieble Institute group rendered a great service to our country with its work in the former Soviet Empire. I am very proud of having played such an important role in its activities.

It may seem strange to people in the United States to think that successive American administrations could have so little appreciation for the hopes and aspirations of people all over this vast country of Russia, who were hoping that the United States would free them from seventy-five years of tyranny, help them establish a rule of law, and restore private property. Instead, the United States government in the first Bush and in the Clinton administrations helped perpetuate a system which was unaccountable, corrupt, and inefficient. I met with many Central Bank officials in various parts of the country. Soon after Gorbachev came to power, they had established a tax treaty with Cyprus providing for maximum security of accounts and used Cyprus from then on as a method through which Russian funds could be laundered into Switzerland and the West. It certainly didn't take long for the Party hierarchy and corrupt officials in the Gorbachev and Yeltsin governments to figure out how to get out of Russia the funds which were coming in from the United States and the IMF. It is hard to understand why the Clinton administration was so willing to accept the corruption of Yeltsin's rule in post-Communist Russia or at least try to control it.

In Khabarosk, the capital of the province of Eastern Siberia, I was invited, along with the two American businessmen who had accompanied me, to a meeting with two local businessmen and a provincial official. They wanted us to participate in a scheme to take advantage of privatization when it came. The suggestion was that we should provide them with funds to rent the principal business buildings in the city. We would be equal partners. When privatization came, they said, those who were renting the buildings would be given priority to purchase the buildings at a very attractive price available only to lessees. This would mean that the partners would reap enormous profits out of eventual resale of what we would have acquired at very discounted values. We cut short the discussion. Shortly thereafter, I received a delegation of the people we had addressed in our lectures. They told me this was going on all over the country. I assured them that we would never participate in this kind of scheme. They were very relieved. Less apparent was the manner in which government-owned businesses were privatized through distribution of shares to Communist managers and their friends in government.

Today there are at least seven billionaires in Russia, men who during the Yeltsin period managed to take personal advantage of a corrupt privatization process to gain great wealth. They are young, ambitious, hard-working, very well-educated, ruthless. Several now have political ambitions. Like the men who ran the Directoire in post-Revolutionary France until Napolean did away with them, these men, if they insist on a political role, run the risk of losing what they have to the new political dictatorship of President Putin, who comes out of the KGB apparatus and will never allow new men with economic power to reduce the political power of the State, which he now runs.

There were many very happy moments during these trips to the former Soviet Empire. I remember a picnic we had one evening on the shores of Lake Baikal with a group of democratic leaders of the province, a trip to a dinner at a remote "tourist" hotel on the Amur River in eastern Siberia, where the washrooms consisted of open spaces for men on one side of the inn and for women on the other. We had caviar and sturgeon for dinner and on the way home on the bus we sang alternately Russian and American folk songs. The Russians, like the Americans, are outgoing and very friendly people. We made many friends even though we did not know if we would ever see each other again. There were dinners at every city we visited, good conversation, vodka that never ran out. We were accepted because our audience knew we had come to help and asked nothing in return. There was no reason to hold anything back. Conversation was open. There was usually singing and laughter and an exchange of jokes. Each city was different. In Rostov, the head of the 3 million Cossacks in the region wore his Cossack uniform to our sessions and took me to the Cossack museum filled with exploits of Cossack actions in Russian wars. In Perm, the center of the Stalin concentration camps, our audience was the progeny of men who had been sent to the camps and died there. We arrived in the dead of night in September in a raging snowstorm. Despite the terrible stories we were told during our stay there, the audience was more interested in knowing what the future might hold in a quite different political and economic environment, rather than to dwell on the past.

Russia and the Krieble Foundation

It is not possible to think that this great people will not extricate itself from the quagmire of the past, rid itself of the current corruption and establish a system based on private property, democracy, and the rule of law. It took a short time in Poland, Hungary, Czechoslovakia and Slovenia because people there still remembered what life was like before these countries became part of the Soviet Empire. But it has to come throughout the region in time.

History has shown that revolutions do not end in democracy and the rule of law but rather in dictatorships which only gradually allow for the creation of a middle class and a more open society. There is no reason to think that the same political evolution will not happen in time in Russia. Since that country has never known anything but dictatorial rule from the whole period of the Tsars through the Communist dictatorship, it may take a long time.

Democracy in Russia will take time.

But Krieble's own dream of hastening the transition in Russia was ended by his death in 1999, while Yeltsin was still in power.

Classes at the Krieble Institute in the former Soviet Union were filled, whether it was a work day or not, because Russians were anxious to learn about the American free enterprise system.

The Krieble Institute headquarters in Moscow was the home of a Russian prince before the Revolution of 1917. It was purchased by Bob Krieble, and shared with a Russian group determined to bring democracy to Russia.

The author with Bob Krieble, and two business executives, Ralph Hosttetter and Louis Andrew, before their class at Tartu University in eastern Estonia. The 15th century university is one of the oldest in Europe.

The author in Rostov on Don in southern Russia, with Bob Krieble and the head of three million Cossacks from the region, one of the two principal Cossack areas, the other being in the Ukraine

XXVII

THE NEW CENTURY

I was born in 1918 during the last great battle by the Allies against the Germans in World War I, the war as it was said to end all wars. After it ended, later that year, the survivors wanted only to forget it and enjoy life. This lasted until the great economic depression of 1929.

New challenges ahead

The generation of which I have been a part suffered greatly in the Depression of 1929 and in World War II which followed. I had had to put myself through school, college and law school while holding a job besides; I had become a millionaire before I was forty; I had taken care of my parents financially; I had served with relative distinction in the war, been decorated, and most importantly, came home physically whole. To succeed in my business activities I had sacrificed much of my family life. I might have done a lot of things differently. I might have tried to live in the suburbs and commuted to work in New York. But my office hours would have remained impossible. Whoever said "the law is a jealous mistress" underestimated the problem by far. There is no easy answer to the demands made on a corporate lawyer in New York City. Any compromise is unsatisfactory. Combined with a practice in two nations with an ocean in between, the demands are too often prohibitive. It does little good to look backward into the past to see how one might have done things better.

In the United States, unlike Europe or other parts of the world, talk of death is unacceptable. One doesn't mention it except in times of crisis, when it occurs to others. When my first wife, Rosamond, was so sick, the doctor taking care of her told me not to talk to her about the consequences of her cancer because she wanted so much to live. Her close women friends told me the same thing. So we made no plans. Her friends told me not to speak to the children either. Looking back, I realize they were wrong. Members of a family should participate together in both good times and bad.

Each generation has to learn for itself. We can give our children love, affection, a sense of duty, a love of God, a respect for others, a code of ethics. Unfortunately, one cannot pass on intellect, talent, a sense of humor, zest for life, curiosity, and most important of all, common sense. Some of us are spendthrifts by nature; others hate to spend money on trifles. Those of us who weathered the Great Depression still hesitate to travel business or first class by air. We learned the value of money through having none.

My colleague and client, Bill Shriver, once told me, "Never worry about money, Thibaut. If you do a good job, the rewards will always follow." I followed his advice and ended up at 72, after an extraordinarily active and varied business life, with no retirement plan in place. So I had to start again. It did me no harm to do so.

I have always considered myself ambitious, but not for many of the things generally associated with ambition: wealth, big houses, tailored suits. When I was young and very poor, I used to dream of having a monogrammed silk shirt and having a Chinese valet who would be my own personal "Jeeves." I finally gained the shirt and found it couldn't be laundered. I also learned to lay out my clothes for the morrow each night before going to bed, as Jeeves himself might have done it.

Much of my life was spent in putting myself in difficult situations simply because I enjoyed the challenge of finding the solution. As a lawyer I enjoyed mastering clients' problems. B-D and St. Croix were also problems to be solved. So was working with Bill Shriver on sick companies. So was trying to teach Russians about competition and the free enterprise system—a people who had experienced two thousand years of tyranny. I might have realized sooner that that was what I enjoyed doing the most. I believe that I have served my country well in every administration from Roosevelt to George Bush. And my special love has been teaching, in part because teaching is the best way to learn. That is how I met Dr. Nasrollah Fatemi, the Iranian scholar with whom I wrote two books on international economics. We taught at Fairleigh Dickinson University together.

I have had interesting teaching assignments: all the way from tutoring the Sulzberger children to get them into college, to helping classmates in law school, to teaching at the Practicing Law Institute, MBA programs at Fairleigh Dickinson University and Wroxton Abbey (a College of Oxford) in England, to serving as Professor of International Finance and International Law at the Management Center of the University of Geneva, to MBA programs at MIT, in Trinidad and Tobago, in Colombia, to say nothing of teaching knife fighting and Chinese culture in 1945 at the OSS camp on an island off the coast of California.

I have enjoyed writing books almost as much as teaching. In addition to *The Dollar Crisis* published in 1963 and *Multinational Corporations* published in 1975, I wrote successive editions of *Trade, Inflation and the Dollar* in 1984 and *The Federal Reserve—an Intentional Mystery* in 1985. Over the past several years, I have been working on a new study on how cultural differences affect economic development. It is a subject on which I have not been able to find any published book. It may take me the rest of my life to finish it because "culture," at least in the United States, is changing so rapidly.

Above all, I have been lucky in life. My failure to work as I should have at Harvard meant that I had to do two years in one at Columbia, but this meant I graduated from law school before the war instead of in 1946 with the rest of my Harvard classmates. After a difficult second marriage I found, in facing blindness for a time, a woman with whom I could very happily spend the rest of my life. In coming home from teaching in Geneva to going back to being counsel to Coudert Brothers in New York, where I no longer wanted to be, I was given the opportunity to serve as a director of the Export-Import Bank of the United States. In 1950, I risked my life for France in Indochina. In 1998, President Chirac made me a member of the French Legion of Honor,

through the intercession of a friend who understood what I had done almost fifty years earlier. Luck was what Napoleon demanded of his generals. I have had more than most. During my time in China a friend taught me how to play serious poker, how to take advantage of a run of luck, how to sense that the cards were turning. He taught me that good luck always comes, but one must be ready to take advantage of it when it calls.

I still look forward to the years to come. I expect to teach again and continue to learn—and write, so long as I can still think of things to say.

In the first years of the new century, we are facing a very different kind of world. Americans were totally unprepared for what happened to the World Trade Center in New York on September 11, 2001. We will all remember where we were that day when the terrorists destroyed these beautiful buildings and the people in them, using two of our jet airplanes and the passengers in them to do so. Mariana and I had just turned on the television set on a beautiful morning in Stratton, Vermont. We watched each plane deliberately fly into each of those buildings. We knew immediately what was happening. It was a horror that was unimaginable. What happened to Americans that day will change America forever. Just as to most of us who remember where we were on December 7, 1941 or November 22, 1963, we will never forget the details of our lives on September 11, 2001. In many ways, the shock of this was even greater than the destruction of the U.S. fleet at Pearl Harbor, because it brought death to civilians going about their normal daily activities. We were not prepared emotionally for what happened that day. That any group of people might plan over a long period of time and then calmly carry out such an act of insanity and self-destruction has to be beyond our capacity to understand, much less accept. Worst of all, for the first time in history, we watched an attack by foreign terrorists occurring in our own home. We had never thought about how vulnerable we might be in our own country.

The New Century

How does one respond to such an act? How can recurrences be prevented? What similar actions lie ahead? How do we prepare ourselves, our children and our grandchildren to face this new era of religious intolerance, which draws no distinctions between civilians and the military, has no justification that we can understand, attacks anyone, anywhere? How does a country which prides itself on having created a free society adjust its rules to cope with such irrational behavior?

When I had my chair at the Georgetown University Center for Strategic and International Studies (CSIS), I wrote a book, with a colleague, on international terrorism. My section dealt with how to control international financial transfers to terrorist organizations. At the time, no one was interested in the subject. Now it has become very important, since so much of our oil money is going to unreliable governments who finance Moslem fundamentalist schools and even directly fund terrorist groups.

There will now certainly be changes in the way Americans conduct their lives. We must expect more government supervision: in financial transactions, to detect transfers to organizations or individuals which may have links to terrorists or to those who finance them; in telecommunications, to monitor exchanges within terrorist networks; in insurance, to spell out under what conditions the government will act as insurer of last resort. We can expect less travel overseas, particularly to areas deemed unsafe. There will be more emphasis on the discovery of new drugs which may protect the public from the spread of disease; religion will play a greater role in people's lives; life will become more serious; government will be much more intrusive; immigration

American conduct must change.

regulations will be tightened appreciably; an attempt may be made to require Americans to carry an identity card as in Europe; foreigners may be required to register with local police, if they have visitors' visas; inspections and controls over travelers will be much stricter and will discourage international travel. As a result, the cost of government will rise greatly.

We need to realize and help others realize that it is our entire civilization that is at stake here, not just our religious freedom.

Since Islam is now the religion of some one-quarter of the world's population, and that number is growing at a rate approaching three percent per year in many areas, what does this phenomenon hold out for the rest of humanity? What is the significance to our civilization that this religious fervor is occurring principally in those areas of the world where reserves of oil are located, the product on which we are wholly dependent in our advanced societies? A great writer, V. S. Naipaul, winner of the Nobel Prize in Literature for 2001, who has written a great deal about Islam, claims that the reason for the rise in Moslem extremism is not their concern by the manner in which the Israelis are treating the Palestinians, but because the people of the oil-rich Moslem countries in the Middle East and Africa were promised so much wealth by their leaders and given so little. In his view, it is not religious fervor that is at the base of extremism, but a desire to participate in a better economic life. They hold the United States accountable because it is our demands for oil that have made the countries rich.

Why is it that Americans always want to be loved? The British, French and Germans don't seem to care what others think of them. If this concerns us so much, why isn't this administration doing a better job of making others understand what our policies are trying to accomplish? We are needlessly arrogant and unresponsive to the concerns of others. We shouldn't expect the culture of other countries to mirror our own. Our society in America is too prone to violence, our children brought up to accept it through television and motion pictures, where the focus is endlessly on sex and violence. We can admire Moslem conservatism here. I gave an instance in chapter IV of how violence and sex in an American movie may give a very unfavorable image of life in America to a Chinese community. We do not export our culture well.

At the start of the 20th century, the civilized world was at peace. Britain was rich. On its empire the sun never set. It controlled transportation, insurance and trade worldwide. Its gold standard made international trade possible. Today Britain has been replaced by the United

States. But are we as prepared as Britain was to exercise that role? Britain taught us that the civilized world needed a government of laws to control the greed of men. Today the world has to accept our military might. We speak endlessly of bringing democracy all over the world. But it is not realistic to expect other countries to be governed as we are. How can democracy exist where there is no middle class to support it? One cannot do away with poverty. But it is never the poor who bring about revolutions. The man who organized the destruction of the Trade Center towers was the son of an Egyptian lawyer.

Revolutions are brought about by middle classes and intellectuals who for one reason or another are not participating in the economic benefits of the rest of society. To understand this, one has only to observe who the followers are of bin Laden.

The Chinese Communist Revolution of Mao Tse-tung was the great exception. His was truly an agrarian revolt, similar to those in 14th century France or Britain, orchestrated by starving men and women prepared to accept in their future communal living and, at most, a bicycle. I have never met a Chinese who was a Communist in the sense that Russian (or French or Italian) intellectuals were who looked upon Communism as a religious faith. China today is ruled by a political dictatorship which has accepted economic capitalism.

It has made me very proud to be both French and American. When I am in France, I see how American I am. When I am in America, I often react as a Frenchman might. I deplore what is quite apparent: that We need a cyclically the French and Americans tend to dislike each other. In the better sense days when Rome ruled the world, Athens was a place where one who of history. could afford it went to study the cultural achievements of the past. It is so today. Our culture comes from Europe and much of it from France. The French envy our power. We should envy their culture, as well as their food and their glorious wines.

We may have the wealth in the United States, but we probably don't live as well as they do in France. In the United States too many of us live to work, and then retire to play golf. In France one works only to live better, with more leisure time to read, to travel, to eat, drink and enjoy conversation. Success there is not measured by wealth as it is here, but how well a man lives with whatever he has.

In China, the ideograph for "happiness" is a woman and a pig under a roof. Not a very sophisticated conclusion but worthy of consideration. I am grateful for the time I had occasion to spend in China during the war. China is like the United States in 1870. In the coming century

China is likely to become the world's most powerful country and economically blessed, as we were.

Mariana and I have tried to create one family out of three segments. I don't know whether we will have succeeded. But if I learned nothing more out of my time in China it is that family is the core of any society and it must be of ours.

Today, my faith is very strong. I remember once my daughter, Thérèse, saying to me: "Daddy, your religion is only a crutch." "Of course it is," I replied. "You are strong and so don't need this crutch as you call it. I do." She hasn't raised the question with me again.

I have not spoken much about religious faith. I was fortunate to have had it implanted in me by my French grandmother. Like my Uncle Père Bernard de Chabannes and my friend, Bob Krieble, I too have had a dream and have sought to achieve it. Since it is ongoing, I cannot know to what extent I have succeeded.

It has been my good fortune along the way to meet a few saints, some sinners, even scalawags. Many are spoken of in this book. They are, each in their own way, the stimulus of life. I agree with Bernard that, perhaps, calumny is the only sin.

Unfortunately, educated people in the United States no longer have a sense of history, as the founders of our country did two hundred years ago. We study economics and statistics, but history is no longer taught, except as "social studies."

When my youngest daughter was married in 1999, she insisted that I wear white tie and tails, which meant decorations as well. At the end of the service, a young man came up to me and asked politely which war I was in.

"Do you remember Picket's charge," I asked him.

He seemed quite satisfied that I might have been at Gettysburg in 1863.

The author's wife,
Mariana de Saint Phalle.
A great cook, for many
years she published a
newsletter—Mariana's
Letter—giving recipes,
cooking advice and
travel notes.

The author dances with his youngest daughter,
Diane, at her wedding in 1999.

GENEALOGY OF THE
SAINT PHALLE FAMILY

Genealogy of the Saint Phalle Family*

St. Fale,[1] Abbot in 530 A.D. of Moustiers-la-Celle in Champagne

↓

Ponthus I de St. Fale starts building large castle above Troyes in Champagne (863 A.D.); has title of Baron

↓

Ponthus II (great grandson); completes castle destroyed in 1830 – *m.* – Judith de Néele in 761

↓

Robert I. – *m.* – Agnes, sister of Thibaut II, count of Champagne and king of Navarre, 1010 A.D

↓

Philippe

↓

Robert II (grandson) – *m.* – Agnes of Champagne in 1106

↓

Etienne Milon

↓

Pierre – *m.* – Jehanne de Brie

↓

Andre–Robert II – *m.* – Jeanne de Seignelay (becomes brother-in-law of Pierre, son of Louis VI, king of France)

↓

Milon – *m.* – Emmeline de Ville-Hardouin in 1135 (goes on 1st Crusade in 1147 with Thibaut III of Champagne)

↓

Pierre Etienne – *m.* – Jeanne de Brie

↓

Andre-Robert IV[2] – *m.* – Alpäis de Seignelay in 1190 (inherits Cudot[3,4] through his wife)

↓

Jobert – *m.* – Matilde

↓

---

*This genealogy traces the male line from father to son, only where confirmed by public and private archives. All collaterals are omitted.

The spelling of the family name has varied over time from Latin, to Medieval French, to the current spelling: *Sancto Fidolo, St. Fiule, St. Fale, St. Phal, Symphal, de St. Phalle.* Notes appear on page 561.

Pierre – *m.*– Brune de Foix

↓

Pierre – *m.*– Alix de la Chapelle (1278), d. 1297, buried at Cudot (crusader with St. Louis IX, king of France, captured at Tunis, ransomed by his serfs, whom he liberates)

↓

Philippe[5] – *m.*– Isabel de Loot (1325) (godson of King Philippe III, whose life he saves at battle of Mons en Pucelle (1304)

↓

Jehan – *m.*– Jehanne de Vaux (wife brings him two large properties, Cuissarts and Vaux)

↓

Philippe – *m.*– Isabelle de Molans (1402) (fights alongside Joan of Arc; made Count by Charles VII)

↓

Philippe – *m.*– Claudine de Bailly (1442); one of the captains of Charles VII and Louis XI; Knight of Malta

↓

Louis – *m.*– Marie de Brichanteau-Nangis (1496), d. in 1509; buried at Cudot

↓

Richard – *m.*– Jeanne le Fort de Villemandor (1528), d. in 1571; buried at Cudot

↓

Eustache – *m.*– Marthe de Blondeau (1567) (wife brings Villefranche[3] to marriage), d. 1602; served Henry II, Charles IX, Henri III, Henri IV; given title of Marquis by King Charles IX

↓

Claude – *m.*– Eleonore de Grivel de Grossove (wife brings Chateau of Montgoublin[4] to marriage); was commander of Musketeers under King Louis XIII; d. 1674 during religious wars; both buried at Cudot

↓

Claude – *m.*– Elizabeth de Chastellux (1650); commander of French cavalry under Louis XIV; becomes Marquis de St. Phalle–Coulanges

↓

Charles – *m.*– Marie Anne le Tonnelierde Breteuil (1693), d. 1711

↓

Claude Lié – *m.*– Louise de Bardin de Champagne, d. 1750 (wife brings Chambrun property[3] to marriage)

↓

Jean-Vincent – *m.* – **Charlotte-Hermine de Boynes** (1790); wife brings large property[3] in Haiti to marriage; emigrated to Holland during Revolution and served in Army of Princes; returned after amnesty

↓

Edouard-Charles, b. 1798 in London, – *m.* – **Louise-Henriette-Pauline de Chabannes**[6], daughter of one of the principal advisors to King Louis XVIII; cousin of king, Pair de France. Wife brings Chateau de Huez into family[4]

↓

Ernest[7], b. 1828 – *m.* – **Genevieve de Man d'Attenrode** (1858); d. 1864; brother of Xavier, midshipman killed by cannibals in New Caledonia in 1850 and of Gaston, commander of French naval squadron engaged in placing Maximilian of Austria on Mexican throne; died and brought back to France on his flagship

↓

Pierre, b. 1859, d. 1934 – *m.* – **Catherine de Chabannes**[6]–La Palice (1884); aide de camp to Marshall Fosh, head of Allied Armies in World War I

↓

Fal, b. 1889-d. 1978, – *m.* – **Marie Duryee** in 1916; d. 1982; was fourth son of Pierre; became American citizen in 1911; fought for France in World War I; decorated with Croix de Guerre; wounded; founder of family bank with his brothers)

↓

Thibaut, b. 1918, – *m.* – **Rosamond Frame** (1946); *m.* **Elene Isles** (1965, divorced 1983); *m.* **Mariana Mann Smith** (1983)

↓

Fal, b. 1946; **Pierre**, b. 1948; **Thérèse**, b. 1951; **Marc**, b. 1966; **Diane**, b. 1970

↓

Robert, b. 1978

NOTES:

1 As a younster in Auvergne in mountainous southern France, Fale was taken as a slave by Huns returning through Gaul from the sack of Rome. He was purchased by an abbot in a monastery in Champagne. In time, Fale succeeded him as abbot and was later canonized. Family by that name in Auvergne before 520 followed the abbot north and settled in the Champagne region near Troyes.

2 Robert inherited through his wife the Chateau of Cudot and became Baron of Cudot. His wife was related to the king of France and Emperor Beaudoin of Constantinople.

3 With each generation, properties were acquired through marriage and others lost through marriages of daughters.

4 Huez and Montgoublin are still in the family: Cudot was sold recently.

5 Phillippe was the godson of King Philippe III of France whose life he saved at the battle of Mons en Pucelle in what is today Belgium (1304).

6 The Chabannes family is one of the most famous in French history as marshals of France, generals, admirals, ministers, etc.

7 Ernest was the brother of Xavier, a midshipman eaten by cannibals in New Caledonia in 1850, and Gaston naval commander of the French fleet that helped to put Maximilian on the Mexican throne in 1862.

Index

Index

ABOUT THE AUTHOR

THIBAUT DE SAINT PHALLE has been a corporate and international lawyer, an investment banker, a corporate executive, professor and author. From 1981 to 1983, he was the first holder of the Scholl Chair in International Business at the Georgetown University Center for Strategic and International Studies. He was also the director of its International Business and Economic Program. From 1977 to 1981 he was a director of the Export-Import Bank of the United States.

Prior to that, he was, successively, financial vice president of a multinational company and responsible for its foreign operations, a senior partner of an international law firm in New York, partner in an investment banking firm in charge of its international operations, and Professor of International Law and Finance at the International Management Institute (C.E.I.) of the University of Geneva, Switzerland.

He has written numerous articles on banking, law, finance and trade. He co-authored two books on international economics, *The Dollar Crisis* (1963) and *Multinational Corporations* (1978). He is the author of *Trade, Inflation and the Dollar* (1981, revised edition 1984), and *The Federal Reserve—An Intentional Mystery* (1985).

He is currently working on a study of the effect of cultural differences on economic development in various parts of the world. He lives with his wife, Mariana, in Boca Grande, Florida.